MyAccountingLab

- Web-based tutorial and assessment software where students have more "I Get It" moments.

- Flexible for instructors to easily integrate into their course.

For Instructors

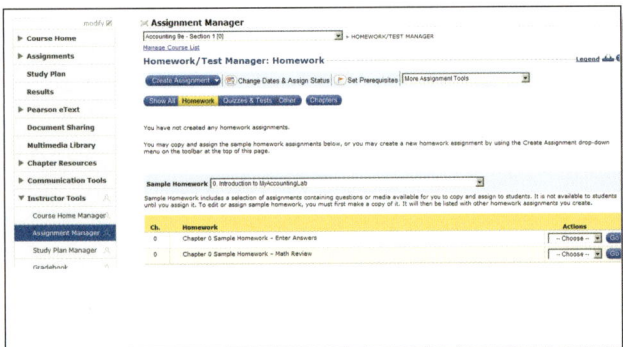

Powerful Homework and Test Manager

- Homework assignments, quizzes, and tests that directly correlate to the textbook.

- Homework guided solutions to help students understand concepts.

- Multiple assignment options including time limits, proctoring, and maximum number of attempts allowed.

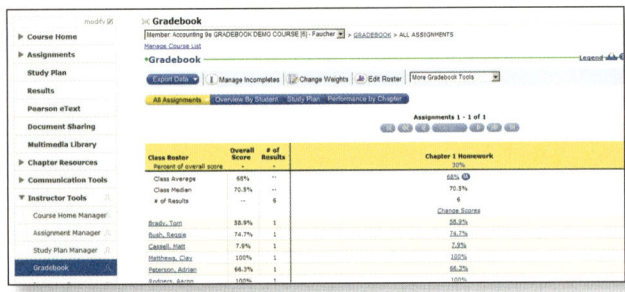

Comprehensive Gradebook Tracking

- Automatic grading that tracks students' results on tests, homework, and tutorials.

- Flexible Gradebook with numerous student data views, weighted assignments, choice on which attempts to include when calculating scores, and the ability to omit results of individual assignments.

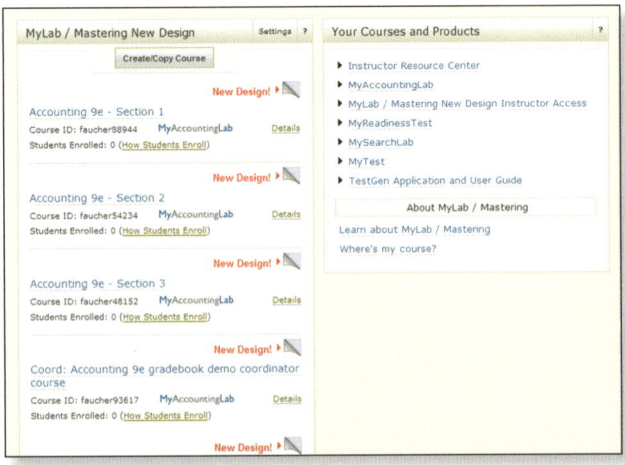

Department-Wide Solutions

- Simplified for departmental implementation with the use of Coordinator Courses—make changes once and they ripple down to all members.

View a guided tour of MyAccountingLab at
http://www.myaccountinglab.com/support/tours

For Students

Interactive Tutorial Exercises

- Homework and practice exercises with additional algorithmic–generated problems for more practice.

- Personalized interactive learning—guided solutions and learning aids for point-of-use help and immediate feedback.

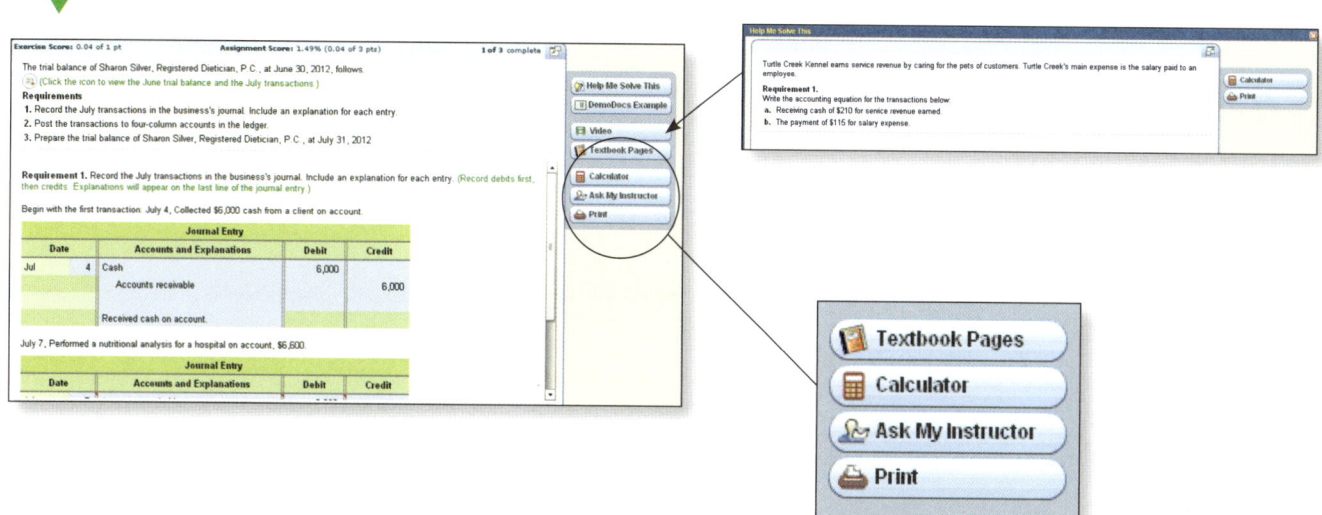

Study Plan for Self-Paced Learning

- Assists students in monitoring their own progress by offering them a customized study plan based on their test results.

- Includes regenerated exercises with new values for unlimited practice and guided multimedia learning aids for extra guidance.

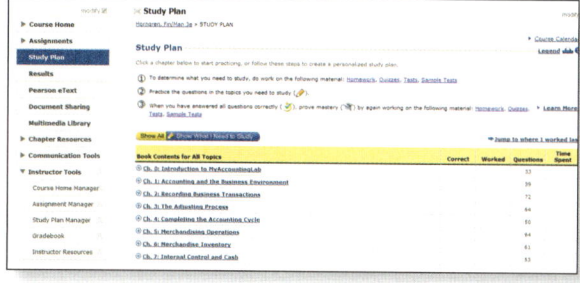

College Accounting

A Practical Approach

CHAPTERS 1–12
with Study Guide and Working Papers

Twelfth Edition

Jeffrey Slater

North Shore Community College
Danvers, Massachusetts

PEARSON

Boston Columbus Indianapolis New York San Francisco Upper Saddle River
Amsterdam Cape Town Dubai London Madrid Milan Munich Paris Montreal Toronto
Delhi Mexico City Sao Paulo Sydney Hong Kong Seoul Singapore Taipei Tokyo

To Nanny Shelley
With Love,
Papa Jeff

Editorial Director: Sally Yagan
Editor in Chief: Donna Battista
Acquisitions Editor: Lacey Vitetta
Development Editor: Mignon Tucker, Brava360° Solutions
Editorial Project Managers: Nicole Sam and Christina Rumbaugh
Editorial Assistants: Jane Avery and Lauren Zanedis
Director of Marketing: Maggie Moylan Leen
Marketing Assistant: Kimberly Lovato
Senior Managing Editor: Nancy Fenton
Senior Production Project Manager: Roberta Sherman
Manufacturing Buyer: Carol Melville
Art Director: Anthony Gemmellaro
Text Designer: Ximena/Tamvakopoulus

Cover Designer: Anthony Gemmellaro
Photo Researcher: Bill Smith Group
Cover Art: © iStockphoto
AVP/Director of Product Development: Lisa Strite
Media Project Manager: Sarah Peterson
Media Production Project Manager: John Cassar
Full-Service Project Management: GEX Publishing Services
Composition: GEX Publishing Services
Printer/Binder: Courier/Kendallville
Cover Printer: Lehigh-Phoenix Color/Hagerstown
Text Font: Sabon Roman 10/12

Credits and acknowledgments borrowed from other sources and reproduced, with permission, in this textbook appear on appropriate page within text and on page C-1.

Cataloging-in-Publication data unavailable at press time.

10 9 8 7 6 5 4 3 2 1

www.pearsonhighered.com

ISBN 13: 978-0-13-277217-4
ISBN 10: 0-13-277217-5

BRIEF CONTENTS

Preface   xi

1   Accounting Concepts and Procedures   1

2   Debits and Credits: Analyzing and Recording Business Transactions   39

3   Beginning the Accounting Cycle   77

4   The Accounting Cycle Continued   119

5   The Accounting Cycle Completed   161

6   Banking Procedure and Control of Cash   221

7   Calculating Pay and Payroll Taxes: The Beginning of the Payroll Process   259

8   Paying, Recording, and Reporting Payroll and Payroll Taxes: The Conclusion of the Payroll Process   289

9   Sales and Cash Receipts   335

10   Purchases and Cash Payments   367

10A   Appendix: Special Journals with Problem Material   413

11   Preparing a Worksheet for a Merchandise Company   423

12   Completion of the Accounting Cycle for a Merchandise Company   455

Glindex   I-1

Credits   C-1

CONTENTS

Preface   xi

1   Accounting Concepts and Procedures   1

Accounting and Business   2
Types of Business Organization   2
Classifying Business Organizations   3
Definition of Accounting   3
Difference between Bookkeeping and Accounting   4

Learning Unit 1-1: The Accounting Equation   4
Assets, Liabilities, and Equities   4

Learning Unit 1-2: The Balance Sheet   9
Points to Remember in Preparing a Balance Sheet   9

Learning Unit 1-3: The Accounting Equation Expanded: Revenue, Expenses, and Withdrawals   11
Revenue   11
Expenses   12
Net Income/Net Loss   12
Withdrawals   12
Expanded Accounting Equation   12

Learning Unit 1-4: Preparing Financial Statements   18
The Income Statement   18
Points to Remember in Preparing an Income Statement   18
The Statement of Owner's Equity   18
The Balance Sheet   19
Main Elements of the Income Statement, the Statement of Owner's Equity, and the Balance Sheet   20

Chapter Assignments
Demonstration Problem   23   •   Blueprint: Financial Statements   26   •   Accounting Coach   27   •   Chapter Summary   28   •   Discussion Questions and Critical Thinking/Ethical Case, Concept Checks, Exercises and Problems   30   •   Financial Report Problem: Reading the Kellogg's Annual Report   36   •   Continuing Problem: On the Job—Sanchez Computer Center   36

SUBWAY CASE: A Fresh Start   37

2   Debits and Credits: Analyzing and Recording Business Transactions   39

Learning Unit 2-1: The T Account   40
Balancing an Account   40

Learning Unit 2-2: Recording Business Transactions: Debits and Credits   42
T Account Entries for Accounting in the Accounting Equation   42
The Transaction Analysis: Five Steps   44
Applying the Transaction Analysis to Mia Wong's Law Practice   45

Learning Unit 2-3: The Trial Balance and Preparation of Financial Statements   53
The Trial Balance   54
Preparing Financial Statements   55

Chapter Assignments
Demonstration Problem Debits and Credits: Analyzing and Recording Business Transactions 59 • Blueprint: Preparing Financial Statements from a Trial Balance 63 • Accounting Coach 64 • Chapter Summary 65 • Discussion Questions and Critical Thinking/Ethical Case, Concept Checks, Exercises and Problems 66 • Financial Report Problem: Reading the Kellogg's Annual Report 75 • Continuing Problem: On the Job—Sanchez Computer Center 75

SUBWAY CASE: Debits on the Left . . . 76

3   Beginning the Accounting Cycle 77

Learning Unit 3-1: Analyzing and Recording Business Transactions into a Journal: Steps 1 and 2 of the Accounting Cycle 78
The General Journal 78

Learning Unit 3-2: Posting to the Ledger: Step 3 of the Accounting Cycle 86
Posting 86

Learning Unit 3-3: Preparing the Trial Balance: Step 4 of the Accounting Cycle 93
What to Do If a Trial Balance Doesn't Balance 94
Some Common Mistakes 94
Making a Correction Before Posting 94
Making a Correction After Posting 95
Correcting an Entry Posted to the Wrong Account 95
Journalizing Transaction, Posting, and Preparing a Trial Balance 98

Chapter Assignments
Demonstration Problem: Journalizing Transaction, Posting, and Preparing a Trial Balance 98 • Blueprint of First Four Steps of Accounting Cycle 102 • Accounting Coach 103 • Chapter Summary 104 • Discussion Questions and Critical Thinking/Ethical Case, Concept Checks, Exercises and Problems 106 • Financial Report Problem: Reading the Kellogg's Annual Report 115 • Continuing Problem: On the Job— Sanchez Computer Center 115

PEACHTREE COMPUTER WORKSHOP:
Computerized Accounting Application for Chapter 3 118

QUICKBOOKS COMPUTER WORKSHOP:
Computerized Accounting Application for Chapter 3 118

4   The Accounting Cycle Continued 119

Learning Unit 4-1: Step 5 of the Accounting Cycle: Preparing a Worksheet 120
The Trial Balance Section 120
The Adjustments Section 120
The Adjusted Trial Balance Section 128
The Income Statement Section 128
The Balance Sheet Section 131

Learning Unit 4-2: Step 6 of the Accounting Cycle: Preparing the Financial Statements from the Worksheet 136
Preparing the Income Statement 136
Preparing the Statement of Owner's Equity 138
Preparing the Balance Sheet 138

Chapter Assignments
Demonstration Problem: Preparing a Worksheet and Financial Statements 141 • Blueprint of Steps 5 and 6 of the Accounting Cycle 146 • Accounting Coach 147 • Chapter Summary 148 • Discussion Questions and Critical Thinking/Ethical Case, Concept Checks, Exercises and Problems 149 • Financial Report Problem: Reading the Kellogg's Annual Report 158 • Continuing Problem: On the Job—Sanchez Computer Center 158

SUBWAY CASE: Where the Dough Goes . . . 159

PEACHTREE COMPUTER WORKSHOP:
Computerized Accounting Application for Chapter 4 160

QUICKBOOKS COMPUTER WORKSHOP:
Computerized Accounting Application for Chapter 4   160

5   The Accounting Cycle Completed   161

Learning Unit 5-1: Journalizing and Posting Adjusting Entries: Step 7 of the Accounting Cycle   162
Recording Journal Entries from the Worksheet   162

Learning Unit 5-2: Journalizing and Posting Closing Entries: Step 8 of the Accounting Cycle   166
How to Journalize Closing Entries   166

Learning Unit 5-3: The Post-Closing Trial Balance: Step 9 of the Accounting Cycle and the Cycle Reviewed   176

Chapter Assignments
Demonstration Problem   179   •   Blueprint of Closing Process from the Worksheet   189   •   Accounting Coach   190   •   Chapter Summary   191   •   Discussion Questions and Critical Thinking/Ethical Case, Concept Checks, Exercises and Problems   192   •   Financial Report Problem: Reading the Kellogg's Annual Report   202   •   Continuing Problem: On the Job—Sanchez Computer Center   202

SUBWAY CASE: Closing Time   203

PEACHTREE COMPUTER WORKSHOP:
Computerized Accounting Application for Chapter 5   219

QUICKBOOKS COMPUTER WORKSHOP:
Computerized Accounting Application for Chapter 5   220

6   Banking Procedure and Control of Cash   221

Learning Unit 6-1: Bank Procedures, Checking Accounts, and Bank Reconciliation   222
Opening a Checking Account   222
Check Endorsement   223
The Checkbook   226
Monthly Recordkeeping: The Bank's Statement of Account and In-Company Records   228
The Bank Reconciliation Process   228
Trends in Banking   231

Learning Unit 6-2: The Establishment of Petty Cash and Change Funds   236
Setting Up the Petty Cash Fund   236
Making Payments from the Petty Cash Fund   237
How to Replenish the Petty Cash Fund   239
Setting Up a Change Fund and Insight into Cash Short and Over   241

Chapter Assignments
Blueprint: A Bank Reconciliation   244   •   Accounting Coach   245   •   Chapter Summary   246   •   Discussion Questions and Critical Thinking/Ethical Case, Concept Checks, Exercises and Problems   248   •   Financial Report Problem: Reading the Kellogg's Annual Report   253   •   Continuing Problem: On the Job—Sanchez Computer Center   253

SUBWAY CASE: Counting Down the Cash   256

7   Calculating Pay and Payroll Taxes: The Beginning of the Payroll Process   259

Learning Unit 7-1: Calculation of Gross Earnings, Employee Withholding Taxes, and Net Pay   260
Gross Earnings   261
Federal Income Tax Withholding   262
State Income Tax Withholding   263

Other Income Tax Withholding   264
Employee Withholding for Social Security Taxes   266
Other Withholdings   267
Net Pay   267

Learning Unit 7-2: Preparing a Payroll Registerand Employee Earning Record   268
The Payroll Register   268
The Employee Earnings Record   270

Learning Unit 7-3: Employer Payroll Tax Expense   270
Employer Payment for Social Security Taxes   270
FUTA and SUTA   272
Workers' Compensation Insurance   273

Chapter Assignments
Blueprint for Recording Transactions in a Payroll Register   275   •   **Accounting Coach   276**   •   Chapter
Summary   278   •   Discussion Questions and Critical Thinking/Ethical Case, Concept Checks, Exercises and
Problems   280   •   Financial Report Problem: Reading the Kellogg's Annual Report   287   •   Continuing
Problem: On the Job—Sanchez Computer Center   287

SUBWAY CASE: Payroll Records: A Full-Time Job?   287

8 Paying, Recording, and Reporting Payroll and Payroll Taxes: The Conclusion of the Payroll Process   289

**Learning Unit 8-1: Recording Payroll and Payroll Tax Expense and
Paying the Payroll   290**
Recording Payroll   291
Recording Payroll Tax Expense   293
Paying the Payroll and Recording the Payment   293

**Learning Unit 8-2: Paying Fit and Fica Taxes and Completing the
Employer's Quarterly Federal Tax Return, Form 941   295**
Paying FIT and FICA Taxes   296
Completing the Employer's Quarterly Federal Tax Return, Form 941   300

**Learning Unit 8-3: Preparing Forms W-2 and W-3, Paying FUTA Tax and Completing
the Employer's Annual Unemployment Tax Return, Form 940, and Paying SUTA Tax
and Workers' Compensation Insurance   304**
Preparing Form W-2: Wage and Tax Statement   304
Preparing Form W-3: Transmittal of Income   305
Paying FUTA Tax   306
Completing the Employer's Annual Federal Unemployment (FUTA) Tax Return, Form 940   307
Paying SUTA Tax   311
Paying Workers' Compensation Insurance   311

Chapter Assignments
Blueprint: Form 941 Tax Deposit Rules   313   •   **Accounting Coach   315**   •   Chapter Summary   317   •
Discussion Questions and Critical Thinking/Ethical Case, Concept Checks, Exercises and Problems   319   •
Financial Report Problem: Reading the Kellogg's Annual Report   330   •   Continuing Problem: On the Job—
Sanchez Computer Center   330

SUBWAY CASE: Hold the Lettuce, Withhold the Taxes   331

PEACHTREE COMPUTER WORKSHOP:
Computerized Accounting Application For Chapter 8   332

QUICKBOOKS COMPUTER WORKSHOP:
Computerized Accounting Application For Chapter 8   333

9 Sales and Cash Receipts   335

Learning Unit 9-1: Chou's Toy Shop: Seller's View of a Merchandise Company   336
Gross Sales   336

Sales Returns and Allowances   336
Sales Discount   337
Sales Tax Payable   338

Learning Unit 9-2: Recording and Posting Sales Transactions on Account* for Art's Wholesale Clothing Company: Introduction to Subsidiary Ledgers and Credit Memorandum   340

Accounts Receivable Subsidiary Ledgers   341
The Credit Memorandum   344
Journalizing, Recording, and Posting the Credit Memorandum   345

Learning Unit 9-3: Recording and Posting Cash Receipt Transactions for Art's Wholesale: Schedule of Accounts Receivable   346

Schedule of Accounts Receivable   349

Chapter Assignments
Blueprint: Transferring Information from the General Journal   351   •   Accounting Coach   352   •   Chapter Summary   354   •   Discussion Questions and Critical Thinking/Ethical Case, Concept Checks, Exercises and Problems   356   •   Financial Report Problem: Reading the Kellogg's Annual Report   364   •   Continuing Problem: On the Job—Sanchez Computer Center   364

10 Purchases and Cash Payments   367

Learning Unit 10-1: Chou's Toy Shop: Buyer's View of a Merchandise Company   368

Purchases   368
Purchases Returns and Allowances   368

Learning Unit 10-2: Recording and Posting Purchases Transactions on Account for Art's Wholesale Clothing Company: Introduction to Subsidiary Ledgers and Debit Memorandum   371

Accounts Payable Subsidiary Ledger   373
Debit Memorandum   376

Learning Unit 10-3: Recording and Posting Cash Payments Transactions for Art's Wholesale: Schedule of Accounts Payable   379

Learning Unit 10-3 Review At This Point   380
Instant Replay Self-Review Quiz 10-3   380

Learning Unit 10-4: Introduction to a Merchandise Company Using a Perpetual Inventory System   383

Introduction to the Merchandise Cycle   383
What Inventory System Walmart Uses   383
Recording Merchandise Transactions   384

Chapter Assignments
Blueprint: Periodic Versus Perpetual   391   •   Accounting Coach   392   •   Chapter Summary   394   •   Discussion Questions and Critical Thinking/Ethical Case, Concept Checks, Exercises and Problems   396   •   Financial Report Problem: Reading the Kellogg's Annual Report   409   •   Continuing Problem: On the Job—Sanchez Computer Center   409

PEACHTREE COMPUTER WORKSHOP:
Computerized Accounting Application for Chapter 10   410

QUICKBOOKS COMPUTER WORKSHOP:
Computerized Accounting Application for Chapter 10   411

10A Appendix: Special Journals With Problem Material   413

Classroom Demonstration Problem: Periodic Method   413

Journalizing Transactions to Special Journals; Posting to Subsidiary and General Ledger Accounts from Special Journals   413
Summary of Solution Tips   418

Appendix A Problems   418

Sales and Cash Receipts Journal Using a Perpetual Inventory System for Art's Wholesale Clothing   421

11 Preparing a Worksheet for a Merchandise Company   423

Learning Unit 11-1: Adjustments for Merchandise Inventory and Unearned Rent   424

Adjustments A and B: Merchandise Inventory, $19,000   425
Adjustment C: Unearned Rent   425

Learning Unit 11-2: Completing the Worksheet   427

Adjustment C: Rental Income Earned by Art's Wholesale, $200   428
Adjustment D: Supplies on Hand, $300   429
Adjustment E: Insurance Expired, $300   430
Adjustment F: Depreciation Expense, $50   430
Adjustment G: Salaries Accrued, $600   430

Chapter Assignments
Blueprint: A Worksheet for a Merchandise Company   438   •   Accounting Coach   439   •   Chapter Summary   440   •   Discussion Questions and Critical Thinking/Ethical Case, Concept Checks, Exercises and Problems   441   •   Financial Report Problem: Reading the Kellogg's Annual Report   450   •   Continuing Problem: On the Job—Sanchez Computer Center   450

Appendix   452

A Worksheet for Art's Wholesale Clothing Co. Using a Perpetual Inventory System   452
Problem for Appendix   452

12 Completion of the Accounting Cycle for a Merchandise Company   455

Learning Unit 12-1: Preparing Financial Statements   456

The Income Statement   456
Operating Expenses   458
Statement of Owner's Equity   458
The Balance Sheet   459

Learning Unit 12-2: Journalizing and Posting Adjusting and Closing Entries; Preparing the Post-Closing Trial Balance   463

Journalizing and Posting Adjusting Entries   463
Journalizing and Posting Closing Entries   467
The Post-Closing Trial Balance   467

Learning Unit 12-3: Reversing Entries (Optional Section)   470

Chapter Assignments
Blueprint: Financial Statements   473   •   Accounting Coach   475   •   Chapter Summary   476   •   Discussion Questions and Critical Thinking/Ethical Case, Concept Checks, Exercises and Problems   477   •   Financial Report Problem: Reading the Kellogg's Annual Report   488   •   Continuing Problem: On the Job—Sanchez Computer Center   489

Mini Practice Set   489

The Corner Dress Shop   489

PEACHTREE COMPUTER WORKSHOP:

Computerized Accounting Application For Chapter 12   494

QUICKBOOKS COMPUTER WORKSHOP:

Computerized Accounting Application For Chapter 12   495

Glindex   I-1
Credits   C-1

GAME PLAN FOR SUCCESS FROM ACCOUNTING COACH JEFF SLATER...

COACHING SUCCESS WITH IN-CHAPTER LEARNING TOOLS

- **Learning Unit Reviews:** Each chapter is organized into small, bite-sized units. Students are introduced to a new concept in the learning unit, and then they can immediately test their understanding in the learning unit review.
- **Instant Replay:** This feature, located in the self-review quiz at the end of each learning unit for the first five chapters, is like a private tutoring session with the author, as he anticipates students' questions and walks them through the provided solution, step by step. These Instant Replay sections are the key to retention.
- **Chapter Opening Game Plan:** Each chapter introduces students to the key concepts that they will learn in the chapter using student-friendly companies and examples.
- **Coaching Tips:** Short, sweet, and to the point. They're not found on every page; instead they are provided only when students may need some coaching.
- **In-Text Practice Set:** The in-text Sullivan Realty Practice Set (Chapter 5) enables students to complete two cycles of transactions (either manually or with Peachtree or Quickbooks).

END-OF-CHAPTER PRACTICE MATERIAL

- **Demonstration Problems:** Demonstration problems walk students through a sample problem as if they were getting one-on-one help from their instructor.
- **Blueprint:** This is a visual summary of the chapter. Students can use it as a roadmap to review what they have learned. It stresses when to perform specific activities.
- **Concept Checks:** Short exercises can be assigned or used in class for difficult topics.
- **Learning Objectives:** A learning objective number and the average time to complete each exercise is now included for all end-of-chapter material.
- **Group A and New Group B Exercises:** Short exercises can be assigned or used in class to focus on building skills. B exercises were added to the text in this edition.
- **Group A and Group B Problems:** All of the problems have been updated for this edition.
- **Financial Report Problem:** Students use the annual financial report of Kellogg Company to apply theory and applications completed in the chapter.
- **Discussion Questions:** These include ethical questions and critical-thinking questions.
- **Computerized Accounting:** Selected end-of-chapter problems can be completed with Peachtree or Quickbooks.

- **Continuing Problem: On The Job: Sanchez Computer Center:** Students follow the activities of a single company and then are asked to apply concepts to solve specific accounting problems for the company. Problems can be found in Chapters 1–12 and can be solved manually or by using Peachtree or Quickbooks.
- **Computer Workshops:** This book contains seven computer workshops (for the most recent versions of Peachtree and QuickBooks) with detailed step-by-step instructions on how to take a manual problem from the end of the chapter and use both types of software.

Students need to do accounting manually before they can use the computer. These workshops allow the student to see how fast accounting procedures can be done on the computer. They will need these computer skills when applying for jobs in the business.

    These workshops assume no computer knowledge and facilitate a step-by-step teaching package. Each step provides the student (or instructor) with detailed explanations. Initial instructions appear in the textbook itself, and then students are directed to the computer to do the actual work online.

MyAccountingLab

NEW TO THIS EDITION

MyAccountingLab® is Web-based tutorial and assessment software for accounting that not only gives students more "I Get It" moments, but also gives instructors the flexibility to make technology an integral part of their course.

With MyAccountingLab students will have…

- **Personalized help** when they need it with the interactive "Help Me Solve This" tool that automatically generates algorithmic versions of the problem the student is working on and provides step-by-step assistance until the solution is obtained. The "Help Me Solve This" tool is personal tutorials to help students understand how to work through accounting problems.
- **Dynamic learning resources** that work with students' individual learning styles. *All Learning Aids can be turned off by the instructor.*
- **Interactive Tutorial Exercises**—found in MyAccountingLab's homework and practice questions—that are correlated to students' Pearson textbook.
- **A personalized Study Plan** for self-paced learning that links students directly to interactive tutorial exercises on the topics they have yet to master.
- **An easy-to-navigate system** so the focus is on what matters the most—learning accounting!
- **Chapter resources** that are in one spot for students so they can quickly access all learning tools associated with each chapter of the book they are using. Examples of the chapter resources include audio PowerPoints, videos, MP3 summaries, e-Study guide, Check Figure for Cost Accounting, working papers, etc.

MyAccountingLab is also reshaping accounting courses for instructors by…

- **Providing flexibility** for any course through its robust course management tools and adaptable course materials.
- **Offering several choices** when it comes to scheduling, item analysis, questions and problems, and grading and assessment.
- **Simplifying instructor and student experiences** from set-up and through day-to-day activity with its easy-to-use interface.
- **Motivating students** by providing learning tools that engage, stimulate, and help students connect online and in the classroom.

Chapter Changes

All Chapters:

- New Accounting Coach feature, which assesses students' understanding of key concepts.
- New chapter summaries which summarize key concepts and terms. This feature provides students with an all-in-one review tool for each chapter.
- All problems and exercises are updated. MyAccountingLab contains an exact match of the A and B sets in the text. In addition, MyAccountingLab provides three additional sets of problems and exercises for endless practice and assignment opportunities.
- An additional set of exercises (Set B) has been added to the text.
- Classroom Demonstration Exercises have been renamed "Concept Checks" and are reproduced in MyAccountingLab.
- The "Play by Play: Extra Help" explanation of solutions to Learning Unit quizzes has been retitled "Instant Replay."

Chapter 1 Accounting Concepts and Procedures

- New chapter opener entitled "Game Plan" with new company information on eBay

Chapter 2 Debits and Credits: Analyzing and Recording Business Transactions

- New chapter opener entitled "Game Plan" with new company information on Subway

Chapter 3 Beginning the Accounting Cycle

- New chapter opener entitled "Game Plan" with new company information on American Airlines

Chapter 4 The Accounting Cycle Continued

- New chapter opener entitled "Game Plan" with new company information on General Motors

Chapter 5 The Accounting Cycle Completed

- New chapter opener entitled "Game Plan" with new company information on Disney
- Updated 2010 numbers for the Sullivan Realty Mini-Practice Set

Chapter 6 Banking Procedure and Control of Cash

- New chapter opener entitled "Game Plan" with a banking example about the latest banking procedures
- Updated information on trends in banking and accounting procedures for debit and credit cards

Chapter 7 Calculating Pay and Payroll Taxes: The Beginning of the Payroll Process

- New chapter opener entitled "Game Plan" with new company information on Sears
- Updated figures and tables throughout include 2010 rates
- Footnote on OASDI rate used and explained
- Continued focus on integrating role of employee and employer

Chapter 8 Paying, Recording, and Reporting Payroll and Payroll Taxes: The Conclusion of the Payroll Process

- New chapter opener entitled "Game Plan" with new company information on Google
- Updated figures and tables throughout include 2010 payroll tax rates
- Updated tax forms

Chapter 9 Sales and Cash Receipts
- New chapter opener entitled "Game Plan" with new company information on Home Depot

Chapter 10 Purchases and Cash Payments
- New chapter opener entitled "Game Plan" with new company information on Best Buy
- Special journal appendix problems included in MyAccountingLab

Chapter 11 Preparing a Worksheet for a Merchandise Company
- New chapter opener entitled "Game Plan" with new company information on Apple

Chapter 12 Completion of the Accounting Cycle for a Merchandise Company
- New chapter opener entitled "Game Plan" with new company information on Toys "R" Us
- New Computer Workshop after Chapter 12

FOR INSTRUCTORS

Instructor's Resource Center (IRC): Register. Redeem. Login.

At www.pearsonhighered.com/slater instructors can access a variety of print, media, and presentation resources available with this text in downloadable, digital format. For most texts, resources are also available for course management platforms such as Blackboard, WebCT, and Course Compass.

It gets better. Once you register, you will not have additional forms to fill out or multiple usernames and passwords to remember to access new titles and/or editions. As a registered faculty member, you can log in directly to download resource files and receive immediate access and instructions for installing course management content to your campus server.

Need help? Our dedicated technical support team is ready to assist instructors with questions about the media supplements that accompany this text. Visit http://247pearsoned.custhelp.com for answers to frequently asked questions and toll-free user support phone numbers.

The following supplements are available to adopting instructors. For detailed descriptions, please visit www.pearsonhighered.com/slater.

Instructor's Resource Center (IRC) online: Login at www.pearsonhighered.com/slater.

Chapters 1–12 with Study Guide and Working Papers: 0-13-277217-5

Study Guide and Working Papers (Chapters 1–12): 0-13-277215-9

Study Guide and Working Papers (Chapters 13–25): 0-13-277216-7

Instructor's Solutions Manual: 0-13-277207-8

Instructor's Manual: Visit the IRC for this supplement.

TestGen Test Generating Software: Visit the IRC for this supplement.

Test Item File: Visit the IRC for this supplement.

Working Papers in Excel format: Visit the IRC for this supplement.

PowerPoint Presentation Slides: Visit the IRC for this supplement.

FOR STUDENTS

Textbook Volumes

Textbook Chapters 1–25: ISBN 0-13-277206-X *Includes payroll and additional blank worksheets

Textbook Chapters 1–12: ISBN 0-13-277217-5 *Includes study guide and working papers for Chapters 1–12

Print Study Aids

Study Guide and Working Papers Chapters 1–12: ISBN 0-13-277215-9
Study Guide and Working Papers Chapters 13–25: ISBN 0-13-277216-7
Who Dun It? Practice Set: ISBN 0-13-277253-1

Online Resources

Valuable resources for both students and professors can be found at www.pearsonhighered.com/slater.

REVIEWERS

Terry Aime, *Delgado Community College*
Cornelia Alsheimer, *Santa Barbara City College*
Julia Angel, *North Arkansas College*
Julie Armstrong, *St. Clair County Community College*
Marjorie Ashton, *Truckee Meadows Community College*
John Babich, *Kankakee Community College*
Cecil Battiste, *Valencia Community College*
Donald Benoit, *Mitchell College*
Peggy A. Berrier, *Ivy Technical State College*
Michelle Berube, *Everest University*
Anne Bikofsky, *College of Westchester*
Michael Bitting, *John A. Logan College*
David Bland, *Cape Fear Community College*
Suzanne Bradford, *Angelina College*
Beverly Bugay, *Tyler Junior College*
Gary Bumgarner, *Mountain Empire Community College*
Betsy Crane, *Victoria College*
Noel Craven, *El Camino College*
Don Curfman, *McHenry County College*
John Daugherty, *Pitt Community College*
Susan Davis, *Green River Community College*
Michael Discello, *Pittsburgh Technical Institute*
Sylvia Dorsey, *Florence-Darlington Technical College*
Sid Downey, *Cochise College*
Donna Eakman, *Great Falls College of Technology*
Steven Ernest, *Baton Rouge Community College*
John Evanson, *Williston State College*
Marilyn Ewing, *Seward County Community College*
Nancy Fallon, *Albertus Magnus College*
Nicole Fife, *Bucks County Community College*
Brian Fink, *Danville Area Community College*
Paul Fisher, *Rogue Community College*
Carolyn Fitzmorris, *Hutchinson Community College*
Trish Glennon, *Central Florida Community College*
Nancy Goehring, *Monterey Peninsula College*
Jane Goforth, *North Seattle Community College*
Lori Grady, *Bucks County Community College*
Gretchen Graham, *Community College of Allegheny County*
Marina Grau, *Houston Community College*
Mary Jane Green, *Des Moines Area Community College*
Joyce Griffin, *Kansas City Kansas Community College*
Becky Hancock, *El Paso Community College*
Toni Hartley, *Laurel Business Institute*
Raymond Hartman, *Triton Community College*
Scott Hays, *Central Oregon Community College*

Kathy Hebert, *Louisiana Technical College*
Sueanne Hely, *West Kentucky Community & Technical College*
Maggie Hilgart, *Mid-State Technical College*
Michele Hill, *Schoolcraft College*
Michelle Hoeflich, *Elgin Community College*
Mary Hollars, *Vincennes University*
Donna Jacobs, *University of New Mexico-Gallup*
Judy Jager, *Pikes Peak Community College*
Jane Jones, *Mountain Empire Community College*
Jenny Jones, *Central Kentucky Technical College*
Patrick Jozefowicz, *Southwest Wisconsin Technical College*
Nancy Kelly, *Middlesex Community College*
Karen Kettelson, *Western Wisconsin Technical College*
Elizabeth King, *Sacramento City College*
Ken Koerber, *Bucks County Community College*
David Krug, *Johnson County Community College*
Christy Land, *Catawba Valley Community College*
Ronald Larner, *John Wood Community College*
Lee Leksell, *Lake Superior College*
Lolita Lockett, *Florida Community College at Jacksonville*
Sue Mardock, *Colby Community College*
John Masserwick, *Five Towns College*
Pam Mattson, *Tulsa Community College*
Bonnie Mayer, *Lakeshore Technical College*
Sally McMillin, *Katharine Gibbs School*
John Miller, *Metropolitan Community College*
Susan L. Miller, *Delaware County Community College*
Cora Newcomb, *Technical College of Lowcountry*
Jon Nitschke, *Great Falls Technical College*
Lorinda Oliver, *Vermont Technical College*
Barbara Pauer, *Gateway Technical College*
Nicholas Peppes, *St. Louis Community College*
Richard Pettit, *Mountain View College*
Lisa Phillips, *City College*
Margaret Pollard, *American River College*
Shirley Powell, *Arkansas State University*
Linda Prescott, *Hillsborough Community College*
Claudia Quinn, *San Joaquin Delta College*
Jerry Rhodes, *Daymar College*
Ed Richter, *Southeast Technical Institute*
Alberta Robinson, *Indiana Business College*
Beth Sanders, *Hawaii Community College*
Bob Sanner, *Central Community College*
Debra Schmidt, *Cerritos College*
Karen Scott, *Bates Technical College*

Carolyn Seefer, *Diablo Valley College*
Jeri Spinner, *Idaho State University*
Alice Steljes, *Illinois Valley Community College*
Jack Stone, *Linn-Benton Community College*
Rick Street, *Spokane Community College*
Domenico Tavella, *Pittsburgh Technical Institute*
Bill Taylor, *Cossatot Community College*

Mary J. Tobaben, *Collin County Community College*
Ron J. Trucks, *Jefferson College*
Elaine Tuttle, *Bellevue Community College*
Ski Vanderlaan, *Delta College*
Andy Williams, *Edmonds Community College*
Jack Williams, *Tulsa Community College*

Supplement Authors and Invaluable Assistance

Test Item File: William Jefferson, *Metropolitan Community College*; Brenda
   Mattison, *TriCounty Technical College*
PowerPoint Presentations: Robin Turner, *Rowan-Cabarrus Community College*
Computerized Workshops: Terri Brunsdon
End-of-chapter Peachtree/QuickBooks problems: Terri Brunsdon
Who Dun It? Practice Set: Toni Hartley, *Laurel Business Institute*
Update of Chapters 7, 8, and Continuing Problem Corner Dress Shop and Who
   Dun It? Practice Sets: Richard Pettit, *Mountain View College*
Text Accuracy Checkers: Richard Pettit, *Mountain View College*; Cornelia
   Alsheimer-Barthel, *Santa Barbara City College*
Solutions Manual Update: Judith Zander, *Grossmont Community College*
Supplement Quality Assurance: Richard Pettit, *Mountain View College*; Michele
   Hill, *Schoolcraft College*

I WANT TO HEAR FROM YOU

How to "get to me": Please e-mail me at jeffslater@aol.com, and I promise to get
back to you within 24 hours or less. You are my customer, and I want to provide you
with the best service possible.

Accounting Concepts and Procedures

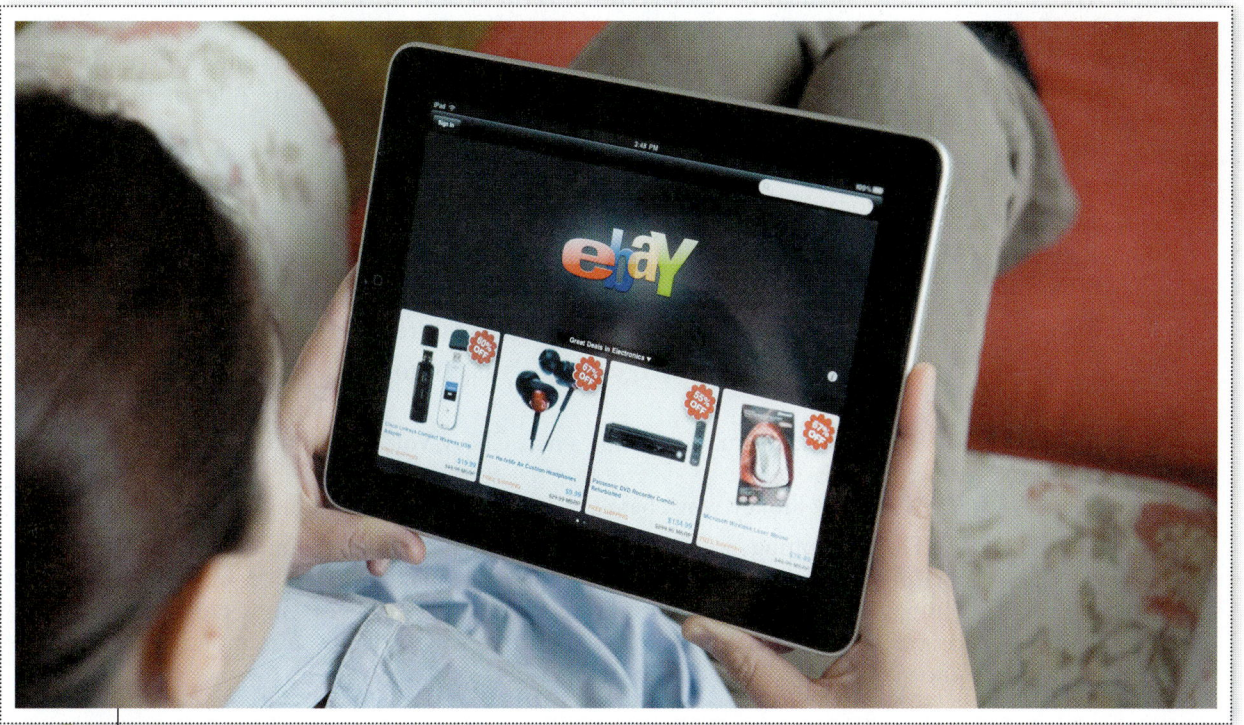

THE GAME PLAN

Did you ever think about how a business with millions of sales each day keeps track of them and why it needs to? When you purchase an item on eBay, accounting surrounds each transaction.

You have a record of your purchase in your PayPal account, and at the same time, eBay tracks the sale in its version of a PayPal account, called the Revenue account. In this chapter, we will see how eBay records all these transactions and how eBay communicates its sales to the business world. If you want to run your own business one day, it is important to understand accounting—"the language of business"—so that you can communicate your performance in the business world like eBay.

LEARNING OBJECTIVES

- **1.** Defining and listing the functions of accounting.
- **2.** Recording transactions in the basic accounting equation.
- **3.** Seeing how revenue, expenses, and withdrawals expand the basic accounting equation.
- **4.** Preparing an income statement, a statement of owner's equity, and a balance sheet.

ACCOUNTING AND BUSINESS

Companies like eBay have to comply with many federal statutes. The Sarbanes-Oxley Act is a federal statute passed to prevent fraud at public companies. This act requires a closer look at the internal controls and the accuracy of the financial results of a company.

Accounting A system that measures the business's activities in financial terms, provides written reports and financial statements about those activities, and communicates these reports to decision makers and others.

Accounting is the language of business; it provides information to managers, owners, investors, government agencies, and others inside and outside the organization. Accounting provides answers and insights to questions like these:

- Should I invest in Google or Apple stock?
- How will increasing fuel costs affect American Airlines?
- Can United Airlines pay its debt obligations?
- What percentage of the Amazon marketing budget is allocated to e-business? How does that percentage compare with the competition? What is the overall financial condition of Amazon?

Smaller businesses also need answers to their financial questions:

- At a local Walgreens, did business increase enough over the last year to warrant hiring a new assistant?
- Should Local Auto Detailing Co. spend more money to design, produce, and send out new brochures in an effort to create more business?
- What role should the Internet play in the future of business spending?

Accounting is as important to individuals as it is to businesses; it answers questions like these:

- Should I take out a loan to buy a new Chevy Volt or wait until I can afford to pay cash for it?
- Would my money work better in a money market or in the stock market?

The accounting process analyzes, records, classifies, summarizes, reports, and interprets financial information for decision makers—whether individuals, small businesses, large corporations, or governmental agencies—in a timely fashion. It is important that students understand the "whys" of this accounting process. Just knowing the mechanics is not enough.

Types of Business Organization

The four main categories of business organization are (1) sole proprietorships, (2) partnerships, (3) corporations, and (4) limited liability corporations. Let's define each of them and look at their advantages and disadvantages. This information also appears in Table 1.1.

Sole proprietorship A type of business organization that has one owner. The owner is personally liable for paying the business's debts.

Sole Proprietorship A sole proprietorship, such as Mona's Nail Care, is a business that has one owner. That person is both the owner and the manager of the business. An advantage of a sole proprietorship is that the owner makes all the decisions for the business. A disadvantage is that if the business cannot pay its obligations, the business owner must pay them, which means that the owner could lose some of his or her personal assets (e.g., house or savings).

Sole proprietorships are easy to form. They end if the business closes or when the owner dies.

Partnership A form of business organization that has at least two owners. The partners usually are personally liable for the partnership's debts.

Partnership A partnership, such as Hope and Sam, is a form of business ownership that has at least two owners (partners). Each partner acts as an owner of the company, which is an advantage because the partners can share the decision making and the risks of the business usually outlined in a partnership agreement. A disadvantage is that, as in a sole proprietorship, the partners' personal assets could be lost if the partnership cannot meet its obligations.

Partnerships are easy to form. They end when a partner dies or leaves the partnership, or when the partners decide to close the business.

TABLE 1.1 Types of Business Organizations

	Sole Proprietorship (Mona's Nail Care)	Partnership (Hope and Sam)	Corporation (eBay)	Limited Liability Corporations (LLC)
Ownership	Business owned by one person.	Business owned by more than one person.	Business owned by stockholders.	Business owned by a limited number of stockholders.
Formation	No formal filing or agreement necesssary to form.	Requires a partnership agreement to define the terms of partnership.	Requires filing with the state to be recognized.	Requires filing with the state a document called articles of incorporation.
Liability	Owner could lose personal assets to meet obligations of business.	Partners could lose personal assets to meet obligations of partnership.	Limited personal risk. Stockholders' loss is limited to their investment in the company.	Limited personal risk. Stockholders' loss is limited to their investment.
Closing	Ends with death of owner or closing of business.	Ends with death of partner or closing of business.	Can continue indefinitely.	May end with death of shareholder.

Corporation A corporation, such as eBay, is a business owned by stockholders. The corporation may have only a few stockholders, or it may have many stockholders. The stockholders are not personally liable for the corporation's debts, and they usually do not have input into the business decisions.

Corporations are more difficult to form than sole proprietorships or partnerships as the corporation must file with the state in order to gain the protections provided by this form of business. Corporations can exist indefinitely.

Liability Corporations (LLC) A limited liability corporation, such as the law firm of Battista, Tucker and Sam, LLC, is a business owned by a few stockholders. The stockholders are liable only to the extent of their investment in the firm and, unlike a corporation, have input in the business decisions. Like corporations, the LLC must file with the state in which it does business in order to gain the liability protection of this form of business.

Classifying Business Organizations

Whether we are looking at a sole proprietorship, a partnership, or a corporation, the business can be classified by what the business does to earn money. Companies are categorized as service, merchandise, or manufacturing businesses.

A limo service is a good example of a service company because it provides a service. The first part of this book focuses on service businesses.

Gap and JCPenney sell products. They are called merchandise companies. Merchandise companies can either make their own products or sell products that are made by another supplier. Companies such as Intel and Ford Motor Company that make their own products are called manufacturers. (See Table 1.2, p. 4.)

Definition of Accounting

Accounting (also called the accounting process) is a system that measures the activities of a business in financial terms. It provides reports and financial statements that show how the various transactions the business undertook (e.g., buying and

Corporation A type of business organization that is owned by stockholders. Stockholders usually are not personally liable for the corporation's debts.

Service company Business that provides a service.

Merchandise company Business that buys a product from a manufacturing company to sell to its customers.

Manufacturer Business that makes a product and sells it to its customers.

● **L01**

TABLE 1.2 Examples of Service, Merchandise, and Manufacturing Businesses

Service Businesses	Merchandise Businesses	Manufacturing Businesses
Mona's Nail Care	Sears	Hershey's
eBay	JCPenney	Ford Motor Company
Dr. Wheeler, M.D.	Amazon.com	Toro
Accountemps	Home Depot	Levi's
Langley Landscaping	Gap	Intel

selling goods) affected the business. This accounting process performs the following functions:

- **Analyzing:** Looking at what happened and how the business was affected.
- **Recording:** Putting the information into the accounting system.
- **Classifying:** Grouping all the same activities (e.g., all purchases) together.
- **Summarizing:** Totaling the results.
- **Reporting:** Issuing the statements that tell the results of the previous functions.
- **Interpreting:** Examining the statements to determine how the various pieces of information they contain relate to each other.
- **Communication:** Providing the reports and financial statements to people who are interested in the information, such as the business's decision makers, investors, creditors, and government agencies (e.g., the Internal Revenue Service).

As you can see, a lot of people use these reports. A set of procedures and guidelines were developed to make sure that everyone prepares and interprets them the same way. These guidelines are known as generally accepted accounting principles (GAAP). International Financial Reporting Standards (IFRS) are a group of guidelines developed by the International Accounting Standards Board. The United States is considering a change from GAAP to IFRS. No final decisions have been made.

Now let's look at the difference between bookkeeping and accounting. Keep in mind that we use the terms *accounting* and the *accounting process* interchangeably.

Difference between Bookkeeping and Accounting

Confusion often arises concerning the difference between bookkeeping and accounting. Bookkeeping is the recording (record keeping) function of the accounting process; a bookkeeper enters accounting information in the company's books. An accountant takes that information and prepares the financial statements that are used to analyze the company's financial position. Accounting involves many complex activities. Often, it includes the preparation of tax and financial reports, budgeting, and analyses of financial information.

Today, computers are used for routine bookkeeping operations that used to take weeks or months to complete. This book explains how the advantages of the computer can be applied to a manual accounting system by using hands-on knowledge of how accounting works. Basic accounting knowledge is needed even though computers can do routine tasks. QuickBooks, Excel, and Peachtree are popular software packages in use today.

LEARNING UNIT 1-1 THE ACCOUNTING EQUATION
Assets, Liabilities, and Equities

Let's begin our study of accounting concepts and procedures by looking at a small business: Mia Wong's law practice. Mia decided to open her practice at the end of August. She consulted her accountant before she made her decision, and he gave her some important information. First, he told her the new business would be considered a separate business entity whose finances had to be kept separate and distinct from

Generally accepted accounting principles (GAAP) The procedures and guidelines that must be followed during the accounting process.

International Financial Reporting Standards (IFRS) A group of accounting standards and procedures that if adopted by the US, could replace GAAP.

Bookkeeping The recording function of the accounting process.

Mia's personal finances. The accountant went on to say that all transactions can be analyzed using the basic accounting equation: Assets = Liabilities + Owner's Equity.

Mia had never heard of the basic accounting equation. She listened carefully as the accountant explained the terms used in the equation and how the equation works.

Assets Cash, land, supplies, office equipment, buildings, and other properties of value *owned* by a firm are called assets.

Equities The rights of financial claim to the assets are called equities. Equities belong to those who supply the assets. If you are the only person to supply assets to the firm, you have the sole rights or financial claims to them. For example, if you supply the law firm with $6,000 in cash and $8,000 in office equipment, your equity in the firm is $14,000.

Relationship between Assets and Equities The relationship between assets and equities is

Assets = Equities
(Total value of items *owned* by business)   (Total claims against the assets)

The total dollar value of the assets of your law firm will be equal to the total dollar value of the financial claims to those assets, that is, equal to the total dollar value of the equities.

The total dollar value is broken down on the left-hand side of the equation to show the specific items of value owned by the business and on the right-hand side to show the types of claims against the assets owned.

Liabilities A firm may have to borrow money to buy more assets; when it does, it *buys assets on account* (buy now, pay later). Suppose the law firm purchases a new computer for $3,000 on account from Dell, and the company is willing to wait 10 days for payment. The law firm has created a liability: an obligation to pay that comes due in the future. Dell is called the creditor. This liability—the amount owed to Dell—gives the store the right, or the financial claim, to $3,000 of the law firm's assets. When Dell is paid, the store's rights to the assets of the law firm will end because the obligation has been paid off.

Basic Accounting Equation To best understand the various claims to a business's assets, accountants divide equities into two parts. The claims of creditors—outside persons or businesses—are labeled *liabilities*. The claim of the business's owner is labeled owner's equity. Let's see how the accounting equation looks now.

Assets =   **Equities**
                    1. Liabilities: rights of creditors
                    2. Owner's equity: rights of owner

Assets = Liabilities + Owner's Equity

The total value of all the assets of a firm equals the combined total value of the financial claims of the creditors (liabilities) and the claims of the owners (owner's equity). This calculation is known as the basic accounting equation. The basic accounting equation provides a basis for understanding the conventional accounting system of a business. The equation records business transactions in a logical and orderly way that shows their impact on the company's assets, liabilities, and owner's equity.

Importance of Creditors Another way of presenting the basic accounting equation is

Assets − Liabilities = Owner's Equity

This form of the equation stresses the importance of creditors. The owner's rights to the business's assets are determined after the rights of the creditors are subtracted. In other words, creditors have first claim to assets. If a firm has no

Assets Properties (resources) of value owned by a business (cash, supplies, equipment, land).

Equities The rights or financial claim of creditors (liabilities) and owners (owner's equity) who supply the assets to a firm.

Liabilities Obligations that come due in the future. Liabilities are the financial rights or claims of creditors to assets.

Creditor Someone who has a claim to assets.

Owner's equity Rights or financial claims to the assets of a business (in the accounting equation, assets minus liabilities).

 L02

Basic accounting equation
Assets = Liabilities + Owner's Equity.

Capital The owner's investment of equity in the company.

liabilities—therefore no creditors—the owner has the total rights to assets. Another term for the owner's current investment, or equity, in the business's assets is capital.

As Mia Wong's law firm engages in business transactions (paying bills, serving customers, and so on), changes will take place in the assets, liabilities, and owner's equity (capital). Let's analyze some of these transactions.

COACHING TIP

In accounting, capital does not mean cash. Capital is the owner's current investment, or equity, in the assets of the business.

Transaction A Aug. 28: Mia invests $6,000 in cash and $200 of office equipment into the business.

On August 28, Mia withdraws $6,000 from her personal bank account and deposits the money in the law firm's newly opened bank account. She also invests $200 of office equipment in the business. She plans to be open for business on September 1. With the help of her accountant, Mia begins to prepare the accounting records for the business. We put this information into the basic accounting equation as follows:

Assets			= Liabilities + Owner's Equity
Cash	+	Office Equipment	=	Mia Wong, Capital
$6,000	+	$200	=	$6,200
		$6,200 = $6,200		

Note that the total value of the assets, cash, and office equipment—$6,200—is equal to the combined total value of liabilities (none, so far) and owner's equity ($6,200). Remember, Mia has supplied all the cash and office equipment, so she has the sole financial claim to the assets. Note how the heading "Mia Wong, Capital" is written under the owner's equity heading. The $6,200 is Mia's investment, or equity, in the firm's assets.

Transaction B Aug. 29: Law practice buys office equipment for cash, $500.

From the initial investment of $6,000 cash, the law firm buys $500 worth of office equipment (such as a computer desk), which lasts a long time, whereas supplies (such as pens) tend to be used up relatively quickly.

Supplies One type of asset acquired by a firm; it has a much shorter life than equipment.

	Assets			= Liabilities + Owner's Equity
	Cash	+	Office Equipment	=	Mia Wong, Capital
Beginning Balance	$6,000	+	$200	=	$6,200
Transaction	−500		+500		
Ending Balance	$5,500	+	$700	=	$6,200
			$6,200 = $6,200		

Shift in assets A shift that occurs when the composition of the assets has changed but the total of the assets remains the same.

Shift in Assets As a result of the last transaction, the law office has less cash but has increased its amount of office equipment. This shift in assets indicates that the makeup of the assets has changed, but the total of the assets remains the same.

Suppose you go food shopping at Walmart with $100 and spend $60. Now you have two assets, food and money. The composition of your assets has *shifted*—you have more food and less money than you did—but the *total* of the assets has not increased or decreased. The total value of the food, $60, plus the cash, $40, is still $100. When you borrow money from the bank, on the other hand, you increase cash (an asset) and increase liabilities at the same time. This action results in an increase in assets, not just a shift.

An accounting equation can remain in balance even if only one side is updated. The key point to remember is that the left-hand-side total of assets must always equal the right-hand-side total of liabilities and owner's equity.

Transaction C Aug. 30: Buys additional office equipment on account, $300.

The law firm purchases an additional $300 worth of chairs and desks from Wilmington Company. Instead of demanding cash right away, Wilmington agrees to deliver the equipment and to allow up to 60 days for the law practice to pay the invoice (bill).

This liability, or obligation to pay in the future, has some interesting effects on the basic accounting equation. Wilmington Company accepts as payment a partial claim against the assets of the law practice. This claim exists until the law firm pays off the bill. This unwritten promise to pay the creditor is a liability called **accounts payable**.

Accounts payable Amounts owed to creditors that result from the purchase of goods or services on account—a liability.

Assets			=	Liabilities	+	Owner's Equity	
Cash	+	Office Equipment	=	Accounts Payable	+	Mia Wong, Capital	
$5,500	+	$ 700	=			$6,200	Beginning Balance
		+300		+$300			Transaction
$5,500	+	$1,000	=	$300	+	$6,200	Ending Balance
			$6,500 = $6,500				

When this information is analyzed, we can see that the law practice increased what it owes (accounts payable) as well as what it owns (office equipment) by $300. The law practice gains $300 in an asset but also takes on an obligation to pay Wilmington Company at a future date.

The owner's equity remains unchanged. This transaction results in an increase of total assets from $6,200 to $6,500.

Finally, note that after each transaction the basic accounting equation remains in balance.

LEARNING UNIT 1-1 REVIEW

AT THIS POINT you should be able to do the following:

- Define and explain the purpose of the Sarbanes-Oxley Act.
- Define and explain the differences between sole proprietorships, partnerships, and corporations.
- Explain the difference between GAAP and IFRS.
- List the functions of accounting.
- Compare and contrast bookkeeping and accounting.
- Explain the role of the computer as an accounting tool.
- State the purpose of the accounting equation.
- Explain the difference between liabilities and owner's equity.
- Define capital.
- Explain the difference between a shift in assets and an increase in assets.

To test your understanding of this material, complete Instant Replay: Self-Review Quiz 1-1. The blank forms you need for all Self-Review quizzes and end-of-chapter material throughout the textbook can be found in the *Study Guide and Working Papers*. The solution to the quiz immediately follows here in the text. If you have difficulty doing the problems, review Learning Unit 1-1 and the solution to the quiz along with a detailed explanation called Play by Play: Extra Help on Self-Review Quiz with Jeff Slater, your author. Be sure to check the Slater Web site for student study aids.

Keep in mind that learning accounting is like learning to type: The more you practice, the better you become. You will not be an expert in one day. Be patient. It will all come together.

Instant Replay ⊙ Self-Review Quiz 1-1

Record the following transactions in the basic accounting equation:

1. Gracie Ryan invests $17,000 cash to begin a real estate company.
2. The real estate company buys $600 of computer equipment from Walmart for cash.
3. The real estate company buys $800 of additional computer equipment on account from Best Buy.

Solution to Instant Replay: Self-Review Quiz 1-1

	Assets		=	Liabilities	+	Owner's Equity
	Cash	+	Computer Equipment	=	Accounts Payable	+	Gracie Ryan, Capital
	+$17,000						+$17,000
1. Balance	17,000			=			17,000
	−600		+$600				
2. Balance	16,400	+	600	=			17,000
			+800		+$800		
3. Ending Balance	$16,400	+	$1,400	=	$800	+	$17,000

$17,800 = $17,800

PLAY BY PLAY: EXTRA HELP ON SELF-REVIEW QUIZ 1-1

Let's review first: The left side of the accounting equation shows what is owned by the business and the right side of the equation shows you who supplied those assets to a business. Now let's look at the transactions in the solution:

Transaction 1: In your head you must say to yourself, "What did the business get and how did it get it?" The business is getting or increasing its cash by $17,000 and that cash is being supplied by Gracie Ryan. Think of Gracie as increasing her rights in the business since she is supplying cash. Keep in mind that capital does not mean cash. Instead it is what the owner supplies to the business. (Gracie may in the future supply other items to the business.)

So the end result is to put $17,000 on the left side of the equation under cash and put $17,000 under Gracie Ryan, Capital on the right side. The sum of the left side must equal the sum on the right side.

Transaction 2: Here we are NOT looking at the personal finances of Gracie. You must focus on the business. What did the business get and who supplied it to the business?

In this transaction the business is getting $600 of computer equipment by using some of its cash. *It is shifting its assets: more equipment for less cash.* Note that capital is not affected since Gracie has not invested anything new into the business.

Note that the right side of the equation is not touched, but the equation still remains in the balance. We are just rearranging the composition of the assets.

Transaction 3: Now the business is getting more equipment but is not paying cash. The equipment is being supplied by a creditor called Accounts Payable. Hopefully in the future the business will be able to pay the creditor back the $800 that it owes. The end result is that the business now has $1,400 in equipment. Note that capital is not affected since no new investments were made by Gracie into the business.

Summary: At the end of these three transactions this company is made up of two assets, Cash $16,400 and Computer Equipment $1,400. The total of the assets was supplied by creditors $800 and the owner Gracie Ryan, Capital $17,000. The sum of the left side ($17,800) must equal the sum of the right side ($17,800).

COACHING TIP

$17,800 $17,800

LEARNING UNIT 1-2 THE BALANCE SHEET

In the first learning unit, the transactions for Mia Wong's law firm were recorded in the accounting equation. The transactions we recorded occurred before the law firm opened for business. A statement called a balance sheet or statement of financial position can show the financial position of a company before it opened. The balance sheet is a formal statement that presents the information from the ending balances of both sides of the accounting equation. Think of the balance sheet as a snapshot of the business's financial position as of a particular date.

Let's look at the balance sheet of Mia Wong's law practice for August 31, 201X, shown in Figure 1.1. The figures in the balance sheet come from the ending balances of the accounting equation for the law practice as shown in Learning Unit 1-1.

Balance sheet A statement, as of a particular date, that shows the amount of assets owned by a business as well as the amount of claims (liabilities and owner's equity) against these assets. Also known as statement of financial position.

COACHING TIP

The balance sheet shows the company's financial position as of a particular date. (In our example, that date is at the end of August.)

FIGURE 1.1
The Balance Sheet

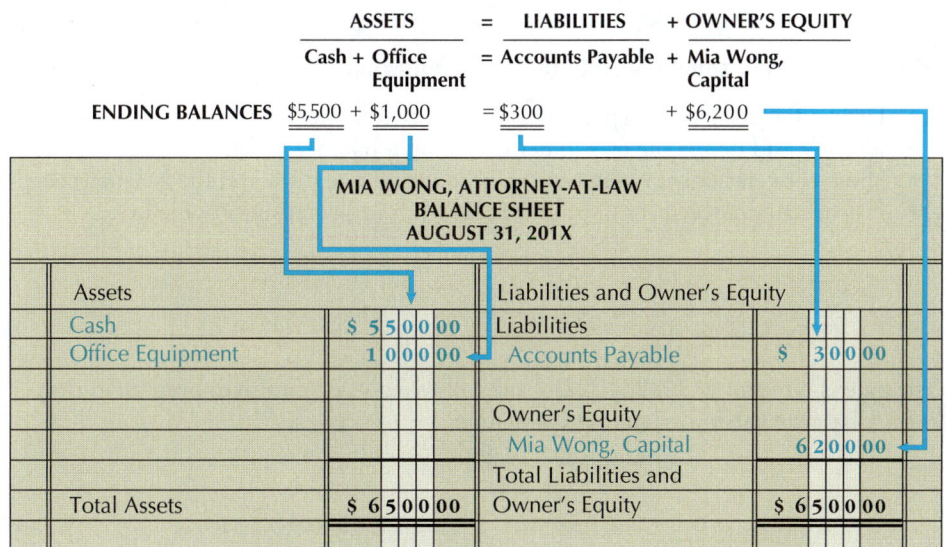

Note in Figure 1.1 that the assets owned by the law practice appear on the left-hand side and that the liabilities and owner's equity appear on the right-hand side. Both sides equal $6,500. This *balance* between left and right gives the balance sheet its name. In later chapters we look at other ways to set up a balance sheet.

Points to Remember in Preparing a Balance Sheet

The Heading The heading of the balance sheet provides the following information:
- The company name: Mia Wong, Attorney-at-Law
- The name of the statement: Balance Sheet
- The date for which the report is prepared: August 31, 201X

Use of the Dollar Sign Note that the dollar sign is not repeated each time a figure appears. As shown in Figure 1.2, the balance sheet for Mia Wong's law practice, it usually is placed to the left of each column's top figure and to the left of the column's total.

Distinguishing the Total When adding numbers down a column, use a single line above the total and a double line beneath it. A single line means that the numbers above it have been added or subtracted. A double line indicates a total. It is important to align the numbers in the column; many errors occur because these figures are not lined up. These rules are the same for all accounting reports.

The balance sheet gives Mia the information she needs to see the law firm's financial position before it opens for business. This information does not tell her, however, whether the firm made a profit.

FIGURE 1.2 Partial Balance Sheet

MIA WONG, ATTORNEY-AT-LAW BALANCE SHEET AUGUST 31, 201X	
Assets	
Cash	$ 5 5 0 0 00
Office Equipment	1 0 0 0 00
Total Assets	$ 6 5 0 0 00

A single line means the numbers above it have been added or subtracted.

A double line indicates a total.

LEARNING UNIT 1-2 REVIEW

AT THIS POINT you should be able to do the following:

- Define and state the purpose of a balance sheet.
- Identify and define the elements making up a balance sheet.
- Show the relationship between the accounting equation and the balance sheet.
- Prepare a balance sheet in proper form from information provided.

Instant Replay ◉ Self-Review Quiz 1-2

The date is November 30, 201X. Use the following information to prepare in proper form a balance sheet for Janning Company:

Accounts Payable	$40,000
Cash	18,000
A. Janning, Capital	9,000
Office Equipment	31,000

Solution to Instant Replay: Self-Review Quiz 1-2

JANNING COMPANY BALANCE SHEET NOVEMBER 30, 201X					
Assets		Liabilities and Owner's Equity			
Cash	$18 000 00	Liabilities			
Office Equipment	31 000 00	Accounts Payable	$ 40 000 00		
		Owner's Equity			
		A. Janning, Capital	9 000 00		
		Total Liabilities and			
Total Assets	$ 4 9 000 00	Owner's Equity	$ 49 000 00		

FIGURE 1.3
Balance Sheet

Capital does not mean cash. The capital amount is the owner's current investment of assets in the business.

PLAY BY PLAY: EXTRA HELP ON SELF-REVIEW QUIZ 1-2

Let's review first: A photo of your family is like a balance sheet: It gives you a history of your family as of a particular date. The balance sheet is a formal report that lists assets, liabilities, and owner's equity for a business as of a particular date.

Before preparing the report, identify whether each item is an asset, liability, or owner's equity. Accounts payable is a liability. Hopefully the business will be able to pay. Cash is an asset, or something of value owned by the business. A. Janning, Capital is owner's equity, representing the value of the assets which the owner is supplying to the business.

The heading of a balance sheet answers three questions:

Who? Janning Company

What report? Balance Sheet

When? November 30, 201X

The left side of the balance sheet lists out the assets: cash, and office equipment.

The right side lists out who supplies the assets to the business: creditors (accounts payable) or the owner, A. Janning, Capital. Use single lines to add and double lines for totals. The sum of the left side must equal the sum of the right side.

LEARNING UNIT 1-3 THE ACCOUNTING EQUATION EXPANDED:
Revenue, Expenses, and Withdrawals

● **LO3**

As soon as Mia Wong's office opened on September 1, she began performing legal services for her clients and earning revenue for the business. At the same time, as a part of doing business, she incurred various expenses such as rent.

When Mia asked her accountant how these transactions fit into the accounting equation, she began by defining some terms.

Revenue

A service company earns revenue when it provides services to its clients. Mia's law firm earned revenue when she provided legal services to her clients for legal fees. When revenue is earned, owner's equity is increased. In effect, revenue is a subdivision of owner's equity.

Revenue An amount earned by performing services for customers or selling goods to customers; it can be in the form of cash or accounts receivable. A subdivision of owner's equity: As revenue increases, owner's equity increases.

Accounts receivable An asset that indicates amounts owed by customers.

Assets are increased. The increase is in the form of cash if the client pays right away. If the client promises to pay in the future, the increase is called accounts receivable. When revenue is earned, the transaction is recorded as an increase in revenue and an increase in assets (either as cash or as accounts receivable, depending on whether it was paid right away or will be paid in the future).

Expenses

Expense A cost incurred in running a business by consuming goods or services in producing revenue. A subdivision of owner's equity.

A business's expenses are the costs the company incurs in carrying on operations in its effort to create revenue. Expenses are also a subdivision of owner's equity; when expenses are incurred, they *decrease* owner's equity. Expenses can be paid for in cash or they can be charged.

Net Income/Net Loss

Net income When revenue totals more than expenses, the result is net income.

Net loss When expenses total more than revenue, the result is net loss.

When revenue totals more than expenses, net income is the result; when expenses total more than revenue, net loss is the result.

Withdrawals

Withdrawals A subdivision of owner's equity that records money or other assets an owner withdraws from a business for personal use.

At some point Mia Wong may need to withdraw cash or other assets from the business to pay living or other personal expenses that do not relate to the business. We will record these transactions in an account called withdrawals. Sometimes this account is called the *owner's drawing account*. Withdrawals is a subdivision of owner's equity that records personal expenses not related to the business. Withdrawals decrease owner's equity (see Figure 1.4 below).

It is important to remember the difference between expenses and withdrawals. Expenses relate to business operations; withdrawals are the result of personal needs outside the normal operations of the business.

Now let's analyze the September transactions for Mia Wong's law firm using an expanded accounting equation that includes withdrawals, revenues, and expenses.

Expanded accounting equation Assets = Liabilities + Capital – Withdrawals + Revenue – Expenses.

Expanded Accounting Equation

Transaction D Sept. 1–30: Provided legal services for cash, $2,000.

Transactions A, B, and C were discussed earlier, when the law office was being formed in August. See Learning Unit 1.1.

FIGURE 1.4
Owner's Equity

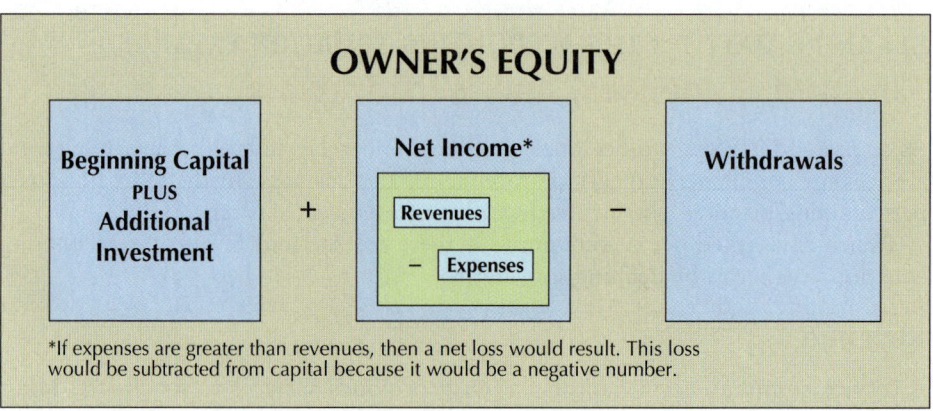

Assets			=	Liabilities	+		Owner's Equity			
Cash	+ Accts. Rec.	+ Office Equip.	=	Accts. Pay.	+ M. Wong, Capital	− M. Wong, Withdr.	+ Revenue	− Expenses		
$5,500		+ $1,000	=	$300	+ $6,200					Balance Forward
+2,000							+ $2,000			
$7,500		+ $1,000	=	$300	+ $6,200		+ $2,000			Ending Balance
		$8,500 = $8,500								

COACHING TIP

In the law firm's first month of operation, a total of $2,000 in cash was received for legal services performed. In the accounting equation, the asset Cash is increased by $2,000. Revenue is also increased by $2,000, resulting in an increase in total owner's equity.

Remember: Accounts receivables result from earning revenue even when cash is not yet received.

Record an expense when it is incurred, whether it is paid immediately or is to be paid later.

A revenue column was added to the basic accounting equation. Amounts are recorded in the revenue column when they are earned. They are also recorded in the assets column under Cash and/or Accounts Receivable (see also Transaction E below). Do not think of revenue as an asset. It is part of owner's equity. It is the revenue that creates an inward flow of cash and accounts receivable.

Transaction E Sept. 1–30: Provided legal services on account, $3,000.

	Assets		=	Liabilities	+		Owner's Equity		
Cash	+ Accts. Rec.	+ Office Equip.	=	Accts. Pay.	+ M. Wong, Capital	− M. Wong, Withdr.	+ Revenue	− Expenses	
$7,500		+ $ 1,000	=	$ 300	+ $6,200		+ $2,000		Bal. for Trans.
	+$3,000						+ 3,000		
$7,500	+ $3,000	+ $ 1,000	=	$ 300	+ $6,200		+ $5,000		End. Bal.
		$11,500	=	$11,500					

Mia's law practice performed legal work on account for $3,000. The firm did not receive the cash for these earned legal fees; it accepted an unwritten promise from these clients that payment would be received in the future.

Transaction F Sept. 1–30: Received $900 cash as partial payment from previous services performed on account.

During September some of Mia's clients who had received services and promised to pay in the future decided to reduce what they owed the practice by making payment of $900. This decision is shown as follows on the expanded accounting equation:

	Assets		=	Liabilities	+		Owner's Equity		
Cash	+ Accts. Rec.	+ Office Equip.	=	Accts. Pay.	+ M. Wong, Capital	− M. Wong, Withdr.	+ Revenue	− Expenses	
$7,500	+ $3,000	+ $ 1,000	=	$ 300	+ $6,200		+ $5,000		Bal. for. Trans.
+900	−900								
$8,400	+ $2,100	+ $ 1,000	=	$ 300	+ $6,200		+ $5,000		End. Bal.
		$11,500	=	$11.500					

The law firm increased the asset Cash by $900 and reduced another asset, Accounts Receivable, by $900. The *total* of assets does not change. The right-hand side of the expanded accounting equation has not been touched because the total on the left-hand side of the equation has not changed. The revenue was recorded when it was earned (see Transaction E), and the *same revenue cannot be recorded twice*. This transaction analyzes the situation *after* the revenue has been previously earned and recorded. Transaction F shows a shift in assets resulting in more cash and less accounts receivable.

Transaction G Sept. 1–30: Paid salaries expense, $700.

	Assets			= Liabilities +		Owner's Equity			
	Cash	+ Accts. Rec.	+ Office Equip.	= Accts. Pay.	+ M. Wong, Capital	− M. Wong, Withdr.	+ Revenue	− Expenses
Bal. for Trans.	$8,400	+ $2,100	+ $ 1,000	= $ 300	+ $6,200		+ $5,000	
	−700							+ $700
End. Bal.	$7,700	+ $2,100	+ $ 1,000	= $ 300	+ $6,200		+ $5,000	− $700
			$10,800	= $10,800				

As expenses increase, they decrease owner's equity. This incurred expense of $700 reduces the cash by $700. Although the expense was paid, the total of our expenses to date has *increased* by $700. Keep in mind that owner's equity decreases as expenses increase, so the accounting equation remains in balance, because expenses are deducted from Owner's Equity.

Transaction H Sept. 1–30: Paid rent expense, $400.

	Assets			= Liabilities +		Owner's Equity			
	Cash	+ Accts. Rec.	+ Office Equip.	= Accts. Pay.	+ M. Wong, Capital	− M. Wong, Withdr.	+ Revenue	− Expenses
Bal. for Trans.	$7,700	+ $2,100	+ $ 1,000	= $ 300	+ $6,200		+ $5,000	− $700
	−400							+400
End. Bal.	$7,300	+ $2,100	+ $ 1,000	= $ 300	+ $6,200		+ $5,000	− $1,100
			$10,400	= $10,400				

During September the practice incurred rent expenses of $400. This rent was not paid in advance; it was paid when it came due. The payment of rent reduces the asset Cash by $400 as well as increases the expenses of the firm, resulting in a decrease in owner's equity. The firm's expenses are now $1,100.

Transaction I Sept. 1–30: Incurred advertising expenses of $200, to be paid next month.

	Assets			= Liabilities +		Owner's Equity			
	Cash	+ Accts. Rec.	+ Office Equip.	= Accts. Pay.	+ M. Wong, Capital	− M. Wong, Withdr.	+ Revenue	− Expenses
Bal. for Trans.	$7,300	+ $2,100	+ $ 1,000	= $ 300	+ $6,200		+ $5,000	− $1,100
				+200				+200
End. Bal.	$7,300	+ $2,100	+ $ 1,000	= $ 500	+ $6,200		+ $5,000	− $1,300
			$10,400	= $10,400				

Mia ran an ad in the local newspaper and incurred an expense of $200. This increase in expenses caused a corresponding decrease in owner's equity. Because Mia has not paid the newspaper for the advertising yet, she owes $200. Thus her liabilities (Accounts Payable) increase by $200. Eventually, when the bill comes in and is paid, both Cash and Accounts Payable will be decreased.

Transaction J Sept. 1–30: Mia withdrew $100 for personal use.

	Assets			=	Liabilities	+		Owner's Equity				
Cash	+ Accts. Rec.	+ Office Equip.		= Accts. Pay.		+ M. Wong, Capital	– M. Wong, Withdr.	+ Revenue	– Expenses		
$7,300	+ $2,100	+ $ 1,000	= $ 500		+ $6,200			+ $5,000	– $1,300	Bal. for Trans.
–100						+$100				
$7,200	+ $2,100	+ $ 1,000	= $ 500		+ $6,200	– $100		+ $5,000	– $1,300	End. Bal.
		$10,300	= $10,300							

By taking $100 for personal use, Mia *increased* her withdrawals from the business by $100 and decreased the asset Cash by $100. Note that as withdrawals increase, the owner's equity *decreases*. Keep in mind that a withdrawal is *not* a business expense. It is a subdivision of owner's equity that records money or other assets an owner withdraws from the business for *personal* use.

Subdivision of Owner's Equity Take a moment to review the subdivisions of owner's equity:

- As capital increases, owner's equity increases (see transaction A).
- As withdrawals increase, owner's equity decreases (see transaction J).
- As revenue increases, owner's equity increases (see transaction D and E).
- As expenses increase, owner's equity decreases (see transaction G through I).

Mia Wong's Expanded Accounting Equation The following is a summary of the expanded accounting equation for Mia Wong's law firm.

Mia Wong Attorney-at-Law Expanded Accounting Equation: A Summary										
Assets			**= Liabilities**	+		**Owner's Equity**				
Cash	+ Accts. Rec.	+ Office Equip.	= Accts. Pay.	+ M. Wong, Capital	– M. Wong, Withdr.	+ Revenue	– Expenses		
$6,000		+$200 =		+$6,200				A.	
6,000	+	200 =		6,200				Balance	
–500		+500						B.	
5,500	+	700 =		6,200				Balance	
		+300	+$300					C.	
5,500 +		1,000 =	300 +	6,200				Balance	
+2,000						+$2,000		D.	
7,500	+	1,000 =	300 +	6,200		+ 2,000		Balance	
+	$3,000					+3,000		E.	
7,500 +	3,000 +	1,000 =	300 +	6,200		+ 5,000		Balance	
+900	–900							F.	
8,400 +	2,100 +	1,000 =	300 +	6,200		+ 5,000		Balance	

(continued on page 16)

Mia Wong													
Attorney-at-Law													
Expanded Accounting Equation: A Summary													
Assets				**= Liabilities**		**+**			**Owner's Equity**				
	Cash	+ Accts. Rec.	+ Office Equip.	=	Accts. Pay.	+ M. Wong, Capital	– M. Wong, Withdr.	+	Revenue	– Expenses			
G.	–700									+$700			
Balance	7,700 +	2,100 +	1,000 =		300 +	6,200		+	5,000 –	700			
H.	–400									+400			
Balance	7,300 +	2,100 +	1,000 =		300 +	6,200		+	5,000 –	1,100			
I.					+200					+200			
Balance	7,300 +	2,100 +	1,000 =		500 +	6,200		+	5,000 –	1,300			
J.	–100						+$100						
End Balance	$7,200 +	$2,100 +	$1,000 =		$500 +	$6,200 –	$100 +		$5,000 –	$1,300			
					$10,300 = $10,300								

LEARNING UNIT 1-3 REVIEW

AT THIS POINT you should be able to do the following:

- Define and explain the difference between revenue and expenses.
- Define and explain the difference between net income and net loss.
- Explain the subdivisions of owner's equity.
- Explain the effects of withdrawals, revenue, and expenses on owner's equity.
- Record transactions in an expanded accounting equation and balance the basic accounting equation as a means of checking the accuracy of your calculations.

▸ Instant Replay ◉ Self-Review Quiz 1-3

Record the following transactions into the expanded accounting equation for the Bing Company. Note that all titles have a beginning balance.

1. Received cash revenue, $4,000.
2. Billed customers for services rendered, $6,000.
3. Received a bill for telephone expenses (to be paid next month), $125.
4. Bob Bing withdrew cash for personal use, $500.
5. Received $1,000 from customers in partial payment for services performed in transaction 2.

Solution to Instant Replay Self-Review Quiz 1-3

Assets			**= Liabilities**		**+**		**Owner's Equity**			
	Cash	+ Accts. Rec.	+ Cleaning Equip.	= Accts. Pay.	+ B. Bing, Capital	– B. Bing, Withdr.	+ Revenue	– Expenses		
Beg. Balance	$10,000 +	$2,500 +	$6,500 =	$1,000 +	$11,800 –	$ 800 +	$9,000	–	$2,000	
1.	+4,000						+4,000			
Balance	14,000 +	2,500 +	6,500 =	1,000 +	11,800 –	800 +	13,000	–	2,000	
2.		+6,000					+6,000			
Balance	14,000 +	8,500 +	6,500 =	1,000 +	11,800 –	800 +	19,000	–	2,000	
3.				+125					+125	
Balance	14,000 +	8,500 +	6,500 =	1,125 +	11,800 –	800 +	19,000	–	2,125	

(continued on page 17)

Assets			= Liabilities		+		Owner's Equity			
Cash	+ Accts. Rec.	+ Cleaning Equip.	= Accts. Pay.	+ B. Bing, Capital	–	B. Bing, Withdr.	+ Revenue	–	Expenses	
–500						+$500				4.
13,500	+ 8,500 +	6,500 =	1,125 +	11,800 –		1,300 +	19,000 –		2,125	Balance
+1,000	–1,000									5.
$14,500	+ $7,500 +	$6,500 =	$1,125 +	$11,800 –		$1,300 +	$19,000 –		$2,125	End. Balance
			$28,500 = $28,500							

PLAY BY PLAY: EXTRA HELP ON SELF-REVIEW QUIZ 1-3

Let's review first: You only record revenue when it is earned. What can the business get? Cash and/or promises from customers called Accounts Receivable. Revenue is not an asset but does provide an inward flow of assets into the business. Revenue is part of owner's equity. Think of expenses as always increasing in a business. The end result will be a decrease in owner's equity. Expenses are recorded when they happen and can be paid for by cash or charged as Accounts Payable.

Withdrawals work just like expenses as they also are deducted from Owner's Equity, but they represent personal withdrawals by the owner. Expenses and withdrawals are not recorded together. Each has a separate title.

Transaction 1: The company has done the work. It now records revenue of $4,000 in the revenue column (we only put numbers in this column when we do the work). This time the inward flow of assets from the revenue is all in the form of cash of $4,000.

Transaction 2: This time the company does the work but is not getting the cash. It is receiving promises that it will be paid in the future. You record the $6,000 in the revenue column because you did the work. The inward flow from this revenue is not cash but promises called Accounts Receivable. Thus, the Accounts Receivable column is increased by $6,000.

Transaction 3: An expense has happened and should be recorded whether money is paid or not. The expenses for telephone have INCREASED by $125, resulting in the total expenses rising to $2,125. As expenses in a business rise, the end result is a reduction in owner's equity.

Since the expense was charged, the $125 is recorded under Accounts Payable because hopefully the expense will be paid in the future. At this point this telephone expense has created a liability. Remember that an expense is not a liability.

Transaction 4: This transaction relates to a personal transaction and does not affect any expenses in the business. Bob Bing takes $500 cash from the business. Think of Bob as receiving the $500, but in reality his owner's rights will be reduced. This is shown by a $500 increase under withdrawals, which now results in a total of $1,300 (a reduction to owner's equity) and a decrease to cash. Note that expenses are not affected since this is a personal transaction.

Transaction 5: No new work is done, so we do not earn or record any new revenue. Here customers are paying part of what they owe. The result is that company cash increased by $1,000 and Accounts Receivable is reduced by $1,000. This is a shift in assets: more cash, less accounts receivable.

Summary: Note the four subdivisions of owner's equity: Capital, Withdrawals, Revenues, and Expenses. As capital and revenue increases, owner's equity will increase. As expenses and withdrawals increase, owner's equity will decrease. Revenue is not an asset. Rather, it provides assets in the form of cash and/or accounts receivable. Only record revenue when work is done. Only record expenses when they happen, regardless of whether cash is paid.

COACHING TIP

Revenue is shown when earned, not when cash is received.

LO4   LEARNING UNIT 1-4 PREPARING FINANCIAL STATEMENTS

Mia Wong would like to be able to find out if her firm is making a profit, so she asks her accountant if he can measure the firm's financial performance on a monthly basis. Her accountant replies that a number of financial statements that he can prepare, such as the income statement, will show Mia how well the law firm has performed over a specific period of time. The accountant can use the information in the income statement to prepare other reports.

The Income Statement

Income statement An accounting statement that details the performance of a firm (revenue minus expenses) for a specific period of time.

An income statement is an accounting statement that shows business results in terms of revenue and expenses. If revenues are greater than expenses, the report shows net income. If expenses are greater than revenues, the report shows net loss. An income statement typically covers 1, 3, 6, or 12 months. It cannot cover more than one year. The statement shows the result of all revenues and expenses throughout the entire period and not just as of a specific date. The income statement for Mia Wong's law firm is shown in Figure 1.5.

Points to Remember in Preparing an Income Statement

Heading The heading of an income statement tells the company's name, the name of the statement, and the period of time the statement covers.

The Setup As you can see on the income statement, the inside column of numbers ($700, $400, and $200) is used to subtotal all expenses ($1,300) before subtracting them from revenue ($5,000 − $1,300 = $3,700).

COACHING TIP

The income statement is prepared from data found in the revenue and expense columns of the expanded accounting equation. The inside column of numbers ($700, $400, $200) is used to subtotal all expenses ($1,300) before subtracting from revenue.

FIGURE 1.5
The Income Statement

MIA WONG, ATTORNEY-AT-LAW INCOME STATEMENT FOR MONTH ENDED SEPTEMBER 30, 201X		
Revenue:		
Legal Fees		$ 5 0 0 0 00
Operating Expenses:		
Salaries Expense	$ 7 0 0 00	
Rent Expense	4 0 0 00	
Advertising Expense	2 0 0 00	
Total Operating Expenses		1 3 0 0 00
Net Income		$ 3 7 0 0 00

Operating expenses may be listed in alphabetical order, in order of largest amounts to smallest, or in a set order established by the accountant.

The Statement of Owner's Equity

Statement of owner's equity A financial statement that reveals the change in capital. The ending figure for capital is then placed on the balance sheet.

As we said, the income statement is a business statement that shows business results in terms of revenue and expenses, but how does net income or net loss affect owner's equity? To find out, we have to look at a second type of statement, the statement of owner's equity.

The statement of owner's equity shows for a certain period of time what changes occurred in Mia Wong, Capital. The statement of owner's equity is shown in Figure 1.6.

The capital of Mia Wong can be

Increased by: Owner Investment
Net Income (Revenue – Expenses) and Revenue Greater Than Expenses
Decreased by: Owner Withdrawals
Net Loss (Revenue – Expenses) and Expenses Greater Than Revenue

Remember, a withdrawal is *not* a business expense and thus, is not involved in the calculation of net income or net loss on the income statement. It appears on the statement of owner's equity. The statement of owner's equity summarizes the effects of all the subdivisions of owner's equity (revenue, expenses, withdrawals) on beginning capital. The ending capital figure ($9,800) will be the beginning figure in the next statement of owner's equity.

Suppose Mia's law firm had operated at a loss in the month of September. Suppose that instead of net income, a $400 net loss occurred and an additional investment of $700 was made on September 15. Figure 1.7 shows how the statement would look with this net loss and additional investment.

COACHING TIP

If this statement of owner's equity is omitted, the information will be included in the owner's equity section of the balance sheet.

FIGURE 1.6
Statement of Owner's Equity—Net Income

MIA WONG, ATTORNEY-AT-LAW STATEMENT OF OWNER'S EQUITY FOR MONTH ENDED SEPTEMBER 30, 201X		
Mia Wong, Capital, September 1, 201X		$ 6 2 0 0 00
Net Income for September	$ 3 7 0 0 00	
Less Withdrawals for September	1 0 0 00	
Increase in Capital		3 6 0 0 00
Mia Wong, Capital, September 30, 201X		$ 9 8 0 0 00

Comes from Income Statement

FIGURE 1.7
Statement of Owner's Equity—Net Loss

MIA WONG, ATTORNEY-AT-LAW STATEMENT OF OWNER'S EQUITY FOR MONTH ENDED SEPTEMBER 30, 201X		
Mia Wong, Capital, September 1, 201X		$ 6 2 0 0 00
Additional Investment, September 15, 201X		7 0 0 00
Total Investment for September*		$ 6 9 0 0 00
Less: Net Loss for September	$ 4 0 0 00	
Withdrawals for September	1 0 0 00	
Decrease in Capital		5 0 0 00
Mia Wong, Capital, September 30, 201X		$ 6 4 0 0 00

*Beginning capital and additional investments.

The Balance Sheet

Now let's look at how to prepare a balance sheet from the expanded accounting equation (see Figure 1.8, p. 20). As you can see, the asset accounts (cash, accounts receivable, and office equipment) appear on the left side of the balance sheet.

Accounts payable and Mia Wong, Capital appear on the right side. Notice that the $9,800 of capital can be calculated within the accounting equation or can be read from the statement of owner's equity.

FIGURE 1.8
The Accounting Equation and the Balance Sheet

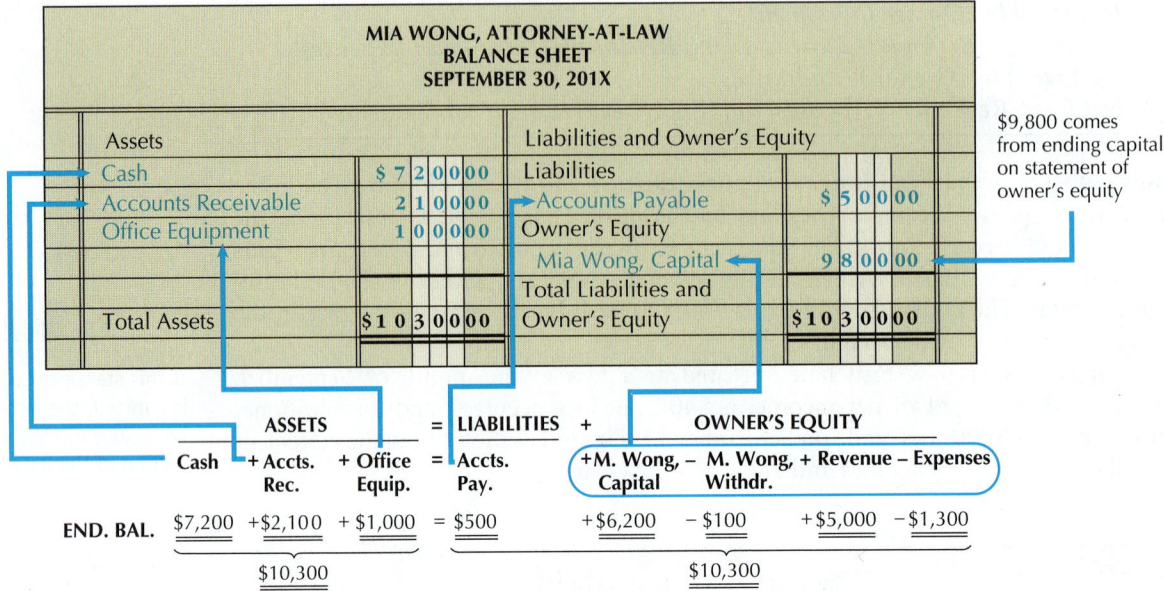

Main Elements of the Income Statement, the Statement of Owner's Equity, and the Balance Sheet

In this chapter we have discussed three financial statements: the income statement, the statement of owner's equity, and the balance sheet. A fourth statement, called the statement of cash flows, will not be covered at this time. Let us review what elements of the expanded accounting equation go into each statement and the usual order in which the statements are prepared. Figure 1.8 presents a diagram of the accounting equation and the balance sheet. Table 1.3 summarizes the following points:

- The income statement is prepared first; it includes revenues and expenses and shows net income or net loss. This net income or net loss is used to update the next statement, the statement of owner's equity.
- The statement of owner's equity is prepared second; it includes beginning capital and any additional investments, the net income or net loss shown on the income statement, withdrawals, and the total, which is the ending capital. The balance in Capital comes from the statement of owner's equity.

Ending capital Beginning Capital + Additional Investments + Net Income Withdrawals = Ending Capital. Or: Beginning Capital + Additional Investments − Net Loss − Withdrawals = Ending Capital.

TABLE 1.3 What Goes on Each Financial Statement

	Income Statement	Statement of Owner's Equity	Balance Sheet
Assets			X
Liabilities			X
Capital* (beg.)		X	
Capital (end)		X	X
Withdrawals		X	
Revenues	X		
Expenses	X		

*Note: Additional Investments go on the statement of owner's equity.

COACHING TIP

Net income is reported separately from capital on the balance sheet in the equity section in both QuickBooks and Peachtree.

- The balance sheet is prepared last; it includes the final balances of each of the elements listed in the accounting equation under Assets and Liabilities. The balance in Capital comes from the statement of owner's equity.

LEARNING UNIT 1-4 REVIEW

AT THIS POINT you should be able to do the following:

- Define and state the purpose of the income statement, the statement of owner's equity, and the balance sheet.
- Discuss why the income statement should be prepared first.
- Show what happens on a statement of owner's equity when a net loss occurs.
- Compare and contrast these three financial statements.
- Calculate a new figure for capital on the statement of owner's equity and the balance sheet.

Instant Replay ⊙ Self-Review Quiz 1-4

From the balances listed next for Rusty Realty prepare the following:

1. Income statement for the month ended November 30, 201X.
2. Statement of owner's equity for the month ended November 30, 201X.
3. Balances as of November 30, 201X.

Cash	$4,000	R. Rusty, Capital	
Accounts Receivable	1,370	November 1, 201X	$5,000
Store Furniture	1,490	R. Rusty, Withdrawals	100
Accounts Payable	900	Commissions Earned	1,500
		Rent Expense	200
		Advertising Expense	150
		Salaries Expense	90

Solution to Instant Replay: Self-Review Quiz 1-4

FIGURE 1.9
Financial Statements

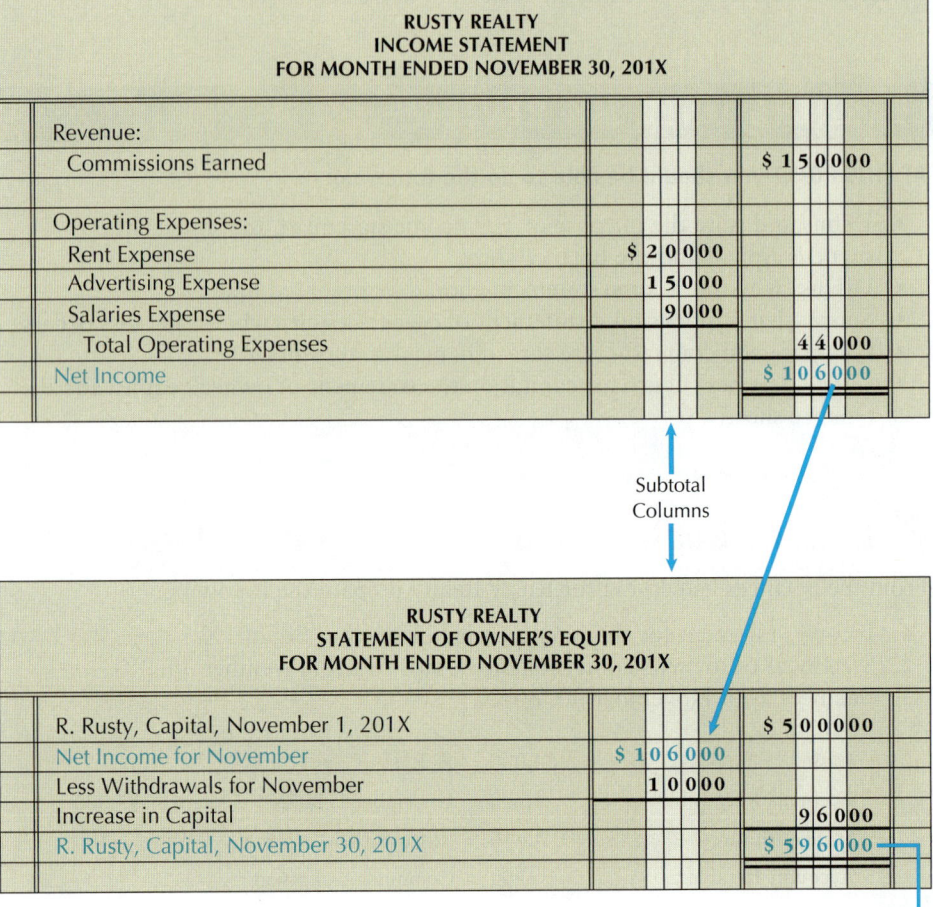

RUSTY REALTY
INCOME STATEMENT
FOR MONTH ENDED NOVEMBER 30, 201X

Revenue:		
Commissions Earned		$ 1 5 0 0 00
Operating Expenses:		
Rent Expense	$ 2 0 0 00	
Advertising Expense	1 5 0 00	
Salaries Expense	9 0 00	
Total Operating Expenses		4 4 0 00
Net Income		$ 1 0 6 0 00

Subtotal
Columns

RUSTY REALTY
STATEMENT OF OWNER'S EQUITY
FOR MONTH ENDED NOVEMBER 30, 201X

R. Rusty, Capital, November 1, 201X		$ 5 0 0 0 00
Net Income for November	$ 1 0 6 0 00	
Less Withdrawals for November	1 0 0 00	
Increase in Capital		9 6 0 00
R. Rusty, Capital, November 30, 201X		$ 5 9 6 0 00

RUSTY REALTY
BALANCE SHEET
NOVEMBER 30, 201X

Assets		Liabilities and Owner's Equity		
Cash	$ 4 0 0 0 00	Liabilities		
Accounts Receivable	1 3 7 0 00	Accounts Payable	$	9 0 0 00
Store Furniture	1 4 9 0 00			
		Owner's Equity		
		R. Rusty, Capital		5 9 6 0 00
		Total Liabilities and		
Total Assets	$ 6 8 6 0 00	Owner's Equity		$ 6 8 6 0 00

PLAY BY PLAY: EXTRA HELP ON SELF-REVIEW QUIZ 1-4

Let's review first: The first formal report is the income statement, which is made up of only revenues and expenses. This report shows how a company is performing for a specific period of time. The second report is the statement of the owner's equity. This report shows how capital has changed from its beginning balance during this period of time. The net income is added to the beginning balance less any personal withdrawals resulting in a new figure for capital, which will also be placed in the balance sheet. This third report, the balance sheet, is made up of assets, liabilities, and the new figure for capital. The balance sheet shows the history of the company as of a particular date.

The Income Statement: Commissions earned is the revenue for Rusty Realty. It is listed to the right since it is the only revenue. The inside column will be used for a subtotal if there is more than one revenue.

Rent, Advertising, and Salaries are expenses that are listed on the income statement. Note that we use the inside column to subtotal them and then list the final figure as total operating expenses of $440 in the right column. The difference between revenue ($1,500) and the total operating expenses ($440) results in a net income of $1,060. Keep in mind that net income is not cash. Remember that some revenue may not have resulted in cash and some of the expenses may not have been paid for in cash.

Statement of Owner's Equity: The beginning balance of Rusty, Capital is $5,000. We place this to the right because it is one number. We then use the inside column to add net income from the income statement ($1,060) and subtract any withdrawals ($100) to get an increase in capital of $960, which is placed in the right column. This figure is then added to beginning capital to arrive at Rusty, Capital (ending) of $5,960.

Balance Sheet: All the assets are listed on the left (cash, accounts receivable, and store furniture), for a total of $6,860. The liability of $900 for accounts payable is listed on the right and will be added to the new figure for Rusty, Capital of $5,960 from the statement of owner's equity.

Summary: The income statement lists out revenue and expenses. No withdrawals are found on this report. The statement of owner's equity will show how capital changes by net income, net loss, and/or withdrawals. The balance shows the new history of the company's assets, liabilities, and a new figure for capital.

COACHING TIP

The balance sheet shows the latest or ending balance in capital.

DEMONSTRATION PROBLEM

L02,3,4

Michael Brown opened his law office on June 1, 201X. During the first month of operations, Michael conducted the following transactions:

a. Invested $6,000 in cash into the law practice.
b. Paid $600 for office equipment.
c. Purchased additional office equipment on account, $1,000.
d. Received cash for performing legal services for clients, $2,000.
e. Paid salaries, $800.
f. Performed legal services for clients on account, $1,000.
g. Paid rent, $1,200.
h. Withdrew $500 from his law practice for personal use.
i. Received $500 from customers in partial payment for legal services performed, transaction 6.

(continued on page 24)

Requirements

1. Record these transactions in the expanded accounting equation.
2. Prepare the financial statements at June 30 for Michael Brown, Attorney-at-Law.

Demonstration Problem Solutions

Requirement 1
Record these transactions in the expanded accounting equation.

	Part 1	Part 2	Demonstration Problem Complete

	Assets			= Liabilities +		Owner's Equity			
A.	Cash	+ Accts. Rec.	+ Office Equip.	= Accounts Payable	+ M. Brown, Capital	– M. Brown, Withdr.	+ Legal Fees	– Expenses	
a.	+$6,000				+$6,000				
BAL.	6,000			=	6,000				
b.	–600		+$600						
BAL.	5,400	+	600 =		6,000				
c.			+1,000	+$1,000					
BAL.	5,400	+	1,600 =	1,000 +	6,000				
d.	+2,000						+$2,000		
BAL.	7,400	+	1,600 =	1,000 +	6,000	+	2,000		
e.	–800							+$800	
BAL.	6,600	+	1,600 =	1,000 +	6,000	+	2,000	–	800
f.	+$1,000						+1,000		
BAL.	6,600 +	1,000 +	1,600 =	1,000 +	6,000	+	3,000	–	800
g.	–1,200							+1,200	
BAL.	5,400 +	1,000 +	1,600 =	1,000 +	6,000	+	3,000	–	2,000
h.	–500					+$500			
BAL.	4,900 +	1,000 +	1,600 =	1,000 +	6,000	– 500	+	3,000	– 2,000
i.	+500	–500							
End. Bal.	$5,400 +	$500 +	$1,600 =	$1,000 +	$6,000	– $500	+	$3,000	– $2,000

$$\$7{,}500 = \$7{,}500$$

Solution Tips to Expanded Accounting Equation

- **Transaction a:** The business increased its Cash by $6,000. Owner's Equity (capital) increased when Michael supplied the cash to the business. Note how the equation is now in balance.
- **Transaction b:** A shift in assets occurred when the equipment was purchased. The business lowered its Cash by $600, and a new column—Office Equipment—was increased for the $600 of equipment that was bought. The amount of capital is not touched because the owner did not supply any new funds. You do not have to touch both sides of the equation to make it balance.
- **Transaction c:** When creditors supply $1,000 of additional equipment, the business Accounts Payable shows the debt. The business had increased what it *owes* the creditors. The end result is an increase in an asset and an increase in a liability.
- **Transaction d:** Legal Fees, a subdivision of Owner's Equity, is increased when the law firm provides a service even if no money is received. The service provides an inward flow of $2,000 to Cash, an asset. Remember that Legal Fees is *not* an asset. As Legal Fees revenue increase, Owner's Equity increases. Keep in mind that revenue can provide an inflow of cash and/or accounts receivable. Cash and accounts receivable are assets. The revenue is part of Owner's Equity.

- **Transaction e:** The salary paid by Michael creates an $800 increase in Expenses and a corresponding decrease in Owner's Equity as well as a decrease in Cash. Keep in mind that as the expenses increase they do in fact lower Owner's Equity.
- **Transaction f:** Michael did the work and earned the $1,000. That $1,000 is recorded as revenue. This time the legal fees create an inward flow of assets called Accounts Receivable for $1,000. Remember that Legal Fees is *not* an asset. It is a subdivision of Owner's Equity.
- **Transaction g:** The $1,200 rent expense reduces Owner's Equity as well as Cash. Remember to think of expenses as increasing. This increase in expenses then causes Owner's Equity to decrease.
- **Transaction h:** Withdrawals are for personal use. Here the business decreases Cash by $500 while Michael's withdrawals increase by $500. Withdrawals decrease the Owner's Equity. Remember to think of withdrawals as increasing. This is the amount withdrawn by the owner for personal use, decreasing Owner's Equity.
- **Transaction i:** This transaction does not reflect new revenue in the form of Legal Fees. It is only a shift in assets: more Cash and less Accounts Receivable.

Requirement 2

Prepare the financial statements at June 30 for Michael Brown, Attorney-at-Law.

Part 1	Part 2	Demonstration Problem Complete

Solution Tips to Financial Statements

a. The income statement lists only revenues and expenses for a period of time. The inside column is for subtotaling. Withdrawals are not listed here.

b. The statement of owner's equity takes the net income figure of $1,000 and adds it to beginning capital less any withdrawals. This new capital figure of $6,500 will go on the balance sheet. This statement shows changes in capital for a period of time.

c. The $5,400, $500, $1,600 (Assets) and $1,000 (Liabilities) came from the totals of the expanded accounting equation. The capital figure of $6,500 came from the statement of owner's equity. This balance sheet reports assets, liabilities, and a new figure for capital at a specific date.

A

MICHAEL BROWN, ATTORNEY-AT-LAW
INCOME STATEMENT
FOR MONTH ENDED JUNE 30, 201X

Revenue:		
Legal Fees		$3,000
Operating Expenses:		
Salaries Expense	$ 800	
Rent Expense	1,200	
Total Operating Expenses		2,000
Net Income		$1,000

B

MICHAEL BROWN, ATTORNEY-AT-LAW
STATEMENT OF OWNER'S EQUITY
FOR MONTH ENDED JUNE 30, 201X

Michael Brown, Capital, June 1, 201X		$6,000
Net income for June	$1,000	
Less withdrawls for June	500	
Increase in Capital		500
Michael Brown, Capital, June 30, 201X		$6,500

(continued on page 26)

C	MICHAEL BROWN, ATTORNEY-AT-LAW BALANCE SHEET JUNE 30, 201X		
Assets	**Liabilities and Owner's Equity**		
Cash	$5,400	Liabilities	
Accounts Receivable	500	Accounts Payable	$1,000
Office Equipment	1,600	Owner's Equity	
		M. Brown, Capital	$6,500
Total Assets	$7,500	Total Liabilities and Owner's Equity	$7,500

Part 1	Part 2	Demonstration Problem Complete

BLUEPRINT: FINANCIAL STATEMENTS

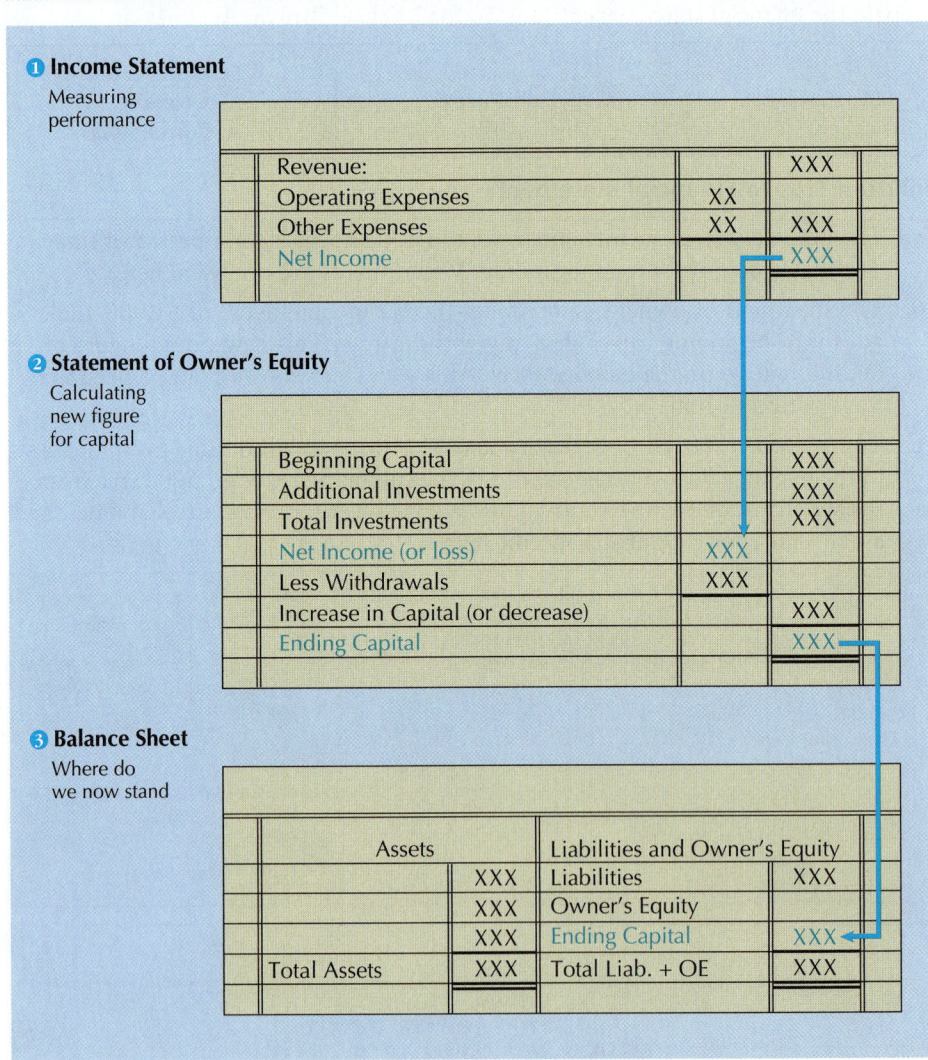

❶ Income Statement

Measuring
performance

			XXX
Revenue:			XXX
Operating Expenses	XX		
Other Expenses	XX	XXX	
Net Income			XXX

❷ Statement of Owner's Equity

Calculating
new figure
for capital

		XXX
Beginning Capital		XXX
Additional Investments		XXX
Total Investments		XXX
Net Income (or loss)	XXX	
Less Withdrawals	XXX	
Increase in Capital (or decrease)		XXX
Ending Capital		XXX

❸ Balance Sheet

Where do
we now stand

Assets		Liabilities and Owner's Equity	
	XXX	Liabilities	XXX
	XXX	Owner's Equity	
	XXX	Ending Capital	XXX
Total Assets	XXX	Total Liab. + OE	XXX

ACCOUNTING COACH

CHAPTER 1

The following Coaching Tips are from Learning Units 1-1 to 1-4. Take the Pre-Game Checkup and use the Check Your Score at the bottom of the page to see how you are doing. The Accounting Coach provides tips before each Checkup to help you avoid common accounting errors.

LU 1-1 The Accounting Equation

Pre-Game Tips: After a transaction is recorded in the accounting equation, the sum of all the assets must equal the total of all the liabilities and owner's equity.

Pre-Game Checkup

Answer true or false to the following statements.

1. Capital is cash.
2. Accounts Payable is a liability.
3. A shift in assets means liabilities will increase.
4. Assets – Liabilities = Owner's Equity.
5. Assets represent what is owned by the business.

LU 1-2 The Balance Sheet

Pre-Game Tips: The Balance Sheet is a formal report listing assets, liabilities, and owner's equity as of a particular date.

Pre-Game Checkup

Answer true or false to the following statements.

1. Cash is a liability.
2. Office Equipment is an asset.
3. Accounts Payable is listed under assets.
4. Capital is listed under liabilities.
5. A heading of a financial report has no particular date.

LU 1-3 The Expanded Accounting Equation

Pre-Game Tips: Revenue is recorded when earned even if cash is not received. Expenses are recorded when they happen (incurred) whether they are paid or to be paid later.

Pre-Game Checkup

Answer true or false to the following statements.

1. Revenue is an asset.
2. Withdrawals increase owner's equity.
3. As expenses go down, owner's equity goes down.
4. An advertising bill incurred but unpaid is recorded as an increase in Advertising Expense and a decrease in liability.
5. Revenue inflows can only be in the form of cash.

LU 1-4 Financial Reports

Pre-Game Tips: Net income from the income statement is used to update the statement of owner's equity. The ending figure for capital on the statement of owner's equity is the one used to update the balance sheet.

Pre-Game Checkup

Answer true or false to the following statements.

1. Net income occurs when expenses are greater than revenue.
2. Withdrawals will reduce owner's capital on the income statement.
3. The balance sheet lists assets, liabilities, and expenses.
4. Withdrawals are listed on the income statement.
5. Assets are listed on the income statement.

CHECK YOUR SCORE: Answers to the Pre-Game Checkup

LU 1-1
1. False—Capital represents the owner's claim to the assets.
2. True.
3. False—A shift in assets means liabilities will stay the same.
4. True.
5. True.

LU 1-2
1. False—Cash is an asset.
2. True.
3. False—Accounts Payable is listed under liabilities.
4. False—Capital is listed under owner's equity.
5. False—A heading of a financial report does have a particular date.

LU 1-3
1. False—Revenue is part of owner's equity.
2. False—Withdrawals decrease owner's equity.
3. False—As expenses go down, owner's equity goes up.
4. False—An advertising bill incurred but unpaid is recorded as an increase in Advertising Expense and an increase in liability.
5. False—Revenue inflows can be in the form of cash and/or accounts receivable.

LU 1-4
1. False—Net income occurs when expenses are less than revenue.
2. False—Withdrawals will reduce owner's capital on the statement of owner's equity.
3. False—Expenses are listed on the income statement.
4. False—Withdrawals are listed on the statement of owner's equity.
5. False—Assets are listed on the balance sheet.

Chapter Summary

MyAccountingLab

Here are all the key concepts and equations to help you understand the concepts of this chapter and prepare you for your exam. After completing this review, go to MyAccountingLab for more practice opportunities.

Concepts You Should Know	Key Terms

L01   **Defining and listing the functions of accounting.**
 	
 1. The functions of accounting involve analyzing, recording, classifying, summarizing, reporting, and interpreting financial information.
 	
 2. Forms of business organization:
 	
    a. A sole proprietorship is a business owned by one person.
 	
    b. A partnership is a business owned by two or more persons.
 	
    c. A corporation is a business owned by stockholders.
 	
    d. An LLC is owned by a limited number of stockholders.
 	
 3. The Sarbanes-Oxley Act helps prevent fraud at trading companies.
 	
 4. GAAP and IFRS are guidelines established by U.S. (GAAP) and international (IFRS) accounting standard boards.
	Accounting (p. 2)
	 Assets (p. 5)
	 Bookkeeping (p. 4)
	 Corporation (p. 3)
	 Creditor (p. 5)
	 Equities (p. 5)
	 Generally accepted accounting principles (GAAP) (p. 4)
	 International Financial Reporting Standards (IFRS) (p. 4)
	 Liabilities (p. 5)
	 Manufacturer (p. 3)
	 Merchandise company (p. 3)
	 Owner's equity (p. 5)
	 Partnership (p. 2)
	 Sole proprietorship (p. 2)
	 Service company (p. 3)

L02 **Recording transactions in the basic accounting equation.** 1. Assets = Liabilities + Owner's Equity is the basic accounting equation. 2. Liabilities represent amounts owed to creditors. 3. Capital does not mean cash. 4. In a shift of assets the composition of assets changes but the total of assets does not change.	Accounts payable (p. 7) Balance sheet (p. 9) Basic accounting equation (p. 5) Capital (p. 6) Shift in assets (p. 6) Supplies (p. 6) Statement of financial position (p. 9) Assets = Liabilities + Owner's Equity (p. 5)

Seeing how revenue, expenses, and withdrawals expand the basic accounting equation.

1. Revenue generates an inward flow of assets. Expenses generate an outward flow of assets or a potential outward flow.

2. When revenue totals more than expenses, net income is the result; when expenses total more than revenue, there is a net loss.

3. Owner's equity can be subdivided into four elements: capital, withdrawals, revenue, and expenses.

4. Withdrawals and expenses will decrease owner's equity.

Accounts receivable (p. 12)

Expanded accounting equation (p. 12)

Expense (p. 12)

Net income (p. 12)

Net loss (p. 12)

Revenue (p. 11)

Withdrawals (p. 12)

Assets = Liabilities + Capital – Withdrawals + Revenue – Expenses (p. 12)

● **L03**

Preparing an income statement, a statement of owner's equity, and a balance sheet.

1. The income statement is a statement written for a specific period of time that lists earned revenue and expenses incurred to produce the earned revenue.

2. The statement of owner's equity is a statement written for a specific period of time that reveals the causes of a change in capital. The ending figure for capital will be used on the balance sheet.

3. The balance sheet is a statement written for a specific point of time that uses the ending balances of assets and liabilities from the accounting equation and the capital from the statement of owner's equity.

4. The income statement should be prepared first because the information on it about net income or net loss is used to prepare the statement of owner's equity, which in turn provides information about capital for the balance sheet.

Ending capital (p. 20)

Income statement (p. 18)

Statement of owner's equity (p. 18)

● **L04**

Discussion Questions and Critical Thinking/Ethical Case

1. What are the functions of accounting?

2. Define, compare, and contrast sole proprietorships, partnerships, and corporations.

3. How are businesses classified?

4. What is the relationship of bookkeeping to accounting?

5. List the three elements of the basic accounting equation.

6. Define capital.

7. The total of the left-hand side of the accounting equation must equal the total of the right-hand side. True or false? Please explain.

8. A balance sheet tells a company where it is going and how well it performs. True or false? Please explain.

9. Revenue is an asset. True or false? Please explain.

10. Owner's equity is subdivided into what categories?

11. A withdrawal is a business expense. True or false? Please explain.

12. As expenses increase they cause owner's equity to increase. Defend or reject.

13. What does an income statement show?

14. The statement of owner's equity only calculates ending withdrawals. True or false? Please explain.

15. Paul Kloss, accountant for Lowe & Co., traveled to New York on company business. His total expenses came to $350. Paul felt that because the trip extended over the weekend he would "pad" his expense account with an additional $100 of expenses. After all, weekends represent his own time, not the company's. What would you do? Write your specific recommendations to Paul.

MyAccountingLab

Concept Checks

● **L01** *(5 MIN)*   **Classifying Accounts**

1. Classify each of the following items as an Asset (A), Liability (L), or part of Owner's Equity (OE).

   a. Computer Tablet   _____
   b. Accounts Payable   _____
   c. Accounts Receivable   _____
   d. Cash   _____
   e. A. Jones, Capital   _____
   f. Verizon Cell Phone   _____

● **L01** *(5 MIN)*   **The Accounting Equation**

2. Complete the following statements.
   a. _____: rights of the creditors
   b. _____ are total value of items owned by a business.
   c. _____ _____ is an unwritten promise to pay the creditor.

Shift versus Increase in Assets

● **L01** *(5 MIN)*

3. Identify which transaction results in a shift in assets (S) and which transaction causes an increase in assets (I).

   a. Target bought computer equipment on account.
   b. Macy's bought office equipment for cash.

The Balance Sheet

●● **L02, 4** *(5 MIN)*

4. From the following, calculate what would be the total of assets on the balance sheet.

B. Fleese, Capital	$12,000
Computer Equipment	21,000
Accounts Payable	8,000
Cash	34,000

The Accounting Equation Expanded

● **L03** *(5 MIN)*

5. From the following, which are subdivisions of owner's equity?

   a. Trees _____
   b. J. Penny, Capital _____
   c. Accounts Payable _____
   d. J. Penny, Withdrawals _____
   e. Accounts Receivable _____
   f. Advertising Expense _____
   g. Taxi Fees Earned _____
   h. Computer Equipment _____

Identifying Assets

6. Identify which of the following are *not* assets.

   a. DVD Player _____
   b. Accounts Receivable _____
   c. Accounts Payable _____
   d. Grooming Fees Earned _____

The Accounting Equation Expanded

7. Which of the following statements are false?

   a. _____ Revenue provides only outward flows of cash.
   b. _____ Revenue is a subdivision of Assets.
   c. _____ Revenue provides an inward flow of cash or accounts receivable.
   d. _____ Expenses are part of Total Assets.

Preparing Financial Statements

8. Indicate whether the following items would appear on the income statement (IS), statement of owner's equity (OE), or balance sheet (BS).

   a. _____ Tutoring Fees Earned
   b. _____ Office Equipment
   c. _____ Accounts Receivable
   d. _____ Office Supplies
   e. _____ Legal Fees Earned

(continued on page 32)

f. _____ Advertising Expenses

g. _____ J. Earl, Capital (Beg.)

h. _____ Accounts Payable

Preparing Financial Statements

9. Indicate next to each statement whether it refers to the income statement (IS), statement of owner's equity (OE), or balance sheet (BS).

a. _____ Withdrawals found on it

b. _____ List total of all assets

c. _____ Statement that is prepared last

d. _____ Statement listing net income

MyAccountingLab **Exercises**

Set A

LO2 *(5 MIN)* **1A-1.** Complete the following table:

	Assets	=	Liabilities	+	Owner's Equity
a.	$27,000	=	?	+	$18,000
b.	?	=	$6,000	+	$69,000
c.	$35,000	=	$10,000	+	?

LO2 *(5 MIN)* **1A-2.** Record the following transactions in the basic accounting equation. Treat each one separately.

Assets = Liabilities + Owner's Equity

a. Micheal invests $112,000 in company.

b. Bought equipment for cash, $1500.

c. Bought equipment on account, $750.

LO2, 4 *(10 MIN)* **1A-3.** From the following, prepare a balance sheet for Rauscher Co. Cleaners at the end of April 201X: Cash, $52,000; Equipment, $28,000; Accounts Payable, $14,000; B. Rauscher, Capital.

LO3 *(15 MIN)* **1A-4.** Record the following transactions in the expanded accounting equation. The running balance may be omitted for simplicity.

Assets			=	Liabilities	+			Owner's Equity		
Cash +	Accounts Receivable	+ Computer Equipment	=	Accounts Payable	+	B. Baker, Capital	– B. Baker, Withdrawals	+	Revenues – Expenses		

a. Baker invested $90,000 in a computer company.

b. Bought computer equipment on account, $10,200.

c. Baker paid personal telephone bill from company checkbook, $50.

d. Received cash for services rendered, $13,700.

e. Billed customers for services rendered for month, $29,000.

f. Paid current rent expense, $4,200.

g. Paid supplies expense, $1,510.

LO4 *(20 MIN)* **1A-5.** From the following account balances, prepare in proper form for September (a) an income statement, (b) a statement of owner's equity, and (c) a balance sheet for Frechette Realty.

Cash	$5,700	S. Frechette, Withdrawals	$ 225
Accounts Receivable	990	Professional Fees	3,500
Office Equipment	7,200	Salaries Expense	600
Accounts Payable	10,000	Utilities Expense	150
S. Frechette, Capital, Sep 1, 201X	1,840	Rent Expense	475

Set B

1B-1. Complete the following table:

	Assets	=	Liabilities	+	Owner's Equity
a.	$ 30,000	=	?	+	$ 15,000
b.	?	=	$ 10,000	+	$ 55,000
c.	$		15,000 = $3,000	+	?

● **L02** *(5 MIN)*

1B-2. Record the following transactions in the basic accounting equation. Treat each one separately.
  a. Morgan invests $118,000 in company.
  b. Bought equipment for cash, $1,100.
  c. Bought equipment on account, $800.

● **L02** *(5 MIN)*

1B-3. From the following, prepare a balance sheet for Rauscher Co. Cleaners at the end of April 201X: Cash, $18,000; Equipment, $40,000; Accounts Payable, $25,000; B. Rauscher, Capital.

●● **L02, 4** *(10 MIN)*

1B-4. Record the following transactions in the expanded accounting equation. The running balance may be omitted for simplicity.
  a. Baker invested $60,000 in a computer company.
  b. Bought computer equipment on account, $10,000.
  c. Baker paid personal telephone bill from company checkbook, $150.
  d. Received cash for services rendered, $14,000.
  e. Billed customers for services rendered for month, $30,000.
  f. Paid current rent expense, $3,500.
  g. Paid supplies expense, $1,470.

● **L03** *(15 MIN)*

1B-5. From the following account balances, prepare in proper form for September (a) an income statement, (b) a statement of owner's equity, and (c) a balance sheet for Frechette Realty.

● **L04** *(20 MIN)*

Cash	$ 7,050	S. Frechette, Withdrawals	$ 800
Accounts Receivable	1,060	Professional Fees	4,000
Office Equipment	6,700	Salaries Expense	400
Accounts Payable	2,000	Utilities Expense	360
S. Frechette, Capital, September 1, 201X	10,770	Rent Expense	400

Problems

MyAccountingLab

Set A

1A-1. Mike Ackerman decided to open Mike's Nail Spa. Mike completed the following transactions:

  a. Invested $17,000 cash from his personal bank account into the business.
  b. Bought store equipment for cash, $3,900.
  c. Bought additional store equipment on account, $6,100.
  d. Paid $700 cash to partially reduce what was owed from transaction C.

  Based on this information, record these transactions into the basic accounting equation.

● **L02** *(15 MIN)*

Check Figure:
Cash $22,400

1A-2. Bob Shire is the accountant for Shire's Internet Service. From the following information, his task is to construct a balance sheet as of September 30, 201X, in proper form. Could you help him?

●● **L02, 4** *(15 MIN)*

Building	$30,000	Cash	$35,000
Accounts Payable	17,000	Equipment	29,000
Shire, Capital	77,000		

Check Figure:
Total Assets $94,000

● **LO3** *(20 MIN)*

1A-3. At the end of September, Ron Ferlito decided to open his own typing service. Analyze the following transactions he completed by recording their effects in the expanded accounting equation.

a. Invested $15,000 in his typing service.
b. Bought new office equipment on account, $6,500.
c. Received cash for typing services rendered, $900.
d. Performed typing services on account, $3,600.
e. Paid secretary's salary, $325.
f. Paid office supplies expense for the month, $150.
g. Rent expenses for office due but unpaid, $900.
h. Withdrew cash for personal use, $600.

● **LO4** *(30 MIN)*

1A-4. Johann Wheldon, owner of Wheldon Stenciling Service, has requested that you prepare from the following balances (a) an income statement for November 201X, (b) a statement of owner's equity for November, and (c) a balance sheet as of November 30, 201X.

Cash	$1,900	Stenciling Fees	$2,600
Accounts Receivable	650	Advertising Expense	110
Equipment	1,025	Repair Expense	20
Accounts Payable	250	Travel Expense	225
J. Wheldon, Capital, Nov. 1, 201X	2,510	Supplies Expense	155
J. Wheldon, Withdrawals	900	Rent Expense	375

●●● **LO2, 3, 4** *(45 MIN)*

PT/QB

1A-5. Jerry Trickett, a retired army officer, opened Trickett's Catering Service. As his accountant, analyze the transactions listed next and present them in proper form.

a. The analysis of the transactions by using the expanded accounting equation.
b. A balance sheet showing the position of the firm before opening for business on March 31, 201X.
c. An income statement for the month of April.
d. A statement of owner's equity for April.
e. A balance sheet as of April 30, 201X.

201X

Mar. 25   Jerry Trickett invested $45,000 in the catering business from his personal savings account.
27   Bought equipment for cash from Small Co., $1,600.
28   Bought additional equipment on account from Aiden Co., $2,200.
29   Paid $100 to Aiden Co. as partial payment of the March 28 transaction.

(You should now prepare your balance sheet as of March 31, 201X.)

Apr. 1   Catered a graduation and immediately collected cash, $1,900.
5   Paid salaries of employees, $700.
8   Prepared desserts for customers on account, $150.
10   Received $75 cash as partial payment of April 8 transaction.
15   Paid telephone bill, $120.
17   Paid his home electric bill from the company's checkbook, $80.
20   Catered a wedding and received cash, $2,700.
25   Bought additional equipment on account, $1000.
28   Rent expense due but unpaid, $500.
30   Paid supplies expense, $550.

Set B

MyAccountingLab

1B-1. Mike Ackerman decided to open Mike's Nail Spa. Mike completed the following transactions:

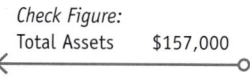
L02 *(15 MIN)*

   a. Invested $24,000 cash from his personal bank account into the business.
   b. Bought store equipment for cash, $3,700.
   c. Bought additional store equipment on account, $6,100.
   d. Paid $900 cash to partially reduce what was owed from transaction C.

Check Figure:
Ending Balance Cash $29,200

Record these transactions into the basic accounting equation.

1B-2. Bob Shire is the accountant for Shire's Internet Service. From the following information, his task is to construct a balance sheet as of September 30, 201X, in proper form. Can you help him?

L02, 4 *(15 MIN)*

Building	$ 55,000
Accounts Payable	15,000
Shire, Capital	142,000
Cash	48,000
Equipment	54,000

Check Figure:
Total Assets $157,000

1B-3. At the end of September, Ron Ferlito decided to open his own typing service. Analyze the following transactions he completed by recording their effects into the expanded accounting equation.

L03 *(20 MIN)*

   a. Invested $30,000 in his typing business.
   b. Bought new office equipment on account, $5,000.
   c. Received cash for typing services rendered, $400.
   d. Performed typing services on account, $3,100.
   e. Paid secretary's salary, $425.
   f. Paid office supplies expense for the month, $130.
   g. Rent expenses for office due but unpaid, $750.
   h. Withdrew cash for personal use, $500.

Check Figure:
Total Assets $37,445

1B-4. Johann Wheldon, owner of Wheldon Stenciling Service, has requested that you prepare from the following balances (a) an income statement for November 201X, (b) a statement of owner's equity for November, and (c) a balance sheet as of November 30, 201X.

L03 *(30 MIN)*

Cash	$2,400	Stenciling Fees	$3000
Accounts Receivable	650	Advertising Expense	110
Equipment	685	Repair Expense	50
Accounts Payable	850	Travel Expense	550
J. Wheldon, Capital, Nov. 1, 201X	1,125	Supplies Expense	55
J. Wheldon, Withdrawals	300	Rent Expense	175

Check Figure:
J. Weldon, Capital, $2,885
Nov. 1, 201X

1B-5. Jerry Trickett, a retired army officer, opened Trickett's Catering Service. As his accountant, analyze the transactions listed and present them in proper form.

   a. The analysis of the transactions by using the expanded accounting equation.
   b. A balance sheet showing the financial position of the firm before opening on March 31, 201X.
   c. An income statement for the month of April.
   d. A statement of owner's equity for April.
   e. A balance sheet as of April 30, 201X.

(continued on page 36)

201X

Mar.	25	Jerry Trickett invested $30,000 in the catering business from his personal savings account.
	27	Bought equipment for cash from Lucas Co., $700.
	28	Bought additional equipment on account from Gavin Co., $3,000.
	29	Paid $1,000 to Gavin Co. as partial payment of the March 28 transaction.
Apr.	1	Catered a graduation and collected cash, $2,500.
	5	Paid salaries of employees, $1,500.
	8	Prepared desserts for customers on account, $200.
	10	Received $100 cash as partial payment of September 8 transaction.
	15	Paid telephone bill, $60.
	17	Paid his home electric bill from the company's checkbook, $90.
	20	Catered a wedding and received cash, $1,400.
	25	Bought additional equipment on account, $900.
	28	Rent expense due but unpaid, $900.
	30	Paid supplies expense, $250.

Check Figure:
Total Liabilities and
Owner's Equity
Apr. 30 $35,100

○○ **LO2, 4** *(5 MIN)*

Financial Report Problem

Reading the Kellogg's Annual Report

Go to http://investor.kelloggs.com/annuals.cfm, to access the Kellogg's 2010 Annual Report. Find the balance sheet and calculate the following: How much did cash increase in 2010 from 2009?

✓ MyAccountingLab

○○ **LO3, 4** *(45 MIN)*

SANCHEZ COMPUTER CENTER

The following problem continues from one chapter to the next, carrying the balances of each month forward. Each chapter focuses on the learning experience of the chapter, adds information as the business grows and shows how critical the knowledge of accounting is to the performance of a business decision-maker.

Assignment

1. Set up an expanded accounting equation spreadsheet using the following accounts:

Assets	**Liabilities**	**Owner's Equity**
Cash	Accounts Payable	Freedman, Capital
Supplies		Freedman, Withdrawal
Computer Shop		Service Revenue
Equipment		Expenses (notate type)
Office Equipment		

2. Analyze and record each transaction in the expanded accounting equation.

3. Prepare the financial statements ending July 31 for Sanchez Computer Center.

    On July 1, 201X, Tony Freedman decided to begin his own computer service business. He named the business the Sanchez Computer Center. During the first month Tony conducted the following business transactions:

a. Invested $4,500 of his savings into the business.

b. Paid $1,200 (check #8095) for the computer from Multi Systems, Inc.

c. Paid $600 (check #8096) for office equipment from Office Furniture, Inc.

d. Set up a new account with Office Depot and purchased $250 in office supplies on credit.

e. Paid July rent, $400 (check #8097).

f. Repaired a system for a customer and collected $250.

g. Collected $200 for system upgrade labor charge from a customer.

h. Electric bill due but unpaid, $85.

i. Collected $1,200 for services performed on Taylor Golf computers.

j. Withdrew $100 (check #8098) to take his wife, Carol, out in celebration of opening the new business.

SUBWAY CASE

A Fresh Start

LO4 *(20 MIN)*

"Hey, Stan the man!" a loud voice boomed. "I never thought I'd see you making sandwiches!" Stan Hernandez stopped layering lettuce in a foot-long submarine sandwich and grinned at his old college buddy, Ron.

"Neither did I. But then again," said Stan, "I never thought I'd own a profitable business either."

That night, catching up on their lives over dinner, Stan told Ron how he became the proud owner of a Subway sandwich restaurant.

"After working like crazy at Xellent Media for five years and *finally* making it to marketing manager, then wham . . . I got laid off," said Stan. "That very day I was having my lunch at the local Subway as usual, when. . . ."

"Hmmm, wait a minute! I did notice you've lost quite a bit of weight," Ron interrupted and began to hum the bars of Subway's latest ad featuring Clay Henry, yet another hefty male who lost weight on a diet of Subway sandwiches.

"Right!" Stan quipped, "Not only was I laid off, but I was 'downsizing!' *Anyway*, I was eating a Dijon horseradish melt when I opened up an *Entrepreneur* magazine someone had left on the table—right to the headline 'Subway Named #1 Franchise in All Categories for 11th Time in 15 Years.'"

Well, to make a foot-long submarine sandwich story short, Stan realized his long-time dream of being his own boss by owning a business with a proven product and highly successful business model. When you look at Stan's restaurant, you are really seeing two businesses. Even though Stan is the sole proprietor of his business, he operates under an agreement with Subway of Milford, Connecticut. Subway supplies the business know-how and support (like training at Subway University, national advertising, and gourmet bread recipes). Stan supplies capital (his $12,500 investment) and his food preparation, management, and elbow grease. Subway and Stan operate interdependent businesses, and both rely on accounting information for their success.

Subway, in business since 1965, has grown dramatically over the years and now has more than 18,000 locations in 73 countries. It has even surpassed McDonald's in the number of locations in the United States and Canada. To manage this enormous service business requires careful control of each of its stores. At a Subway regional office, Mariah Washington, a field consultant for Stan's territory, monitors Stan's restaurant closely. In addition to making monthly visits to check whether Stan is complying with Subway's model in everything from décor to uniforms to food quality and safety, she also looks closely at Stan's weekly sales and inventory reports. When Stan's sales go up, Subway's do too, because each Subway franchisee, like Stan, pays Subway, the franchiser, a percentage of sales in the form of royalties.

Why does headquarters require accounting reports? Accounting reports give the information both Stan and the company need to make business decisions in a number of vital areas. For example:

- Before Stan could buy his Subway restaurant, the company needed to know how much cash Stan had and his assets and liabilities (such as credit card debt). Stan prepared a personal balance sheet to give them this information.
- Stan must have the right amount of supplies on hand. If he has too few, he can't make the sandwiches. If he has too many for the amount he expects to sell, items such as sandwich meats and bread dough may spoil. The inventory report tells Mariah what supplies are on hand. In combination with the sales report, it also alerts Mariah to potential red flags: If Stan is reporting that he is using far too much bread dough for the amount of sandwiches he is selling, a problem would be indicated.
- Although Subway does not require its restaurant owners to report operating costs and profit information, Subway gives them the option and most franchisees take it. Information on profitability helps Mariah and Stan make decisions such as whether and when to remodel or buy new equipment.

So that its restaurant owners can make business decisions in a timely manner, Subway requires them to submit the weekly sales and inventory report to headquarters electronically every Thursday by 2:00 P.M. Stan has his latest report in mind as he makes a move to pay the bill for his dinner with Ron. "We had a great week. Let me get this," he says. "Thanks, Stan the Man. I'm going to keep in touch because I may just be ready for a business opportunity of my own!"

Discussion Questions

1. What makes Stan a sole proprietor?
2. Why are Stan and Subway interdependent businesses?
3. Why did Stan have to share his personal balance sheet with Subway? Do you think most interdependent businesses operate this way?
4. What does Subway learn from Stan's weekly sales and inventory reports?

Debits and Credits: Analyzing and Recording Business Transactions

THE GAME PLAN

Do you ever wonder when making a purchase at the mall how a shop will know if the cash taken in at the register will equal the sales at the end of the day? For example, if you go to Subway and purchase a sub, how will Subway know that the money collected for your sale will equal the amount in the register at day's end? In this chapter, we learn how businesses small and large like Subway are required to use the accounting equation to ensure this balance. By following the rules associated with the accounting equation, investors and creditors, when reviewing financial statements, can have confidence that businesses like Subway are accurately reporting their financial activities.

LEARNING OBJECTIVES

1. Setting up and organizing a chart of accounts.
2. Recording transactions in T accounts according to the rules of debit and credit.
3. Preparing a trial balance.
4. Preparing financial statements from a trial balance.

In Chapter 1 we used the expanded accounting equation to document the financial transactions performed by Mia Wong's law firm. Remember how long it was: The cash column had a long list of pluses and minuses, with no quick system of recording and summarizing the increases and decreases of cash or other items. Can you imagine the problem Subway would have if it used the expanded accounting equation to track the thousands of business transactions it makes each day?

LEARNING UNIT 2-1 THE T ACCOUNT

Let's look at the problem a little more closely. Each business transaction is recorded in the accounting equation under a specific account. Different accounts are used for each of the subdivisions of the accounting equation: asset accounts, liabilities accounts, expense accounts, revenue accounts, and so on. What is needed is a way to record the increases and decreases in specific account *categories* and yet keep them together in one place. The answer is the standard account form (see Figure 2.1). A standard account is a formal account that includes columns for date, item, posting reference, debit, and credit. Each account has a separate form, and all transactions affecting that account are recorded on the form. All the business's account forms (which often are referred to as *ledger accounts*) are then placed in a ledger. Each page of the ledger contains one account. The ledger may be in the form of a bound or a loose-leaf book. If computers are used, the ledger may be part of a computer file. For simplicity's sake, we use the T account form. This form got its name because it looks like the letter T. Generally, T accounts are used for demonstration purposes. Each T account contains three basic parts:

1
Title of Account

2 Left side | Right side **3**

All T accounts have this structure.

In accounting, the left side of any T account is called the debit side.

Left side
Dr. (debit)

Just as the word *left* has many meanings, the word *debit* for now in accounting means a position, the left side of an account. Do not think of it as good (+) or bad (−).

Amounts entered on the left side of any account are said to be *debited* to an account. The abbreviation for debit, Dr., is from the Latin *debere*.

The right side of any T account is called the credit side.

Right side
Cr. (credit)

Amounts entered on the right side of an account are said to be *credited* to an account. The abbreviation for credit, Cr., is from the Latin *credere*.

At this point do not associate the definition of debit and credit with the words *increase* or *decrease*. Think of debit or credit as only indicating a *position* (left or right side) of a T account.

Balancing an Account

No matter which individual account is being balanced, the procedure used to balance it is the same.

Account An accounting device used in bookkeeping to record increases and decreases of business transactions relating to individual assets, liabilities, capital, withdrawals, revenue, expenses, and so on.

Standard account A formal account that includes columns for date, explanation, posting reference, debit, and credit.

Ledger A group of accounts that records data from business transactions.

T account A skeleton version of a standard account, used for demonstration purposes.

Debit The left-hand side of any account. A number entered on the left side of any account is said to be debited to an account.

Credit The right-hand side of any account. A number entered on the right side of any account is said to be credited to an account.

Account Title								Account No.	
Date	Item	PR	Debit	Date	Item	PR	Credit		

FIGURE 2.1
The Standard Account Form Is the Source of the T Account's Shape

COACHING TIP

If the balance is greater on the credit side, that is the side the ending balance would be on.

	Dr.	Cr.
Entries →	5,000	400
	600	500
Footings →	5,600	900
Balance 4,700		

In the "real" world, the T account would also include the date of the transaction. The date would appear to the left of the entry:

		Dr.	Cr.	
4/2		5,000	4/3	400
4/20		600	4/25	500
		5,600		900
Bal	4,700			

Footings The totals of each side of a T account.

Ending balance The difference between footings in a T account.

Note that on the debit (left) side the numbers add up to $5,600. On the credit (right) side the numbers add up to $900. The $5,600 and the $900 written in small type are called **footings**. Footings help in calculating the new (or ending) balance. The **ending balance** ($4,700) is placed on the debit or left side, because the balance of the debit side is greater than that of the credit side.

Remember that the ending balance does not tell us anything about increase or decrease. It only tells us that we have an ending balance of $4,700 on the debit side.

LEARNING UNIT 2-1 REVIEW

AT THIS POINT you should be able to do the following:

- Define ledger.
- State the purpose of a T account.
- Identify the three parts of a T account.
- Define debit.
- Define credit.
- Explain footings and calculate the balance of an account.

Instant Replay ⊙ Self-Review Quiz 2-1

Respond True or False to the following:

1.

	Dr.	Cr.	
	3,000	200	
	200	600	

The balance of the account is $2,400 Cr.

(continued on page 42)

   2. A credit always means increase.
   3. A debit is the left side of any account.
   4. A ledger can be prepared manually or by computer.
   5. Footings replace the need for debits and credits.

Solutions to Instant Replay: Self-Review Quiz 2-1

   1. False
   2. False
   3. True
   4. True
   5. False

PLAY BY PLAY: EXTRA HELP ON SELF-REVIEW QUIZ 2-1

Let's review first: "Debit" does not mean good or bad. Instead, it represents a position, the left side of any account. "Credit" does not mean good or bad either. It represents a position, the right side of any account.

   1. It is false because if you add the two debits of 3,000 and 200 you get 3,200 on the debit, or left side. A dr. + dr. = Debit balance. Now if you add the credit side of 200 and 600 you get a balance of 800 on the credit side. A cr. + cr. = Credit balance. To find the ending balance we take 3,200 less the 800 to arrive at a balance that is still larger on the DEBIT side by 2,400.
   2. A credit is a position. It is the right side of any account.
   3. Yes, the debit is always the left side of any account. It does not mean good or bad.
   4. In the past, the ledger, a group of accounts, was prepared manually; however, today most ledgers are prepared (not only updated) by computer software.
   5. Footings are used to add debits and credits to arrive at a new balance. Think of footings as the totals of a column.

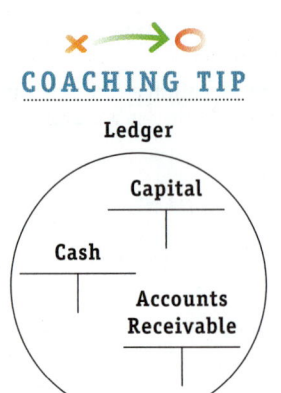

COACHING TIP

LEARNING UNIT 2-2 RECORDING BUSINESS TRANSACTIONS:
Debits and Credits

Can you get a queen in checkers? In a baseball game, does a runner rounding first base skip second base and run over the pitcher's mound to get to third? No; most of us don't do such things because we follow the rules of the game. Usually we learn the rules first and reflect on the reasons for them afterward. The same is true in accounting.

   Instead of first trying to understand all the rules of debit and credit and how they were developed in accounting, it is easier to learn the rules by "playing the game."

T Account Entries for Accounting in the Accounting Equation

Have patience. Learning the rules of debit and credit is like learning to play any game: The more you play, the easier it becomes. Table 2.1 shows the rules for the side on which you enter an increase or a decrease for each of the separate accounts in the accounting equation. For example, an increase is entered on the debit side in the asset account but on the credit side for a liability account.

TABLE 2.1 Rules of Debit and Credit

● L02

Account Category	Increase (Normal Balance)	Decrease
Assets	Debit	Credit
Liabilities	Credit	Debit
Owner's Equity		
Capital	Credit	Debit
Withdrawals	Debit	Credit
Revenue	Credit	Debit
Expenses	Debit	Credit

It might be easier to visualize these rules of debit and credit if we look at them in the T account form, using + to show increase and − to show decrease.

Normal balance of an account
The side of an account that increases by the rules of debit and credit.

Assets	=	Liabilities	+	Owner's Equity						
				+ Capital − Withdrawals + Revenue − Expenses						

Assets		Liabilities		Capital		Withdrawals		Revenue		Expenses	
Dr.	Cr.	Dr.	Cr.	Dr.	Cr.	Dr.	Cr.	Dr.	Cr.	Dr.	Cr.
+	−	−	+	−	+	+	−	−	+	+	−

Rules for Assets Work in the Opposite Direction to Those for Liabilities When you look at the equation you can see that the rules for assets work in the opposite direction to those for liabilities. That is, for assets the increases appear on the debit side and the decreases are shown on the credit side; the opposite is true for liabilities. As for the owner's equity, the rules for withdrawals and expenses, which *decrease* owner's equity, work in the opposite direction to the rules for capital and revenue, which *increase* owner's equity.

Assets		Withdrawals		Expenses		Liabilities		Capital		Revenue	
Dr.	Cr.	Dr.	Cr.	Dr.	Cr.	Dr.	Cr.	Dr.	Cr.	Dr.	Cr.
+	−	+	−	+	−	−	+	−	+	−	+

This setup may help you visualize how the rules for withdrawals and expenses are just the opposite of those for capital and revenue.

A normal balance of an account is the side that increases by the rules of debit and credit. For example, the balance of cash is a debit balance, because an asset is increased by a debit. We discuss normal balances further in Chapter 3.

Balancing the Equation It is important to remember that any amount(s) entered on the debit side of a T account or accounts also must appear on the credit side of another T account or accounts. This approach ensures that the total amount added to the debit side will equal the total amount added to the credit side, thereby keeping the accounting equation in balance.

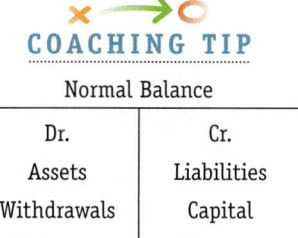

COACHING TIP

Normal Balance

Dr.	Cr.
Assets	Liabilities
Withdrawals	Capital
Expenses	Revenue

LO1

Chart of accounts A numbering system of accounts that lists the account titles and account numbers to be used by a company.

Chart of Accounts Our job is to analyze Mia Wong's business transactions—the transactions we looked at in Chapter 1—using a system of accounts guided by the rules of debit and credit that will summarize increases and decreases of individual accounts in the ledger. The goal is to prepare an income statement, statement of owner's equity, and balance sheet for Mia Wong. Sound familiar? If this system works, the rules of debit and credit and the use of accounts will give us the same answers as in Chapter 1, but with greater ease.

Mia's accountant developed what is called a chart of accounts. The chart of accounts is a numbered list of all of the business's accounts. It allows accounts to be located quickly. In Mia's business, for example, 100s are assets, 200s are liabilities, and so on. As you see in Table 2.2, each separate asset and liability account has its own number. Note that the chart may be expanded as the business grows.

TABLE 2.2 Chart of Accounts for Mia Wong, Attorney-at-Law

Balance Sheet Accounts	
Assets	**Liabilities**
111 Cash	211 Accounts Payable
112 Accounts Receivable	**Owner's Equity**
121 Office Equipment	311 Mia Wong, Capital
	312 Mia Wong, Withdrawals
Income Statement Accounts	
Revenue	**Expenses**
411 Legal Fees	511 Salaries Expense
	512 Rent Expense
	513 Advertising Expense

The Transaction Analysis: Five Steps

We will analyze the transactions in Mia Wong's law firm using a teaching device called a *transaction analysis chart* to record these five steps. (Keep in mind that the transaction analysis chart is not a part of any formal accounting system.) The five steps to analyzing each business transaction include the following:

STEP 1: Determine which accounts are affected. Example: Cash, Accounts Payable, Rent Expense. A transaction always affects at least two accounts.

STEP 2: Determine which categories the accounts belong to: assets, liabilities, capital, withdrawals, revenue, or expenses. Example: Cash is an asset.

STEP 3: Determine whether the accounts increase or decrease. Example: If you receive cash, that account increases.

STEP 4: What do the rules of debit and credit say (Table 2.1)?

STEP 5: What does the T account look like? Place amounts into accounts either on the left or right side depending on the rules in Table 2.1.

The following chart shows the five-step analysis from another perspective.

COACHING TIP

Remember that the rules of debit and credit only tell us on which side to place information. Whether the debit or credit represents increases or decreases depends on the account category: assets, liabilities, capital, and so on. Think of a business transaction as an exchange: You get something and you give or part with something.

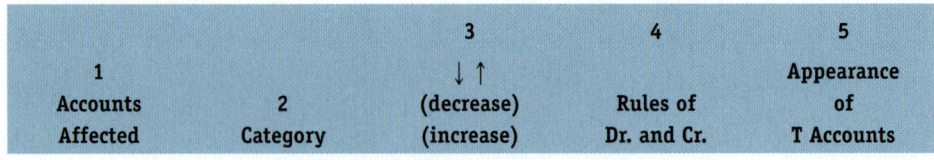

1 Accounts Affected	2 Category	3 ↓ ↑ (decrease) (increase)	4 Rules of Dr. and Cr.	5 Appearance of T Accounts

Let us emphasize a major point: *Do not try to debit or credit an account until you go through the first three steps of the transaction analysis.*

Applying the Transaction Analysis to Mia Wong's Law Practice

Transaction A August 28: Mia Wong invests $6,000 cash and $200 of office equipment in the business.

1 Accounts Affected	2 Category	3 ↓ ↑	4 Rules of Dr. and Cr.	5 Appearance of T Accounts
Cash	Asset	↑	Dr.	Cash 111
				(A) 6,000
Office Equipment	Asset	↑	Dr.	Office Equipment 121
				(A) 200
Mia Wong, Capital	Capital	↑	Cr.	Mia Wong, Capital 311
				6,200 (A)

COACHING TIP

Note that in column 3 of the chart it doesn't matter if both arrows go up, as long as the sum of the debits equals the sum of the credits in the T accounts in column 5.

Note again that every transaction affects at least two T accounts and that the total amount added to the debit side(s) must equal the total amount added to the credit side(s) of the T accounts of each transaction.

Analysis of Transaction A

STEP 1: Which accounts are affected? The law firm receives its cash and office equipment, so three accounts are involved: Cash, Office Equipment, and Mia Wong, Capital. These account titles come from the chart of accounts.

STEP 2: Which categories do these accounts belong to? Cash and Office Equipment are assets. Mia Wong, Capital is capital.

STEP 3: Are the accounts increasing or decreasing? Cash and Office Equipment, both assets, are increasing in the business. The rights or claims of Mia Wong, Capital are also increasing because she invested money and office equipment in the business.

STEP 4: What do the rules say? According to the rules of debit and credit, an increase in assets (Cash and Office Equipment) is a debit. An increase in Capital is a credit. Note that the total dollar amount of debits will equal the total dollar amount of credits when the T accounts are updated in column 5.

STEP 5: What does the T account look like? The amount for Cash and Office Equipment is entered on the debit side. The amount for Mia Wong, Capital goes on the credit side.

A transaction that involves more than one debit or more than one credit is called a compound entry. This first transaction of Mia Wong's law firm is a compound entry; it involves a debit of $6,000 to Cash and a debit of $200 to Office Equipment (as well as a credit of $6,200 to Mia Wong, Capital).

The name for this double-entry analysis of transactions, where two or more accounts are affected and the total of debits and credits is equal, is double-entry bookkeeping. This double-entry system helps in checking the recording of business transactions.

As we continue, the explanations will be brief, but do not forget to apply the five steps in analyzing and recording each business transaction.

Compound entry A transaction involving more than one debit or credit.

Double-entry bookkeeping An accounting system in which the recording of each transaction affects two or more accounts and the total of the debits is equal to the total of the credits.

Transaction B Aug. 29: Law practice bought office equipment for cash, $500.

1 Accounts Affected	2 Category	3 ↓ ↑	4 Rules of Dr. and Cr.	5 T Account Update
Office Equipment	Asset	↑	Dr.	Office Equipment 121
				(A) 200
				(B) 500
Cash	Asset	↓	Cr.	Cash 111
				(A) 6,000 | 500 (B)

Analysis of Transaction B

STEP 1: The law firm paid $500 cash for the office equipment it purchased. The accounts involved in the transaction are Cash and Office Equipment.

STEP 2: The accounts belong to these categories: Office Equipment is an asset; Cash is an asset.

STEP 3: The asset Office Equipment is increasing. The asset Cash is decreasing; it is being reduced to buy the office equipment.

STEP 4: An increase in the asset Office Equipment is a debit; a decrease in the asset Cash is a credit.

STEP 5: When the amounts are placed in the T accounts, the amount for Office Equipment is entered on the debit side and the amount for Cash on the credit side.

Transaction C Aug. 30: Bought more office equipment on account, $300.

1 Accounts Affected	2 Category	3 ↓ ↑	4 Rules of Dr. and Cr.	5 T Account Update
Office Equipment	Asset	↑	Dr.	Office Equipment 121
				(A) 200
				(B) 500
				(C) 300
Accounts Payable	Liability	↑	Cr.	Accounts Payable 211
				300 (C)

Analysis of Transaction C

STEP 1: The law firm receives office equipment totaling $300 by promising to pay in the future. An obligation or liability, Accounts Payable, is created. The accounts affected are Office Equipment and Accounts Payable.

STEP 2: Office Equipment is an asset. Accounts Payable is a liability.

STEP 3: The asset Office Equipment is increasing; the liability Accounts Payable is increasing because the law firm is increasing what it owes.

STEP 4: An increase in the asset Office Equipment is a debit. An increase in the liability Accounts Payable is a credit.

STEP 5: Enter the amount for Office Equipment on the debit side of the T account. The amount for the Accounts Payable goes on the credit side.

Transaction D Sept. 1–30: Provided legal services for cash, $2,000.

1 Accounts Affected	2 Category	3 ↓ ↑	4 Rules of Dr. and Cr.	5 T Account Update			
Cash	Asset	↑	Dr.	Cash 111			
				(A)	6,000	500	(B)
				(D)	2,000		
Legal Fees	Revenue	↑	Cr.	Legal Fees 411			
						2,000	(D)

Analysis of Transaction D

STEP 1: The firm earned revenue from legal services and received $2,000 in cash. The accounts affected are Legal Fees and Cash.

STEP 2: Cash is an asset. Legal Fees is revenue.

STEP 3: Cash, an asset, is increasing. Legal Fees, or revenue, is also increasing.

STEP 4: An increase in Cash, an asset, is debited. An increase in Legal Fees, or revenue, is credited.

STEP 5: Enter the amount for Cash on the debit side of the T account. Enter the amount for Legal Fees on the credit side.

Transaction E Sept. 1–30: Provided legal services on account, $3,000.

1 Accounts Affected	2 Category	3 ↓ ↑	4 Rules of Dr. and Cr.	5 T Account Update			
Accounts Receivable	Asset	↑	Dr.	Accounts Receivable 112			
				(E)	3,000		
Legal Fees	Revenue	↑	Cr.	Legal Fees 411			
						2,000	(D)
						3,000	(E)

Analysis of Transaction E

STEP 1: The law practice has earned revenue of $3,000 but has not yet received payment (cash). The amounts owed by these clients are called Accounts Receivable. Revenue is earned at the time the legal services are provided, whether payment is received then or will be received some time in the future. The accounts affected are Accounts Receivable and Legal Fees.

STEP 2: Accounts Receivable is an asset. Legal Fees is revenue.

STEP 3: Accounts Receivable is increasing because the law practice increased the amount owed to it for legal fees earned but not yet paid. Legal Fees, or revenue, is increasing.

STEP 4: An increase in the asset Accounts Receivable is a debit. An increase in Revenue is a credit.

STEP 5: Enter the amount for Accounts Receivable on the debit side of the T account. The amount for Legal Fees goes on the credit side.

Transaction F Sept. 1–30: Received $900 cash from clients for services rendered previously on account.

---

1 Accounts Affected	2 Category	3 ↓ ↑	4 Rules of Dr. and Cr.	5 T Account Update
Cash	Asset	↑	Dr.	Cash 111
				(A) 6,000 | 500 (B)
				(D) 2,000
				(F) 900
Accounts Receivable	Asset	↓	Cr.	Accounts Receivable 112
				(E) 3,000 | 900 (F)

Analysis of Transaction F

STEP 1: The law firm collects $900 in cash from previous revenue earned. Because the revenue is recorded at the time it is earned, and not when the collection is received, in this transaction we are concerned only with the collection, which affects the Cash and Accounts Receivable accounts.

STEP 2: Cash is an asset. Accounts Receivable is an asset.

STEP 3: Because clients are paying what is owed, Cash (asset) is increasing and the amount owed (Accounts Receivable) is decreasing (the total amount owed by clients to Wong is going down). This transaction results in a shift in assets, more Cash for less Accounts Receivable.

STEP 4: An increase in Cash, an asset, is a debit. A decrease in Accounts Receivable, an asset, is a credit.

STEP 5: Enter the amount for Cash on the debit side of the T account. The amount for Accounts Receivable goes on the credit side.

Transaction G Sept. 1–30: Paid salaries expense, $700.

---

1 Accounts Affected	2 Category	3 ↓ ↑	4 Rules of Dr. and Cr.	5 T Account Update
Salaries Expense	Expense	↑	Dr.	Salaries Expense 511
				(G) 700 |
Cash	Asset	↓	Cr.	Cash 111
				(A) 6,000 | 500 (B)
				(D) 2,000 | 700 (G)
				(F) 900 |

Analysis of Transaction G

STEP 1: The law firm pays $700 of salaries expense by cash. The accounts affected are Salaries Expense and Cash.

STEP 2: Salaries Expense is an expense. Cash is an asset.

STEP 3: The Salaries Expense of the law firm is increasing, which results in a decrease in Cash.

STEP 4: An increase in Salaries Expense, an expense, is a debit. A decrease in Cash, an asset, is a credit.

STEP 5: Enter the amount for Salaries Expense on the debit side of the T account. The amount for Cash goes on the credit side.

Transaction H Sept. 1–30: Paid rent expense, $400.

---

1 Accounts Affected	2 Category	3 ↓ ↑	4 Rules of Dr. and Cr.	5 T Account Update
Rent Expense	Expense	↑	Dr.	Rent Expense 512
				(H) 400 |
Cash	Asset	↓	Cr.	Cash 111
				(A) 6,000 | 500 (B)
				(D) 2,000 | 700 (G)
				(F) 900 | 400 (H)

Analysis of Transaction H

STEP 1: The law firm's rent expenses of $400 are paid in cash. The accounts affected are Rent Expense and Cash.

STEP 2: Rent is an expense. Cash is an asset.

STEP 3: The Rent Expense increases the expenses, and the payment for the Rent Expense decreases the cash.

STEP 4: An increase in Rent Expense, an expense, is a debit. A decrease in Cash, an asset, is a credit.

STEP 5: Enter the amount for Rent Expense on the debit side of the T account. Place the amount for Cash on the credit side.

Transaction I Sept. 1–30: Received a bill for Advertising Expense (to be paid next month), $200.

---

1 Accounts Affected	2 Category	3 ↓ ↑	4 Rules of Dr. and Cr.	5 T Account Update
Advertising Expense	Expense	↑	Dr.	Advertising Expense 513
				(I) 200 |
Accounts Payable	Liability	↑	Cr.	Accounts Payable 211
				| 300 (C)
				| 200 (I)

Analysis of Transaction I

STEP 1: The advertising bill in the amount of $200 has come in and payment is due but has not yet been made. Therefore, the accounts involved here are Advertising Expense and Accounts Payable; the expense has created a liability.

(continued on page 50)

STEP 2: Advertising Expense is an expense. Accounts Payable is a liability.

STEP 3: Both the expense and the liability are increasing.

STEP 4: An increase in an expense is a debit. An increase in a liability is a credit.

STEP 5: Enter the amount for Advertising Expense on the debit side of the T account. Enter the amount for Accounts Payable on the credit side.

Transaction J Sept. 1–30: Wong withdrew cash for personal use, $100.

1 Accounts Affected	2 Category	3 ↓ ↑	4 Rules of Dr. and Cr.	5 T Account Update
Mia Wong, Withdrawals	Withdrawals	↑	Dr.	Mia Wong, Withdrawals 312 (J) 100 |
Cash	Asset	↑	Cr.	Cash 111 (A) 6,000 | 500 (B) (D) 2,000 | 700 (G) (F) 900 | 400 (H) | 100 (J)

Analysis of Transaction J

STEP 1: Mia Wong withdraws $100 cash from business for *personal* use. This withdrawal is not a business expense. The accounts affected are Withdrawals and Cash.

STEP 2: This transaction affects the Withdrawals and Cash accounts.

STEP 3: Mia has increased what she has withdrawn from the business for personal use. The business cash decreased.

STEP 4: An increase in Withdrawals is a debit. A decrease in Cash is a credit. (*Remember:* Withdrawals go on the statement of owner's equity; expenses go on the income statement.)

STEP 5: Enter the amount for Mia Wong, Withdrawals, on the debit side of the T account. The amount for Cash goes on the credit side.

COACHING TIP

Withdrawals are always increased by debits.

Summary of Transactions for Mia Wong						
Assets	=	**Liabilities**	+	**Owner's Equity**		
Cash 111	=	Accounts	+ **Capital**	− **Withdrawals**	+ **Revenue**	− **Expenses**
(A) 6,000 | 500 (B)		Payable 211	Mia Wong,	Mia Wong,	Legal	Salaries
(D) 2,000 | 700 (G)	=	| 300 (C) +	Capital 311 −	Withdrawals 312 +	Fees 411 −	Expense 511
(F) 900 | 400 (H)		| 200 (I)	| 6,200 (A)	(J) 100 |	2,000 (D)	(G) 700 |
| 100 (J)					3,000 (E)	
Accounts						Rent
Receivable 112						Expense 512
(E) 3,000 | 900 (F)					−	(H) 400 |
Office						Advertising
Equipment 121						Expense 513
(A) 200 |					−	(I) 200 |
(B) 500 |						
(C) 300 |						

LEARNING UNIT 2-2 REVIEW

AT THIS POINT you should be able to do the following:

- State the rules of debit and credit.
- List the five steps of a transaction analysis.
- Fill out a transaction analysis chart.
- Explain double-entry bookkeeping.

Instant Replay ⊙ Self-Review Quiz 2-2

King Company uses the following accounts from its chart of accounts: Cash (111), Accounts Receivable (112), Equipment (121), Accounts Payable (211), Jamie King, Capital (311), Jamie King, Withdrawals (312), Professional Fees (411), Utilities Expense (511), and Salaries Expense (512).

Record the following transactions into transaction analysis charts.

a. Jamie King invested in the business $1,000 cash and equipment worth $700 from his personal assets.
b. Billed clients for services rendered, $12,000.
c. Utilities bill due but unpaid, $150.
d. Withdrew cash for personal use, $120.
e. Paid salaries expense, $250.

Solution to Instant Replay: Self-Review Quiz 2-2

a.

1 Accounts Affected	2 Category	3 ↓ ↑	4 Rules of Dr. and Cr.	5 T Account Update
Cash	Asset	↑	Dr.	Cash 111
				(A) 1,000 |
Equipment	Asset	↑	Dr.	Equipment 121
				(A) 700 |
Jamie King, Capital	Capital	↑	Cr.	Jamie King, Capital 311
				| 1,700 (A)

b.

1 Accounts Affected	2 Category	3 ↓ ↑	4 Rules of Dr. and Cr.	5 T Account Update
Accounts Receivable	Asset	↑	Dr.	Accounts Receivable 112
				(B) 12,000 |
Professional Fees	Revenue	↑	Cr.	Professional Fees 411
				| 12,000 (B)

(continued on page 52)

c.

1			4	5
Accounts Affected	2 Category	3 ↓ ↑	Rules of Dr. and Cr.	T Account Update
Utilities Expense	Expense	↑	Dr.	Utilities Expense 511 (C) 150 |
Accounts Payable	Liability	↑	Cr.	Accounts Payable 211 | 150 (C)

d.

1			4	5
Accounts Affected	2 Category	3 ↓ ↑	Rules of Dr. and Cr.	T Account Update
Jamie King, Withdrawals	Withdrawals	↑	Dr.	Jamie King, Withdrawals 312 (D) 120 |
Cash	Asset	↓	Cr.	Cash 111 (A) 1,000 | 120 (D)

e.

1			4	5
Accounts Affected	2 Category	3 ↓ ↑	Rules of Dr. and Cr.	T Account Update
Salaries Expense	Expense	↑	Dr.	Salaries Expense 512 (E) 250 |
Cash	Asset	↓	Cr.	Cash 111 (A) 1,000 | 120 (D) | 250 (E)

PLAY BY PLAY: EXTRA HELP ON SELF-REVIEW QUIZ 2-2

Let's review first: Make up a note card of the rules of debit and credit from Table 2.1. You will notice that assets, withdrawals, and expenses increase when you put amounts on the left, or debit, side of these accounts. The accounting system balances because liabilities, capital, and revenue increase when you put amounts on the right, or credit, side of these accounts. The increase side of any account will represent its normal balance. Think of a chart of accounts as a roadmap to all account titles a company will use. *All accounts affected must come from the chart of accounts.*

Transaction A: In column 1 all titles must come from the chart of accounts. The order listed does not matter as long as the sum of the left side equals the sum of the right side. In this transaction we see that accounts affected include Cash, Equipment, and Jamie King, Capital. Cash and Equipment are assets, while Capital is categorized as capital. Remember that the six category choices are as follows:

assets   liabilities
capital   withdrawals
revenue   expenses

The cash and equipment in business are increasing (thus arrows up) and because the owner supplied them Jamie King, Capital rights are increasing. Assets are increased by putting amounts on the debit side and capital is increased by putting amounts on the credit side (See table 2.3).

TABLE 2.3 Rules of Debit and Credit

Account Category	Increase (Normal Balance)	Decrease
Assets	Debit	Credit
Liabilities	Credit	Debit
Owner's Equity		
Capital	Credit	Debit
Withdrawals	Debit	Credit
Revenue	Credit	Debit
Expenses	Debit	Credit

Transaction B: Here we do the work but do not get the money yet. We see from the chart of accounts that revenue is called Professional Fees and customers owing money is called Accounts Receivable. Revenue for King Co. is going up, and customers owe the company more money. Increase in an asset is a debit, and increase in revenue is a credit.

Transaction C: Here we record Utilities Expense before it is paid. The expenses have increased for King Co. and it has increased what it owes the utility company. An increase in an expense is a debit and an increase in a liability is a credit. Here an expense has created a liability.

Transaction D: This is not a business expense since this is a personal withdrawal of cash by the owner. Jamie King, Withdrawals are increasing since King is taking the withdrawal but the business is lowering its cash from the withdrawal. An increase in withdrawal is a debit and a decrease in cash is a credit. Note the "dr" in the middle of "withdrawal." A withdrawal always increases by a debit.

Transaction E: In this transaction the business has another expense increasing and is paying for it in cash. The end result is that expenses increase on the debit side and cash, which is an asset, decreases on the credit side. Remember that we record expenses when they happen whether they are paid or not. Here they were paid. In transaction C they were not paid.

Summary: The transaction analysis charts are a great way to organize your information before deciding on what to debit or credit. Column 1 must come from the chart of accounts. In the category column you have six choices: assets, liabilities, capital, revenue, withdrawals, and expenses. The arrows tell you if the business accounts are increasing or decreasing. Note in column 5 that if an account is repeated a running summary of all transactions is accumulated in the account.

LEARNING UNIT 2-3 THE TRIAL BALANCE AND PREPARATION OF FINANCIAL STATEMENTS

Let us look at all the transactions we have discussed, arranged by T accounts and recorded using the rules of debit and credit. This grouping of accounts is much easier to use than the expanded accounting equation because all the transactions that affect a particular account are in one place.

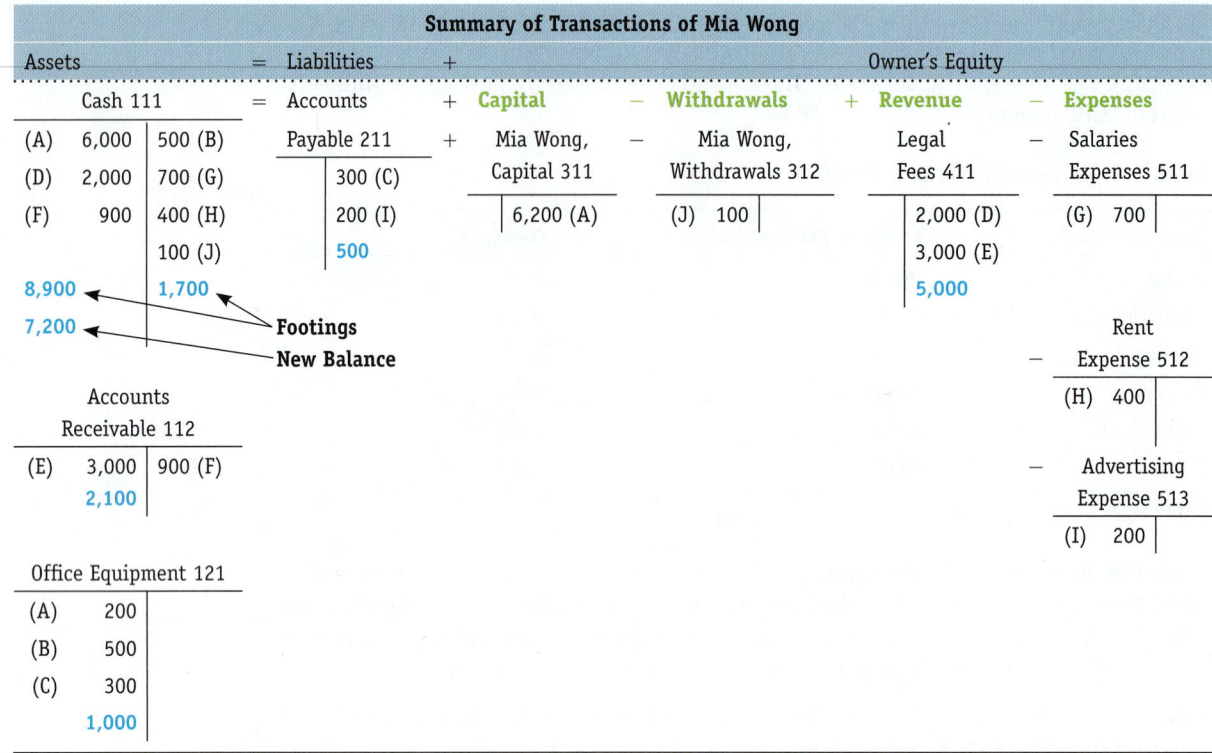

As we saw in Learning Unit 2-2, when all the transactions are recorded in the accounts, the total of all the debits should be equal to the total of all the credits. (If they are not, the accountant must go back and find the error by checking the numbers and adding every column again.)

○ LO3   The Trial Balance

Trial balance A list of the ending balances of all the accounts in a ledger. The total of the debits should equal the total of the credits.

Footings are used to obtain the totals of each side of every T account that has more than one entry. The footings are used to find the ending balance. The ending balances are used to prepare a **trial balance**. The trial balance is not a financial statement, although it is used to prepare financial statements. The trial balance lists all the accounts with their balances in the same order as they appear in the chart of accounts. It proves the accuracy of the ledger. For example, look at the preceding Cash account. The footing for the debit side is $8,900, and the footing for the credit side is $1,700. Because the debit side is larger, we subtract $1,700 from $8,900 to arrive at an *ending debit balance* of $7,200. Now look at the Rent Expense account. It doesn't need a footing because it has only one entry. The amount itself is the ending balance. When the ending balance has been found for every account, we should be able to show that the total of all debits equals the total of all credits.

In the ideal situation, businesses would take a trial balance every day. The large number of transactions most businesses conduct each day makes this impractical. Instead, trial balances are prepared periodically.

Keep in mind that the figure for Capital might not be the beginning figure if any additional investment has taken place during the period. You can tell by looking at the Capital account in the ledger.

A more detailed discussion of the trial balance is provided in the next chapter. For now, notice the heading, how the accounts are listed, the debits in the left column, the credits in the right, and that the total of debits is equal to the total of credits.

A trial balance of Mia Wong's accounts is shown in Figure 2.2.

MIA WONG, ATTORNEY-AT-LAW TRIAL BALANCE SEPTEMBER 30, 201X		
	Dr.	Cr.
Cash	7 2 0 0 00	
Accounts Receivable	2 1 0 0 00	
Office Equipment	1 0 0 0 00	
Accounts Payable		5 0 0 00
Mia Wong, Capital		6 2 0 0 00
Mia Wong, Withdrawals	1 0 0 00	
Legal Fees		5 0 0 0 00
Salaries Expense	7 0 0 00	
Rent Expense	4 0 0 00	
Advertising Expense	2 0 0 00	
Totals	11 7 0 0 00	11 7 0 0 00

FIGURE 2.2
Trial Balance for Mia Wong's
Law Firm

COACHING TIP

Because this statement is not a
formal one, it doesn't need dollar
signs; the single and double lines
under subtotals and final totals,
however, are still used for clarity.

Preparing Financial Statements

● L04

The trial balance is used to prepare the financial statements. The diagram in Figure 2.3 (p. 56) shows how financial statements can be prepared from a trial balance. Statements do not have debit or credit columns. The left column is used only to subtotal numbers.

LEARNING UNIT 2-3 REVIEW

AT THIS POINT you should be able to do the following:

* Explain the role of footings.
* Prepare a trial balance from a set of accounts.
* Prepare financial statements from a trial balance.

Instant Replay ● Self-Review Quiz 2-3

As the bookkeeper of Pam's Hair Salon, you are to prepare from the accounts that follow on June 30, 201X (1) a trial balance as of June 30, (2) an income statement for the month ended June 30, (3) a statement of owner's equity for the month ended June 30, and (4) a balance sheet as of June 30, 201X.

Cash 111	
4,500	300
2,000	100
1,000	1,200
300	1,300
	2,600

Accounts Payable 211	
300	700

Salon Fees 411	
	3,500
	1,000

Accounts Receivable 121	
1,000	300

Pam Jay, Capital 311	
	4,000*

Rent Expense 511	
1,200	

Salon Equipment 131	
700	

Pam Jay, Withdrawals 321	
100	

Salon Supplies Expense 521	
1,300	

Salaries Expense 531	
2,600	

*No additional investments.

(solution page 57)

FIGURE 2.3
Steps in Preparing Financial Statements
from a Trial Balance

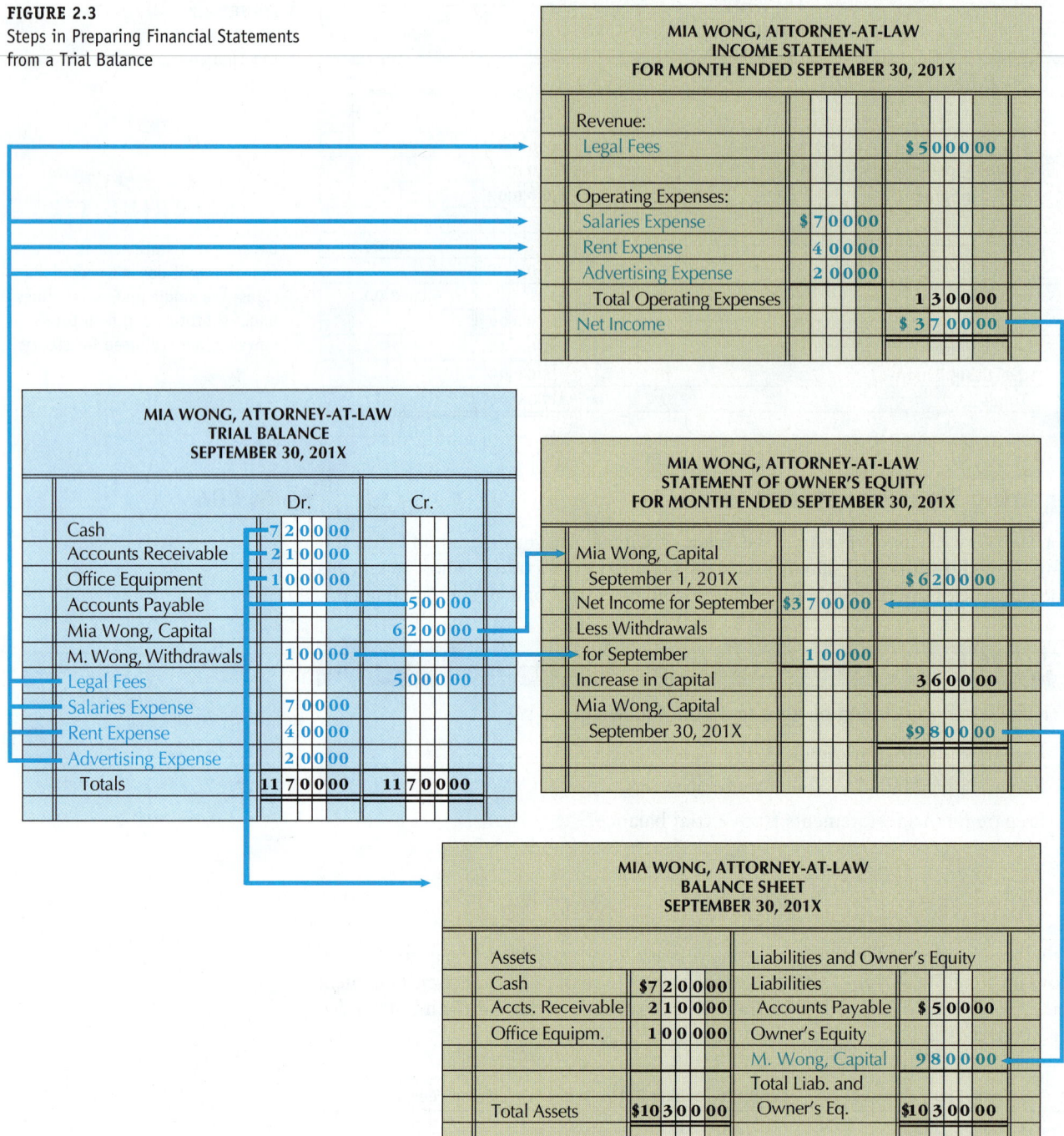

Solution to Instant Replay: Self-Review Quiz 2-3

FIGURE 2.4

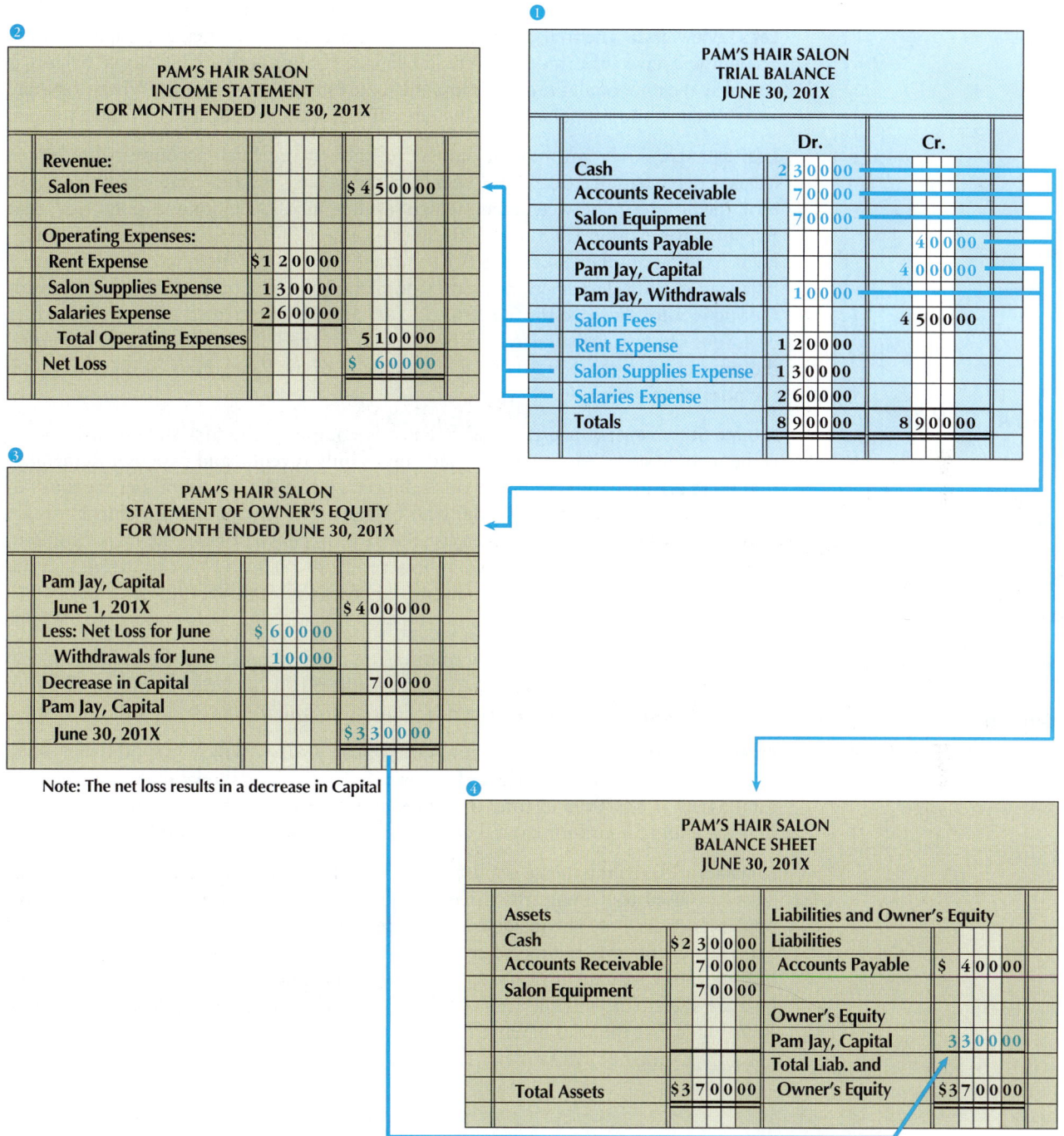

PAM'S HAIR SALON
INCOME STATEMENT
FOR MONTH ENDED JUNE 30, 201X

Revenue:		
Salon Fees		$ 4 5 0 00
Operating Expenses:		
Rent Expense	$1 2 0 00	
Salon Supplies Expense	1 3 0 00	
Salaries Expense	2 6 0 00	
Total Operating Expenses		5 1 0 00
Net Loss		$ 6 0 00

PAM'S HAIR SALON
TRIAL BALANCE
JUNE 30, 201X

	Dr.	Cr.
Cash	2 3 0 00	
Accounts Receivable	7 0 00	
Salon Equipment	7 0 00	
Accounts Payable		4 0 00
Pam Jay, Capital		4 0 0 00
Pam Jay, Withdrawals	1 0 00	
Salon Fees		4 5 0 00
Rent Expense	1 2 0 00	
Salon Supplies Expense	1 3 0 00	
Salaries Expense	2 6 0 00	
Totals	8 9 0 00	8 9 0 00

PAM'S HAIR SALON
STATEMENT OF OWNER'S EQUITY
FOR MONTH ENDED JUNE 30, 201X

Pam Jay, Capital		
June 1, 201X		$ 4 0 0 00
Less: Net Loss for June	$ 6 0 00	
Withdrawals for June	1 0 00	
Decrease in Capital		7 0 00
Pam Jay, Capital		
June 30, 201X		$ 3 3 0 00

Note: The net loss results in a decrease in Capital

PAM'S HAIR SALON
BALANCE SHEET
JUNE 30, 201X

Assets		Liabilities and Owner's Equity	
Cash	$ 2 3 0 00	Liabilities	
Accounts Receivable	7 0 00	Accounts Payable	$ 4 0 00
Salon Equipment	7 0 00		
		Owner's Equity	
		Pam Jay, Capital	3 3 0 00
		Total Liab. and	
Total Assets	$ 3 7 0 00	Owner's Equity	$ 3 7 0 00

PLAY BY PLAY: EXTRA HELP ON SELF-REVIEW QUIZ 2-3

Let's review first: The trial balance is a list of accounts and their ending balances. Each account will have either a debit or credit balance (but not both). When a trial balance is complete the total of all the debits must equal the total of all the credits. When preparing a trial balance you list out assets, liabilities, capital, withdrawals, revenue, and expenses.

Trial balance: After you have taken the balance of the Cash account in the ledger, it has a debit balance of 2,300 (we added the debits, we added the credits, and we took the difference between them, which resulted in 2,300 more on the left side). For Accounts Receivable 1,000 less 300 leaves us with a 700 debit balance. Salon Equipment has one number, so that is the balance (700 debit). Once Accounts Payable is balanced it is 400 larger on the credit side (700–300). The only other title that needs footing is Salon Fees, so the 3,500 and 1,000 are added together for a credit balance of 4,500. Once each balance is listed the sum on the left (8,900) does indeed equal the sum on the right (8,900). Each ending balance for Pam's Hair Salon ends up on the normal balance side.

Income Statement: Once the trial balance is complete, the first statement to make is the income statement, which is made up of only revenue and expense. Remember that there are no debits or credits on financial reports. All we are taking are the ending balances of each title from the trial balance. For the income statement, we list salon fees as the revenue and then list the three expense titles in the inside column. Total operating expenses are then subtracted from the salon fees to arrive at a net loss. Here revenue is less than operating expenses ($4,500–$5,100).

Statement of Owner's Equity: The second statement to prepare is the statement of owner's equity, which shows how to calculate a new figure for capital. Note that in this case the net loss of $600 is ADDED to the $100 of withdrawals, resulting in a decrease of $700 to capital. The new figure for capital is $3,300 ($4,000–$700).

Balance Sheet: The third statement is the balance sheet, which lists out each asset, each liability, and the new figure for capital. This report shows that as of June 30 total assets is $3,700 and total liabilities and owner's equity is $3,700. Remember that the ending figure for capital comes from the statement of owner's equity.

Summary: The trial balance is a list of ending balances of ledger accounts. These balances are used to prepare the three financial statements. Financial statements have no debits or credits. The inside columns are used to subtotal numbers. Revenue and expenses go on the income statement. Withdrawals and either net income or net loss go on the statement of owner's equity to calculate a new figure for capital. The balance sheet is a list of assets, liabilities, and the new amount for ending capital. Remember that the trial balance has debit or credits, not the financial statements.

COACHING TIP

	Dr.	Cr.
Cash	x	
Acc. Rec.	x	
Salon Equip.	x	
Accounts Pay.		x
Pam Jay, Cap.		x
Pam Jay, Withd.	x	
Salon Fees		x
Rent Expense	x	
Salon Supp. Exp.	x	
Salaries Exp.	x	

Note that titles on the trial balance are not indented.

DEMONSTRATION PROBLEM

MyAccountingLab

Debits and Credits: Analyzing and Recording Business Transactions

●●●○ L01, 2, 3, 4

56 29

The chart of accounts of Mel's Delivery Service includes the following: Cash, 111; Accounts Receivable, 112; Office Equipment, 121; Delivery Trucks, 122; Accounts Payable, 211; Mel Free, Capital, 311; Mel Free, Withdrawals, 312; Delivery Fees Earned, 411; Advertising Expense, 511; Gas Expense, 512; Salaries Expense, 513; and Telephone Expense, 514. The following transactions resulted for Mel's Delivery Service during the month of July:

Transaction A:	Mel invested $10,000 in the business from his personal savings account.
Transaction B:	Bought delivery trucks on account, $17,000.
Transaction C:	Advertising bill received but unpaid, $700.
Transaction D:	Bought office equipment for cash, $1,200.
Transaction E:	Received cash for delivery services rendered, $15,000.
Transaction F:	Paid salaries expense, $3,000.
Transaction G:	Paid gas expense for company trucks, $1,250.
Transaction H:	Billed customers for delivery services rendered, $4,000.
Transaction I:	Paid telephone bill, $300.
Transaction J:	Received $3,000 as partial payment of transaction H.
Transaction K:	Mel paid home telephone bill from company checkbook, $150.

Requirements

As Mel's newly employed accountant, you must do the following:

1. Set up T accounts in a ledger.

2. Record transactions in the T accounts. (Place the letter of the transaction next to the entry.)

3. Foot and take the balance of each account where appropriate.

4. Prepare a trial balance at the end of July.

5. Prepare from the trial balance, in proper form, (a) an income statement for the month of July, (b) a statement of owner's equity, and (c) a balance sheet as of July 31, 201X.

Demonstration Problem Solution

Requirements 1, 2, 3, 4

Set up T accounts, record transactions, foot each account, and prepare a trial balance.

		Demonstration Problem Complete
Part 1	Part 2	

GENERAL LEDGER

Cash 111			
(A)	10,000	1,200	(D)
(E)	15,000	3,000	(F)
(J)	3,000	1,250	(G)
		300	(I)
		150	(K)
	28,000	5,900	
	22,100		

Accts. Payable 211		
	17,000	(B)
	700	(C)
	17,700	

Advertising Expense 511		
(C)	700	

Accts. Receivable 112		
(H)	4,000	3,000	(J)
	1,000		

Mel Free, Capital 311		
	10,000	(A)

Gas Expense 512		
(G)	1,250	

Office Equipment 121	
(D)	1,200

Mel Free, Withdrawals 312	
(K)	150

Salaries Expense 513	
(F)	3,000

Delivery Trucks 122	
(B)	17,000

Delivery Fees Earned 411		
	15,000	(E)
	4,000	(H)
	19,000	

Telephone Expense 514	
(I)	300

Solution Tips to Recording Transactions

A. Cash	A	↑	Dr.
Mel Free, Capital	Cap.	↑	Cr.
B. Delivery Trucks	A	↑	Dr.
Accts. Payable	L	↑	Cr.
C. Advertising Expense	Exp.	↑	Dr.
Accts. Payable	L	↑	Cr.
D. Office Equipment	A	↑	Dr.
Cash	A	↓	Cr.
E. Cash	A	↑	Dr.
Del. Fees Earned	Rev.	↑	Cr.
F. Salaries Expense	Exp.	↑	Dr.
Cash	A	↓	Cr.
G. Gas Expense	Exp.	↑	Dr.
Cash	A	↓	Cr.
H. Acc. Receivable	A	↑	Dr.
Del. Fees Earned	Rev.	↑	Cr.
I. Tel. Expense	Exp.	↑	Dr.
Cash	A	↓	Cr.
J. Cash	A	↑	Dr.
Accts. Receivable	A	↓	Cr.
K. Mel Free, Withd.	Withd.	↑	Dr.
Cash	A	↓	Cr.

Mel's Delivery Service
Trial Balance
July 31, 201X

	Dr.	Cr.
Cash	22,100	
Accounts Receivable	1,000	
Office Equipment	1,200	
Delivery Trucks	17,000	
Accounts Payable		17,700
Mel Free, Capital		10,000
Mel Free, Withdrawals	150	
Delivery Fees Earned		19,000
Advertising Expense	700	
Gas Expense	1,250	
Salaries Expense	3,000	
Telephone Expense	300	
TOTALS	46,700	46,700

Solution Tips to Taking the Balance of an Account and Preparation of a Trial Balance

3. Footings: Cash   Add left side, $28,000.

Add right side, $5,900.

Take difference, $22,100, and stay on side that is larger.

Accounts Payable   Add $17,000 + $700 and stay on same side.

Total is $17,700.

4. Trial balance is a list of the ledger's ending balances. The list is in the same order as the chart of accounts. Each title has only one number listed either as a debit or credit balance.

Requirement 5

Prepare an Income Statement, Statement of Owner's Equity, and a Balance Sheet from the Trial Balance.

Part 1	Part 2	Demonstration Problem Complete

FIGURE 2.5
Financial Statements

5a.

MEL'S DELIVERY SERVICE
INCOME STATEMENT
FOR MONTH ENDED JULY 31, 201X

Revenue:		
Delivery Fees Earned		$19 0 0 0 00
Operating Expenses:		
Advertising Expense	$ 7 0 0 00	
Gas Expense	1 2 5 0 00	
Salaries Expense	3 0 0 0 00	
Telephone Expense	3 0 0 00	
Total Operating Expenses		5 2 5 0 00
Net Income		$13 7 5 0 00

b.

MEL'S DELIVERY SERVICE
STATEMENT OF OWNER'S EQUITY
FOR MONTH ENDED JULY 31, 201X

Mel Free, Capital		
July 1, 201X		$10 0 0 0 00
Net Income for July	$13 7 5 0 00	
Less Withdrawals for July	1 5 0 00	
Increase in Capital		$13 6 0 0 00
Mel Free, Capital		
July 31, 201X		$23 6 0 0 00

c.

MEL'S DELIVERY SERVICE
BALANCE SHEET
JULY 31, 201X

Assets		Liabilities and Owner's Equity	
Cash	$22 1 0 0 00	Liabilities	
Accounts Receivable	1 0 0 0 00	Accounts Payable	$17 7 0 0 00
Office Equipment	1 2 0 0 00		
Delivery Trucks	17 0 0 0 00		
		Owner's Equity	
		Mel Free, Capital	23 6 0 0 00
		Total Liab. and	
Total Assets	$41 3 0 0 00	Owner's Equity	$41 3 0 0 00

Solution Tips to Prepare Financial Statements from a Trial Balance

		Trial Balance	
		Dr.	Cr.
Balance Sheet	Assets	X	
	Liabilities		X
Statement of Equity	Capital		X
	Withdrawals	X	
Income Statement	Revenues		X
	Expenses	X	
		XX	XX

Net income of $13,750 on the income statement goes on the statement of owner's equity.

Ending capital of $23,600 on the statement of owner's equity goes on the balance sheet as the new figure for capital.

Note: Financial statements do not show debits or credits. The inside column is used for subtotaling.

Part 1	Part 2	Demonstration Problem Complete

BLUEPRINT: PREPARING FINANCIAL STATEMENTS FROM A TRIAL BALANCE

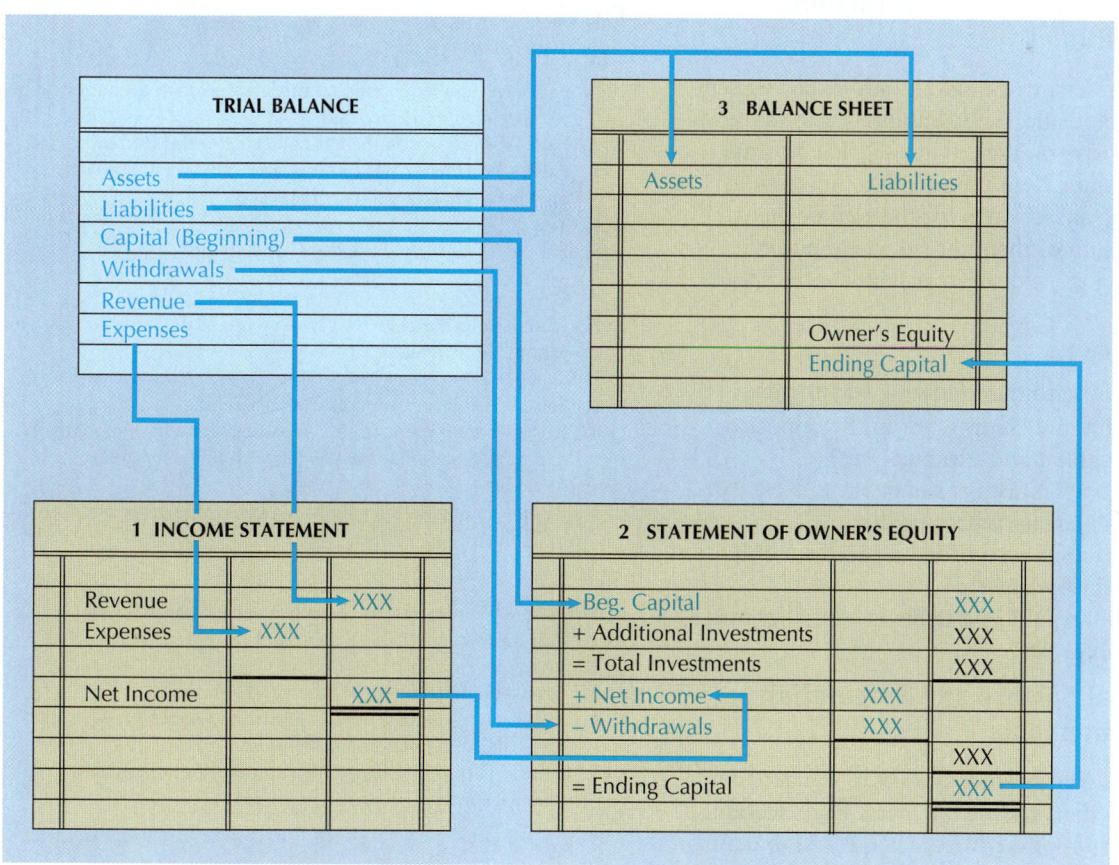

ACCOUNTING COACH

The following Coaching Tips are from Learning Units 2-1 to 2-3. Take the Pre-Game Checkup and use the Check Your Score at the bottom of the page to see how you are doing. The Accounting Coach provides tips before each Checkup to help you avoid common accounting errors.

LU 2-1 The T Account

Pre-Game Tips: Think of "debit" or "credit" as only indicating a position (left or right). To balance an account, total the left (debit) side and the right (credit) side and take the difference between the two totals. This ending balance is placed on the side that is greater. Do not think at this point of "debit" or "credit" as being good or bad. They simply indicate a position, left or right.

Pre-Game Checkup

Answer true or false to the following statements.
1. A number entered on the left side of an account is said to be credited to the account.
2. Debits always are positive.
3. Footings are always a credit balance.
4. "Credit" always means the number should be put on the right side.
5. A ledger does not use debits or credits.

LU 2-2 Recording Business Transactions: Debits and Credits

Pre-Game Tips: Assets, withdrawals, and expenses will increase on the debit side, while liabilities, capital, and revenues will increase on the credit side. The normal balance of an account is on the side that increases it. The goal of each transaction is for the sum of the left side to equal the sum of the right side. Compound entries result when three or more accounts affect a transaction.

Pre-Game Checkup

Answer true or false to the following statements.
1. Rules for debit and credit work in the opposite direction as capital and revenue.
2. Increase in an asset always is a debit.
3. Withdrawals increase with a credit.
4. After a transaction is recorded it can have only one debit and one credit.
5. An unpaid bill results in a debit to a liability and a credit to an expense.

LU 2-3 The Trial Balance and Preparation of Financial Statements

Pre-Game Tips: A trial balance is a list of the accounts in the ledger with their ending balances. Each account can only have a debit or credit balance. A trial balance will list assets, liabilities, capital, withdrawals, revenue, and expenses. When the financial statements are prepared there are no debits or credits on the financial reports. It is the ending balance of each account that is listed. The inside columns of financial reports are used for subtotaling.

Pre-Game Checkup

Answer true or false to the following statements.
1. Withdrawals are usually a credit balance on the trial balance.
2. A balance sheet will list only debit accounts.
3. The balance sheet is always prepared before the income statement.
4. Subtotaling is only used on the trial balance.
5. The beginning balance of capital is shown on the balance sheet.

CHECK YOUR SCORE: Answers to the Pre-Game Checkup

LU 2-1
1. False—A number entered on the left side of an account is said to be debited to the account.
2. False—Debits are on the left-hand side of the account.
3. False—Whether or not footings are a credit balance depends on which side is larger after balancing.
4. True.
5. False—A ledger does use debits and credits.

LU 2-2
1. False—Rules for debit and credit work in the same direction as capital and revenue.
2. True.
3. False—Withdrawals increase with a debit.
4. False—After a transaction is recorded it can have more than one debit or credit as long as the total of debits equals the total of credits.
5. False—An unpaid bill results in a debit to expense and a credit to liability.

LU 2-3
1. False—Withdrawals are usually a debit balance on the trial balance.
2. True.
3. False—prepared after the income statement.
4. False—Subtotaling is used in preparing financial reports; the trial balance is not a financial report.
5. False—The ending figure for capital is shown on the balance sheet.

Chapter Summary

Here are all the key concepts and equations to help you understand the concepts of this chapter and prepare you for your exam. After completing this review, go to MyAccountingLab for more practice opportunities.

MyAccountingLab

Concepts You Should Know	Key Terms	
Setting up and organizing a chart of accounts. 1. A T account is a simplified version of a standard account. 2. A ledger is a group of accounts. 3. A debit is the left-hand position (side) of an account, and a credit is the right-hand position (side). 4. A footing is the total of one side of an account. The ending balance is the difference between the footings.	Chart of accounts (p. 44) Compound entry (p. 45) Double-entry book-keeping (p. 45)	🔴 **L01**
Recording transactions in T accounts according to the rules of debit and credit. 1. A chart of accounts lists the account titles and their numbers for a company. 2. The transaction analysis chart is a teaching device. 3. A compound entry is a transaction involving more than one debit or credit. 4. In double-entry bookkeeping, the recording of each business transaction affects two or more accounts, and the total of debits equals the total of credits. 5. A trial balance is a list of the ending balances of all accounts, listed in the same order as the chart of accounts. 6. Any additional investments during the period result in the Capital balance on the trial balance not being the beginning figure. 7. No debit or credit columns are used in the three financial statements.	Account (p. 40) Credit (p. 40) Debit (p. 40) Ending balance (p. 41) Footings (p. 41) Ledger (p. 40) Normal balance of an account (p. 43) Standard account (p. 40) T account (p. 40)	🟢 **L02**
Preparing a trial balance. 1. A trial balance is a list of the ending balances of all accounts, listed in the same order as chart of accounts. 2. Any additional investments during the period result in the Capital balance on the trial balance not being the beginning figure.	Trial balance (p. 54)	🔵 **L03**
Preparing financial statements from a trial balance. 1. No debit or credit columns are used in the three financial statements. 2. To prepare the financial statements, take the balances of each ledger account to prepare the income statement, statement of owner's equity, and balance sheet.		🟡 **L04**

Discussion Questions and Critical Thinking/Ethical Case

1. Define a ledger.

2. Why is the left-hand side of an account called a debit?

3. Footings are used in balancing all accounts. True or false? Please explain.

4. What is the end product of the accounting process?

5. What do we mean when we say that a transaction analysis chart is a teaching device?

6. What are the five steps of the transaction analysis chart?

7. Explain the concept of double-entry bookkeeping.

8. A trial balance is a formal statement. True or false? Please explain.

9. Why are there no debit or credit columns on financial statements?

10. Compare the financial statements prepared from the expanded accounting equation with those prepared from a trial balance.

11. Audrey Flet, the bookkeeper of ALN Co., was scheduled to leave on a three-week vacation at 5:00 on Friday. She couldn't get the company's trial balance to balance. At 4:30, she decided to put in fictitious figures to make it balance. Audrey told herself she would fix it when she got back from her vacation. Was Audrey right or wrong to do this? Why?

MyAccountingLab

Concept Checks

LO1, 2 *(5 MIN)*

The T Account

1. From the following, foot and balance each account.

Cash 110				Ken Dalton, Capital 311	
7/24	3,000	7/25	100	7/3	11,000
7/26	11,000			7/11	6,000
				7/21	7,000

LO2 *(5 MIN)*

Transaction Analysis

2. Complete the following:

Account	Category	↑	↓	Normal Balance
A. Accounts Payable				
B. Taxable Fees Earned				
C. Accounts Receivable				
D. M. Blanc, Capital				
E. M. Blanc, Withdrawals				
F. Prepaid Advertising				
G. Rent Expense				

Transaction Analysis

L02 *(5 MIN)*

3. Record the following transaction in the transaction analysis chart:
Provided legal fees for $5,000, receiving $500 cash with the remainder
to be paid next month.

Accounts Affected	Category	↓	↑	Rules of Dr. and Cr.	T Accounts

Trial Balance

L04 *(5 MIN)*

4. Rearrange the following titles in the order they would appear on a trial
balance:

B. O'Mally, Withdrawals   Hair Salon Fees Earned

Accounts Receivable   Selling Expense

Cash   Salary Expense

B. O'Mally, Capital   Advertising Expense

Office Equipment   Accounts Payable

Trial Balance/Financial Statements

L03 *(10 MIN)*

5. From the following trial balance, identify which statement each title will
appear on:

- Income statement (IS)
- Statement of owner's equity (OE)
- Balance sheet (BS)

Bradford Co.
Trial Balance
Nov. 30, 201X

		Dr.	Cr.
A. _____	Cash	600	
B. _____	Computer	100	
C. _____	Computer Equipment	1,000	
D. _____	Accounts Payable		800
E. _____	L. Bradford, Capital		200
F. _____	L. Bradford, Withdrawals	500	
G. _____	Legal Fees Earned		1,500
H. _____	Consulting Fees Earned		300
I. _____	Wage Expense	200	
J. _____	Supplies Expense	250	
K. _____	Internet Advertising Expense	150	
	Totals	2,800	2,800

✓ MyAccountingLab   **Exercises**

Set A

● **L01** *(10 MIN)*   **2A-1.** From the following, prepare a chart of accounts.

Panasonic HD Television   Legal Fees

Salary Expense   L. Janas, Capital

Accounts Payable   Cash

Accounts Receivable   Advertising Expense

Repair Expense   L. Janas, Withdrawals

● **L02** *(5 MIN)*   **2A-2.** Record the following transaction in the transaction analysis chart: Shaylin Princeton bought a new piece of computer equipment for $26,000, paying $9,000 down and charging the rest.

● **L02** *(5 MIN)*   **2A-3.** Complete the following table. For each account listed on the left, fill in what category it belongs to, whether increases and decreases in the account are marked on the debit or credit sides, and on which financial statement the account appears. A sample is provided.

Accounts Affected	Category	↑	↓	Appears on Which Financial Statements
Computer Supplies	Asset	Dr.	Cr.	Balance Sheet
Legal Fees Earned				
P. Roy, Withdrawals				
Accounts Payable				
Salaries Expense				
Auto				

● **L02** *(20 MIN)*   **2A-4.** Given the following accounts, complete the table by inserting appropriate numbers next to the individual transaction to indicate which account is debited and which account is credited.

1. Cash
2. Accounts Receivable
3. Equipment
4. Accounts Payable
5. B. Barker, Capital
6. B. Barker, Withdrawals
7. Plumbing Fees Earned
8. Salaries Expense
9. Advertising Expense
10. Supplies Expenses

		Transaction	Rules Dr.	Cr.
Example:	**A.**	Paid salaries expense.	8	1
	B.	Bob paid personal utilities bill from the company checkbook.		
	C.	Advertising bill received but unpaid.		
	D.	Received cash from plumbing fees.		
	E.	Paid supplies expense.		
	F.	Bob invested in additional equipment for the business.		
	G.	Billed customers for plumbing services rendered.		
	H.	Received one-half the balance from transaction G.		
	I.	Bought equipment on account.		

2A-5. From the following trial balance of Hill's Cleaners (Figure 2.6), prepare the following:

- Income statement
- Statement of owner's equity
- Balance sheet

● L04 *(20 MIN)*

FIGURE 2.6

HILL'S CLEANERS TRIAL BALANCE MAY 31, 201X	Dr.	Cr.
Cash	8 0 0 00	
Equipment	7 0 0 00	
Accounts Payable		5 0 0 00
J. Hill, Capital		10 8 6 00
J. Hill, Withdrawals	2 3 0 00	
Cleaning Fees		4 1 5 00
Salaries Expense	1 0 0 00	
Utilities Expense	1 7 1 00	
Totals	20 0 1 00	20 0 1 00

Set B

2B-1. From the following, prepare a chart of accounts.

● L01 *(10 MIN)*

Copy machine	Legal Fees Earned
Salary Expense	L. Jones, Capital
Accounts Payable	Cash
Accounts Receivable	Advertising Expense
Rent Expense	L. Jones, Withdrawals

2B-2. Record the following transaction in the transaction analysis chart: Sally Pallermo bought a new piece of computer equipment for $11,000, paying $10,000 down and charging the rest.

● L02 *(5 MIN)*

2B-3. Complete the following table. For each account listed on the left, fill in what category it belongs to, whether increases and decreases in the account are marked on the debit or credit sides, and on which financial statement the account appears. A sample is provided.

● L02 *(5 MIN)*

Accounts Affected	Category	Increases	Decreases	Appears on Which Financial Statement
Office Supplies	Asset	Dr.	Cr.	Balance Sheet
Rental Fees Earned				
A. Troy, Withdrawals				
Accounts Payable				
Wage Expense				
Computer				

2B-4. Given the following accounts, complete the table by inserting appropriate numbers next to the individual transaction to indicate which account is debited and which account is credited.

● L02 *(20 MIN)*

1. Cash
2. Accounts Receivable
3. Furniture
4. Accounts Payable
5. B. Martin, Capital

6. B. Martin, Withdrawals
7. Photography Fees Earned
8. Salaries Expense
9. Advertising Expense
10. Supplies Expenses

	Transaction		Rules Dr.	Rules Cr.
Example:	A.	Paid salaries expense.	8	1
	B.	Bill paid personal utilities bill from the company checkbook.		
	C.	Advertising bill received but unpaid.		
	D.	Received cash from photography fees.		
	E.	Paid supplies expense.		
	F.	Bill invested in additional furniture for the business.		
	G.	Billed customers for photography services rendered.		
	H.	Received one-half the balance from transaction G.		
	I.	Bought furniture on account.		

● L04 *(20 MIN)*

2B-5. From the following trial balance of Hill's Cleaners (Figure 2.7), prepare the following:

- Income statement
- Statement of owner's equity
- Balance sheet

FIGURE 2.7

HILL'S CLEANERS TRIAL BALANCE MAY 31, 201X		
	Dr.	**Cr.**
Cash	8 0 0 00	
Equipment	7 0 0 00	
Accounts Payable		5 0 0 00
J. Hill, Capital		1 0 8 6 00
J. Hill, Withdrawals	2 3 0 00	
Cleaning Fees		4 1 5 00
Salaries Expense	1 0 0 00	
Utilities Expense	1 7 1 00	
Totals	2 0 0 1 00	2 0 0 1 00

MyAccountingLab

Problems

Set A

● L02 *(20 MIN)*

2A-1. The following transactions occurred in the opening and operation of Bryce's Delivery Service.

a. Bryce Orwell opened the delivery service by investing $28,000 from his personal savings account.

Check Figure:
After F:

Cash	
(A) 28,000	800 (F)
(D) 2,100	

b. Purchased used delivery trucks on account, $12,000.
c. Rent expense due but unpaid, $1,200.
d. Received cash for delivery, $2,100.
e. Billed a client on account, $300.
f. Bryce withdrew cash for personal use, $800.

Complete a transaction analysis chart for each of the transactions. The chart of accounts includes Cash; Accounts Receivable; Delivery Trucks; Accounts Payable; Bryce Orwell, Capital; Bryce Orwell, Withdrawals; Delivery Fees Earned; and Rent Expense.

2A-2. Brian Pud opened a consulting company, and the following transactions resulted:

● L02 *(20 MIN)*

    a. Brian invested $40,000 in the consulting agency.

    b. Bought office equipment on account, $7,000.

    c. Agency received cash for consulting work that it completed for a client, $2,000.

    d. Brian paid a personal bill from the company checkbook, $150.

    e. Paid advertising expense for the month, $300.

    f. Rent expense for the month due but unpaid, $1,000.

    g. Paid $1,100 as partial payment of what was owed from transaction B.

As Brian's accountant, analyze and record the transactions in T account form. Set up the T accounts and label each entry with the letter of the transaction.

Check Figure:
After G:

Cash		
(A) 40,000	150	(D)
(C) 2,000	300	(E)
	1,100	(G)

Chart of Accounts

Assets	Revenue
Cash 111	Consulting Fees Earned 411
Office Equipment 121	
Liabilities	**Expenses**
Accounts Payable 211	Advertising Expense 511
	Rent Expense 512
Owner's Equity	
Brian Pud, Capital 311	
Brian Pud, Withdrawals 312	

2A-3. From the following T accounts of Brad's Cleaning Service, (a) record and foot the balances, and (b) prepare a trial balance in proper form for October 31, 201X.

● L03 *(20 MIN)*

Check Figure:
Trial Balance Total $19,000

Cash 111		
(A) 10,000	(D)	300
(G) 4,000	(E)	400
	(F)	200
	(H)	300
	(I)	1,000

Accounts Payable 211		
(D) 300	(C)	2,300

Cleaning Fees Earned 411	
	(B) 7,000

Accounts Receivable 112		
(B) 7,000	(G)	4,000

Brad Joy, Capital 311	
	(A) 10,000

Rent Expense 511	
(F) 200	

Office Equipment 121	
(C) 2,300	
(H) 300	

Brad Joy, Withdrawals 312	
(I) 1,000	

Utilities Expense 512	
(E) 400	

2A-4. From the trial balance of Gail Lucas, Attorney-at-Law (Figure 2.8), prepare (a) an income statement for the month of May, (b) a statement of owner's equity for the month ended May 31, and (c) a balance sheet at May 31, 201X.

● L04 *(40 MIN)*

FIGURE 2.8

Check Figure:
Total Assets $7,350

GAIL LUCAS, ATTORNEY-AT-LAW TRIAL BALANCE MAY 31, 201X	Dr.	Cr.
Cash	5 0 0 0 00	
Accounts Receivable	1 1 0 0 00	
Office Equipment	1 2 5 0 00	
Accounts Payable		3 0 0 0 00
Salaries Payable		7 6 0 00
G. Lucas, Capital		3 6 9 0 00
G. Lucas, Withdrawals	6 0 0 00	
Revenue from Legal Fees		1 6 5 0 0 0
Utilities Expense	3 5 0 00	
Rent Expense	6 5 0 00	
Salaries Expense	1 5 0 00	
Totals	9 1 0 0 00	9 1 0 0 00

●●● **L02, 3, 4** *(60 MIN)*

Check Figure:
Total Trial Balance $45,200

2A-5. The chart of accounts for Annis's Delivery Service is as follows:

Chart of Accounts

Assets
Cash 111
Accounts Receivable 112
Office Equipment 121
Delivery Trucks 122

Liabilities
Accounts Payable 211

Owner's Equity
Avery Annis, Capital 311
Avery Annis, Withdrawals 312

Revenue
Delivery Fees Earned 411

Expenses
Advertising Expense 511
Gas Expense 512
Salaries Expense 513
Telephone Expense 514

Annis's Delivery Service completed the following transactions during the month of August:

Transaction A:	Avery Annis invested $29,000 in the delivery service from her personal savings account.
Transaction B:	Bought delivery trucks on account, $12,000.
Transaction C:	Bought office equipment for cash, $600.
Transaction D:	Paid advertising expense, $650.
Transaction E:	Collected cash for delivery services rendered, $2,300.
Transaction F:	Paid drivers' salaries, $600.
Transaction G:	Paid gas expense for trucks, $1,600.
Transaction H:	Performed delivery services for a customer on account, $1,700.
Transaction I:	Telephone expense due but unpaid, $200.
Transaction J:	Received $250 as partial payment of transaction H.
Transaction K:	Avery withdrew cash for personal use, $300.

As Avery's newly hired accountant, you must perform the following:

1. The T accounts in the ledger have been set up for you. Record transactions in the T accounts. (Place the letter of the transaction next to the entry.)
2. Foot the T accounts where appropriate.
3. Prepare a trial balance at the end of August.
4. Prepare from the trial balance, in proper form, (a) an income statement for the month of August, (b) a statement of owner's equity, and (c) a balance sheet as of August 31, 201X.

Set B

2B-1. The following transactions occurred in the opening and operation of Bryon's Delivery Service. Complete a transaction analysis chart for each of the transactions.

● **L02** *(20 MIN)*

Transaction A:	Bryon Orn opened the delivery service by investing $50,000 from his personal savings account.
Transaction B:	Purchased used delivery trucks on account, $7,000.
Transaction C:	Rent expense due but unpaid, $1,200.
Transaction D:	Received cash for delivery, $1,700.
Transaction E:	Billed a client on account, $150.
Transaction F:	Bryon withdrew cash for personal use, $100.

The chart of accounts for the shop includes Cash; Accounts Receivable; Delivery Truck; Accounts Payable; Bryon Orn, Capital; Bryon Orn, Withdrawals; Delivery Fees Earned; and Rent Expense.

Check Figure:
After F:

Cash	
(A) 50,000	100 (F)
(D) 1,700	

2B-2. Brian Pud opened a consulting company, and the following transactions resulted. As Brian's accountant, analyze and record the transactions in T account form. Label each entry with the letter of the transaction.

● **L02** *(20 MIN)*

Transaction A:	Brian invested $18,000 in the consulting agency.
Transaction B:	Bought office equipment on account, $4,000.
Transaction C:	Agency received cash for consulting work that it completed for a client, $2,400.
Transaction D:	Brian paid a personal bill from the company checkbook, $50.
Transaction E:	Paid advertising expense for the month, $200.
Transaction F:	Rent expense for the month due but unpaid, $1,200.
Transaction G:	Paid $900 as partial payment of what was owed from transaction B.

The chart of accounts includes Cash, 111; Office Equipment, 121; Accounts Payable, 211; Brian Pud, Capital, 311; Brian Pud, Withdrawals, 312; Consulting Fees Earned, 411; Advertising Expense, 511; and Rent Expense, 512.

Check Figure:
After G:

Cash	
(A) 18,000	50 (D)
(C) 2,400	200 (E)
	900 (G)

2B-3. From the following T accounts of Brad's Cleaning Service, (a) record and foot the balances, and (b) prepare a trial balance in proper form for October 31, 201X.

● **L03** *(20 MIN)*

Cash 111			
(A)	12,000	(D)	1,000
(G)	3,500	(E)	150
		(F)	100
		(H)	250
		(I)	600

Accounts Receivable 112			
(B)	14,000	(G)	3,500

Office Equipment 121		
(C)	1,400	
(H)	250	

Accounts Payable 211			
(D)	1,000	(C)	1,400

Brad Joy, Capital 311		
	(A)	12,000

Brad Joy, Withdrawals 312		
(I)	600	

Check Figure:
Trial Balance Total $26,400

Cleaning Fees Earned 411		
	(B)	14,000

Rent Expense 511		
(F)	100	

Utilities Expense 512		
(E)	150	

L04 *(40 MIN)*

FIGURE 2.9

Check Figure:
Total Assets $8,000

2B-4. From the trial balance of Gail Lucas, Attorney-at-Law (Figure 2.9), prepare (a) an income statement for the month of May, (b) a statement of owner's equity for the month ended May 31, and (c) a balance sheet at May 31, 201X.

GAIL LUCAS, ATTORNEY-AT-LAW TRIAL BALANCE MAY 31, 201X	Debit	Credit
Cash	6 0 0 0 00	
Accounts Receivable	7 5 0 00	
Office Equipment	1 2 5 0 00	
Accounts Payable		6 2 0 0 00
Salaries Payable		7 7 0 00
G. Lucas, Capital		1 1 8 0 00
G. Lucas, Withdrawals	8 0 0 00	
Revenue from Legal Fees		1 8 0 0 00
Utilities Expense	1 5 0 00	
Rent Expense	5 0 0 00	
Salaries Expense	5 0 0 00	
Totals	9 9 5 0 00	9 9 5 0 00

L02, 3, 4 *(60 MIN)*

Check Figure:
Trial Balance Total $33,700

2B-5. The chart of accounts of Annis's Delivery Service is as follows: Cash, 111; Accounts Receivable, 112; Office Equipment, 121; Delivery Trucks, 122; Accounts Payable, 211; Avery Annis, Capital, 311; Avery Annis, Withdrawals, 312; Delivery Fees Earned, 411; Advertising Expense, 511; Gas Expense, 512; Salaries Expense, 513; and Telephone Expense, 514. Annis's Delivery Service completed the following transactions during the month of August:

Transaction A:	Avery invested $17,000 in the delivery service from her personal savings account.
Transaction B:	Bought delivery trucks on account, $11,000.
Transaction C:	Bought office equipment for cash, $600.
Transaction D:	Paid advertising expense, $350.
Transaction E:	Collected cash for delivery services rendered, $3,500.
Transaction F:	Paid drivers' salaries, $900.
Transaction G:	Paid gas expense for trucks, $1,700.
Transaction H:	Performed delivery services for a customer on account, $1,600.
Transaction I:	Telephone expense due but unpaid, $600.
Transaction J:	Received $400 as partial payment of transaction H.
Transaction K:	Avery withdrew cash for personal use, $250.

As Avery's newly hired accountant, you must perform the following:

1. The T accounts in the ledger have been set up for you. Record transactions in the T accounts. (Place the letter of the transaction next to the entry.)
2. Foot the T accounts where appropriate.
3. Prepare a trial balance at the end of August.
4. Prepare from the trial balance, in proper form, (a) an income statement for the month of August, (b) a statement of owner's equity, and (c) a balance sheet as of August 31, 201X.

Financial Report Problem

Reading the Kellogg's Annual Report

● L04 (5 min)

Go to http://investor.kelloggs.com/annuals.cfm, to access the Kellogg's 2010 Annual Report and find the balance sheet of Kellogg's. Did Kellogg's Accounts Payable go up or down from 2009 to 2010? What does this change mean? Into what category does Accounts Payable fall by rules of debit and credit? Which side of the T account would make Accounts Payable increase?

ON the JOB |||||||||||||||||||||

SANCHEZ COMPUTER CENTER

●●● L02, 3, 4 (60 MIN)

The Sanchez Computer Center created its chart of accounts as follows:

Chart of Accounts as of July 1, 201X

Assets		Revenue	
1000	Cash	4000	Service Revenue
1020	Accounts Receivable	**Expenses**	
1030	Supplies	5010	Advertising Expense
1080	Computer Shop Equipment	5020	Rent Expense
1090	Office Equipment	5030	Utilities Expense
Liabilities		5040	Phone Expense
2000	Accounts Payable	5050	Supplies Expense
Owner's Equity		5060	Insurance Expense
3000	Freedman, Capital	5070	Postage Expense
3010	Freedman, Withdrawals		

You will use this chart of accounts to complete the Continuing Problem.

The following problem continues from Chapter 1. The balances as of July 31 have been brought forward in the working papers that accompany this text.

Assignment

1. Set up T accounts in a ledger.

2. Record transactions k through s in the appropriate T accounts.

3. Foot and take the balances of the T accounts where appropriate.

4. Prepare a trial balance at the end of August.

5. Prepare from the trial balance an income statement, statement of owner's equity, and a balance sheet for the two months ending with August 31, 201X.

   k. Received the phone bill for the month of July, $155.

   l. Paid $150 (check #8099) for insurance for the month.

   m. Paid $200 (check #8100) of the amount due from transaction d in Chapter 1.

   n. Paid advertising expense for the month, $1,400 (check #8101).

   o. Billed a client (Jeannine Sparks) for services rendered, $850.

   p. Collected $900 for services rendered.

   q. Paid the electric bill in full for the month of July (check #8102, transaction h, Chapter 1).

   r. Paid cash (check #8103) for $50 in stamps.

   s. Purchased $200 worth of supplies from Computer Connection on credit.

SUBWAY CASE

Debits on the Left . . .

When Stan took the big leap from being an employee to a Subway owner, the thing that terrified him most was *not* the part about managing people—that was one of his strengths as a marketing manager. Why, at Xellent Media, 40 sales reps reported to him! No, Stan was terrified of having to manage the accounts. Subway restaurant owners have so many accounts to deal with: food costs, payroll, rent, utilities, supplies, advertising, promotion, and, biggest of all, cash. It's critical for them to keep debits and credits straight. If not, both they and Subway could lose a lot of money, quickly.

LO2 *(20 MIN)*

Even though Stan got some intense training in accounting and bookkeeping at Subway University, he still felt shaky about doing his own books. When he confided his fears to Mariah Washington, his field consultant, she suggested he hire an accountant. "You need to play to your strengths," said Mariah, and she told Stan, "More and more owners are using accountants, and almost all owners of multiple franchises do. In fact, some accountants actually specialize in handling Subway accounts for these multirestaurant owners."

Even though Stan decided to hire his cousin, Lila, to do his accounting, he still needs to feed her the right data so she can calculate his T accounts. Like many small business owners, Stan enters data into an accounting software program such as QuickBooks or Peachtree, which he then uploads to his accountant, who edits it and reviews it for accuracy. Several times in the beginning Stan mistakenly debited both cash and supplies when he paid for orders of paper cups, bread dough, and other supplies.

Lila urged Stan to review the rules for recording debits and credits. She even told him to practice for a while using a paper ledger. "On the computer debits and credits are not as visible as they are with your paper system. Since you only enter the payables, the computer does the other side of the balance sheet. So you have to bone up on debits and credits to ensure that your Peachtree data are correct."

Discussion Questions

1. Why is the cash account so important in Stan's business?
2. Why do you think that most owners of the larger shops use accountants to do their books instead of doing the accounting themselves?
3. Is the difference between debits and credits important to Subway restaurant owners who don't do their own books?

Beginning the Accounting Cycle

THE GAME PLAN

Did you ever go to the airport late at night and wonder how an airline gets all its planes ready and safe for the next day's flights? American Airlines completes a checklist for its airplanes' maintenance and cleaning. Day in and day out, these checklists must be followed. Just like the American Airlines maintenance and cleaning procedures, specific steps must be completed in accounting for American Airlines to properly maintain its accounting records over a period of time. These procedures or steps are referred to as the **accounting cycle**. Once one cycle is completed (usually called a fiscal year), another cycle is begun. Learning the accounting procedures necessary during an accounting cycle will help you understand how businesses like American Airlines maintain consistent accounting records.

LEARNING OBJECTIVES

1. Journalizing: analyzing and recording business transactions into a journal.
2. Posting: transferring information from a journal to a ledger.
3. Preparing a trial balance.

Accounting cycle For each accounting period, the process that begins with the recording of business transactions or procedures into a journal and ends with the completion of a post-closing trial balance.

Accounting period The period of time for which an income statement is prepared.

Calendar year The 12-month period a business chooses for its accounting year. Alternatively known as fiscal year and natural business year.

Interim reports Financial statements that are prepared for a month, quarter, or some other portion of the fiscal year.

Companies like American Airlines have to perform certain accounting procedures. The normal accounting procedures that are performed over a period of time are called the accounting cycle. The accounting cycle takes place in a period of time called an accounting period. An accounting period is the period of time covered by the income statement. Although it can be any time period up to one year (e.g., one month or three months), most businesses use a one-year accounting period. The year can be either a calendar year (January 1 through December 31) or a fiscal year.

A fiscal year is an accounting period that runs for any 12 consecutive months, so it can be the same as a calendar year. Big Dollar and Aeropostale, Inc., end their accounting periods on January 31. A business can choose any fiscal year that is convenient. For example, some retailers may decide to end their fiscal year when inventories and business activity are at a low point, such as after the Christmas season. This period is called a natural business year. Using a natural business year allows the business to count its year-end inventory when it is easiest to do so.

Businesses would not be able to operate successfully if they only prepared financial reports at the end of their calendar or fiscal year. For more timely information, most businesses prepare interim reports on a monthly, quarterly, or semiannual basis.

In this chapter, as well as in Chapters 4 and 5, we follow Brenda Clark's new business, Clark's Word Processing Services. We follow the normal accounting procedures that the business performs over a period of time. Clark has chosen to use a fiscal period of January 1 to December 31, which also is the calendar year.

● **LO1**   **LEARNING UNIT 3-1 ANALYZING AND RECORDING BUSINESS TRANSACTIONS INTO A JOURNAL:**

Steps 1 and 2 of the Accounting Cycle

The General Journal

Chapter 2 taught us how to analyze and record business transactions into T accounts, or ledger accounts. Recording a debit in an account on one page of the ledger and recording the corresponding credit on a different page of the ledger, however, can make it difficult to find errors. It would be much easier if all the business's transactions were located in the same place. That is the function of the journal or general journal. Transactions are entered in the journal in chronological order (January 1, 8, 15, etc.), and then this recorded information is used to update the ledger accounts. In computerized accounting, a journal may be stored on disk.

Journal A listing of business transactions in chronological order. The journal links on one page the debit and credit parts of transactions. Alternatively known as general journal.

Journal entry The transaction (debits and credits) that is recorded into a journal once it is analyzed.

Journalizing The process of recording a transaction entry into the journal.

Book of original entry Book that records the first formal information about business transactions. Example: a journal.

Book of final entry Book that receives information about business transactions from a book of original entry (a journal). Example: a ledger.

We will use a general journal, the simplest form of a journal, to record the transactions of Clark's Word Processing Services. A transaction [debit(s) + credit(s)] that has been analyzed and recorded in a journal is called a journal entry. The process of recording the journal entry into the journal is called journalizing.

The journal is called the book of original entry because it contains the first formal information about the business transactions. The ledger is known as the book of final entry because the information the journal contains will be transferred to the ledger. Like the ledger, the journal may be a bound or loose-leaf book. Each of the journal pages looks like or similar to the one in Figure 3.1. The pages of the journal are numbered consecutively from page 1. Keep in mind that the journal and the ledger are separate books.

Relationship between the Journal and the Chart of Accounts The accountant must refer to the business's chart of accounts for the account name that is to be used in the journal. Every company has its own "unique" chart of accounts.

The following chart of accounts for Clark's Word Processing Services lists the accounts used in the business. By the end of Chapter 5, we will have discussed each of these accounts.

Date	Account Titles and Description	PR	Dr.	Cr.

**CLARK'S WORD PROCESSING SERVICES
GENERAL JOURNAL**

Page 1

FIGURE 3.1
The General Journal

Note that we will continue to use transaction analysis charts as a teaching aid in the journalizing process.

Clark's Word Processing Services
Chart of Accounts

Assets (100–199)

111 Cash
112 Accounts Receivable
114 Office Supplies
115 Prepaid Rent
121 Word Processing Equipment
122 Accumulated Depreciation,
Word Processing Equipment

Liabilities (200–299)
211 Accounts Payable
212 Salaries Payable

Owner's Equity (300–399)

311 Brenda Clark, Capital
312 Brenda Clark, Withdrawals
313 Income Summary
Revenue (400–499)
411 Word Processing Fees
Expenses (500–599)
511 Office Salaries Expense
512 Advertising Expense
513 Telephone Expense
514 Office Supplies Expense
515 Rent Expense
516 Depreciation Expense,
Word Processing Equipment

Journalizing the Transactions of Clark's Word Processing Services Certain formalities must be followed in making journal entries:

- The debit portion of the transaction always is recorded first.
- The credit portion of a transaction is indented a ½ inch and placed below the debit portion.
- The explanation of the journal entry follows immediately after the credit and is indented 1 inch from the date column.
- A one-line space follows each transaction and explanation. This makes the journal easier to read, and there is less chance of mixing transactions.
- Each transaction must affect at least two different accounts.
- Finally, as always, the total amount of debits must equal the total amount of credits. The same format is used for each of the entries in the journal.

MAY 1, 201X: BRENDA CLARK BEGAN THE BUSINESS BY INVESTING $10,000 IN CASH			
1	2	3	4
Accounts Affected	Category	↓↑	Rules of Dr. and Cr.
Cash	Asset	↑	Dr.
Brenda Clark, Capital	Capital	↑	Cr.

COACHING TIP

For now the PR (posting reference) column is blank; we discuss it later.

	CLARK'S WORD PROCESSING SERVICES GENERAL JOURNAL				
					Page 1
Date	Account Titles and Description	PR	Dr.	Cr.	
201X May 1	Cash		10000 00		
	Brenda Clark, Capital			10000 00	
	Initial investment of cash by owner				

Let's now look at the structure of this journal entry (Figure 3.2). The entry contains the following information:

1. Year of the journal entry   201X
2. Month of the journal entry   May
3. Day of the journal entry   1
4. Name(s) of accounts debited   Cash
5. Name(s) of accounts credited   Brenda Clark, Capital
6. Explanation of transaction   Investment of cash
7. Amount of debit(s) $10,000
8. Amount of credit(s) $10,000

MAY 1: PURCHASED WORD PROCESSING EQUIPMENT FROM BEN CO. FOR $6,000, PAYING $1,000 AND PROMISING TO PAY THE BALANCE WITHIN 30 DAYS			
1	2	3	4
Accounts Affected	Category	↓↑	Rules of Dr. and Cr.
Word Processing Equipment	Asset	↑	Dr.
Cash	Asset	↓	Cr.
Accounts Payable	Liability	↑	Cr.

This transaction affects three accounts. When a journal entry has more than two accounts, it is called a compound journal entry.

In this entry (Figure 3.3), only the day is entered in the date column because the year and month were entered at the top of the page from the first transaction. This information doesn't need to be repeated until a new page is needed or a change of months occurs.

Compound journal entry A journal entry that affects more than two accounts.

1	Word Processing Equipment	6000 00		
	Cash		1000 00	
	Accounts Payable		5000 00	
	Purchase of equipment from Ben Co.			

MAY 1: RENTED OFFICE SPACE, PAYING $1,200 IN ADVANCE FOR THE FIRST THREE MONTHS			
1	2	3	4
Accounts Affected	Category	↓↑	Rules of Dr. and Cr.
Prepaid Rent	Asset	↑	Dr.
Cash	Asset	↓	Cr.

COACHING TIP

Rent paid in advance is an asset.

In this transaction (Figure 3.4) Clark gains an asset called prepaid rent and gives up an asset, cash. The prepaid rent does not become an expense until it expires.

	1	Prepaid Rent		1	2	0	0	00			
		Cash						1	2	0	0	00
		Rent paid in advance—(3 months)							

FIGURE 3.4
Paid Rent in Advance

MAY 3: PURCHASED OFFICE SUPPLIES FROM NORRIS CO. ON ACCOUNT, $600			
1	2	3	4
Accounts Affected	Category	↓↑	Rules of Dr. and Cr.
Office Supplies	Asset	↑	Dr.
Accounts Payable	Liability	↑	Cr.

Remember, supplies are an asset when they are purchased. Once they are used up or consumed in the operation of business, they become an expense (Figure 3.5).

COACHING TIP

Supplies become an expense when used up.

	3	Office Supplies		6	0	0	00		
		Accounts Payable				6	0	0	00
		Purchase of supplies on account				
		from Norris				

FIGURE 3.5
Purchased Supplies on Account

MAY 7: COMPLETED SALES PROMOTION PIECES FOR A CLIENT AND IMMEDIATELY COLLECTED $3,000			
1	2	3	4
Accounts Affected	Category	↓↑	Rules of Dr. and Cr.
Cash	Asset	↑	Dr.
Word Processing Fees	Revenue	↑	Cr.

	7	Cash		3	0	0	0	00		
		Word Processing Fees				3	0	0	0	00
		Cash received for services rendered				

FIGURE 3.6
Services Rendered

MAY 13: PAID OFFICE SALARIES, $650			
1	2	3	4
Accounts Affected	Category	↓↑	Rules of Dr. and Cr.
Office Salaries Expense	Expense	↑	Dr.
Cash	Asset	↓	Cr.

	13	Office Salaries Expense		6	5	0	00		
		Cash				6	5	0	00
		Payment of office salaries				

FIGURE 3.7
Paid Salaries

MAY 18: ADVERTISING BILL FROM AL'S NEWS CO. COMES IN BUT IS NOT PAID, $250			
1	2	3	4
Accounts Affected	Category	↓↑	Rules of Dr. and Cr.
Advertising Expense	Expense	↑	Dr.
Accounts Payable	Liability	↑	Cr.

COACHING TIP

Remember, expenses are recorded when they are incurred, no matter when they are paid.

FIGURE 3.8
Received Advertising Bill

	18	Advertising Expense		2 5 0 00	
		Accounts Payable			2 5 0 00
		Bill in but not paid from Al's News			

COACHING TIP

Keep in mind that as withdrawals increase, owner's equity decreases.

MAY 20: BRENDA CLARK WROTE A CHECK ON THE BANK ACCOUNT OF THE BUSINESS TO PAY HER HOME MORTGAGE PAYMENT OF $625

1 Accounts Affected	2 Category	3 ↓↑	4 Rules of Dr. and Cr.
Brenda Clark, Withdrawals	Withdrawals	↑	Dr.
Cash	Asset	↓	Cr.

FIGURE 3.9
Personal Withdrawal

	20	Brenda Clark, Withdrawals		6 2 5 00	
		Cash			6 2 5 00
		Personal withdrawal of cash			

COACHING TIP

Reminder: Revenue is recorded when it is earned, no matter when the cash is actually received.

MAY 22: BILLED MORRIS COMPANY FOR A SOPHISTICATED WORD PROCESSING JOB, $5,000

1 Accounts Affected	2 Category	3 ↓↑	4 Rules of Dr. and Cr.
Accounts Receivable	Asset	↑	Dr.
Word Processing Fees	Revenue	↑	Cr.

FIGURE 3.10
Fees Earned

	22	Accounts Receivable		5 0 0 0 00	
		Word Processing Fees			5 0 0 0 00
		Billed Morris Co. for fees earned			

MAY 27: PAID OFFICE SALARIES, $650

1 Accounts Affected	2 Category	3 ↓↑	4 Rules of Dr. and Cr.
Office Salaries Expense	Expense	↑	Dr.
Cash	Asset	↓	Cr.

FIGURE 3.11
Paid Salaries

CLARK'S WORD PROCESSING SERVICES GENERAL JOURNAL					
					Page 2
Date		Account Titles and Description	PR	Dr.	Cr.
201X May	27*	Office Salaries Expense		6 5 0 00	
		Cash			6 5 0 00
		Payment of office salaries			

*Note that this is a new page, so the year and month are repeated.

MAY 28: PAID HALF THE AMOUNT OWED FOR WORD PROCESSING EQUIPMENT PURCHASED MAY 1 FROM BEN CO., $2,500			
1	**2**	**3**	**4**
Accounts Affected	**Category**	**↓↑**	**Rules of Dr. and Cr.**
Accounts Payable	Liability	↓	Dr.
Cash	Asset	↓	Cr.

	28	Accounts Payable		2 5 0 0 00	
		Cash			2 5 0 0 00
		Paid half the amount owed Ben Co.			

FIGURE 3.12
Partial Payment

MAY 29: RECEIVED AND PAID TELEPHONE BILL, $220			
1	**2**	**3**	**4**
Accounts Affected	**Category**	**↓↑**	**Rules of Dr. and Cr.**
Telephone Expense	Expense	↑	Dr.
Cash	Asset	↓	Cr.

	29	Telephone Expense		2 2 0 00	
		Cash			2 2 0 00
		Paid telephone bill			

FIGURE 3.13
Paid Telephone Bill

This concludes the journal transactions of Clark's Word Processing Services for the month of May.

LEARNING UNIT 3-1 REVIEW

AT THIS POINT you should be able to do the following:

- Define an accounting cycle.
- Define and explain the relationship of the accounting period to the income statement.
- Compare and contrast a calendar year to a fiscal year.
- Explain the term *natural business year*.
- Explain the function of interim reports.
- Define and state the purpose of a journal.
- Compare and contrast a book of original entry to a book of final entry.
- Differentiate between a chart of accounts and a journal.
- Journalize a business transaction.
- Explain a compound entry.

Instant Replay ◉ Self-Review Quiz 3-1

The following are the transactions of Lowe's Repair Service for the month of June 201X. Journalize the transactions in proper form. The chart of accounts includes Cash; Accounts Receivable; Prepaid Rent; Repair Supplies; Repair Equipment; Accounts Payable; A. Lowe, Capital; A. Lowe, Withdrawals; Repair Fees Earned; Salaries Expense; Advertising Expense; and Supplies Expense.

201X

June 1	A. Lowe invested $7,000 cash and $5,000 of repair equipment in the business.
1	Paid two months' rent in advance, $1,200.
4	Bought repair supplies from Melvin Co. on account, $600. (These supplies have not yet been consumed or used up.)
15	Performed repair work, received $600 in cash, and had to bill Doe Co. for remaining balance of $300.
18	A. Lowe paid his home telephone bill, $50, with a check from the company.
20	Advertising bill for $400 from Jones Co. received but payment not due yet. (Advertising has already appeared in the newspaper.)
24	Paid salaries, $1,400.

Solution to Instant Replay: Self-Review Quiz 3-1

FIGURE 3.14
Transactions Journalized

LOWE'S REPAIR SERVICE
GENERAL JOURNAL

Page 1

Date		Account Titles and Description	PR	Dr.	Cr.
201X June	1	Cash		7 0 0 0 00	
		Repair Equipment		5 0 0 0 00	
		A. Lowe, Capital			12 0 0 0 00
		Owner investment			
	1	Prepaid Rent		1 2 0 0 00	
		Cash			1 2 0 0 00
		Rent paid in advance—2 mos.			
	4	Repair Supplies		6 0 0 00	
		Accounts Payable			6 0 0 00
		Purchase on account from Melvin Co.			
	15	Cash		6 0 0 00	
		Accounts Receivable		3 0 0 00	
		Repair Fees Earned			9 0 0 00
		Performed repairs for Doe Co.			
	18	A. Lowe, Withdrawals		5 0 00	
		Cash			5 0 00
		Personal withdrawal			
	20	Advertising Expense		4 0 0 00	
		Accounts Payable			4 0 0 00
		Advertising bill from Jones Co.			
	24	Salaries Expense		1 4 0 0 00	
		Cash			1 4 0 0 00
		Paid salaries			

PLAY BY PLAY: EXTRA HELP ON SELF-REVIEW QUIZ 3-1

Let's review first: When recording transactions into a general journal, the accounts debited will be aligned to the date column and the credit(s) will be indented. These titles will come from the chart of accounts. The explanation line will then be indented below the last credit entry. The sum of the left side (Dr.) must equal the sum of the right side (Cr.) for each transaction.

Here are the transaction analysis charts for each transaction. Be sure to remember that the accounts affected come from the chart of accounts. You have six categories: assets, liabilities, capital, withdrawals, revenues, and expenses. You must ask yourself what the company is getting and how it is getting it. Remember to think of expenses and withdrawals as increasing, resulting in a decrease to owner's equity.

June 1	Cash	Asset	↑	Dr.
	Repair Equip.	Asset	↑	Dr.
	A. Lowe, Cap.	Capital	↑	Cr.

Debits are listed first against the date column and credits are indented. This is an investment by the owner. The month is written because the month starts a new page.

1	Prepaid Rent	Asset	↑	Dr.
	Cash	Asset	↓	Cr.

This is a shift in assets, more rent paid in advance by cash. Note that the month is not repeated.

4	Repair Supplies	Asset	↑	Dr.
	Accounts Payable	Liability	↑	Cr.

This is an example of buy now and pay later. Supplies will not be an expense until they are used up.

15	Cash	Asset	↑	Dr.
	Acc. Receiv.	Asset	↑	Dr.
	Rep. Fees Earn.	Revenue	↑	Cr.

Here we did the work and got some money as well as some promises that the customer will pay later. Note how the two debits are against the date column and the credit is indented.

18	A. Lowe, Withd.	Withdr.	↑	Dr.
	Cash	Asset	↓	Cr.

The owner increases her withdrawals for personal use, and the end result is that the business has less cash.

20	Advertising Exp.	Expense	↑	Dr.
	Accounts Pay.	Liability	↑	Cr.

An expense has been incurred but is not paid for. This expense has created a liability. Think of expenses as always increasing.

24	Salaries Exp.	Expense	↑	Dr.
	Cash	Asset	↓	Cr.

Here the expense is increasing and it is being paid for in cash.

COACHING TIP

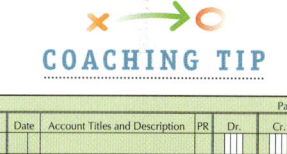

The journal (green) is the book of original entry and the ledger (blue) is the book of final entry.

LO2

LEARNING UNIT 3-2 POSTING TO THE LEDGER:
Step 3 of the Accounting Cycle

The general journal serves a particular purpose: It puts every transaction the business does in one place. It cannot do certain things, though. For example, if you were asked to find the balance of the cash account from the general journal, you would have to go through the entire journal and look for only the cash entries. Then you would have to add up the debits and credits for the Cash account and determine the difference between the two.

Posting The transferring, copying, or recording of information from a journal to a ledger.

What we really need to do to find balances of accounts is to transfer the information from the journal to the ledger. This process is called posting. In the ledger we accumulate an ending balance for each account so that we can prepare financial statements.

FIGURE 3.15
Four-Column Account

COACHING TIP

$5,000 Cr. + $600 Cr. = $5,600 Cr.

Accounts Payable						Account No. 211		
			Post.				Balance	
Date	Explanation		Ref.	Debit	Credit		Debit	Credit
201X May	1		GJ1		5 0 0 0 00			5 0 0 0 00
	3		GJ1		6 0 0 00			5 6 0 0 00
	18		GJ1		2 5 0 00			5 8 5 0 00
	28		GJ2	2 5 0 0 00				3 3 5 0 00

In Chapter 2 we used the T account form to make our ledger entries. T accounts are simple, but they are not used in the real business world; they are only used for demonstration purposes. In practice, accountants often use a four-column account form that includes a column for the business's running balance. Figure 3.15 shows a standard four-column account. We use this format in the text from now on.

Four-column account A running balance account that records debits and credits and has a column for an ending balance (debit or credit). It replaces the standard two-column account we used earlier.

Posting

Now let's look at how to post the transactions of Clark's Word Processing Services from its journal. The diagram in Figure 3.16 shows how to post the cash line from the journal to the ledger. The steps in the posting process are numbered and illustrated in the figure.

> **STEP 1:** In the Cash account in the ledger, record the date (May 1, 201X) and the amount of the entry ($10,000).
>
> **STEP 2:** Record the page number of the journal "GJ1" in the posting reference (PR) column of the Cash account.
>
> **STEP 3:** Calculate the new balance of the account. To keep a running balance in each account, as you would in your personal checkbook, take the present balance in the account on the previous line and add or subtract the transaction as necessary to arrive at your new balance.
>
> **STEP 4:** Record the account number of Cash (111) in the posting reference (PR) column of the journal. This listing is known as cross-referencing.

Cross-referencing Adding to the PR column of the journal the account number of the ledger account that was updated from the journal.

The same sequence of steps occurs for each line in the journal. In a manual system like Clark's, the debits and credits in the journal may be posted in the order they were recorded, or all the debits may be posted first and then all the credits. If Clark's used a computer with an accounting software the program menu would post at the press of a button.

FIGURE 3.16
How to Post from Journal to Ledger

CLARK'S WORD PROCESSING SERVICES
GENERAL JOURNAL

Page 1

Date	Account Titles and Description	PR	Dr.	Cr.
201X May 1	Cash	111	10 00 000	
	Brenda Clark, Capital	311		10 00 000
	Initial investment of cash by owner			

① **②** **③** **④**

CLARK'S WORD PROCESSING SERVICES
GENERAL LEDGER

Cash   Account No. 111

Date	Explanation	Post. Ref.	Debit	Credit	Balance Debit	Balance Credit
201X May 1		GJ1	10 00 000		10 00 000	

③

Brenda Clark, Capital   Account No. 311

Date	Explanation	Post. Ref.	Debit	Credit	Balance Debit	Balance Credit
201X May 1		GJ1		10 00 000		10 00 000

Using Posting References The posting references are helpful. In the journal, the PR column tells us which transactions have or have not been posted and also to which accounts they were posted. In the ledger, the posting reference leads us back to the original transaction in its entirety, so we can see why the debit or credit was recorded and what other accounts were affected. (It leads us back to the original transaction by identifying the journal and the page in the journal from which the information came.)

LEARNING UNIT 3-2 REVIEW

AT THIS POINT you should be able to do the following:

- State the purpose of posting.
- Discuss the advantages of the four-column account.
- Identify the elements to be posted.
- From journalized transactions, post to the general ledger.

↙ Instant Replay ◉ Self-Review Quiz 3-2

Figure 3.17 shows the journalized transactions of Clark's Word Processing Services. Your task is to post information to the ledger. The ledger in your workbook has all the account titles and numbers that were used from Clark's chart of accounts.

FIGURE 3.17
Journalized Entries

CLARK'S WORD PROCESSING SERVICES						
GENERAL JOURNAL						
						Page 1
Date		Account Titles and Description	PR	Dr.	Cr.	
201X May	1	Cash		10 0 0 0 00		
		Brenda Clark, Capital			10 0 0 0 00	
		Initial investment of cash by owner				
	1	Word Processing Equipment		6 0 0 0 00		
		Cash			1 0 0 0 00	
		Accounts Payable			5 0 0 0 00	
		Purchase of equip. from Ben Co.				
	1	Prepaid Rent		1 2 0 0 00		
		Cash			1 2 0 0 00	
		Rent paid in advance (3 months)				
	3	Office Supplies		6 0 0 00		
		Accounts Payable			6 0 0 00	
		Purchase of supplies on acct. from Norris				
	7	Cash		3 0 0 0 00		
		Word Processing Fees			3 0 0 0 00	
		Cash received for services rendered				
	13	Office Salaries Expense		6 5 0 00		
		Cash			6 5 0 00	
		Payment of office salaries				
	18	Advertising Expense		2 5 0 00		
		Accounts Payable			2 5 0 00	
		Bill received but not paid from Al's News				
	20	Brenda Clark, Withdrawals		6 2 5 00		
		Cash			6 2 5 00	
		Personal withdrawal of cash				
	22	Accounts Receivable		5 0 0 0 00		
		Word Processing Fees			5 0 0 0 00	
		Billed Morris Co. for fees earned				

CLARK'S WORD PROCESSING SERVICES
GENERAL JOURNAL

Page 2

Date	Account Titles and Description	PR	Dr.	Cr.
201X May 27	Office Salaries Expense		65000	
	Cash			65000
	Payment of office salaries			
28	Accounts Payable		250000	
	Cash			250000
	Paid half the amount owed Ben Co.			
29	Telephone Expense		22000	
	Cash			22000
	Paid telephone bill			

Solution to Instant Replay: Self-Review Quiz 3-2

FIGURE 3.18
Posting from Journal to the Ledger Using PR Columns

CLARK'S WORD PROCESSING SERVICES
GENERAL JOURNAL

Page 1

Date	Account Titles and Description	PR	Dr.	Cr.
201X May 1	Cash	111	1000000	
	Brenda Clark, Capital	311		1000000
	Initial investment of cash by owner			
1	Word Processing Equipment	121	600000	
	Cash	111		100000
	Accounts Payable	211		500000
	Purchase of equip. from Ben Co.			
1	Prepaid Rent	115	120000	
	Cash	111		120000
	Rent paid in advance (3 months)			
3	Office Supplies	114	60000	
	Accounts Payable	211		60000
	Purchase of supplies on acct. from Norris			
7	Cash	111	300000	
	Word Processing Fees	411		300000
	Cash received from services rendered			
13	Office Salaries Expense	511	65000	
	Cash	111		65000
	Payment of office salaries			
18	Advertising Expense	512	25000	
	Accounts Payable	211		25000
	Bill received but not paid from Al's News			

FIGURE 3.18 (continued)

CLARK'S WORD PROCESSING SERVICES
GENERAL JOURNAL

Page 1

Date		Account Titles and Description	PR	Dr.	Cr.
	20	Brenda Clark, Withdrawals	312	6 2 5 00	
		Cash	111		6 2 5 00
		Personal withdrawal of cash			
	22	Accounts Receivable	112	5 0 0 0 00	
		Word Processing Fees	411		5 0 0 0 00
		Billed Morris Co. for fees earned			

CLARK'S WORD PROCESSING SERVICES
GENERAL JOURNAL

Page 2

Date		Account Titles and Description	PR	Dr.	Cr.
201X May	27	Office Salaries Expense	511	6 5 0 00	
		Cash	111		6 5 0 00
		Payment of office salaries			
	28	Accounts Payable	211	2 5 0 0 00	
		Cash	111		2 5 0 0 00
		Paid half the amount owed Ben Co.			
	29	Telephone Expense	513	2 2 0 00	
		Cash	111		2 2 0 00
		Paid telephone bill			

FIGURE 3.18 (continued)

CLARK'S WORD PROCESSING SERVICES
PARTIAL GENERAL LEDGER

Cash   Account No. 111

Date		Explanation	Post. Ref.	Debit	Credit	Balance Debit	Balance Credit
201X May	1		GJ1	10 0 0 0 00		10 0 0 0 00	
	1		GJ1		1 0 0 0 00	9 0 0 0 00	
	1		GJ1		1 2 0 0 00	7 8 0 0 00	
	7		GJ1	3 0 0 0 00		10 8 0 0 00	
	13		GJ1		6 5 0 00	10 1 5 0 00	
	20		GJ1		6 2 5 00	9 5 2 5 00	
	27		GJ2		6 5 0 00	8 8 7 5 00	
	28		GJ2		2 5 0 0 00	6 3 7 5 00	
	29		GJ2		2 2 0 00	6 1 5 5 00	

Accounts Receivable   Account No. 112

Date		Explanation	Post. Ref.	Debit	Credit	Balance Debit	Balance Credit
201X May	22		GJ1	5 0 0 0 00		5 0 0 0 00	

FIGURE 3.18 (continued)

Office Supplies   Account No. 114

Date	Explanation	Post. Ref.	Debit	Credit	Balance Debit	Balance Credit
201X May 3		GJ1	6 0 0 00		6 0 0 00	

Prepaid Rent   Account No. 115

Date	Explanation	Post. Ref.	Debit	Credit	Balance Debit	Balance Credit
201X May 1		GJ1	1 2 0 0 00		1 2 0 0 00	

Word Processing Equipment   Account No. 121

Date	Explanation	Post. Ref.	Debit	Credit	Balance Debit	Balance Credit
201X May 1		GJ1	6 0 0 0 00		6 0 0 0 00	

Accounts Payable   Account No. 211

Date	Explanation	Post. Ref.	Debit	Credit	Balance Debit	Balance Credit
201X May 1		GJ1		5 0 0 0 00		5 0 0 0 00
3		GJ1		6 0 0 00		5 6 0 0 00
18		GJ1		2 5 0 00		5 8 5 0 00
28		GJ2	2 5 0 0 00			3 3 5 0 00

Brenda Clark, Capital   Account No. 311

Date	Explanation	Post. Ref.	Debit	Credit	Balance Debit	Balance Credit
201X May 1		GJ1		1 0 0 0 0 00		1 0 0 0 0 00

Brenda Clark, Withdrawals   Account No. 312

Date	Explanation	Post. Ref.	Debit	Credit	Balance Debit	Balance Credit
201X May 20		GJ1	6 2 5 00		6 2 5 00	

Word Processing Fees   Account No. 411

Date	Explanation	Post. Ref.	Debit	Credit	Balance Debit	Balance Credit
201X May 7		GJ1		3 0 0 0 00		3 0 0 0 00
22		GJ1		5 0 0 0 00		8 0 0 0 00

FIGURE 3.18 *(continued)*

Office Salaries Expense					Account No. 511	
		Post. Ref.	Debit	Credit	Balance	
Date	Explanation				Debit	Credit
201X May 13		GJ1	6 5 0 00		6 5 0 00	
27		GJ2	6 5 0 00		1 3 0 0 00	

Advertising Expense					Account No. 512	
		Post. Ref.	Debit	Credit	Balance	
Date	Explanation				Debit	Credit
201X May 18		GJ1	2 5 0 00		2 5 0 00	

Telephone Expense					Account No. 513	
		Post. Ref.	Debit	Credit	Balance	
Date	Explanation				Debit	Credit
201X May 29		GJ2	2 2 0 00		2 2 0 00	

PLAY BY PLAY: EXTRA HELP ON SELF-REVIEW QUIZ 3-2

Let's review first: The PR column of the journal will show to which account information has been posting. The PR column in the ledger accounts show from which page of the journal the information came. When updating ledger accounts, two debits added equals a debit balance. Two credits added would be a credit balance. If you have a debit and a credit, take the difference between them; whichever side is larger is the balance (be it a debit or credit).

Partial General Ledger:

Cash: There are nine postings from the journal to the cash account. GJ1 means that posting came from the general journal, page 1. In the second line the credit of 1,000 is subtracted from the debit balance in line 1 (10,000) to show a new balance of 9,000 in line 2. In line 3 the 1,200 credit is then subtracted from the 9,000 debit for a current balance of 7,800. Normally the balance is on the side that causes it to increase. Thus cash is normally a debit balance.

Accounts Payable: In this account the first three postings were credits from the general journal. Note that the month is written only once. Since all three are credits we add each together, arriving at a credit balance of 5,850. On May 28 a debit of 2,500 is posted and we take the difference between a 5,850 credit balance and a 2,500 debit balance to arrive at a 3,350 ending credit balance.

Office Salaries Expense: Note that here we have two debit postings, so they are added together to arrive at a 1,300 debit balance.

Summary: Posting is copying from the journal to the ledger. The ledger will accumulate information in the form of debits and credits. The last line in the balance column will show whether it is a debit or credit balance. The general journal does not show a running balance like the ledger accounts do.

COACHING TIP

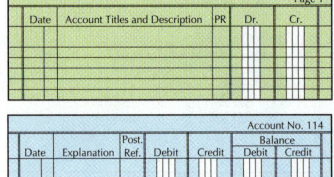

Posting is done from journal (green) to ledger (blue).

LEARNING UNIT 3-3 PREPARING THE TRIAL BALANCE:
Step 4 of the Accounting Cycle

● **L03**

Did you note in Quiz 3-2 how each account had a running balance figure? Did you know the normal balance of each account in Clark's ledger? As we discussed in Chapter 2, the list of the individual accounts with their balances taken from the ledger is called a trial balance.

The trial balance shown in Figure 3.19 was developed from the ledger accounts of Clark's Word Processing Services that were posted and balanced in Quiz 3-2. If the information is journalized or posted incorrectly, the trial balance will not be correct.

Trial balance An informal listing of the ledger accounts and their balances in the ledger to aid in proving the equality of debits and credits.

TRIAL BALANCE

Debits	Credits
Assets	Liabilities
Expenses	Revenue
Withdrawals	Capital

The trial balance will not show everything:

- The capital figure on the trial balance may not be the beginning capital figure. For instance, if Brenda Clark had made additional investments during the period, the additional investment would have been journalized and posted to the Capital account. The only way to tell if the capital balance on the trial balance is the original balance is to check the ledger Capital account to see whether any additional investments were made. This confirmation of beginning capital will be important when we make financial reports.

CLARK'S WORD PROCESSING SERVICE
TRIAL BALANCE
MAY 31, 201X

	Debit	Credit
Cash	6 1 5 5 00	
Accounts Receivable	5 0 0 0 00	
Office Supplies	6 0 0 00	
Prepaid Rent	1 2 0 0 00	
Word Processing Equipment	6 0 0 0 00	
Accounts Payable		3 3 5 0 00
Brenda Clark, Capital		10 0 0 0 00
Brenda Clark, Withdrawals	6 2 5 00	
Word Processing Fees		8 0 0 0 00
Office Salaries Expense	1 3 0 0 00	
Advertising Expense	2 5 0 00	
Telephone Expense	2 2 0 00	
Totals	21 3 5 0 00	21 3 5 0 00

FIGURE 3.19
Trial Balance

The trial balance lists the accounts in the same order as in the ledger. The $6,155 figure of cash came from the ledger.

- Even careful cross-referencing does not guarantee that transactions have been properly recorded. For example, the following errors would remain undetected: (1) a transaction that may have been omitted in the journalizing process, (2) a transaction incorrectly analyzed and recorded in the journal, and (3) a journal entry journalized or posted twice.

COACHING TIP

The totals of a trial balance can balance and yet be incorrect.

What to Do If a Trial Balance Doesn't Balance

The trial balance of Clark's Word Processing Services shows that the total of debits is equal to the total of credits. What happens, however, if the trial balance is in balance but the correct amount is not recorded in each ledger account? Accuracy in the journalizing and posting process will help ensure that no errors are made.

Even if you find an error, the first rule is "don't panic." Everyone makes mistakes, and accepted ways of correcting them are available. Once an entry has been made in ink, correcting an error in it must always show that the entry has been changed and who changed it. Sometimes the change has to be explained.

Some Common Mistakes

If the trial balance does not balance, the cause could be something relatively simple. Here are some common errors and how they can be fixed:

- If the difference (the amount you are off) is 10, 100, 1,000, and so forth, it is probably a mathematical error in addition.
- If the difference is equal to an individual account balance in the ledger, the amount could have been omitted. It is also possible the figure was not posted from the general journal.
- Divide the difference by two, then check to see whether a debit should have been a credit, or vice versa, in the ledger or trial balance. Example: $150 difference ÷ 2 = $75 means you may have placed $75 as a debit to an account instead of a credit, or vice versa.
- If the difference is evenly divisible by nine, a slide or transposition may have occurred. A slide is an error resulting from adding or deleting zeros in writing numbers. For example, $4,175.00 may have been copied as $41.75. A transposition is the accidental rearrangement of digits of a number. For example, $4,175 might have been accidentally written as $4,157.
- Compare the balances in the trial balance with the ledger accounts to check for copying errors.
- Recompute balances in each ledger account.
- Trace all postings from journal to ledger.

If you cannot find the error after taking all these steps, take a coffee break. Then start all over again.

Slide The error that results in adding or deleting zeros in the writing of a number. Example: 79,200 → 7,920.

Transposition The accidental rearrangement of digits of a number. Example: 152 → 125.

Making a Correction Before Posting

Before posting, error correction is straightforward. Simply draw a line through the incorrect entry, write the correct information above the line, and write your initials near the change. Keep in mind that accounting software may provide their own methods for making corrections.

Correcting an Error in an Account Title Figure 3.20 shows an error and its correction in an account title:

FIGURE 3.20
Account Error

Correcting a Numerical Error Numbers are handled the same way as account titles, as the next change from 520 to 250 in Figure 3.21 shows:

18	Advertising Expense		2 5 0 00		
	Accounts Payable			amp 2 5 0 00 / 5 2 0 00	
	Bill from Al's News				

FIGURE 3.21
Number Error

Correcting an Entry Error If a number has been entered in the wrong column, a straight line is drawn through it. The number is then written in the correct column, as shown in Figure 3.22:

1	Word Processing Equipment		6 0 0 00		
	Cash			1 0 0 0 00	
	Accounts Payable		amp 5 0 0 0 00	5 0 0 0 00	
	Purchase of equip. from Ben Co.				

FIGURE 3.22
Correcting Entry

Making a Correction After Posting

It is also possible to correct an amount that is correctly entered in the journal but posted incorrectly to the ledger of the proper account. The first step is to draw a line through the error and write the correct figure above it. The next step is changing the running balance to reflect the corrected posting. Here, too, a line is drawn through the balance and the corrected balance is written above it. Both changes must be initialed, as shown in Figure 3.23.

FIGURE 3.23
Correction After Posting

		Word Processing Fees				Account No. 411	
			Post.			Balance	
Date		Explanation	Ref.	Debit	Credit	Debit	Credit
201X May	7		GJ1		2 5 0 0 00		2 5 0 0 00
	22		GJ1		4 1 0 0 00 / 1 0 0 00 amp		6 6 0 0 00 / 2 6 0 0 00 amp

Correcting an Entry Posted to the Wrong Account

Drawing a line through an error and writing the correction above it is possible when a mistake has occurred within the proper account, but when an error involves a posting to the wrong account, the journal must include a correction accompanied by an explanation. In addition, the correct information must be posted to the appropriate ledgers.

Suppose, for example, that as a result of tracing postings from journal entries to ledgers you find that a $180 telephone bill was incorrectly debited as an advertising expense. The following illustration shows how this correction is done.

STEP 1: The journal entry is corrected and the correction is explained (Figure 3.24):

FIGURE 3.24
Corrected Entry for Telephone

		GENERAL JOURNAL			Page 3
Date		Account Titles and Description	PR	Dr.	Cr.
201X May	29	Telephone Expense	513	1 8 0 0 0	
		Advertising Expense	512		1 8 0 0 0
		To correct error in which			
		Advertising Exp. was debited			
		for charges to Telephone Exp.			

STEP 2: The Advertising Expense ledger account is corrected (Figure 3.25):

FIGURE 3.25
Ledger Update for Advertising

						Balance	
				Advertising Expense		Account No. 512	
Date	Explanation	Post. Ref.	Debit	Credit	Debit	Credit
201X May	18		GJ1	1 7 5 00		1 7 5 00	
	23		GJ1	1 8 0 00		3 5 5 00	
	29	Correcting entry	GJ3		1 8 0 00	1 7 5 00	

STEP 3: The Telephone Expense ledger is corrected (Figure 3.26):

FIGURE 3.26
Ledger Update for Telephone

				Telephone Expense		Account No. 513	
						Balance	
Date	Explanation	Post. Ref.	Debit	Credit	Debit	Credit
201X May	29		GJ3	1 8 0 00		1 8 0 00	

LEARNING UNIT 3-3 REVIEW

AT THIS POINT you should be able to do the following:

- Prepare a trial balance with a ledger, using four-column accounts.
- Analyze and correct a trial balance that doesn't balance.
- Correct journalizing and posting errors.

Instant Replay ⊙ Self-Review Quiz 3-3

1.

MEMO

TO: Al Vincent
FROM: Professor Jones
RE: Trial Balance

You have submitted to me an incorrect trial balance (Figure 3.28). Could you please rework and turn in to me before next Friday?

Note: Individual amounts look OK.

FIGURE 3.27
Incorrect Trial Balance

A. RICE
TRIAL BALANCE
OCTOBER 31, 201X

		Dr.	Cr.
Cash	✓	←	8 0 6 0 00
Operating Expenses	✓	←	1 7 0 0 00
A. Rice, Withdrawals	✓	←	4 0 0 00
Service Revenue			5 4 0 0 00
Equipment		5 0 0 0 00	
Accounts Receivable		3 5 4 0 00	
Accounts Payable	→	2 0 0 0 00	
Supplies		3 0 0 00	
A. Rice, Capital			11 6 0 0 00

19,000   19,000

2. An $8,000 debit to Office Equipment was mistakenly journalized and posted on June 9, 201X, to Office Supplies. Prepare the appropriate journal entry to correct this error.

Solution to Instant Replay: Self-Review Quiz 3-3

1.

FIGURE 3.28
Correct Trial Balance

A. RICE
TRIAL BALANCE
OCTOBER 31, 201X

	Dr.	Cr.
Cash	8 0 6 0 00	
Accounts Receivable	3 5 4 0 00	
Supplies	3 0 0 00	
Equipment	5 0 0 0 00	
Accounts Payable		2 0 0 0 00
A. Rice, Capital		11 6 0 0 00
A. Rice, Withdrawals	4 0 0 00	
Service Revenue		5 4 0 0 00
Operating Expenses	1 7 0 0 00	
Totals	19 0 0 0 00	19 0 0 0 00

2.

FIGURE 3.29
Correcting Entry

GENERAL JOURNAL   Page 4

Date		Account Titles and Description	PR	Dr.	Cr.
201X June	9	Office Equipment		8 0 0 0 00	
		Office Supplies			8 0 0 0 00
		To correct error in which office supplies			
		had been debited for purchase of			
		office equipment			

PLAY BY PLAY: EXTRA HELP ON SELF-REVIEW QUIZ 3-3

Let's review first: Items in a trial balance are listed in the same order as in the ledger or chart of accounts. Expect each account to have its normal balance (either a debit or credit). No title in the trial list balance can have both a debit and credit balance.

List the ending balance of each ledger account (last number listed in the balance columns) and list them in the order of the ledger. They should follow this pattern:

Assets	Dr.
Liabilities	Cr.
Capital	Cr.
Withdrawals	Dr.
Revenues	Cr.
Expenses	Dr.

When complete, the total of all debits will equal the total of the credits. In this case the total is 19,000.

Summary: The trial balance lists the accounts in the same order as the ledger. Be sure to refer to the learning unit for what to do if the trial balance does not balance. It could be a posting mistake or just a math error.

DEMONSTRATION PROBLEM

LO1,2,3

Journalizing Transaction, Posting, and Preparing a Trial Balance

In March, Abby's Employment Agency had the following transactions:

201X

Mar.	1	Abby Todd invested $5,000 cash in the new employment agency.
	4	Bought equipment for cash, $200.
	5	Earned employment fee commission, $200, but payment from Blue Co. will not be received until June.
	6	Paid wages expense, $300.
	7	Abby paid her home utility bill from the company checkbook, $75.
	9	Placed Rick Wool at VCR Corporation, receiving $1,200 cash.
	15	Paid cash for supplies, $200.
	28	Telephone bill received but not paid, $180.
	29	Advertising bill received but not paid, $400.

The chart of accounts includes Cash, 111; Accounts Receivable, 112; Supplies, 131; Equipment, 141; Accounts Payable, 211; A. Todd, Capital, 311; A. Todd, Withdrawals, 321; Employment Fees Earned, 411; Wage Expense, 511; Telephone Expense, 521; and Advertising Expense, 531.

Requirements

Your tasks are to do the following:

1. Journalize business transactions in General Journal (all page 1).

2. Set up a ledger based on the chart of accounts.

3. Journalize (all page 1) and post transactions.

4. Prepare a trial balance for March 31.

Demonstration Problem Solution

Requirements 1 and 2

Set up ledger based on chart of accounts. Journalize (all page 1) and post transactions.

Part 1	Part 2	Demonstration Problem Complete

a.

FIGURE 3.30
General Ledger

Cash   111

Date		PR	Dr.	Cr.	Balance Dr.	Balance Cr.
201X Mar.	1	GJ1	5,000		5,000	
	4	GJ1		200	4,800	
	6	GJ1		300	4,500	
	7	GJ1		75	4,425	
	9	GJ1	1,200		5,625	
	15	GJ1		200	5,425	

Accounts Receivable   112

Date		PR	Dr.	Cr.	Balance Dr.	Balance Cr.
201X Mar.	5	GJ1	200		200	

Supplies   131

Date		PR	Dr.	Cr.	Balance Dr.	Balance Cr.
201X Mar.	15	GJ1	200		200	

Equipment   141

Date		PR	Dr.	Cr.	Balance Dr.	Balance Cr.
201X Mar.	4	GJ1	200		200	

Accounts Payable   211

Date		PR	Dr.	Cr.	Balance Dr.	Balance Cr.
201X Mar.	28	GJ1		180		180
	29	GJ1		400		580

A. Todd, Capital   311

Date		PR	Dr.	Cr.	Balance Dr.	Balance Cr.
201X Mar.	1	GJ1		5,000		5,000

A. Todd, Withdrawals   321

Date		PR	Dr.	Cr.	Balance Dr.	Balance Cr.
201X Mar.	7	GJ1	75		75	

Employment Fees Earned   411

Date		PR	Dr.	Cr.	Balance Dr.	Balance Cr.
201X Mar.	5	GJ1		200		200
	9	GJ1		1,200		1,400

Wage Expense   511

Date		PR	Dr.	Cr.	Balance Dr.	Balance Cr.
201X Mar.	6	GJ1	300		300	

Telephone Expense   521

Date		PR	Dr.	Cr.	Balance Dr.	Balance Cr.
201X Mar.	28	GJ1	180		180	

Advertising Expense   531

Date		PR	Dr.	Cr.	Balance Dr.	Balance Cr.
201X Mar.	29	GJ1	400		400	

b.

FIGURE 3.31
Journal Entries and Post References

	Date		Account Titles and Description	PR	Dr.	Cr.
	201X Mar.	1	Cash	111	5 0 0 0 00	
			A. Todd, Capital	311		5 0 0 0 00
			Owner investment			
		4	Equipment	141	2 0 0 00	
			Cash	111		2 0 0 00
			Bought equipment for cash			
		5	Accounts Receivable	112	2 0 0 00	
			Employment Fees Earned	411		2 0 0 00
			Fees on account from Blue Co.			
		6	Wage Expense	511	3 0 0 00	
			Cash	111		3 0 0 00
			Paid wages			
		7	A. Todd, Withdrawals	321	7 5 00	
			Cash	111		7 5 00
			Personal withdrawals			
		9	Cash	111	1 2 0 0 00	
			Employment Fees Earned	411		1 2 0 0 00
			Cash fees			
		15	Supplies	131	2 0 0 00	
			Cash	111		2 0 0 00
			Bought supplies for cash			
		28	Telephone Expense	521	1 8 0 00	
			Accounts Payable	211		1 8 0 00
			Telephone bill owed			
		29	Advertising Expense	531	4 0 0 00	
			Accounts Payable	211		4 0 0 00
			Advertising bill received			

ABBY'S EMPLOYMENT AGENCY — Page 1

Solution Tips to Journalizing

1. When journalizing, the PR column is not filled in.
2. Write the name of the debit against the date column. Indent credits and list them below debits. Be sure total debits for each transaction equal total credits.
3. Skip a line between each transaction.

The Analysis of the Journal Entries

Mar.	1	Cash	A	↑	Dr.	$5,000
		A. Todd, Capital	Capital	↑	Cr.	$5,000
	4	Equipment	A	↑	Dr.	$ 200
		Cash	A	↓	Cr.	$ 200
	5	Accts. Receivable	A	↑	Dr.	$ 200
		Empl. Fees Earned	Rev.	↑	Cr.	$ 200
	6	Wage Expense	Exp.	↑	Dr.	$ 300
		Cash	A	↓	Cr.	$ 300
	7	A. Todd, Withdrawals	Withd.	↑	Dr.	$ 75
		Cash	A	↓	Cr.	$ 75
	9	Cash	A	↑	Dr.	$1,200
		Empl. Fees Earned	Rev.	↑	Cr.	$1,200
	15	Supplies	A	↑	Dr.	$ 200
		Cash	A	↓	Cr.	$ 200
	28	Telephone Expense	Exp.	↑	Dr.	$ 180
		Accounts Payable	L	↑	Cr.	$ 180
	28	Advertising Expense	Exp.	↑	Dr.	$ 400
		Accounts Payable	L	↑	Cr.	$ 400

COACHING TIP

This analysis is what should be going through your head before determining debit or credit.

Solution Tips to Posting

The PR column in the ledger cash account tells you from which page journal information came. After the ledger cash account is posted, account number 111 is put in the PR column of the journal for cross-referencing.

Note how we keep a running balance in the cash account. A $5,000 debit balance and a $200 credit entry result in a new debit balance of $4,800.

Requirement 3

Preparing a Trial Balance from the Ledger

Part 1	Part 2	Demonstration Problem Complete

FIGURE 3.32

ABBY'S EMPLOYMENT AGENCY TRIAL BALANCE MARCH 31, 201X		
	Dr.	Cr.
Cash	5 4 2 5 00	
Accounts Receivable	2 0 0 00	
Supplies	2 0 0 00	
Equipment	2 0 0 00	
Accounts Payable		5 8 0 00
A. Todd, Capital		5 0 0 0 00
A. Todd, Withdrawals	7 5 00	
Employment Fees Earned		1 4 0 0 00
Wage Expense	3 0 0 00	
Telephone Expense	1 8 0 00	
Advertising Expense	4 0 0 00	
Totals	6 9 8 0 00	6 9 8 0 00

Solution Tip to Trial Balance
The trial balance lists the ending balances of the titles in the order in which they appear in the ledger. The total of 6,980 on the left equals 6,980 on the right in Figure 3.33.

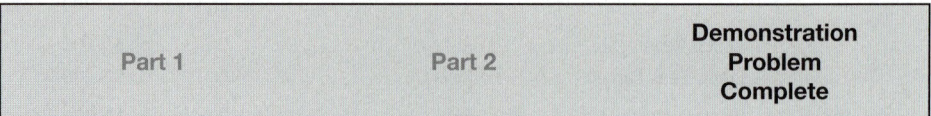

Part 1	Part 2	Demonstration Problem Complete

BLUEPRINT OF FIRST FOUR STEPS OF ACCOUNTING CYCLE

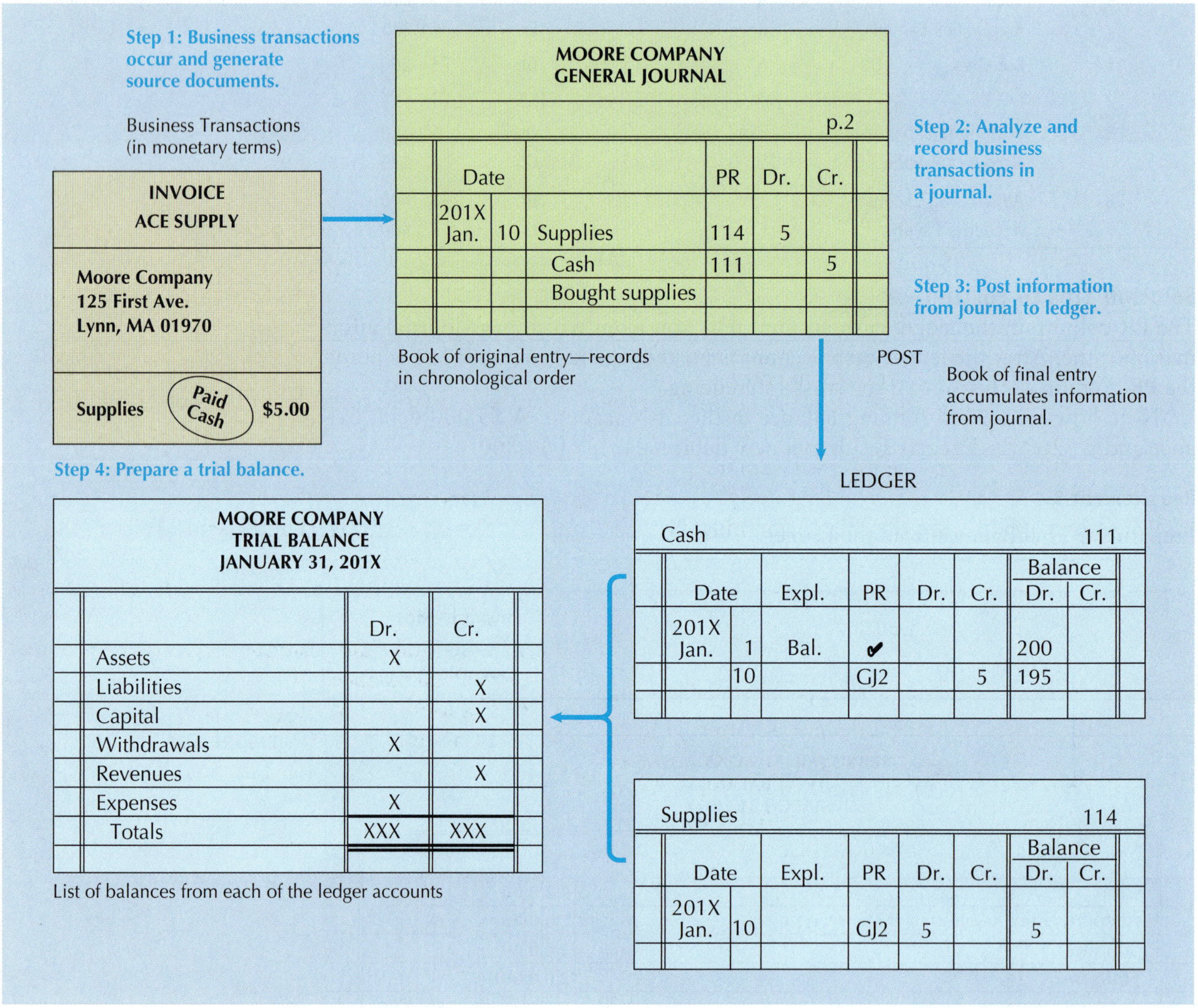

Step 1: Business transactions occur and generate source documents.

Business Transactions (in monetary terms)

INVOICE
ACE SUPPLY

Moore Company
125 First Ave.
Lynn, MA 01970

Supplies   *Paid Cash*   **$5.00**

MOORE COMPANY
GENERAL JOURNAL

p.2

Date			PR	Dr.	Cr.
201X Jan.	10	Supplies	114	5	
		Cash	111		5
		Bought supplies			

Book of original entry—records in chronological order

Step 2: Analyze and record business transactions in a journal.

Step 3: Post information from journal to ledger.

POST

Book of final entry accumulates information from journal.

Step 4: Prepare a trial balance.

LEDGER

MOORE COMPANY **TRIAL BALANCE** **JANUARY 31, 201X**		
	Dr.	Cr.
Assets	X	
Liabilities		X
Capital		X
Withdrawals	X	
Revenues		X
Expenses	X	
Totals	XXX	XXX

List of balances from each of the ledger accounts

Cash   111

Date		Expl.	PR	Dr.	Cr.	Balance Dr.	Balance Cr.
201X Jan.	1	Bal.	✔			200	
	10		GJ2		5	195	

Supplies   114

Date		Expl.	PR	Dr.	Cr.	Balance Dr.	Balance Cr.
201X Jan.	10		GJ2	5		5	

ACCOUNTING COACH

The following Coaching Tips are from Learning Units 3-1 to 3-3. Take the Pre-Game Checkup and use the Check Your Score at the bottom of the page to see how you are doing. The Accounting Coach provides tips before each Checkup to help you avoid common accounting errors.

LU 3-1 Analyzing and Recording Business Transactions into a Journal: Steps 1 and 2 of the Accounting Cycle

Pre-Game Tips: When journalizing transactions be sure to use the Chart of Accounts. It provides the specific titles you will use for either debit(s) or credit(s). You will not use the Chart of Accounts for the explanations in the journal. In the journal, the debit portion of the transaction is listed first, followed by the credit portion. Remember that these titles come from the Chart of Accounts. The total of all debits must equal the total of all credits for each individual transaction.

Pre-Game Checkup
1. The ledger is the book of original entry.
2. Compound journal entries must have no more than three credits.
3. Billing a company for services on account would result in a debit to cash.
4. When you journalize, the PR column must be completed.
5. Rent paid in advance is an expense.

LU 3-2 Posting to the Ledger: Step 3 of the Accounting Cycle

Pre-Game Tips: Posting is transferring information from the journal to the ledger. The ledger accounts keep a running balance of each title, while the journal does not. Cross-referencing helps to fill in the PR column of the journal to show the account number that was posted from that line. With computer software, today's posting could be just a click away.

Pre-Game Checkup
1. Posting can only be done manually.
2. Posting means transferring information from the ledger to the journal.
3. Cross-referencing means the PR column in the ledger is up to date.
4. Posting can only be done once a month.
5. Posting results in information being accumulated in the journal.

LU 3-3 Preparing the Trial Balance: Step 4 of the Accounting Cycle

Pre-Game Tips: The trial balance is listed in the same order as the general ledger. Only one balance is shown for each account in the trial balance. Keep in mind that the trial balance could be in balance and still be incorrect due to posting twice, missing transactions, or analyzing them incorrectly.

Pre-Game Checkup
1. The trial balance is in the same order as the journal.
2. A trial balance can have two balances for some accounts.
3. Slides and transpositions can help locate errors in the trial balance.
4. If a journal entry is posted, no corrections can be made.
5. Account titles that have credit balances are indented.

CHECK YOUR SCORE: Answers to the Pre-Game Checkup

LU 3-1
1. False—The ledger is the book of final entry.
2. False—Compound journal entries must have more than two accounts.
3. False—Billing a company for services on account would result in a debit to accounts receivable.
4. False—When you post, the PR column is completed.
5. False—Rent paid in advance is an asset.

LU 3-2
1. False—Posting can be done by computer.
2. False—Posting means transferring information from the journal to the ledger.

3. False—Cross-referencing means the PR column is updated in the journal.
4. False—Posting can be done at various times.
5. False—Posting results in information being accumulated in the ledger.

LU 3-3
1. False—The trial balance is in the same order as the ledger.
2. False—A trial balance can have only one balance per title.
3. True.
4. False—If a journal entry is posted, corrections can still be made.
5. False—All account titles are listed with no indentations.

Chapter Summary

Here are all the key concepts and equations to help you understand the concepts of this chapter and prepare you for your exam. After completing this review, go to MyAccountingLab for more practice opportunities.

Concepts You Should Know	Key Terms
● **L01** Journalizing: analyzing and recording business transactions into a journal. 1. The accounting cycle is a sequence of accounting procedures that are usually performed during an accounting period. 2. An accounting period is the time period (up to one year) for which the income statement is prepared. 3. A calendar year is from January 1 to December 31. The fiscal year is any 12-month period. 4. Interim statements are statements that are usually prepared for a portion of the business's calendar or fiscal year. 5. A general journal is a book that records transactions in chronological order. It is the book of original entry. 6. The ledger is a collection of accounts in which information is accumulated from the postings of the journal. The ledger is the book of final entry. 7. Journalizing is the process of recording journal entries. 8. The chart of accounts provides the specific titles of accounts to be entered in the journal. 9. When journalizing, the post reference (PR) column is left blank. 10. A compound journal entry occurs when more than two accounts are affected in the journalizing process of a business transaction.	**Accounting cycle** (p. 78) **Accounting period** (p. 78) **Book of final entry** (p. 78) **Book of original entry** (p. 78) **Calendar year** (p. 78) **Compound journal entry** (p. 80) **Fiscal year** (p. 78) **General journal** (p. 78) **Interim reports** (p. 78) **Journal** (p. 78) **Journal entry** (p. 78) **Journalizing** (p. 78) **Natural business year** (p. 78)

Posting: transferring information from a journal to a ledger.

1. Posting is the process of transferring information from the journal to the ledger.

2. The journal and ledger contain the same information but in a different form.

3. The four-column account aids in keeping a running balance of an account.

4. The normal balance of an account will be located on the side that increases it according to the rules of debit and credit.

5. The mechanical process of posting requires care in transferring to the appropriate account the dates, post references, and amounts.

Cross-referencing (p. 86)

Four-column account (p. 86)

Posting (p. 86)

● **L02**

Preparing a trial balance

1. A trial balance can balance but be incorrect.

2. If a trial balance doesn't balance, check for errors in addition, omission of postings, slides, transpositions, copying errors, and so on.

Slide (p. 94)

Trial balance (p. 93)

Transposition (p. 94)

● **L03**

Discussion Questions and Critical Thinking/Ethical Case

1. Explain the concept of the accounting cycle.

2. An accounting period is based on the balance sheet. Agree or disagree?

3. Compare and contrast a calendar year versus a fiscal year.

4. What are interim statements?

5. Why is the ledger called the book of final entry?

6. How do transactions get "linked" in a general journal?

7. What is the relationship of the chart of accounts to the general journal?

8. What is a compound journal entry?

9. Posting means updating the journal. Agree or disagree? Please comment.

10. The side that decreases an account is the normal balance. True or false?

11. The PR column of a general journal is the last item to be filled in during the posting process. Agree or disagree?

12. Discuss the concept of cross-referencing.

13. What is the difference between a transposition and a slide?

14. Jay Simons, the accountant of See Co., would like to buy a new software package for his general ledger. He couldn't do it because all funds were frozen for the rest of the fiscal period. Jay called his friend at Joor Industries and asked whether he could copy its software. Comment on why it is or is not okay for Jay to make such a request.

MyAccountingLab

Concept Checks

LO1 *(5 MIN)*   **General Journal**

1. Complete the following from the general journal of Mueller Co.:
   a. Year of journal entry   _____
   b. Month of journal entry   _____
   c. Day of journal entry   _____
   d. Name(s) of accounts debited _____
   e. Name(s) of accounts credited _____
   f. Explanation of transaction   _____
   g. Amount of debit(s)   _____
   h. Amount of credit(s)   _____
   i. Page of journal   _____

FIGURE 3.33
General Journal

MUELLER COMPANY
GENERAL JOURNAL   Page 1

Date	Account Titles and Descriptions	PR	Dr.	Cr.
201X Oct. 3	Cash		9 000 00	
	Equipment		37 000 00	
	B. Mueller, Capital			46 000 00
	Initial Investment by Owner			

General Journal

⬤ **LO2** *(5 MIN)*

2.   Provide the explanation for each of the general journal entries in Figure 3.34.

			GENERAL JOURNAL				Page 4	
	Date		Account Titles and Descriptions	PR	Debit		Credit	
201X								
Jan.	10		Cash		7 0 0 0 00			
			Computer Equipment		10 0 0 0 00			
			B. Babson, Capital				17 0 0 0 00	
			(A)					
	11		Cash		4 0 00			
			Accounts Receivable		6 0 00			
			Consulting Fees Earned				1 0 0 00	
			(B)					
	14		Advertising Expense		1 7 0 00			
			Accounts Payable				1 7 0 00	
			(C)					

FIGURE 3.34
Journal Entries

Posting and Balancing

⬤ **LO2** *(5 MIN)*

3.   Balance this four-column account. What function does the PR column serve? When will Account 111 be used in the journalizing and posting process?

		Cash			Acct. 111 Balance	
Date	Explanation	PR	Dr.	Cr.	Dr.	Cr.
201X						
Nov.	7	GJ 1	70			
	10	GJ 1	12			
	18	GJ 2		3		
	22	GJ 3	20			

The Trial Balance

⬤ **LO4** *(15 MIN)*

4.   The following trial balance (Figure 3.35) was prepared *incorrectly*.

   a.   Rearrange the accounts in proper order.

FIGURE 3.35

TIMMONY CO. TRIAL BALANCE DECEMBER 31, 201X		
	Dr.	Cr.
D. Timmony, Capital	4 8 00	
Equipment	1 6 00	
Rent Expense		2 5 00
Advertising Expense		5 00
Accounts Payable		8 00
Taxi Fees	1 6 00	
Cash	1 5 00	
D. Timmony, Withdrawals	—	1 1 00
Totals	9 5 00	4 9 00

    b. Calculate the total of the trial balance. (Small numbers are used intentionally so that you can do the calculations in your head.) Assume each account has a normal balance.

LO3 *(5 MIN)*   **Correcting Entry**

5. On June 1, 2010, a telephone expense for $250 was debited to Repair Expense. On June 10, 2010, this error was found. Prepare the corrected journal entry. When would a correcting entry *not* be needed?

MyAccountingLab   **Exercises**

Set A

LO1 *(10 MIN)*   **3A-1.** Prepare journal entries for the following transactions that occurred during July:

201X	
July 1	Jodi Wills invested $90,000 cash and $11,000 of equipment into her new business.
3	Purchased building for $120,000 on account.
12	Purchased a truck from Liberty Co. for $9,000 cash.
18	Bought supplies from McVey Co. on account, $800.

LO1 *(10 MIN)*   **3A-2.** Record the following into the general journal of Raymond's Auto Shop.

201X	
Jan. 1	Raymond Tucci invested $100,000 cash in the auto shop.
5	Paid $12,000 for auto equipment.
8	Bought from Leominster Co. auto equipment for 1,000 on account.
14	Received $1,500 for repair fees earned.
18	Billed Thompson Co. $900 for services rendered.
20	Raymond withdrew $150 for personal use.

LO2 *(10 MIN)*   **3A-3.** Post the transactions in Figure 3.36 to the ledger of Koskorous Company. The partial ledger of Koskorous Company is Cash, 111; Equipment, 121; Accounts Payable, 211; and A. Koskorous, Capital, 311. Please use four-column accounts in the posting process.

FIGURE 3.36
Journal Entries

Date 201X			PR	Dr.	Cr.
					Page 4
Jan. 6	Cash			9 0 0 0 00	
	A. Koskorous, Capital				9 0 0 0 00
	Cash investment				
14	Equipment			3 7 0 0 00	
	Cash				3 0 0 0 00
	Accounts Payable				7 0 0 00
	Purchase of equipment				

3A-4. From the following transactions for Long Company for the month of January, (a) prepare journal entries (assume that it is page 1 of the journal), (b) post to the ledger (use a four-column account), and (c) prepare a trial balance.

L01, 2, 3 *(20 MIN)*

201X		
Jan.	1	Jan Long invested $12,000 in the business.
	4	Bought from Mesa Co. equipment on account, $2,300.
	15	Billed Buddy Co. for services rendered, $1,000.
	18	Received $2,000 cash for services rendered.
	24	Paid salaries expense, $1,400.
	28	Jan withdrew $500 for personal use.

A partial chart of accounts includes Cash, 111; Accounts Receivable, 112; Equipment, 121; Accounts Payable, 211; J. Long, Capital, 311; J. Long, Withdrawals, 312; Fees Earned, 411; and Salaries Expense, 511.

3A-5. You have been hired to correct the trial balance in Figure 3.37 that has been recorded improperly from the ledger to the trial balance.

L03 *(15 MIN)*

FIGURE 3.37
Incorrect Trial Balance

SANDY CO. TRIAL BALANCE JANUARY 31, 201X	Dr.	Cr.
Accounts Payable	9 0 0 00	
A. Sandy, Capital		9 2 5 0 00
A. Sandy, Withdrawals		2 5 0 00
Services Earned		5 1 0 0 00
Concessions Earned	1 4 0 0 00	
Rent Expense	7 0 0 00	
Salaries Expense	2 1 0 0 00	
Miscellaneous Expense		1 2 0 0 00
Cash	10 0 0 0 00	
Accounts Receivable		2 4 0 0 00
Totals	15 1 0 0 00	18 2 0 0 00

3A-6. On February 6, 201X, Mark Sullivan made the journal entry in Figure 3.38 to record the purchase on account of office equipment priced at $1,200. This transaction had not yet been posted when the error was discovered. Make the appropriate correction.

L03 *(10 MIN)*

FIGURE 3.38
Recording Error

	Date	Account Titles and Description	PR	Dr.	Cr.
	201X Feb. 6	Office Equipment		8 0 0 00	
		Accounts Payable			8 0 0 00
		Purchase of office equip. on account			

GENERAL JOURNAL

Set B

LO1 *(10 MIN)* **3B-1.** Prepare journal entries for the following transactions that occurred during March:

201X		
Mar. 1	Jordan Doxbury invested $50,000 cash and $5,000 of equipment into her new business.	
3	Purchased building for $20,000 on account.	
12	Purchased a truck from Lancaster Co. for $15,000 cash.	
18	Bought supplies from Roger Co. on account, $1,000.	

LO1 *(10 MIN)* **3B-2.** Record the following into the general journal of Rick's Auto Shop.

201X		
Sep. 1	Rick Stone invested $110,000 cash in the auto shop.	
5	Paid $9,000 for auto equipment.	
8	Bought from Lexington Co. auto equipment for $8,000 on account.	
14	Received $1,600 for repair fees earned.	
18	Billed Franklin Co. $675 for services rendered.	
20	Rick withdrew $200 for personal use.	

LO2 *(10 MIN)* **3B-3.** Post the transactions to the ledger of Koskorous Company. The partial ledger of Koskorous Company is Cash, 111; Equipment, 121; Accounts Payable, 211; and A. Koskorous, Capital, 311. Please use four-column accounts in the posting process.

				PR	Dr.	Cr.	Page 4
Date							
201X Feb.	6	Cash			3 0 0 00		
			A. Koskorous, Capital			3 0 0 00	
			Cash investment				
	14	Equipment			6 0 00		
			Cash			3 0 00	
			Accounts Payable			3 0 00	
			Purchase of equipment				

LO1, 2, 3 *(20 MIN)* **3B-4.** From the following transactions for Long Company for the month of January,
a. prepare journal entries (assume that it is page 1 of the journal),
b. post to the ledger (use a four-column account), and
c. prepare a trial balance.

A partial chart of accounts includes

Cash, 111	J. Long, Capital, 311
Accounts Receivable, 112	J. Long, Withdrawals, 312
Equipment, 121	Fees Earned, 411
Accounts Payable, 211	Salaries Expense, 511

201X

Jan. 1 Jan Long invested $25,000 in the business.

4 Bought from Lind Co. equipment on account, $800.

15 Billed Parent Co. for services rendered, $5,000.

18 Received $8,000 cash for services rendered.

24 Paid salary expense, $1,200.

28 Jan withdrew $800 for personal use.

3B-5. You have been hired to correct the trial balance below that has been recorded improperly from the ledger to the trial balance.

● **L03** (15 MIN)

SANDY CO.
TRIAL BALANCE
JANUARY 31, 201X

	Dr.	Cr.
Accounts Payable	1 7 00	
A. Sandy, Capital		5 7 5 0
A. Sandy, Withdrawals		9 5 0
Services Earned		8 0 00
Concessions Earned	1 8 00	
Rent Expense	6 00	
Salaries Expense	2 4 00	
Miscellaneous Expense		8 00
Cash	1 1 0 00	
Accounts Receivable		1 5 00
Totals	1 7 5 00	1 7 0 00

3B-6. On February 6, 201X, Morris Sanford made the journal entry below to record the purchase on account of office equipment priced at $1,000.

● **L03** (10 MIN)

GENERAL JOURNAL

Date	Account Titles and Description	PR	Dr.	Cr.
201X Feb. 6	Office Equipment		9 00	
	Accounts Payable			9 00
	Purchase of office equipment on account			

Problems

Set A

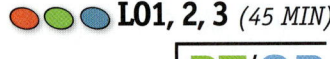 **L01** *(30 MIN)*   **3A-1.** Jarome Tacks operates Jarome's Cleaning Service. As the bookkeeper, you have been requested to journalize the following transactions:

201X		
Aug. 1	Paid rent for two months in advance, $10,000.	
6	Purchased cleaning equipment on account from Aiden's Supply House, $5,000.	
12	Purchased cleaning supplies from Lowell's Wholesale for $200 cash.	
14	Received $1,400 cash from cleaning fees earned.	
20	Jarome withdrew $900 for his personal use.	
21	Advertising bill received from *Sary News* but unpaid, $500.	
25	Paid electrical expense, $50.	
28	Paid salaries expense, $1,100.	
29	Performed cleaning work for $2,500, but payment will not be received until April.	
30	Paid Aiden's Supply House half the amount owed from Aug. 6 transaction.	

Check Figure:
Aug. 21
Dr. Advertising expense $500
Cr. Accounts Payable $500

Your task is to journalize the preceding transactions. The chart of accounts for Jarome's Cleaning Service is as follows:

Chart of Accounts

Assets		**Owner's Equity**	
111	Cash	311	Jarome Tacks, Capital
112	Accounts Receivable	312	Jarome Tacks, Withdrawals
114	Prepaid Rent	**Revenue**	
116	Cleaning Supplies	411	Cleaning Fees Earned
120	Cleaning Equipment	**Expenses**	
121	Office Equipment	511	Advertising Expense
Liabilities		512	Electrical Expense
211	Accounts Payable	514	Salaries Expense

 **L01, 2, 3** *(45 MIN)*

3A-2. On November 1, 201X, Barbie Riley opened Barbie's Art Studio. The following transactions occurred in November:

201X		
Nov. 1	Barbie Riley invested $6,000 in the art studio.	
1	Paid three months' rent in advance, $3,600.	
3	Purchased $1,800 of equipment from Brasa Co. on account.	
5	Received $8,000 cash for art-training workshop for teachers.	
8	Purchased $350 of art supplies for cash.	
9	Billed Walter Co. $4,000 for group art lesson for its employees.	
10	Paid salaries of assistants, $500.	
15	Barbie withdrew $300 from the business for her personal use.	
28	Paid electrical bill, $130.	
29	Paid telephone bill for November, $210.	

Your tasks are to do the following:

   a. Set up the ledger based on the following chart of accounts.
   b. Journalize (journal is page 1) and post the November transactions.
   c. Prepare a trial balance as of November 30, 201X.

Check Figure:
Trial Balance
Total $19,800

The chart of accounts for Barbie's Art Studio is as follows:

Chart of Accounts

Assets		Owner's Equity	
111	Cash	311	Barbie Riley, Capital
112	Accounts Receivable	312	Barbie Riley, Withdrawals
114	Prepaid Rent	**Revenue**	
121	Art Supplies	411	Art Fees Earned
131	Equipment	**Expenses**	
Liabilities		511	Electrical Expense
211	Accounts Payable	521	Salaries Expense
		531	Telephone Expense

3A-3. The following transactions occurred in November 201X for A. Glover's Placement Agency:

L01, 2, 3 *(45 MIN)*

201X	
Nov. 1	A. Glover invested $6,000 cash in the placement agency.
1	Bought equipment on account from Cinder Co., $2,100.
3	Earned placement fees of $2,000, but payment will not be received until December.
5	A. Glover withdrew $400 for his personal use.
7	Paid wages expense, $1,400.
9	Placed a client on a local TV show, receiving $5,000 cash.
15	Bought supplies on account from Holly Co., $400.
28	Paid telephone bill for November, $110.
29	Advertising bill from Shimmer Co. received but not paid, $800.

Check Figure:
Tiral Balance
Total $16,300

The chart of accounts for A. Glover Placement Agency is as follows:

Chart of Accounts

Assets		Owner's Equity	
111	Cash	311	A. Glover, Capital
112	Accounts Receivable	312	A. Glover, Withdrawals
131	Supplies	**Revenue**	
141	Equipment	411	Placement Fees Earned
Liabilities		**Expenses**	
211	Accounts Payable	511	Wage Expense
		521	Telephone Expense
		531	Advertising Expense

Your tasks are to do the following:

   a. Set up the ledger based on the chart of accounts.
   b. Journalize (page 1) and post the November transactions.
   c. Prepare a trial balance as of November 30, 201X.

Set B

3B-1. Jarome Tacks operates Jarome's Cleaning Service. As the bookkeeper, you have been requested to journalize the following transactions:

● **L01** *(30 MIN)*

201X		
Aug.	1	Paid rent for two months in advance, $3,000.
	6	Purchased cleaning equipment on account from Brian's Supply House, $15,000.
	12	Purchased cleaning supplies from Liberty's Wholesale for $700 cash.
	14	Received $1,800 cash from cleaning fees earned.
	20	Jason withdrew $150 for his personal use.
	21	Advertising bill received from *Morning News* but unpaid, $500.
	25	Paid electrical expense, $60.
	28	Paid salaries expense, $500.
	29	Performed cleaning work for $1,900, but payment will not be received until April.
	30	Paid Brian's Supply House half the amount owed from the Aug. 6 transaction.

Check Figure:
Aug. 21
Dr. Advertising expense $500
Cr. Accounts payable $500

The chart of accounts for Jarome's Cleaning Service includes Cash, 111; Accounts Receivable, 112; Prepaid Rent, 114; Cleaning Supplies, 116; Cleaning Equipment, 120; Office Equipment, 121; Accounts Payable, 211; Jarome Tacks, Capital, 311; Jarome Tacks, Withdrawals, 312; Cleaning Fees Earned, 411; Advertising Expense, 511; Electrical Expense, 512; and Salaries Expense, 514.

3B-2. On November 1, 201X, Barbie Riley opened Barbie's Art Studio. The following transactions occurred in November.

●●● **L01, 2, 3** *(45 MIN)*

201X		
Nov.	1	Barbie Riley invested $8,000 in the art studio.
	1	Paid ten months' rent in advance, $2,800.
	3	Purchased $1,200 of equipment from Omni Co. on account.
	5	Purchased $900 cash for art-training workshop for teachers.
	8	Purchased $450 of art supplies for cash.
	9	Billed Howie Co. $2,500 for group art lessons for its employees.
	10	Paid salaries of assistants, $1,300.
	15	Barbie withdrew $100 from the business for personal use.
	28	Paid electrical bill, $110.
	29	Paid telephone bill for November, $140.

Check Figure:
Total Trial Balance $12,600

Your tasks are to do the following:

a. Set up a ledger.

b. Journalize (all page 1) and post the November transactions.

c. Prepare a trial balance as of November 30, 201X.

The chart of accounts includes Cash, 111; Accounts Receivable, 112; Prepaid Rent, 114; Art Supplies, 121; Equipment, 131; Accounts Payable, 211; Barbie Riley, Capital, 311; Barbie Riley, Withdrawals, 312; Art Fees Earned, 411; Electrical Expense, 511; Salaries Expense, 521; and Telephone Expense, 531.

3B-3. The following transactions occurred in November 201X for A. Glover's Placement Agency:

L01, 2, 3 *(45 MIN)*

201X		
Nov.	1	A. Glover invested $5,000 cash in the placement agency.
	1	Bought equipment on account from Tinker Co., $1,200.
	3	Earned placement fees of $2,500, but payment from Avon Co. will not be received until July.
	5	A. Glover withdrew $1,000 for his personal use.
	7	Paid wages expense, $1,300.
	9	Placed a client on a local TV show, receiving $900 cash.
	15	Bought supplies on account from Reindeer Co., $300.
	28	Paid telephone bill for November, $190.
	29	Advertising bill from Shimmer Co. received but not paid, $400.

Check Figure:
Total Trial Balance $10,300

The chart of accounts includes Cash, 111; Accounts Receivable, 112; Supplies, 131; Equipment, 141; Accounts Payable, 211; A. Glover, Capital, 311; A. Glover, Withdrawals, 312; Placement Fees Earned, 411; Wage Expense, 511; Telephone Expense, 521; and Advertising Expense, 531.

Your task is to do the following:

a. Set up a ledger based on the chart of accounts.

b. Journalize (all page 1) and post the November transactions.

c. Prepare a trial balance at November 30, 201X.

Financial Report Problem

Reading the Kellogg's Annual Report

Go to http://investor.kelloggs.com/annuals.cfm, to access the Kellogg's 2010 Annual Report, and find the statement of earnings. Sales are the revenue for a merchandise company. How much did Kellogg's sales increase or decrease from 2009 to 2010? What inward flows could result from these net sales?

L03 *(5 MIN)*

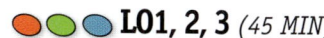

SANCHEZ COMPUTER CENTER

L01, 2, 3 *(45 MIN)*

Tony's computer center is picking up in business, so he has decided to expand his bookkeeping system to a general journal/ledger system. The balances from August have been forwarded to the ledger accounts.

Assignment

1. Use the chart of accounts in Chapter 2 to record the following transactions in Figures 3.39 through 3.49.

FIGURE 3.39
Prepaid Rent

Sanchez Computer Center	8104
385 N. Escondido Blvd.	*September 1, --201X-----*
Escondido CA 92025	

Pay
To the
Order of— *Capital Management* --- $ *1200.00* ------

One thousand two hundred and 00/100

First Union Bank
322 Glen Ave.
Escondido, CA 92025
memo *Prepaid Rent— Aug. Sept. Oct.**   -------- *Tony Freedman* --------
0611 062 78 72

*One check is written for 3 months' rent on September 1. That included August rent. For this problem, consider it all prepaid.

FIGURE 3.40
Service Revenue

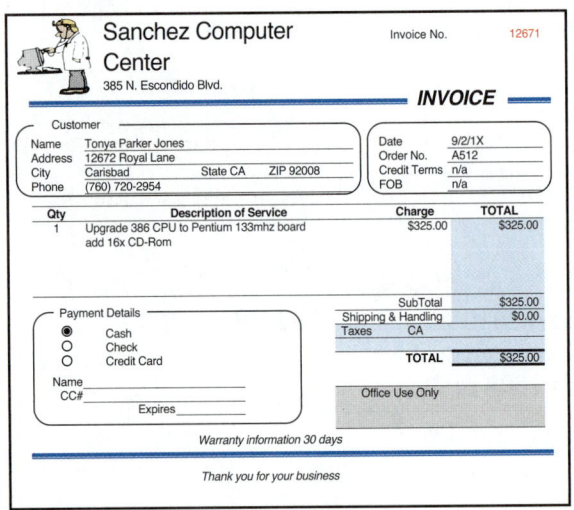

FIGURE 3.41
Service Revenue

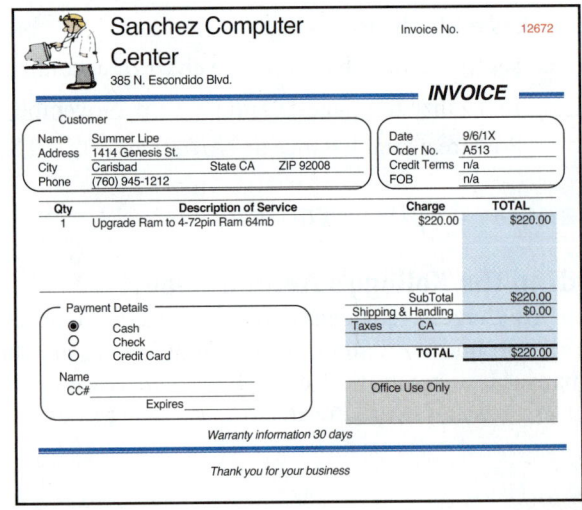

FIGURE 3.42
Phone Bill

Sanchez Computer Center	8105
385 N. Escondido Blvd.	*September 8, --201X-----*
Escondido CA 92025	

Pay
To the
Order of— *Pacific Bell* ------------------------------- $ *155.00* -----

One hundred fifty five and 00/100

First Union Bank
322 Glen Ave.
Escondido, CA 92025
memo *August phone bill transaction (k) Chpt. 2*   ------ *Tony Freedman* ------
0611 062 78 72

Refer back to Chapter 2, transaction k.

FIGURE 3.43
Sparks Collection

Jeannine Sparks	251
1919 Sierra St.	*September 12, --201X-----*
Escondido CA 92025	

Pay
To the
Order of— *Sanchez Computer Center* ----------------------------- $ *850.00* -----

Eight hundred fifty dollars and 00/100

Bank First
322 Cardiff Ave.
Escondido, CA 92025
memo *Computer Fixed, Transaction (o) Chpt. 2*   ------ *Jeannine Sparks* ------
0611 062 78 72

Refer back to Chapter 2, transaction o.

FIGURE 3.44
Paid Computer Connection

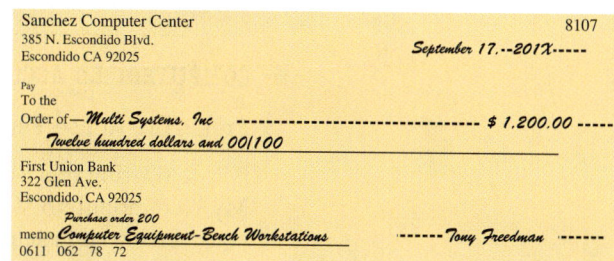

FIGURE 3.45
Purchased Computer Equipment

Refer back to Chapter 2, transaction s.

FIGURE 3.46
Received Phone Bill

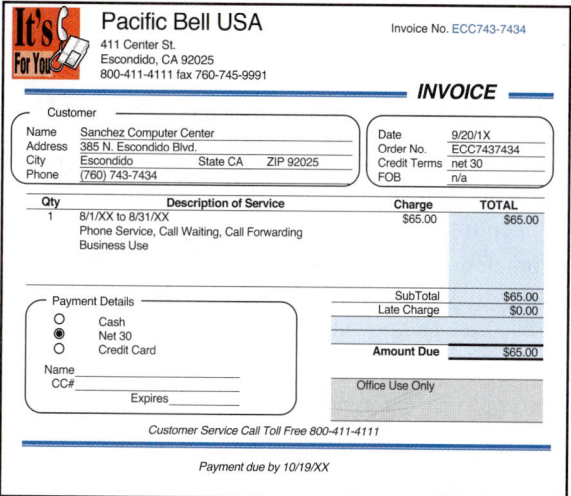

FIGURE 3.47
Received Electric Bill

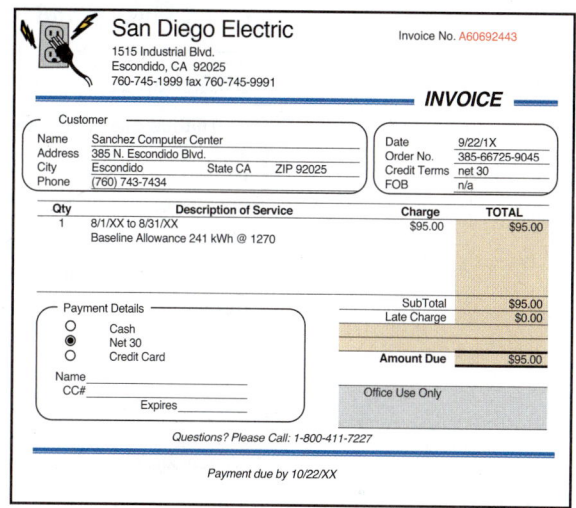

FIGURE 3.48
Service Revenue

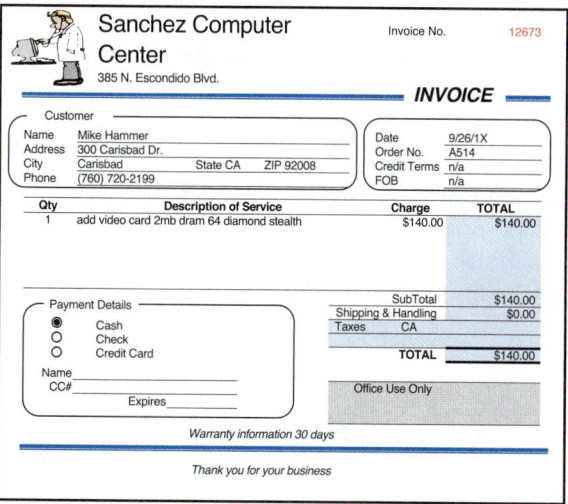

FIGURE 3.49
Service Revenue

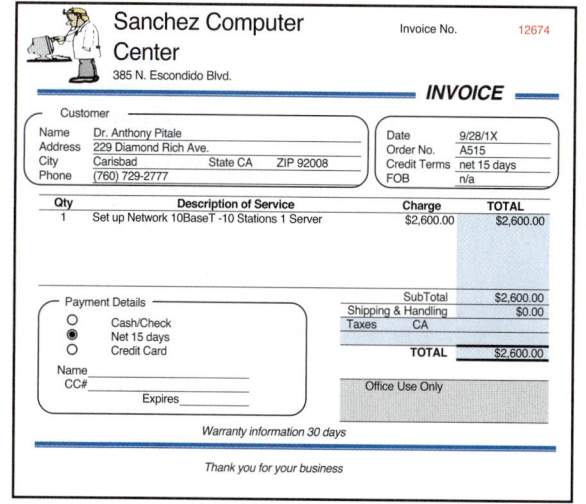

2. Post all transactions to the general ledger accounts (the Prepaid Rent Account #1025 has been added to the chart of accounts).

3. Prepare a trial balance for September 30, 201X.

4. Prepare the financial statements for the three months ended September 30, 201X.

PEACHTREE COMPUTER WORKSHOP

COMPUTERIZED ACCOUNTING APPLICATION FOR CHAPTER 3

Preparing to use Peachtree Complete Accounting

Before starting this assignment, visit the multimedia library of the MyAccountingLab Web site and read the following PDF documents for your version of Peachtree.

1. An Introduction to Computerized Accounting
2. Installing Peachtree Complete Accounting and Student Data Files
3. An Introduction to Peachtree Complete Accounting
4. Correcting Peachtree Transactions
5. How to Repeat or Restart a Peachtree Assignment
6. Backing Up and Restoring Your Work in Peachtree

Workshop 1:

Journalizing, Posting, General Ledger, Trial Balance, and Chart of Accounts

In this workshop you enter, post, and edit journal entries for the Atlas Company using Peachtree Complete Accounting. You will also print the general journal report, trial balance, and chart of accounts.

Instructions and data files for completing this assignment are in the multimedia library of the MyAccountingLab Web site. Open the *Workshop 1 Atlas Company* PDF document for your version of Peachtree and download the *Atlas Company* data file for your version of Peachtree.

QUICKBOOKS COMPUTER WORKSHOP

COMPUTERIZED ACCOUNTING APPLICATION FOR CHAPTER 3

Preparing to use QuickBooks Pro

Before starting this assignment, visit the multimedia library of the MyAccountingLab Web site and read the following PDF documents for your version of QuickBooks.

1. An Introduction to Computerized Accounting
2. Installing QuickBooks Pro and Student Data Files
3. An Introduction to QuickBooks Pro
4. Correcting QuickBooks Transactions
5. How to Repeat or Restart a QuickBooks Assignment
6. Backing Up and Restoring Your Work in QuickBooks

Workshop 1:

Journalizing, Posting, General Ledger, Trial Balance, and Chart of Accounts

In this workshop, you enter, post, and edit journal entries for the Atlas Company using QuickBooks Pro. You will also print the general journal report, trial balance, and chart of accounts.

Instructions and data files for completing this assignment are in the multimedia library of the MyAccountingLab Web site. Open the *Workshop 1 Atlas Company* PDF document for your version of QuickBooks and download the *Atlas Company* data file for your version of QuickBooks.

The Accounting Cycle Continued 4

THE GAME PLAN: THE ACCOUNTING CYCLE CONTINUED

When driving a new car like the Chevrolet Volt, do you ever wonder how many steps it takes to design a car from the idea to the finished product? Designers at General Motors first sketched the concept of the Volt using design software and then considered how this new electrical car could be manufactured. While accountants do not design cars, they do use a sketch pad called a worksheet to make changes and adjustments to the trial balance and financial statements. Today, whether in the accounting department at General Motors or a small business, these "design sheets" or worksheets are "sketched" by accounting software. Laying out a worksheet will provide you with a tool to aid you in understanding the "design"—the financial statements generated by your computerized accounting software. Using these worksheets, you will learn how to complete the accounting cycle.

LEARNING OBJECTIVES

1. Adjustments: prepaid rent, office supplies, depreciation on equipment, and accrued salaries.

2. Preparing the adjusted trial balance on the worksheet.

3. Preparing the income statement and balance sheet sections of the worksheet.

4. Preparing financial statements from the worksheet.

Each year General Motors completes an accounting cycle. In Figure 4.1, steps 1–4 show the parts of the manual accounting cycle that were completed for Clark's Word Processing Services in the previous chapter. This chapter continues the cycle with steps 5–6: the preparation of a worksheet and the three financial statements.

LEARNING UNIT 4-1 STEP 5 OF THE ACCOUNTING CYCLE:
Preparing a Worksheet

Worksheet A columnar device used by accountants to aid them in completing the accounting cycle—often just referred to as "spreadsheet." It is not a formal report.

An accountant uses a **worksheet** to organize and check data before preparing financial statements necessary to complete the accounting cycle. When an accounting software package is used, a worksheet is not needed. The most important function of the worksheet is to allow the accountant to find and correct errors before financial statements are prepared. In a way, a financial statement acts as the accountant's scratch pad. No one sees the worksheet once the financial statements are prepared. A sample worksheet is shown in Figure 4.2.

The accounts listed on the far left of the worksheet are taken from the ledger. The rest of the worksheet has five sections: the trial balance, adjustments, adjusted trial balance, income statement, and balance sheet. Each of these sections is divided into debit and credit columns.

The Trial Balance Section

We discussed how to prepare a trial balance in Chapter 2. Some companies prepare a separate trial balance; others, such as Clark's Word Processing Services, prepare the trial balance directly on the worksheet. A trial balance is taken on every account listed in the ledger that has a balance. Additional titles from the ledger are added as they are needed. (We will show how to add account titles later.)

LO1 The Adjustments Section

Chapters 1–3 discussed transactions that occurred with outside suppliers and companies. In a business, also inside transactions occur during the accounting cycle.

FIGURE 4.1

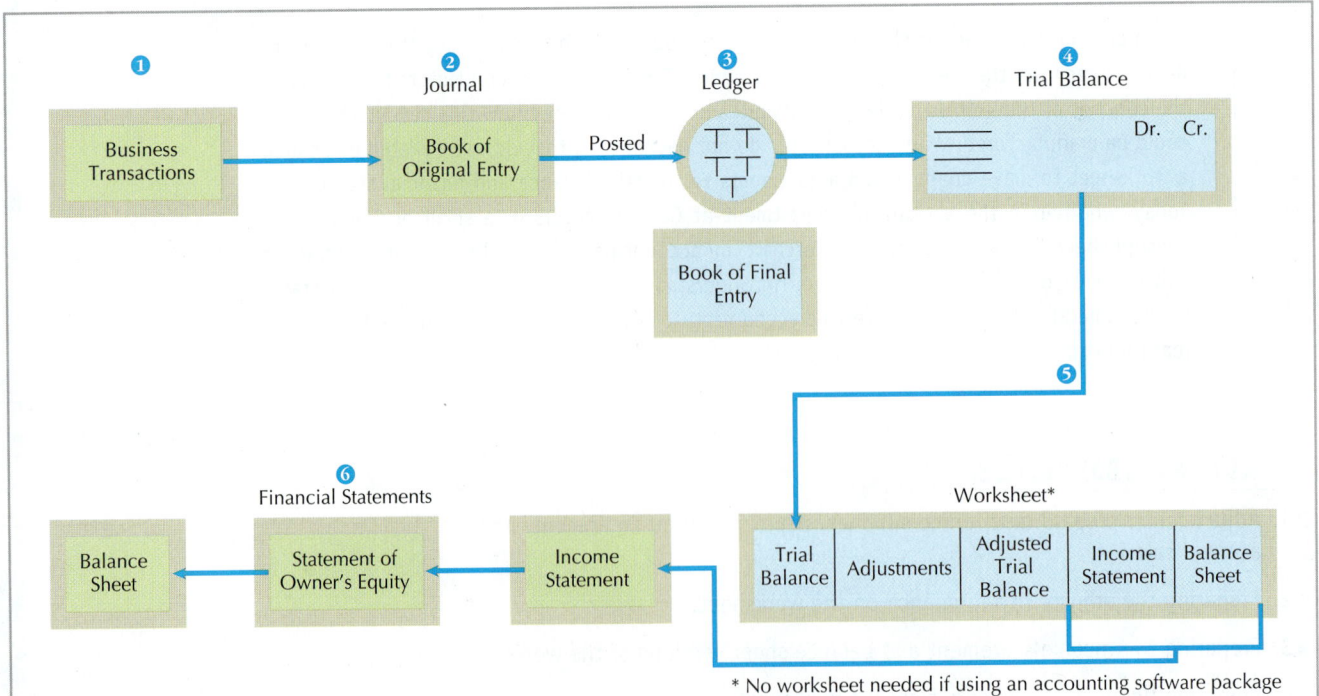

* No worksheet needed if using an accounting software package

FIGURE 4.2
Sample Worksheet

			Trial Balance		Adjustments		Adjusted Trial Balance		Income Statement	
Account Titles			Dr.	Cr.	Dr.	Cr.	Dr.	Cr.	Dr.	Cr.
Cash			6 1 5 5 00							
Accounts Receivable			5 0 0 0 00							
Office Supplies			6 0 0 00							
Prepaid Rent			1 2 0 0 00							
Word Processing Equipment			6 0 0 0 00							
Accounts Payable				3 3 5 0 00						
Brenda Clark, Capital				10 0 0 0 00						
Brenda Clark, Withdrawals			6 2 5 00							
Word Processing Fees				8 0 0 0 00						
Office Salaries Expense			1 3 0 0 00							
Advertising Expense			2 5 0 00							
Telephone Expense			2 2 0 00							
			21 3 5 0 00	21 3 5 0 00						

CLARK'S WORD PROCESSING SERVICES
WORKSHEET
FOR MONTH ENDING MAY 31, 201X

These transactions must be recorded, too. At the end of the worksheet process, the accountant will have all of the business's accounts up-to-date and ready to be used to prepare the formal financial reports. The Sarbanes-Oxley Act specifically states the need to have accurate financial statements. By analyzing each of Clark's accounts on the worksheet, the accountant will be able to identify specific accounts that must be adjusted to bring them up-to-date. The accountant for Clark's Word Processing Services needs to adjust the following accounts:

a. Office Supplies
b. Prepaid Rent
c. Word Processing Equipment
d. Office Salaries Expense

Let's look at how to analyze and adjust each of these accounts.

A. Adjusting the Office Supplies Account On May 31, the accountant found out that the company had only $100 worth of office supplies on hand. When the company had originally purchased the $600 of office supplies, they were considered an asset. As the supplies were used up, they became an expense.

- Office supplies available: $600 on trial balance.
- Office supplies left or on hand as of May 31: $100 will end up on adjusted trial balance.
- Office supplies used up in the operation of the business for the month of May: $500 is shown in the adjustments column.

As a result, the asset Office Supplies is too high on the trial balance (it should be $100, not $600). At the same time, if we don't show the additional expense of supplies used, the company's *net income* will be too high.

If Clark's accountant does not adjust the trial balance to reflect the change, the company's net income will be too high on the income statement and both sides (Assets and Owner's Equity) of the balance sheet will be too high.

Now let's look at the adjustment for office supplies in terms of the transaction analysis chart.

Will go on income statement

Accounts Affected	Category	↓↑	Rules
Office Supplies Expense	Expense	↑	Dr.
Office Supplies	Asset	↑	Cr.

Will go on balance sheet

Office Supplies Exp. 514

500

This amount is supplies used up.

Office Supplies 114

| 600 | 500 |
| 100 | |

↑

This amount is supplies on hand.

The Office Supplies Expense account comes from the chart of accounts in Chapter 3. Because it is not listed in the account titles, it must be listed below the trial balance. Let's see how we enter this adjustment in the worksheet in Figure 4.3.

Place $500 in the debit column of the adjustments section on the same line as Office Supplies Expense. Place $500 in the credit column of the adjustments section on the same line as Office Supplies. The numbers in the adjustment column show what is used, *not* what is on hand.

COACHING TIP

The adjustment for supplies deals with the amount of supplies *used up*.

FIGURE 4.3

Note: Amount "used up" for supplies, $500, goes in adjustments section.

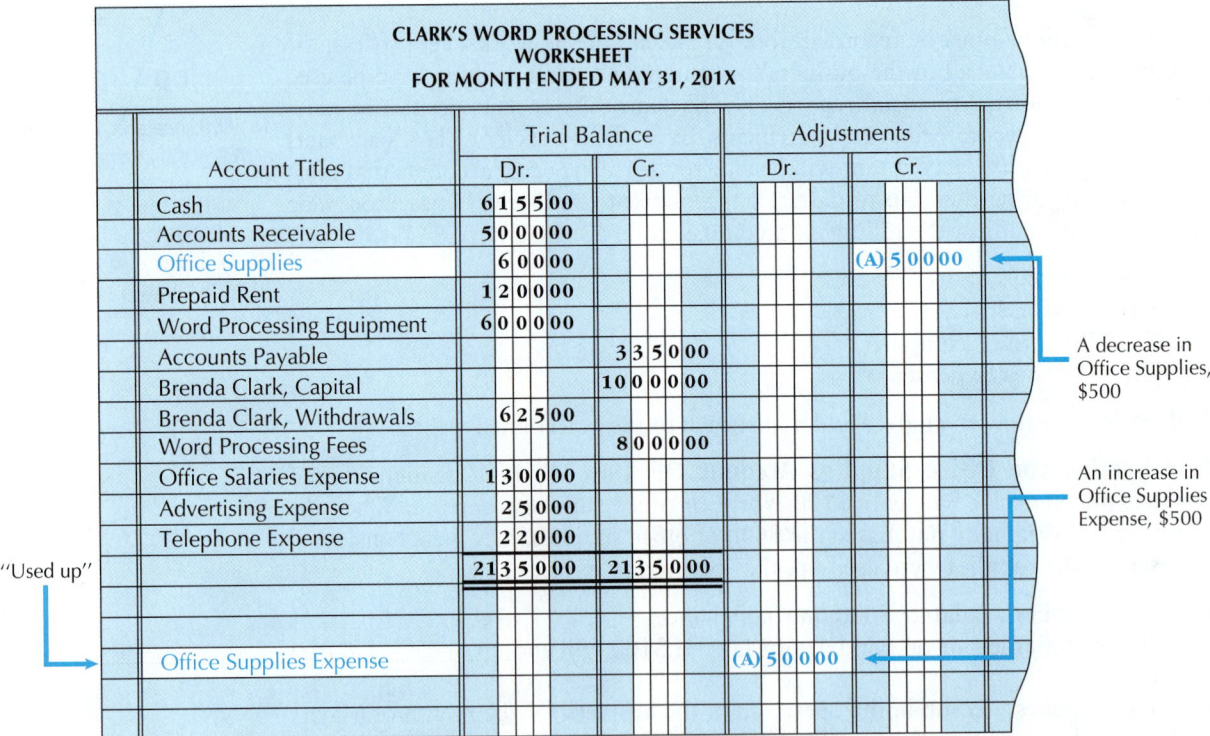

CLARK'S WORD PROCESSING SERVICES
WORKSHEET
FOR MONTH ENDED MAY 31, 201X

Account Titles	Trial Balance Dr.	Trial Balance Cr.	Adjustments Dr.	Adjustments Cr.
Cash	6 1 5 5 00			
Accounts Receivable	5 0 0 0 00			
Office Supplies	6 0 0 00			(A) 5 0 0 00
Prepaid Rent	1 2 0 0 00			
Word Processing Equipment	6 0 0 0 00			
Accounts Payable		3 3 5 0 00		
Brenda Clark, Capital		10 0 0 0 00		
Brenda Clark, Withdrawals	6 2 5 00			
Word Processing Fees		8 0 0 0 00		
Office Salaries Expense	1 3 0 0 00			
Advertising Expense	2 5 0 00			
Telephone Expense	2 2 0 00			
	21 3 5 0 00	21 3 5 0 00		
Office Supplies Expense			(A) 5 0 0 00	

"Used up"

A decrease in Office Supplies, $500

An increase in Office Supplies Expense, $500

B. Adjusting the Prepaid Rent Account Back on May 1, Clark's Word Processing Services paid three months' rent in advance. The accountant realized that the rent expense would be $400 per month ($1,200 ÷ 3 months = $400).

Remember, when rent is paid in advance, it is considered an asset called *prepaid rent*. When the asset, prepaid rent, begins to expire or be used up, it becomes an expense. Now it is May 31, and one month's prepaid rent has become an expense.

How is this type of rent handled? Should the account be $1,200, or is only $800 of prepaid rent left as of May 31? What do we need to do to bring Prepaid Rent to the "true" balance? The answer is that we must increase Rent Expense by $400 and decrease Prepaid Rent by $400 (so that there is only $800 left (see Figure 4.4)).

Without this adjustment, the expenses for Clark's Word Processing Services for May will be too low, and the asset prepaid rent will be too high. If unadjusted amounts were used in the formal reports, the net income shown on the income statement would be too high, and both sides (Assets and Owner's Equity) would be too high on the balance sheet. In terms of our transaction analysis chart, the adjustment would look like this:

Will go on income statement

Accounts Affected	Category	↓↑	Rules
Rent Expense	Expense	↑	Dr.
Prepaid Rent	Asset	↓	Cr.

Will go on balance sheet

Rent Expense 515		Prepaid Rent 115	
400		1200	400
		800	

Like the Office Supplies Expense account, the Rent Expense account comes from the chart of accounts in Chapter 3.

Figure 4.4 shows how to enter an adjustment to Prepaid Rent.

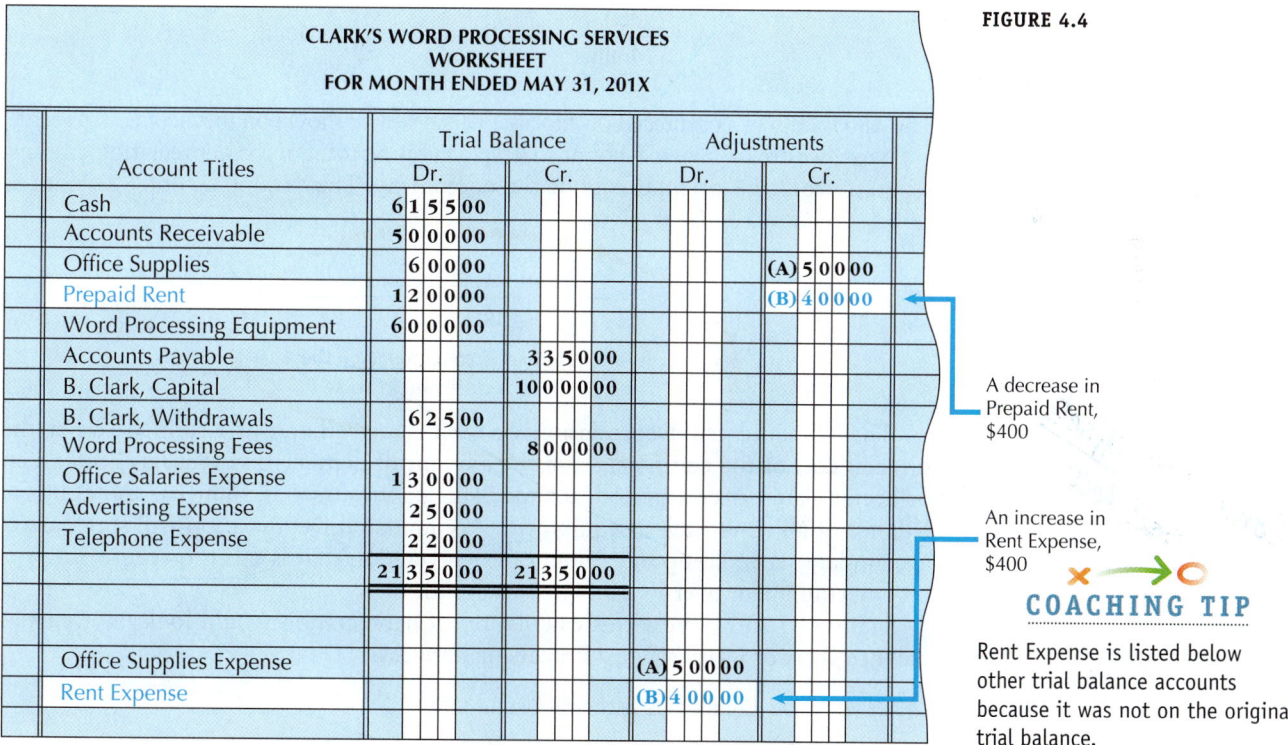

FIGURE 4.4

CLARK'S WORD PROCESSING SERVICES
WORKSHEET
FOR MONTH ENDED MAY 31, 201X

Account Titles	Trial Balance Dr.	Trial Balance Cr.	Adjustments Dr.	Adjustments Cr.
Cash	6 1 5 5 00			
Accounts Receivable	5 0 0 0 00			
Office Supplies	6 0 0 00			(A) 5 0 0 00
Prepaid Rent	1 2 0 0 00			(B) 4 0 0 00
Word Processing Equipment	6 0 0 0 00			
Accounts Payable		3 3 5 0 00		
B. Clark, Capital		10 0 0 0 00		
B. Clark, Withdrawals	6 2 5 00			
Word Processing Fees		8 0 0 0 00		
Office Salaries Expense	1 3 0 0 00			
Advertising Expense	2 5 0 00			
Telephone Expense	2 2 0 00			
	21 3 5 0 00	21 3 5 0 00		
Office Supplies Expense			(A) 5 0 0 00	
Rent Expense			(B) 4 0 0 00	

A decrease in Prepaid Rent, $400

An increase in Rent Expense, $400

COACHING TIP

Rent Expense is listed below other trial balance accounts because it was not on the original trial balance.

C. Adjusting the Word Processing Equipment Account for Depreciation
The life of the asset affects how it is adjusted. The two accounts we just discussed, Office Supplies and Prepaid Rent, involve things that are used up relatively quickly. Equipment—like word processing equipment—is expected to last much longer. Equipment is expected to help produce revenue over a longer period. For that reason accountants treat it differently. The balance sheet reports the historical cost, or original cost, of the equipment. The original cost also is reflected in the ledger. The adjustment shows how the cost of the equipment is allocated (spread) over its expected useful life. This spreading is called depreciation.

LO2

Historical cost The actual cost of an asset at time of purchase.

Depreciation The allocation (spreading) of the cost of an asset (such as an auto or equipment) over its expected useful life.

To depreciate the equipment, we have to figure out how much its cost goes down each month. Then we have to keep a running total of how that depreciation mounts up over time. The Internal Revenue Service (IRS) issues guidelines, tables, and formulas that must be used to estimate the amount of depreciation. Different methods can be used to calculate depreciation. We will use the simplest method—straight-line depreciation—to calculate the depreciation of Clark's Word Processing Services' equipment. Under the straight-line method, equal amounts are taken over successive periods of time. Table 4-1 shows how some companies estimate life of equipment using the straight-line method.

The calculation of depreciation for the year for Clark's Word Processing Services is as follows:

$$\frac{\text{Cost of Equipment} - \text{Residual Value}}{\text{Estimated Years of Usefulness}} = (\text{Trade-In or Salvage Value})$$

According to the IRS, word processing equipment has an expected life of five years. At the end of that time, the property's value is called its "residual value." Think of residual value as the estimated value of the equipment at the end of the fifth year. For Clark, the equipment has an estimated residual value of $1,200.

Residual value Estimated value of an asset after all the allowable depreciation has been taken.

$$\frac{\$6,000 - \$1,200}{5 \text{ Years}} = \frac{\$4,800}{5} = \$960 \text{ Depreciation per Year}$$

Our trial balance is for one month, so we must determine the adjustment for that month:

$$\frac{\$960}{12 \text{ Months}} = \$80 \text{ Depreciation per Month}$$

This $80 is known as depreciation expense, which will be shown on the income statement.

Next, we create a new account to keep a running total of the depreciation amount separate from the original cost of the equipment. The "running total" account is called Accumulated Depreciation.

Accumulated Depreciation
A contra-asset account that summarizes or accumulates the amount of depreciation that has been taken on an asset.

Accumulated Depreciation	
Dr.	Cr.

is a contra-asset account found on the balance sheet. A credit will increase it.

The Accumulated Depreciation account shows the relationship between the original cost of the equipment and the amount of depreciation that has been taken or accumulated over a period of time. This *contra-asset* account has the opposite balance of an asset such as equipment. Accumulated Depreciation will summarize, accumulate, or build up the amount of depreciation that is taken on the word processing equipment over its estimated useful life.

Figure 4.5 shows how this calculation of depreciation would look on a partial balance sheet of Clark's Word Processing Services.

Contra Acct offsets Asset Acct

TABLE 4.1 How Companies Estimate Useful Life

Company	Method of Depreciation	Estimated Life of Equipment
Claire's Stores	Straight-Line	Furniture: 3–25 years
Merck	Straight-Line	Building: 10–50 years
		Office Equip.: 3–15 years
Big Lots	Straight-Line	Building: 40 years
		Equipment: 3–15 years
Dollar General	Straight-Line	Building: 39–40 years
		Furniture: 3–10 years

FIGURE 4.5

❶ Historical cost of $6,000 of equipment is not changed.

❷ Amount of accumulated depreciation is $80 after one month.

❸ This figure shows the unused amount of the equipment that may be depreciated in future periods of time. This figure, the cost of the asset less its accumulated depreciation, is often termed *book value* or *carrying value*.

CLARK'S WORD PROCESSING SERVICES BALANCE SHEET MAY 31, 201X		
Assets		
- - - - - - -		XXXX
Word Processing Equip.	$6,000	
Less Accumulated Depreciation	80	5,920

Let's summarize the key points before going on to mark the adjustment on the worksheet:

1. Depreciation Expense goes on the income statement, which results in
   - an increase in total expenses,
   - a decrease in net income, and, therefore,
   - less to be paid in taxes.
2. Accumulated Depreciation is a contra-asset account found on the balance sheet next to its related equipment account. Accumulated depreciation increases with a credit.
3. The original cost of equipment is not reduced; it stays the same until the equipment is sold or removed.
4. Each month the amount in the Accumulated Depreciation account grows larger while the cost of the equipment remains the same.

Now, let's analyze the adjustment on the transaction analysis chart:

			Will go on income statement
Accounts Affected	**Category**	**↓↑**	**Rules**
Depreciation Expense, Word Processing Equipment	Expense	↑	Dr.
Accumulated Depreciation, Word Processing Equipment	Contra-Asset	↑	Cr.
			Will go on balance sheet

Dep. Expense, W. P. 516	Accum. Dep., W. P. 122
80		80

Remember, the original cost of the equipment never changes: (1) The Equipment account is not included among the affected accounts because the original cost of equipment remains the same, and (2) the original cost does not change. As the accumulated depreciation increases (as a credit), the equipment's book value decreases.

Figure 4.6 (p. 126) shows how we enter the adjustment for depreciation of word processing equipment.

Because it is a new business, neither account had a previous balance. Therefore, neither is listed in the account titles of the trial balance. We need to list both accounts below Rent Expense in the account titles section. On the worksheet, put $80 in the debit column of the adjustments section on the same line as Depreciation Expense, W. P. Equipment, and put $80 in the credit column of the adjustments section on the same line as Accumulated Depreciation, W. P. Equipment.

Next month, on June 30, $80 would be entered under Depreciation Expense and Accumulated Depreciation would show a balance of $160. Remember, in May, Clark's was a new company so no previous depreciation had been taken.

Now let's look at the last adjustment for Clark's Word Processing Services.

COACHING TIP

Note that the original cost of the equipment on the worksheet has *not* been changed ($6,000).

Book value Cost of equipment less accumulated depreciation.

FIGURE 4.6

	Trial Balance		Adjustments	
Account Titles	Dr.	Cr.	Dr.	Cr.
Cash	6 1 5 5 00			
Accounts Receivable	5 0 0 0 00			
Office Supplies	6 0 0 00			(A) 5 0 0 00
Prepaid Rent	1 2 0 0 00			(B) 4 0 0 00
Word Processing Equipment	6 0 0 0 00			
Accounts Payable		3 3 5 0 00		
B. Clark, Capital		10 0 0 0 00		
B. Clark, Withdrawals	6 2 5 00			
Word Processing Fees		8 0 0 0 00		
Office Salaries Expense	1 3 0 0 00			
Advertising Expense	2 5 0 00			
Telephone Expense	2 2 0 00			
	21 3 5 0 00	21 3 5 0 00		
Office Supplies Expense			(A) 5 0 0 00	
Rent Expense			(B) 4 0 0 00	
Depreciation Exp., W. P. Equip.			(C) 8 0 00	
Accum. Deprec., W. P. Equip.				(C) 8 0 00

Table title: CLARK'S WORD PROCESSING SERVICES — WORKSHEET — FOR MONTH ENDED MAY 31, 201X

An increase in Depreciation Expense, W. P. Equipment

An increase in Accumulated Depreciation, W. P. Equipment

Accrued salaries payable

Salaries that are earned by employees but unpaid and unrecorded during the period (and thus need to be recorded by an adjustment) and will not come due for payment until the next accounting period.

D. Adjusting the Salaries Accrued Account Clark's Word Processing Services paid $1,300 in office salaries expense (see the trial balance of any previous worksheet in this chapter). The last salary checks for the month were paid on May 27. How can we update this account to show the salary expense as of May 31?

John Murray worked for Clark on May 28, 29, 30, and 31 (see Figure 4.7). His next paycheck is not due until June 3. John earned $350 for these four days. Is the $350 an expense to Clark in May when it was earned, or in June when it is due and is paid?

Think back to Chapter 1, in which we first discussed revenue and expenses. We noted then that revenue is recorded when it is earned and expenses are recorded when they are incurred, not when they are actually paid. This principle will be discussed further in a later chapter. For now, it is enough to remember that we record revenue and expenses when they occur because we want to match earned revenue with the expenses that resulted in earning those revenues. In this case, by working those four days, John Murray created some revenue for Clark in May. Therefore, the office salaries expense must be shown in May—the month the revenue was earned.

The results are as follows:

- **Office Salaries Expense** is increased by $350. This unpaid and unrecorded expense for salaries for which payment is not yet due is called **accrued salaries payable**. In effect, we now show the true expense for salaries ($1,650 instead of $1,300):

Office Salaries Expense	
1,300	
350	

- **Salaries Payable** is also increased by $350. Clark's created a liability called salaries payable, which means that the firm owes money for salaries. When the firm pays John Murray, it will reduce its liability salaries payable as well as decrease its cash.

FIGURE 4.7

May						
Sunday	Monday	Tuesday	Wednesday	Thursday	Friday	Saturday
						1
2	3	4	5	6	7	8
9	10	11	12	13	14	15
16	17	18	19	20	21	22
23	24	25	26	27	28	29
30	31					

In terms of the transaction analysis chart, the following would be done:

Will go on income statement

Accounts Affected	Category	↓↑	Rules
Office Salaries Expense	Expense	↑	Dr.
Salaries Payable	Liability	↑	Cr.

Will go on balance sheet

Office Salaries Exp. 511		Salaries Payable 212	
1,300			350
350			

How the adjustment for accrued salaries is entered in the worksheet is shown in Figure 4.8.

FIGURE 4.8

CLARK'S WORD PROCESSING SERVICES
WORKSHEET
FOR MONTH ENDED MAY 31, 201X

Account Titles	Trial Balance Dr.	Trial Balance Cr.	Adjustments Dr.	Adjustments Cr.
Cash	6 1 5 5 00			
Accounts Receivable	5 0 0 0 00			
Office Supplies	6 0 0 00			(A) 5 0 0 00
Prepaid Rent	1 2 0 0 00			(B) 4 0 0 00
Word Processing Equipment	6 0 0 0 00			
Accounts Payable		3 3 5 0 00		
B. Clark, Capital		10 0 0 0 00		
B. Clark, Withdrawals	6 2 5 00			
Word Processing Fees		8 0 0 0 00		
Office Salaries Expense	1 3 0 0 00		(D) 3 5 0 00	
Advertising Expense	2 5 0 00			
Telephone Expense	2 2 0 00			
	21 3 5 0 00	21 3 5 0 00		
Office Supplies Expense			(A) 5 0 0 00	
Rent Expense			(B) 4 0 0 00	
Depreciation Exp., W. P. Equip.			(C) 8 0 00	
Accum. Deprec., W. P. Equip.				(C) 8 0 00
Salaries Payable				(D) 3 5 0 00

An increase in Office Salaries Expense, $350

An increase in Salaries Payable, $350

The account Office Salaries Expense is already listed in the account titles, so $350 is placed in the debit column of the adjustments section on the same line as Office Salaries Expense. However, because Salaries Payable is not listed in the account titles, it is added below the trial balance after Accumulated Depreciation, W. P. Equipment. The amount $350 is also placed in the credit column of the adjustments section on the same line as Salaries Payable.

Now that we have finished all the adjustments that we intended to make, we total the adjustments section, as shown in Figure 4.9.

FIGURE 4.9
The Adjustments Section of the Worksheet

CLARK'S WORD PROCESSING SERVICES
WORKSHEET
FOR MONTH ENDED MAY 31, 201X

Account Titles	Trial Balance Dr.	Trial Balance Cr.	Adjustments Dr.	Adjustments Cr.
Cash	6 1 5 5 00			
Accounts Receivable	5 0 0 0 00			
Office Supplies	6 0 0 00			(A) 5 0 0 00
Prepaid Rent	1 2 0 0 00			(B) 4 0 0 00
Word Processing Equipment	6 0 0 0 00			
Accounts Payable		3 3 5 0 00		
B. Clark, Capital		10 0 0 0 00		
B. Clark, Withdrawals	6 2 5 00			
Word Processing Fees		8 0 0 0 00		
Office Salaries Expense	1 3 0 0 00		(D) 3 5 0 00	
Advertising Expense	2 5 0 00			
Telephone Expense	2 2 0 00			
	21 3 5 0 00	21 3 5 0 00		
Office Supplies Expense			(A) 5 0 0 00	
Rent Expense			(B) 4 0 0 00	
Depreciation Exp., W. P. Equip.			(C) 8 0 00	
Accum. Deprec., W. P. Equip.				(C) 8 0 00
Salaries Payable				(D) 3 5 0 00
			1 3 3 0 00	1 3 3 0 00

The Adjusted Trial Balance Section

The adjusted trial balance is the next section on the worksheet. To fill it out we must summarize the information in the trial balance and adjustments sections, as shown in Figure 4.10 (p. 129).

Note that when the numbers are brought across from the trial balance to the adjusted trial balance, two debits will be added together and two credits will be added together. If the numbers include a debit and a credit, take the difference between the two and place it on the side that is larger.

Now that we have completed the adjustments and adjusted trial balance sections of the worksheet, it is time to move on to the income statement and the balance sheet sections. Before we tackle the statements, look at the chart shown in Table 4.2. This table should be used as a reference to help you in filling out the next two sections of the worksheet.

Keep in mind that the numbers from the adjusted trial balance are carried over to one of the last four columns of the worksheet before the bottom section is completed.

LO3   The Income Statement Section

As shown in Figure 4.11 (p. 130), the income statement section lists only revenue and expenses from the adjusted trial balance. Note that Accumulated Depreciation and Salaries Payable do not go on the income statement. Accumulated Depreciation is a contra-asset found on the balance sheet. Salaries Payable is a liability found on the balance sheet.

The revenue ($8,000) and all the individual expenses are listed in the income statement section. The revenue is placed in the credit column of the income statement section because it has a credit balance. The expenses have debit balances so

FIGURE 4.10
The Adjusted Trial Balance Section of the Worksheet

CLARK'S WORD PROCESSING SERVICES
WORKSHEET
FOR MONTH ENDED MAY 31, 201X

Account Titles	Trial Balance Dr.	Trial Balance Cr.	Adjustments Dr.	Adjustments Cr.	Adjusted Trial Balance Dr.	Adjusted Trial Balance Cr.
Cash	615500				615500	
Accounts Receivable	500000				500000	
Office Supplies	60000			(A) 50000	10000	
Prepaid Rent	120000			(B) 40000	80000	
Word Processing Equipment	600000				600000	
Accounts Payable		335000				335000
Brenda Clark, Capital		1000000				1000000
Brenda Clark, Withdrawals	62500				62500	
Word Processing Fees		800000				800000
Office Salaries Expense	130000		(D) 35000		165000	
Advertising Expense	25000				25000	
Telephone Expense	22000				22000	
	2135000	2135000				
Office Supplies Expense			(A) 50000		50000	
Rent Expense			(B) 40000		40000	
Depreciation Exp., W. P. Equip.			(C) 8000		8000	
Accum. Deprec., W. P. Equip.				(C) 8000		8000
Salaries Payable				(D) 35000		35000
			133000	133000	2178000	2178000

If no adjustment is made, just carry over amount from trial balance on same side.

Supplies were $600, but we used up $500, leaving us with a $100 balance (on hand) in Supplies. *Note:* If the account lists both a debit and a credit, take the *difference* between the two and place it on the side that is larger.

Note: Equipment is *not* adjusted here.

Two debits are added together. If there were two credits, they also would be added together.

Carry these amounts over to adjusted trial balance in the same positions.

Note: The total of the left (debit) must equal the total of the right (credit) ($21,780).

Trial Balance only good for making certain LEFT matches RIGHT

Normal Balances and Account Categories

Account Titles	Category	Normal Balance on Adjusted Trial Balance	Income Statement		Balance Sheet	
			Dr.	Cr.	Dr.	Cr.
Cash	Asset	Dr.			X	
Accounts Receivable	Asset	Dr.			X	
Office Supplies	Asset	Dr.			X	
Prepaid Rent	Asset	Dr.			X	
Word Proc. Equip.	Asset	Dr.			X	
Accounts Payable	Liability	Cr.				X
Brenda Clark, Capital	Capital	Cr.				X
Brenda Clark, Withdrawals	Withdrawal	Dr.			X	
Word Proc. Fees	Revenue	Cr.		X		
Office Salaries Exp.	Expense	Dr.	X			
Advertising Expense	Expense	Dr.	X			
Telephone Expense	Expense	Dr.	X			
Office Supplies Exp.	Expense	Dr.	X			
Rent Expense	Expense	Dr.	X			
Dep. Exp., W. P. Equip.	Expense	Dr.	X			
Acc. Dep., W. P. Equip.	Contra-Asset	Cr.				X
Salaries Payable	Liability	Cr.				X

FIGURE 4.11
The Income Statement Section of the Worksheet

CLARK'S WORD PROCESSING SERVICES
WORKSHEET
FOR MONTH ENDED MAY 31, 201X

Account Titles	Adjusted Trial Balance		Income Statement	
	Dr.	Cr.	Dr.	Cr.
Cash	6 1 5 5 00			
Accounts Receivable	5 0 0 0 00			
Office Supplies	1 0 0 00			
Prepaid Rent	8 0 0 00			
Word Processing Equipment	6 0 0 0 00			
Accounts Payable		3 3 5 0 00		
B. Clark, Capital		1 0 0 0 0 00		
B. Clark, Withdrawals	6 2 5 00			
Word Processing Fees		8 0 0 0 00		8 0 0 0 00
Office Salaries Expense	1 6 5 0 00		1 6 5 0 00	
Advertising Expense	2 5 0 00		2 5 0 00	
Telephone Expense	2 2 0 00		2 2 0 00	
Office Supplies Expense	5 0 0 00		5 0 0 00	
Rent Expense	4 0 0 00		4 0 0 00	
Depreciation Exp., W. P. Equip.	8 0 00		8 0 00	
Accum. Deprec., W. P. Equip.		8 0 00		
Salaries Payable		3 5 0 00		
	21 7 8 0 00	21 7 8 0 00	3 1 0 0 00	8 0 0 0 00
Net Income			4 9 0 0 00	
			8 0 0 0 00	8 0 0 0 00

$8,000
−3,100
─────
$4,900

they are placed in the debit column of the income statement section. The following steps must be taken after the debits and credits are placed in the correct columns:

STEP 1: Total the debits and credits.

STEP 2: Calculate the balance between the debit and credit columns and place the difference on the smaller side.

STEP 3: Total the columns.

The worksheet in Figure 4.11 shows that the label Net Income is added in the account title column on the same line as $4,900. When the figures result in a net income, it will be placed in the debit column of the income statement section of the worksheet. A net loss is placed in the credit column. The $8,000 total indicates that the two columns are in balance.

The Balance Sheet Section

To fill out the balance sheet section of the worksheet, the following are carried over from the adjusted trial balance section: assets, contra-assets, liabilities, capital, and withdrawals. Because the beginning figure for Capital* is used on the worksheet, Net Income is brought over to the credit column of the balance sheet so both columns balance.

Let's now look at the completed worksheet in Figure 4.12 (p. 132) to see how the balance sheet section is completed. Note how the Net Income of $4,900 is brought over to the credit column of the balance sheet section. The figure for Capital is also in the credit column while the figure for Withdrawals is in the debit column. By placing Net Income in the credit column, both sides total $18,680. If a net loss were to occur it would be placed in the debit column of the balance sheet section.

Now that we have completed the worksheet, we can go on to the three financial statements. But first let's summarize our progress.

COA

The differ
and $8,000 Cr. indi...
of $4,900. The $4,900 is place...
the debit column to balance both columns to $8,000. Actually, the credit side is larger by $4,900.

COACHING TIP

Remember: The ending figure for Capital is not on the worksheet.

LEARNING UNIT 4-1 REVIEW

AT THIS POINT you should be able to do the following:

- Define and explain the purpose of a worksheet.
- Explain the need as well as the process for adjustments.
- Explain the concept of depreciation.
- Explain the difference between depreciation expense and accumulated depreciation.
- Prepare a worksheet from a trial balance and adjustment data.

*We assume no additional investments during the period.

CHAPTER 4   The Accounting Cycle Continued

Original cost of $6,000 is *not* adjusted

"Used up"   "On hand"

CLARK'S WORD PROCESSING SERVICES
WORKSHEET
FOR MONTH ENDED MAY 31, 201X

Account Titles	Trial Balance Dr.	Trial Balance Cr.	Adjustments Dr.	Adjustments Cr.	Adjusted Trial Balance Dr.	Adjusted Trial Balance Cr.	Income Statement Dr.	Income Statement Cr.	Balance Sheet Dr.	Balance Sheet Cr.
Cash	6 1 5 5 00				6 1 5 5 00				6 1 5 5 00	
Accounts Receivable	5 0 0 0 00				5 0 0 0 00				5 0 0 0 00	
Office Supplies	6 0 0 00			(A) 5 0 0 00	1 0 0 00				1 0 0 00	
Prepaid Rent	1 2 0 0 00			(B) 4 0 0 00	8 0 0 00				8 0 0 00	
Word Processing Equipment	6 0 0 0 00				6 0 0 0 00				6 0 0 0 00	
Accounts Payable		3 3 5 0 00				3 3 5 0 00				3 3 5 0 00
B. Clark, Capital		1 0 0 0 0 00				1 0 0 0 0 00				1 0 0 0 0 00
B. Clark, Withdrawals	6 2 5 00				6 2 5 00				6 2 5 00	
Word Processing Fees		8 0 0 0 00				8 0 0 0 00		8 0 0 0 00		
Office Salaries Expense	1 3 0 0 00		(D) 3 5 0 00		1 6 5 0 00		1 6 5 0 00			
Advertising Expense	2 5 0 00				2 5 0 00		2 5 0 00			
Telephone Expense	2 2 0 00				2 2 0 00		2 2 0 00			
	2 1 3 5 0 00	2 1 3 5 0 00								
Office Supplies Expense			(A) 5 0 0 00		5 0 0 00		5 0 0 00			
Rent Expense			(B) 4 0 0 00		4 0 0 00		4 0 0 00			
Depreciation Exp., W. P. Equip.			(C) 8 0 00		8 0 00		8 0 00			
Accum. Deprec., W. P. Equip.				(C) 8 0 00		8 0 00				8 0 00
Salaries Payable				(D) 3 5 0 00		3 5 0 00				3 5 0 00
			1 3 3 0 00	1 3 3 0 00	2 1 7 8 0 00	2 1 7 8 0 00	3 1 0 0 00	8 0 0 0 00	1 8 6 8 0 00	1 3 7 8 0 00
Net Income							4 9 0 0 00			4 9 0 0 00
							8 0 0 0 00	8 0 0 0 00	1 8 6 8 0 00	1 8 6 8 0 00

contra-asset

FIGURE 4.12

Instant Replay ○ Self-Review Quiz 4-1

From the accompanying trial balance and adjustment data in Figure 4.13 and the adjustment data below, complete a worksheet for P. Logan Co. for the month ended Dec. 31, 201X. (You can use the blank fold-out worksheet located at the end of the textbook.)

Note: The numbers used on this quiz may seem impossibly small, but we have done that on purpose, so that at this point you don't have to worry about arithmetic, just about preparing the worksheet correctly.

Adjustment Data

a. Depreciation Expense, Store Equipment, $1.
b. Insurance Expired, $2.
c. Supplies on hand, $1.
d. Salaries owed but not paid to employees, $3.

FIGURE 4.13

P. LOGAN COMPANY
TRIAL BALANCE
DECEMBER 31, 201X

	Dr.	Cr.
Cash	15 00	
Accounts Receivable	3 00	
Prepaid Insurance	3 00	
Store Supplies	5 00	
Store Equipment	6 00	
Accumulated Depreciation, Store Equipment		4 00
Accounts Payable		2 00
P. Logan, Capital		14 00
P. Logan, Withdrawals	3 00	
Revenue from Clients		25 00
Rent Expense	2 00	
Salaries Expense	8 00	
	45 00	45 00

Solution to Instant Replay: Self-Review Quiz 4-1

Don't adjust this line! Store Equipment always contains the historical cost.

Amount used up

Note that supplies on hand end up on the adjusted trial balance.

P. LOGAN COMPANY
WORKSHEET
FOR MONTH ENDED DECEMBER 31, 201X

Account Titles	Trial Balance Dr.	Trial Balance Cr.	Adjustments Dr.	Adjustments Cr.	Adjusted Trial Balance Dr.	Adjusted Trial Balance Cr.	Income Statement Dr.	Income Statement Cr.	Balance Sheet Dr.	Balance Sheet Cr.
Cash	1500				1500				1500	
Accounts Receivable	300				300				300	
Prepaid Insurance	300			(B) 200	100				100	
Store Supplies	500			(C) 400	100				100	
Store Equipment	600				600				600	
Accum. Depr., Store Equipment		400		(A) 100		500				500
Accounts Payable		200				200				200
P. Logan, Capital		1400				1400				1400
P. Logan, Withdrawals	300				300				300	
Revenue from Clients		2500				2500		2500		
Rent Expense	200				200		200			
Salaries Expense	800		(D) 300		1100		1100			
	4500	4500								
Depr. Exp., Store Equipment			(A) 100		100		100			
Insurance Expense			(B) 200		200		200			
Supplies Expense			(C) 400		400		400			
Salaries Payable				(D) 300		300				300
			1000	1000	4900	4900	2000	2500	2900	2400
Net Income							500			500
							2500	2500	2900	2900

Note that Accumulated Depreciation is listed in the trial balance because the company is not new. Store Equipment has already been depreciated $4.00 from earlier periods.

FIGURE 4.14

PLAY BY PLAY: EXTRA HELP ON SELF-REVIEW QUIZ 4-1

Let's review first: When completing a worksheet, we list the original trial balance, add adjustments, complete an adjusted trial balance, and then decide which titles go on the income statement and balance sheet. Since we do not have columns for statement of owner's equity, withdrawals and net income will be placed on the balance sheet columns. Remember, it is the old figure for Capital that is placed on the worksheet.

Account title column: Any item not listed on the original trial balance will be listed below the trial balance. This will happen when we make adjustments. Note that when we list each title below the trial balance it will be increasing in value.

Adjustment column:

A. Depreciation:

In this adjustment Accumulated Depreciation is already listed on the trial balance so we only have to add Depreciation Expense below the trial balance. Here is the transaction analysis chart for this adjustment:

Depr. Exp. Store Equipm.	Expense	↑	Dr. $1
Acc. Deprec. Store Equip.	Contra-asset	↑	Cr. $1

Note that the original cost of Store Equipment of $6 is not touched.

B. Insurance Expired:

In this adjustment Prepaid Insurance is already listed on the trial balance so we only have to add Insurance Expense below the trial balance. Here is the transaction analysis chart for this adjustment:

Insurance Expense	Expense	↑	Dr. $2
Prepaid Insurance	Asset	↓	Cr. $2

Expired means used up and thus we use the amount of $2.

C. Supplies On Hand:

In this adjustment we have to calculate the amount of supplies used up. We take the beginning amount of supplies of $5 less the amount on hand of $1 to find the amount used up of $4. This is the amount of the adjustment. Since we have Office Supplies listed on the trial balance we only have to add Supplies Expense below the trial balance. Here is the transaction analysis chart for this adjustment:

Supplies Expense	Expense	↑	Dr. $4
Office Supplies	Asset	↓	Cr. $4

D. Salaries Owed:

In this adjustment we have Salaries Expense already listed on the trial balance. Here we have to add Salaries Payable below the trial balance. The following transaction analysis chart shows the new expense that has been incurred but has not been paid:

Salaries Expense	Expense	↑	Dr. $3
Salaries Payable	Liability	↑	Cr. $3

The sum of all the debits on the adjustments equals the sum of the credits.

COACHING TIP

Think of the person as an asset and the dog as a contra-asset. They both stick together (like an asset and a contra-asset on the balance sheet) but have opposite personalities. The dog's name is AC—always a credit.

Adjusted Trial Balance Columns: Accounts that were not adjusted or added below the trial balance have their balances carried over to the adjusted trial balance. Accounts that were adjusted will have their combined balances carried over to the adjusted trial balance.

For example, Salaries Expense is adjusted by adding the debit balance of $8 and the adjustment of $3 to equal an $11 debit balance on the adjusted trial balance. Every account in the adjusted trial balance will end up either on the Income Statement or Balance Sheet columns of the worksheet.

Income Statement Columns: From the adjusted trial balance, all revenue and expense accounts are listed. Note that when we total the debit and credit columns they do not equal each other until we calculate the difference between revenues and expenses. In this case, the ($5) difference will be added to the debit column of the income statement section so both columns will total $25.

Balance Sheet Columns: From the adjusted trial balance, assets and withdrawals will end up in the debit column. The old figures for Capital, liabilities, and contra-assets are in the credit column. Note that the totals of the columns will not balance until a net income of $5 is placed under the $24. This is done because we use the old figure for Capital on the worksheet and there is no column on the worksheet for the statement of owner's equity.

Summary: On the worksheet, items in accounts listed below the trial balance are increasing. Adjustments for supplies must be used up. The original cost of equipment is never touched in the adjustment process. Capital is the old balance on the worksheet. Net income is the difference between revenue and expenses and is carried over to the credit column of the balance sheet. Net losses will be in opposite columns. Income Statement columns and Balance Sheet columns will be out of balance by the amount of Net Income.

LO4   LEARNING UNIT 4-2 STEP 6 OF THE ACCOUNTING CYCLE:
Preparing the Financial Statements from the Worksheet

The formal financial statements can be prepared from the worksheet completed in Learning Unit 4-1. Before beginning, we must check that the entries on the worksheet are correct and in balance. To ensure the accuracy of the figures, we double-check that (1) all entries are recorded in the appropriate column, (2) the correct amounts are entered in the proper places, (3) the addition is correct across the columns (i.e., from the trial balance to the adjusted trial balance to the financial statements), and (4) the columns are added correctly.

Preparing the Income Statement

The first statement to be prepared for Clark's Word Processing Services is the income statement. When preparing the income statement it is important to remember the following:

1. Every figure on the formal statement is on the worksheet. Figure 4.15 (p. 137) shows where each of these figures goes on the income statement.
2. No debit or credit columns appear on the formal statement.
3. The inside column on financial statements is used for subtotaling.
4. Withdrawals do not go on the income statement; they go on the statement of owner's equity.

FIGURE 4.15 From Worksheet to Income Statement

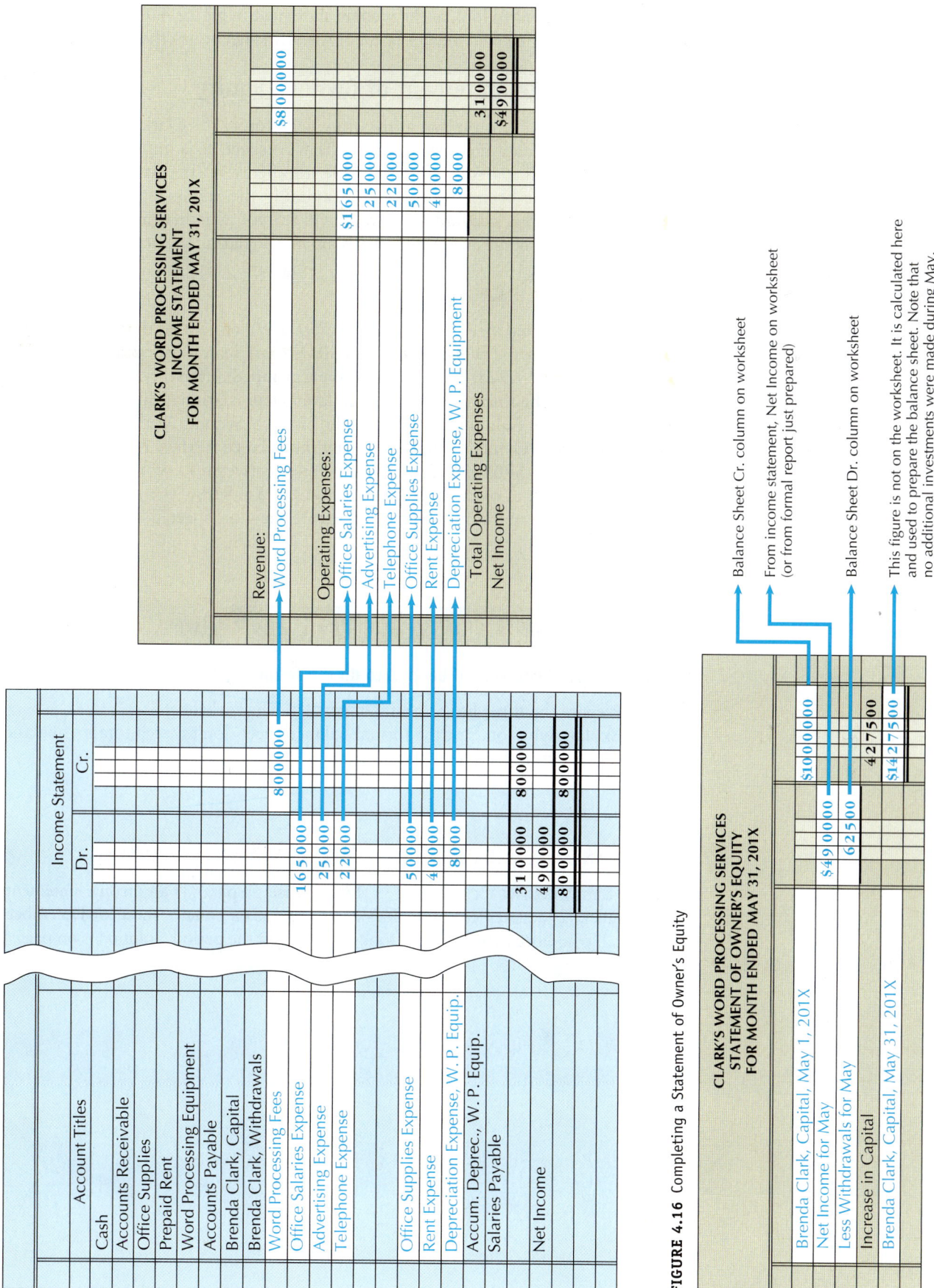

Account Titles	Income Statement Dr.	Income Statement Cr.
Cash		
Accounts Receivable		
Office Supplies		
Prepaid Rent		
Word Processing Equipment		
Accounts Payable		
Brenda Clark, Capital		
Brenda Clark, Withdrawals		
Word Processing Fees		8 0 0 0 00
Office Salaries Expense	1 6 5 0 00	
Advertising Expense	2 5 0 00	
Telephone Expense	2 2 0 00	
Office Supplies Expense	5 0 0 00	
Rent Expense	4 0 0 00	
Depreciation Expense, W. P. Equip.	8 0 00	
Accum. Deprec., W. P. Equip.		
Salaries Payable		
	3 1 0 0 00	8 0 0 0 00
Net Income	4 9 0 0 00	
	8 0 0 0 00	8 0 0 0 00

CLARK'S WORD PROCESSING SERVICES
INCOME STATEMENT
FOR MONTH ENDED MAY 31, 201X

Revenue:			
Word Processing Fees			$8 0 0 0 00
Operating Expenses:			
Office Salaries Expense		$1 6 5 0 00	
Advertising Expense		2 5 0 00	
Telephone Expense		2 2 0 00	
Office Supplies Expense		5 0 0 00	
Rent Expense		4 0 0 00	
Depreciation Expense, W. P. Equipment		8 0 00	
Total Operating Expenses			3 1 0 0 00
Net Income			$4 9 0 0 00

FIGURE 4.16 Completing a Statement of Owner's Equity

CLARK'S WORD PROCESSING SERVICES
STATEMENT OF OWNER'S EQUITY
FOR MONTH ENDED MAY 31, 201X

Brenda Clark, Capital, May 1, 201X			$10 0 0 0 00
Net Income for May		$4 9 0 0 00	
Less Withdrawals for May		6 2 5 00	
Increase in Capital			4 2 7 5 00
Brenda Clark, Capital, May 31, 201X			$14 2 7 5 00

Balance Sheet Cr. column on worksheet

From income statement, Net Income on worksheet (or from formal report just prepared)

Balance Sheet Dr. column on worksheet

This figure is not on the worksheet. It is calculated here and used to prepare the balance sheet. Note that no additional investments were made during May.

Take a moment to look at the income statement in Figure 4.15. Note where items go from the income statement section of the worksheet onto the formal statement.

Preparing the Statement of Owner's Equity

Figure 4.16 (p. 137) is the statement of owner's equity for Clark's. The figure shows where the information comes from on the worksheet. It is important to remember that if additional investments were made, the figure on the worksheet for Capital would not be the beginning figure for Capital in the Statement of Owner's Equity. Checking the ledger account for Capital will tell you whether the amount is correct. Note how Net Income and Withdrawals aid in calculating the new figure for Capital.

Preparing the Balance Sheet

In preparing the balance sheet (Figure 4.17, p. 139), remember that the balance sheet section totals on the worksheet ($18,680) do *not* match the totals on the formal balance sheet ($17,975). This information is grouped differently on the formal statement. First, in the formal report Accumulated Depreciation ($80) is subtracted from Word Processing Equipment, reducing the balance. Second, Withdrawals ($625) are subtracted from Owner's Equity, reducing the balance further. These two reductions (–$80 – $625 = –$705) represent the difference between the worksheet total and the total on the formal of the balance sheet ($17,975 – $18,680 = –$705). Figure 4.17 shows how to prepare the balance sheet from the worksheet.

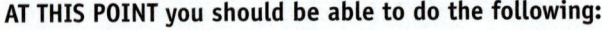

LEARNING UNIT 4-2 REVIEW

AT THIS POINT you should be able to do the following:

- Prepare the three financial statements from a worksheet.
- Explain why totals of the formal balance sheet don't match totals of balance sheet columns on the worksheet.

Instant Replay ⊙ Self-Review Quiz 4-2

From the worksheet for P. Logan (p. 134), please prepare (1) an income statement for December, (2) a statement of owner's equity, and (3) a balance sheet for December 31, 201X. No additional investments took place during the period. Solution is on page 140.

FIGURE 4.17
From Worksheet to Balance Sheet

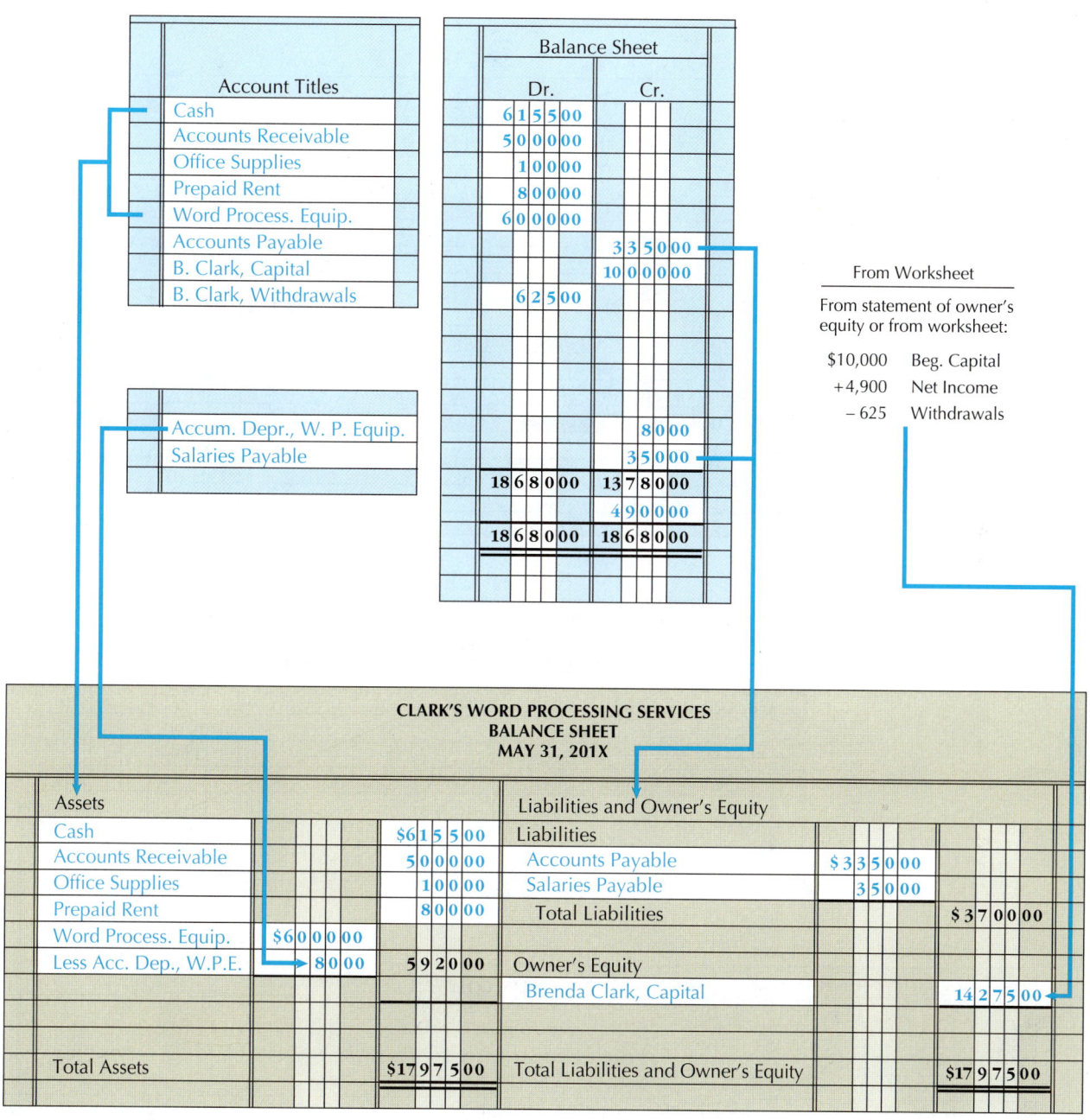

Solution to Instant Replay: Self-Review Quiz 4-2

FIGURE 4.18

P. LOGAN COMPANY
INCOME STATEMENT
FOR THE MONTH ENDED DECEMBER 31, 201X

Revenue:		
Revenue from clients		$2500
Operating Expenses:		
Rent Expense	$200	
Salaries Expense	1100	
Depreciation Expense, Store Equipment	100	
Insurance Expense	200	
Supplies Expense	400	
Total Operating Expenses		2000
Net Income		$500

P. LOGAN COMPANY
STATEMENT OF OWNER'S EQUITY
FOR THE MONTH ENDED DECEMBER 31, 201X

P. Logan, Capital, December 1, 201X		$1400
Net Income for December	$500	
Less Withdrawals for December	300	
Increase in Capital		200
P. Logan, Capital, December 31, 201X		$1600

P. LOGAN COMPANY
BALANCE SHEET
DECEMBER 31, 201X

Assets			Liabilities and Owner's Equity		
Cash		$1500	Liabilities		
Accounts Receivable		300	Accounts Payable	$200	
Prepaid Insurance		100	Salaries Payable	300	
Store Supplies		100	Total Liabilities		$500
Store Equipment	$600		Owner's Equity		
Less Acc. Dep., St. Eq.	500	100	P. Logan, Capital		1600
			Total Liabilities and		
Total Assets		$2100	Owner's Equity		$2100

PLAY BY PLAY: EXTRA HELP ON SELF-REVIEW QUIZ LU4-2

Let's review first: There are no debits or credits on the formal financial statements. The three financial statements are made from the last four columns of the worksheet.

Income Statement: The income statement is made up of revenues and expenses. Use the inside column for subtotaling. All numbers found on the income statement are also found on the worksheet.

Statement of Owner's Equity: The net income of $5 is used from the income statement to update the statement of owner's equity. Note that the $14 is the old figure from the worksheet. The increase in capital of $2 is not found on the worksheet. Logan's ending figure of $16 is not found on the worksheet.

Balance Sheet: Logan's ending figure of $16 from the statement of owner's equity is used as the Capital figure on the balance sheet. Note under Assets how the inside column is used to calculate store equipment less accumulated depreciation. Note that the totals of $21 from the balance sheet are not found on the worksheet. When the financial statement is prepared there are no debits or credits.

Summary: The worksheet was prepared in terms of debits and credits, not the formal financial statements. The inside column of the financial statements is for subtotaling. The worksheet used the old figure for Capital while the balance sheet uses the figure from the statement of owner's equity for the new figure of Capital. Many of the numbers on the statement of owner's equity and balance sheet will not be found on the worksheet since there are no debits or credits on formal financial statements.

DEMONSTRATION PROBLEM

Preparing a Worksheet and Financial Statements

From the following trial balance and adjustment data complete (1) a worksheet and (2) the three financial statements (numbers are intentionally small so you may concentrate on the theory).

● ● ● ○ **LO1, 2, 3, 4**

FROST COMPANY
TRIAL BALANCE
DECEMBER 31, 201X

	Dr.	Cr.
Cash	14	
Accounts Receivable	4	
Prepaid Insurance	5	
Plumbing Supplies	3	
Plumbing Equipment	7	
Accumulated Depreciation, Plumbing Equipment		5
Accounts Payable		1
J. Frost, Capital		12
J. Frost, Withdrawals	3	
Plumbing Fees		27
Rent Expense	4	
Salaries Expense	5	
Totals	45	45

Adjustment Data

a. Insurance Expired, $3.
b. Plumbing Supplies on hand, $1.
c. Depreciation Expense, Plumbing Equipment, $1.
d. Salaries owed but not paid to employees, $2.

Requirements:

1. Prepare a worksheet
2. Prepare financial statments

Demonstration Problem Solutions

Requirement 1

Preparing a worksheet

Part 1	Part 2	Demonstration Problem Complete

Adjustments

a.

Insurance Expense	Expense	↑	Dr.	$3
Prepaid Insurance	Asset	↓	Cr.	$3

Expired means used up.

b.

Plumbing Supplies Expense	Expense	↑	Dr.	$2
Plumbing Supplies	Asset	↓	Cr.	$2

$3 – 1 = $2 *used up*

c.

Depreciation Expense, Plumbing Equipment	Expense	↑	Dr.	$1
Contra-Asset Accumulated Depreciation, Plumbing Equipment	Contra-Asset	↑	Cr.	$1

The original cost of equipment of $7 is not "touched."

d.

Salaries Expense	Expense	↑	Dr.	$2
Salaries Payable	Liability	↑	Cr.	$2

FIGURE 4.19
Solution to Worksheet

Original cost not adjusted

"Used up" "On hand"

FROST COMPANY
WORKSHEET
FOR MONTH ENDED DECEMBER 31, 201X

Account Titles	Trial Balance Dr.	Trial Balance Cr.	Adjustments Dr.	Adjustments Cr.	Adjusted Trial Balance Dr.	Adjusted Trial Balance Cr.	Income Statement Dr.	Income Statement Cr.	Balance Sheet Dr.	Balance Sheet Cr.
Cash	1400				1400				1400	
Accounts Receivable	400				400				400	
Prepaid Insurance	500			(A) 300	200				200	
Plumbing Supplies	300			(B) 200	100				100	
Plumbing Equipment	700				700				700	
Accum. Depr., Plumb. Equip.		500		(C) 100		600				600
Accounts Payable		100				100				100
J. Frost, Capital		1200				1200				1200
J. Frost, Withdrawals	300				300				300	
Plumbing Fees		2700				2700		2700		
Rent Expense	400				400		400			
Salaries Expense	500		(D) 200		700		700			
	4500	4500								
Insurance Expense			(A) 300		300		300			
Plumbing Supplies Expense			(B) 200		200		200			
Depr. Exp. Plumb. Equip.			(C) 100		100		100			
Salaries Payable				(D) 200		200				200
			800	800	4800	4800	1700	2700	3100	2100
Net Income							1000			1000
							2700	2700	3100	3100

The last four columns of the worksheet (Figure 4.19) are prepared from Adjusted Trial Balance.

Capital of $12 is the old figure. Net income of $10 (revenue – expenses) is brought over to same side as Capital on the balance sheet Cr. column to balance columns. This is done because the worksheet contains the old figure for Capital.

Requirement 2

Preparing financial statements

Part 1	Part 2	Demonstration Problem Complete

FROST COMPANY
INCOME STATEMENT
FOR MONTH ENDED DECEMBER 31, 201X

Revenue:		
Plumbing Fees		$27
Operating Expenses:		
Rent Expense	$4	
Salaries Expense	7	
Insurance Expense	3	
Plumbing Supplies Expense	2	
Depreciation Expense, Plumbing Equipment	1	
Total Operating Expenses		17
Net Income		$10

FROST COMPANY
STATEMENT OF OWNER'S EQUITY
FOR MONTH ENDED DECEMBER 31, 201X

J. Frost, Capital, Dec. 1, 201X		$12
Net Income for December	$10	
Less Withdrawals for December	3	
Increase in Capital		7
J. Frost, Capital, Dec. 31, 201X		$19

FROST COMPANY
BALANCE SHEET
DECEMBER 31, 201X

Assets			Liabilities and Owner's Equity		
Cash		$14	Liabilities		
Accounts Receivable		4	Accounts Payable	$1	
Prepaid Insurance		2	Salaries Payable	2	
Plumbing Supplies		1	Total Liabilities		$3
Plumbing Equipment	$7				
Less Accumulated Dep.	6	1	Owner's Equity		
			J. Frost, Capital		19
			Total Liabilities and		
Total Assets		$22	Owner's Equity		$22

Solution Tips for Preparing Financial Statements from a Worksheet

The inside columns of the three financial statements are used for subtotaling. No debits or credits appear on the formal statements.

	Statements
Income Statement	From Income Statement columns of worksheet for revenue and expenses.
Statement of Owner's Equity	Beginning figure for Capital from Balance Sheet worksheet Cr. column. Net Income from income statement. Withdrawal figure from Balance Sheet worksheet Dr. column.
Balance Sheet	Assets from Balance Sheet worksheet Dr. column. Liabilities and Accumulated Depreciation from Balance Sheet worksheet Cr. Column. New figure for Capital from statement of owner's equity.

Note how Plumbing Equipment $7 and Accumulated Depreciation $6 are rearranged on the formal balance sheet. The Total Assets of $22 is not on the worksheet. Remember, no debits or credits appear on formal statements.

Part 1	Part 2	**Demonstration Problem Complete**

Blueprint of Steps 5 and 6 of the Accounting Cycle

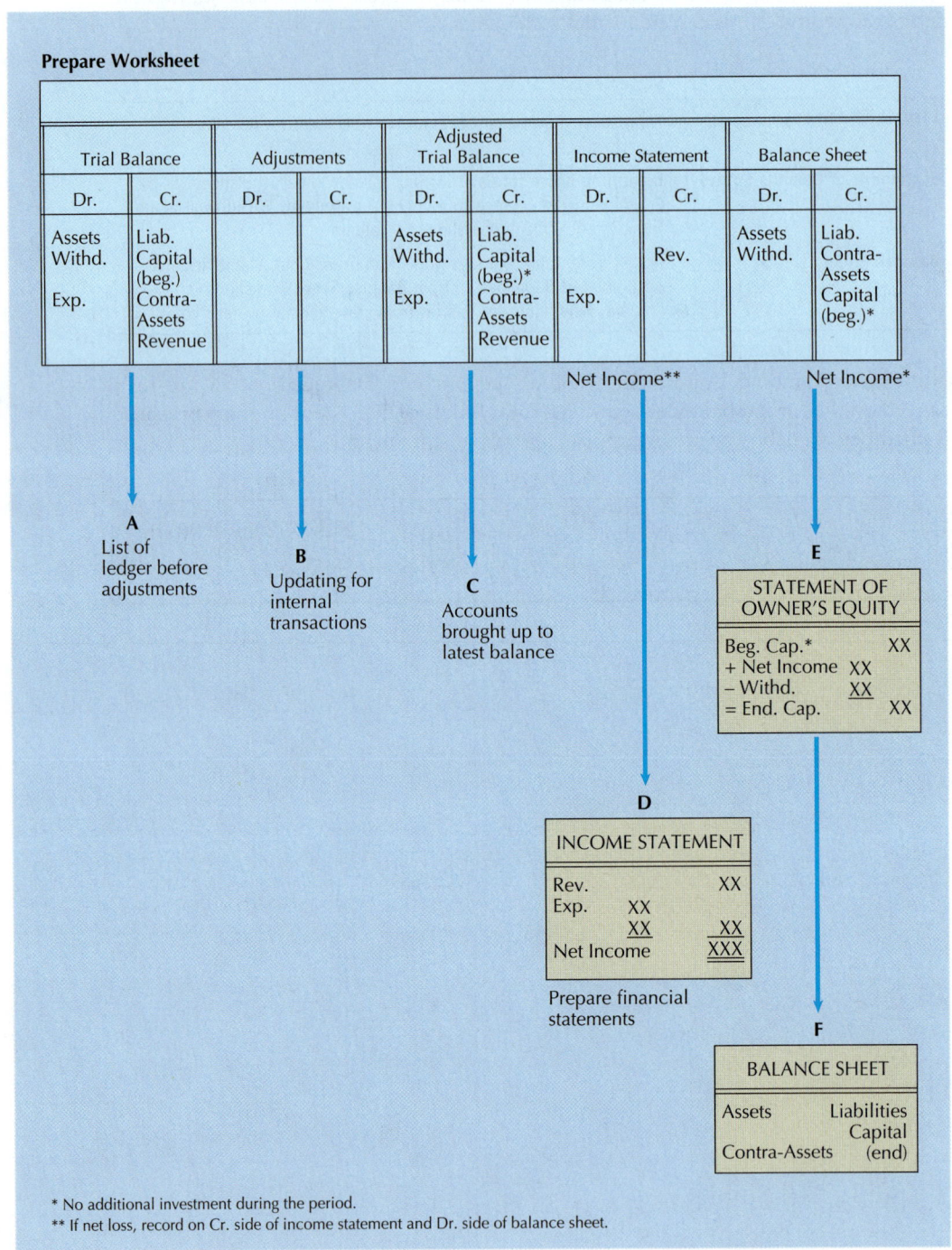

Prepare Worksheet

	Trial Balance		Adjustments		Adjusted Trial Balance		Income Statement		Balance Sheet	
	Dr.	Cr.	Dr.	Cr.	Dr.	Cr.	Dr.	Cr.	Dr.	Cr.
	Assets Withd. Exp.	Liab. Capital (beg.) Contra-Assets Revenue			Assets Withd. Exp.	Liab. Capital (beg.)* Contra-Assets Revenue	Exp.	Rev.	Assets Withd.	Liab. Contra-Assets Capital (beg.)*

Net Income**   Net Income*

A
List of ledger before adjustments

B
Updating for internal transactions

C
Accounts brought up to latest balance

E

STATEMENT OF OWNER'S EQUITY	
Beg. Cap.*	XX
+ Net Income	XX
– Withd.	XX
= End. Cap.	XX

D

INCOME STATEMENT		
Rev.		XX
Exp.	XX	
	XX	XX
Net Income		XXX

Prepare financial statements

F

BALANCE SHEET	
Assets	Liabilities
	Capital
Contra-Assets	(end)

* No additional investment during the period.
** If net loss, record on Cr. side of income statement and Dr. side of balance sheet.

 ACCOUNTING COACH

The following Coaching Tips are from Learning Units 4-1 and 4-2. Take the Pre-Game Checkup and use the Check Your Score at the bottom of the page to see how you are doing. The Accounting Coach provides tips before each Checkup to help you avoid common accounting errors.

LU 4-1 Step 5 of the Accounting Cycle: Preparing a Worksheet

Pre-Game Tips: When preparing adjustments on a worksheet, the accounts listed below the trial balance will always be increasing. In the adjustment for supplies, the adjustment is the amount of supplies used—not what is on hand. Keep in mind that for the adjustment for depreciation the original cost of the asset is not touched. The adjustment is an increase in Depreciation Expense and an increase in Accumulated Depreciation. Depreciation Expense goes on the income statement as an expense, and accumulated depreciation goes on the balance sheet as a contra-asset account. Keep in mind that the original costs of the asset and accumulated depreciation are both listed on the balance sheet.

Pre-Game Checkup
Answer true or false to the following statements.

1. A worksheet is a formal report.
2. Accumulated Depreciation is a contra-liability.
3. The adjustment for supplies is the amount of supplies on hand.
4. The normal balance of Accumulated Depreciation is a debit.
5. The old figure for Capital is on the worksheet, so Net Income must be brought over at the bottom to the balance sheet credit column so totals will balance.

LU 4-2 Step 6 of the Accounting Cycle: Preparing the Financial Statements from the Worksheet

Pre-Game Tips: The worksheet uses debits and credits; however, when the three formal financial statements are prepared they do not use debits and credits. The worksheet uses the beginning figure for Capital (no additional investment during the month), but when the financial statements are complete the formal balance sheet will list the figure for ending Capital from the statement of owner's equity.

Pre-Game Checkup
Answer true or false to the following statements.

1. Subtotaling is not used in preparing the formal financial statements from a worksheet.
2. Withdrawals are listed on the income statement.
3. Accumulated Depreciation is added to the cost of the asset on the balance sheet.
4. Debits are the inside column on the formal reports.
5. Totals on the formal balance sheet will match totals on the worksheet.

CHECK YOUR SCORE: ANSWERS TO THE PRE-GAME CHECKUP

LU 4-1
1. False—A worksheet is an informal report.
2. False—Accumulated Depreciation is a contra-asset.
3. False—The adjustment for Supplies is the amount of supplies used up.
4. False—The normal balance of Accumulated Depreciation is a credit.
5. True.

LU 4-2
1. False—Subtotaling *is* used in preparing the formal financial statements from a worksheet.
2. False—Withdrawals are listed on the statement of owner's equity.
3. False—Accumulated depreciation is subtracted from the cost of the asset on the balance sheet.
4. False—There are no debits or credits on financial statements.
5. False—Totals on formal reports do not match totals on the worksheet since there are no debits and credits on financial reports and subtotaling is used.

Chapter Summary

Here are all the key concepts and equations to help you understand the concepts of this chapter and prepare you for your exam. After completing this review, go to MyAccountingLab for more practice opportunities.

Concepts You Should Know	Key Terms
L01 Preparing Adjustments: prepaid rent, office supplies, depreciation on equipment, and accrued salaries.	Adjusting (p. 121) Worksheet (p. 120)
1. The worksheet is not a formal statement.	
2. Adjustments update certain accounts so that they will reflect their latest balance before financial statements are prepared.	
3. Adjustments will affect both the income statement and the balance sheet.	
4. The original cost of a piece of equipment is not adjusted; historical cost is not lost.	
5. Depreciation is the process of spreading the original cost of the asset over its expected useful life.	
6. Accumulated depreciation is a contra-asset on the balance sheet.	
L02 Preparing the adjusted trial balance on the worksheet.	Accrued salaries payable (p. 126)
1. Accounts listed below the account titles on the trial balance of the worksheet are increasing. Supplies adjustment is amount used up. Rent adjustment is amount expired. Original cost of equipment is not adjusted.	Accumulated Depreciation (p. 124) Book value (p. 125) Depreciation (p. 123) Historical cost (p. 123) Residual value (p. 124)
L03 Preparing the income statement and balance sheet sections of the worksheet.	
1. Revenue and expenses go on income statement sections of the worksheet.	
2. Assets, contra-assets, liabilities, capital, and withdrawals go on balance sheet sections of the worksheet.	
L04 Preparing financial statements from the worksheet.	
1. The formal statements prepared from a worksheet do not have debit or credit columns.	
2. Revenue and expenses go on the income statement.	
3. Beginning capital plus net income less withdrawals (or, beginning capital minus net loss less withdrawals) go on the statement of owner's equity.	
4. Assets, contra-assets, liabilities, and the new figure for capital go on the balance sheet.	

Discussion Questions and Critical Thinking/Ethical Case

1. Worksheets are required in every company's accounting cycle. Please agree or disagree and explain why.

2. What is the purpose of adjusting accounts?

3. What is the relationship of internal transactions to the adjusting process?

4. Explain how an adjustment can affect both the income statement and balance sheet. Please give an example.

5. Why do we need the Accumulated Depreciation account?

6. Depreciation expense goes on the balance sheet. True or false. Why?

7. Each month Accumulated Depreciation grows while Equipment goes up. Agree or disagree? Defend your position.

8. Define the term *accrued salaries*.

9. Why don't the formal financial statements contain debit or credit columns?

10. Explain how the financial statements are prepared from the worksheet.

11. Janet Fox, president of Angel Co., went to a tax seminar. One of the speakers at the seminar advised the audience to put off showing expenses until next year because doing so would allow them to take advantage of a new tax law. When Janet returned to the office, she called in her accountant, Frieda O'Riley. She told Frieda to forget about making any adjustments for salaries in the old year so more expenses could be shown in the new year. Frieda told her that putting off these expenses would not follow generally accepted accounting procedures. Janet said she should do it anyway. You make the call. Write your specific recommendations to Frieda.

Concept Check

MyAccountingLab

Adjustment for Supplies

● **L01** *(5 MIN)*

1. *Before Adjustment*

Computer Supplies	Computer Supplies Expense
750	

Given: At year end, an inventory of Computer Supplies showed $200.
a. How much is the adjustment for Computer Supplies?
b. Complete a transaction analysis box for this adjustment.
c. What will the balance of Computer Supplies be on the adjusted trial balance?

Adjustment for Prepaid Rent

● **L01** *(10 MIN)*

2. *Before Adjustment*

Prepaid Rent	Rent Expense
500	

Given: At year end, rent expired is $50.
a. How much is the adjustment for Prepaid Rent?
b. Complete a transaction analysis box for this adjustment.
c. What will be the balance of Prepaid Rent on the adjusted trial balance?

LO1 *(10 MIN)*   **Adjustment for Depreciation**

3.   *Before Adjustment*

Equip.	Acc. Dep., Equip.	Dep. Exp., Equip.
10,200	1,000	

Given: At year end, depreciation on Equipment is $700.

a.   Which of these three T accounts is not affected?
b.   Which account is a contra-asset?
c.   Draw a transaction analysis box for this adjustment.
d.   What will be the balance of these three accounts on the adjusted trial balance?

LO1 *(10 MIN)*   **Adjustment for Accrued Salaries**

4.   *Before Adjustment*

Salaries Expense	Salaries Payable
1,800	

Given: Accrued Salaries, $50.

a.   Complete a transaction analysis box for this adjustment.
b.   What will be the balance of these two accounts on the adjusted trial balance?

LO2, 3 *(15 MIN)*   **Worksheet**

5.   From the following adjusted trial balance titles of a worksheet, identify in which column each account will be listed on the last four columns of the worksheet:

(ID) Income Statement Dr. Column
(IC) Income Statement Cr. Column
(BD) Balance Sheet Dr. Column
(BC) Balance Sheet Cr. Column

			ATB		IS	BS
A.	Ex: Legal Fees	~~~	~~~		IC	_____
B.	Accts. Payable	~~~	~~~		_____	_____
C.	Cash	~~~	~~~		_____	_____
D.	Prepaid Advertising	~~~	~~~		_____	_____
E.	Salaries Payable	~~~	~~~		_____	_____
F.	Dep. Expense	~~~	~~~		_____	_____
G.	V., Capital	~~~	~~~		_____	_____
H.	V., Withdrawals	~~~	~~~		_____	_____
I.	Computer Supplies	~~~	~~~		_____	_____
J.	Rent Expense	~~~	~~~		_____	_____
K.	Supplies Payable	~~~	~~~		_____	_____
L.	Advertising Expense	~~~	~~~		_____	_____
M.	Accum. Depreciation	~~~	~~~		_____	_____
N.	Wages Payable	~~~	~~~		_____	_____

6. From the following balance sheet (which was made from the worksheet and other financial statements), explain why the lettered numbers were not found on the worksheet. *Hint:* No debits or credits appear on the formal financial statements.

● **L04** *(15 MIN)*

LAZE CO.
BALANCE SHEET
DECEMBER 31, 201X

Assets			Liabilities and Owner's Equity		
Cash		$6	Liabilities		
Acc. Receivable		2	Accounts Payable	$2	
Supplies		2	Salaries Payable	1	
Equipment	$10		Total Liabilities		$3 (B)
Less Acc. Dep.	4	6 (A)	Owner's Equity		
			J. Laze, Capital		13
			Total Liabilities and		
Total Assets		$16	**Owner's Equity**		$16

●● **L02, 3** *(15 MIN)*

H. WELLS
BALANCE SHEET
DECEMBER 31, 201X

Assets			Liabilities and Owner's Equity		
Cash		$6	Liabilities		
Acc. Receivable		2	Accounts Payable	$2	
Supplies		2	Salaries Payable	1	
Equipment	$10		Total Liabilities		$3
Less Acc. Dep.	4	6	Owner's Equity		
			H. Wells, Capital		13 (B)
			Total Liabilities and		
Total Assets		$16 (A)	**Owner's Equity**		$16

Exercises

MyAccountingLab

Set A

4A-1. Complete the following table.

● **L04** *(5 MIN)*

Account	Category	Normal Balance	Which Financial Statement(s) Found
Accounts Payable			
Prepaid Rent			
Office Equipment			
Depreciation Expense			
B. Reel, Capital			
B. Reel, Withdrawals			
Wages Payable			
Accumulated Depreciation			

● **L01** *(10 MIN)*   **4A-2.** Use transaction analysis charts to analyze the following adjustments:

   a. Depreciation on equipment, $500.
   b. Rent expired, $200.

● **L01** *(10 MIN)*   **4A-3.** From the following adjustment data, calculate the adjustment amount and record appropriate debits or credits:

   a. Supplies purchased, $1,300.
   Supplies on hand, $100.
   b. Office equipment, $10,500.
   Accumulated depreciation before adjustment, $1,200.
   Depreciation expense, $800.

● **L03** *(20 MIN)*   **4A-4.** From the following trial balance (Figure 4.20) and adjustment data, complete a worksheet for J. Tripp as of October 31, 201X:

   a. Depreciation expense, equipment, $1.
   b. Insurance expired, $5.
   c. Store supplies on hand, $7.
   d. Wages owed, but not paid for (they are an expense in the old year), $6.

FIGURE 4.20

J. TRIPP TRIAL BALANCE OCTOBER 31, 201X		
	Dr.	Cr.
Cash	32 00	
Accounts Receivable	2 00	
Prepaid Insurance	9 00	
Store Supplies	8 00	
Store Equipment	10 00	
Accumulated Depreciation, Equipment		5 00
Accounts Payable		10 00
J. Tripp, Capital		41 00
J. Tripp, Withdrawals	10 00	
Revenue from Clients		27 00
Rent Expense	10 00	
Wage Expense	2 00	
	83 00	83 00

● **L04** *(20 MIN)*   **4A-5.** From the completed worksheet in Exercise 4A-4, prepare

   a. an income statement for October.
   b. a statement of owner's equity for October.
   c. a balance sheet as of October 31, 201X.

Set B

● **L04** *(5 MIN)*   **4B-1.** Complete the following table.

Account	Category	Normal Balance	Which Financial Statement(s) Found
Accounts Payable			
Prepaid Insurance			
Computer Equipment			
Depreciation Expense			
B. Free, Capital			
B. Free, Withdrawals			
Salaries Payable			
Accumulated Depreciation			

4B-2. Use transaction analysis charts to analyze the following adjustments: 🔴 **L01** *(5 MIN)*

   a. Depreciation on equipment, $700.

   b. Rent expired, $300.

4B-3. From the following adjustment data, calculate the adjustment amount and   🔴 **L01** *(10 MIN)*
record appropriate debits or credits:

   Data Table

   a. Supplies purchased, $900.
      Supplies on hand, $150.

   b. Office equipment, $14,500.
      Accumulated depreciation before adjustment, $600.
      Depreciation expense, $1,100.

4B-4. From the following trial balance (Figure 4.21) and adjustment data, complete   🔵 **L03** *(20 MIN)*
a worksheet for J. Tripp as of October 31, 201X:

   More Info

   a. Depreciation expense, equipment, $3.

   b. Insurance expired, $3.

   c. Store supplies on hand, $4.

   d. Wages owed but not paid for (they are an expense in the old year), $10.

   Data Table

J. TRIPP TRIAL BALANCE OCTOBER 31, 201X	Dr.	Cr.
Cash	6 00	
Accounts Receivable	2 00	
Prepaid Insurance	4 00	
Store Supplies	7 00	
Store Equipment	9 00	
Accumulated Depreciation, Equipment		3 00
Accounts Payable		4 00
J. Tripp, Capital		1 0 00
J. Tripp, Withdrawals	9 00	
Revenue from Clients		2 5 00
Rent Expense	3 00	
Wage Expense	2 00	
	4 2 00	4 2 00

4B-5. From the completed worksheet in Exercise 4B-4, prepare   🟡 **L04** *(20 MIN)*

   a. an income statement for October.

   b. a statement of owner's equity for October.

   c. a balance sheet as of October 31, 201X.

Problems

MyAccountingLab

Set A

🔴🟢 **L01, 2** *(15 MIN)*

4A-1. Use the following adjustment data on December 31 to complete a partial
worksheet (Figure 4.22, p. 154) up to the adjusted trial balance.

   a. Fitness supplies on hand, $2,700.

   b. Depreciation taken on fitness equipment, $500.

FIGURE 4.22

JEANETTE'S FITNESS CENTER TRIAL BALANCE MARCH 31, 201X		
	Debit	Credit
Cash in Bank	10 5 0 0 00	
Accounts Receivable	5 8 0 0 00	
Fitness Supplies	5 7 0 0 00	
Fitness Equipment	11 2 0 0 00	
Accumulated Depreciation, Fitness Equipment		5 5 0 0 00
J. Woodrich, Capital		14 5 7 5 00
J. Woodrich, Withdrawals	1 5 0 0 00	
Fitness Fees		15 3 0 0 00
Rent Expense	4 5 0 00	
Advertising Expense	2 2 5 00	
	35 3 7 5 00	35 3 7 5 00

Check Figure:
Total of adjusted
trial balance $35,875

L02, 3 *(30 MIN)*

4A-2. Update the trial balance for Lancing Landscaping Service (Figure 4.23) for March 31, 201X.

Adjustment Data to Update the Trial Balance

a. Rent expired, $350.
b. Landscaping supplies on hand (remaining), $150.
c. Depreciation expense, Landscaping equipment, $400.
d. Wages earned by workers but not paid or due until April, $600.

FIGURE 4.23

LANCING'S LANDSCAPING SERVICE TRIAL BALANCE MARCH 31, 201X		
	Dr.	Cr.
Cash in Bank	6 7 0 0 00	
Accounts Receivable	4 0 0 00	
Prepaid Rent	1 6 0 0 00	
Landscaping Supplies	1 1 2 2 00	
Landscaping Equipment	1 6 0 0 00	
Accumulated Depreciation, Landscaping Equipment		1 0 2 0 00
Accounts Payable		1 0 3 2 00
A. Lancing, Capital		2 4 0 5 00
Landscaping Revenue		8 7 0 0 00
Heat Expense	2 7 5 00	
Advertising Expense	1 0 0 00	
Wage Expense	1 3 6 0 00	
	13 1 5 7 00	13 1 5 7 00

Check Figure:
Adjusted Trial Balance total $14,157

Your task is to prepare a worksheet for Lancing's Landscaping Service for the month of March.

L01 *(60 MIN)*

4A-3. Update the trial balance for Kyler's Moving Co. (Figure 4.24, p. 155) for January 31, 201X.

Adjustment Data to Update Trial Balance

a. Insurance expired, $550.
b. Moving supplies on hand, $700.

c. Depreciation on moving truck, $400.

d. Wages earned but unpaid, $200.

Your task is to

1. complete a worksheet for Kyler's Moving Co. for the month of January.

2. prepare an income statement for January, a statement of owner's equity for January, and a balance sheet as of January 31, 201X.

FIGURE 4.24

KYLER'S MOVING CO. TRIAL BALANCE JANUARY 31, 201X		
	Dr.	Cr.
Cash	2 0 0 0 00	
Prepaid Insurance	2 0 0 0 00	
Moving Supplies	1 7 0 0 00	
Moving Truck	11 0 0 0 00	
Accumulated Depreciation, Moving Truck		6 0 0 0 00
Accounts Payable		2 2 0 9 00
K. Hilton, Capital		8 6 0 0 00
K. Hilton, Withdrawals	1 9 0 0 00	
Revenue from Moving		8 6 0 0 00
Wage Expense	3 1 5 0 00	
Rent Expense	5 5 0 00	
Advertising Expense	7 0 3 00	
	23 0 0 3 00	23 0 0 3 00

Check Figure:
Net Income $2,047

4A-4. The trial balance for Daniel's Repair Service appears in Figure 4.25.

Adjustment Data to Update Trial Balance

a. Insurance expired, $450.

b. Repair supplies on hand, $2,300.

c. Depreciation on repair equipment, $200.

d. Wages earned but unpaid, $400.

Your task is to

1. complete a worksheet for Daniel's Repair Service for the month of April.

2. prepare an income statement for April, a statement of owner's equity for April, and a balance sheet as of April 30, 201X.

●●○ **L02, 3, 4**
(60 MIN)

PT/QB

FIGURE 4.25

DANIEL'S REPAIR SERVICE TRIAL BALANCE APRIL 30, 201X		
	Dr.	Cr.
Cash	2 4 0 0 00	
Prepaid Insurance	3 5 0 0 00	
Repair Supplies	5 0 0 0 00	
Repair Equipment	7 0 0 0 00	
Accumulated Depreciation, Repair Equipment		1 1 0 0 00
Accounts Payable		5 5 7 0 00
D. Heines, Capital		5 5 2 0 00
Revenue from Repairs		8 4 0 0 00
Wages Expense	1 9 0 0 00	
Rent Expense	7 2 0 00	
Advertising Expense	7 0 00	
	20 5 9 0 00	20 5 9 0 00

Check Figure:
Net Income $1,960

MyAccountingLab

Set B

L01, 2 *(15 MIN)*

4B-1. Please complete a partial worksheet (Figure 4.26) up to the adjusted trial balance for Jeremy's Fitness Center using the following adjustment data:

   a. Fitness supplies on hand, $2,900.

   b. Depreciation taken on fitness equipment, $1,000.

FIGURE 4.26

JEREMY'S FITNESS CENTER TRIAL BALANCE OCTOBER 31, 201X		
	Dr.	Cr.
Cash	9 5 0 0 00	
Accounts Receivable	6 1 0 0 00	
Fitness Supplies	5 8 0 0 00	
Fitness Equipment	7 2 0 0 00	
Accumulated Depreciation, Fitness Equipment		4 5 0 0 00
J. Wickers, Capital		13 9 2 5 00
J. Wickers, Withdrawals	2 2 5 0 00	
Fitness Fees		13 3 0 0 00
Rent Expense	7 5 0 00	
Advertising Expense	1 2 5 00	
	31 7 2 5 00	31 7 2 5 00

Check Figure:
Total of Adjusted
Trial Balance $32,725

L02, 3 *(30 MIN)*

4B-2. Given the trial balance in Figure 4.27 and adjustment data of Lan's Landscaping Service, your task is to prepare a worksheet for the month of October.

Adjustment Data to Update the Trial Balance

   a. Rent expired, $650.

   b. Landscaping supplies on hand (remaining), $300.

   c. Depreciation expense, landscaping equipment, $150.

   d. Wages earned by workers but not paid or due until November, $550.

FIGURE 4.27

LAN'S LANDSCAPING SERVICE TRIAL BALANCE OCTOBER 31, 201X		
	Dr.	Cr.
Cash in Bank	4 6 0 0 00	
Accounts Receivable	1 0 0 0 00	
Prepaid Rent	1 0 0 0 00	
Landscaping Supplies	1 1 9 5 00	
Landscaping Equipment	3 2 0 0 00	
Accumulated Depreciation, Landscaping Equipment		7 8 0 00
Accounts Payable		1 0 7 5 00
A. Lan, Capital		3 3 6 5 00
Landscaping Revenue		7 7 0 0 00
Heat Expense	3 2 5 00	
Advertising Expense	1 6 0 00	
Wage Expense	1 4 4 0 00	
	12 9 2 0 00	12 9 2 0 00

Check Figure:
Adjusted Trial Balance total $13,620

4B-3. Using the trial balance in Figure 4.28, and adjustment data of Kyler's Moving Co., prepare

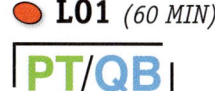
● **L01** *(60 MIN)*

1. a worksheet for the month of January.
2. an income statement for January, a statement of owner's equity for January, and a balance sheet as of January 31, 201X.

Adjustment Data to Update Trial Balance

a. Insurance expired, $450.
b. Moving supplies on hand, $400.
c. Depreciation on moving truck, $350.
d. Wages earned but unpaid, $180.

FIGURE 4.28

KYLER'S MOVING CO. TRIAL BALANCE JANUARY 31, 201X	Dr.	Cr.
Cash	11 000 00	
Prepaid Insurance	1 800 00	
Moving Supplies	1 000 00	
Moving Truck	16 000 00	
Accumulated Depreciation, Moving Truck		5 500 00
Accounts Payable		2 700 00
K. Hilton, Capital		19 228 00
K. Hilton, Withdrawals	1 300 00	
Revenue from Moving		8 300 00
Wages Expense	3 150 00	
Rent Expense	775 00	
Advertising Expense	703 00	
	35 728 00	35 728 00

Check Figure:
Net Income $2,092

4B-4. As the bookkeeper of Daniel's Repair Service, use the information in Figure 4.29 (p. 158), to prepare

●●● **L02, 3, 4**
(60 MIN)

1. a worksheet for the month of April.
2. an income statement for April, a statement of owner's equity for April, and a balance sheet as of April 30, 201X.

Adjustment Data to Update Trial Balance

a. Insurance expired, $200.
b. Repair supplies on hand, $2,600.
c. Depreciation on repair equipment, $500.
d. Wages earned but unpaid, $180.

FIGURE 4.29

DANIEL'S REPAIR SERVICE TRIAL BALANCE APRIL 30, 201X		
	Dr.	Cr.
Cash	3 4 0 0 00	
Prepaid Insurance	5 0 0 0 00	
Repair Supplies	4 9 0 0 00	
Repair Equipment	3 5 0 0 00	
Accumulated Depreciation, Repair Equipment		9 0 0 00
Accounts Payable		5 0 4 0 00
D. Heins, Capital		5 7 4 0 00
Revenue from Repairs		7 6 0 0 00
Wages Expense	1 5 0 0 00	
Rent Expense	7 5 0 00	
Advertising Expense	2 3 0 00	
	19 2 8 0 00	19 2 8 0 00

Check Figure:
Net Income $1,940

Financial Report Problem

 **L01** *(20 MIN)*

Reading the Kellogg's Annual Report

Go to http://investor.kelloggs.com/annuals.cfm, to access the Kellogg's 2010 Annual Report, and look at Note 1 under Property. Find out how Kellogg's depreciates its equipment. How is the equipment recorded?

MyAccountingLab

L02, 3, 4 *(45 MIN)*

SANCHEZ COMPUTER CENTER

At the end of September, Tony took a complete inventory of his supplies and found the following:

  5 dozen ¼" screws at a cost of $8.00 a dozen

  2 dozen ½" screws at a cost of $5.00 a dozen

  2 cartons of computer inventory paper at a cost of $14 a carton

  3 feet of coaxial cable at a cost of $4.00 per foot

After speaking to his accountant, he found that a reasonable depreciation amount for each of his long-term assets is as follows:

3 mos	Computer purchased July 5, 201X	Depreciation $33 a month
2 mos	Office equipment purchased July 17, 201X	Depreciation $10 a month
NO	Computer workstations purchased Sept. 17, 201X	Depreciation $20 a month

Tony uses the straight-line method of depreciation and declares no salvage value for any of the assets. If any long-term asset is purchased in the first 15 days of the month, he will charge depreciation for the full month. If an asset is purchased on the 16th of the month, or later, he will not charge depreciation in the month it was purchased.

August and September's rent has now expired.

ASSIGNMENT

Use your trial balance from the completed problem in Chapter 3 and the adjusting information given here to complete the worksheet for the three months ended September 30, 201X. From the worksheets, prepare the financial statements.

SUBWAY CASE

Where the Dough Goes . . .

●●● **L01, 2, 3** *(20 MIN)*

No matter how harried Stan Hernandez feels as the owner of his own Subway restaurant, the aroma of his fresh-baked gourmet breads *always* perks him up. However, the sales generated by Subway's line of gourmet seasoned breads perks Stan up even more. Subway restaurants introduced freshly baked bread in 1983, a practice that made it stand out from other fast-food chains and helped build its reputation for made-to-order freshness. Since then Subway franchisees have introduced many types of gourmet seasoned breads—such as Hearty Italian or Monterey Cheddar—according to a schedule determined by headquarters.

Stan was one month into the "limited-time promotion" for the chain's new Roasted Garlic seasoned bread when his bake oven started faltering. "The temperature controls just don't seem quite right," said his employee and "sandwich artist," Rashid. "It's taking incrementally longer to bake the bread."

"This couldn't happen at a worse time," moaned Stan. "We're baking enough Roasted Garlic bread to keep a whole town of vampires away, but if we don't get it out of the oven fast enough, we'll keep our customers away!"

That very day Stan called his field consultant, Mariah, to discuss what to do about his bake oven. Mariah reminded Stan that his oven trouble illustrated the flip side of buying an existing store from a retired franchisee—having to repair or replace worn or old equipment. After receiving a rather expensive repair estimate and considering the age of the oven, Stan ultimately decided it would make sense for him to purchase a new one. Mariah concurred, "At the rate your sales are going, Stan, you're going to need that roomier new model."

"Wow, do you realize how much this new bake oven is going to cost me?—$3,000!" Stan exclaimed while meeting with his cousin-turned-Subway-accountant, Lila Hernandez. "Yes, it's a lot to lay out, Stan," said Lila, "but you'll be depreciating the cost over a period of 10 years, which will help you at tax time. Let's do the adjustment on your worksheet, so you can see it."

The two of them were sitting in Stan's small office behind the Subway kitchen, and they pulled up this month's worksheet on Stan's Peachtree program. Lila laughed, "I'm sure glad you started entering your worksheets on Peachtree again! The figures on those old ones were so doodled over and crossed out that I could barely decipher them! We may need your worksheets at tax time."

"Anything for you, *mi prima*," Stan said. "I may depreciate my bake oven, but my gratitude for your accounting skills only appreciates with time!"

Discussion Questions

1. If you are using a straight-line method of depreciation and Stan's bake oven has a residual value of $1,000, how much depreciation will he account for each year and what would the adjustment be for each month?
2. Where does Lila get the information on the useful life of Stan's bake oven and the estimate for its residual value? Why do you think she gets her information from this particular source?
3. Why is a clear worksheet helpful even after that month's statements have been prepared?

PEACHTREE COMPUTER WORKSHOP

COMPUTERIZED ACCOUNTING APPLICATION FOR CHAPTER 4

Refresher on using Peachtree Complete Accounting

Before starting this assignment, you may want to refresh your memory by reading the following PDF documents found in the multimedia library on the MyAccountingLab Web site. Remember to choose the PDF document for your version of Peachtree.

1. An Introduction to Peachtree Complete Accounting
2. Correcting Peachtree Transactions
3. How to Repeat or Restart a Peachtree Assignment
4. Backing Up and Restoring Your Work in Peachtree

You also should have completed Workshop 1 for the Atlas Company in Chapter 3.

Workshop 2:

Compound Journal Entries, Adjusting Entries, and Financial Reports

In this workshop you will post compound journal entries and adjusting journal entries for Zell Company using Peachtree. You will also print the general journal report, trial balance, income statement, and balance sheet.

Instructions and the data file for completing this assignment are in the multimedia library of the MyAccountingLab Web site. Open the *Workshop 2 Zell Company* PDF document for your version of Peachtree and download the *Zell Company* data file for your version of Peachtree.

QUICKBOOKS COMPUTER WORKSHOP

COMPUTERIZED ACCOUNTING APPLICATION FOR CHAPTER 4

Refresher on using QuickBooks Pro

Before starting this assignment, you may want to refresh your memory by reading the following PDF documents found in the multimedia library on the MyAccountingLab Web site. Remember to choose the PDF document for your version of QuickBooks.

1. An Introduction to Computerized Accounting
2. Installing QuickBooks Pro and Student Data Files
3. An Introduction to QuickBooks Pro
4. Correcting QuickBooks Transactions
5. How to Repeat or Restart a QuickBooks Assignment
6. Backing Up and Restoring Your Work in QuickBooks. You also should have completed Workshop 1 for the Atlas Company in Chapter 3.

Workshop 2:

Compound Journal Entries, Adjusting Entries, and Financial Reports

In this workshop you will post compound journal entries and adjusting journal entries for Zell Company using Quickbooks. You will also print the general journal report, trial balance, income statement, and balance sheet.

Instructions and the data file for completing this assignment are in the multimedia library of the MyAccountingLab Web site. Open the *Workshop 2 Zell Company* PDF document for your version of Quickbooks and download the *Zell Company* data file for your version of Quickbooks.

The Accounting Cycle Completed

THE GAME PLAN

By April 15 of every year, you send in your Federal Income Tax form to the IRS. What a relief! But the truth is that you have to go through this process year after year. Each year you gather your financial information and provide a report of your earnings and expenses to the government. The same concept holds true in accounting for companies as well. For example, Disney must report to investors and government regulators how operations performed during its accounting cycle. When one accounting cycle is closed the next one begins. This period of time is called the fiscal year. Many companies end their fiscal years in March, July, or October. Other companies, like retailers, end on December 31 so holiday sales can be included in the final results. No matter when companies end their fiscal years, the accounting cycle must be completed and financial reports prepared so that companies can report to the appropriate governmental authorities, like the SEC and IRS, investors, and creditors.

LEARNING OBJECTIVES

- 1. Journalizing and posting adjusting entries.
- 2. Journalizing and posting closing entries.
- 3. Preparing a post-closing trial balance.

Each accounting cycle completed by Disney will end with the preparation of a post-closing trial balance. In Chapters 3 and 4 we completed these steps of the manual accounting cycle for Clark's Word Processing Services:

STEP 1: Business transactions occurred and generated source documents.

STEP 2: Business transactions were analyzed and recorded in a journal.

STEP 3: Information was posted or transferred from journal to ledger.

STEP 4: A trial balance was prepared.

STEP 5: A worksheet was completed.

STEP 6: Financial statements were prepared.

This chapter covers the following steps to complete Clark's accounting cycle for the month of May:

STEP 7: Journalizing and posting adjusting entries.

STEP 8: Journalizing and posting closing entries.

STEP 9: Preparing a post-closing trial balance.

● L01   LEARNING UNIT 5-1 JOURNALIZING AND POSTING ADJUSTING ENTRIES:
Step 7 of the Accounting Cycle

Recording Journal Entries from the Worksheet

The information in the worksheet is up-to-date. The financial reports prepared from that information can give the business's management and other interested parties a good idea of where the business stands as of a particular date. However, the worksheet is only an informal report. The information concerning the adjustments has not been placed into the journal or posted to the ledger accounts yet, which means that the books are not up-to-date and ready for the next accounting cycle to begin. For example, the ledger shows $1,200 of Prepaid Rent, but the balance sheet we prepared in Chapter 4 shows an $800 balance. Essentially, the worksheet is a tool for preparing financial statements. Now we must use the adjustment columns of the worksheet as a basis for bringing the ledger up-to-date. To update the ledger, we use adjusting journal entries (see Figures 5.1 and 5.2). Again, the updating must be done before the next accounting period starts. For Clark's Word Processing Services, the next period begins on June 1.

Figure 5.2 shows the adjusting journal entries for Clark's taken from the adjustments section of the worksheet. Once the adjusting journal entries are posted to the ledger, the accounts making up the financial statements that were prepared from the worksheet will equal the updated ledger. (Keep in mind that we are using the same journal and ledger as in the previous chapters.) Let's look at some simplified T accounts to show how Clark's ledger looked before and after the adjustments (A–D) were posted.

Adjusting journal entries
Journal entries that are needed in order to update specific ledger accounts to reflect correct balances at the end of an accounting period.

Adjustment (A)

	Office Supplies 114	Office Supplies Expense 514
Before Posting:	600	
After Posting:	Office Supplies 114	Office Supplies Expense 514
	600 | 500	500

Account Titles	Trial Balance		Adjustments	
	Dr.	Cr.	Dr.	Cr.
Cash	6 1 5 5 00			
Accounts Receivable	5 0 0 0 00			
Office Supplies	6 0 0 00			(A) 5 0 0 00
Prepaid Rent	1 2 0 0 00			(B) 4 0 0 00
Word Processing Equipment	6 0 0 0 00			
Accounts Payable		3 3 5 0 00		
Brenda Clark, Capital		10 0 0 0 00		
Brenda Clark, Withdrawals	6 2 5 00			
Word Processing Fees		8 0 0 0 00		
Office Salaries Expense	1 3 0 0 00		(D) 3 5 0 00	
Advertising Expense	2 5 0 00			
Telephone Expense	2 2 0 00			
	21 3 5 0 00	21 3 5 0 00		
Office Supplies Expense			(A) 5 0 0 00	
Rent Expense			(B) 4 0 0 00	
Depreciation Exp., W. P. Equip.			(C) 8 0 00	
Accum. Deprec., W. P. Equip.				(C) 8 0 00
Salaries Payable				(D) 3 5 0 00
			1 3 3 0 00	1 3 3 0 00

FIGURE 5.1
Adjustments A–D in the Adjustments Section of the Worksheet Must Be Recorded in the Journal and Posted to the Ledger.

CLARK'S WORD PROCESSING SERVICES
GENERAL JOURNAL

Page 2

Date		Account Titles and Description	PR	Dr.	Cr.
		Adjusting Entries			
May	31	Office Supplies Expense	514	5 0 0 00	
		Office Supplies	114		5 0 0 00
	31	Rent Expense	515	4 0 0 00	
		Prepaid Rent	115		4 0 0 00
	31	Depreciation Expense, W. P. Equip.	516	8 0 00	
		Accumulated Depreciation, W. P. Equip.	122		8 0 00
	31	Office Salaries Expense	511	3 5 0 00	
		Salaries Payable	212		3 5 0 00

FIGURE 5.2
Journalizing and Posting Adjustments from the Adjustment Section of the Worksheet

COACHING TIP

Each adjustment affects both the income statement and balance sheet.

Adjustment (B)

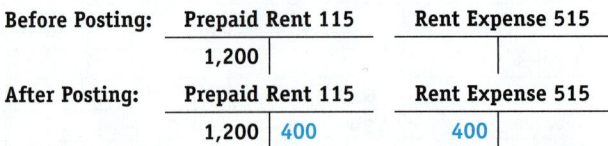

	Before Posting:	Prepaid Rent 115	Rent Expense 515
		1,200	
	After Posting:	Prepaid Rent 115	Rent Expense 515
		1,200	400	400	

Adjustment (C)

Before Posting:

Word Processing Equipment 121	Depreciation Expense, W. P. Equipment 516	Accumulated Depreciation, W. P. Equipment 122
6,000		

After Posting:

Word Processing Equipment 121	Depreciation Expense, W. P. Equipment 516	Accumulated Depreciation, W. P. Equipment 122
6,000	80	80

The first adjustment in (C) shows the same balances for Depreciation Expense and Accumulated Depreciation. However, in subsequent adjustments the Accumulated Depreciation balance will keep getting larger, but the debit to Depreciation Expense and the credit to Accumulated Depreciation will stay the same. We will see why in a moment.

Adjustment (D)

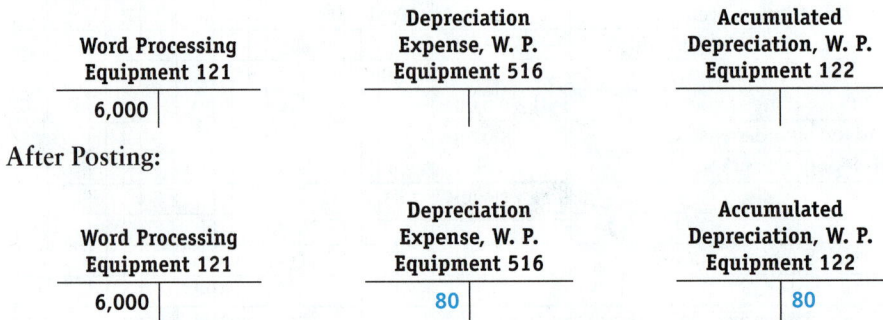

	Before Posting:	Office Salaries Expense 511	Salaries Payable 212
		650	
		650	
	After Posting:	Office Salaries Expense 511	Salaries Payable 212
		650	350
		650	
		350	

LEARNING UNIT 5-1 REVIEW

AT THIS POINT you should be able to do the following:

- Define and state the purpose of adjusting entries.
- Journalize adjusting entries from the worksheet.
- Post journalized adjusting entries to the ledger.
- Compare specific ledger accounts before and after posting of the journalized adjusting entries.

Instant Replay ⊙ Self-Review Quiz 5-1

Turn to the worksheet for P. Logan Company (Figure 4.14, p. 134 in Chapter 4) and (1) journalize and post the adjusting entries and (2) compare the adjusted ledger accounts before and after the adjustments are posted. T accounts are provided in your study guide with beginning balances.

Solution to Instant Replay: Self-Review Quiz 5-1

FIGURE 5.3
Journalized Adjusting Entries

Date		Account Titles and Description	PR	Dr.	Cr.
		Adjusting Entries			
Dec.	31	Depreciation Expense, Store Equip.	511	1 00	
		Accumulated Depreciation, Store Equip.	122		1 00
	31	Insurance Expense	516	2 00	
		Prepaid Insurance	116		2 00
	31	Supplies Expense	514	4 00	
		Store Supplies	114		4 00
	31	Salaries Expense	512	3 00	
		Salaries Payable	212		3 00

Page 2

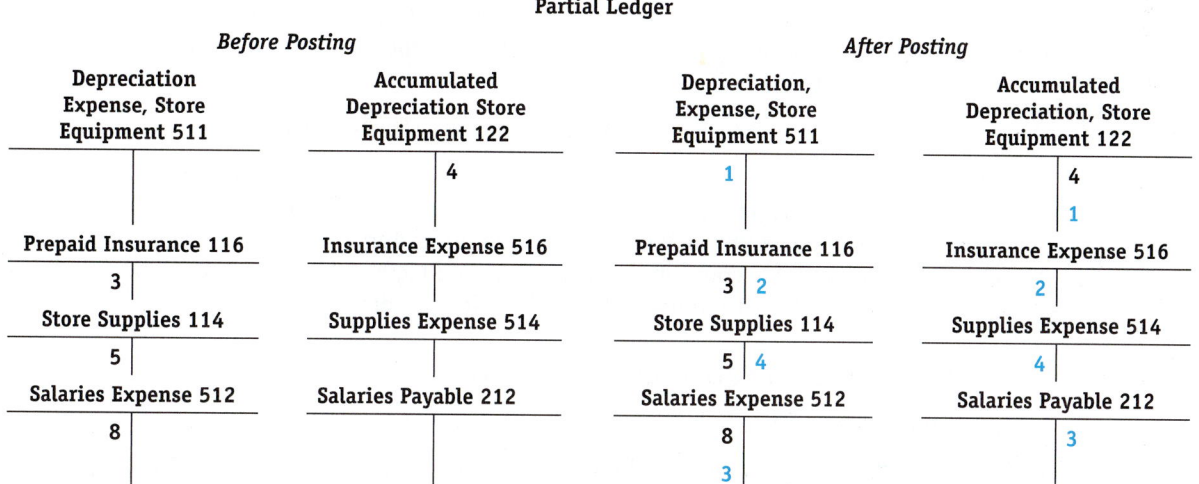

Partial Ledger

Before Posting

Depreciation Expense, Store Equipment 511

Accumulated Depreciation Store Equipment 122
4

Prepaid Insurance 116
3

Insurance Expense 516

Store Supplies 114
5

Supplies Expense 514

Salaries Expense 512
8

Salaries Payable 212

After Posting

Depreciation, Expense, Store Equipment 511
1

Accumulated Depreciation, Store Equipment 122
4
1

Prepaid Insurance 116
3   2

Insurance Expense 516
2

Store Supplies 114
5   4

Supplies Expense 514
4

Salaries Expense 512
8
3

Salaries Payable 212
3

PLAY BY PLAY: EXTRA HELP ON SELF-REVIEW QUIZ 5-1

Let's review first: Once the financial statements are prepared from the worksheet our ledger is still not up-to-date. Information about the adjustments on the worksheet have not been journalized or posted to the ledger.

How to update the ledger with adjustments on the worksheet: Using the worksheet of Logan Company, go to the adjustments section and journalize the four adjusting entries. Once the adjustments are journalized they must be posted to the ledger. When the postings are complete, the titles for depreciation expense, accumulated depreciation, insurance expense, prepaid insurance, supplies expense, store supplies, salaries expense, and salaries payable will have the latest, up-to-date balances.

Summary: The ending balances in the ledger after posting adjustments will be the same amounts that were found on the adjusted trial balance.

LO2   **LEARNING UNIT 5-2 JOURNALIZING AND POSTING CLOSING ENTRIES:**
Step 8 of the Accounting Cycle

To make recording of the next period's transactions easier, a mechanical step, called *closing,* is taken by Clark's accountant. Closing is intended to end—or close off—the revenue, expense, and withdrawal accounts at the end of the accounting period. The information needed to complete closing entries will be found in the income statement and balance sheet sections of the worksheet.

To make it easier to understand this process, we will first look at the difference between temporary (nominal) accounts and permanent (real) accounts.

Here is the expanded accounting equation we used in an earlier chapter:

$$\text{Assets} = \text{Liabilities} + \text{Capital} - \text{Withdrawals} + \text{Revenues} - \text{Expenses}$$

Permanent (real) accounts
Accounts whose balances are carried over to the next accounting period. Examples: Assets, Liabilities, Capital.

Temporary (nominal) accounts Accounts whose balances at the end of an accounting period are not carried over to the next accounting period.

Three of the items in that equation—Assets, Liabilities, and Capital—are known as real or permanent accounts because their balances are carried over from one accounting period to another. The other three items—Withdrawals, Revenues, Expenses, and Income Summary—are called nominal or temporary accounts because their balances are not carried over from one accounting period to another. Instead, their "balances" are reset at zero at the beginning of each accounting period by closing their balances at the end of the prior period. This process allows us to accumulate new data about revenue, expenses, and withdrawals in the new accounting period. The process of closing summarizes the effects of the temporary accounts on Capital for that period using closing journal entries. When the closing process is complete, the accounting equation will be reduced to

Closing journal entries
Journal entries that are prepared to (a) reset all temporary accounts to a zero balance and (b) update Capital to a new balance.

$$\text{Assets} = \text{Liabilities} + \text{Ending Capital}$$

If you look back to Figure 4.16 in Chapter 4, you will see that we already calculated the new capital on the balance sheet to be $14,275 for Clark's Word Processing Services. Before the mechanical closing procedures are journalized and posted, Clark's Capital account in the ledger is only $10,000 (Chapter 3, Figure 3.19). Let's look now at how to journalize and post closing entries.

How to Journalize Closing Entries

Four steps are needed in journalizing closing entries:

Income Summary A temporary account in the ledger that summarizes revenue and expenses and transfers the balance (net income or net loss) to Capital. This account does not have a normal balance, i.e. it could have a debit or a credit balance.

> **STEP 1:** Clear to zero the revenue balance and transfer it to Income Summary. Income Summary is a temporary account in the ledger needed for closing. At the end of the closing process, Income Summary will no longer hold a balance.

Revenue → Income Summary

> **STEP 2:** Clear to zero the individual expense balances and transfer them to Income Summary.

Expenses → Income Summary

COACHING TIP

After all closing entries are journalized and posted to the ledger, all temporary accounts have a zero balance in the ledger. Closing is a step-by-step process.

> **STEP 3:** Clear to zero the balance in Income Summary and transfer it to Capital.

Income Summary → Capital

> **STEP 4:** Clear to zero the balance in Withdrawals and transfer it to Capital.

Withdrawals → Capital

Figure 5.4 is a visual representation of these four steps. Keep in mind that this information must first be journalized and then posted to the appropriate ledger accounts. The worksheet presented in Figure 5.5 contains all the figures we will need for the closing process.

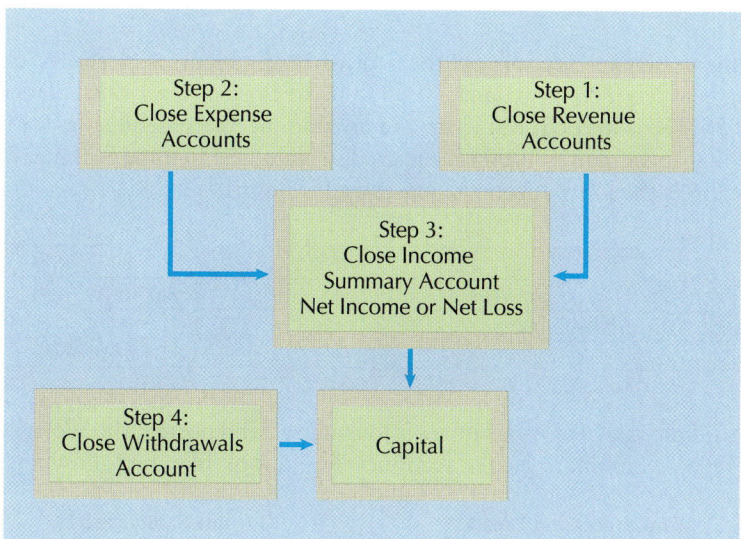

FIGURE 5.4
Four Steps in Journalizing Closing Entries (All numbers can be found on the worksheet in Figure 5.5.)

COACHING TIP

Don't forget two goals of closing:

1. Clear all temporary accounts in ledger.

2. Update Capital to a new balance that reflects a summary of all the temporary accounts.

FIGURE 5.5
Closing Figures on the Worksheet

Account Titles	Income Statement Dr.	Income Statement Cr.	Balance Sheet Dr.	Balance Sheet Cr.
Cash			6 1 5 5 00	
Accounts Receivable			5 0 0 0 00	
Office Supplies			1 0 0 00	
Prepaid Rent			8 0 0 00	
Word Processing Equipment			6 0 0 0 00	
Accounts Payable				3 3 5 0 00
B. Clark, Capital		For Step 1		10 0 0 0 00
B. Clark, Withdrawals	For Step 2		6 2 5 00	
Word Processing Fees		8 0 0 0 00		
Office Salaries Expense	1 6 5 0 00		For Step 4	
Advertising Expense	2 5 0 00			
Telephone Expense	2 2 0 00			
Office Supplies Expense	5 0 0 00			
Rent Expense	4 0 0 00			
Depreciation Exp., W. P. Equip.	8 0 00			
Acc. Depreciation, W. P. Equip.		For Step 3		8 0 00
Salaries Payable				3 5 0 00
	3 1 0 0 00	8 0 0 0 00	18 6 8 0 00	13 7 8 0 00
Net Income	4 9 0 0 00			4 9 0 0 00
	8 0 0 0 00	8 0 0 0 00	18 6 8 0 00	18 6 8 0 00

COACHING TIP

All numbers used in the closing process can be found on the worksheet.

Step 1: Clear Revenue Balance and Transfer to Income Summary Here is what is in the ledger before closing entries are journalized and posted:

Word Processing Fees 411	Income Summary 313
8,000	

The income statement section on the worksheet in Figure 5.5 shows that Word Processing Fees has a credit balance of $8,000. To close or clear this balance to zero, a debit of $8,000 is needed. But if we add an amount to the debit side, we must also add a credit—so we add $8,000 on the credit side of the Income Summary.

Figure 5.6 is the journalized closing entry for Step 1:

FIGURE 5.6
Closing Revenue to Income Summary

May	31	Word Processing Fees	411	8 0 0 0 00		
		Income Summary	313		8 0 0 0 00	

After the first step of closing entries is journalized and posted, the Word Processing Fees and Income Summary ledger accounts should look like the following:

Word Processing Fees 411		Income Summary 313	
8,000	8,000		8,000
Closing	**Revenue**		**Revenue**

Note that the revenue balance is cleared to zero and transferred to Income Summary, a temporary account also located in the ledger.

Step 2: Clear Individual Expense Balances and Transfer the Total to Income Summary The ledger for each expense account is shown here before closing entries are journalized and posted. Each expense is listed on the worksheet in the debit column of the income statement section in Figure 5.5.

Office Salaries Expense 511		Advertising Expense 512	
650		250	
650			
350			

Telephone Expense 513		Office Supplies Expense 514	
220		500	

Rent Expense 515		Depreciation Expense, W. P. Equipment 516	
400		80	

The income statement section of the worksheet lists all the expenses as debits. If we want to reduce each expense to zero, each one must be credited.

Figure 5.7 is the journalized closing entry for Step 2:

FIGURE 5.7
Closing Each Expense Account Balance to Income Summary

	31	Income Summary	313	3 1 0 0 00		
		Office Salaries Expense	511		1 6 5 0 00	
		Advertising Expense	512		2 5 0 00	
		Telephone Expense	513		2 2 0 00	
		Office Supplies Expense	514		5 0 0 00	
		Rent Expense	515		4 0 0 00	
		Depreciation Expense, W. P. Equip.	516		8 0 00	

COACHING TIP

Remember, the worksheet is a tool. The accountant realizes that the information about the total of the expenses will be transferred to the Income Summary account.

COACHING TIP

The $3,100 is the total of all expense account balances.

Individual expenses and Income Summary accounts should look like the following after closing entries are journalized and posted:

Office Salaries Expense 511		
650	Closing	1,650
650		
350		

Advertising Expense 512		
250	Closing	250

Telephone Expense 513		
220	Closing	220

Office Supplies Expense 514		
500	Closing	500

Rent Expense 515		
400	Closing	400

Depreciation Expense, W. P. Equipment 516		
80	Closing	80

Income Summary 313		
	Expenses	Revenue
Step 2	3,100	8,000	Step 1

Step 3: Clear Balance in Income Summary (Net Income) and Transfer It to Capital

The Income Summary and B. Clark, Capital accounts look this way before Step 3:

Income Summary 313	
3,100	8,000
	4,900

B. Clark, Capital 311	
	10,000

Note that the balance of Income Summary (Revenues minus Expenses, or $8,000 Cr − $3,100 Dr = $4,900 Cr. We must clear that amount from the Income Summary account and transfer to the B. Clark, Capital account.

In order to transfer the Credit Balance of $4,900 from Income Summary to Capital, it will be necessary to debit Income Summary for $4,900 and credit or increase Capital of B. Clark for $4,900.

Figure 5.8 is the journalized closing entry for Step 3:

	31	Income Summary	313	4 9 0 0 00	
		B. Clark, Capital	311		4 9 0 0 00

FIGURE 5.8
Closing Net Income to B. Clark, Capital

The Income Summary and B. Clark, Capital accounts will look like the following in the ledger after the closing entries of Step 3 are journalized and posted:

	Income Summary 313		
Total of Expenses →	3,100	8,000	← Revenue
Debit to close account →	4,900	4,900	← Net Income

B. Clark, Capital 311	
	10,000
	4,900 ← Net Income

Step 4: Clear the Withdrawals Balance and Transfer It to Capital

Next, we must close the Withdrawals account. The B. Clark, Withdrawals and B. Clark, Capital accounts currently look like this:

B. Clark, Withdrawals 312	
625	

B. Clark, Capital 311	
	10,000
	4,900

COACHING TIP

At the end of these three steps, the Income Summary has a zero balance. If we had a net loss, the end result would be to decrease Capital. The entry would be debit Capital and credit Income Summary for the loss.

To bring the Withdrawals account to a zero balance and summarize its effect on Capital, we must credit Withdrawals and debit Capital.

Remember, withdrawals are a nonbusiness expense and thus are not transferred to Income Summary. The closing entry is journalized as shown in Figure 5.9.

	31	B. Clark, Capital	311	6 2 5 00	
		B. Clark, Withdrawals	312		6 2 5 00

At this point the B. Clark, Withdrawals and B. Clark, Capital accounts would look this way in the ledger.

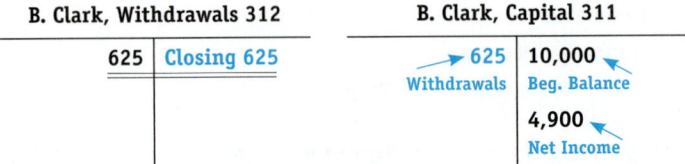

COACHING TIP

Note that the $10,000 is a beginning balance because no additional investments were made during the period.

Now let's look at a summary of the closing entries in Figure 5.10.

FIGURE 5.10
Four Closing Entries

	Date		Account Titles and Description	PR	Dr.	Cr.	
			SUMMARY OF CLOSING ENTRIES				
			Closing Entries				
201X							
May	31		Word Processing Fees	411	8 0 0 0 00		
			Income Summary	313		8 0 0 0 00	
	31		Income Summary	313	3 1 0 0 00		
			Office Salaries Expense	511		1 6 5 0 00	
			Advertising Expense	512		2 5 0 00	
			Telephone Expense	513		2 2 0 00	
			Office Supplies Expense	514		5 0 0 00	
			Rent Expense	515		4 0 0 00	
			Depreciation Expense, W. P. Equip.	516		8 0 00	
	31		Income Summary	313	4 9 0 0 00		
			B. Clark, Capital	311		4 9 0 0 00	
	31		B. Clark, Capital	311	6 2 5 00		
			B. Clark, Withdrawals	312		6 2 5 00	

The following figure shows the complete ledger for Clark's Word Processing Services (see Figure 5.11). Note how "adjusting" or "closing" is written in the explanation column of individual ledgers, as, for example, in the one for Office Supplies. If the goals of closing have been achieved, only permanent accounts will have balances carried to the next accounting period. All temporary accounts should have zero balances.

FIGURE 5.11
Complete Ledger

CLARK'S WORD PROCESSING SERVICES
GENERAL LEDGER

Cash   Account No. 111

Date		Explanation	Post. Ref.	Debit	Credit	Balance	
						Debit	Credit
201X May	1		GJ1	10 0 0 0 00		10 0 0 0 00	
	1		GJ1		1 0 0 0 00	9 0 0 0 00	
	1		GJ1		1 2 0 0 00	7 8 0 0 00	
	7		GJ1	3 0 0 0 00		10 8 0 0 00	
	15		GJ1		6 5 0 00	10 1 5 0 00	
	20		GJ1		6 2 5 00	9 5 2 5 00	
	27		GJ2		6 5 0 00	8 8 7 5 00	
	28		GJ2		2 5 0 0 00	6 3 7 5 00	
	29		GJ2		2 2 0 00	6 1 5 5 00	

Accounts Receivable   Account No. 112

Date		Explanation	Post. Ref.	Debit	Credit	Balance	
						Debit	Credit
201X May	22		GJ1	5 0 0 0 00		5 0 0 0 00	

Office Supplies   Account No. 114

Date		Explanation	Post. Ref.	Debit	Credit	Balance	
						Debit	Credit
201X May	3		GJ1	6 0 0 00		6 0 0 00	
	31	Adjusting	GJ2		5 0 0 00	1 0 0 00	

(Continued on next page)

Figure 5.11 *(continued)*

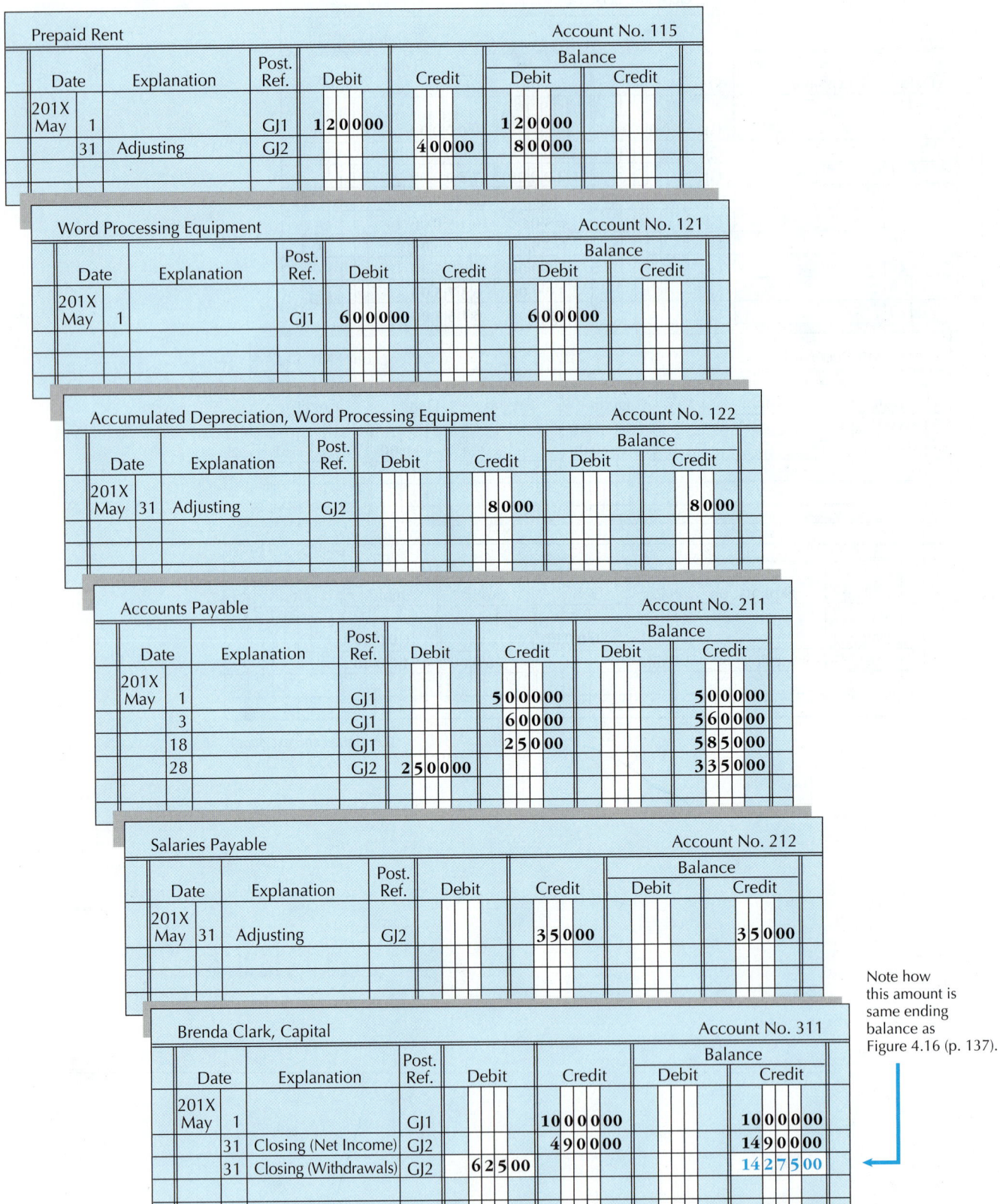

Prepaid Rent   Account No. 115

Date		Explanation	Post. Ref.	Debit	Credit	Balance Debit	Balance Credit
201X May	1		GJ1	1 2 0 0 00		1 2 0 0 00	
	31	Adjusting	GJ2		4 0 0 00	8 0 0 00	

Word Processing Equipment   Account No. 121

Date		Explanation	Post. Ref.	Debit	Credit	Balance Debit	Balance Credit
201X May	1		GJ1	6 0 0 0 00		6 0 0 0 00	

Accumulated Depreciation, Word Processing Equipment   Account No. 122

Date		Explanation	Post. Ref.	Debit	Credit	Balance Debit	Balance Credit
201X May	31	Adjusting	GJ2		8 0 00		8 0 00

Accounts Payable   Account No. 211

Date		Explanation	Post. Ref.	Debit	Credit	Balance Debit	Balance Credit
201X May	1		GJ1		5 0 0 0 00		5 0 0 0 00
	3		GJ1		6 0 0 00		5 6 0 0 00
	18		GJ1		2 5 0 00		5 8 5 0 00
	28		GJ2	2 5 0 0 00			3 3 5 0 00

Salaries Payable   Account No. 212

Date		Explanation	Post. Ref.	Debit	Credit	Balance Debit	Balance Credit
201X May	31	Adjusting	GJ2		3 5 0 00		3 5 0 00

Brenda Clark, Capital   Account No. 311

Date		Explanation	Post. Ref.	Debit	Credit	Balance Debit	Balance Credit
201X May	1		GJ1		1 0 0 0 0 00		1 0 0 0 0 00
	31	Closing (Net Income)	GJ2		4 9 0 0 00		1 4 9 0 0 00
	31	Closing (Withdrawals)	GJ2	6 2 5 00			1 4 2 7 5 00

Note how this amount is same ending balance as Figure 4.16 (p. 137).

Figure 5.11 *(continued)*

Brenda Clark, Withdrawals — Account No. 312

Date		Explanation	Post. Ref.	Debit	Credit	Balance Debit	Balance Credit
201X May	20		GJ1	6 2 5 00		6 2 5 00	
	31	Closing	GJ2		6 2 5 00	—	—

Income Summary — Account No. 313

Date		Explanation	Post. Ref.	Debit	Credit	Balance Debit	Balance Credit
201X May	31	Closing (Revenue)	GJ2		8 0 0 0 00		8 0 0 0 00
	31	Closing (Expenses)	GJ2	3 1 0 0 00			4 9 0 0 00
	31	Closing (Net Income)	GJ2	4 9 0 0 00		—	—

Word Processing Fees — Account No. 411

Date		Explanation	Post. Ref.	Debit	Credit	Balance Debit	Balance Credit
201X May	7		GJ1		3 0 0 0 00		3 0 0 0 00
	22		GJ1		5 0 0 0 00		8 0 0 0 00
	31	Closing	GJ2	8 0 0 0 00		—	—

Office Salaries Expense — Account No. 511

Date		Explanation	Post. Ref.	Debit	Credit	Balance Debit	Balance Credit
201X May	13		GJ1	6 5 0 00		6 5 0 00	
	27		GJ2	6 5 0 00		1 3 0 0 00	
	31	Adjusting	GJ2	3 5 0 00		1 6 5 0 00	
	31	Closing	GJ2		1 6 5 0 00	—	

Advertising Expense — Account No. 512

Date		Explanation	Post. Ref.	Debit	Credit	Balance Debit	Balance Credit
201X May	18		GJ1	2 5 0 00		2 5 0 00	
	31	Closing	GJ2		2 5 0 00	—	

Figure 5.11 *(continued)*

Telephone Expense   Account No. 513

Date		Explanation	Post. Ref.	Debit	Credit	Balance Debit	Balance Credit
201X May	29		GJ2	2 2 0 00		2 2 0 00	
	31	Closing	GJ2		2 2 0 00	—	

Office Supplies Expense   Account No. 514

Date		Explanation	Post. Ref.	Debit	Credit	Balance Debit	Balance Credit
201X May	31	Adjusting	GJ2	5 0 0 00		5 0 0 00	
	31	Closing	GJ2		5 0 0 00	—	

Note: Accounts 312 to 516 are temporary and are closed to zero.

Rent Expense   Account No. 515

Date		Explanation	Post. Ref.	Debit	Credit	Balance Debit	Balance Credit
201X May	31	Adjusting	GJ2	4 0 0 00		4 0 0 00	
	31	Closing	GJ2		4 0 0 00	—	

Depreciation Expense, Word Processing Equipment   Account No. 516

Date		Explanation	Post. Ref.	Debit	Credit	Balance Debit	Balance Credit
201X May	31	Adjusting	GJ2	8 0 00		8 0 00	
	31	Closing	GJ2		8 0 00	—	

LEARNING UNIT 5-2 REVIEW

AT THIS POINT you should be able to do the following:

- Define the goals of the closing process.
- Differentiate between temporary (nominal) and permanent (real) accounts.
- List the four mechanical steps of closing.
- Explain the role of the Income Summary account.
- Explain the role of the worksheet in the closing process.

 **Instant Replay** ○ **Self-Review Quiz 5-2**

Go to the worksheet for P. Logan in Figure 4.14 (p. 134 in Chapter 4). Then (1) journalize and post the closing entries and (2) calculate the new balance for P. Logan, Capital.

Solution to Instant Replay: Self-Review Quiz 5-2

		Closing Entries						
Dec.	31	Revenue from Clients	410		25 00			
		Income Summary	312				25 00	
	31	Income Summary	312		20 00			
		Rent Expense	518				2 00	
		Salaries Expense	512				11 00	
		Depreciation Expense, Store Equip.	510				1 00	
		Insurance Expense	516				2 00	
		Supplies Expense	514				4 00	
	31	Income Summary	312		5 00			
		P. Logan, Capital	310				5 00	
	31	P. Logan, Capital	310		3 00			
		P. Logan, Withdrawals	311				3 00	

FIGURE 5.12
Closing Entries for Logan

Partial Ledger

P. Logan, Capital 310		Revenue from Clients 410		Supplies Expense 514	
	3 14	25	25	4	4
	5				
	16				

P. Logan, Withdrawals 311		Dep. Exp., Store Equip. 510		Insurance Expense 516	
3	3	1	1	2	2

Income Summary 312		Salaries Expense 512		Rent Expense 518	
20	25	11	11	2	2
5	5				

P. Logan, (Beginning) Capital		$14
Net Income	$5	
Less Withdrawals	3	
Increase in Capital		2
P. Logan, Capital (ending)		$16

PLAY BY PLAY: EXTRA HELP ON SELF-REVIEW QUIZ 5-2

Let's review first: Why are closing entries necessary? In the ledger we need to get the new balance in the Capital account. When financial statements were prepared, the ledger for Capital had only the old balance. Also, to get ready for the next accounting period we must close all temporary accounts to zero so they will be ready to collect new data regarding revenues, expenses, and withdrawals. Without the closing process each year, financial statements would run into the next period and financial analysis would be difficult. Keep in mind that the Income Summary account that will be used in the closing process is a temporary account (like a storage area for revenues and expenses).

Why use four steps to closing?

Because you need to do the following:

1. Clear all temporary accounts to zero.
2. Update the Capital account in the ledger to its new balance.

Steps to closing:

1. Close revenue account(s) to Income Summary.
2. Close each INDIVIDUAL expense to Income Summary.
3. Remove the balance in Income Summary (net income or net loss) and transfer it to the Capital account.
4. Close any withdrawals directly to Capital.

All the closing entries can be journalized directly from the last four columns of the worksheet. Each individual expense along with the total of expenses is found on the worksheet. Once these four closing entries are journalized and posted, all temporary accounts have a zero balance and P. Logan, Capital now has an ending balance of $16. This is same amount of ending capital that was used to make the formal balance sheet.

Summary: If you look at the T account in the solution you will see four numbers in Income Summary. Can you explain them?

20...this represents the total of all the expenses.

25...this represents the total revenue of all the revenues.

5 on the credit side...this is net income (25–20).

5 on the debit side...this comes from the third closing entry, which transfers the balance in Income Summary to Capital.

COACHING TIP

Sweep or clear all revenue and expenses into a dustpan (Income Summary) and then place the balance into a barrel (like Capital).

● L03   LEARNING UNIT 5-3 THE POST-CLOSING TRIAL BALANCE:
Step 9 of the Accounting Cycle and the Cycle Reviewed

Preparing a Post-Closing Trial Balance

Post-closing trial balance The final step in the accounting cycle that lists only permanent accounts in the ledger and their balances after adjusting and closing entries have been posted.

The last step in the accounting cycle is the preparation of a post-closing trial balance, which lists only permanent accounts in the ledger and their balances after adjusting and closing entries have been posted. This post-closing trial balance aids in checking whether the ledger is in balance. This checking is important because so many new postings go to the ledger from the adjusting and closing process.

The procedure for taking a post-closing trial balance is the same as for a trial balance, except that, because closing entries have closed all temporary accounts, the post-closing trial balances will contain only permanent accounts (balance sheet). We will walk through this procedure in the Learning Unit 5-3 quiz coming up after we review the accounting cycle.

The Accounting Cycle Reviewed

Table 5.1 lists the steps we completed in the manual accounting cycle for Clark's Word Processing Services for the month of May.

TABLE 5.1 Steps of the Manual Accounting Cycle

Steps	Explanation
1. Collect source documents from business transactions as they occur.	Cash register tape, sales tickets, bills, checks, payroll cards
2. Analyze and record business transactions in a journal.	Called journalizing
3. Post or transfer information from journal to ledger.	Copying the debits and credits of the journal entries into the ledger accounts
4. Prepare a trial balance.	Summarizing each individual ledger account and listing those accounts to test for mathematical accuracy in recording transactions
5. Prepare a worksheet.	A multicolumn form that summarizes accounting information to complete the accounting cycle
6. Prepare financial statements.	Income statement, statement of owner's equity, and balance sheet
7. Journalize and post adjusting entries.	Using figures in the adjustment columns of worksheet
8. Journalize and post closing entries.	Using figures in the income statement and balance sheet sections of worksheet
9. Prepare a post-closing trial balance.	Proving the mathematical accuracy of the adjusting and closing process of the accounting cycle

COACHING TIP

Remember: No worksheet is needed when using accounting software.

Insight Most companies journalize and post adjusting and closing entries only at the end of their fiscal year. A company that prepares interim statements may complete only the first six steps of the cycle. Worksheets allow the preparation of interim reports without the formal adjusting and closing of the books. In this case, footnotes on the interim report will indicate the extent to which adjusting and closing were completed.

LEARNING UNIT 5-3 REVIEW

AT THIS POINT you should be able to do the following:

- Prepare a post-closing trial balance.
- Explain the relationship of interim statements to the accounting cycle.

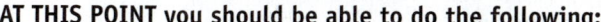

Instant Replay ◉ Self-Review Quiz 5-3

From the ledger in Figure 5.11 (p. 171), prepare a post-closing trial balance.

Solution to Instant Replay: Self-Review Quiz 5-3

FIGURE 5.13
Post-Closing Trial Balance for Clark's Word Processing Services

CLARK'S WORD PROCESSING SERVICES
POST-CLOSING TRIAL BALANCE
MAY 31, 201X

	Dr.	Cr.
Cash	6 1 5 5 00	
Accounts Receivable	5 0 0 0 00	
Office Supplies	1 0 0 00	
Prepaid Rent	8 0 0 00	
Word Processing Equipment	6 0 0 0 00	
Accumulated Depreciation, Word Processing Equip.		8 0 00
Accounts Payable		3 3 5 0 00
Salaries Payable		3 5 0 00
Brenda Clark, Capital		14 2 7 5 00
Totals	18 0 5 5 00	18 0 5 5 00

COACHING TIP

Each day when the park closes, the employees clean and restock it to get ready for the next "cycle" of customers.

PLAY BY PLAY: EXTRA HELP ON SELF-REVIEW QUIZ 5-3

Let's review first: The post-closing trial balance contains only permanent accounts because all temporary accounts have been closed. All temporary accounts are summarized in the Capital account. Remember that Income Summary is a temporary account.

Post-Closing Trial Balance: Once all the closing entries have been journalized and posted we can then prepare a post-closing trial balance. Since only permanent accounts are left after closing, the structure of the post-closing trial balance should look as follows:

Assets .... Dr.

Contra-Assets .... Cr.

Liabilities .... Cr.

Ending Capital .... Cr.

Summary: To begin the next accounting cycle, only permanent accounts with balances are brought forward. In the new cycle transactions will be journalized and posted. Adjustments will be made and new financial statements will be prepared. By the end of the cycle all temporary accounts will be closed to get a new ending figure for capital in the ledger. The end result will be to prepare a new post-closing trial balance.

DEMONSTRATION PROBLEM

MyAccountingLab

 **L01, 2, 3**

Requirements:

1. Journalize transactions and post to ledger.
2. Prepare a worksheet.
3. Prepare financial statements.
4. Journalize adjusting and closing entries and prepare a post-closing trial balance.

Assets	**Owner's Equity**
111 Cash	311 Rolo Kern, Capital
112 Accounts Receivable	312 Rolo Kern, Withdrawals
114 Prepaid Rent	313 Income Summary
115 Office Supplies	**Revenue**
121 Office Equipment	411 Fees Earned
122 Accumulated Depreciation, Office Equipment	**Expenses**
Liabilities	511 Salaries Expense
211 Accounts Payable	512 Advertising Expense
212 Salaries Payable	513 Rent Expense
	514 Office Supplies Expense
	515 Depreciation Expense, Office Equipment

COACHING TIP

Note: Accounts 312 to 515 are temporary accounts.

We will use unusually small numbers to simplify calculation and emphasize the theory.

201X

Jan.	1	Rolo Kern invested $1,200 cash and $100 of office equipment to open Rolo Co.
	1	Paid rent for three months in advance, $300.
	4	Purchased office equipment on account, $50.
	6	Bought office supplies for cash, $40.
	8	Collected $400 for services rendered.
	12	Rolo paid his home electric bill from the company checkbook, $20.
	14	Provided $100 worth of services to clients who will not pay until next month.
	16	Paid salaries, $60.
	18	Advertising bill received for $70 but will not be paid until next month.

Adjustment Data on January 31

a. Supplies on hand, $6.
b. Rent expired, $100.
c. Depreciation, Office Equipment, $20.
d. Salaries accrued, $50.

Demonstration Problem Solutions

Requirement 1
Journalize transactions and post to ledger

Part 1	Part 2	Part 3	Part 4	Demonstration Problem Complete

FIGURE 5.14
Journal Entries for Rolo Company

General Journal					Page 1
Date	Account Titles and Description	PR	Dr.	Cr.	
201X Jan 1	Cash	111	1 2 0 0 00		
	Office Equipment	121	1 0 0 00		
	R. Kern, Capital	311		1 3 0 0 00	
	Initial Investment				
1	Prepaid Rent	114	3 0 0 00		
	Cash	111		3 0 0 00	
	Rent Paid in Advance—3 months				
4	Office Equipment	121	5 0 00		
	Accounts Payable	211		5 0 00	
	Purchased Equipment on Account				
6	Office Supplies	115	4 0 00		
	Cash	111		4 0 00	
	Supplies purchased for cash				
8	Cash	111	4 0 0 00		
	Fees Earned	411		4 0 0 00	
	Services rendered				
12	R. Kern, Withdrawals	312	2 0 00		
	Cash	111		2 0 00	
	Personal payment of a bill				
14	Accounts Receivable	112	1 0 0 00		
	Fees Earned	411		1 0 0 00	
	Services rendered on account				
16	Salaries Expense	511	6 0 00		
	Cash	111		6 0 00	
	Paid salaries				
18	Advertising Expense	512	7 0 00		
	Accounts Payable	211		7 0 00	
	Advertising bill, but not paid				

Solution Tips to Journalizing and Posting Transactions

Jan 1	Cash	Asset	↑	Dr.	$1,200
	Office Equipment	Asset	↑	Dr.	$ 100
	R. Kern, Capital	Capital	↑	Cr.	$1,300

1	Prepaid Rent	Asset	↑	Dr.	$300	
	Cash	Asset	↓	Cr.	$300	
4	Office Equipment	Asset	↑	Dr.	$ 50	
	Accounts Payable	Liability	↑	Cr.	$ 50	
6	Office Supplies	Asset	↑	Dr.	$ 40	
	Cash	Asset	↓	Cr.	$ 40	
8	Cash	Asset	↑	Dr.	$400	
	Fees Earned	Revenue	↑	Cr.	$400	
12	R. Kern, Withdrawals	Withdrawals	↑	Dr.	$ 20	
	Cash	Asset	↓	Cr.	$ 20	
14	Accounts Receivable	Asset	↑	Dr.	$100	
	Fees Earned	Revenue	↑	Cr.	$100	
16	Salaries Expense	Expense	↑	Dr.	$ 60	
	Cash	Asset	↓	Cr.	$ 60	
18	Advertising Expense	Expense	↑	Dr.	$ 70	
	Accounts Payable	Liability	↑	Cr.	$ 70	

Note: All account titles come from the chart of accounts. When journalizing, the PR column of the general journal is blank. It is in the posting process that we update the ledger. The PR column in the ledger accounts tells us from what journal page the information came. After the title in the ledger is posted to, we fill in the PR column of the journal, telling us to what account number the information was transferred.

Requirement 2
Preparing a worksheet (Figure 5.15, p. 183)

Part 1	**Part 2**	Part 3	Part 4	Demonstration Problem Complete

Solution Tips to the Trial Balance and Completion of the Worksheet

After the posting process is complete from the journal to the ledger, we take the ending balance in each account and prepare a trial balance on the worksheet (see Figure 5.15). If a title has no balance, it is not listed on the trial balance. New titles on the worksheet will be added as needed.

Adjustments

Office Supplies Expense	Expense	↑	Dr.	$ 34	($40 – $6)
Office Supplies	Asset	↓	Cr.	$ 34	
Rent Expense	Expense	↑	Dr.	$100	
Prepaid Rent	Asset	↓	Cr.	$100	

COACHING TIP

Supplies on hand of $6 is not the adjustment. You need to calculate amount used up.

Do not touch original cost of equipment.	Depr. Exp., Office Equip.	Expense	↑	Dr.	$ 20
○————————→	Accum. Dep., Office Equip.	Contra-Asset	↑	Cr.	$ 20
	Salaries Expense	Expense	↑	Dr.	$ 50
	Salaries Payable	Liability	↑	Cr.	$ 50

Note: This information on the worksheet has *not* been updated in the ledger. (Updating happens when we journalize and post adjustments at the end of the cycle.)

Note that the last four columns of the worksheet come from numbers on the adjusted trial balance.

On the worksheet we copy the Net Income of $166 to the Balance Sheet credit column in order to make it balance, because the Capital figure there is the old one, hence the net income has not yet been included.

FIGURE 5.15
Completed Worksheet for Rolo Company

ROLO CO.
WORKSHEET
FOR MONTH ENDED JANUARY 31, 201X

Account Titles	Trial Balance Dr.	Trial Balance Cr.	Adjustments Dr.	Adjustments Cr.	Adjusted Trial Balance Dr.	Adjusted Trial Balance Cr.	Income Statement Dr.	Income Statement Cr.	Balance Sheet Dr.	Balance Sheet Cr.
Cash	118000				118000				118000	
Accounts Receivable	10000				10000				10000	
Prepaid Rent	30000			(B) 10000	20000				20000	
Office Supplies	4000			(A) 3400	600				600	
Office Equipment	15000				15000				15000	
Accounts Payable		12000				12000				12000
R. Kern, Capital		130000				130000				130000
R. Kern, Withdrawals	2000				2000				2000	
Fees Earned		50000				50000		50000		
Salaries Expense	6000		(D) 5000		11000		11000			
Advertising Expense	7000				7000		7000			
	192000	192000								
Office Supplies Expense			(A) 3400		3400		3400			
Rent Expense			(B) 10000		10000		10000			
Depr. Exp., Office Equip.			(C) 2000		2000		2000			
Acc. Dep., Office Equip.				(C) 2000		2000				2000
Salaries Payable				(D) 5000		5000				5000
			20400	20400	199000	199000	33400	50000	165600	149000
Net Income							16600			16600
							50000	50000	165600	165600

Supplies used up

Supplies on hand

Requirement 3

Preparing the financial statements

Part 1	Part 2	**Part 3**	Part 4	Demonstration Problem Complete

FIGURE 5.16
Income Statement for Rolo Company

ROLO CO.
INCOME STATEMENT
FOR MONTH ENDED JANUARY 31, 201X

Revenue:		
Fees Earned		$5 0 0 00
Operating Expenses		
Salaries Expense	$11 0 00	
Advertising Expense	7 0 00	
Office Supplies Expense	3 4 00	
Rent Expense	10 0 00	
Depreciation Expense, Office Equipment	2 0 00	
Total Operating Expenses		3 3 4 00
Net Income		$1 6 6 00

FIGURE 5.17
Statement of Owner's
Equity for Rolo Company

ROLO CO.
STATEMENT OF OWNER'S EQUITY
FOR MONTH ENDED JANUARY 31, 201X

R. Kern, Capital, January 1, 201X		$13 0 0 00
Net Income for January	$1 6 6 00	
Less Withdrawals for January	2 0 00	
Increase in Capital		1 4 6 00
R. Kern, Capital, January 31, 201X		$1 4 4 6 00

FIGURE 5.18
Balance Sheet for Rolo Company

ROLO CO.
BALANCE SHEET
JANUARY 31, 201X

Assets			Liabilities & Owner's Equity		
Cash		$11 8 0 00	Liabilities		
Accounts Receivable		1 0 0 00	Accounts Payable	$1 2 0 00	
Prepaid Rent		2 0 0 00	Salaries Payable	5 0 00	
Office Supplies		6 00	Total Liabilities		$ 1 7 0 00
Office Equipment	$1 5 0 00		Owner's Equity		
Less Accum. Depr.	2 0 00	1 3 0 00	R. Kern, Capital		1 4 4 6 00
			Total Liabilities &		
Total Assets		$1 6 1 6 00	Owner's Equity		$1 6 1 6 00

Solution Tips to Preparing the Financial Statements

The statements are prepared from the worksheet. (Many of the ledger accounts are not up-to-date.) The income statement (Figure 5.16) lists revenue and expenses. The Net Income figure of $166 is used to update the statement of owner's equity. The statement of owner's equity (Figure 5.17) calculates a new figure for Capital, $1,446 (Beginning Capital + Net Income – Withdrawals). This new figure is then listed on the balance sheet (Figure 5.18) (Assets, Liabilities, and a new figure for Capital).

Requirement 4

Journalize and post adjusting and closing entries and prepare a post-closing trial balance (Figure 5.19).

Part 1	Part 2	Part 3	**Part 4**	Demonstration Problem Complete

FIGURE 5.19
Adjusting and Closing Entries Journalized and Posted

	Date		Account Titles and Description	PR	Dr.	Cr.
General Journal						Page 2
			ADJUSTING ENTRIES			
	Jan.	31	Office Supplies Expense	514	3400	
			Office Supplies	115		3400
		31	Rent Expense	513	10000	
			Prepaid Rent	114		10000
		31	Depr. Expense, Office Equipment	515	2000	
			Accum. Depr., Office Equip.	122		2000
		31	Salaries Expense	511	5000	
			Salaries Payable	212		5000
			CLOSING ENTRIES			
Step 1 →		31	Fees Earned	411	50000	
			Income Summary	313		50000
Step 2 →		31	Income Summary	313	33400	
			Salaries Expense	511		11000
			Advertising Expense	512		7000
			Office Supplies Expense	514		3400
			Rent Expense	513		10000
			Depr. Expense, Office Equip.	515		2000
Step 3 →		31	Income Summary	313	16600	
			R. Kern, Capital	311		16600
Step 4 →		31	R. Kern, Capital	311	2000	
			R. Kern, Withdrawals	312		2000

Closing {

Solution Tips to Journalizing and Posting Adjusting and Closing Entries

Adjustments

The adjustments from the worksheet are journalized (same journal as transactions) and posted to the ledger. Now ledger accounts will be brought up-to-date. Remember, we have already prepared the financial statements from the worksheet. Our goal now is to get the ledger up-to-date.

Closing

Note that Income Summary is a temporary account located in the ledger.

Goals

1. Wipe out all temporary accounts in the ledger to zero balances.
2. Get a new figure for Capital in the ledger.

Steps in the Closing Process

STEP 1: Close revenue accounts to Income Summary.

STEP 2: Close expense accounts to Income Summary.

STEP 3: Close balance of Income Summary to Capital. (This amount really is the Net Income and equal to the figure on the worksheet.)

STEP 4: Close balance of Withdrawals to Capital.

All the journal closing entries are posted. (No new calculations are needed because all figures are on the worksheet.) The result in the ledger is that all temporary accounts have a zero balance (Figure 5.20).

FIGURE 5.20
General Ledger for Rolo Company

GENERAL LEDGER

Cash 111

Date	PR	Dr.	Cr.	Balance Dr.	Balance Cr.
1/1	GJ1	1,200		1,200	
1/1	GJ1		300	900	
1/6	GJ1		40	860	
1/8	GJ1	400		1,260	
1/12	GJ1		20	1,240	
1/16	GJ1		60	1,180	

Accounts Receivable 112

Date	PR	Dr.	Cr.	Balance Dr.	Balance Cr.
1/14	GJ1	100		100	

Accumulated Depreciation, Equipment 122

Date	PR	Dr.	Cr.	Balance Dr.	Balance Cr.
1/31 Adj.	GJ2		20		20

Accounts Payable 211

Date	PR	Dr.	Cr.	Balance Dr.	Balance Cr.
1/4	GJ1		50		50
1/18	GJ1		70		120

Salaries Payable 212

Date	PR	Dr.	Cr.	Balance Dr.	Balance Cr.
1/31 Adj.	GJ2		50		50

FIGURE 5.20 *(Continued)*

Prepaid Rent   114

Date	PR	Dr.	Cr.	Balance Dr.	Balance Cr.
1/1	GJ1	300		300	
1/31 Adj.	GJ2		100	200	

Office Supplies   115

Date	PR	Dr.	Cr.	Balance Dr.	Balance Cr.
1/6	GJ1	40		40	
1/31 Adj	GJ2		34	6	

Office Equipment   121

Date	PR	Dr.	Cr.	Balance Dr.	Balance Cr.
1/1	GJ1	100		100	
1/4	GJ1	50		150	

Fees Earned   411

Date	PR	Dr.	Cr.	Balance Dr.	Balance Cr.
1/8	GJ1		400		400
1/14	GJ1		100		500
1/31 Clos.	GJ2	500		—	

Salaries Expense   511

Date	PR	Dr.	Cr.	Balance Dr.	Balance Cr.
1/16	GJ1	60		60	
1/31 Adj.	GJ2	50		110	
1/31 Clos.	GJ2		110	—	

Advertising Expense   512

Date	PR	Dr.	Cr.	Balance Dr.	Balance Cr.
1/18	GJ1	70		70	
1/31 Clos.	GJ2		70	—	

Rolo Kern, Capital   311

Date	PR	Dr.	Cr.	Balance Dr.	Balance Cr.
1/1	GJ1		1,300		1,300
1/31 Clos.	GJ2		166		1,466
1/31 Clos.	GJ2	20			1,446

Rolo Kern, Withdrawals   312

Date	PR	Dr.	Cr.	Balance Dr.	Balance Cr.
1/12	GJ1	20		20	
1/31 Clos.	GJ2		20	—	

Income Summary   313

Date	PR	Dr.	Cr.	Balance Dr.	Balance Cr.
1/31 Clos.	GJ2		500		500
1/31 Clos.	GJ2	334			166
1/31 Clos.	GJ2	166		—	

Rent Expense   513

Date	PR	Dr.	Cr.	Balance Dr.	Balance Cr.
1/31 Adj.	GJ2	100		100	
1/31 Clos.	GJ2		100	—	

Office Supplies Expense   514

Date	PR	Dr.	Cr.	Balance Dr.	Balance Cr.
1/31 Adj.	GJ2	34		34	
1/31 Clos.	GJ2		34	—	

Depreciation Expenses Office Equipment   515

Date	PR	Dr.	Cr.	Balance Dr.	Balance Cr.
1/31 Adj.	GJ2	20		20	
1/31 Clos.	GJ2		20	—	

Solution Tips for the Post-Closing Trial Balance

The post-closing trial balance is a list of the ledger *after* adjusting and closing entries have been completed. Note that the figure for Capital, $1,446, is the new figure (see Figure 5.21).

FIGURE 5.21
Post-Closing Trial Balance for
Rolo Company

COACHING TIP

The post-closing trial balance contains all permanent accounts.

ROLO CO. POST-CLOSING TRIAL BALANCE JANUARY 31, 201X		
	Dr.	Cr.
Cash	1 1 8 0 00	
Accounts Receivable	1 0 0 00	
Prepaid Rent	2 0 0 00	
Office Supplies	6 00	
Office Equipment	1 5 0 00	
Accum. Dep., Office Equipment		2 0 00
Accounts Payable		1 2 0 00
Salaries Payable		5 0 00
R. Kern, Capital		1 4 4 6 00
TOTAL	1 6 3 6 00	1 6 3 6 00

Beginning Capital	$1,300
+ Net Income	166
– Withdrawals	20
= Ending Capital	$1,446

The post-closing trial balance is made up of permanent accounts only. Next accounting period we will enter new amounts in the Revenues, Expenses, and Withdrawal accounts.

Part 1	Part 2	Part 3	Part 4	Demonstration Problem Complete

BLUEPRINT OF CLOSING PROCESS FROM THE WORKSHEET

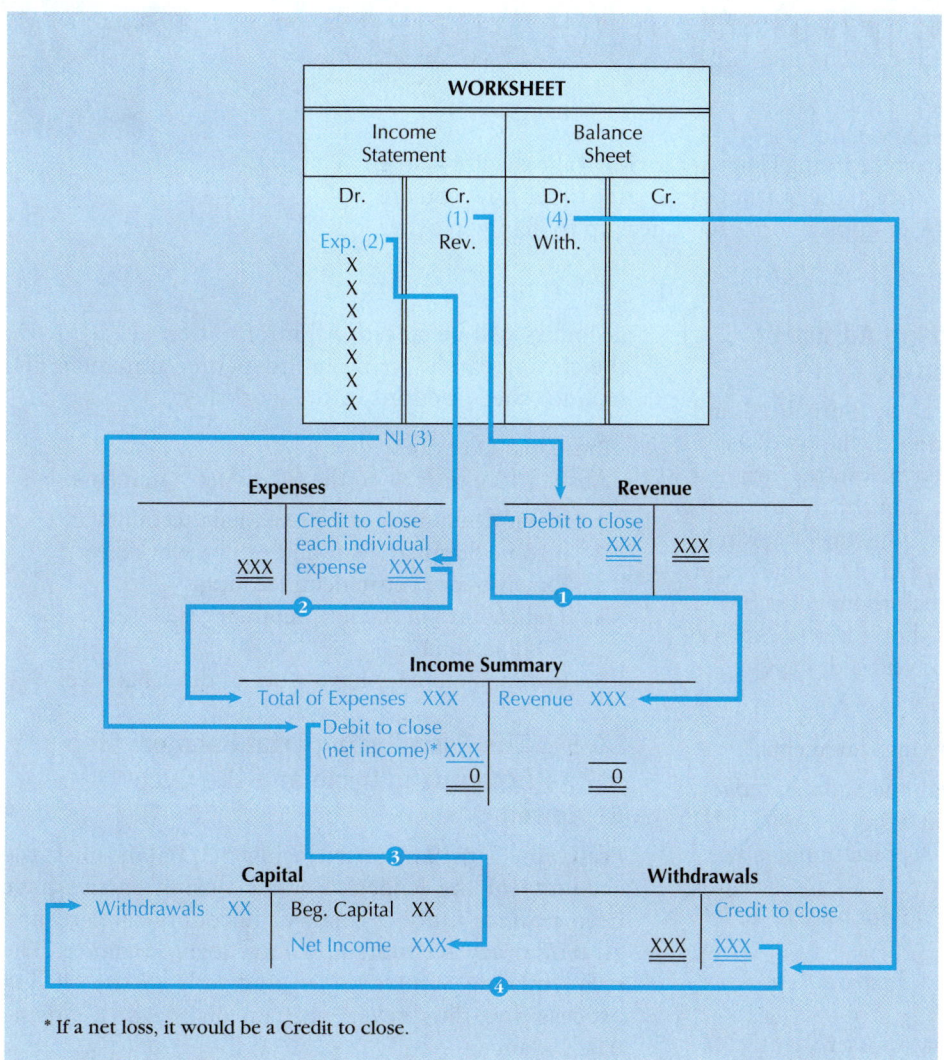

* If a net loss, it would be a Credit to close.

The Closing Steps

1. Close revenue ($) balance to Income Summary.
2. Close each *individual* expense and transfer *total* of all expenses to Income Summary.
3. Transfer balance in Income Summary (net income or net loss) to Capital.
4. Close Withdrawals to Capital.

ACCOUNTING COACH

The following Coaching Tips are from Learning Units 5-1 to 5-3. Take the Pre-Game Checkup and use the Check Your Score at the bottom of the page to see how you are doing. The Accounting Coach provides tips before each Checkup to help you avoid common accounting errors.

LU 5-1 Journalizing and Posting Adjusting Entries: Step 7 of the Accounting Cycle

Pre-Game Tips: All adjustments can be journalized and posted from the adjustments section of the worksheet. Remember that all accounts listed below the original trial balance are increasing. The adjustment for supplies is the amount used up. The adjustment for rent is the amount of rent that has expired. The adjustment for depreciation does not affect the original cost of the asset. The adjustment for salaries shows a new expense creating a liability because it is not yet paid.

Pre-Game Checkup
Answer true or false to the following statements.

1. After the adjustment is posted, the Supplies ledger account shows the amount on hand.
2. After posting, Accumulated Depreciation has a debit balance.
3. Adjustments on a worksheet do not have to be journalized and posted.
4. After the adjustment is posted, Prepaid Rent shows the amount expired.
5. Depreciation Expense is a contra-asset.

LU 5-2 Journalizing and Posting Closing Entries: Step 8 of the Accounting Cycle

Pre-Game Tips: The goal of closing is to update the ledger for the next accounting cycle. All temporary accounts need to be cleared, and a new figure for capital results. In the process, Income Summary is a temporary account that helps closing revenues and expenses to Capital. Withdrawals will be closed directly to Capital since it is not a business expense. When the closing process is complete, all temporary accounts will be closed. All information needed to do the closing can be found in the income statement and balance sheet sections of the worksheet.

Pre-Game Checkup
Answer true or false to the following statements.

1. Income Summary is a permanent account.
2. Income Summary is found on the worksheet.
3. Expenses are permanent accounts.
4. The balance in Income Summary is closed to the Cash account.
5. Income Summary has a normal debit balance.

LU 5-3 The Post-Closing Trial Balance: Step 9 of the Accounting Cycle and the Cycle Reviewed

Pre-Game Tips: The post-closing trial balance lists the accounts of the ledger after all closing entries have been posted. Only permanent accounts remain, and all temporary accounts now have a zero balance. The title "Income Summary" is used only in the closing process and thus never ends up on the post-closing trial balance.

Pre-Game Checkup
Answer true or false to the following statements.

1. Income Summary is listed on the post-closing trial balance.
2. Interim reports are always prepared each month.
3. Capital on the post-closing trial balance is the beginning balance for the next accounting cycle.
4. Accumulated Depreciation is a temporary account.
5. Supplies on the post-closing trial balance represent the amount of supplies used up.

CHECK YOUR SCORE: Answers to the Pre-Game Checkup

LU 5-1
1. True.
2. False—After posting, Accumulated Depreciation has a credit balance.
3. False—Adjustments on a worksheet have to be journalized and posted.
4. False—After the adjustment is posted, Prepaid Rent shows the amount that has not expired yet.
5. False—Depreciation Expense is an expense.

Chapter Summary

Here are all the key concepts and equations to help you understand the concepts of this chapter and prepare you for your exam. After completing this review, go to MyAccountingLab for more practice opportunities.

MyAccountingLab

Concepts You Should Know	Key Terms	
Journalizing and posting adjusting entries. 1. After formal financial statements have been prepared, the ledger has still not been brought up-to-date. 2. Information for journalizing adjusting entries comes from the adjustments section of the worksheet.	Adjusting journal entries (p. 162)	● **L01**
Journalizing and posting closing entries. 1. Closing is a mechanical process that aids the accountant in recording transactions for the next period. 2. Assets, Liabilities, and Capital are permanent (real) accounts; their balances are carried over from one accounting period to another. Withdrawals, Revenue, and Expenses are temporary (nominal) accounts; their balances are not carried over from one accounting period to another. 3. Income Summary is a temporary account in the general ledger and does not have a normal balance. It will summarize revenue and expenses and transfer the balance to Capital. Withdrawals do not go into Income Summary. 4. All information for closing can be obtained from the worksheet or ledger. 5. When closing is complete, all temporary accounts in the ledger will have a zero balance, and all this information will be updated in the Capital account.	Closing journal entries (p. 166) Income Summary (p. 166) Permanent (real) accounts (p. 166) Temporary (nominal) accounts (p. 166)	● **L02**
Preparing a post-closing trial balance. 1. Closing entries are usually done only at year-end. Interim reports can be prepared from worksheets that are prepared monthly, quarterly, or at some other regular interval. 2. The post-closing trial balance is prepared from the ledger accounts after the adjusting and closing entries have been posted. 3. The accounts on the post-closing trial balance are all permanent titles.	Post-closing trial balance (p. 176)	● **L03**

Discussion and Critical Thinking Questions/Ethical Case

1. When a worksheet is completed, what balances are found in the general ledger?

2. Why must adjusting entries be journalized even though the formal statements have already been prepared?

3. "Closing slows down the recording of next year's transactions." Defend or reject this statement with supporting evidence.

4. What is the difference between temporary and permanent accounts?

5. What are the two major goals of the closing process?

6. List the four steps of closing.

7. What is the purpose of Income Summary and where is it located?

8. How can a worksheet aid the closing process?

9. What accounts are usually listed on a post-closing trial balance?

10. Closing entries are always prepared once a month. Agree or disagree? Why?

11. Todd Silver is the purchasing agent for Moore Co. One of his suppliers, Gem Co., offers Todd a free vacation to France if he buys at least 75% of Moore's supplies from Gem Co. Todd, who is angry because Moore Co. has not given him a raise in over a year, is considering the offer. Write your recommendation to Todd.

Concept Checks

MyAccountingLab

● **L01** *(5 MIN)*

Journalizing and Posting Adjusting Entries

1. Post the following adjusting entries that came from the adjustments section of the worksheet to the T accounts and be sure to cross-reference back to the journal. (Use Figure 5.22.)

LEDGER ACCOUNTS BEFORE ADJUSTING ENTRIES POSTED

Prepaid Insurance 115	Insurance Expense 510
105	
Store Supplies 116	**Dep. Exp., Store Equip. 512**
75	
Acc. Dep., Store Equip. 119	**Supplies Expense 514**
52	
Salaries Payable 210	**Salaries Expense 516**
	95

General Journal			Page 3			

FIGURE 5.22
Journalized Adjusting Entries

Date		Account Titles and Description	PR	Dr.	Cr.
Aug.	31	Insurance Expense		8 00	
		Prepaid Insurance			8 00
	31	Supplies Expense		2 5 00	
		Store Supplies			2 5 00
	31	Depr. Exp., Store Equipment		1 5 00	
		Accum. Depr., Store Equipment			1 5 00
	31	Salaries Expense		8 2 00	
		Salaries Payable			8 2 00

Steps of Closing and Journalizing Closing Entries

L02 *(10 MIN)*

2. Explain the four steps of the closing process given the following:

Aug. 31 ending balance, before closing	
Fees Earned	$1,000
Rent Expense	150
Advertising Expense	110
J. Roulette, Capital	5,000
J. Roulette, Withdrawals	50

Journalizing Closing Entries

L02 *(15 MIN)*

3. From the following accounts, journalize the closing entries (assume January 31).

Max Benson, Capital 310
	250

Max Benson, Withdr. 312
105	

Income Summary 314

Taxi Fees 410
	115

Gas Expense 510
5	

Advertising Exp. 512
101	

Dep. Exp., Taxi 516
6	

Posting to Income Summary

L02 *(10 MIN)*

4. Draw a T account of Income Summary and post to it all entries from Question 3 that affect it. Is Income Summary a temporary or permanent account?

Posting to Capital

L02 *(10 MIN)*

5. Draw a T account for Max Benson, Capital, and post to it all entries from Question 3 that affect it. What is the final balance of the Capital account?

Exercises

● **L01** *(15 MIN)*   **Set A**

5A-1. From the adjustments section of a worksheet presented in Figure 5.23, prepare adjusting journal entries for the end of July.

FIGURE 5.23
Adjustments on Worksheet

	Adjustments	
	Dr.	Cr.
Prepaid Rent		(A) 1 2 0 0 00
Office Supplies		(B) 3 5 0 00
Accumulated Depreciation, Equipment		(C) 2 2 5 00
Salaries Payable		(D) 4 0 0 00
Rent Expense	(A) 1 2 0 0 00	
Office Supplies Expense	(B) 3 5 0 00	
Depreciation Expense, Equipment	(C) 2 2 5 00	
Salaries Expense	(D) 4 0 0 00	
	2 1 7 5 00	2 1 7 5 00

●● **L01, 2** *(10 MIN)*   **5A-2.** Complete the following table by placing an X in the correct column.

	Temporary	Permanent	Will Be Closed
Ex. Accounts Receivable		X	
1. Income Summary			
2. Jen Rich, Capital			
3. Salary Expense			
4. Jen Rich, Withdrawals			
5. Fees Earned			
6. Accounts Payable			
7. Cash			

● **L02** *(15 MIN)*   **5A-3.** From the following T accounts, journalize the four closing entries on December 31, 201X.

J. Konnor, Capital		Rent Expense	
	18,800	7,000	

J. Konnor, Withdrawals		Wage Expense	
2,500		8,200	

Income Summary		Insurance Expense	
		2,800	

Fees Earned		Dep. Expense, Office Equipment	
	40,000	2,800	

5A-4. From the following posted T accounts, reconstruct the closing journal entries for July 31, 201X.

LO2 *(20 MIN)*

M. Fitzgerald, Capital

Withdrawals 1,700	5,000 (July 1)
	1,000 Net Income

M. Fitzgerald, Withdrawals

1,700	Closing 1,700

Income Summary

Expenses 2,800	Revenue 3,800
Closing 1,000	

Salon Fees

Closing 3,800	3,800

Insurance Expense

250	Closing 250

Wage Expense

900	Closing 900

Rent Expense

1,400	Closing 1,400

Depreciation Expense, Equipment

250	Closing 250

5A-5. From the following accounts (not in order), prepare a post-closing trial balance for Winter Co. on October 31, 201X. *Note:* These balances are *before* closing.

LO3 *(20 MIN)*

Accounts Receivable	$19,950	P. Winter, Capital	$45,300
Legal Supplies	9,700	P. Winter, Withdrawals	3,000
Office Equipment	54,400	Legal Fees Earned	28,000
Repair Expense	2,700	Accounts Payable	48,000
Salaries Expense	1,550	Cash	30,000

Set B

5B-1. From the adjustments section of a worksheet presented in Figure 5.24, prepare adjusting journal entries for the end of January.

LO1 *(15 MIN)*

FIGURE 5.24
Adjustments Section of Worksheet

Adjustments	Dr.	Cr.
Prepaid Rent		(A) 17 00
Office Supplies		(B) 5 00
Accumulated Depreciation, Equipment		(C) 4 25
Salaries Payable		(D) 10 00
Rent Expense	(A) 17 00	
Office Supplies Expense	(B) 5 00	
Depreciation Expense, Equipment	(C) 4 25	
Salaries Expense	(D) 10 00	
	36 25	36 25

LO1, 2 *(10 MIN)*   **5B-2.** Complete the following table by placing an X in the correct column.

		Temporary	Permanent	Will Be Closed
Ex.	Accounts Receivable		X	
1.	Income Summary			
2.	Jan Ralls, Capital			
3.	Rent Expense			
4.	Jan Ralls, Withdrawals			
5.	Fees Earned			
6.	Accounts Payable			
7.	Cash			

LO2 *(15 MIN)*   **5B-3.** From the following T accounts, journalize the four closing entries on January 31, 201X.

J. Kris, Capital		Rent Expense	
	37,000	10,000	

J. Kris, Withdrawals		Wage Expense	
5,000		8,300	

Income Summary		Insurance Expense	
		1,300	

Fees Earned		Depr. Expense, Office Equipment	
	42,000	2,500	

LO2 *(20 MIN)*   **5B-4.** From the following posted T accounts, reconstruct the closing journal entries for December 31, 201X.

M. Ferron, Capital		Insurance Expense	
Withdrawals 700	4,000 (Dec. 1)	275	Closing 275
	2,425 Net Income		

M. Ferron, Withdrawals		Wage Expense	
700	Closing 700	200	Closing 200

Income Summary		Rent Expense	
Expenses 2,375	Revenue 4,800	1,400	Closing 1,400
Closing 2,425			

Salon Fees		Depreciation Expense, Equipment	
Closing 4,800	4,800	500	Closing 500

5B-5. From the following accounts (not in order), prepare a post-closing trial balance for Winter Co. on October 31, 201X. *Note:* These balances are *before* closing.

● **L03** (20 MIN)

Accounts Receivable	$ 28,500	P. Winter, Capital	$ 47,790
Legal Supplies	5,300	P. Winter, Withdrawals	6,000
Office Equipment	28,500	Legal Fees Earned	8,000
Repair Expense	1,740	Accounts Payable	47,000
Salaries Expense	1,750	Cash	31,000

Problems

MyAccountingLab

Set A

●●**L01, 2** (40 MIN)

5A-1. Consider the data in Figure 5.25 for Daisy's Dance Studio:

DAISY'S DANCE STUDIO
TRIAL BALANCE
SEPTEMBER 30, 201X

	Dr.	Cr.
Cash	60 00 00	
Accounts Receivable	11 00 00	
Prepaid Insurance	8 00 00	
Dance Supplies	1 40 00	
Dance Equipment	19 00 00	
Accumulated Depreciation, Dance Equipment		10 20 00
Accounts Payable		18 00 00
D. Dalia, Capital		45 50 00
D. Dalia, Withdrawals	4 00 00	
Dance Fees Earned		21 80 00
Salaries Expense	1 70 00	
Telephone Expense	7 00 00	
Advertising Expense	5 00 00	
	95 50 00	95 50 00

FIGURE 5.25
Trial Balance for Daisy's Dance Studio

Check Figure:
Net Income $15,500

Adjustment Data

a. Insurance expired, $100.
b. Dance supplies on hand, $1,100.
c. Depreciation on dance equipment, $2,000.
d. Salaries earned by employees but not to be paid until October, $1,000.

Your task is to do the following:

1. Prepare a worksheet.
2. Journalize adjusting and closing entries.

L01, 2, 3

(35 MIN)

Check Figure:
Post-closing
trial balance $4,094

5A-2. Enter the beginning balance in each account in your working papers from the Trial Balance columns of the worksheet (Figure 5.26, p. 199). From that worksheet, (1) journalize and post adjusting and closing entries and (2) prepare from the ledger a post-closing trial balance for the month of January.

5A-3. As the bookkeeper of Parker's Plowing, you have been asked to complete the entire accounting cycle for Parker from the following information.

L01, 2, 3

(150 MIN)

PT/QB

201X		
Jan.	1	Parker invested $14,000 cash and $9,000 worth of snow equipment into the plowing company.
	1	Paid rent for five months in advance for garage space, $3,500.
	4	Purchased office equipment on account from Liliis Corp., $12,600.
	6	Purchased snow supplies for $500 cash.
	8	Collected $15,000 from plowing local shopping centers.
	12	Parker Muroney withdrew $5,000 from the business for his own personal use.
	20	Plowed Holiday Co. parking lots, payment not to be received until March, $7,000.
	26	Paid salaries to employees, $1,400.
	28	Paid Liliis Corp. one-half amount owed for office equipment.
	29	Advertising bill received from Carter Co. but will not be paid until March, $600.
	30	Paid telephone bill, $200.

Use the following chart of accounts.

Chart of Accounts

Assets	Owner's Equity
111 Cash	311 Parker Muroney, Capital
112 Accounts Receivable	312 Parker Muroney, Withdrawals
114 Prepaid Rent	313 Income Summary
115 Snow Supplies	**Revenue**
121 Office Equipment	411 Plowing Fees
122 Accumulated Depreciation, Office Equipment	**Expenses**
123 Snow Equipment	511 Salaries Expense
124 Accumulated Depreciation Snow Equipment	512 Advertising Expense
Liabilities	513 Telephone Expense
211 Accounts Payable	514 Rent Expense
212 Salaries Payable	515 Snow Supplies Expense
	516 Depreciation Expense, Office Equipment
	517 Depreciation Expense, Snow Equipment

Problem 5A-3 continued on p. 200.

FIGURE 5.26
Worksheet for Palmer Cleaning Service

PALMER CLEANING SERVICE
WORKSHEET
FOR MONTH ENDED JANUARY 31, 201X

Account Titles	Trial Balance Dr.	Trial Balance Cr.	Adjustments Dr.	Adjustments Cr.	Adjusted Trial Balance Dr.	Adjusted Trial Balance Cr.	Income Statement Dr.	Income Statement Cr.	Balance Sheet Dr.	Balance Sheet Cr.
Cash	50000				50000				50000	
Prepaid Insurance	52000			(A) 26000	26000				26000	
Cleaning Supplies	29000			(B) 24600	4400				4400	
Auto	329000				329000				329000	
Accum. Depr., Auto		46000		(C) 75000		121000				121000
Accounts Payable		38400				38400				38400
B. Palmer, Capital		44100				44100				44100
B. Palmer, Withdrawals	101000				101000				101000	
Cleaning Fees		586000				586000		586000		
Salaries Expense	99000		(D) 16000		115000		115000			
Telephone Expense	11000				11000		11000			
Advertising Expense	22500				22500		22500			
Gas Expense	21000				21000		21000			
	714500	714500								
Insurance Expense			(A) 26000		26000		26000			
Cleaning Supplies Expense			(B) 24600		24600		24600			
Depr. Expense, Auto			(C) 75000		75000		75000			
Salaries Payable				(D) 16000		16000				16000
			141600	141600	805500	805500	295100	586000	510400	219500
Net Income							290900			290900
							586000	586000	510400	510400

Adjustment Data

a. Snow supplies on hand, $400.
b. Rent expired, $700.
c. Depreciation on office equipment, $210: ($12,600/5 yr. = $2,520/12 mo. = $210).
d. Depreciation on snow equipment, $150: ($9,000/5 yr. = $1,800/12 mo. = $150).
e. Accrued salaries, $380.

MyAccountingLab

LO1, 2 *(40 MIN)*

Set B

5B-1.

MEMO

TO: *Matt Kaminsky*

FROM: *Abby Ellen*

RE: *Accounting Needs*

Please prepare ASAP from the following information (Figure 5.27 on the following page) (1) a worksheet along with (2) journalized adjusting and closing entries.

Adjustment Data

a. Insurance expired, $700.
b. Dance supplies on hand, $300.
c. Depreciation on dance equipment, $400.
d. Salaries earned by employees but not due to be paid until October, $1,000.

FIGURE 5.27
Trial Balance for Daisy's
Dance Studio

DAISY'S DANCE STUDIO TRIAL BALANCE SEPTEMBER 30, 201X		
	Dr.	Cr.
Cash	30 00 00	
Accounts Receivable	8 00 00	
Prepaid Insurance	8 00 00	
Dance Supplies	1 00 00	
Dance Equipment	21 00 00	
Accumulated Depreciation, Dance Equipment		8 90 00
Accounts Payable		27 00 00
D. Dalia, Capital		4 50 00
D. Dalia, Withdrawals	9 00 00	
Dance Fees Earned		23 80 00
Salaries Expense	1 10 00	
Telephone Expense	5 00 00	
Advertising Expense	9 00 00	
	64 20 00	64 20 00

LO1, 2 *(35 MIN)*

5B-2. Enter the beginning balance in each account in your working papers from the Trial Balance columns of the worksheet (Figure 5.28, p. 201). From the worksheet, (1) journalize and post adjusting and closing entries and (2) prepare from the ledger a post-closing trial balance at the end of September.

FIGURE 5.28
Worksheet for Palmer Cleaning Service

PALMER CLEANING SERVICE
WORKSHEET
FOR MONTH ENDED JANUARY 31, 201X

Account Titles	Trial Balance Dr.	Trial Balance Cr.	Adjustments Dr.	Adjustments Cr.	Adjusted Trial Balance Dr.	Adjusted Trial Balance Cr.	Income Statement Dr.	Income Statement Cr.	Balance Sheet Dr.	Balance Sheet Cr.
Cash	50000				50000				50000	
Prepaid Insurance	74000			(A) 31000	43000				43000	
Cleaning Supplies	32600			(B) 15200	17400				17400	
Auto	357000				357000				357000	
Accumulated Depreciation, Auto		44000		(C) 85000		129000				129000
Accounts Payable		61000				61000				61000
B. Palmer, Capital		193600				193600				193600
B. Palmer, Withdrawals	71000				71000				71000	
Cleaning Fees		468000				468000		468000		
Salaries Expense	105000		(D) 21000		126000		126000			
Telephone Expense	17000				17000		17000			
Advertising Expense	31000				31000		31000			
Gas Expense	29000				29000		29000			
	766600	766600								
Insurance Expense			(A) 31000		31000		31000			
Cleaning Supplies Expense			(B) 15200		15200		15200			
Depreciation Expense, Auto			(C) 85000		85000		85000			
Salaries Payable				(D) 21000		21000				21000
			152200	152200	872600	872600	334200	468000	538400	404600
Net Loss							133800			133800
							468000	468000	538400	538400

L01, 2, 3
(150 MIN)

PT/QB

Check Figure:
Net Income $10,880

5B-3. From the following transactions as well as additional data, please complete the entire accounting cycle for Parker's Plowing (use the chart of accounts for 5A-3).

201X

Jan.	1	Parker invested $10,000 cash and $12,000 worth of snow equipment into the plowing company.
	1	Paid rent for six months in advance for garage space, $6,000.
	4	Purchased office equipment on account from Lumen Corp., $12,600.
	6	Purchased snow supplies for $800 cash.
	8	Collected $14,000 from plowing local shopping centers.
	12	Parker Muroney withdrew $4,000 from the business for his own personal use.
	20	Plowed Alton Co. parking lots, payment not to be received until May, $1,500.
	26	Paid salaries to employees, $1,900.
	28	Paid Lumen Corp. one-half amount owed for office equipment.
	29	Advertising bill received from Washington Co. but will not be paid until May, $700.
	30	Paid telephone bill, $130.

Adjustment Data

a. Snow supplies on hand, $700.

b. Rent expired, $1,000.

c. Depreciation on office equipment, $210: ($12,600/5 yr = $2,520/12 mo. = $210).

d. Depreciation on snow equipment, $200: ($12,000/5 yr = $2,400/12 mo. = $200).

e. Accrued salaries, $380.

Financial Report Problem

L03 *(15 MIN)*

Reading the Kellogg's Annual Report

Go to http://investor.kelloggs.com/annuals.cfm, to access the Kellogg's 2010 Annual Report and find Note 1 in Basis of Presentation. What is the fiscal year for Kellogg's Company?

MyAccountingLab

the JOB ||||||||||||||||||||||||||

L01, 2, 3
(60 MIN)

SANCHEZ COMPUTER CENTER

Tony decided to end the Sanchez Computer Center's first year as of September 30, 201X. Following is an updated chart of accounts.

Assets	Revenue
1000 Cash	4000 Service Revenue
1020 Accounts Receivable	**Expenses**
1025 Prepaid Rent	5010 Advertising Expense
1030 Supplies	5020 Rent Expense
1080 Computer Shop Equip.	5030 Utilities Expense
1081 Accum. Depr., C.S. Equip.	5040 Phone Expense
1090 Office Equipment	5050 Supplies Expense
1091 Accum. Depr., Office Equip.	5060 Insurance Expense
Liabilities	5070 Postage Expense
2000 Accounts Payable	5080 Depr. Exp., C.S. Equip.

Assets	Revenue
Owner's Equity	5090 Depr. Exp., Office Equip.
3000 T. Freedman, Capital	
3010 T. Freedman, Withdrawals	
3020 Income Summary	

Assignment

1. Journalize the adjusting entries from Chapter 4.
2. Post the adjusting entries to the ledger.
3. Journalize the closing entries.
4. Post the closing entries to the ledger.
5. Prepare a post-closing trial balance.

SUBWAY CASE

Closing Time

●● **L02, 3** *(20 MIN)*

"You wait and see," Stan told his new sandwich artist Wanda Kurtz. "Everything will fall into place soon." Wanda had a tough time serving customers quickly enough, and Stan was in the middle of giving her a pep talk when the phone rang.

"I'll let the machine pick up," Stan reassured Wanda, as he proceeded to train her in some crucial POS touch-screen maneuvers.

"Stan!" an urgent voice came over the message machine. "I think you've forgotten something!" Stan picked up the phone and said, "Lila, can I get back to you tomorrow? I'm in the middle of an important talk with Wanda." One of Stan's strong points as an employer was his ability to focus 100 percent on his employees' concerns. Yet, Lila simply would not wait.

"Stan," Lila said impatiently, "you absolutely must get me your worksheet by noon tomorrow so I can close your books. Tomorrow's the 31st of March and we close on the last day of the month!"

"*Ay caramba!*" Stan sighed. "Looks like I'm going to be up till the wee hours," he confided to Wanda when he put down the phone.

Although Subway company policy doesn't require a closing every month, closing the books is a key part of their accounting training for all new franchisees. By closing their books, business owners can clearly measure their net profit and loss for each period separate from all other periods. This practice makes activities such as budgeting and comparing performance with similar businesses (or performance over time) possible.

At 9:00 A.M. the next morning, an exhausted Stan opened up the restaurant and e-mailed his worksheet to Lila. He was feeling quite pleased with himself—that is, until he heard Lila's urgent-sounding voice coming over the message machine 10 minutes later.

"I've been over and over this," said Lila after Stan picked up, "and I can't get it to balance. I know it's hard for you to do this during working hours, but I need you to go back over the figures."

Stan opened up Peachtree and pored over his worksheets. Errors are hard to find when closing the books and, unfortunately, the process doesn't offer a set way to detect errors or any set place to start. Stan chose payroll because it is one of the largest expenses and because of the new hire.

At 11:45 he called Lila, who sounded both exasperated and relieved to hear from him. "I think I've got it! It looks like I messed up on adjusting the Salaries Expense account. I looked at the payroll register and compared the total to the Salaries Payable account. It didn't match! When I hired Wanda Kurtz on the 26th, I should have increased both the Salaries Expense and the Salaries Payable lines because she has accrued wages."

"Yes," said Lila, "Salaries Expense is a debit and Salaries Payable is a credit, and you skipped the payable. Great! With this adjusting entry in the general journal, the worksheet will balance."

Stan's sigh of relief turned into a big yawn, and they both laughed. "I guess I just find it easier to hire people and train them than to account for them," said Stan.

Discussion Questions

1. How would the adjustment be made if Wanda Kurtz received $7.00 per hour and worked 25 additional hours? Where do you place her accrued wages?
2. Stan bought three new Subway aprons and hats for Wanda Smith for $20 each but forgot to post it to the Uniforms account. How much will the closing balance be off? In what way will it be off?
3. Put yourself in Stan's shoes: What is the value of doing a monthly closing, no matter how much—or little—business you do?

Mini Practice Set

Sullivan Realty

Est Time 5 hours

Reviewing the Accounting Cycle Twice

This comprehensive review problem requires you to complete the accounting cycle for Sullivan Realty twice. This practice set allows you to review Chapters 1–5 while reinforcing the relationships between all parts of the accounting cycle. By completing two cycles, you will see how the ending June balances in the ledger are used to accumulate data in July.

First, look at the chart of accounts for Sullivan Realty.

Sullivan Realty
Chart of Accounts

Assets	Revenue
111 Cash	411 Commissions Earned
112 Accounts Receivable	**Expenses**
114 Prepaid Rent	511 Rent Expense
115 Office Supplies	512 Salaries Expense
121 Office Equipment	513 Gas Expense
122 Accumulated Depreciation, Office Equipment	514 Repairs Expense
123 Automobile	515 Telephone Expense
124 Accumulated Depreciation, Automobile	516 Advertising Expense
Liabilities	517 Office Supplies Expense
211 Accounts Payable	518 Depreciation Expense, Office Equipment
212 Salaries Payable	519 Depreciation Expense, Automobile
Owner's Equity	524 Miscellaneous Expense
311 John Sullivan, Capital	
312 John Sullivan, Withdrawals	
313 Income Summary	

On June 1, 201X, John Sullivan opened a real estate office called Sullivan Realty. The following transactions were completed for the month of June:

201X

June   1   John Sullivan invested $9,000 cash in the real estate agency along with $4,000 of office equipment.

June   1   Rented and paid three months rent in advance to Miller Property Management, $3,000.

June   1   Bought an automobile on account from Volvo West, $14,000.

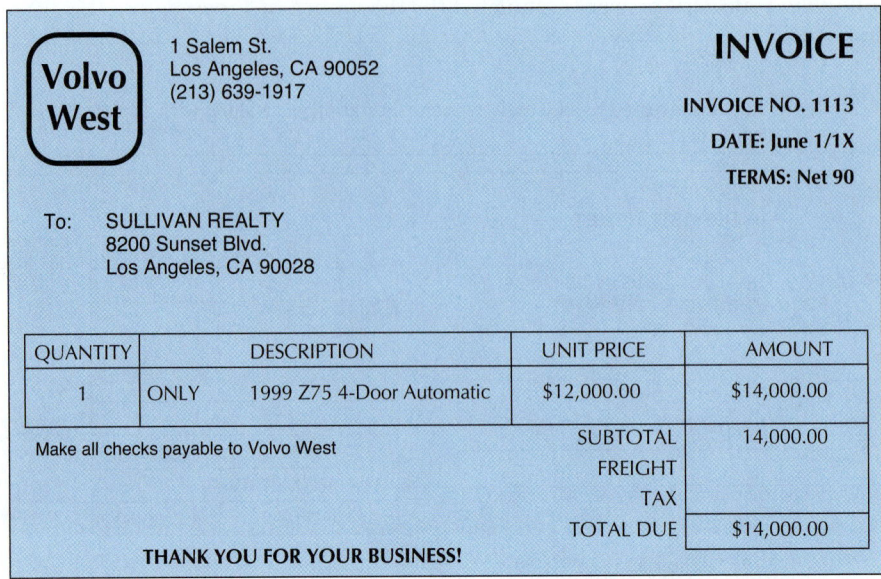

	Volvo West	1 Salem St. Los Angeles, CA 90052 (213) 639-1917		**INVOICE**

INVOICE NO. 1113

DATE: June 1/1X

TERMS: Net 90

To: SULLIVAN REALTY
        8200 Sunset Blvd.
        Los Angeles, CA 90028

QUANTITY	DESCRIPTION		UNIT PRICE	AMOUNT
1	ONLY	1999 Z75 4-Door Automatic	$12,000.00	$14,000.00

Make all checks payable to Volvo West

SUBTOTAL	14,000.00
FREIGHT	
TAX	
TOTAL DUE	$14,000.00

THANK YOU FOR YOUR BUSINESS!

June   4   Purchased office supplies from Office Supply Direct for cash, $300.

Office Supply Direct   **INVOICE**

1 Ferncroft Rd.
Los Angeles, CA 90052
Phone (213) 631-0288

DATE: June 4/1X
NUMBER: D198795
TERMS: Cash

SOLD TO:	SHIPPED TO:
Sullivan Realty 8200 Sunset Blvd. Los Angeles, CA 90028	Sullivan Realty 8200 Sunset Blvd. Los Angeles, CA 90028

DATE	DESCRIPTION	UNIT PRICE	AMOUNT
Jun 4/1X	Office supplies PAYMENT RECEIVED - - CHK #0002 - THANK YOU		$300.00
		Subtotal	300.00
		Total	$300.00

Business Number: 115555559

THANK YOU FOR YOUR BUSINESS

PLEASE PAY
THE ABOVE

SULLIVAN REALTY (213) 478-3584	0002

8200 SUNSET BOULEVARD
LOS ANGELES, CA 90028

June 4   201X

PAY TO THE
ORDER OF   Office Supply Direct $ 300 XX/100

Three Hundred and XX/100   DOLLARS

BAY BANK
Box 1739 Terminal Annex
Los Angeles, CA 90052

MEMO   Office supplies   *John Sullivan*

June   5   Purchased additional office supplies from Office Supply Direct on account, $150.

Office Supply Direct   **INVOICE**

1 Ferncroft Rd.
Los Angeles, CA 90052   **DATE:**   June 5/1X
Phone (213) 631-0288   **NUMBER:**   D198825
                                        TERMS: net 60

SOLD TO:	SHIPPED TO:
Sullivan Realty 8200 Sunset Blvd. Los Angeles, CA 90028	Sullivan Realty 8200 Sunset Blvd. Los Angeles, CA 90028

DATE	DESCRIPTION	UNIT PRICE	AMOUNT
Jun 5/1X	Office supplies		$150.00
		Subtotal	150.00
		Total	$150.00

Business Number: 115555559

PLEASE PAY
THE ABOVE

THANK YOU FOR YOUR BUSINESS

June   6   Sold a house to Bill Barnes and collected a $6,000 commission.

—| **DEPOSIT TICKET** |—

SULLIVAN REALTY (213)478-3584
8200 SUNSET BOULEVARD
Los Angeles, CA 90028

CASH	CURRENCY		
	COIN		
LIST CHECKS SINGLY 250-99		6,000	00
TOTAL FROM OTHER SIDE			
TOTAL			
LESS CASH RECEIVED			
NET DEPOSIT		6,000	00

16-66/1220

A hold for uncollected funds may be placed on funds deposited by check or similar instruments. This could delay your ability to withdraw such funds. The delay if any would not exceed the period of time permitted by law.

DATE   June 6   201X

SIGN HERE IN PRESENCE OF TELLER FOR CASH RET'D FROM DEP.

BAY BANK
Box 1739 Terminal Annex
Los Angeles, CA 90052

⑆122000661⑆1400॥03857॥013621॥

SULLIVAN REALTY COMMISSION REPORT				*Date:* June 6, 201X
Name: Bill Barnes				
Date:	*Sales Description*	*Sales No.*	*Commission Amount*	
Jun 6/1X	Home at 66 Sullivan St.	A1001	$6,000.00	*Paid in full.*
C001		*Remarks:*		

June   8   Paid gas bill to Petro Petroleum, $22.

SULLIVAN REALTY (213) 478-3584	0003
8200 SUNSET BOULEVARD LOS ANGELES, CA 90028	June 8 201X

PAY TO THE ORDER OF _Petro Petroleum_ $ 22 XX/100

Twenty-two and XX/100 ————————————————————— DOLLARS

BAY BANK
Box 1739 Terminal Annex
Los Angeles, CA 90052

MEMO _Gas Bill – June 6_   _John Sullivan_

June   15   Paid Betty Long, office secretary, $350.

SULLIVAN REALTY (213) 478-3584	0004
8200 SUNSET BOULEVARD LOS ANGELES, CA 90028	June 15 201X

PAY TO THE ORDER OF _Betty Long_ $ 350 XX/100

Three Hundred fifty and XX/100 ———————————————— DOLLARS

BAY BANK
Box 1739 Terminal Annex
Los Angeles, CA 90052

MEMO _Salary – June 1–15_   _John Sullivan_

June   17   Sold a building lot to West Land Developers and earned a commission, $6,500; payment to be received on July 8.

SULLIVAN REALTY **COMMISSION REPORT**			**Date:**	June 17, 201X	
Name: West Land Developers					
Date:	**Sales Description**	**Sales No.**	**Commission Amount**		
Jun 17/1X	Lot at 8 Ridge Rd.	A1002	$6,500.00		
C002		**Remarks:** Payment due July 8, 201X			

June 20 John Sullivan withdrew $1,000 from the business to pay personal expenses.

SULLIVAN REALTY (213) 478-3584   0005

8200 SUNSET BOULEVARD
LOS ANGELES, CA 90028   *June 20*   *201X*

PAY TO THE
ORDER OF *John Sullivan* $ *1,000 XX/100*

One Thousand and XX/100 ———————— DOLLARS

BAY BANK
Box 1739 Terminal Annex
Los Angeles, CA 90052

MEMO *Withdrawal*   *John Sullivan*

June 21 Sold a house to Laura Harrison and collected a $3,500 commission.

— DEPOSIT TICKET —

SULLIVAN REALTY (213)478-3584
8200 SUNSET BOULEVARD
Los Angeles, CA 90028

DATE *June 21* *201X*

SIGN HERE IN PRESENCE OF TELLER FOR CASH RET'D FROM DEP.

BAY BANK
Box 1739 Terminal Annex
Los Angeles, CA 90052

CASH	CURRENCY		
	COIN		
LIST CHECKS SINGLY 270-88		3,500	00
TOTAL FROM OTHER SIDE			
TOTAL			
LESS CASH RECEIVED			
NET DEPOSIT		3,500	00

16-66/1220

A hold for uncollected funds may be placed on funds deposited by check or similar instruments. This could delay your ability to withdraw such funds. The delay if any would not exceed the period of time permitted by law.

⑆ 1 2 2 0 0 0 6 6 ⑈ 1 4 0 0 ⑆ 0 3 8 5 7 ⑆ 0 1 3 6 2 ⑈

SULLIVAN REALTY
     COMMISSION REPORT   *Date:*   June 21, 201X

Name: Ms. Laura Harrison

Date:	*Sales Description*	*Sales No.*	*Commission Amount*	
Jun 21/1X	Home at 666 Jersey St.	A1003	$3,500.00	Paid in full.
C003			*Remarks:*	

June   22   Paid gas bill, $25, to Petro Petroleum.

SULLIVAN REALTY (213) 478-3584   0006

8200 SUNSET BOULEVARD   *June 22*   *201X*
LOS ANGELES, CA 90028

PAY TO THE
ORDER OF *Petro Petroleum* $ *25 XX/100*

Twenty-five and XX/100 ————————————————————— DOLLARS

BAY BANK
Box 1739 Terminal Annex
Los Angeles, CA 90052

MEMO *Gas Bill–June 22*   *John Sullivan*

June   24   Paid Volvo West $600 to repair automobile.

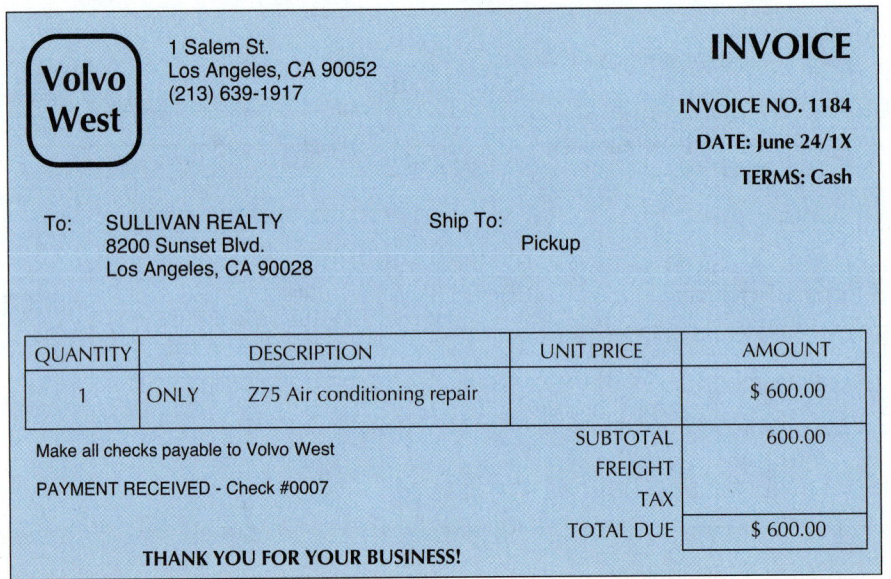

INVOICE

Volvo West
1 Salem St.
Los Angeles, CA 90052
(213) 639-1917

INVOICE NO. 1184
DATE: June 24/1X
TERMS: Cash

To: SULLIVAN REALTY   Ship To:
       8200 Sunset Blvd.
       Los Angeles, CA 90028   Pickup

QUANTITY	DESCRIPTION	UNIT PRICE	AMOUNT
1	ONLY Z75 Air conditioning repair		$ 600.00

Make all checks payable to Volvo West

PAYMENT RECEIVED - Check #0007

SUBTOTAL	600.00
FREIGHT	
TAX	
TOTAL DUE	$ 600.00

THANK YOU FOR YOUR BUSINESS!

SULLIVAN REALTY (213) 478-3584   0007

8200 SUNSET BOULEVARD   *June 24*   *201X*
LOS ANGELES, CA 90028

PAY TO THE
ORDER OF *Volvo West* $ *600 XX/100*

Six Hundred and XX/100 ————————————————————— DOLLARS

BAY BANK
Box 1739 Terminal Annex
Los Angeles, CA 90052

MEMO *Auto Repairs – Inv. 1184*   *John Sullivan*

June 30 Paid Betty Long, office secretary, $350.

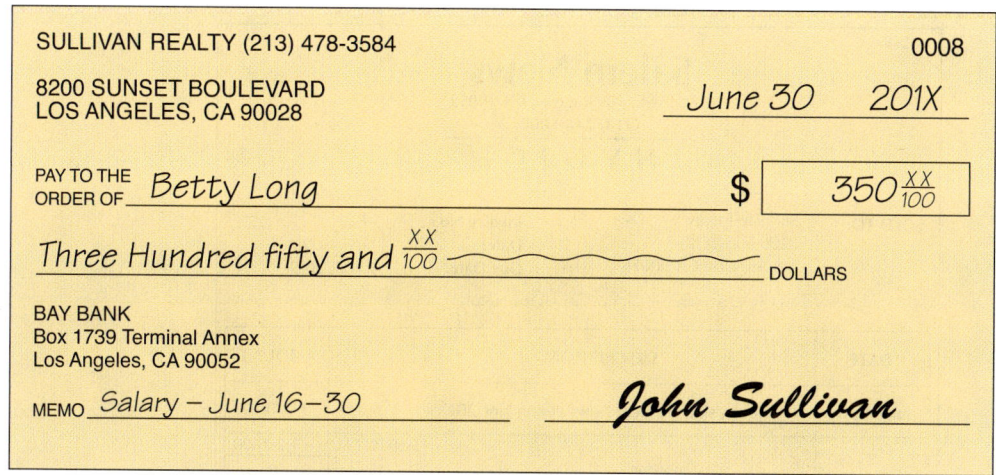

June 30 Paid CellService Inc. June telephone bill, $510.

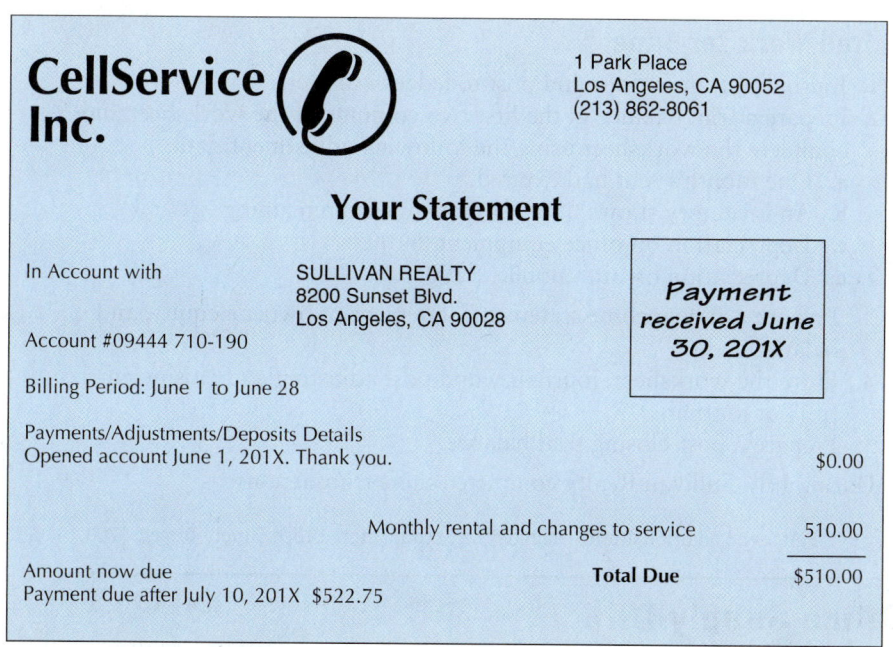

June 30   Received advertising bill for June, $1,200, from Salem News. The bill is to be paid on July 2.

Salem News
1 Main St., Los Angeles, CA 90052
(213) 744-1000
I N V O I C E

SOLD TO:	Sullivan Realty	**Invoice No.:**	4879
	8200 Sunset Blvd.	**Date:**	June 30, 201X
	Los Angeles, CA 90028	**Due Date:**	July 2, 201X

DATE	DESCRIPTION		AMOUNT
June 26/1X	Advertising in Salem News during June 201X		$1,200.00
		SUBTOTAL	1,200.00
Business Number 944122338		TOTAL	$1,200.00

MAKE ALL CHECKS PAYABLE TO SALEM NEWS

Required Work for June

1. Journalize transactions and post to ledger accounts.
2. Prepare a trial balance in the first two columns of the worksheet and complete the worksheet using the following adjustment data:
   a. One month's rent had expired.
   b. An inventory shows $50 of office supplies remaining.
   c. Depreciation on office equipment, $100.
   d. Depreciation on automobile, $200.
3. Prepare a June income statement, statement of owner's equity, and balance sheet.
4. From the worksheet, journalize and post adjusting and closing entries (p. 3 of journal).
5. Prepare a post-closing trial balance.

During July, Sullivan Realty completed these transactions:

Check Figure:
June post closing
trial balance $38,893

July   1   Purchased additional office supplies on account from Office Supply Direct, $700.

Office Supply Direct   INVOICE

1 Ferncroft Rd.
Los Angeles, CA 90052
Phone (213) 631-0288

DATE: Jul 1/1X
NUMBER: D1996035
TERMS: Net 60

SOLD TO:	SHIPPED TO:
Sullivan Realty	Sullivan Realty
8200 Sunset Blvd.	8200 Sunset Blvd.
Los Angeles, CA 90028	Los Angeles, CA 90028

DATE	DESCRIPTION	UNIT PRICE	AMOUNT
Jul 2/1X	Office supplies		$700.00
		Subtotal	700.00
		Total	$700.00

Business Number: 115555559

THANK YOU FOR YOUR BUSINESS

PLEASE PAY
THE ABOVE

July   2   Paid Salem News advertising bill for June.

SULLIVAN REALTY (213) 478-3584	0010
8200 SUNSET BOULEVARD LOS ANGELES, CA 90028	July 2 201X

PAY TO THE
ORDER OF _Salem News_ $ | 1,200 XX/100 |

One Thousand Two Hundred and XX/100 ———————— DOLLARS

BAY BANK
Box 1739 Terminal Annex
Los Angeles, CA 90052

MEMO _Invoice # 4879_   _John Sullivan_

⑆1 2 2000 66 1⑆ 1400 ⑈0 3 85 7⑈ 0 13 6 2⑈0010

July   3   Sold a house to Melissa King and collected a commission of $6,600.

SULLIVAN REALTY					
	COMMISSION REPORT		**Date:**	July 3, 201X	
Name:	Melissa King				
Date:	**Sales Description**	**Sales No.**	**Commission Amount**		
July 3/1X	Home at 800 Rose Ave.	A1004	$6,600.00	Paid in full.	
C004		**Remarks:**			

⊢ **DEPOSIT TICKET** ⊢			
SULLIVAN REALTY (213) 478-3584 8200 SUNSET BOULEVARD Los Angeles, CA 90028	**CASH**	CURRENCY	
		COIN	
	LIST CHECKS SINGLY 278-92	6,600	00
DATE July 3 201X	TOTAL FROM OTHER SIDE		
	TOTAL		
SIGN HERE IN PRESENCE OF TELLER FOR CASH RET'D FROM DEP. →	LESS CASH RECEIVED		
	NET DEPOSIT	6,600	00
BAY BANK Box 1739 Terminal Annex Los Angeles, CA 90052			

16-66/1220

A hold for uncollected funds may be placed on funds deposited by check or similar instruments. This could delay your ability to withdraw such funds. The delay if any would not exceed the period of time permitted by law.

⑆1 2 2000 66 1⑆ 1400 ⑈0 3 85 7⑈ 0 13 6 2⑈

July   6   Paid gas bill to Petro Petroleum, $29.

SULLIVAN REALTY (213) 478-3584   0011

8200 SUNSET BOULEVARD   _July 6_   _201X_
LOS ANGELES, CA 90028

PAY TO THE
ORDER OF _Petro Petroleum_ $ | 29 XX/100 |

Twenty-nine and XX/100 ————————————— DOLLARS

BAY BANK
Box 1739 Terminal Annex
Los Angeles, CA 90052

MEMO _Gas Bill – July 6_   _John Sullivan_

July   8   Collected commission from West Land Developers for sale of building lot on June 17.

⊢ DEPOSIT TICKET ⊢

	CURRENCY		
CASH	COIN		
LIST CHECKS SINGLY 228-114		6,500	00

SULLIVAN REALTY (213) 478-3584
8200 SUNSET BOULEVARD
Los Angeles, CA 90028

16-66/1220

TOTAL FROM OTHER SIDE			
TOTAL			
LESS CASH RECEIVED			
NET DEPOSIT		6,500	00

DATE _____ _July 8_   _201X_ _____

SIGN HERE IN PRESENCE OF TELLER FOR CASH RET'D FROM DEP.

A hold for uncollected funds may be placed on funds deposited by check or similar instruments. This could delay your ability to withdraw such funds. The delay if any would not exceed the period of time permitted by law.

BAY BANK
Box 1739 Terminal Annex
Los Angeles, CA 90052

⑆122000661⑆1400⑈03857⑈0136 2⑈

July   12   Paid $300 to Regan Realtors Assoc. to send employees to realtors' workshop.

SULLIVAN REALTY (213) 478-3584   0012

8200 SUNSET BOULEVARD   _July 12_   _201X_
LOS ANGELES, CA 90028

PAY TO THE
ORDER OF _Regan Realtors Assoc._ $ | 300 XX/100 |

Three Hundred and XX/100 ————————————— DOLLARS

BAY BANK
Box 1739 Terminal Annex
Los Angeles, CA 90052

MEMO _Workshop Registration_   _John Sullivan_

July 15 Paid Betty Long, office secretary, $350.

SULLIVAN REALTY (213) 478-3584	0013
8200 SUNSET BOULEVARD LOS ANGELES, CA 90028	July 15 201X

PAY TO THE ORDER OF _Betty Long_ $ | 350 XX/100

Three Hundred fifty and XX/100 —————————— DOLLARS

BAY BANK
Box 1739 Terminal Annex
Los Angeles, CA 90052

MEMO _Salary July 1–15_   _John Sullivan_

July 17 Sold a house to Matt Karminsky and earned a commission of $2,400. Commission to be received on August 10.

SULLIVAN REALTY **COMMISSION REPORT**			**Date:** July 17, 201X	
Name: Matt Karminsky				
Date:	**Sales Description**	**Sales No.**	**Commission Amount**	
July 17/1X	Home at RR2, Site 3	A1010	$2,400.00	
C005		**Remarks:** Payment due August 10, 201X		

July 18 Sold a building lot to DiBiasi Builders and collected a commission of $7,000.

—⊢ DEPOSIT TICKET ⊢—				
SULLIVAN REALTY (213)478-3584 8200 SUNSET BOULEVARD Los Angeles, CA 90028	CASH	CURRENCY		
		COIN		
	LIST CHECKS SINGLY 269-10	7,000	00	
DATE July 18 201X				16-66/1220
	TOTAL FROM OTHER SIDE			
	TOTAL			
SIGN HERE IN PRESENCE OF TELLER FOR CASH RET'D FROM DEP.	LESS CASH RECEIVED			
BAY BANK Box 1739 Terminal Annex Los Angeles, CA 90052	NET DEPOSIT	7,000	00	

A hold for uncollected funds may be placed on funds deposited by check or similar instruments. This could delay your ability to withdraw such funds. The delay if any would not exceed the period of time permitted by law.

⑈122000661⑈1400⑈03857⑈01362⑈

SULLIVAN REALTY					
	COMMISSION REPORT			Date:	July 18, 201X
Name:	DiBiasi Builders				
Date:	*Sales Description*	*Sales No.*	*Commission Amount*		
July 18/1X	Building lot at 5004 King St. E	A1005	$7,000.00	*Paid in full.*	
C006		*Remarks:*			

July   22   Sent a check to Catholic Charities for $40 to help sponsor a local road race to aid the poor. (This amount is not to be considered an advertising expense; it is a business expense and is posted to Miscellaneous Expense.)

SULLIVAN REALTY (213) 478-3584   0014

8200 SUNSET BOULEVARD   *July 22   201X*
LOS ANGELES, CA 90028

PAY TO THE
ORDER OF   *Catholic Charities* $ 40 $\frac{XX}{100}$

Forty and $\frac{XX}{100}$ _____ DOLLARS

BAY BANK
Box 1739 Terminal Annex
Los Angeles, CA 90052

MEMO *Aid to Poor*   *John Sullivan*

⑆122000661⑈1400⑇03857⑇0136 2⑆0014

July   24   Paid Volvo West $590 for repairs to automobile due to accident.

Volvo West   1 Salem St.
Los Angeles, CA 90052
(213) 639-1917

INVOICE

INVOICE NO. 2119

DATE: July 24/1X

TERMS: Cash

To: SULLIVAN REALTY
8200 Sunset Blvd.
Los Angeles, CA 90028

QUANTITY	DESCRIPTION	UNIT PRICE	AMOUNT
	Accident Repairs		$ 590.00
		SUBTOTAL	590.00
Make all checks payable to Volvo West		FREIGHT	
PAYMENT RECEIVED - Check #0015		TAX	
		TOTAL DUE	$ 590.00

SULLIVAN REALTY (213) 478-3584   0015

8200 SUNSET BOULEVARD
LOS ANGELES, CA 90028   July 24   201X

PAY TO THE
ORDER OF   Volvo West $ 590 XX/100

Five Hundred Ninety and XX/100 ———————————— DOLLARS

BAY BANK
Box 1739 Terminal Annex
Los Angeles, CA 90052

MEMO Auto Repairs – Inv. 2119   John Sullivan

July 28   John Sullivan withdrew $1,800 from the business to pay personal expenses.

SULLIVAN REALTY (213) 478-3584   0016

8200 SUNSET BOULEVARD
LOS ANGELES, CA 90028   July 28   201X

PAY TO THE
ORDER OF   John Sullivan $ 1,800 XX/100

One Thousand Eight hundred and XX/100 ———————————— DOLLARS

BAY BANK
Box 1739 Terminal Annex
Los Angeles, CA 90052

MEMO Withdrawal   John Sullivan

July 30   Paid Betty Long, office secretary, $350.

SULLIVAN REALTY (213) 478-3584   0017

8200 SUNSET BOULEVARD
LOS ANGELES, CA 90028   July 30   201X

PAY TO THE
ORDER OF   Betty Long $ 350 XX/100

Three Hundred fifty and XX/100 ———————————— DOLLARS

BAY BANK
Box 1739 Terminal Annex
Los Angeles, CA 90052

MEMO Salary – July 16–31   John Sullivan

July   30   Paid CellService Inc. telephone bill, $590.

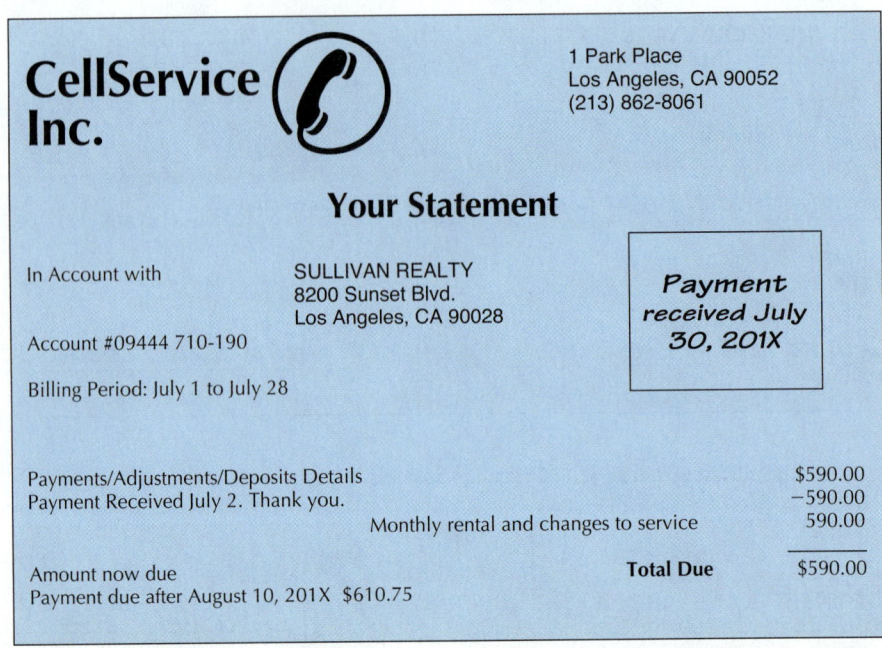

CellService Inc.

1 Park Place
Los Angeles, CA 90052
(213) 862-8061

Your Statement

In Account with

SULLIVAN REALTY
8200 Sunset Blvd.
Los Angeles, CA 90028

Payment received July 30, 201X

Account #09444 710-190

Billing Period: July 1 to July 28

Payments/Adjustments/Deposits Details	$590.00
Payment Received July 2. Thank you.	−590.00
Monthly rental and changes to service	590.00
Total Due	$590.00

Amount now due
Payment due after August 10, 201X $610.75

SULLIVAN REALTY (213) 478-3584   0018

8200 SUNSET BOULEVARD
LOS ANGELES, CA 90028   *July 30   201X*

PAY TO THE
ORDER OF   *CellService Inc.* $ 590 XX/100

Five Hundred Ninety and XX/100 ———————— DOLLARS

BAY BANK
Box 1739 Terminal Annex
Los Angeles, CA 90052

MEMO   *July Phone Bill*   *John Sullivan*

July   30   Advertising bill from *Salem News* for July, $1,400. The bill is to be paid on August 2.

Salem News
1 Main St., Los Angeles, CA 90052
(213) 744-1000
INVOICE

SOLD TO:	Sullivan Realty	Invoice No.:	5400
	8200 Sunset Blvd.	Date:	July 30, 201X
	Los Angeles, CA 90028	Due Date:	August 2, 201X

DATE	DESCRIPTION		AMOUNT
July 30/1X	Advertising in Salem News during July 201X		$1,400.00
		SUBTOTAL	1,400.00
Business Number 944122338		TOTAL	$1,400.00

MAKE ALL CHECKS PAYABLE TO SALEM NEWS

Required Work for July

1. Journalize transactions in a general journal (p. 4) and post to ledger accounts.
2. Prepare a trial balance in the first two columns of a blank, fold-out work-sheet located at the end of your textbook and complete the worksheet using the following adjustment data:
   a. One month's rent had expired.
   b. An inventory shows $90 of office supplies remaining.
   c. Depreciation on office equipment, $100.
   d. Depreciation on automobile, $200.
3. Prepare a July income statement, statement of owner's equity, and balance sheet.
4. From the worksheet, journalize and post adjusting and closing entries (p. 6 of journal).
5. Prepare a post-closing trial balance.

PEACHTREE COMPUTER WORKSHOP

COMPUTERIZED ACCOUNTING APPLICATION FOR CHAPTER 5

Refresher on using Peachtree Complete Accounting

Before starting this assignment, you may want to refresh your memory by reading the following PDF documents in the multimedia library of the MyAccountingLab Web site. Remember to choose the PDF document for your version of Peachtree.

1. An Introduction to Peachtree Complete Accounting
2. Correcting Peachtree Transactions
3. How to Repeat or Restart a Peachtree Assignment
4. Backing Up and Restoring Your Work in Peachtree

You also should have completed the following workshops:

1. Workshop 1 Atlas Company from Chapter 3
2. Workshop 2 Zell Company from Chapter 4

Workshop 3:

Accounting Cycle Mini Practice Set

In this workshop you will complete the June and July accounting cycles for Sullivan Realty using Peachtree. Tasks include posting journal entries and adjusting journal entries, printing reports and financial statements, and closing the accounting period.

Instructions and the data file for completing this assignment are in the multimedia library of the MyAccountingLab Web site. Open the *Workshop 3 Sullivan Realty* PDF document for your version of Peachtree and download the *Sullivan Realty* data file for your version of Peachtree.

QUICKBOOKS COMPUTER WORKSHOP

COMPUTERIZED ACCOUNTING APPLICATION FOR CHAPTER 5

Refresher on using QuickBooks Pro

Before starting this assignment, you may want to refresh your memory by reading the following PDF documents in the multimedia library of the MyAccountingLab Web site. Remember to choose the PDF document for your version of QuickBooks.

1. An Introduction to QuickBooks Pro
2. Correcting QuickBooks Transactions
3. How to Repeat or Restart a QuickBooks Assignment
4. Backing Up and Restoring Your Work in QuickBooks

You also should have completed the following workshops:

1. Workshop 1 Atlas Company from Chapter 3
2. Workshop 2 Zell Company from Chapter 4

Workshop 3:

Accounting Cycle Mini Practice Set

In this workshop you will complete the June and July accounting cycles for Sullivan Realty using QuickBooks. Tasks include posting journal entries and adjusting journal entries, printing reports and financial statements, and closing the accounting period.

Instructions and the data file for completing this assignment are in the multimedia library of the MyAccountingLab Web site. Open the **Workshop 3 Sullivan Realty** PDF document for your version of QuickBooks and download the **Sullivan Realty** data file for your version of QuickBooks.

Banking Procedure and Control of Cash

THE GAME PLAN

Denied. Have you ever been shopping and given the clerk your credit or debit card, only to be told that the transaction has been denied for lack of funds? You cannot understand it since you just sent a check to the credit card company yesterday! You know you have a zero dollar balance on your card but the credit card company shows a negative balance. How could this happen? In this chapter, we will look at banking procedures, the reconciliation of bank statements with company accounting records, and the control of cash. Maintaining accurate records of transactions, rather than just relying on bank-prepared statements, is important to the control of cash and shows the importance of accounting in business.

LEARNING OBJECTIVES

1. Depositing, writing, and endorsing checks for a checking account.
2. Reconciling a bank statement.
3. Establishing and replenishing a petty cash fund; setting up an auxiliary petty cash record.
4. Establishing and replenishing a change fund.
5. Handling transactions involving cash short and over.

Bank Rate, Inc., helps you monitor how interest rates change. Be it in business or your personal life, you need to make wise financial decisions. In the first five chapters of this book, we analyzed the accounting cycle for businesses that perform personal services (e.g., word processing or legal services). In this chapter we turn our attention to Becca's Jewelry Store, a merchandising company that earns revenue by selling goods (or merchandise) to customers. When Becca's business began to increase, she became concerned that she was not monitoring the business's cash closely. She understood that a business with good internal control systems safeguards cash. Cash is the asset that is most easily stolen, lost, or mishandled. Therefore, it is important to protect all cash receipts and to control cash payments so that payments are made only for authorized business purposes.

Internal control system
Procedures and methods to control a firm's assets as well as monitor its operations.

After studying the situation carefully, Becca began a series of procedures that were to be followed by all company employees. The new company policies that Becca's Jewelry Store put into place are as follows:

1. Responsibilities and duties of employees will be divided. For example, the person receiving the cash, whether at the register or by opening the mail, will not record this information into the accounting records. The accountant will not be handling the cash receipts.
2. All cash receipts of Becca's Jewelry Store will be deposited into the bank the same day they arrive.
3. All cash payments will be made by check (except petty cash, which is discussed later in this chapter).
4. Employees will be rotated. This change allows workers to become acquainted with the work of others as well as to prepare for a possible changeover of jobs.
5. Becca Baker will sign all checks after receiving authorization to pay from the departments concerned.
6. At time of payment, all supporting invoices or documents will be stamped "paid." The stamp will show when the invoice or document is paid as well as the number of the check used.
7. All checks will be prenumbered. Periodically, the number of the checks that were issued and the numbers of the blank check forms remaining will be verified to make sure that all check numbers are accounted for. This change will control the use of checks and make it difficult to use a check fraudulently without its being revealed at some point.
8. Monthly bank statements will be sent to and reconciled by someone other than the employees who handle, record, or deposit the cash.

LO1 LEARNING UNIT 6-1 BANK PROCEDURES, CHECKING ACCOUNTS, AND BANK RECONCILIATION

Becca knew that a checking account is one of the most useful and common banking services available, but she had many questions and decisions to make. She wanted to know about account options, monthly service charges, check-printing charges, minimum balance requirements, interest paid on the account, availability of automatic teller machines (ATMs), line of credit, and debit cards. Before Becca's Jewelry opened on April 1, 201X, she met with the manager of Sunshine Bank to discuss opening and using a checking account for the company.

Opening a Checking Account

Signature card A form signed by a bank customer that the bank uses to verify signature authenticity on all checks.

COACHING TIP

A signature card is another safeguard.

The bank manager gave Becca a signature card to fill out. The bank uses the signature card to verify the authenticity of the signature on company checks. Because Becca would be signing all the checks for her company, she was the only person who needed to sign the card.

The bank account enabled Becca to implement two of the basic internal control procedures. First, all revenue sources (cash and checks from cash sales and accounts receivable collections as well as credit card and debit card proceeds) were deposited in the bank account. Second, all withdrawals were to be made by check.

After Becca completed the initial paperwork, she received deposit slips and a set of checks. A deposit slip is a form that is used when making deposits of currency, coins, or checks in a bank or other financial institution. When filling out a deposit slip, you list the total amount of currency, coins, and checks that you are depositing (see Figure 6.1, p. 224).

You list each check that you are depositing individually. Also, alongside each check you list its American Bankers Association (ABA) code. The ABA code is found in the upper-right corner of each check, below the check number. In Figure 6.1, the *16* identifies the large city or state the bank is located in, and the *21* identifies the bank. The *112* is split into two parts: *1* represents the First Federal Reserve District, and *12* is a routing number used by the Federal Reserve Bank. When completing a deposit slip, only the first two numbers are required.

When a deposit is completed, the depositor receives a copy of the deposit slip as a receipt or proof of the transaction. The deposit should also be recorded on the current check stub. The bank manager told Becca that she could give the deposits to a bank teller or she could use an ATM. Often, Becca makes her deposits after business hours when the bank is closed. At those times, she puts the deposit into a locked bag (provided by the bank) and places the bag in the night depository. The bank will credit Becca's account when the deposit is processed. Becca plans to make all business payments by written check (except petty cash) and deposit all money received (cash and checks) in the bank account.

Check Endorsement

Checks have to be *endorsed* (signed) by the person to whom the check is made out before they can be deposited or cashed. Endorsement is the signing or stamping of one's name on the back left-hand side of the check. This signature means that the payee has transferred the right to deposit or cash the check to someone else (the bank). The bank can then collect the money from the person or company that issued the check.

Three different types of endorsement can be used (see Figure 6.2, p. 225). The first is a *blank endorsement*. A blank endorsement does not specify that a particular person or firm must endorse it. It can be further endorsed by someone else. The bank will pay the last person who signs the check. This type of endorsement is not very safe. If the check is lost, the person who finds it can sign it and get the money.

The second type of endorsement is a *full endorsement*. The person or company signing (or stamping) the back of the check indicates the name of the company or the person to whom the check is to be paid. Only the person or company named in the endorsement can transfer the check to someone else.

Restrictive endorsements, the third type of endorsement, are the safest for businesses. Becca's Jewelry Store stamps the back of the check so that it must be deposited in the firm's account. This stamp limits any further use of the check.

Deposit slip A form provided by a bank for use in depositing money or checks into a checking account.

COACHING TIP

When a bank credits your account, it is increasing the balance.

Endorsement *Blank:* Could be further endorsed. *Full:* Restricts further endorsement to only the person or company named. *Restrictive:* Restricts any further endorsement.

COACHING TIP

Endorsements can be made by using a rubber stamp instead of a handwritten signature.

COACHING TIP

The regulations require the endorsement to be within the top 1½ inches to speed up the check-clearing process.

FIGURE 6.1
Deposit Slip

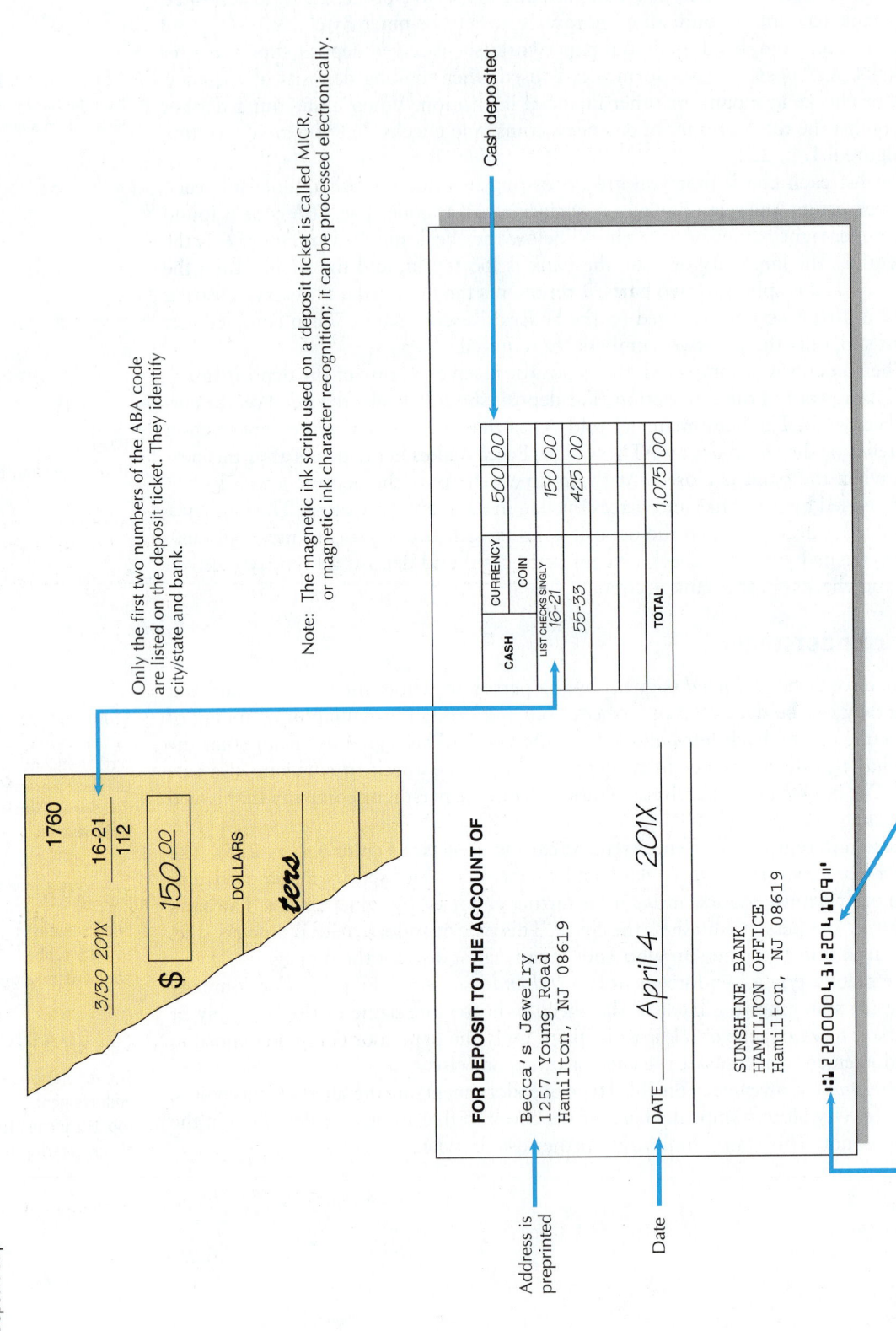

Only the first two numbers of the ABA code are listed on the deposit ticket. They identify city/state and bank.

Note: The magnetic ink script used on a deposit ticket is called MICR, or magnetic ink character recognition; it can be processed electronically.

Cash deposited

Address is preprinted

Date

Becca's account number is usually preprinted.

Preprinted numbers in magnetic ink identify bank number and routing and sorting of check.

Types of Check Endorsement

FIGURE 6.2
Types of Check Endorsement

Blank Endorsement

Becca Baker

204109

A signature on the back left side of a check of the person or firm the check is payable to. This check can be *further* endorsed by someone else; the bank will give the money to the last person who signs the check. This type of endorsement is not very safe. If the check is lost, anyone who picks it up can sign it and get the money.

Full Endorsement

Pay to the order of
Sunshine Bank

Becca's Jewelry Store
204109

This type of endorsement is safer than a simple signature, because the person or company signing (or stamping) the back of the check indicates the name of the company or person to whom the check is to be paid. Only the person or company named in the endorsement can transfer the check to someone else.

Restrictive Endorsement

Payable to the order of
Sunshine Bank
for deposit only.

Becca's Jewelry Store
204109

This endorsement is the safest for businesses. Becca's Jewelry Store stamps the back of the check so that it must be deposited in the firm's account. This endorsement limits any further use of the check (it can only be deposited in the specified account).

In the past and to a lesser extent in the present the primary sources of cash were cash sales and the collection of company accounts receivable. The journal entries to record the collection and deposit of cash in a bank vary only by the source. If the deposit is composed of the proceeds of cash sales, the journal entry is as follows (see Figure 6.3).

	Date	Accounts	PR	Dr.	Cr.	
		Cash		500 00		
		Sales			500 00	

If the deposit is composed of collections of company accounts receivable, the journal entry would be as follows:

	Date	Accounts	PR	Dr.	Cr.	
		Cash		750 00		
		Accounts Receivable			750 00	

There are two other sources of revenue that have taken on greater importance to businessmen and businesswomen: the credit card and the debit card. There are two categories of credit cards: those issued by financial institutions and those issued by credit card companies. Many of those issued by financial institutions, such as MasterCard, VISA, and Discover, are co-branded by other institutions such as airlines, NFL teams, and colleges and universities. These credit cards offer revolving credit facilities. Other credit cards such as American Express are issued by credit card companies. These companies generally extend credit for 30 days at a time. There are several good reasons for a merchant to accept credit cards in payment for its goods or services. The seller does not have to make a decision as to whether it should grant credit or the amount of the credit to be granted. The seller also avoids the risk that the purchaser cannot or will not pay. Additionally, the seller does not have to maintain an accounts receivable system. Credit cards offer a greater number of repayment plans than do merchants, and this may actually increase sales. A credit card may facilitate purchases over the phone or Internet as cash does not need to change hands at the time of sale, and the seller usually receives payment to the company's bank account within 24 hours from VISA, MasterCard, or Discover. American Express typically takes longer than one day to credit the merchant's bank account. A drawback is that merchants typically must pay a service fee associated with the cost of processing the credit card transaction. The following example reflects a 1.5% service charge (Figure 6.4).

FIGURE 6.4
Journal Entry to Record the Deposit of the Proceeds of Credit Card Sales

Date	Account	PR	Dr.	Cr.
	Cash		985 00	
	Service Charge Expense		15 00	
	Sales			1000 00

A debit card is an instrument very similar to the credit card that is used by the buyer to purchase goods and services. Debit cards are issued by banks, savings and loan institutions, and credit unions on behalf of depositors having an account with the institution. In addition, a debit card is not an extension of credit, as the debit card holder cannot spend more than the balance currently in his or her institutional account. As far as the merchant accepting the card is concerned, a debit card, with minor exceptions, is the same as a credit card. Both eliminate the need for the buyer to carry cash or checks to complete a purchase. Within 24 hours the merchant usually receives payment that is reduced by the amount of the service charge fee associated with the debit card transaction. The journal entry to record a debit card transaction is the same as the one shown in Figure 6.4.

The Checkbook

Check A form used to indicate a specific amount of money that is to be paid by the bank to a named person or company.

Drawer Person who writes a check.

Drawee Bank that drawer has an account with.

Payee The person or company to whom the check is payable.

When Becca opened her business's checking account, she received checks. These checks can be used to buy items for the business or to pay bills or salaries.

A **check** is a written order signed by a **drawer** (the person who writes the check) instructing a **drawee** (the person who pays the check) to pay a specific sum of money to the **payee** (the person to whom the check is payable). Figure 6.5 shows a check issued by Becca's Jewelry Store. Becca Baker is the drawer, Sunshine Bank is the drawee, and Ziegler Wholesalers is the payee.

Look at the check in Figure 6.5. Notice that certain features, such as the company's name and address and the check number, are preprinted. Also notice (1) the line drawn after xx/100, which is to fill up the empty space and ensure that the amount cannot be changed, and (2) the word *and*, which should be used only to differentiate between dollars and cents.

Figure 6.5 includes a check stub. The check stub is used to record transactions, and it is kept for future reference. The information found on the stub includes the beginning balance ($3,441), the amount of any deposits ($0), the total amount in the account ($3,441), the amount of the check being written ($580), and the ending balance ($2,861). The check stub should be filled out before the check is written.

FIGURE 6.5
A Company Check

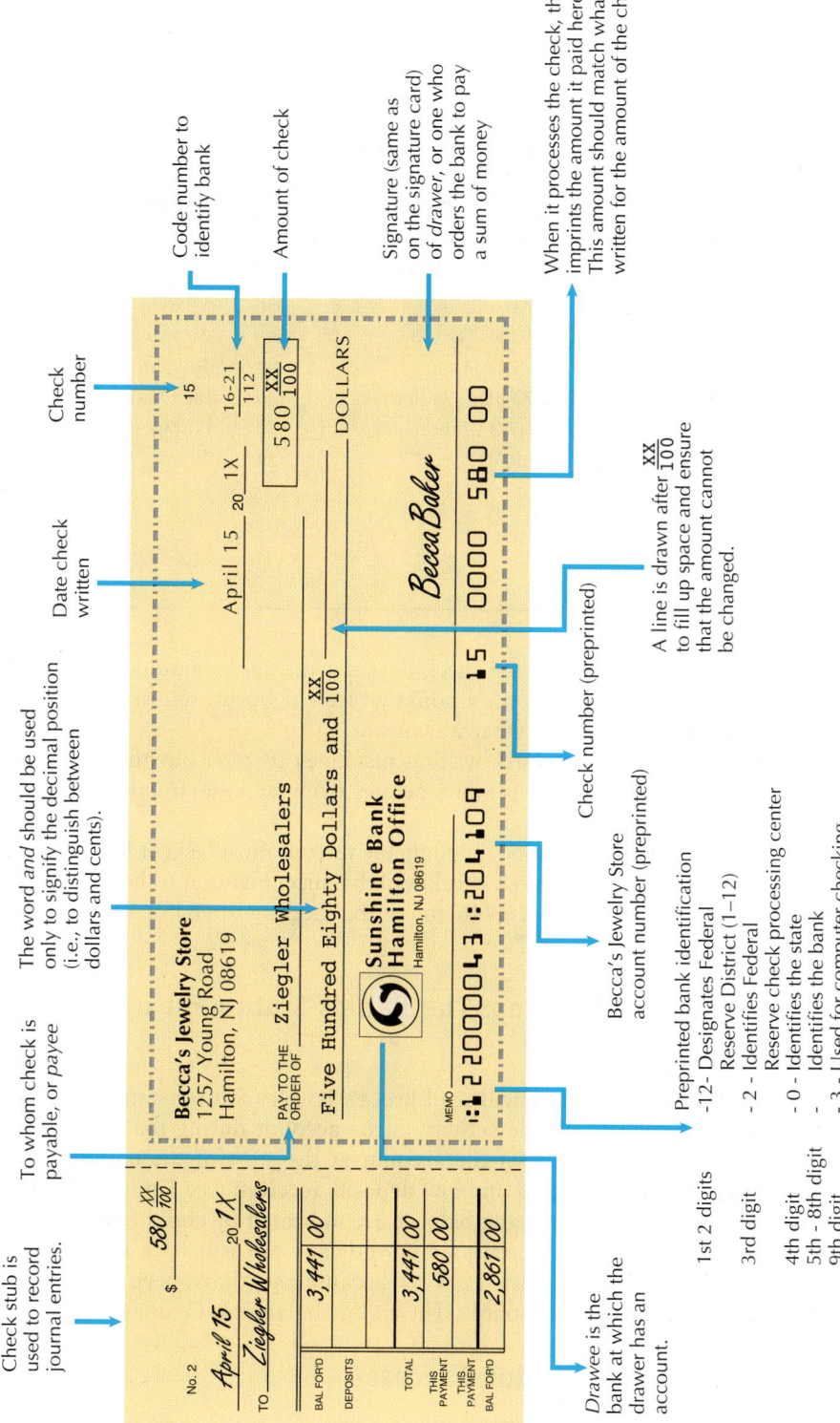

Check stub is used to record journal entries.

To whom check is payable, or *payee*

The word *and* should be used only to signify the decimal position (i.e., to distinguish between dollars and cents).

Check number

Date check written

Code number to identify bank

Amount of check

Signature (same as on the signature card) of *drawer*, or one who orders the bank to pay a sum of money

When it processes the check, the bank imprints the amount it paid here. This amount should match what is written for the amount of the check.

A line is drawn after $\frac{XX}{100}$ to fill up space and ensure that the amount cannot be changed.

Check number (preprinted)

Becca's Jewelry Store account number (preprinted)

Preprinted bank identification

1st 2 digits — 12 - Designates Federal Reserve District (1–12)

3rd digit — 2 - Identifies Federal Reserve check processing center

4th digit — 0 - Identifies the state

5th - 8th digit — Identifies the bank

9th digit — 3 - Used for computer checking

Drawee is the bank at which the drawer has an account.

FIGURE 6.6
Transaction (In-Company Records)
Affecting Checkbook Balance

Bank Deposits Made for April		
Date of Deposit	Amount	Received From
Apr. 1	$5,000	Becca Baker, Capital
4	340	Jennifer Leung
16	89	Mary Figueroa
27	117	Carl Jones
28	900	Cash Sales
Total deposits for month:	$6,446	

Checks Written for the Month of April				
Date	Check No.	Payment To	Amount	Description
Apr. 2	10	Quality Insurance	$ 500	Insurance paid in advance
7	11	ABC Wholesalers	400	Merchandise
9	12	Payroll	800	Salaries
10	13	Times Newspaper	100	Advertising
12	14	Verizon	99	Telephone
15	15	Ziegler Wholesalers	580	Merchandise
15		ATM Withdrawal	50	Postage
Total Amount of Checks Written:			$2,529	
Deposits and Credits			$6,446	
Withdrawals and Fees			−2,529	
Balance in Account			$3,917	

COACHING TIP

Figure 6.7 shows one format for a bank statement. Different banks use different formats.

If the written amount on the check does not match the amount expressed in figures, Sunshine Bank may pay the amount written in words, return the check unpaid, or contact the drawer to see what was meant.

Many companies use check-writing machines to type out the information on the check. These machines prevent people from making fraudulent changes on handwritten checks.

During the same time period, in-company records must be kept for all transactions affecting Becca's Jewelry Store's checkbook balance. Figure 6.6 shows these records. Note that the bank deposits ($6,446) minus the checks written ($2,529) give an ending checkbook balance of $3,917.

Monthly Recordkeeping: The Bank's Statement of Account and In-Company Records

Each month, Sunshine Bank will send Becca's Jewelry Store a statement of account. This statement reflects all the activity in the account during that period. It begins with the beginning balance of the account at the start of the month, along with the checks the bank has paid and any deposits received (see Figure 6.7). Any other charges or additions to the bank balance are indicated by codes found on the statement. All checks that have been paid by the bank are sent back to Becca's Jewelry Store. They are called cancelled checks because they have been processed by the bank and are no longer negotiable. The ending balance in Figure 6.7 is $3,592.

Cancelled check A check that has been processed by a bank and is no longer negotiable.

● L02 The Bank Reconciliation Process

COACHING TIP

Online banking and computer software has made the reconciliation process even easier.

The problem is that the ending bank balance of $3,592 does not agree with the amount in Becca's checkbook, $3,917, or the balance in the cash amount in the ledger, $3,917. Such differences are caused partly by the time a bank takes to process a company's transactions. A company records a transaction when it occurs, but a bank

FIGURE 6.7
A Bank Statement

Sunshine Bank

Becca's Jewelry Store
1257 Young Road
Hamilton, NJ 08619

ACCOUNT
NUMBER   20   410   9

CLOSING
PERIOD   4/30/1X

AMOUNT
ENCLOSED $ _____

RETURN THIS PORTION WITH YOUR PAYMENT IF YOU ARE NOT USING OUR AUTOMATIC PAYMENT PLAN   Address Correction on Reverse Side ☐

CHECKING ACCOUNT

ON	YOUR BALANCE WAS	NO.	WE SUBTRACTED CHECKS TOTALING	LESS SERVICE CHARGE	NO.	WE ADDED DEPOSITS OF	MAKING YOUR PRESENT BALANCE
	0	5	1,949.00	5.00	4	5,546.00	3,592.00

DATE	CHECKS • WITHDRAWALS • PAYMENTS			DEPOSITS • INTEREST • ADVANCES	BALANCE
4/1				5,000.00	5,000.00
4/2	500.00				4,500.00
4/4				340.00	4,840.00
4/7	400.00				4,440.00
4/9	800.00				3,640.00
4/10	100.00				3,540.00
4/12	99.00				3,441.00
4/15				89.00	3,530.00
4/15	50.00 ATM				3,480.00
4/27				117.00	3,597.00
4/30	5.00 SC				3,592.00

FIGURE 6.8
Bank Reconciliation Using Back of the Bank Statement

CHECKS OUTSTANDING		
NUMBER	AMOUNT	
15	580	00
TOTAL OF CHECKS OUTSTANDING	580	00

1. Enter balance shown on this statement	3,592	00
2. If you have made deposits since the date of this statement add them to the above balance.	900	00
3. SUBTOTAL	4,492	00
4. Deduct total of checks outstanding	580	00
5. ADJUSTED BALANCE This should agree with your check-book.	3,912	00*

TO VERIFY YOUR CHECKING BALANCE
1. Sort checks by number or by date issued and compare with your check stubs and prior outstanding list. Make certain all checks paid have been recorded in your checkbook. If any of your checks were not included with this statement, list the numbers and amounts under "CHECKS OUTSTAND-ING."
2. Deduct the Service Charge as shown on the statement from your checkbook balance.
3. Review copies of charge advices included with this statement and check for proper entry in your checkbook.

IF THE ADJUSTED BALANCE DOES NOT AGREE WITH YOUR CHECKBOOK BALANCE, THE FOLLOWING SUGGESTIONS ARE OFFERED FOR YOUR ASSISTANCE.

• Recheck additions and subtractions in your checkbook and figures to the left.
• Make certain checkbook balances have been carried forward properly.
• Verify deposits recorded on statement against deposits entered in checkbook.
• Compare amount on each checkbook stub.

COACHING TIP

Keep in mind that both the bank and the depositor can make mistakes that will not be discovered until the reconciliation process.

*Note that the $5 service charge is included

cannot record a deposit until it receives that deposit, and it cannot pay a check until the check is presented by the payee. In addition, the bank statement will report fees and transactions that the company did not know about.

Becca's accountant has to find out why there is a $325 difference between the balances and how the records can be brought into balance. The process of reconciling the bank balance on the bank statement versus the company's checkbook balance is called a bank reconciliation. Bank reconciliations involve several steps, including calculating the deposits in transit and the outstanding checks. The bank reconciliation usually is done on the back of the bank statement (see Figure 6.8). However, it can also be done by computer software.

Deposits in Transit In comparing the list of deposits received by the bank with the checkbook, the accountant notices that a deposit made on April 28 for $900 was not on the bank's statement. The accountant realizes that to prepare this statement, the bank only included information about Becca's Jewelry Store up to April 27. This deposit made by Becca was not shown on the monthly bank statement because it arrived at the bank after the statement was printed after April 30. Thus, timing becomes a consideration in the reconciliation process. Deposits not yet added to the bank balance are called deposits in transit. This deposit needs to be added to the bank balance shown on the bank statement. Becca's check-book is not affected, because the deposit has already been added to its balance. The bank has no way of knowing that the deposit is coming until it receives it.

Outstanding Checks The first thing the accountant does when the bank statement is received is put the checks in numerical order (1, 2, 3, etc.). In doing so, the accountant notices that one payment was not made by the bank and check no. 15 was not returned by the bank.

Becca's books showed that this check had been deducted from the checkbook balance. The outstanding check, however, had not yet been presented to the bank for payment or deducted from the bank balance. When this check does reach the bank, the bank will reduce the amount of the balance.

Service Charges Becca's accountant also notices a bank service charge of $5. Becca's book balance will be lowered by $5.

Nonsufficient Funds While Becca's Jewelry Store did not experience either of the following two transactions, both may occur in the normal course of business. An NSF (nonsufficient funds) check is a check that has been returned because the drawer did not have enough money in its account to pay the check. Accountants are continually on the lookout for NSF checks. An NSF check means less money in the checking account than was thought. Becca will have to (1) lower the checkbook balance and (2) try to collect the amount from the customer. The bank will notify Becca's Jewelry of an NSF check (or other deductions) by a debit memorandum. Think of a debit memorandum as a deduction from the account holder's balance.

If the bank acts as a collecting agent for Becca's Jewelry, say in collecting notes, it will charge Becca a small fee and the net amount collected will be added to Becca's bank balance. The bank will send to Becca a credit memorandum verifying the increase in the depositor's balance.

A journal entry is also needed to bring the ledger accounts of Cash and Service Charge expense up-to-date. Any adjustment to the checkbook balance results in a journal entry. The entry in Figure 6.9 was made to accomplish this step.

Bank reconciliation The process of reconciling the checkbook balance with the bank balance given on the bank statement.

Bank statement A report sent by a bank to a customer indicating the previous balance, atm transactions, nonsufficient funds, individual checks processed, individual deposits received, service charges, and ending bank balance.

Deposits in transit Deposits that were made by customers of a bank but did not reach, or were not processed by, the bank before the preparation of the bank statement.

COACHING TIP

Check no. 15 is outstanding in Figure 6.8.

Outstanding checks Checks written by a company or person that were not received or not processed by the bank before the preparation of the bank statement.

NSF (nonsufficient funds) Notation indicating that a check has been written on an account that lacks sufficient funds to back it up.

Debit memorandum Decrease in depositor's balance.

Credit memorandum Increase in depositor's balance.

FIGURE 6.9
Service Charge Journalized

Apr.	30	Service Charge Expense		5 00		
		Cash			5 00	
		Bank service charge for April				

It is important for Becca to prepare a bank reconciliation when she receives her bank statement every month as part of the cash control procedure. It verifies the amount of cash in her checking account. Another important reason to do a bank reconciliation is that it may uncover irregularities such as employee theft of funds.

Here are step-by-step instructions for preparing a bank reconciliation:

1. **Prepare a list of deposits in transit.** Compare the deposits listed on your bank statement with the bank deposits shown in your checkbook. On your bank reconciliation, list any deposits that have not yet cleared the bank statement. Also, take a look at the bank reconciliation you prepared last month. Did all of last month's deposits in transit clear on this month's bank statement? If not, you should find out what happened.

2. **Prepare a list of outstanding checks.** In your checkbook, mark each check that cleared the bank statement this month. On your bank reconciliation, list all the checks in your checkbook that did not clear. Also, take a look at the bank reconciliation you prepared last month. Did any checks outstanding from last month still not clear the bank? If so, be sure they are on your list of outstanding checks this month. If a check is several months old and still has not cleared the bank, you may want to investigate further.

3. **Record any bank charges or credits.** Take a close look at your bank statement. Are all special charges made by the bank recorded in your books? If not, journalize them now as if you had just written a check for that amount. By the same token, any credits made to your account by the bank should be journalized as well. Post the entries to your general ledger.

4. **Compute the cash balance per your books.**

5. **Enter bank balance on the reconciliation.** At the top of the bank reconciliation statement, enter the ending balance from the bank statement.

6. **Total the deposits in transit.** Add up the deposits in transit and enter the total on the reconciliation. Add the total deposits in transit to the bank balance to arrive at a subtotal.

7. **Total the outstanding checks.** Add up the outstanding checks, and enter the total on the reconciliation.

8. **Compute the balance per the reconciliation.** Subtract the total outstanding checks (see step 7) from the subtotal in step 6. The result should equal the balance shown in your general ledger.

Before we look at a more comprehensive bank statement, let's look at trends in banking.

Trends in Banking

The Internet is changing how people bank. In the past, banking took place on the main street of your town. The branches were open from 9 A.M. to 3 P.M. Monday through Thursday. They were probably open from 9 A.M. to 6 P.M. on Friday and possibly from 9 A.M. to noon on Saturday. These times were not always convenient for people who worked full time.

Many financial institutions have developed ways to transfer funds electronically, without the use of paper checks. Such systems are called **electronic funds transfers (EFTs)**. Most EFTs are established to save money and avoid theft.

Financial institutions use powerful computer networks to automate millions of daily transactions. Today, banks are able to use computer technology to give you the option of bypassing the time-consuming, paper-based aspects of traditional banking so that you can manage your finances more quickly and efficiently.

The first step toward online banking, **automatic teller machines (ATMs)**, were first installed in banks about 40 years ago. For the first time, customers could make deposits, withdraw money, and obtain account balances without having to stand in line during the times that the bank was open. Today, customers are able to use an ATM in banks, supermarkets, malls, and possibly even at a college student center.

COACHING TIP

Adjustments to the checkbook balance must be journalized and posted. These steps keep the depositor's ledger accounts (especially Cash) up-to-date. This charge could be recorded as a miscellaneous expense.

Electronic funds transfer (EFT) An electronic system that transfers funds without the use of paper checks.

ATM Automatic teller machine that allows for depositing, withdrawal, and advanced banking transactions.

Call centers were the next major step forward for banks. Customers could now telephone the center using either a toll-free number or local number and find out information about their accounts without leaving their home.

The latest development in banking is internet or online banking. Most of the large banks offer fully secure, fully functional online banking for free or for a small fee. Some smaller banks offer limited access; for instance, you may be able to view your account balance and history but may not be able to initiate transactions online. As more banks succeed online and more customers use their sites, fully functional online banking is becoming as common as ATMs.

With a debit card and personal identification number (PIN), you can use an ATM to withdraw cash, make deposits, or transfer funds between accounts. Some ATMs charge a fee if you are not a member of their ATM network or are making a transaction at a remote location.

Retail purchases can also be made with a debit card. You enter your PIN or sign for the purchase. Some banks that issue debit cards are charging customers a fee for a debit card purchase made with a PIN. Although a debit card looks like a credit card, the money for the purchase is transferred from your bank account to the store's account at the time of the purchase. The purchase will be shown on your bank account statement.

Immediately call the card issuer when you suspect a debit card may be lost or stolen. Most companies have toll-free numbers and a 24-hour service to deal with such emergencies. Although federal law limits your liability for a stolen credit card to $50, your liability for unauthorized use of your ATM or debit card can be much greater—depending on how quickly you report the loss. Also, it is important to remember that when you use a debit card, federal law does not give you the right to stop payment. You must resolve the problem with the seller.

If you don't mind foregoing the teller window and the lobby cookie, a virtual bank or e-bank, such as Virtual Bank or Giant Bank, may save you real money. Virtual banks are banks without bricks. They exist entirely online and offer much of the same range of services and adhere to the same regulations as your corner bank. Virtual banks pass the money that they save on overhead, such as buildings and tellers, along to you in the form of higher yields and lower fees. Banking is available everywhere, all the time. Your finances are at your fingertips. With the advent of "smart phones" such as the iPhone, Droid, Nexus, and Palm Pre, internet banking is available regardless of location. Almost every major and many minor bank has developed "banking apps," which are provided to enable customers to access their accounts from almost any location.

Advantages of Online Banking   Customers who use online banking services enjoy many advantages. They can do almost everything from the comfort of their own homes at convenient times and without standing in long lines.

- *Convenience:* Unlike your corner site, online banks never close. They are available 24 hours a day, seven days a week.
- *Availability:* If you are out of state or even out of the country when a money problem arises, you can log on instantly to your online bank and take care of business, 24/7.
- *Transaction speed:* Online bank sites generally execute and confirm transactions as quickly or even faster than ATM processing speeds.
- *Efficiency:* You can access and manage all of your bank accounts, including IRAs and CDs, from one secure site.
- *Effectiveness:* Many online banking sites now offer sophisticated tools to help you manage all of your assets more effectively. Most of these tools are compatible with money managing programs such as Quicken and Microsoft Money.

Disadvantages of Online Banking Although online banking has many advantages, it also has some disadvantages.

- *Start-up may take time:* In order to register for your bank's online program, you will probably have to provide some personal identification and sign a form at a branch bank.
- *Learning curve:* Banking sites can be difficult to navigate at first. Plan to invest time to read the tutorials in order to become comfortable in your virtual lobby.
- *Bank site changes:* Even the largest banks periodically upgrade their online programs, adding new features in unfamiliar places. In some cases, you may need to reenter account information.
- *Trust:* For many people, the biggest hurdle to online banking is learning to trust it. Did my transaction go through? Did I push the transfer button once or twice? Best bet: Always print the transaction receipt and keep it with your bank records until it shows up on your personal site or your bank statement.

When problems arise, it is usually much easier to sort them out face to face rather than to use e-mail or the telephone. Perhaps the biggest problem with online banking is security. It is important to keep passwords safe and to be aware of fake e-mails arriving in your inbox. These e-mails pretend to be from your bank and attempt to obtain log in information from you. This kind of fraud is called phishing.

Phishing Fake e-mails that attempt to obtain information about online banking customers.

Fraudulent practices can happen at cash registers when you make a purchase or at restaurants when you pay with a credit card and the waiter is out of your sight. Skimming is the theft of credit card information used in an otherwise legitimate debit card or credit card transaction. Skimming at ATMs can be much more damaging because of the number of accounts and the amount of money that can be quickly accessed. Card-based purchases—online, debit, and credit—are convenient for consumers. For example, tens of thousands of ATMs are swipe-based. The large number of ATMs contributes to the skimming problem. In a way, we've become victims of the convenience we demand.

Here are some tips to help you avoid becoming a skimming victim.

- Keep your PIN safe. Don't give it to anyone.
- Watch out for people who try to "help" you at an ATM.
- Look at the ATM before using it. If it doesn't look right, don't use it.
- If an ATM has any unusual signage, don't use it. No bank would hang a sign that says, "Swipe your ATM here before inserting it in the card reader" or something to that effect.
- If your card is not returned after the transaction or after pressing cancel, immediately contact the institution that issued the card.
- Check your statement to be sure that no unusual withdrawals appear on it.

Check Truncation (Safekeeping) Some banks do not return cancelled checks to the depositor but instead use a procedure called check truncation or safekeeping. This practice is increasing rapidly. The bank holds a cancelled check for a specific period of time (usually 90 days) and then keeps a microfilm copy handy and destroys the original check. In Texas, for example, some credit unions and savings and loan institutions do not send back checks. Instead, the check date, number, and amount are listed on the bank statement. If the customer needs a copy of a check, the bank will provide the check or a photocopy for a small fee. (Photocopies are accepted as evidence in Internal Revenue Service tax returns and audits.)

Check truncation (safekeeping) Procedure whereby checks are not returned to the drawer with the bank statement but are instead kept at the bank for a certain amount of time before being first transferred to microfilm and then destroyed.

Truncation cuts down on the amount of "paper" that is returned to customers and thus provides substantial cost savings. It is estimated that more than 80 million checks are written each day in the United States.

Example of a More Comprehensive Bank Statement The bank reconciliation of Becca's Jewelry was not as complicated as it is for many companies, even using today's computer technology. Let's look at a reconciliation for Matty's Supermarket (Figures 6.10 and 6.11), which is based on the following business transactions:

Matty's checkbook balance	$13,176.84
Bank balance	23,726.04
Leased space to Subway	8,456.00
Leased space to Dunkin' Donuts	3,616.12
Both lease payments are deposited by electronic transfer.	
Matty pays a health insurance payment each month by electronic transfer	1,444.00
Deposits in transit 5/30	6,766.52

Checks outstanding

Ck # 738	$1,144.00
739	1,277.88
740	332.00
741	812.56
742	1,834.12
	1,440.00

Check # 734 was overstated in company's books

FIGURE 6.10
Bank Statement for Matty's Supermarket

Ranger Bank
1 Left St.
Marblehead, MA 01945

ACCOUNT STATEMENT

Matty's Supermarket
20 Sullivan St.
Lynn, MA 01917

Checking Account: 775800061

Checking Account Summary as of 6/30/1X

Beginning Balance	Total Deposits	Total Withdrawals	Service Charge	Ending Balance
$26,224.48	$17,410.56	$19,852.00	$57.00	$23,726.04

Checking Accounts Transactions

Deposits	Date	Amount
Deposit	6/05	4,000.00
Deposit	6/05	448.00
Deposit	6/09	778.40
EFT leasing: Dunkin' Donuts	6/18	3,616.12
EFT leasing: Subway	6/27	8,456.00
Interest	6/30	112.04

Charges	Date	Amount
Service charge: Check printing	6/30	57.00
EFT: Blue Cross/Blue Shield	6/21	1,444.00
NSF	6/21	208.00

Checks			Daily Balance			
Number	Date	Amount	Date	Balance	Date	Balance
401	6/07	400.00	5/28	26,224.48	6/18	21,059.00
733	6/13	12,000.00	6/05	30,464.48	6/21	19,615.00
734	6/13	600.00	6/07	29,664.48	6/28	28,071.00
735	6/11	400.00	6/09	30,442.88	6/30	23,726.04
736	6/18	400.00	6/11	30,042.88		
737	6/30	4,400.00	6/13	17,442.88		

Note that in Figure 6.11 each adjustment to Matty's checkbook is the reconciliation process that would result in general journal entries in the company's accounting records.

FIGURE 6.11
Bank Reconciliation for Matty's Supermarket

MATTY'S SUPERMARKET Bank Reconciliation as of June 30, 201X				
Checkbook balance			**Bank balance**	
Matty's checkbook balance	$13,176.84	Bank balance		$23,726.04
Add:		Add:		
EFT leasing: Dunkin' Donuts		Deposits in transit, 5/30		6,766.52
$ 3,616.12				$30,492.56
EFT leasing: Subway				
8,456.00				
Interest	112.04			
Error: Overstated				
check no. 734	1,440.00	13,624.16		
		$26,801.00		
Deduct:		Deduct:		
Service charge	$ 57.00	Outstanding checks:		
NSF check	208.00	No. 738	$1,144.00	
EFT health insurance		No. 739	1,277.88	
payment	1,444.00	1,709.00	No. 740	332.00
			No. 741	812.56
			No. 742	1,834.12	5,400.56
Reconciled balance		$25,092.00	Reconciled balance	$25,092.00

LEARNING UNIT 6-1 REVIEW

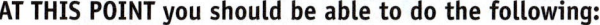

AT THIS POINT you should be able to do the following:

- Define and explain the need for deposit slips.
- Explain where the American Bankers Association transit number is located on the check and what its purpose is.
- List as well as compare and contrast the three common types of check endorsements.
- Explain the structure of a check.
- Define and state the purpose of a bank statement.
- Explain deposits in transit, checks outstanding, service charge, and NSF checks.
- Explain the difference between a debit memorandum and a credit memorandum.
- Prepare a bank reconciliation.
- Explain electronic funds transfer and check truncation.
- Explain the advantages and disadvantages of online banking.

Instant Replay • Self-Review Quiz 6-1

Indicate, by placing an X under it, the heading that describes the appropriate action in a bank reconciliation for each of the following situations:

Situation	Add to Bank Balance	Deduct from Bank Balance	Add to Checkbook Balance	Deduct from Checkbook Balance
1. Check printing charge				
2. Deposits in transit				

(continued on page 236)

Situation	Add to Bank Balance	Deduct from Bank Balance	Add to Checkbook Balance	Deduct from Checkbook Balance
3. NSF check				
4. A $75 check was written and recorded by the company as $85				
5. Proceeds of a note collected by the bank				
6. Check outstanding				
7. Forgot to record ATM withdrawal				
8. Forgot to record direct deposit				

Solution to Instant Replay: Self-Review Quiz 6-1

Situation	Add to Bank Balance	Deduct from Bank Balance	Add to Checkbook Balance	Deduct from Checkbook Balance
1				X
2	X			
3				X
4			X	
5			X	
6		X		
7				X
8			X	

Deposits in transit are added to the bank balance, whereas checks outstanding are subtracted from the bank balance.

LO3

LEARNING UNIT 6-2 THE ESTABLISHMENT OF PETTY CASH AND CHANGE FUNDS

Becca realized how time-consuming and expensive it would be to write checks for small amounts to pay for postage, small supplies, and so forth, so she set up a petty cash fund. Similarly, she established a *change fund* to make cash transactions more convenient. This unit explains how to manage petty cash and change funds.

Setting Up the Petty Cash Fund

The petty cash fund is an account dedicated to paying small day-to-day expenses. These petty cash expenses are recorded in an auxiliary record and later summarized, journalized, and posted. Becca estimated that the company would need a fund of $60 to cover small expenditures during the month of May. This petty cash was not expected to last longer than one month. She gave one of her employees responsibility for overseeing the fund. This person is called the *custodian*.

Petty cash fund Fund (source) that allows payment of small amounts without the writing of checks.

COACHING TIP

Petty Cash is an asset on the balance sheet that is established by writing a new check. The Petty Cash account is debited only once unless a greater or lesser amount of petty cash is needed on a regular basis.

Becca named her office manager, John Sullivan, as custodian. In other companies, the cashier or secretary may be in charge of petty cash. Check no. 6 was drawn to the order of the custodian and cashed to establish the fund. John keeps the petty cash fund in a small tin box in the office safe.

Shown here is the transaction analysis chart for the establishment of a $60 petty cash fund, which would be journalized on May 1, 201X, as shown in Figure 6.12.

Accounts Affected	Category	↓ ↑	Rules
Petty Cash	Asset	↑	Dr.
Cash (checks)	Asset	↓	Cr.

Note that the new asset called Petty Cash, which was created by writing check no. 6, reduced the asset Cash. In reality, the total assets stay the same; what has occurred is a shift from the asset Cash (check no. 6) to a new asset account called Petty Cash.

The Petty Cash account is not debited or credited again if the size of the fund is not changed. If the $60 fund is used up quickly, the fund should be increased. If the fund is too large, the Petty Cash account should be reduced. We take a closer look at this issue when we discuss replenishment of petty cash.

	GENERAL JOURNAL			Page 1	
Date	Account Title and Description	PR	Dr.	Cr.	
201X May 1	Petty Cash		60 00		
	Cash			60 00	
	Establishment of petty cash and change fund.				

FIGURE 6.12
Establishing Petty Cash

Making Payments from the Petty Cash Fund

John Sullivan has the responsibility for filling out a **petty cash voucher** for each cash payment made from the petty cash fund. The petty cash vouchers are numbered in sequence.

Note that when the voucher (shown in Figure 6.13, p. 238) is completed, it will include

- the voucher number (which will be in sequence),
- the date,
- the person or organization to whom the payment was made,
- the amount of payment,
- the reason for payment (in this case, cleaning),
- the signature of the person who approved the payment,
- the signature of the person who received the payment from petty cash, and
- the account to which the expense will be charged.

The completed vouchers are placed in the petty cash box. No matter how many vouchers John Sullivan fills out, the total of the vouchers in the box and the cash on hand should equal the original amount of petty cash with which the fund was established ($60).

Petty cash voucher A petty cash form to be completed when money is taken out of petty cash.

COACHING TIP

The check for $60 is usually drawn to the order of the custodian and is cashed, and the proceeds are turned over to John Sullivan, the custodian.

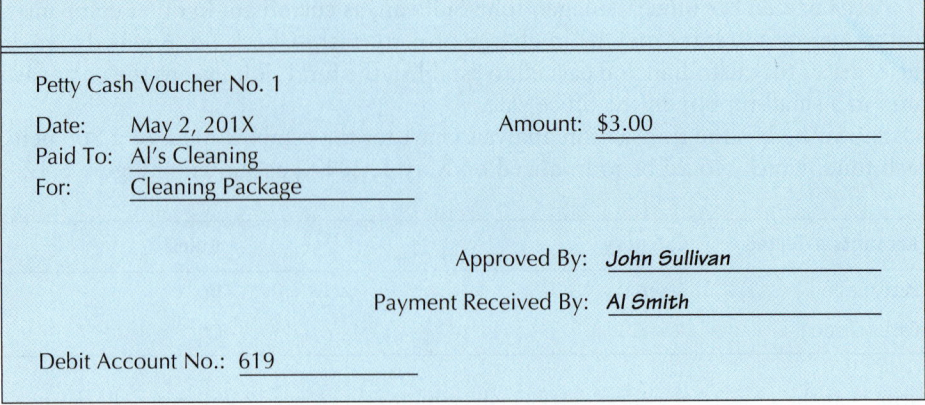

Petty Cash Voucher No. 1

Date: May 2, 201X   Amount: $3.00
Paid To: Al's Cleaning
For: Cleaning Package

                                    Approved By: *John Sullivan*

                                    Payment Received By: *Al Smith*

Debit Account No.: 619

Assume that at the end of May the following items are documented by petty cash vouchers in the petty cash box as having been paid by John Sullivan:

201X			
May	2	Cleaning package, $3.00
	5	Postage stamps, $9.00
	8	First-aid supplies, $15.00
	9	Delivery expense, $6.00
	14	Delivery expense, $15.00
	27	Postage stamps, $6.00

Auxiliary petty cash record
A supplementary record for summarizing petty cash information.

John records this information in the **auxiliary petty cash record** shown in Figure 6.14. It is not a required record but is an aid to John. In other words, it is an auxiliary record that is not essential but that is quite helpful as part of the petty cash system. You may want to think of the auxiliary petty cash record as an optional worksheet. Let's look at how to replenish the petty cash fund.

						Category of Payments			
								Sundry	
Date	Voucher No.	Description	Receipts	Payments	Postage Expense	Delivery Expense	Account	Amount
201X May 1		Establishment	60 00					
2	1	Cleaning		3 00			Cleaning	3 00
5	2	Postage		9 00	9 00			
8	3	First Aid		15 00			Misc.	15 00
9	4	Delivery		6 00		6 00		
14	5	Delivery		15 00		15 00		
27	6	Postage		6 00	6 00			
		Total	60 00	54 00	15 00	21 00		18 00

How to Replenish the Petty Cash Fund

No postings are done from the auxiliary record because it is not a journal. At some point the summarized information found in the auxiliary petty cash record is used as a basis for a journal entry in the general journal and eventually posted to appropriate ledger accounts to reflect up-to-date balances.

The $54 of expenses (see Figure 6.14) is recorded in the general journal (Figure 6.15) and a new check, no. 17, for $54 is cashed and returned to John Sullivan. In replenishment, old expenses are updated in the journal and ledger to show where money has gone. The petty cash box now once again reflects $60 cash. The old vouchers that were used are stamped to indicate that they have been processed and the fund replenished.

Note that in the replenishment process the debits are a summary of the totals (except sundry, because individual items are different) of expenses or other items from the auxiliary petty cash record. Posting these specific expenses will ensure that the expenses will not be understated on the income statement. The credit to Cash allows us to draw a check for $54 to put money back in the petty cash box. The $60 in the box now agrees with the Petty Cash account balance. The end result is that our petty cash box is filled, and we have justified for which accounts the petty cash money was spent. Think of replenishment as a single, summarizing entry.

COACHING TIP

A new check, which is payable to the custodian and is cashed by John, is written in the replenishment process, and the cash is placed in the petty cash box.

FIGURE 6.15
Establishment and Replenishment of Petty Cash Fund

Petty cash is an asset. ➡

Note that the Petty Cash account is not listed in replenishment unless we raise or lower the basic amount. To raise it we would debit it; to lower it we would credit it. ➡

	Date		Account Title and Description	PR	Dr.	Cr.
	201X May	1	Petty Cash		60 00	
			Cash			60 00
			Establishment			
		31	Postage Expense		15 00	
			Delivery Expense		21 00	
			Cleaning Expense		3 00	
			Miscellaneous Expense		15 00	
			Cash			54 00
			Replenishment			

GENERAL JOURNAL — Page 1

Remember that if at some point the petty cash fund is to be greater than $60, a check can be written that will increase Petty Cash and decrease Cash. If the Petty Cash account balance is to be reduced, we can credit or reduce Petty Cash. For our present purpose, however, Petty Cash will remain at $60.

The auxiliary petty cash record after replenishment would look as shown in Figure 6.16, p. 240 (keep in mind that no postings are made from the auxiliary).

FIGURE 6.16
Auxiliary Petty Cash Record with Replenishment

						Category of Payments			
						Postage Expense	Delivery Expense	Sundry	
Date	Voucher No.	Description	Receipts	Payments				Account	Amount
201X May 1		Establishment	60 00						
2	1	Cleaning		3 00				Cleaning	3 00
5	2	Postage		9 00		9 00			
8	3	First Aid		15 00				Misc.	15 00
9	4	Delivery		6 00			6 00		
14	5	Delivery		15 00			15 00		
27	6	Postage		6 00		6 00			
		Total	60 00	54 00		15 00	21 00		18 00
		Ending Balance		6 00					
			60 00	60 00					
		Ending Balance	6 00						
	31	Replenishment	54 00						
	31	Balance (New)	60 00						

Figure 6.17 may help you put the sequence together.

FIGURE 6.17
Which Transactions Involve Petty Cash and How to Record Them

Date	Description	New Check Written	Petty Cash Voucher Prepared	Recorded in Auxiliary Petty Cash Record	
201X May 1	Establishment of petty cash for $60	X		X	Dr. Petty Cash Cr. Cash
2	Paid salaries, $2,000	X			
10	Paid $10 from petty cash for Band-Aids		X	X	No journal entries
19	Paid $8 from petty cash for postage		X	X	
24	Paid light bill, $200	X			
29	Replenishment of petty cash to $60	X		X	Dr. individual expenses Cr. Cash

Has nothing to do with petty cash (amounts too great)

In this step the old expenses are listed in the general journal and a new check is written to replenish. All old vouchers are removed from the petty cash box.

Before concluding this unit, let's look at how Becca will handle setting up a change fund and problems with cash shortages and overages.

Setting Up a Change Fund and Insight into Cash Short and Over

 L04

If a company such as Becca's Jewelry expects to have many cash transactions occurring, it may be a good idea to establish a change fund. This fund is placed in the cash register drawer and used to make change for customers who pay cash. Becca decides to put $120 in the change fund, made up of various denominations of bills and coins. Let's look at a transaction analysis chart and the journal entry (Figure 6.18) for this sort of transaction.

Change fund Fund made up of various denominations that are used to make change for customers.

COACHING TIP

Beg. change fund

+ Cash register total

= Cash should have on hand

− Counted cash

= Shortage or overage of cash

FIGURE 6.18
Change Fund Established

Accounts Affected	Category	↓ ↑	Rules
Change Fund	Asset	↑	Dr.
Cash	Asset	↓	Cr.

Apr.	1	Change Fund		1 2 0 00	
		Cash			1 2 0 00
		Establish change fund			

At the close of the business day, Becca will place the amount of the change fund back in the safe in the office. She will prepare the change fund (the same $120) in the appropriate denominations for the next business day. She will deposit in the bank the *remainder* of the cash taken in for the day.

In the next section, we look at how to record errors that are made in making change, called cash short and over.

Cash Short and Over In a local pizza shop the total sales for the day did not match the amount of cash on hand. Errors often happen in making change. To record and summarize the differences in cash, an account called *Cash Short and Over* is used. This account records both overages (too much money) and shortages (not enough money). Let's first look at the account (in T account form).

 L05

Cash Short and Over The account that records cash shortages and overages. If the ending balance is a debit, it is recorded on the income statement as a miscellaneous expense; if it is a credit, it is recorded as miscellaneous income.

Cash Short and Over

Dr.	Cr.
shortage	overage

All shortages will be recorded as debits and all overages will be recorded as credits. This account is temporary. If the ending balance of the account is a debit (a shortage), it is considered a miscellaneous expense that would be reported on the income statement. If the balance of the account is a credit (an overage), it is considered as other-income reported on the income statement. Let's look at how the Cash Short and Over account could be used to record shortages or overages in sales as well as in the petty cash process.

Example 1: Shortages and Overages in Sales On December 5 a pizza shop rang up sales of $560 for the day but only had $530 in cash.

Accounts Affected	Category	↓ ↑	Rules
Cash	Asset	↑	Debit $530
Cash Short and Over	Misc. Exp.	↑	Debit $30
Sales	Revenue	↑	Credit $560

The journal entry would be as shown in Figure 6.19

FIGURE 6.19
Cash Shortage

Dec.	5	Cash			5 3 0 00					
		Cash Short and Over			3 0 00					
		Sales					5 6 0 00			
		Cash shortage								

Note that the shortage of $30 is a debit and would be recorded on the income state-ment as a miscellaneous expense.

What would the entry look like if the pizza shop showed a $50 overage, i.e. if the cash at the end of the day was $610?

Accounts Affected	Category	↓ ↑	Rules
Cash	Asset	↑	Debit $610
Cash Short and Over	Other Income	↑	Credit $50
Sales	Revenue	↑	Credit $560

The journal entry would be as shown in Figure 6.20.

FIGURE 6.20
Cash Overage

Dec.	5	Cash			6 1 0 00					
		Cash Short and Over					5 0 00			
		Sales					5 6 0 00			
		Cash overage								

Note that the Cash Short and Over account would be reported as other income on the income statement. Now let's look at how to use this Cash Short and Over account to record petty cash transactions.

Example 2: Cash Short and Over in Petty Cash A local computer company estab-lished petty cash for $200. On November 30, the petty cash box had $160 in vouchers as well as $32 in coin and currency. What would be the journal entry to replenish petty cash? Assume the vouchers were made up of $90 for postage and $70 for supplies expense.

If you add up the vouchers and cash in the box, cash is short by $8.

COACHING TIP

NOTE: The account Petty Cash is not used since the level in petty cash is not raised or lowered.

Accounts Affected	Category	↓ ↑	Rules
Postage Expense	Expense	↑	Debit $90
Supplies Expense	Expense	↑	Debit $70
Cash Short and Over	Misc. Expense	↑	Debit $8
Cash	Asset	↓	Credit $168

The journal entry is shown in Figure 6.21

FIGURE 6.21
Petty Cash Replenished with Shortage

Nov.	30	Postage Expense			9 0 00					
		Supplies Expense			7 0 00					
		Cash Short and Over			8 00					
		Cash					1 6 8 00			

In the case of an overage, the Cash Short and Over would be a credit as other income. The solution to Instant Replay: Self Review Quiz 6-2 shows how a fund shortage would be recorded in the auxiliary record.

LEARNING UNIT 6-2 REVIEW

AT THIS POINT you should be able to do the following:

- State the purpose of a petty cash fund.
- Prepare a journal entry to establish a petty cash fund.
- Prepare a petty cash voucher.
- Explain the relationship of the auxiliary petty cash record to the petty cash process.
- Prepare a journal entry to replenish Petty Cash to its original amount.
- Explain why individual expenses are debited in the replenishment process.
- Explain how a change fund is established.
- Explain how Cash Short and Over could be a miscellaneous expense.

Instant Replay ⊙ Self-Review Quiz 6-2

As the custodian of the petty cash fund, it is your task to prepare journal entries to establish the fund on October 1 as well as to replenish the fund on October 31. Please keep an auxiliary petty cash record.

201X		
Oct.	1	Establish petty cash fund for $90, check no. 8.
	5	Voucher 11, delivery expense, $21.
	9	Voucher 12, delivery expense, $15.
	10	Voucher 13, office repair expense, $24.
	17	Voucher 14, general expense, $12.
	30	Replenishment of petty cash fund, $78, check no. 108. (Check would be payable to the custodian.)

COACHING TIP

How to calculate shortage: $21 + $15 + $24 + $12 = $72 of vouchers. Replenished with $78 check. Thus there was a $6 shortage. Note how cash short and over was entered in the auxiliary petty cash record.

Solution to Instant Replay: Self-Review Quiz 6-2

FIGURE 6.22
Establishment and Replenishment of Petty Cash

GENERAL JOURNAL				Page 6	
Date	Account Title and Description	PR	Dr.	Cr.	
201X Oct. 1	Petty Cash		90 00		
	Cash			90 00	
	Establishment, Check 8				
31	Delivery Expense		36 00		
	General Expense		12 00		
	Office Repair Expense		24 00		
	Cash Short and Over		6 00		
	Cash			78 00	
	Replenishment, Check 108				

FIGURE 6.23
Auxiliary Petty Cash Received

	Date	Voucher No.	Description	Receipts	Payments	Delivery Expense	General Expense	Sundry Account	Sundry Amount
				AUXILIARY PETTY CASH RECORD		Category of Payments			
201X Oct.	1		Establishment	90 00					
	5	11	Delivery		21 00	21 00			
	9	12	Delivery		15 00	15 00			
	10	13	Repairs		24 00			Office Repair	24 00
	17	14	General		12 00		12 00		
	25		Fund Shortage		6 00			Cash Short and Over	6 00
			Totals	90 00	78 00	36 00	12 00		30 00
			Ending Balance		12 00				
					90 00				
	30		Ending Balance	12 00					
	31		Replenishment	78 00					
Nov.	1		New Balance	90 00					

BLUEPRINT: A BANK RECONCILIATION

Checkbook Balance	Bank Balance
+ EFT (electronic funds transfer)	+ Deposits in transit
+ Interest earned	− Outstanding checks
+ Notes collected	± Bank errors
+ Direct deposits	
− ATM withdrawals	
− Check redeposits	
− NSF check	
− Online fees	
− Automatic withdrawals	
− Overdrafts	
− Service charges	
− Stop payments	
± Book errors*	
+ Credit Memo—adds to balance	
− Debit Memo—deducts from balance	

*If a $60 check is recorded as $50, we must decrease the checkbook balance by $10.

ACCOUNTING COACH

The following Coaching Tips are from Learning Units 6-1 and 6-2. Take the Pre-Game Checkup and use the Check Your Score at the bottom of the page to see how you are doing. The Accounting Coach provides tips before each Checkup to help you avoid common accounting errors.

LU 6-1 Bank Procedures, Checking Accounts, and Bank Reconciliation

Pre-Game Tips: When reconciling a bank statement, timing is a key consideration. Deposits in transit would be added to the bank balance while checks outstanding would be subtracted. Sometimes on the bank statement, interest is shown and must be updated on the checkbook side. If you forget to record a withdrawal from an ATM, you must update your book balance. Keep in mind that any adjustments to the checkbook will require journal entries so the cash ledger account will be correct. Today, online banking is taking over many of the manual tasks, but the accounting theory remains the same.

Pre-Game Checkup
Answer true or false to the following statements.

1. A credit memo from the bank means that it is decreasing your balance.
2. NSF results in an increase to your checkbook balance.
3. Blank endorsements are the safest type of endorsement.
4. The drawer is the one receiving a check.
5. A service charge must be adjusted on the bank balance.

LU 6-2 The Establishment of Petty Cash and Change Funds

Pre-Game Tips: Petty cash is an asset. When petty cash is replenished to the same level, all of the old expenses are shown and a new check is written. The account Petty Cash is not touched. When a new level of petty cash is desired, the account Petty Cash will be debited to increase it or credited to decrease it. Keep in mind that the account Cash Short and Over is a miscellaneous account found on the income statement. A debit balance on Cash Short and Over means that you have a shortage, and a credit balance means you have an overage.

Pre-Game Checkup

Answer true or false to the following statements.

1. Petty cash is an expense.
2. Increasing the Petty Cash account means that you have to credit it.
3. In the replenishment process, cash is not involved.
4. When petty cash is established, the Petty Cash account is debited.
5. A shortage in the Cash Short and Over account results in a credit balance.

CHECK YOUR SCORE: Answers to the Pre-Game Checkup

LU 6-1

1. False—A credit memo from the bank means that it is increasing your balance.
2. False—NSF results in a decrease to your checkbook balance.
3. False—Restrictive endorsements are the safest type of endorsement.
4. False—The payee is to whom a check is payable.
5. False—A service charge must be adjusted on the checkbook balance.

LU 6-2

1. False—Petty cash is an asset.
2. False—Increasing the Petty Cash account means that you have to debit it.
3. False—In the replenishment process, a new check (cash) needs to be written.
4. True.
5. False—A shortage in the Cash Short and Over account results in a debit balance.

Chapter Summary

MyAccountingLab

Here are all the key concepts and equations to help you understand the concepts of this chapter and prepare you for your exam. After completing this review, go to MyAccountingLab for more practice opportunities.

Concepts You Should Know	Key Terms
L01 **Depositing, writing, and endorsing checks for a checking account.** 1. Restrictive endorsement limits any further negotiation of a check. 2. The payee is the person to whom the check is payable. The drawer is the one who orders the bank to pay a sum of money. The drawee is the bank with which the drawer has an account.	Check (p. 226) Cancelled check (p. 228) Deposit slip (p. 223) Drawee (p. 226) Drawer (p. 226) Endorsement (p. 223) Internal control system (p. 222) Payee (p. 226) Signature card (p. 222)
L02 **Reconciling a bank statement.** 1. The process of reconciling the bank balance with the company's cash balance is called the bank reconciliation. 2. Deposits in transit are added to the bank balance. 3. Checks outstanding are subtracted from the bank balance. 4. NSF means that a check previously deposited has non-sufficient funds to be credited (deposited) to a checking account; therefore, the amount is not included in the bank balance and thus the checking account balance is lowered. 5. When a bank debits your account, it is deducting an amount from your balance. A credit to the account is an increase to your balance. 6. All adjustments to the checkbook balance require journal entries. 7. The Internet has created online banking options.	ATM (p. 231) Bank reconciliation (p. 230) Bank statement (p. 230) Credit memorandum (p. 230) Check truncation (safekeeping) (p. 233) Debit memorandum (p. 230) Deposits in transit (p. 230) Electronic funds transfer (EFT) (p. 231) NSF (nonsufficient funds) (p. 230) Outstanding checks (p. 230) Phishing (p. 233)

Establishing and replenishing a petty cash fund; setting up an auxiliary petty cash record.

1. Petty Cash is an asset found on the balance sheet.

2. The auxiliary petty cash record is an auxiliary book; therefore, no postings are done from this record.

3. When a petty cash fund is established, the amount is entered as a debit to Petty Cash and a credit to Cash.

4. At the time of replenishment of the petty cash fund, all expenses are debited (by category) and a credit to Cash (a new check) results. This replenishment, when journalized and posted, updates the ledger from the journal.

5. The only time the Petty Cash account is used is to establish the fund initially or to bring the fund to a higher or lower level.

Auxiliary petty cash record (p. 238)

Petty cash fund (p. 236)

Petty cash voucher (p. 237)

L03

Establishing and replenishing a change fund.

1. A change fund is an asset that is used to give change to cash customers.

Change fund (p. 241)

L04

Handling transactions involving cash short and over.

1. Cash Short and Over is an account that is either a miscellaneous expense or miscellaneous income, depending on whether the ending balance is a shortage or overage.

Cash Short and Over (p. 241)

L05

Discussion Questions and Critical Thinking/Ethical Case

1. What is the purpose of internal control?

2. What is the advantage of having preprinted deposit slips?

3. Explain the difference between a blank endorsement and a restrictive endorsement.

4. Explain the difference between payee, drawer, and drawee.

5. Why should check stubs be filled out first, before the check itself is written?

6. A bank statement is sent twice a month. True or false? Please explain.

7. Explain the end product of a bank reconciliation.

8. Why are outstanding checks subtracted from the bank balance?

9. An NSF check results in a bank issuing the depositor a credit memorandum. Agree or disagree? Please explain your response.

10. Why do adjustments to the checkbook balance in the reconciliation process need to be journalized?

11. What is EFT?

12. What are the major advantages and disadvantages of online banking?

13. What is meant by check truncation or safekeeping?

14. Petty cash is a liability. Agree or disagree? Explain.

15. Explain the relationship of the auxiliary petty cash record to the recording of the cash payment.

16. At the time of replenishment, why are the totals of individual expenses debited?

17. Explain the purpose of a change fund.

18. Explain how Cash Short and Over can be a miscellaneous expense.

19. Sean Nah, the bookkeeper of Revell Co., received a bank statement from Lone Bank. Sean noticed a $250 mistake made by the bank in the company's favor. Sean called his supervisor, who said that as long as it benefits the company, he should not tell the bank about the error. You make the call. Write your specific recommendations to Sean.

Concept Checks

● **LO2** *(10 MIN)*   **Bank Reconciliation**

1. Indicate what effect (#1 – 4) each situation (#a – f) will have on the bank reconciliation process.
    1. Add to bank balance.
    2. Deduct from bank balance.
    3. Add to checkbook balance.
    4. Deduct from checkbook balance.
        _____ **a.** Check no. 150 was outstanding for $120.
        _____ **b.** $200 deposit in transit.
        _____ **c.** $155 NSF check.
        _____ **d.** A check written for $15 was recorded in the company's books as $25.
        _____ **e.** Bank collected a $1,000 note less a $50 collection fee.
        _____ **f.** $12 bank service charge.

Journal Entries in Reconciliation Process

⬤ **LO2** *(5 MIN)*

2. Which of the transactions in Exercise 1 would require a journal entry?

Bank Reconciliation

⬤ **LO2** *(10 MIN)*

3. From the following, construct a bank reconciliation for King Co. as of November 30, 201X.

Checkbook balance	$1,907.10
Bank statement balance	1,938.20
Deposits in transit	283.70
Outstanding checks	389.50
Bank service charge	15.80
NSF check	58.90

Petty Cash

⬤ **LO3** *(10 MIN)*

4. Indicate what effects (#1 – 4) each situation (#a – f) will have. (Note: There might be more than one effect applicable for a situation.)

   1. New check written.
   2. Recorded in general journal.
   3. Petty cash voucher prepared.
   4. Recorded in auxiliary petty cash record.
      _____ a. Established petty cash.
      _____ b. Paid $1,200 bill.
      _____ c. Paid $3 for Band-Aids from petty cash.
      _____ d. Paid $4 for stamps from petty cash.
      _____ e. Paid electric bill, $270.
      _____ f. Replenished petty cash.

Replenishment of Petty Cash

⬤ **LO3** *(15 MIN)*

5. Petty cash was originally established for $25. During the month, $4 was paid out for stamps and $5 for floor wax. During replenishment, the custodian discovered that the balance in petty cash was $8. Record, using a general journal entry, the replenishment of petty cash back to $25.

Increasing Petty Cash

⬤ **LO3** *(10 MIN)*

6. In Exercise 5, if the custodian decided to raise the level of petty cash to $35, what would be the journal entry to replenish? (Use a general journal entry.)

Exercises

Set A

6A-1. From the following information, construct a bank reconciliation for Zing Co. as of March 31, 201X. Then prepare journal entries if needed.

⬤ **LO2** *(15 MIN)*

Checkbook balance	$1,851	Outstanding checks	$642
Bank statement balance	1,400	Bank service charge	55
Deposits (in transit)	1,000	NSF: Mia Kaminsky's check in payment of account was returned for insufficient funds.	38

● **LO3** *(15 MIN)*   **6A-2.** In general journal form, prepare journal entries to establish a petty cash fund on October 1 and replenish it on October 31.

201X		
Oct.	1	A $109 petty cash fund is established.
	31	At the end of the month, $23 cash plus the following paid vouchers exist: donations expense, $23; postage expense, $19; office supplies expense, $27; miscellaneous expense, $17.

● **LO3** *(15 MIN)*   **6A-3.** If in Exercise 6A-2 cash on hand is $17, prepare the entry to replenish the petty cash on October 31.

● **LO3** *(15 MIN)*   **6A-4.** If in Exercise 6A-2 cash on hand is $29, prepare the entry to replenish the petty cash on October 31.

● **LO5** *(15 MIN)*   **6A-5.** At the end of the day the clerk for Bill's Variety Shop noticed an error in the amount of cash he should have. Total cash sales from the sales tape were $1,190, whereas the total cash in the register was $1,149. Bill keeps a $21 change fund in his shop. Prepare an appropriate general journal entry to record the cash sale as well as reveal the cash shortage.

Set B

● **LO2** *(15 MIN)*   **6B-1.** From the following information, construct a bank reconciliation for Zing Co. as of March 31, 201X. Then prepare journal entries if needed.

Checkbook balance	$1,563	Outstanding checks	$654
Bank statement balance	1,200	Bank service charge	45
Deposits (in transit)	900	NSF: Mia Kaminsky's check in payment of account was returned for insufficient funds.	72

● **LO3** *(15 MIN)*   **6B-2.** In general journal form, prepare journal entries to establish a petty cash fund on January 1 and replenish it on January 31.

201X		
Jan.	1	A $107 petty cash fund is established.
	31	At the end of the month, $32 cash plus the following paid vouchers exist: donations expense, $22; postage expense, $13; office supplies expense, $22; miscellaneous expense, $18.

● **LO3** *(15 MIN)*   **6B-3.** If in Exercise 6B-2 cash on hand is $29, prepare the entry to replenish the petty cash on January 31.

● **LO3** *(15 MIN)*   **6B-4.** If in Exercise 6B-2 cash on hand is $35, prepare the entry to replenish the petty cash on January 31.

● **LO5** *(15 MIN)*   **6B-5.** At the end of the day the clerk for Jack's Variety Shop noticed an error in the amount of cash he should have. Total cash sales from the sales tape were $1,208, whereas the total cash in the register was $1,156. Jack keeps a $28 change fund in his shop. Prepare an appropriate general journal entry to record the cash sale as well as reveal the cash shortage.

Problems

Set A

6A-1. Slacks.com received a bank statement from Italian Bank indicating a bank balance of $7,600. Based on Slacks.com's check stubs, the ending checkbook balance was $8,767. Your task is to prepare a bank reconciliation for Slacks.com as of July 31, 201X, from the following information (journalize entries as needed):

● L02 *(20 MIN)*

Check Figure:
Reconciled Balance $8,500

  a. Checks outstanding: no. 122, $810; no. 130, $690.
  b. Deposits in transit, $2,400.
  c. Slacks.com forgot to record a $1,260 equipment purchase made with a debit card.
  d. Bank service charges, $40.
  e. Italian Bank collected a note for Slacks.com, $1,040, less a $7 collection fee.

6A-2. From the following bank statement, please (1) complete the bank reconciliation for Jimmy's Deli found on the reverse of the following bank statement and (2) journalize the appropriate entries as needed.

● L02 *(20 MIN)*

  a. A deposit of $1,600 is in transit.
  b. Jimmy's Deli has an ending checkbook balance of $5,730.
  c. Checks outstanding: no. 111, $450; no. 119, $1,400; no. 121, $390.
  d. Jim Rice's check for $1,000 bounced due to lack of sufficient funds.
  e. Bank Service Charge $10.

Check Figure:
Reconciled Balance $4,720

Bourne National Bank
Rio Mean Branch
Bugna, Texas
Jimmy's Deli
8811 2nd St.
Bugna, Texas

Old Balance	Checks and Other Withdrawals in Order of Payment		Deposits	Date	New Balance
6,700				2/2	6,700
	60.00	200.00		2/3	6,440
	90.00		320.00	2/10	6,670
	630.00		620.00	2/15	6,660
	1,000.00	NSF	240.00	2/20	5,900
	1,250.00		1,180.00	2/24	5,830
	680.00	10.00 SC	220.00	2/28	5,360

6A-3. The following transactions occurred in April for Joyous Co.:

● L03 *(30 MIN)*

Check Figure:
Cash Replenishment $69

201X
Apr.

  1 Issued check no. 14 for $125 to establish a petty cash fund.

  5 Paid $13 from petty cash for postage, voucher no. 1.

  8 Paid $16 from petty cash for office supplies, voucher no. 2.

 15 Issued check no. 15 to Real Bell Corp. for $240 from past purchases on account.

 17 Paid $16 from petty cash for office supplies, voucher no. 3.

 20 Issued check no. 16 to Angell Corp., $625 for past purchases on account.

 24 Paid $13 from petty cash for postage, voucher no. 4.

 26 Paid $11 from petty cash for local church donation, voucher no. 5 (a miscellaneous payment).

 28 Issued check no. 17 to Jay Moon to pay for office equipment, $725.

 30 Replenished petty cash, check no. 18.

Your tasks are to do the following:

1. Record the appropriate entries in the general journal as well as the auxiliary petty cash record as needed.
2. Replenish the petty cash fund on April 30 (check no. 18).

LO3, 4, 5 *(40 MIN)*

6A-4. From the following, record the transactions in Burbanks's auxiliary petty cash record and general journal as needed:

201X		
Oct.	1	A check was drawn (no. 444) payable to Jane Janiak, petty cashier, to establish a $180 petty cash fund.

Check Figure:
Cash Replenishment $137

	5	Paid $26 for postage stamps, voucher no. 1.
	9	Paid $10 for delivery charges on goods for resale, voucher no. 2.
	12	Paid $18 for donation to a church (miscellaneous expense), voucher no. 3.
	14	Paid $12 for postage stamps, voucher no. 4.
	17	Paid $21 for delivery charges on goods for resale, voucher no. 5.
	27	Purchased computer supplies from petty cash for $18; voucher no. 6.
	28	Paid $20 for postage, voucher no. 7.
	29	Drew check no. 592 to replenish petty cash and a $12 shortage.

Set B

LO2 *(20 MIN)*

6B-1. Slacks.com received a bank statement from French Bank indicating a balance of $8,200. Based on Slacks.com's check stubs, the ending checkbook balance was $9,000. Your task is to prepare a bank reconciliation for Slacks.com as of July 31, 201X, from the following information (journalize as needed):

Check Figure:
Reconciled Balance $8,730

a. Checks outstanding: no. 122, $850; no. 130, $720.
b. Deposits in transit, $2,100.
c. Slacks.com forgot to record a $1,300 equipment purchase made with a debit card.
d. Bank service charges, $55.
e. French bank collected a note for Slacks.com, $1,090, less a $5 collection fee.

LO2 *(20 MIN)*

6B-2. From the following statement, please (1) complete the bank reconciliation for Jimmy's Deli found on the reverse of the bank statement and (2) journalize the appropriate entries as needed.

a. A deposit of $2,300 is in transit.
b. Jimmy's Deli has an ending checkbook balance of $4,470.
c. Checks outstanding: no. 111, $950; no. 119, $1,600; no. 121, $280.
d. Stanley Pennant's check for $1,500 bounced due to lack of sufficient funds.

Check Figure:
Reconciled Balance $2,910

Bourne National Bank
Rio Mean Branch
Bugna, Texas
Jimmy's Deli
8811 2nd St.
Bugna, Texas

Old Balance	Checks and Other Withdrawals in Order of Payment		Deposits	Date	New Balance
5,300				2/2	5,300
	70.00	230.00		2/3	5,000
	110.00		360.00	2/10	5,250
	540.00		530.00	2/15	5,240
	1,500.00	NSF	270.00	2/20	4,010
	1,350.00		1,250.00	2/24	3,910
	570.00	60.00 SC	160.00	2/28	3,440

6B-3. The following transactions occurred in April for Joyous Co.:

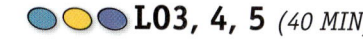 **L03** *(30 MIN)*

201X		
Apr.	1	Issued check no. 14 for $120 to establish a petty cash fund.
	5	Paid $10 from petty cash for postage, voucher no. 1.
	8	Paid $16 from petty cash for office supplies, voucher no. 2.
	15	Issued check no. 15 to Upright Corp. for $240 for past purchases on account.
	17	Paid $17 from petty cash for office supplies, voucher no. 3.
	20	Issued check no. 16 to Federer Corp. $500 for past purchases on account.
	24	Paid $15 from petty cash for postage, voucher no. 4.
	26	Paid $12 from petty cash for local church donation, voucher no. 5 (a miscellaneous payment).
	28	Issued check no. 17 to Josh Loon to pay for office equipment, $600.
	30	Replenished petty cash, check no. 18.

Check Figure:
Cash Replenishment $70

Your tasks are to do the following:

a.   Record the appropriate entries in the general journal as well as the auxiliary petty cash record as needed

b.   Be sure to replenish the petty cash fund on April 30 (check no. 18).

6B-4. From the following, record the transactions in Burbank's auxiliary petty cash record and general journal as needed:

 **L03, 4, 5** *(40 MIN)*

201X		
Oct.	1	A check was drawn (no. 444) payable to Eileen Cooper, petty cashier, to establish a $200 petty cash fund.
	5	Paid $20 for postage stamps, voucher no. 1.
	9	Paid $11 for delivery charges on goods for resale, voucher no. 2.
	12	Paid $16 for donation to a church (miscellaneous expense), voucher no. 3.
	14	Paid $10 for postage stamps, voucher no. 4.
	17	Paid $20 for delivery charges on goods for resale, voucher no. 5.
	27	Purchased computer supplies from petty cash for $25, voucher no. 6.
	28	Paid $13 for postage, voucher no. 7.
	29	Drew check no. 715 to replenish petty cash and a $5 shortage.

Check Figure:
Cash Replenishment $120

Financial Report Problem

 **L02** *(15 MIN)*

Reading the Kellogg's Annual Report

Go to http://investor.kelloggs.com/annuals.cfm, to access the Kellogg's 2010 Annual Report. How often do you think Kellogg's reconciles its bank statement? What type of security control may be in place? Support your position.

ON the JOB |||||||||||||||||||||||||||||||

MyAccountingLab

SANCHEZ COMPUTER CENTER

L02, 3, 4 *(60 MIN)*

The books have been closed for the first year of business for Sanchez Computer Center. The company ended up with a marginal profit for the first three months in operation. Tony expects faster growth as he enters a busy season.

Following is a list of transactions for the month of October. Petty Cash account #1010 and Miscellaneous Expense account #5100 have been added to the chart of accounts.

Oct.	1	Paid rent for November, December, and January, $1,200 (check no. 8108).
	2	Established a petty cash fund for $100.
	4	Collected $3,600 from a cash customer for building five systems.
	5	Collected $2,600, the amount due from A. Pitale's invoice no. 12674, customer on account.
	6	Purchased $25 worth of stamps using petty cash voucher no. 101.
	7	Withdrew $2,000 (check no. 8109) for personal use.
	8	Purchased $22 worth of supplies using petty cash voucher no. 102.
	12	Paid the newspaper carrier $10 using petty cash voucher no. 103.
	16	Paid the amount due on the September phone bill, $65 (check no. 8110).
	17	Paid the amount due on the September electric bill, $95 (check no. 8111).
	22	Performed computer services for Taylor Golf; billed the client $4,200 (invoice no. 12675).
	23	Paid $20 for computer paper using petty cash voucher no. 104.
	30	Took $15 out of petty cash for lunch, voucher no. 105.
	31	Replenished the petty cash. Coin and currency in drawer total $8.

Because Tony was so busy trying to close his books, he forgot to reconcile his last three months of bank statements. A list of all deposits and checks written for the past three months (each entry is identified by chapter, transaction date, or transaction letter) and the bank statements for July through September are provided. The statement for October won't arrive until the first week of November.

Assignment

1. Record the transactions in general journal or petty cash format.

2. Post the transactions to the general ledger accounts.

3. Prepare a trial balance.

4. Compare the Computer Center's deposits and checks with the bank statements and complete a bank reconciliation as of September 30, 201X.

Sanchez Computer Center Summary of Deposits and Checks

Chapter	Transaction	Payor/Payee	Amount
		Deposits	
1	a	Tony Freedman	$4,500
1	f	Cash customer	250
1	i	Taylor Golf	1,200
1	g	Cash customer	200
2	p	Cash customer	900
3	Sept. 2	Tonya Parker Jones	325
3	Sept. 6	Summer Lipe	220
3	Sept. 12	Jeannine Sparks	850
3	Sept. 26	Mike Hammer	140

Chapter	Transaction	Check #	Payor/Payee	Amount
			Checks	
1	b	8095	Multi Systems, Inc.	$1,200
1	c	8096	Office Furniture, Inc.	600
1	e	8097	Capital Management	400
1	j	8098	Tony Freedman	100
2	l	8099	Insurance Protection, Inc.	150
2	m	8100	Office Depot	200
2	n	8101	Computer Edge Magazine	1,400
2	q	8102	San Diego Electric	85
2	r	8103	U.S. Postmaster	50
3	Sept. 1	8104	Capital Management	1,200
3	Sept. 8	8105	Pacific Bell USA	155
3	Sept. 15	8106	Computer Connection	200
3	Sept. 16	8107	Multi Systems, Inc.	1,200

Bank Statement

First Union Bank 322 Glen Ave. Escondido, CA 92025

Sanchez Computer Center			Statement Date: July 22, 201X	
Checks Paid:			Deposits and Credits:	
Date paid	Number	Amount	Date received	Amount
7-4	8095	1,200.00	7-1	4,500.00
7-7	8096	600.00	7-10	250.00
7-15	8097	400.00	7-20	1,200.00
			7-21	200.00
Total 3 checks paid for $2,200.00			Total Deposits	$6,150.00
Ending balance on July 22—$3,950.00				

Received statement July 29, 201X.

Bank Statement

First Union Bank 322 Glen Ave. Escondido, CA 92025

Sanchez Computer Center			Statement Date: August 21, 201X	
Checks Paid:			Deposits and Credits:	
Date paid	Number	Amount	Date received	Amount
8-2	8098	100.00	8-12	900.00
8-3	8099	150.00		
8-10	8100	200.00		
8-15	8101	1,400.00		
8-20	8102	85.00		
Total 5 checks paid for $1,935.00			Total Deposits	$900.00
Beginning balance on July 22—$3,950.00			Ending balance on August 21—$2,915.00	

Received statement August 27, 201X.

Bank Statement

First Union Bank 322 Glen Ave. Escondido, CA 92025				
Sanchez Computer Center			**Statement Date: September 20, 201X**	
Checks Paid:			Deposits and Credits:	
Date paid	Number	Amount	Date received	Amount
9-2	8103	50.00	9-4	325.00
9-6	8104	1,200.00	9-7	220.00
9-12	8105	155.00	9-14	850.00
Total 3 checks paid for $1,405.00			Total Deposits	$1,395.00
Beginning balance on August 21			Ending balance on September 20	
$2,915.00			$2,905.00	

Received statement September 29, 201X.

SUBWAY CASE

Counting Down the Cash

Subway now requires all of its franchisees to submit their weekly sales and inventory reports electronically using new point-of-sale (POS) touch-screen cash registers. With the new POS registers, clerks use a touch screen to punch in the number and type of items bought. Franchisees can quickly reconfigure prices and products to match new promotions. Not only is this POS method faster than using the old cash registers, but it also allows franchisees to view every transaction as it occurs—from their own back office computers or even from home. Also, individual POS terminals within the restaurant are linked, so franchisees are able to see consolidated data quickly.

L01,2,3,4
(20 MIN)

The transition to electronic reporting and networked POS terminals, however, has not been without bumps, as Stan can testify. About six months before the deadline for all Subway franchisees to "go electronic," Stan attended a heated meeting on the topic at his local chapter of the North American Association of Subway Franchisees (NAASF). The NAASF is an independent organization of franchisees that serves as an advisory council on Subway policies and issues of common concern. Everyone seemed to be talking at once.

"I just don't trust these machines. What am I supposed to do when the system crashes?" complained one man.

"Yeah, and I don't like the idea of a bunch of kids knowing more about how to run the software than I do," said one older franchisee.

"Don't be so quick to assume that our sandwich artists will love POS," said one woman. "I overheard one of my employees say to another, 'POS means **P**eeking **O**ver **S**houlders.' These young kids we hire have more reason to be resistant than we do!"

"I'll say they do!" rejoined Jay Harden, the president of Stan's local NAASF. "Employee theft is one of the largest problems we face as franchisees. I, for one, really welcome the cash control we get with POS."

Stan had to agree with Jay. Training staff to record every sale and record it correctly is a critical component of a cash business such as Subway. In Stan's view, the POS machines would only make that training easier. Cash control is built into the new system, which also provides the owners with information that will help them spot problems—such as employee theft—and track trends. Of course, thought Stan, the chore of counting down the cash at the end of a shift remained. No matter what type of computer program you install, cash still must be counted down and rectified with the register tape at the end of each shift.

As the voices rang louder around him, Stan thought about what had happened that day when Ellen closed out her cash register drawer. He had spent hours figuring out a discrepancy between the cash in the drawer and the register tape. Ellen had forgotten to void a mistaken entry for $99.99. Stan had first suspected that she had made a huge error in counting change.

Thinking of errors in counting brought him back to the topic of the meeting. Stan raised his hand to speak.

"One thing that concerns me is the potential for accounting errors. I still have to key in data from the POS terminals into my Peachtree accounting software. Every time I have to reenter data, the potential for error multiplies."

"That shows good foresight, Stan," said Jay Harden. "We're actually exploring computer programs that will feed the data directly from the POS terminals into our accounting programs." Even some of the technophobes and POS skeptics in the group had to agree that it would be a great idea.

Discussion Questions

1. What is an advisory council? Why do you think franchisees need one?
2. Why do you think some small business owners fear computerization?
3. How would Stan catch a discrepancy in the Cash account? How would he record a loss?
4. Why does Subway invest time, money, and effort in investigating new cash handling systems such as its new POS terminals?

The internal control policies of a company will depend on things such as number of employees, company size, sources of cash, and usage of the Internet.

Calculating Pay and Payroll Taxes: The Beginning of the Payroll Process

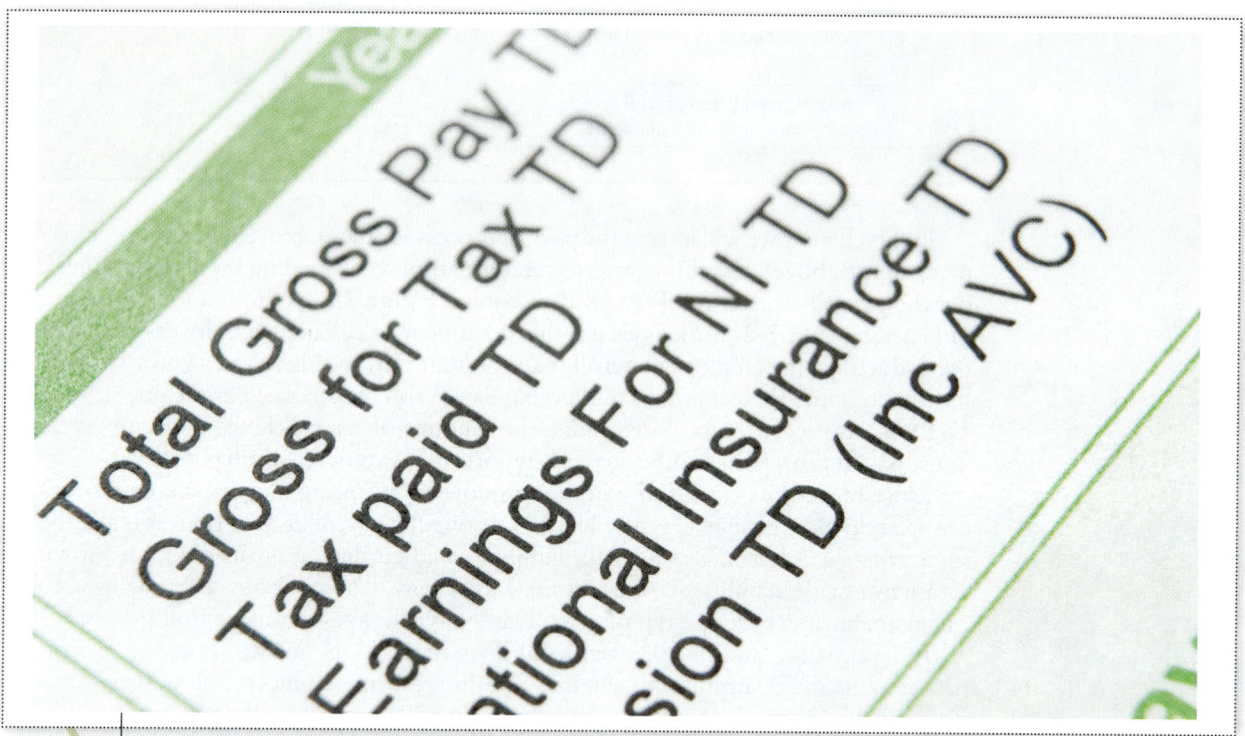

THE GAME PLAN

Wow! You just got your first paycheck from your new job at Sears. You had expected a check for $500 but were disappointed when you saw the check was for much less. You had forgotten about all the taxes withheld from your paycheck. Sears, like many other companies, has payroll departments that prepare its payrolls, which calculate employee earnings and proper amounts to be withheld for Social Security and Medicare, as well as state and federal income tax. Through the understanding of the payroll process in this chapter, you will learn the difference between gross pay and net pay. Generally speaking, gross pay is what you wish you had and net pay is what you actually get!

LEARNING OBJECTIVES

1. Calculating gross pay, employee payroll tax deductions for federal income tax withholding, state income tax withholding, FICA (OASDI, Medicare), and net pay.

2. Preparing a payroll register.

3. Maintaining an employee earnings record.

4. Calculating employer taxes for FICA (OASDI, Medicare), FUTA, SUTA, and workers' compensation insurance.

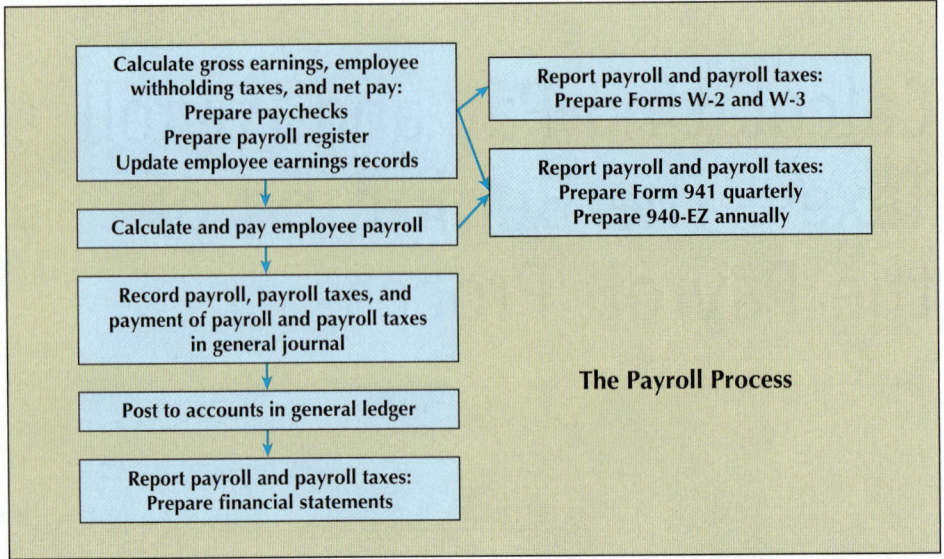

In this chapter we will look at the payroll process for the employer (see the accompanying figure above). Use this chart as a reference tool when reading the chapter. Check out the payroll register for Travelwithus.com in Figure 7.3 (p. 269) at the beginning of Learning Unit 7-2. Businesses use this document to calculate employees' pay and the deductions for employee payroll taxes on that pay. In this chapter you will learn how to compute these amounts and prepare a payroll register such as the one shown. You will also learn how to determine the amount of payroll taxes that employers must pay and prepare another payroll report, the employee earnings record.

Most businesses can't run without employees, so hiring and paying employees are pretty typical business events. The accounting for payroll transactions is really the same whether a business is a small, family-owned gardening business in your town or a nationwide retail department store. Either way, it's important to know how to calculate, pay, record, and report payroll and payroll taxes in this payroll process.

Federal, state, and maybe even local laws regulate the payroll process. A business may be fined substantial penalties and interest for failing to follow these laws properly. For example, a business may be fined $50 per statement up to a maximum of $250,000, or $100,000 for a small business, for failing to give its employees their W-2 forms, Wage and Tax Statements after August 31 of the calendar year following the tax year. Because of this, there are many companies, such as ADP, Paychex, and Ceridian, that will handle payroll for a fee. However, it is often less costly for the business to do these tasks itself.

In this chapter we take a close look at the employees of Travelwithus.com, a new Internet-based company that makes travel arrangements for its customers, to see how a payroll is figured and recorded. Travelwithus.com specializes in two types of travel, cruises and business travel. We look at how its payroll is affected by federal, state, and local taxes and how the accountant at Travelwithus.com handles payroll transactions for the company.

● LO1   LEARNING UNIT 7-1 CALCULATION OF GROSS EARNINGS, EMPLOYEE WITHHOLDING TAXES, AND NET PAY

Katherine Kurtz is the accountant for Travelwithus.com who calculates and records each payroll for the company. Several parts of Katherine's job are especially important. First, Katherine must be accurate in everything she does, because any mistake she makes in working with the payroll may affect both the employee and the company. Second, Katherine needs to be on time when working on the company's payroll so that employees get their paychecks as expected and governments receive payroll taxes when due. Third, Katherine must at all times obey the appropriate federal, state, and local laws governing payroll matters. Fourth, because processing payroll involves personal employee information such as pay rates and marital status, Katherine always needs to keep payroll data confidential.

Gross Earnings

To begin the payroll process, Katherine must first calculate the earnings for Travelwithus.com's employees. To make the correct calculations, Katherine must know how each employee has been classified for payroll purposes. As a rule, a company will classify every employee either as "hourly" or "salaried." If an employee is an hourly employee, that employee only will be paid for the hours he or she worked. Employees classified as salaried employees receive a fixed dollar amount for the time period worked.

Travelwithus.com classified three of its six employees as hourly. For these three employees, Katherine must compute the hours they worked during a specific time period known as a pay period; the number of hours determines how much each has earned. For payroll purposes, pay periods are defined as daily, weekly, biweekly (every two weeks), semimonthly (twice each month), monthly, quarterly, or annually. A pay period can start on any day of the week and must end after the specified period of time has passed. Most companies use weekly, biweekly, semimonthly, or monthly pay periods when calculating their payrolls.

Companies can use different pay periods for different groups of employees. Travelwithus.com chose a biweekly pay period for its hourly employees and a monthly pay period for its salaried employees. The biweekly pay period starts on Monday and ends two weeks later on a Sunday. Hourly employees actually receive their paychecks on the following Friday because it takes Katherine a few days to calculate all of the amounts involved in paying an hourly payroll. The monthly pay period starts on the first day of the calendar month and ends on the last day of that month. Salaried employees will be paid on the last day of the month. Because they receive a fixed amount of pay, Katherine is able to calculate these payroll amounts much faster than the hourly ones and can even start these calculations before the month ends.

Now that Katherine knows the pay period for Travelwithus.com's hourly employees, she calculates their total or gross earnings. Gross earnings are calculated by adding the regular earnings for an employee for the period to any overtime earnings the employee has earned for that period.

Overtime earnings must be computed according to federal law. The federal law that governs overtime earnings is called the Fair Labor Standards Act and is sometimes referred to as the **Federal Wage and Hour Law.** An employer must follow the Fair Labor Standards Act if it is involved in interstate commerce, in other words, if it is doing business in more than one state. For most employers, this law says that an hourly employee must be paid at least one and a half times his or her regular pay rate for any hours he or she works over 40 in one workweek. A workweek, according to the law, is a seven-day (or 168-hour) period that can start at any time, but once the starting time for the week is determined, it must stay the same for each week.

It is important to know that some states also have payroll laws that need to be followed in determining pay. For example, California requires employers to pay overtime pay to hourly employees who have worked more than 8 hours in any day, even if they work less than 40 hours total for that week. Employers must follow both sets of laws, and in this case, Travelwithus.com would pay overtime if an employee works more than 8 hours in one day and if an employee works more than 40 hours in one week.

Hourly employees of Travelwithus.com have two workweeks in each biweekly pay period. Travelwithus.com's hourly workweek starts on Monday morning at 12:01 A.M. each week and ends seven days later on Sunday evening at 12:00 midnight. Thus, Katherine must calculate overtime pay for any employee who worked more than 40 hours in each week of this two-week period.

Stephanie Higuera is one of the three hourly employees working for Travelwithus. com. Travelwithus.com's most recent biweekly pay period began on Monday, October 16, at 12:01 A.M. and ended on Sunday, October 29 at 12:00 midnight. The first week of this period ended on Sunday, October 22, and during this week Stephanie worked 44 hours. During the second week that ended on October 29, Stephanie worked 38 hours.

Pay or payroll period A length of time used by an employer to calculate the amount of an employee's earnings. Pay periods can be daily, weekly, biweekly (once every two weeks), semimonthly (twice each month), monthly, quarterly, or annual.

Gross earnings (gross pay) Amount of pay received before any deductions.

Fair Labor Standards Act (Federal Wage and Hour Law) A law the majority of employers must follow that contains rules stating the minimum hourly rate of pay and the maximum number of hours a worker will work before being paid time and a half for overtime hours worked. This law also has other rules and regulations that employers must follow for payroll purposes.

Interstate commerce A test that is applied to determine whether an employer must follow the rules of the Fair Labor Standards Act. If an employer communicates or does business with another business in some other state, it is usually considered to be involved in interstate commerce.

Workweek A seven-day (168-hour) period used to determine overtime hours for employees. A workweek can begin on any given day, but must end seven days later.

How much should she be paid? Katherine will answer this question by first calculating both Stephanie's regular hours and her overtime hours. According to the federal law, Katherine must look at each week separately. Stephanie worked 44 hours during the first week, which means that she worked 40 regular hours and 4 overtime hours. Because she worked fewer than 40 hours in the second week, all of these hours are regular hours.

Week No.	Week Ending	Regular Hours	Overtime Hours	Total Hours
1	October 22	40	4	44
2	October 29	38	0	38
Total		78	4	82

Stephanie earns $11.40 for each hour she works, so Katherine computes Stephanie's pay as follows:

$11.40 regular rate × 1.5 = $17.10 overtime rate
78 regular hours × $11.40 regular rate = $889.20 regular earnings
4 overtime hours × $17.10 overtime rate =   68.40 overtime earnings

$889.20 regular earnings + $68.40 overtime earnings = $957.60 gross earnings

Or, Katherine could figure Stephanie's pay this way: SAME

$11.40 regular rate × 0.5 = $5.70 extra pay for
    each overtime hour
82 total hours × $11.40 regular rate = $934.80 earnings at the regular rate
4 overtime hours × $5.70 extra pay for each
    overtime hour =   22.80 extra earnings

$934.80 earnings at the regular rate + $22.80
    extra earnings = $957.60 gross earnings

Notice that either way, Katherine computed exactly the same amount of gross earnings. The advantage of using the first method is that it clearly shows the amount of extra money that Stephanie earned from working those additional overtime hours. The advantage of the second is that it shows the effect of being paid at a higher, overtime rate for those extra hours worked.

Julia Regan also works for Travelwithus.com. She, however, is a salaried employee, and earns $4,875 per month. As a salaried (one example of an exempt) employee, she is not eligible for overtime pay, and Katherine will list her total earnings for the month of October as $4,875. To be considered a salaried employee, Julia must qualify as a salaried employee according to the specifics of the Fair Labor Standards Act. Thus, Travelwithus.com can't decide to classify employees as salaried just to avoid paying the overtime pay; these employees must be salaried persons according to this law.

Federal Income Tax Withholding

After Katherine determines Stephanie's and Julia's gross earnings, she figures out how much each of them will actually receive in their paychecks after several different taxes have been withheld. These taxes are called payroll taxes and must be paid by the employees. Employees pay these amounts by having them taken out, or withheld, from their paychecks. Their employer then sends them to the Internal Revenue Service (IRS), state governments, and maybe even local governments so they count against the amount of federal, state, and possible local income taxes that the employees will owe for the year.

In this way, Stephanie and Julia pay their taxes on a "pay as you go basis." In other words, when Stephanie and Julia complete their federal income tax returns at the end of the year, they will deduct the amount of income tax withheld during the year from the total amount owed for the year. How and when Travelwithus.com turns these amounts over to the federal, state, and local governments will be discussed in Chapter 8. Katherine computes the amount of taxes to be withheld based on each employee's gross earnings for the pay period.

Katherine starts figuring out how much to withhold from each employee's pay by looking at the W-4 that he or she completed. The IRS Form W-4, Employee's Withholding Allowance Certificate, is completed by every employee and provides information that will be used to determine the amount of federal income tax (FIT) withholdings. Figure 7.1 (p. 264) is Stephanie's W-4 form. Notice that it shows Stephanie's marital status and total number of allowances she claims for federal income tax purposes. Usually, an employee may claim one allowance for himself or herself, one for his or her spouse, and one for each of his or her dependents, such as a child. Employees who want more withheld from their paychecks can claim fewer allowances than they really have. However, they are not allowed to claim more allowances than they really have to avoid underpaying taxes owed, which may also result in them owing the government amounts for penalties and interest.

To look up the amount of federal income tax that needs to be withheld from Stephanie's paycheck, Katherine uses Stephanie's marital status and the number of claimed allowances listed on her Form W-4. She also uses Stephanie's gross earnings for the pay period and the length of the pay period. The amount of federal income tax that needs to be withheld is listed in a wage bracket table that can be found in the IRS publication called Circular E, *Employer's Tax Guide*, also known as Publication 15. Check out one of the tables from the Circular that's shown in Figure 7.2. Notice from the heading "SINGLE Persons—BIWEEKLY Payroll Period" that this table applies to single persons who are paid biweekly. Wage bracket tables are prepared according to marital status and pay period; Circular E has a similar table for married persons who are paid biweekly, as well as tables for single and married persons who are paid daily, weekly, monthly, semimonthly, monthly, quarterly, and annually. Also notice that the table has rows for different ranges of gross pay, starting from lower amounts of pay in the top rows of the table to higher amounts in the bottom rows.

Katherine determines the amount of federal income tax that needs to be withheld from Stephanie's paycheck by first locating the correct table in Circular E. She finds the table for single persons who are paid biweekly. Then, she locates the row that says "At least $940 but less than $960." Stephanie's gross pay for this pay period is $957.60, so this row applies to her. Katherine traces this row to the column for one withholding allowance, and finds that the amount of withholding tax is $93. Based on Stephanie's gross earnings of $957.60 and her one claimed allowance, Katherine will withhold $93 in federal income taxes from Stephanie's pay.

What if Stephanie had earned $960 instead of 957.60? Would the amount of federal income tax withheld be the same? No, Katherine would have withheld $96. To see this, check out the heading for the columns showing the wages. Notice that it says, "If the wages are—." Katherine will look at the rows of wage ranges, stopping when she sees the line that says, "At least $940 but less than $960." If Stephanie's gross wages are exactly $960—not less than $960—Katherine must go to the next line, which says, "At least $960 but less than $980" and withhold the amount in the column for one withholding allowance, which is $96.

State Income Tax Withholding

Most states also charge their residents an income tax based on the amount of money they earn from their employers. In 2011, only Alaska, Florida, Nevada, South Dakota, Texas, Washington, and Wyoming do not. (Technically, New Hampshire and Tennessee also do not have a state income tax; it is only imposed on interest and dividends.) So, in addition to withholding federal income taxes, Katherine may also have to determine amounts for state income tax (SIT) withholding. Fortunately for Katherine, the process for withholding state income tax is much the same as it is for withholding federal income tax. In many states, withholding amounts are based on the same information that is listed in the employee's W-4, although some states do have their own versions of this form that are used instead. Employers use state publications similar to the federal Publication 15 to figure the amount to be withheld

Form W-4 (Employee's Withholding Allowance Certificate) A form filled out by employees and used by employers to supply needed information about the number of allowances claimed, marital status, and so forth. The form is used for payroll purposes to determine federal income tax withholding from an employee's paycheck.

Federal income tax (FIT) withholding Amount of federal income tax withheld by the employer from the employee's gross pay; the amount withheld is determined by the employee's gross pay, the pay period, the number of allowances claimed by the employee on the W-4 form, and the marital status indicated on the W-4 form.

Allowances (also called exemptions) Certain dollar amounts of a person's income tax that will be considered nontaxable for income tax withholding purposes.

Circular E An IRS tax publication of tax tables.

Wage bracket table One of various charts in IRS Circular E that provide information about deductions for federal income tax based on earnings and data supplied on the W-4 form.

State income tax (SIT) withholding Amount of state income tax withheld by the employer from the employee's gross pay.

FIGURE 7.1
Completed Form W-4

Cut here and give Form W-4 to your employer. Keep the top part for your records.

Form **W-4**	**Employee's Withholding Allowance Certificate**	OMB No. 1545-0074
Department of the Treasury Internal Revenue Service	▶ Whether you are entitled to claim a certain number of allowances or exemption from withholding is subject to review by the IRS. Your employer may be required to send a copy of this form to the IRS.	**201X**

1 Type or print your first name and middle initial.   Last name
Stephanie A.   Higuera

2 Your social security number
123 : 45 : 6789

Home address (number and street or rural route)
1014 Inverness Way

3 ☒ Single ☐ Married ☐ Married, but withhold at higher Single rate.
Note. If married, but legally separated, or spouse is a nonresident alien, check the "Single" box.

City or town, state, and ZIP code
Southside, MA 01945

4 If your last name differs from that shown on your social security card, check here. You must call 1-800-772-1213 for a new card. ▶ ☐

5 Total number of allowances you are claiming (from line **H** above **or** from the applicable worksheet on page 2)   **5** 1

6 Additional amount, if any, you want withheld from each paycheck   **6** $

7 I claim exemption from withholding for 2006, and I certify that I meet **both** of the following conditions for exemption.
• Last year I had a right to a refund of **all** federal income tax withheld because I had **no** tax liability **and**
• This year I expect a refund of **all** federal income tax withheld because I expect to have **no** tax liability.
If you meet both conditions, write "Exempt" here   ▲   **7**

Under penalties of perjury, I declare that I have examined this certificate and to the best of my knowledge and belief, it is true, correct, and complete.

Employee's signature
(Form is not valid
unless you sign it.) ▶ Stephanie A. Higuera   Date ▶ January 3, 201X

8 Employer's name and address (Employer: Complete lines 8 and 10 only if sending to the IRS.)   **9** Office code (optional)   **10** Employer identification number (EIN)

For Privacy Act and Paperwork Reduction Act Notice, see page 2.   Cat. No. 10220Q   Form **W-4** (201X)

for state income taxes. However, because the 43 states can differ significantly in the way they calculate income tax, we will keep our discussion simple by assuming that state income tax is a fixed percentage of employee earnings. For our example we use an 8% tax rate. So Katherine calculates Stephanie's SIT withholding at $76.61.

Other Income Tax Withholding

We pointed out previously that employees would have state income taxes withheld from their paychecks if they live in one of the 43 states that charges such a tax. In addition, many cities and counties tax employee earnings. Sometimes the tax will be a percentage of gross earnings much like federal income tax, or it may be a fixed dollar amount that the employer will withhold from every pay period. These cities and counties have their own rules regarding payroll tax deposits and tax reports for this type of withholding tax. A state tax rate of 8% will be used in the example in this chapter.

FIGURE 7.2

Wage Bracket Tables: Single Persons—Biweekly Payroll Period

(For Wages Paid through December 2011)

And the wages are –		And the number of withholding allowances claimed is —										
At least	But less than	0	1	2	3	4	5	6	7	8	9	10
		The amount of income tax to be withheld is —										
$800	$820	$93	$72	$50	$30	$16	$2	$0	$0	$0	$0	$0
820	840	96	75	53	32	18	4	0	0	0	0	0
840	860	99	78	56	35	20	6	0	0	0	0	0
860	880	102	81	59	38	22	8	0	0	0	0	0
880	900	105	84	62	41	24	10	0	0	0	0	0
900	920	108	87	65	44	26	12	0	0	0	0	0
920	940	111	90	68	47	28	14	0	0	0	0	0
940	960	114	93	71	50	30	16	2	0	0	0	0
960	980	117	96	74	53	32	18	4	0	0	0	0
980	1,000	120	99	77	56	35	20	6	0	0	0	0
1,000	1,020	123	102	80	59	38	22	8	0	0	0	0
1,020	1,040	126	105	83	62	41	24	10	0	0	0	0
1,040	1,060	129	108	86	65	44	26	12	0	0	0	0
1,060	1,080	132	111	89	68	47	28	14	0	0	0	0
1,080	1,100	135	114	92	71	50	30	16	1	0	0	0
1,100	1,120	138	117	95	74	53	32	18	3	0	0	0
1,120	1,140	141	120	98	77	56	34	20	5	0	0	0
1,140	1,160	144	123	101	80	59	37	22	7	0	0	0
1,160	1,180	147	126	104	83	62	40	24	9	0	0	0
1,180	1,200	150	129	107	86	65	43	26	11	0	0	0
1,200	1,220	153	132	110	89	68	46	28	13	0	0	0
1,220	1,240	156	135	113	92	71	49	30	15	1	0	0
1,240	1,260	159	138	116	95	74	52	32	17	3	0	0
1,260	1,280	162	141	119	98	77	55	34	19	5	0	0
1,280	1,300	165	144	122	101	80	58	37	21	7	0	0
1,300	1,320	168	147	125	104	83	61	40	23	9	0	0
1,320	1,340	171	150	128	107	86	64	43	25	11	0	0
1,340	1,360	174	153	131	110	89	67	46	27	13	0	0
1,360	1,380	177	156	134	113	92	70	49	29	15	1	0
1,380	1,400	180	159	137	116	95	73	52	31	17	3	0
1,400	1,420	183	162	140	119	98	76	55	34	19	5	0
1,420	1,440	188	165	143	122	101	79	58	37	21	7	0
1,440	1,460	193	168	146	125	104	82	61	40	23	9	0
1,460	1,480	198	171	149	128	107	85	64	43	25	11	0
1,480	1,500	203	174	152	131	110	88	67	46	27	13	0
1,500	1,520	208	177	155	134	113	91	70	49	29	15	1
1,520	1,540	213	180	158	137	116	94	73	52	31	17	3
1,540	1,560	218	183	161	140	119	97	76	55	33	19	5
1,560	1,580	223	188	164	143	122	100	79	58	36	21	7
1,580	1,600	228	193	167	146	125	103	82	61	39	23	9
1,600	1,620	233	198	170	149	128	106	85	64	42	25	11
1,620	1,640	238	203	173	152	131	109	88	67	45	27	13
1,640	1,660	243	208	176	155	134	112	91	70	48	29	15
1,660	1,680	248	213	179	158	137	115	94	73	51	31	17
1,680	1,700	253	218	182	161	140	118	97	76	54	33	19
1,700	1,720	258	223	187	164	143	121	100	79	57	36	21
1,720	1,740	263	228	192	167	146	124	103	82	60	39	23
1,740	1,760	268	233	197	170	149	127	106	85	63	42	25
1,760	1,780	273	238	202	173	152	130	109	88	66	45	27
1,780	1,800	278	243	207	176	155	133	112	91	69	48	29
1,800	1,820	283	248	212	179	158	136	115	94	72	51	31
1,820	1,840	288	253	217	182	161	139	118	97	75	54	33
1,840	1,860	293	258	222	187	164	142	121	100	78	57	36
1,860	1,880	298	263	227	192	167	145	124	103	81	60	39
1,880	1,900	303	268	232	197	170	148	127	106	84	63	42
1,900	1,920	308	273	237	202	173	151	130	109	87	66	45
1,920	1,940	313	278	242	207	176	154	133	112	90	69	48
1,940	1,960	318	283	247	212	179	157	136	115	93	72	51
1,960	1,980	323	288	252	217	182	160	139	118	96	75	54
1,980	2,000	328	293	257	222	186	163	142	121	99	78	57
2,000	2,020	333	298	262	227	191	166	145	124	102	81	60
2,020	2,040	338	303	267	232	196	169	148	127	105	84	63
2,040	2,060	343	308	272	237	201	172	151	130	108	87	66
2,060	2,080	348	313	277	242	206	175	154	133	111	90	69
2,080	2,100	353	318	282	247	211	178	157	136	114	93	72

$2,100 and over Use Table 2(a) for a **SINGLE person** on page 36. Also see the instructions on page 35.

Employee Withholding for Social Security Taxes

FICA (Federal Insurance Contributions Act) Part of the Social Security Act of 1935, this law taxes both the employer and employee up to a certain maximum rate and wage base for OASDI tax purposes. It also taxes both the employer and employee for Medicare purposes, but this tax has no wage base maximum.

In addition to withholding federal and, probably, state income tax, Katherine must also compute and withhold Social Security tax from Travelwithus.com employees. Social Security tax is also known as FICA because it was created by a 1935 federal law called the Federal Insurance Contribution Act. The law became effective in 1937. Ever since then, employers have been required to withhold amounts from employees' pay and turn them over to the federal government. The government then uses these amounts to make the following payments:

- Monthly retirement benefits for persons over 62 years old
- Medical benefits for persons over 65 years old
- Benefits for persons who have become disabled
- Benefits for families of deceased workers who were covered by this law

Before the amount of taxes withheld from employees' pay can be calculated, we need to know a few things about the Social Security (or FICA) tax. First, the tax is really two taxes. One tax is called the old-age, survivor's, and disability insurance (OASDI) tax and the other is known as Medicare. Sometimes people talk about the two taxes as though they were one, but it is key to know that they are actually separate, because each tax is calculated differently. Also know that OASDI puts a limit on the amount of tax that an employee must pay by setting a maximum dollar amount of earnings that can be taxed, and this amount is called the wage base. The same is not true of Medicare; all wages earned are subject to the Medicare tax. The OASDI and Medicare tax rates and the OASDI wage base amount are all set by the federal government; the OASDI wage base increases as the federal government calculated cost-of-living increases in each calendar year. The amounts for 2011 are as follows:

Calendar year A one-year period beginning on January 1 and ending on December 31. Employers must use a calendar year for payroll purposes, even if the employer uses a fiscal year for financial statements and for any other reason.

Tax	2011 Tax Rate	2011 Wage Base**
OASDI	6.2%*	$106,800
Medicare	1.45%	None

COACHING TIP

Medicare unlike OASDI does not have a wage base, all gross earnings are subject to taxation.

Katherine begins to calculate the amount of Social Security tax that needs to be withheld from Stephanie's pay by looking at Stephanie's current and year-to-date (YTD) gross earnings. She needs to know the amount of earnings from the current pay period so that she can calculate the current amount of taxes. However, she also needs to know the YTD earnings so that she can see whether Stephanie has reached the maximum amount of OASDI tax yet or if Stephanie will reach it in this pay period. So far in this calendar year, Stephanie has earned a total of $19,471.20. This amount includes the $957.60 that she has earned for the most recent biweekly pay period.

Katherine calculates Stephanie's OASDI and Medicare taxes as follows:

$957.60 gross earnings × 6.2% OASDI tax rate = $59.37 OASDI tax

$957.60 gross earnings × 1.45% Medicare tax rate = $13.89 Medicare tax

Because Stephanie has earned less than the wage base limit of $106,800, all of her earnings for the current pay period are taxable. But what if Stephanie had earned more this year so far? Suppose she had earned $106,140 before this pay period. With her current earnings of $957.60, she would have earned a total of $107,097.60 for the year thus far, which is more than the wage base limit of $106,800. In that case, Katherine would have calculated the amount of OASDI tax to be withheld from Stephanie's pay by first calculating the amount of taxable earnings for the current period:

Stephanie's YTD earnings before this pay period	$106,140.00
Plus: Stephanie's current earnings	957.60
Stephanie's YTD earnings after this pay period	$107,097.60

---

*The OASDI employee tax rate has been reduced to 4.2% for calendar year 2011 as a part of an economic stimulus plan. All calculations in this textbook will be based on the tax rate of 6.2%.

**The OASDI wage base in 2011 is $106,800 and is scheduled to increase to $110,100 on January 1, 2012.

Less: 2011 OASDI tax wage base limit	106,800.00
Stephanie's earnings above the limit, and thus, not taxable	$297.60
Stephanie's current earnings	$957.60
Less: Stephanie's earnings above the limit, and thus, not OASDI taxable	297.60
Stephanie's current OASDI taxable earnings	$660.00

Now Katherine would calculate the amount of OASDI tax as follows:

$660.00 current taxable earnings × 6.2% OASDI tax rate = $40.92 OASDI tax

Stephanie has now reached the maximum amount of taxable wages (taxable earnings), which means she is done paying OASDI tax for the calendar year. What if Stephanie had already earned $106,800 or more before the current pay period? In that case, none of Stephanie's current gross earnings would be subject to OASDI tax. In other words, Stephanie would already have paid her maximum OASDI tax for the year by paying tax on the money she made up to this $106,800 wage base limit. What about next year? Both Social Security taxes are calculated on a calendar year basis, and Stephanie would have to start paying the OASDI tax again until she reached the maximum for that year.

What about the Medicare tax? Would the current amount tax that Stephanie needs to pay for this tax change too? No. Because the Medicare tax does not limit the amount of earnings that can be taxed, all of Stephanie's earnings will be taxable. In other words, even if Stephanie had already earned $106,800 this year, all of her current earnings of $957.60 would be taxable and she would still have $13.89 withheld from her current paycheck for the Medicare tax.

Taxable earnings Shows amount of earnings subject to a tax. The tax itself is not shown.

Other Withholdings

Sometimes employees have additional amounts withheld from their paychecks for various reasons. For example, they may choose to buy medical insurance for themselves and maybe even their spouse and dependents through an insurance plan offered by their employer. Sometimes the employer pays the premium for this insurance coverage, or at least pays for the part of the premium that covers the employee. Even if the employer pays some of the premium, however, it is common for the employee to pay the rest. The employee pays this premium by having it withheld from his or her pay, just as the employee pays income and Social Security taxes by having these amounts withheld by the employer. Travelwithus.com currently offers this opportunity to its employees, and the cost to the hourly employee is $33 for each pay period. Other companies may allow their employees to have funds withheld from their paychecks for union dues, retirement plan contributions, or lfe insurance premiums.

Medical insurance Health care insurance for which premiums may be paid through a deduction from an employee's paycheck.

Net Pay

Katherine's next step in the payroll accounting process is to calculate the amount of pay that Stephanie will actually receive as her paycheck; this amount is called net pay. At this point, Katherine has computed all of the amounts necessary to determine Stephanie's net pay. Now she simply needs to combine them as follows:

Net pay Gross earnings, less deductions. Net pay, or take-home pay, is what the worker actually takes home.

Gross earnings for the current biweekly pay period:		$957.60
Deductions for employee withholding taxes:		
Federal income tax	$93.00	
State income tax	76.61	
OASDI tax	59.37	
Medicare tax	13.89	
Medical insurance	33.00	
Total deductions		275.87
Net pay		$681.73

LEARNING UNIT 7-1 REVIEW

AT THIS POINT you should be able to do the following:

- Explain the purpose of the Fair Labor Standards Act (i.e., the Federal Wage and Hour Law).
- Calculate regular, overtime, and total gross pay.
- Complete a W-4 form.
- Discuss the term *claiming an allowance*.
- Use a wage-bracket tax table to determine the amount of federal income tax withholding.
- Define the purpose of the Social Security (FICA) taxes, OASDI, and Medicare.
- Calculate withholdings for OASDI and Medicare taxes.
- Calculate net pay.

Instant Replay ◉ Self-Review Quiz 7-1

Tony Kagaragis is an hourly software engineer who is paid biweekly. He earns $23.00 per hour. In the first week of the most recent pay period, he worked 39 hours, and during the second week of the period he worked 46 hours. Please calculate his regular, overtime, and gross earnings.

Solutions to Instant Replay: Self-Review Quiz 7-1

1. $23.00 regular rate × 79 regular hours = $1,817.00 regular earnings
2. $23.00 regular rate × 1½ = $34.50 overtime rate. $34.50 overtime rate × 6 overtime hours = $207.00 overtime earnings
3. $1,817.00 + $207.00 = $2,024.00 gross earnings

LEARNING UNIT 7-2 PREPARING A PAYROLL REGISTER AND EMPLOYEE EARNING RECORDLO3. $34.50 overtime rate

At this point, Katherine Kurtz, the accountant for Travelwithus.com, knows how much each of the three hourly employees earned for the most recent biweekly pay period and how many dollars of taxes need to be withheld from their paychecks. She now needs to enter this information into the accounting records for the company. Two primary records are used in accounting systems to keep track of payroll information for a company. The first of these records is a worksheet, known as a payroll register, which shows all information related to an entire pay period. The second record is called the employee earnings record and is used to keep track of an individual employee's payroll history for an entire calendar year.

 **L02**

The Payroll Register

Payroll register A multicolumn form that is used to record payroll data.

Katherine enters information about the current payroll period for hourly employees in a **payroll register**. The register includes each employee's gross earnings, employee withholding taxes, net pay, taxable earnings, cumulative earnings, and the accounts to be charged (Business Scheduling or Cruise Scheduling) for the salary and wage expense for that pay period. Travelwithus.com will actually have two registers, a biweekly one for its hourly employees and a monthly one for its salaried personnel. Figure 7.3 shows the completed payroll register for the hourly payroll covering the biweekly pay period from October 16 through October 29.

FIGURE 7.3
Payroll Register

TRAVELWITHUS.COM INC.
HOURLY EMPLOYEE PAYROLL REGISTER
OCTOBER 16–29

Employee / Social Security No.	Allowances and Marital Status	Previous Earnings (YTD)	Regular Hours	Regular Rate	Regular Amount	Overtime Hours	Overtime Rate	Overtime Amount	Gross	Current Earnings (YTD)
Higuera, Stephanie 123-45-6789	S-1	18 513 60	78	11 40	889 20	4	17 10	68 40	957 60	19 471 20
Sui, Annie 123-45-6788	S-0	21 211 00	80	15 15	1212 00	4	22 73	90 90	1302 90	3423 90
Taylor, Harold 123-45-6787	S-2	19 043 70	78	12 10	943 80	4	18 15	72 60	1016 40	20 060 10
TOTALS					3045 00			231 90	3276 90	42 955 20

TRAVELWITHUS.COM INC.
HOURLY EMPLOYEE PAYROLL REGISTER
OCTOBER 16–29

Employee / Social Security No.	Taxable Earnings FUTA/SUTA	Taxable Earnings OASDI	FIT	SIT	FICA OASDI	FICA Medicare	Medical Insurance	Net Pay	Check No.	Business Scheduling Expense	Cruise Scheduling Expense
Higuera, Stephanie 123-45-6789	—	957 60	93 00	76 61	59 37	13 89	33 00	681 73	820	957 60	
Sui, Annie 123-45-6788	1302 90	1302 90	168 00	104 23	80 78	18 89	33 00	898 00	821		1302 90
Taylor, Harold 123-45-6787	—	1016 40	80 00	81 31	63 02	14 74	33 00	744 33	822		1016 40
TOTALS	1302 90	3276 90	341 00	262 15	203 17	47 52	99 00	2324 06		957 60	2319 30

Marital Status and No. of allowances are from Employee's W-4.
Previous YTD earnings = the employee's total earnings for the year before this pay period.
Regular Hours x Regular Rate = Regular Amount.
Overtime Hours x Overtime Rate = Overtime Amount.
Regular Amount + Overtime Amount = Gross Current Earnings.
Previous YTD Earnings + Gross Current Earnings = Current YTD Earnings.

Taxable Earnings, FUTA/SUTA = Gross Current Earnings < FUTA/SUTA limit of $7,000.
Taxable Earnings, OASDI = GrossCurrent Earnings < OASDI Limit of $$106,800.
FIT = FIT from wage Bracket Table in Circular E.
SIT = Gross Current Earnings x 8%.
FICA, OASDI = Taxable Earnings, OASDI x 6.2%.
FICA, Medicare =Gross Current Earnings x 1.45%.
Medical Insurance = $33 per employee.
Net Pay = Gross Current Earnings – FIT – SIT – OASDI – Medicare – Medical Insurance.

L03   The Employee Earnings Record

Individual employee earnings record An accounting document that summarizes the total amount of wages paid and the deductions for the calendar year. It aids in preparing governmental reports. A new record is prepared for each employee each year.

After Katherine prepares the payroll register for the period, and in order to comply with all applicable employment laws and regulations, she also completes a payroll record known as the individual employee earnings record. This record provides a summary of each employee's earnings, withholding taxes, net pay, and cumulative earnings during each calendar year, as shown in Figure 7.4 on page 271. Katherine uses the information summarized in this record to prepare quarterly and annual payroll tax reports. Thus, the employee earnings record is split into calendar quarters, with each quarter being 13 weeks long.

LEARNING UNIT 7-2 REVIEW

AT THIS POINT you should be able to do the following:

- Explain and prepare a payroll register.
- Explain the purpose of the taxable earnings columns of the register and explain how they relate to the cumulative earnings column.
- Update an individual employee earnings record.

COACHING TIP

The Payroll Register is prepared first and provides data for the preparation of the Employee Earnings Record.

Instant Replay ⊙ Self-Review Quiz 7-2

Mike Chen is an hourly employee who is paid biweekly. He is paid overtime at a rate of 1½ times his hourly rate for any hours he works over 40 in a workweek. Mike worked many overtime hours this year to develop a Web site for his employer, and as of December 10 his cumulative earnings total $105,578.06. For the pay period ending on December 24, Mike's gross earnings are $1,940.85. Calculate Mike's net pay based on the following facts:

- Mike is single and claims three withholding allowances per his Form W-4. Use the tax table in Figure 7.2 on page 265. to find Mike's federal income tax withholding amount.
- The state income tax rate is 8% with no wage base limit.
- The OASDI tax rate is 6.2% with a wage base limit of $106,800 for the year; the Medicare rate is 1.45% with no wage base limit.
- Mike pays $44.00 for medical insurance for the pay period.

Solutions to Instant Replay: Self-Review Quiz 7-2

1. Federal income tax = $212.00 (Look at the "At least $1,940" line and trace it into the "3" withholding allowance column.)
2. State income tax is $155.27 ($1,940.85 × .08)
3. FICA OASDI tax is $75.76 ($106,800 − $105,578.06 = $1,221.94 taxable; $1,221.94 × .062)
4. FICA Medicare tax is $28.14 ($1,940.85 × .0145)
5. Mike Chen's net pay is $1,425.68 ($1,940.85 − $212.00 − $155.27 − $75.76 − $28.14 − $44.00)

L04   LEARNING UNIT 7-3 EMPLOYER PAYROLL TAX EXPENSE

Employer Payment for Social Security Taxes

As we discussed, employees pay payroll taxes including federal income tax, Social Security taxes, probably state income tax, and maybe even a city or county income tax. It surprises some employees to find that their employers pay payroll taxes, too. As a matter of fact, employers pay exactly the same amount of Social Security

FIGURE 7.4
Employee Earnings Record

TRAVELWITHUS.COM INC.
EMPLOYEE EARNINGS RECORD

Stephanie Higuera Social Security No. 123-45-6789

Pay Period	Hours		Earnings			Deductions					Net Pay	Check No.	YTD Earnings
	Regular	Overtime	Regular	Overtime	Gross	FIT	SIT	FICA OASDI	FICA Medicare	Medical Insurance			
10/2–10/15	80	0	91200	000	91200	8700	7296	5654	1322	3300	64927	806	1851360
10/16–10/29	78	4	88920	6840	95760	9300	7661	5937	1389	3300	68173	820	1947120
10/30–11/12	76	0	86640	000	86640	8100	6931	5372	1256	3300	61681	825	2033760
11/13–11/26	80	2	91200	3420	94620	9300	7570	5866	1372	3300	67212	839	2128380
11/27–12/10	80	4	91200	6840	98040	9900	7843	6078	1422	3300	69457	844	2226420
12/11–12/24	80	0	91200	000	91200	8700	7296	5654	1322	3300	64728	858	2317620
12/25–12/31	48	0	54720	000	54720	3300	4378	3393	793	3300	39556	863	2372340
4th Quarter Totals			595080	17100	612180	57300	48975	37954	8876	23100	435734		
YTD Totals			2314200	58140	2372340	224886	189787	147085	34399	85800	1690383		

taxes (OASDI and Medicare) for each employee as the employee pays. In 2011 the employee's OASDI rate was decreased from 6.2% to 4.2% as part of an economic stimulus plan. The employer's rate remained at 6.2%. The reduced employee rate is not used in any calculations in this text. In addition to paying OASDI and Medicare taxes for each employee, employers also pay unemployment taxes that are used to provide unemployed workers with benefits while they are looking for work.

As Travelwithus.com's accountant, Katherine calculates the amount of Social Security taxes that the company must pay as an employer much the same way that she calculated them for each employee. She first determines the amount of current gross earnings for all employees that fall below the wage base limit of $106,800. She looks at the OASDI Taxable Earnings total in the payroll register for the current period. She then multiplies this total by the OASDI tax rate of 6.2% to determine the OASDI tax that Travelwithus.com must pay:

$3,276.90 gross earnings × 6.2% OASDI tax rate = $203.17 OASDI tax

Katherine then calculates Travelwithus.com's Medicare tax by taking the current gross earnings for all employees and multiplying this total by the Medicare tax rate of 1.45%. Remember that the amount of Medicare tax for each employee is not subject to any limit; every dollar that an employee earns is taxed at the Medicare tax rate of 1.45%.

$3,276.90 gross earnings × 1.45% Medicare tax rate = $47.52 Medicare tax

The way Katherine computes these taxes differs in only one way compared to how she computed them for each employee. Because Katherine is now calculating Travelwithus.com's share of these taxes, Katherine uses current gross earnings for the company in total instead of using each employee's current gross earnings as she did when she was determining the amount to withhold from each employee's paycheck.

FUTA and SUTA

In addition to paying its employer share of FICA taxes, Travelwithus.com must also pay unemployment taxes. Unemployment tax, or unemployment insurance as it is sometimes called, was created by the same 1935 law that created Social Security. This federal law requires all 50 states, the District of Columbia, and U.S. territories to run unemployment compensation programs that are approved and monitored by the federal government. Unemployment taxes are paid by employers based on wages paid to employees. Federal Unemployment Tax Act (FUTA) taxes pay the costs of administering the federal and state programs but do not pay benefits to employees. State Unemployment Tax Act (SUTA) taxes pay the benefits to unemployed persons.

Currently, employers pay FUTA tax at a rate of 6.2%* on wages earned by each employee up to a wage base limit of $7,000. However, the federal government allows employers to take a tax credit for SUTA tax against this tax, up to a maximum credit of 5.4%.

COACHING TIP

Only employers, not employees, must calculate and pay both FUTA and SUTA taxes.

FUTA tax rate	6.2%
Less: Normal FUTA tax credit	5.4%
Net FUTA tax rate	0.8%

*Effective July 1, 2011, the federal unemployment tax rate decreased from 6.2% to 6.0% and the FUTA portion rate decreased from 0.8% to 0.6%. The expiring levy of 0.2% was established as a surcharge in 1977 and has been extended several times since that date. At present it is not known if the surcharge will be extended. The IRS is in the process of revising the Form 940 (Employer's Annual Federal Unemployment [FUTA] tax return to accommodate the two different FUTA tax rates for 2011. However, it is possible that the surcharge will be extended at a later date in 2011, retroactive to July 1, 2011.

Because of the uncertainty associated with the extension of the surcharge and the complexity that may be added to the Form 940, the author has decided to treat FUTA in the text and the associated problems as though the surcharge has not expired. The federal unemployment tax rate will remain at 6.2% and the FUTA portion will remain at 0.8%.

Employers are allowed to take this credit as long as they have paid all amounts that they owe for SUTA taxes and have paid them on time. In other words, the federal law essentially says to employers, "Comply with your state's unemployment tax laws and your total tax will not exceed a maximum of 6.2%: 0.8% to the federal government and a state rate that will vary up to maximum of 5.4%." Remember that employers alone are responsible for paying FUTA tax; it is never withheld from the earnings of employees.

Katherine calculates FUTA tax by referring to the FUTA Taxable Earnings total in the current payroll register. This column tells her how much, in total, Travelwithus.com's employees have earned this period that falls below the FUTA wage base limit of $7,000. She uses this amount to calculate the FUTA tax by multiplying it by the net FUTA tax rate as follows:

$$\$1,302.90 \text{ FUTA taxable earnings} \times 0.8\% \text{ FUTA tax rate} = \$10.42 \text{ FUTA tax}$$

Because states run their own unemployment programs, each state may use a different SUTA wage base limit. These amounts are based on the needs of the unemployment funds in each state. In 2011 the wage base limits for states ranged from $7,000 to $37,300. Different states have different SUTA tax rates for the same reason that the wage base limits vary; they are based on the needs of the unemployment funds in each state.

Additionally, the SUTA tax rate can vary from employer to employer within a state. In any state, an employer's SUTA tax rate will be based on how many dollars it contributes to the state unemployment fund and the dollar amount of claims that its employees make against that fund. In other words, the rate is tied to the employer's employment history. The more frequently an employer lays off its employees, the more unemployment benefits the state will have to pay and the higher the tax rate for that employer. In other words, employers who rarely lay off their workers will be charged a lower SUTA rate than employers who lay off workers often. In this way, the SUTA tax rate motivates employers to stabilize their workforce.

Travelwithus.com's current SUTA rate is 5.4% and the wage base limit for the state in which it is located is $7,000. Katherine calculates Travelwithus.com's SUTA tax similar to the way she calculated its FUTA tax. She first looks at the SUTA Taxable Earnings total in the current payroll register to see how much, in total, Travelwithus.com's employees earned this period below the SUTA wage base limit of $7,000. She then calculates the SUTA tax by multiplying this amount by the SUTA tax rate as follows:

$$\$1,302.90 \text{ SUTA taxable earnings} \times 5.4\% \text{ SUTA tax rate} = \$70.36$$

Workers' Compensation Insurance

Workers' compensation insurance insures employees against losses they may incur due to work caused injury or death while on the job. Each employer must purchase this insurance either through an insurance broker or state agency. In most states, this tax is paid completely by the employer, not the employee.

Travelwithus.com's premium for this insurance is based on its total estimated gross payroll, and the rate is calculated for each $100 of weekly payroll. By estimating payroll before the beginning of the year, the insurance company can determine the amount of the premium to charge Travelwithus.com. If actual payroll for the year turns out to differ from estimated payroll, then the insurance company will either credit Travelwithus.com for any overpayment or bill it for any underpayment. The rate for Travelwithus.com is based on the type of work that its employees perform as well as the amount and extent of any on-the-job injuries that its employees experience.

Travelwithus.com has two groups of employees: travel schedulers and managers. It estimated that it would have $50,000 of gross payroll for its schedulers in the next year, and its rate is $1.80 for every $100 of this payroll. The company also estimated

Workers' compensation insurance A benefit plan required by federal regulations in which employers must purchase insurance to protect their employees against losses due to injury or death incurred while on the job.

COACHING TIP

Workers' Compensation Insurance is based on the type of work each employee performs (more hazardous jobs have higher rates) and the extent of any previous on-the-job injuries.

that it will incur $190,000 of payroll for managers, and its rate for this group is $.22 for every $100 of payroll. Travelwithus.com then calculated its premium as follows:

Workers' compensation premium for schedulers:	$50,000/$100 = 500	500 × $1.80 =	$ 900.00
Workers' compensation premium for managers:	$190,000/$100 = 1,900	1,900 × $.22 =	418.00
Total workers' compensation premium =			$1,318.00

Suppose, however, that at the end of the year, Travelwithus.com's scheduler payroll totaled $57,977.14 and its manager payroll totaled $220,648.16. The actual premiums for the year would be calculated in the following manner:

Workers' compensation premium for schedulers:	$57,977.14/$100 = 580	580 × $1.80 =	$1,044.00
Workers' compensation premium for managers:	$220,648.16/$100 = 2,206	2,206 × $.22 =	485.32
Total workers' compensation premium =			$1,529.32

Travelwithus.com would then owe an additional amount of premium:

Workers' compensation premium based on actual gross payroll	$1,529.32
Workers' compensation premium based on estimated gross payroll	1,318.00
Additional workers' compensation premium owed =	$ 211.32

LEARNING UNIT 7-3 REVIEW

AT THIS POINT you should be able to do the following:

- Explain the use of the taxable earnings column of the payroll register in calculating the employer's payroll tax expense.
- Calculate the employer's payroll taxes of OASDI, Medicare, FUTA, and SUTA.
- Explain the difference between FUTA and SUTA taxes.
- Understand the purpose of workers' compensation insurance.
- Calculate the estimated premium for workers' compensation insurance.

Instant Replay ◎ Self-Review Quiz 7-3

Given the following, calculate the employer FICA OASDI, FICA Medicare, FUTA, and SUTA for Farmington Co. for the weekly payroll of July 8. Assume the following:

- FUTA tax is paid at the net rate of 0.8% on the first $7,000 of earnings.
- SUTA tax is paid at a rate of 5.6% on the first $7,000 of earnings.
- FICA tax rate for Social Security is 6.2% on $106,800, and Medicare is 1.45% on all earnings.

Employee	Cumulative Pay Before This Week's Payroll	Gross Pay for Week
Bill Jones	$6,000	$800
Julie Warner	$6,600	$400
Al Brooks	$7,900	$700

Solutions to Instant Replay: Self-Review Quiz 7-3

1. FICA OASDI   = $1,900 × .062 = $117.80
2. FICA Medicare = $1,900 × .0145 = $27.55
3. FUTA   = $1,200 × .008 = $9.60
4. SUTA   = $1,200 × .056 = $67.20

Blueprint for Recording Transactions in a Payroll Register

Current Earnings (YTD)

Current Earnings

Gross — *Amounts used to look up the applicable FIT in Circular E*

Overtime: Amount | Rate | Hours

Regular: Amount | Rate | Hours

Previous Earnings (YTD)

Allowances and Marital Status

Employee Name / Social Security No.

Account Charged: Business Scheduling Expense | Cruise Scheduling Expense — *Gross pay allocated to applicable expense catagory.*

Check No.

Net Pay — *Gross pay − deductions = net pay*

Deductions

Medical Insurance

FICA: Medicare | OASDI

SIT

FIT

Taxable Earnings: OASDI | FUTA/SUTA — *Not the tax but the wages subject to the tax*

Employee Name / Social Security No.

ACCOUNTING COACH

The following Coaching Tips are from Learning Units 7-1 through 7-3. Take the Pre-Game Checkup and use the Check Your Score to see how you are doing. The Accounting Coach provides tips before each Checkup to help you avoid common accounting errors.

LU 7-1 Calculation of Gross Earnings, Employee Withholding, Taxes, and Net Pay

Pre-Game Tips: The maximum amount of Social Security (OASDI) tax is capped by a wage base of $106,800*, while the Social Security (Medicare) tax has no limit on the amount that may be collected.

Pre-Game Checkup

Answer true or false to the following statements.

1. A pay period is always defined as a two-week period.
2. The Fair Labor Standards Act states that an employee must be paid overtime pay if he or she works over 40 hours in a work week.
3. An employee may claim fewer allowances on his or her IRS Form-4, Employee's Withholding Allowance Certificate than he or she really has.
4. Withholding of Social Security taxes (OASDI and Medicare) are limited to the amount due on all earnings below $106,800 (the wage base) in 2011.
5. Gross pay is the amount the employee receives in his or her paycheck.

LU 7-2 Preparing a Payroll Register and Employee Earning Record

Pre-Game Tips: Following the calculation of gross and net pay, records must be maintained on both a pay period and individual employee basis to ensure that appropriate reports are prepared on a timely and accurate basis.

Pre-Game Checkup

Answer true or false to the following statements.

1. The employee earnings record shows gross earnings, deductions, net pay, and taxable earnings for a payroll period.

2. The individual employee earnings record is used to update the payroll register.
3. The taxable earnings columns of the payroll register do not show the amount of tax owed.
4. The employee earnings record indicates the employee's marital status and the number of allowances claimed.
5. The payroll register shows gross earnings, deductions, net pay, and taxable earnings for a payroll period.

LU 7-3 Employer Payroll Tax Expense

Pre-Game Tips: Not only must employees pay a variety of payroll taxes, but their employers must also pay a number of payroll taxes.

Pre-Game Checkup

Answer true or false to the following statements.

1. Employers must pay FICA (OASDI and Medicare) equal to 1½ times the employee payment.
2. Only employers, not employees, must calculate and pay both FUTA and SUTA taxes.
3. FUTA and SUTA taxes are calculated on a wage base of $106,800.
4. Workers' Compensation Insurance is paid by the employer to insure that each employee is fairly compensated.
5. Workers' Compensation Insurance has a single rate for each employee of a firm, much like Social Security.

---

*The OASDI Wage base in 2011 is $106,800 and is scheduled to increase to $110,100 on January 1, 2012.

CHECK YOUR SCORE: Answers to the Pre-Game Checkup

LU 7-1

1. False—Pay periods are defined as daily, weekly, biweekly, semi-monthly, monthly, quarterly, or annually.
2. True.
3. True.
4. False—(OASDI) tax is limited by a wage base of $106,800. (Medicare) tax does not have a wage base limit therefore all wages earned are subject to the Medicare tax.
5. False—Gross pay is the amount calculated as earned by the employee before employee withholdings such as FIT, SIT and FICA (OASDI and Medicare). After these deductions from gross pay, the employee receives his or her net pay.

LU 7-2

1. False—The employee earnings record shows gross earnings, deductions, and net pay for the employee for each calendar quarter and the entire calendar year.
2. False—The payroll register is used to update the employee earnings record.
3. True. They show the amount of earnings to be taxed for unemployment taxes and Social Security (OASDI).
4. False—The employee's marital status and the number of allowances are found on the payroll register.
5. True.

LU 7-3

1. False—The employer pays exactly the same amount of Social Security taxes (OASDI and Medicare) as do its employees.
2. True.
3. False—Both FUTA and SUTA are calculated on a wage base of $7,000 for each employee.
4. False—Workers' Compensation Insurance is paid by the employer to insure employees against work related death or injury.
5. False—The rate paid by the employer is based on the type of work each employee performs (more hazardous jobs have higher rates) and the extent of any previous on-the-job injuries or deaths.

Chapter Summary

MyAccountingLab

Here are all the key concepts and equations to help you understand the concepts of this chapter and prepare you for your exam. After completing this review, go to MyAccountingLab for more practice opportunities.

Concepts You Should Know	Key Terms
● **L01** Calculating gross pay, employee payroll tax deductions for federal income tax withholding, state income tax withholding, FICA (OASDI, Medicare), and net pay. 1. The Fair Labor Standards Act states that hourly workers will receive a minimum of one and a half times their regular hourly rate of pay for all hours they work over 40 hours during a workweek. 2. Salaried employees are employees who are classified as salaried according to the provisions of the Fair Labor Standards Act. 3. For the rules of the Fair Labor Standards Act to apply to an employer, the employer must be involved in interstate commerce. 4. Employees and employers pay equal amounts of Social Security tax. Note that Social Security, or FICA tax, is made up of two taxes: OASDI and Medicare. The OASDI tax is based on a tax rate and wage base amount that is set for each calendar year. 5. Gross earnings minus deductions equals net pay. 6. Federal income tax withholding amounts are listed in tax tables found in IRS Circular E, Employer's Tax Guide, also known as Publication 15.	**Allowances (also called exemptions)** (p. 263) **Calendar year** (p. 266) **Circular E** (p. 263) **Fair Labor Standards Act (Federal Wage and Hour Law)** (p. 261) **Federal income tax (FIT) withholding** (p. 263) **FICA (Federal Insurance Contributions Act)** (p. 266) **Form W-4 (Employee's Withholding Allowance Certificate)** (p. 263) **Gross earnings (gross pay)** (p. 261) **Interstate commerce** (p. 261) **Medical insurance** (p. 267) **Net pay** (p. 267) **Pay or payroll period** (p. 261) **State income tax (SIT) withholding** (p. 263) **Taxable earnings** (p. 267) **Wage bracket table** (p. 263) **Workweek** (p. 261)
● **L02** Preparing a payroll register. 1. The two primary accounting records used to keep track of payroll amounts are the payroll register and employee earnings record. The payroll register shows gross earnings, deductions, net pay, and taxable earnings for a payroll period. 2. The taxable earnings columns of the payroll register do not show the tax. They show the amount of earnings to be taxed for unemployment taxes, OASDI, and Medicare.	**Payroll register** (p. 268)

Maintaining an employee earnings record.	Individual employee earnings record (p. 270)	● **L03**
1. The employee earnings record shows the gross earnings, deductions, and net pay for an employee for an entire calendar year.		
2. The individual employee earnings records are updated soon after the payroll register is prepared.		

Calculating employer taxes for FICA (OASDI, Medicare), FUTA, SUTA, and workers' compensation insurance.	Workers' compensation insurance (p. 273)	● **L04**
1. The payroll tax expense for an employer is made up of FICA OASDI, FICA Medicare, FUTA, and SUTA.		
2. The OASDI tax rate for 2011 is 6.2%, and the wage base limit for this year is $106,800.		
3. Medicare has no wage base limit, so an employee and employer will pay this tax on all of an employee's earnings during the calendar year, at a rate of 1.45% for 2011.		
4. The maximum amount of credit given for state unemployment taxes paid against the FUTA tax is 5.4%. This figure is known as the normal FUTA tax credit. The normal FUTA tax credit typically results in employers paying 0.8% for FUTA tax.		
5. Employers pay workers' compensation insurance premiums based on estimated payroll. At the end of the year, estimated payroll is compared to actual payroll, and the employer either pays any additional premium or receives a credit for any overpayment of premium.		

Discussion and Critical Thinking Questions/Ethical Case

1. What is the purpose of the Fair Labor Standards Act (also called the Federal Wage and Hour Law)?

2. Explain how to calculate overtime pay.

3. Explain how a W-4 form, called the Employee's Withholding Allowance Certificate, is used to determine Federal Income Tax (FIT) withheld.

4. The more allowances an employee claims on a W-4 form, the more take-home pay the employee gets with each paycheck. Agree or disagree?

5. Explain how federal and state income tax withholdings are determined.

6. Explain why a business should prepare a payroll register before employees are paid.

7. The taxable earnings column of a payroll register records the amount of tax due. Agree or disagree?

8. Define and state the purpose of FICA taxes.

9. Explain how to calculate OASDI and Medicare taxes.

10. The employer doesn't have to contribute to Social Security. Agree or disagree? Please explain.

11. What purpose does the individual employee earnings record serve?

12. Please draw a diagram showing how the following items relate to each other: (a) weekly payroll, (b) payroll register, (c) individual employee earnings record, and (d) general journal entries for payroll.

13. If you earned $130,000 this year, you would pay more OASDI and Medicare than your partner who earned $75,000. Do you agree or disagree? Please provide calculations to support your answer.

14. Explain how an employer can receive a credit against the FUTA tax due.

15. Explain what an experience or merit rating is and how it affects the amount paid by an employer for state unemployment insurance.

16. Who pays workers' compensation insurance, the employee or the employer? What types of benefits does this insurance provide? How are premiums calculated?

17. An employee for Repairs to Go, Inc., works different numbers of hours each week depending on the needs of the business. To simplify the accounting, the bookkeeper for Repairs to Go classifies this employee as a salaried person. Is this practice appropriate? Please explain.

Concept Check

MyAccountingLab

Calculating Gross Earnings

● **LO1** *(10 MIN)*

1. Calculate the total wages earned (assume an overtime rate of time and a half over 40 hours).

Employee	Hourly Rate	No. of Hours Worked
Karen Black	$14	30
Peter Rogers	$12	50

FIT and FICA

● **LO1** *(15 MIN)*

2. Devon Mark, single, claiming one exemption, has cumulative earnings before this biweekly pay period of $105,800. If he is paid $1,940 this period, what will his deductions be for FIT and FICA (OASDI and Medicare)? The FICA tax rate for Social Security is 6.2% on $106,800 and Medicare is 1.45% on all earnings.

Net Pay

● **LO1** *(15 MIN)*

3. From Exercise 2, calculate Devon's net pay. The state income tax rate is 5% and health insurance is $35.

Payroll Register

● **LO2** *(10 MIN)*

4. Match the following:
   1. Total gross pay
   2. A deduction
   3. Net pay
      a. _____ Office Salary
      b. _____ FICA OASDI Payable
      c. _____ FICA Medicare
      d. _____ Federal Income Tax
      e. _____ Medical Insurance
      f. _____ Wages and Salaries

Employer and Employee Taxes

● **LO2** *(10 MIN)*

5. Identify which of the following taxes are paid by the employee (EE) and which are paid by the employer (ER):
   a. _____ FICA Medicare
   b. _____ FIT
   c. _____ FUTA
   d. _____ SUTA

Exercises

Set A

7A-1. Calculate the total wages earned for each hourly employee assuming an overtime rate of time and a half over 40 hours.

● **LO1** *(15 MIN)*

Employee	Hourly Rate	No. of Hours Worked
Lucky Mars	$13	32
Pam Valley	$14	44
Louis Jones	$15	44

L01 *(20 MIN)*   **7A-2.** Compute the net pay for each employee using the federal income tax withholding table in Figure 7.2. Assume that FICA OASDI tax is 6.2% on a wage base limit of $106,800, Medicare is 1.45% on all earnings, the payroll is paid biweekly, and no state income tax applies.

Employee	Status	Allowances	Cumulative Pay	Biweekly Pay
Zhu Rui	Single	2	$61,000	$1,670
Tilla Palmer	Single	1	$58,500	$1,620

L04 *(20 MIN)*   **7A-3.** From the following information, calculate the payroll tax expense for Gray Company for the payroll of August 9:

Employee	Cumulative Earnings before Weekly Payroll	Gross Pay for the Week
U. Acorn	$3,900	$875
F. Jackson	6,100	825
R. Robins	7,100	300

The FICA tax rate for OASDI is 6.2% on the first $106,800 earned, and Medicare is 1.45% on all earnings. Federal unemployment tax is 0.8% on the first $7,000 earned by each employee. The SUTA tax rate for Gray is 5.2% on the first $7,000 of employee earnings for state unemployment purposes.

L04 *(15 MIN)*   **7A-4.** Refer to Exercise 7A-3 and assume that the state changed Gray's SUTA tax rate to 4.0%. What effect would this change have on the total payroll tax expense?

L04 *(15 MIN)*   **7A-5.** Refer to Exercise 7A-3. If R. Robins earned $2,500 for the week instead of $300, what effect would this change have on the total payroll tax expense?

L02 *(20 MIN)*   **7A-6.** The total wage expense for Carol Co. was $156,000. Of this total, $28,000 was above the OASDI wage base limit and not subject to this tax. All earnings are subject to Medicare tax, and $59,000 was above the federal and state unemployment wage base limits and not subject to unemployment taxes. Please calculate the total payroll tax expense for Carol Co. given the following rates and wage base limits:

    a. FICA tax rate: OASDI, 6.2% with a wage base limit of $106,800; Medicare, 1.45% with no wage base limit

    b. State unemployment tax rate: 5.5% with a wage base limit of $7,000

    c. Federal unemployment tax rate (after credit): 0.8% with a wage base limit of $7,000

L04 *(20 MIN)*   **7A-7.** At the end of the first quarter of 201X, you are asked to determine the FUTA tax liability for Carter Company. The FUTA tax rate is 0.8% on the first $7,000 each employee earns during the year (assuming 13 weeks for the first quarter) and each employee earned the same gross weekly pay for all 13 weeks).

Employee	Gross Pay Per Week
R. Frank	$680
G. Jill	810
L. Peter	600
Y. Ralph	410

7A-8. From the following data, estimate the annual premium for workers' compensation insurance:

L04 *(10 MIN)*

Type of Work	Estimated Payroll	Rate per $100
Office	$20,000	$0.17
Repairs	80,000	1.82

Set B

7B-1. Calculate the total wages earned for each employee assuming an overtime rate of time and a half over 40 hours.

L01 *(15 MIN)*

Employee	Hourly Rate	No. of Hours Worked
Lucky Mars	$17	39
Pam Valley	$16	42
Louis Jones	$20	45

7B-2. Compute the net pay for each employee using the federal income tax withholding table included. Assume that FICA OASDI tax is 6.2% on a wage base limit of $106,800; Medicare is 1.45% on all earnings, the payroll is paid biweekly, and no state income tax applies.

L01 *(20 MIN)*

Employee	Status	Allowances	Cumulative Pay	Biweekly Pay
Chen Rong	Single	1	$63,300	$1,710
Mary Pinney	Single	0	$63,700	$1,630

7B-3. From the following information, calculate the payroll tax expense for Aim Company for the payroll of June 9:

L04 *(20 MIN)*

Employee	Cumulative Earnings Before Weekly Payroll	Gross Pay for the Week
O. Barns	$3,300	$800
O. Hienze	6,200	650
D. Toll	7,800	320

The FICA tax rate for OASDI is 6.2% on the first $106,800 earned, and Medicare is 1.45% on all earnings. Federal unemployment tax is 0.8% on the first $7,000 earned by each employee. The SUTA tax rate for Aim is 5.1% on the first $7,000 of earnings for state unemployment purposes.

7B-4. Refer to Exercise 7B-3 and assume that the state changed Aim's SUTA tax rate to 3.5%. What effect would this change have on the total payroll tax expense?

L04 *(15 MIN)*

7B-5. Refer to Exercise 7B-3. If D. Toll earned $3,000 for the week instead of $320, what effect would this change have on the total payroll tax expense?

L04 *(15 MIN)*

7B-6. The total wage expense for Orange Co. was $150,000. Of this total, $26,000 was above the OASDI wage base limit and not subject to this tax. All earnings are subject to Medicare tax, and $62,000 was above the federal and state unemployment wage base limits and not subject to unemployment

L02 *(20 MIN)*

taxes. Please calculate the total payroll tax expense for Orange Co. given the following rates and wage base limits:

a. FICA tax rate: OASDI, 6.2% with a wage base limit of $106,800; Medicare, 1.45% with no wage base limit.

b. State unemployment tax rate 5.6% with a wage base limit of $7,000.

c. Federal unemployment tax rate (after credit): 0.8% with a wage base limit of $7,000.

LO4 *(20 MIN)*   **7B-7.** At the end of the first quarter of 201X, you are asked to determine the FUTA tax liability for Ali Company. The FUTA tax rate is 0.8% on the first $7,000 each employee earns during the year (assuming 13 weeks for the first quarter and each employee earned the same gross weekly pay for all 13 weeks).

Employee	Gross Pay Per Week
T. Bork	$650
G. Jill	770
L. Steven	590
Q. Watson	420

LO4 *(10 MIN)*   **7B-8.** From the following data, estimate the annual premium for worker's compensation insurance:

Type of Work	Estimated Payroll	Rate per $100
Office	$28,000	$0.15
Repairs	85,000	1.86

MyAccountingLab   # Problems

....

Set A

LO1 *(20 MIN)*   **7A-1.** From the following information, please complete the chart for gross earnings for the week. (Assume an overtime rate of time and a half over 40 hours.)

Check Figure:
Dave Johnson: $1,016.50 Gross
Earnings

Employee	Hourly Rate	No. of Hours Worked	Gross Earnings
Jaden Vasquez	$10	48	
Lucy Ferris	$14	37	
Nicolette Patt	$13	39	
Dave Johnson	$19	49	

LO1 *(30 MIN)*   **7A-2.** May Company has five salaried employees. Your task is to use the following information to calculate net pay for each employee:

Employee	Allowance and Marital Status	Cumulative Earnings before This Payroll	Biweekly Salary	Department
Dixie, Dylan	S-1	$46,000	$1,100	Customer Service
Fry, Marc	S-1	28,000	1,250	Office
Ricard, Alison	S-2	59,200	1,300	Office
Hammel, Audrey	S-3	105,880	1,690	Customer Service
Clinton, Lionel	S-3	26,000	1,110	Customer Service

Assume the following:

1. FICA OASDI is 6.2% on $106,800; FICA Medicare is 1.45% on all earnings.
2. Each employee contributes $45 biweekly for medical insurance.
3. State income tax is 4% of gross pay.
4. FIT is calculated from Figure 7.2.

Check Figure:
Total Net Pay $4,905.30

7A-3. The bookkeeper of Samba Co. gathered the following data from individual employee earnings records and daily time cards. Your task is to complete a payroll register on March 17.

LO1, 2 *(40 MIN)*

Employee	Allowance and Marital Status	Cumulative Earnings before This Payroll	M	T	W	T	F	Hourly Rate of Pay	FIT
					Daily Time				
Keys, Pam	M-1	$64,100	6	6	13	6	10	$11	$27
Hale, Don	S-0	14,000	8	12	7	12	7	16	113
Dean, Ria	M-3	70,000	7	8	13	6	13	25	118
Vent, Jane	S-1	22,500	10	5	9	11	5	19	91

Assume the following:

1. FICA OASDI is 6.2% on $106,800; FICA Medicare is 1.45% on all earnings.
2. Federal income tax has been calculated from a weekly table for you.
3. Each employee contributes $26 weekly for health insurance.
4. Overtime is paid at a rate of time and a half over 40 hours.
5. Keys and Dean work in the office; the other employees work in sales.

Check Figure:
Total Net Pay $2,560.37

7A-4. You gathered the following data from time cards and individual employee earnings records. Your tasks are as follows:

1. On December 5, 201X, prepare a payroll register for this biweekly payroll.
2. Calculate the employer taxes of FICA OASDI, FICA Medicare, FUTA, and SUTA.

LO1, 2, 3, 4 *(40 MIN)*

Employee	Allowance and Marital Status	Cumulative Earnings before This Payroll	Biweekly Salary	Check No.	Department
Abood, John	S-3	$36,900	$1,580	30	Production
Gallant, Nicki	S-1	47,600	2,010	31	Office
Malone, Jeff	S-2	64,800	2,090	32	Production
Scott, Paul	S-1	4,800	900	33	Office

Assume the following:

1. FICA OASDI is 6.2% on $106,800; FICA Medicare is 1.45% on all earnings.
2. Federal income tax is calculated from Figure 7.2.
3. State income tax is 8% of gross pay.
4. Union dues are $13 biweekly.
5. The SUTA rate is 5.4% and the FUTA rate is 0.8% on earnings up to $7,000.

Check Figure:
Total Net Pay $4,685.22

Set B

7B-1. From the following information, please complete the chart for gross earnings for the week. (Assume an overtime rate of time and a half over 40 hours.)

LO1 *(20 MIN)*

Employee	Hourly Rate	No. of Hours Worked	Gross Earnings
Jacoby Vasquez	$15	47	
Leena Ferris	$13	45	
Nicolette Patt	$17	42	
Danyl Johnson	$18	50	

Check Figure:
Danyl Johnson Gross Pay $990

LO1 *(30 MIN)*

7B-2. October Company employs five salaried employees. Your task is to use the following information to calculate net pay for each employee:

Employee	Allowance and Marital Status	Cumulative Earnings before This Payroll	Biweekly Salary	Department
Bristow, Dylan	S-0	$45,000	$1,500	Customer Service
Herman, Marc	S-0	30,000	1,350	Office
Sears, Alison	S-1	54,700	1,050	Office
Flaherty, Audrey	S-3	105,800	1,790	Customer Service
Ackerman, Lionel	S-3	34,000	860	Customer Service

Assume the following:

1. FICA OASDI is 6.2% on $106,800; FICA Medicare is 1.45% on all earnings.
2. Each employee contributes $20 biweekly for medical insurance.
3. State income tax is 5% of gross pay.
4. FIT is calculated from Figure 7.2.

Check Figure:
Total Net Pay $4,966.39

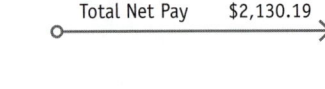

LO1, 2 *(40 MIN)*

7B-3. The bookkeeper of Coast Co. gathered the following data from individual employee earnings records and daily time cards. Your task is to complete a payroll register on November 17.

Employee	Allowance and Marital Status	Cumulative Earnings before This Payroll	Daily Time M	T	W	T	F	Hourly Rate of Pay	FIT
Ryan, Pam	M-1	$65,400	9	10	6	5	5	$17	$40
Badu, Don	S-0	17,500	8	7	12	11	3	13	65
Dean, Ria	M-3	107,150	9	8	11	6	9	16	37
Gray, Jane	S-1	21,000	8	10	6	9	7	20	104

Assume the following:

1. FICA OASDI is 6.2% on $106,800; FICA Medicare is 1.45% on all earnings.
2. Federal income tax has been calculated from a weekly table for you.
3. Each employee contributes $28 weekly for health insurance.
4. Overtime is paid at a rate of time and a half over 40 hours.
5. Ryan and Dean work in the office; the other employees work in sales.

Check Figure:
Total Net Pay $2,130.19

LO1, 2, 3, 4 *(40 MIN)*

PT/QB

7B-4. You gathered the following data from time cards and individual employee earnings records. Your tasks are as follows:

1. On December 5, 201X, prepare a payroll register for this biweekly payroll.
2. Calculate the employer taxes of FICA OASDI, FICA Medicare, FUTA, and SUTA.

Employee	Allowance and Marital Status	Cumulative Earnings before This Payroll	Biweekly Salary	Check No.	Department
Alvin, John	S-3	$37,400	$1,510	30	Production
Gale, Nicki	S-1	47,500	2,040	31	Office
Malone, Jeff	S-2	64,800	2,080	32	Production
Seaver, Paul	S-1	4,600	810	33	Office

Assume the following:

1. FICA OASDI is 6.2% on $106,800; FICA Medicare is 1.45% on all earnings.
2. Federal income tax is calculated from Figure 7.2.
3. State income tax is 3% of gross pay.
4. Union dues are $18 biweekly.
5. The SUTA rate is 5.4%, and the FUTA rate is 0.8% on earnings below $7,000.

Check Figure:
Total Net Pay $4,886.13

Financial Report Problem

● ● **LO1, 2** *(10 MIN)*

Reading the Kellogg's Annual Report

Go to http://investor.kelloggs.com/annuals.cfm, to access the Kellogg's 2010 Annual Report. Go to Notes to Consolidated Financial Statements and calculate from Note 16 how much Advertising Expense has increased from 2009 to 2010.

ON the JOB ||||||||||||||||||||||||||

SANCHEZ COMPUTER CENTER

● **LO1** *(60 MIN)*

During the month of November the following transactions occurred.

Assignment

1. Record the following transactions in the general journal and post them to the general ledger.

2. Prepare a trial balance as of November 30, 201X.

Assume the following transactions:

Nov.	1	Billed Vita Needle Company $6,800, invoice no. 12675, for services rendered.
	3	Billed Accu Pac, Inc., $3,900, invoice no. 12676, for services rendered.
	5	Purchased new shop benches for $1,400 on account from System Design Furniture.
	9	Received the phone bill, $150.
	12	Collected $500 of the amount due from Taylor Golf.
	18	Collected $800 of the amount due from Taylor Golf.
	20	Purchased a fax machine for the office from Multi Systems, Inc., on credit, $450.00.

Payroll Records: A Full-Time Job?

● ● ● ● **LO1, 2, 3, 4**
(30 MIN)

Like every Subway restaurant owner, Stan needs to keep a master file of important employee information. This file contains every employee's name, address, phone number, Social Security number, rate of pay, hours worked per week, and W-4 form.

Stan employs two part-time "sandwich artists" and no full-time managers—yet. If his sales continue to be high, he'll need to hire someone to manage operations so that he can spend more time analyzing the financials—with Lila's help—and growing his business. Most restaurants hire primarily part-timers with a core of full-time employees, but the numbers vary from restaurant to restaurant. Benefits vary too. Stan, for instance, plans to offer health and dental benefits when he hires a manager. He knows what a great incentive these benefits are, with health costs so high. He pays his sandwich artists, Rashid and Ellen, the minimum wage because they both have less than a year's experience. However, he's talking to Mariah Washington about creating some incentives to keep them motivated. If Rashid and Ellen are with him for a full year, they'll see a nice raise in their biweekly paychecks. Both the frequency of pay and the tax rates vary by state and sometimes by city or county.

Stan must record all this vital information and report it to the various state, local, and federal authorities. In addition, Stan includes total payroll expenses on the weekly sales and inventory report, which he submits electronically to headquarters from his point-of-sale (POS) screen.

Scheduling workers and keeping payroll records are the bane of Stan's existence. These tasks are so incredibly time consuming. He was pleased to hear, then, at the last meeting of his local North American Association of Subway Franchisees (NAASF) that the new POS terminals will soon offer an electronic scheduling package.

"Wow! That will really help," said Stan cheerfully to another franchisee. "No more different colors of ink just to keep track of who will work when! Now I can plan around Rashid and Ellen's exam schedules without a hassle. Scheduling might just become my favorite module in the new system."

"Sure," said Javier Gonzalez, another owner. "Now you can concentrate on payroll records. What fun!"

"Ay. Que lata," Stan groaned. What a drag!

Discussion Questions

1. What payroll records does Stan need to keep for his Subway restaurant?
2. What other information might Stan want in order to schedule working hours for each employee?
3. How does the payroll register help Stan prepare the payroll? (Consult the process outlined at the beginning of the chapter.)

Paying, Recording, and Reporting Payroll and Payroll Taxes: The Conclusion of the Payroll Process

THE GAME PLAN

Every month or every two weeks you might receive a paycheck. When reviewing all the deductions, did you ever wonder what they were for? Your company must report these deductions in order to meet its state and federal reporting requirements. For example, Google must take taxes out of its employees' paychecks and report the amounts to the federal and state authorities. By law, Google will have to make periodic payroll deposits of these taxes along with some matching requirements like Social Security. Google and other companies also are required by law to contribute to unemployment programs. This chapter will focus on the payroll reporting responsibilities of the employer. For both small and large businesses the payroll process is an inseparable part of the accounting process.

LEARNING OBJECTIVES

- **1.** Recording payroll and payroll taxes.
- **2.** Recording the payroll and the paying of the payroll taxes.
- **3.** Recording employer taxes for FICA OASDI, FICA Medicare, FUTA, SUTA, and workers' compensation insurance.
- **4.** Preparing Forms W-2, W-3, 941, and 940.
- **5.** Paying FUTA, SUTA, and workers' compensation insurance.

289

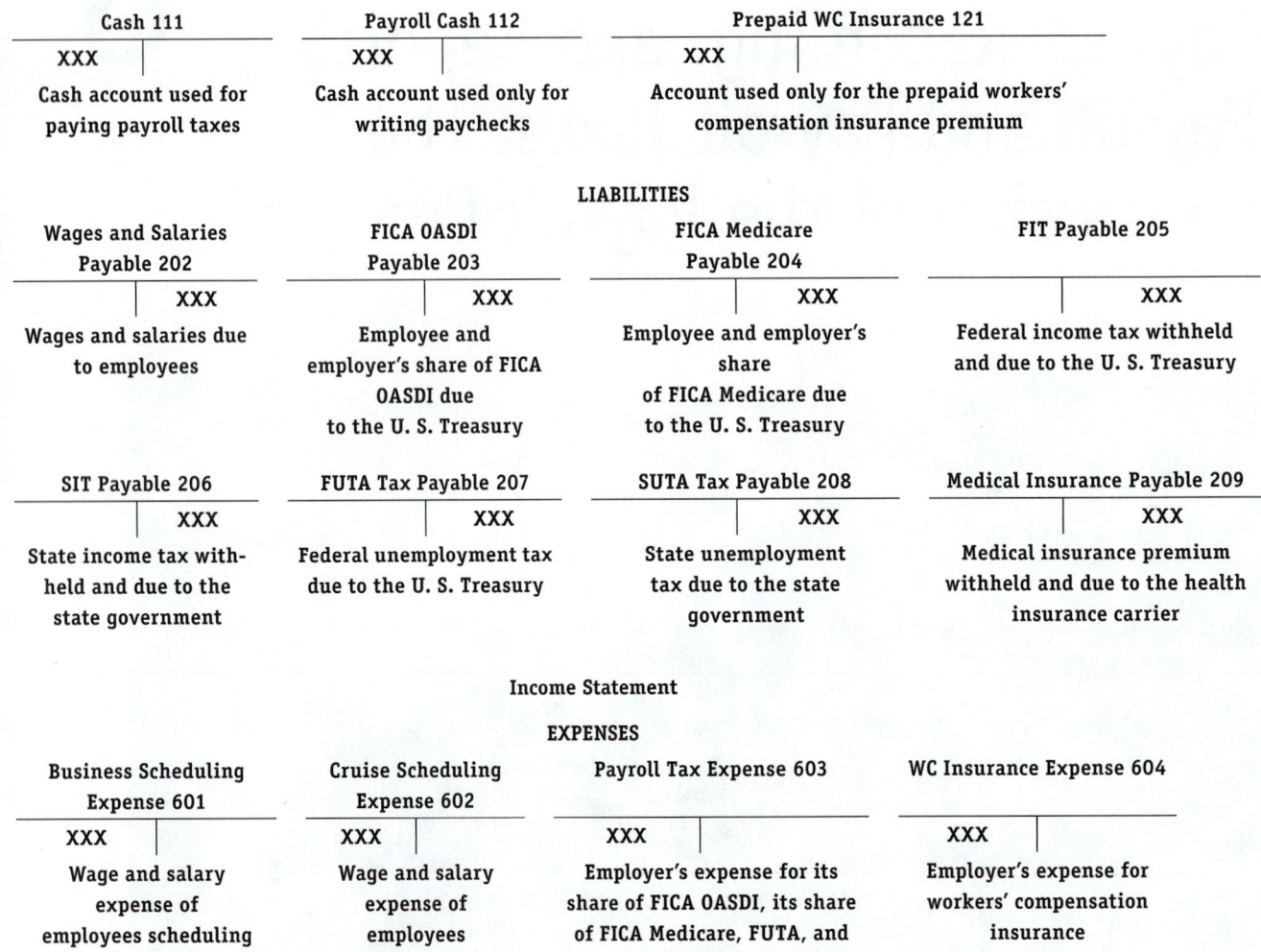

Balance Sheet

ASSETS

Cash 111	Payroll Cash 112	Prepaid WC Insurance 121
XXX		XXX		XXX	
Cash account used for paying payroll taxes	Cash account used only for writing paychecks	Account used only for the prepaid workers' compensation insurance premium

LIABILITIES

Wages and Salaries Payable 202	FICA OASDI Payable 203	FICA Medicare Payable 204	FIT Payable 205
	XXX		XXX		XXX		XXX
Wages and salaries due to employees	Employee and employer's share of FICA OASDI due to the U. S. Treasury	Employee and employer's share of FICA Medicare due to the U. S. Treasury	Federal income tax withheld and due to the U. S. Treasury

SIT Payable 206	FUTA Tax Payable 207	SUTA Tax Payable 208	Medical Insurance Payable 209
	XXX		XXX		XXX		XXX
State income tax withheld and due to the state government	Federal unemployment tax due to the U. S. Treasury	State unemployment tax due to the state government	Medical insurance premium withheld and due to the health insurance carrier

Income Statement

EXPENSES

Business Scheduling Expense 601	Cruise Scheduling Expense 602	Payroll Tax Expense 603	WC Insurance Expense 604
XXX		XXX		XXX		XXX	
Wage and salary expense of employees scheduling business travel	Wage and salary expense of employees scheduling cruises	Employer's expense for its share of FICA OASDI, its share of FICA Medicare, FUTA, and SUTA	Employer's expense for workers' compensation insurance

Google has many thousands of employees. With the aid of computers, the accounting department of Google must monitor as well as complete in a timely manner its employer tax responsibilities. In Chapter 7 we learned how to calculate gross earnings, employee withholding taxes, net pay, and employer payroll taxes. We now look at how businesses pay, record, and report these amounts. The journal entries necessary to record all of the payroll transactions for Travelwithus.com appear in the next section. Use the preceding T accounts as a reference guide. They will be covered as part of our discussion on completing the payroll process.

LO1 LEARNING UNIT 8-1 RECORDING PAYROLL AND PAYROLL TAX EXPENSE AND PAYING THE PAYROLL

At this point in the payroll process, Katherine Kurtz, the accountant for Travelwithus. com, has calculated gross earnings, deductions for employee withholding taxes, and net pay for each of Travelwithus.com's employees. She entered these amounts into two accounting records for Travelwithus.com called the payroll register and the employee earnings record. She also computed the amount of payroll taxes that Travelwithus.com must pay as an employer. At this point, Katherine must record these payroll amounts in the accounts of Travelwithus.com by making journal entries in the general journal and posting these entries to accounts in the general ledger. By entering these amounts into Travelwithus.com's accounting system, Travelwithus.com's financial statements will include these payroll transactions.

Recording Payroll

Before we discuss how payroll transactions are recorded, let's first review the accounts that we will be using and the rules for increasing and decreasing these accounts:

Accounts Affected	Category	↑↓	Rules	Financial Statement
Business Scheduling Expense	Expense	↑	Dr.	Income Statement
Cruise Scheduling Expense	Expense	↑	Dr.	Income Statement
Payroll Tax Expense	Expense	↑	Dr.	Income Statement
Workers' Compensation	Expense	↑	Dr.	Income Statement
Insurance Expense	Expense	↑	Dr.	Income Statement
Payroll Cash	Asset	↑	Dr.	Balance Sheet
Prepaid Workers' Compensation Insurance	Asset	↑	Dr.	Balance Sheet
FICA OASDI Payable	Liability	↑	Cr.	Balance Sheet
FICA Medicare Payable	Liability	↑	Cr.	Balance Sheet
FIT Payable	Liability	↑	Cr.	Balance Sheet
SIT Payable	Liability	↑	Cr.	Balance Sheet
FUTA Payable	Liability	↑	Cr.	Balance Sheet
SUTA Payable	Liability	↑	Cr.	Balance Sheet
Medical Insurance Payable	Liability	↑	Cr.	Balance Sheet
Wages and Salaries Payable	Liability	↑	Cr.	Balance Sheet

Katherine needs to record the expense of wages and salaries. The information needed to make these journal entries comes from the hourly and salaried payroll registers. Figure 8.1 shows the hourly payroll register for the current payroll period. Katherine locates this register and uses totals from it to make the following journal entry:

	Date			PR	Dr.	Cr.
			GENERAL JOURNAL			
	201X					
	Oct.	29	Business Scheduling Expense		9 5 7 60	
			Cruise Scheduling Expense		2 3 1 9 30	
			FIT Payable			3 4 1 00
			SIT Payable			2 6 2 15
			FICA OASDI Payable			2 0 3 17
			FICA Medicare Payable			4 7 52
			Medical Insurance Payable			9 9 00
			Wages and Salaries Payable			2 3 2 4 06
			To record payroll for the pay period			
			ending October 29, 201X			

FIGURE 8.1 Payroll Register

TRAVELWITHUS.COM INC.
HOURLY EMPLOYEE PAYROLL REGISTER
OCTOBER 16–29

Employee / Social Security No.	Allowances and Marital Status	Previous Earnings (YTD)	Current Earnings Regular Hours	Regular Rate	Regular Amount	Overtime Hours	Overtime Rate	Overtime Amount	Gross	Current Earnings (YTD)
Higuera, Stephanie 123-45-6789	S-1	1851360	78	1140	88920	4	1710	6840	95760	1947120
Sui, Annie 123-45-6788	S-0	212100	80	1515	121200	4	22725	9090	130290	342390
Taylor, Harold 123-45-6787	S-2	1904370	78	1210	94380	4	1815	7260	101640	2006010
TOTALS					304500			23190	327690	4295520

TRAVELWITHUS.COM INC.
HOURLY EMPLOYEE PAYROLL REGISTER
OCTOBER 16–29

Employee / Social Security No.	Taxable Earnings FUTA/SUTA	Taxable Earnings OASDI	FIT	SIT	FICA OASDI	FICA Medicare	Medical Insurance	Net Pay	Check No.	Account Charged Business Scheduling Expense	Account Charged Cruise Scheduling Expense
Higuera, Stephanie 123-45-6789	—	95760	9300	7661	5937	1389	3300	68173	820	95760	
Sui, Annie 123-45-6788	130290	130290	16800	10423	8078	1889	3300	89800	821		130290
Taylor, Harold 123-45-6787	—	101640	8000	8131	6302	1474	3300	74433	822		101640
TOTALS	130290	327690	34100	26215	20317	4752	9900	232406		95760	231930

A couple things may be surprising about the journal entry. First, notice that the gross earnings, not the net pay, are recorded as expenses for the two different departments that the employees worked in. This total amount of earnings is the real expense to Travelwithus.com. Employees will actually only receive the lower, net pay; the difference relates to deductions that are made for OASDI, HI, FIT, state and local income taxes, and other deductions authorized by the employee.

Also notice that the amounts of taxes withheld are recorded in "Payable" accounts, which means that they are liabilities of Travelwithus.com. How can Travelwithus.com be liable for these taxes if the taxes are paid by employees? The answer is that Travelwithus.com collects these amounts by withholding them from the paychecks of its employees and then turns them over to the federal and, in this case, state governments. In other words, Travelwithus.com is the intermediary in this process. Until it does pay these amounts to the governments, Travelwithus.com owes these taxes to the governments. The same is true of the medical insurance premiums that the employees pay; the company collects them and then pays them to the insurance company.

Recording Payroll Tax Expense

Katherine's next task is to record the employer payroll taxes for Travelwithus.com. The entry to record the taxes for the current hourly payroll follows:

GENERAL JOURNAL				
Date		PR	Dr.	Cr.
201X				
Oct. 29	Payroll Tax Expense		331 47	
	FICA OASDI Payable			203 17
	FICA Medicare Payable			47 52
	FUTA Payable			10 42
	SUTA Payable			70 36
	To record payroll tax expense for the			
	pay period ending October 29, 201X			

Notice that FICA OASDI, FICA Medicare, FUTA, and SUTA were recorded in separate liability accounts because they are different taxes and, except for the FICA taxes, are paid to different government agencies. Also note that the amount of all of these taxes are added together and recorded as one amount for Travelwithus.com's payroll tax expense. These amounts are an expense to Travelwithus.com because they represent the cost of the payroll taxes that it must pay as an employer.

Payroll tax expense The cost to employers that includes the total of the employer's FICA OASDI, FICA Medicare, FUTA, and SUTA taxes.

Paying the Payroll and Recording the Payment

 **L02**

Katherine next must record the payment of payroll to Travelwithus.com's employees:

GENERAL JOURNAL				
Date		PR	Dr.	Cr.
201X				
Nov. 3	Wages and Salaries Payable		2324 06	
	Payroll Cash			2324 06
	To record the payment of hourly payroll			
	for the pay period ending October 29,			
	201X			

Travelwithus.com, like most companies, uses a special checking account for paying its payroll. This account is called Payroll Cash and only paychecks are written from this account. A company with a substantial number of employees might want to use an extra account just for payroll for a number of reasons. First, having a separate account just for paychecks provides much better internal control over the funds deposited to pay employees. Also, because only payroll checks are written from this account, it is easier to reconcile it to the bank statement each month and determine whether someone has not cashed his or her paycheck for some reason. Finally, the business can still manage its cash effectively even with this extra bank account; the business simply deposits the total net pay amount in this account and thus has enough money to pay every paycheck without leaving extra in the account that could be used for other purposes.

The paychecks that Travelwithus.com gives to its employees are, like the paychecks of most companies, attached to pay stubs that show the employee's gross earnings, deductions for employee withholding taxes, and net pay. Stephanie Higuera's current paycheck and stub look like this:

Travelwithus.com Inc.

Employee	Social Security	Check	Net Pay	Pay Date	Marital Status	Allowances
Stephanie Higuera	123-45-6789	820	$681.73	11/03/201X	S	1

Earnings	Current			Deductions		
	Pay Rate	Hours	Earnings	Item	Current	YTD
Regular Earnings	11.40	78	889.20	FIT	93.00	2,067.00
Overtime Earnings	17.10	4	68.40	SIT	76.61	1,557.70
Current Gross Earnings			957.60	OASDI	59.37	1,207.21
				Medicare	13.89	282.33
				Medical insurance	33.00	693.00
				Total	275.87	6,807.24

Travelwithus.com Inc.
504 Washington Blvd.
Salem, MA 01970

11-325/1210

No. 820

November 3,   201X

PAY TO THE
ORDER OF   Stephanie Higuera $681.73

Six hundred eighty one and 73/100   DOLLARS

BC   Bank of Commerce

MEMO   October 16–29 payroll   *Julia Regan*

LEARNING UNIT 8-1 REVIEW

AT THIS POINT you should be able to do the following:

- Explain how to use the payroll register to record the payroll.
- Journalize the payroll.
- Journalize the employer's payroll tax expense.
- Journalize the payment of a payroll.

Instant Replay ⊙ Self-Review Quiz 8-1

Given the following information, prepare the general journal entry to record the payroll tax expense for Bill Co. for the weekly payroll of Oct 29. Assume the following:

- SUTA tax is paid at a rate of 5.6% on the first $7,000 of earnings.
- FUTA tax is paid at the net rate of 0.8% on the first $7,000 of earnings.
- FICA tax rate for OASDI is 6.2% on $106,800, and Medicare is 1.45% on all earnings.

Employee	Cumulative Pay Before This Week's Payroll	Gross Pay for the Week
Bill Jones	$6,000	$800
Julie Warner	$6,600	$400
Al Brooks	$7,900	$700

Solution to Instant Replay: Self-Review Quiz 8-1

		GENERAL JOURNAL			
Date		Account	PR	Dr.	Cr.
201X					
Oct.	29	Payroll Tax Expense		222 15	
		FICA OASDI Payable			117 80
		FICA Medicare Payable			27 55
		FUTA Payable			9 60
		SUTA Payable			67 20
		To record payroll tax expense for the pay period ending October 29, 201X			

FICA OASDI	= $1,900 × 0.062	= $117.80
FICA Medicare	= $1,900 × 0.0145	= $ 27.55
FUTA	= $1,200 × 0.008	= $ 9.60
SUTA	= $1,200 × 0.056	= $ 67.20

COACHING TIP

Remember that OASDI and Medicare are employer payroll taxes even though employees pay these taxes, too.

LEARNING UNIT 8-2 PAYING FIT AND FICA TAXES AND COMPLETING THE EMPLOYER'S QUARTERLY FEDERAL TAX RETURN, FORM 941

As we discussed in Chapter 7, both employers and employees pay payroll taxes. Employees pay these amounts not by writing checks to the different levels of government, but by having the amounts of these taxes taken out, or withheld, from

Employer identification number (EIN) A number assigned by the IRS that is used by an employer when recording and paying payroll and income taxes.

Form SS-4 The form filled out by an employer to get an EIN. The form is sent to the IRS, which assigns the number to the business.

Federal Insurance Contribution Act (FICA) Part of the Social Security law that requires employees and employers to pay OASDI taxes and Medicare taxes.

⬤ **L03**

Federal Unemployment Tax Act (FUTA) A tax paid by employers to the federal government. The current rate is 0.8% on the first $7,000 of earnings of each employee after the normal SUTA tax credit is applied.

Calendar quarter A three-month, 13-week time period. Four calendar quarters occur during a calendar year that runs from January 1 through December 31. The first quarter is January through March, the second is April through June, the third is July through September, and the fourth is October through December.

the amount of pay that they actually receive. Employers withhold these amounts, report them and the related earnings to federal, state, and sometimes local governments, and then turn them over to those levels of government. Let's now discuss how Travelwithus.com carries out these responsibilities.

For Travelwithus.com, the process began when the business opened. When opening a business, every employer must get a federal identification number. This number is also called an employer identification number (EIN) and is like a Social Security number for businesses in the sense that it identifies businesses to the government. To get an EIN, an employer fills out Form SS-4, much like individuals fill out Form SS-5 to get a Social Security number. Travelwithus.com will use its EIN, 58-1213479, to report employee earnings and payroll taxes.

Travelwithus.com must next determine when its payroll taxes are due to the government. Due dates vary according to the type of tax being paid.

Paying FIT and FICA Taxes

As required by law, Travelwithus.com withholds federal income tax from employees' paychecks, along with Social Security (OASDI) and Medicare taxes as established by the Federal Insurance Contributions Act or FICA. As the employer, Travelwithus.com reports and pays these taxes to the federal government. The Federal Unemployment Tax Act (FUTA) tax is the unemployment tax paid and reported separately that employers pay to the federal government. To see how Travelwithus.com reports the FIT and FICA taxes to the federal government, let's look at its payroll information for the last calendar quarter of the year, which covers October, November, and December.

To comply with federal law, Travelwithus.com must do two things: First, it must determine when FIT and FICA taxes need to be paid to the federal government and make this payment on time. Second, it must report these taxes on Form 941, the Employer's Quarterly Federal Tax Return. Figure 8.2 contains a worksheet that Katherine prepared from payroll registers to make sure that these two tasks happen the way they should.

FIGURE 8.2 Form 941 Worksheet

TRAVELWITHUS.COM INC.
Form 941 Taxes
4th Quarter

Payroll Period		Pay Check Date	Earnings	FIT	Taxable FICA Wages for		FICA		Total Tax	Cumulative Tax
					OASDI	Medicare	OASDI EE + ER*	Medicare EE + ER		
October	2–15	Oct. 20	3680 75	393 84	3680 75	3680 75	456 41	106 74	956 99	956 99
October	16–29	Nov. 3	3276 90	341 00	3276 90	3276 90	406 34	95 04	842 38	1799 37
October	31	Oct. 31	18387 33	3493 59	18387 33	18387 33	2280 03	533 23	6306 85	8106 22
Oct./Nov.	30–12	Nov. 17	3276 90	352 00	3276 90	3276 90	406 34	95 03	853 37	8959 59
November	13–26	Dec. 1	3870 02	414 09	3870 02	3870 02	479 88	112 23	1006 20	9965 79
November	30	Nov. 30	18387 33	3493 59	18387 33	18387 33	2280 03	533 23	6306 85	16272 64
Nov./Dec.	27–10	Dec. 15	3340 60	357 44	3340 60	3340 60	414 23	96 88	868 55	17141 19
December	11–24	Dec. 29	3214 50	343 95	3214 50	3214 50	398 60	93 22	835 77	17976 96
December	25–31	Dec. 29	1578 90	168 94	1578 90	1578 90	195 78	45 79	410 51	18387 47
December	31	Dec. 29	18387 33	3493 59	16887 33	18387 33	2094 03	533 23	6120 85	24508 32
4th Quarter Totals			77400 56	12852 03	75900 56	77400 56	9411 67	2244 62	24508 32	24508 32
			(a)	(b)	(c)	(d)	(e)	(f)	(g)	(h)

*EE stands for employee; ER stands for employer

Notice a few things about this worksheet. First, look at the payroll period dates and see that some cover two-week periods and others show the last day of the month. Remember that the two types of dates relate to the two types of payroll that Travelwithus.com has, hourly and salaried. Next, observe that the quarter is 13 weeks long. By putting 13 weeks into each quarter, companies report all 52 weeks of a calendar year. Also, FIT and FICA are shown in separate columns because the IRS wants those amounts reported separately. Finally, notice that for the December 31 monthly payroll not all of the wages earned are taxable for OASDI, because an employee has reached the $106,800 wage base limit by this point in the year.

The total amount of taxes due must be transmitted to the Treasury Department using the Electronic Federal Tax Payment System (EFTPS) unless the quarterly deposit is less than $2,500. If the quarterly payment is less than $2,500 the deposit may be paid by check submitted with the quarterly Form 941.

Types of Payroll Tax Depositors To determine when payroll taxes are due, for payroll tax deposit purposes, employers are usually classified as either monthly or semiweekly depositors. Rarely a company will owe less than $2,500 in total taxes for the quarter, but in this case the taxes may be deposited quarterly. A monthly depositor is an employer who has to deposit Form 941 taxes (federal income tax withholdings, OASDI, and Medicare) on the 15th day of the month following the payday(s). Semiweekly depositors must deposit their Form 941 taxes once or twice each week, depending on when payroll is paid. These classifications last for an entire calendar year, and employers are reevaluated every year.

Employers are classified according to the dollar amount of the Form 941 taxes that they have paid in the past. The IRS developed a rule known as the look-back period rule to determine how to classify an employer for payroll tax deposits. Under this rule, the IRS looks back to a one-year time period that begins on July 1 and ends the following June 30 of the previous year. If during this look-back period an employer paid less than $50,000 of Form 941 taxes, then it is classified as a monthly depositor. Alternately, if the employer paid $50,000 or more during this period, then it is considered a semiweekly depositor. New companies are automatically classified as monthly depositors until they have been in business long enough to have a look-back period that can be used to classify them. Figure 8.3 shows how the look-back period works.

Travelwithus.com is a semiweekly depositor because it made more than $50,000 of FIT and FICA deposits during the most recent look-back period.

Rules for Monthly Depositors If an employer is classified as a monthly depositor, the FIT and both the employee and employer OASDI and Medicare taxes accumulated during any month must be deposited by the 15th day of the next month. If the 15th is a Saturday, Sunday, or bank holiday, then the deposit must be made on the next banking day.

Form 941, Employer's Quarterly Federal Tax Return A tax report that a business will complete after the end of each calendar quarter indicating the total FICA (OASDI and Medicare) taxes owed plus the amount of FIT withheld from employees' pay for the quarter. If federal tax deposits have been made correctly and on time, the total amount deposited should equal the amount due on Form 941. Any difference results in a payment due or a refund.

Form 941 taxes Another term used to describe FIT, OASDI, and Medicare. This name comes from the form used to report these taxes.

Monthly depositor A business classified as a monthly depositor will make its payroll tax deposits only once each month for the amount of Form 941 taxes due from the prior month.

Semiweekly depositor A business classified as a semiweekly depositor may have to make its payroll tax deposits up to twice in one week, depending on when payroll is paid.

Look-back period A period of time used to determine whether a business should make its Form 941 tax deposits on a monthly or semiweekly basis. The IRS defines this period as July 1 through June 30 of the year prior to the year in which Form 941 tax deposits will be made.

Banking day A banking day is any day that a bank is open to the public for business. Generally, a banking day will end at 2:00 or 3:00 P.M. local time. Banking business transacted after this time is usually considered to be the next day's business. Saturdays, Sundays, and federal holidays are usually not considered banking days.

FIGURE 8.3
Look-Back Illustration

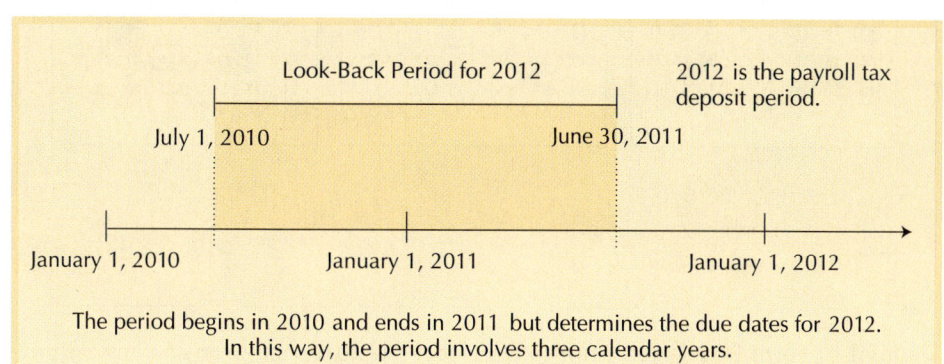

The period begins in 2010 and ends in 2011 but determines the due dates for 2012. In this way, the period involves three calendar years.

Rules for Semiweekly Depositors If an employer is classified as a semiweekly depositor, as a general rule it always has three banking days to make its payroll tax deposit. However, semiweekly depositors like Travelwithus.com may have to make up to two payroll tax deposits every week, depending on when they pay their employees. According to the IRS, for this purpose, each week begins on Wednesday and ends on the following Tuesday. This week is broken into two parts, Wednesday through Friday, and Saturday through Tuesday. If the company's payday is a Wednesday, Thursday, or Friday, the payroll tax deposit is due on the following Wednesday. If the company's payday is a Saturday, Sunday, Monday, or Tuesday, the payroll tax deposit is due on the following Friday.

Thus, if an employer pays its employees on a Thursday and a Monday, it must make two payroll tax deposits, one on Wednesday for the Thursday payday, and one on Friday for the Monday payday. If a bank holiday occurs between a payday and the day when the payroll tax deposit is due, the employer gets an extra day to make the deposit. So, a deposit due on a Wednesday will be due on Thursday, or a Friday deposit will be due on the following Monday.

The diagram in Figure 8.4 shows how these rules work:

FIGURE 8.4
Semiweekly Deposit Rules
Illustration

	Sat	Sun	Mon	Tues	Wed	Thurs	Fri	Sat	Sun	Mon	Tues	Wed
If payday is												
Then deposit is due												

See Figure 8.5 to see how the rules apply to Travelwithus.com. Remember that Travelwithus.com's hourly payroll is always paid on a Friday. Because Travelwithus.com is a semiweekly payroll tax depositor, its FIT, OASDI and Medicare tax deposits for its hourly payroll are due on the following Wednesday. Because its hourly payroll is paid on a biweekly, or every other week, basis, Travelwithus.com will need to make a deposit every other Wednesday. However, if we look at week 52, the payday for this week is Friday, December 29, which is two days before New Year's Day. Under the law, January 1 is a federal holiday, so Katherine must apply the rule regarding a holiday that falls between a payday and a tax deposit day and will make the Form 941 tax deposit not on Wednesday but on Thursday, January 4, of the next year.

Travelwithus.com also has a salaried payroll, and this payroll is paid on the last day of the month. In October, the last day of the month is a Tuesday, so Travelwithus.com will make its Form 941 tax deposit for this payroll on the following Friday.

FIGURE 8.5
Third Quarter Payroll Calendar
for Travelwithus.com

Deposit of Form 941 Taxes Prior to December 31, 2010, employers paying the government less than $200,000 per year in Form 941 taxes were permitted to pay these taxes (FICA and FIT) by check. The IRS required the employer to use Form 8901,

Federal Tax Deposit Coupon to make these deposits. The Form 8901 is very similar to a deposit slip used to make a deposit in a bank account. Employers owing more than $200,000 of deposits of Form 941 taxes in a year were required to pay these taxes using the Electronic Federal Tax Payment System (EFTPS).

Effective January 1, 2011, all employers paying Form 941 taxes must use the Electronic Federal Tax Payment System (EFTPS) except for those that owe less than $2,500 per quarter. Failure to use the EFTPS could result in a 10% failure-to-deposit penalty. Those employers owing less than $2,500 per quarter will be permitted to remit Form 941 taxes with their quarterly or annual Form 941 submission.

The EFTPS is a communications network that facilitates the direct transfer of funds from the employer's bank to the Treasury Department. These transfers may be transacted by touchtone phone, by personal computer, or online. The EFTPS requirement does not change existing rules for determining a depositor's status as either a monthly or semiweekly depositor for employment taxes.

Enrollment in the EFTPS program is accomplished online at http://www.eftps.gov. It takes several days to obtain the necessary documentation in the mail. Once enrolled in the program the employer can use either of the following two methods to make the required deposit. The employer may instruct the Treasury Financial Agent for that area to withdraw funds from the employer's bank account and route them to the Treasury's account at the Federal Reserve Bank. The employer may also instruct his or her bank to send each payment directly to the Treasury's account at the Federal Reserve Bank.

Once Travelwithus.com has enrolled in EFTPS, all Katherine needs to do is contact the IRS via either the Internet or phone. Katherine must notify the IRS before 8:00 p.m., at least one day in advance of the payment due date, of the amount to be transferred. The EFTPS will provide Travelwithus.com with a confirmation number called an "EFT Number," which guarantees the depositor that the tax deposit has been scheduled and allows the transaction to be traced if necessary.

The last task that Katherine must perform is to record the payment of the FIT and FICA taxes. The journal entry that she makes looks like this:

GENERAL JOURNAL						
Date			PR	Dr.	Cr.	
201X						
Nov.	8	FICA OASDI Payable		4 0 6 34		
		FICA Medicare Payable		9 5 04		
		FIT Payable		3 4 1 00		
		Cash			8 4 2 38	
		To record payment of FIT and FICA				
		taxes for pay period ending				
		October 29, 201X				

To get a better idea of how payroll tax amounts appear in the accounting system of Travelwithus.com, let's check out its general ledger for the FICA OASDI Payable and FICA Medicare Payable accounts:

FICA OASDI Payable						Account No. 203	
Date		PR	Dr.	Cr.	Cr. Bal.		
201X							
Oct.	15	GJ28		4 5 6 41	4 5 6 41		
	25	GJ28	4 5 6 41		0		
	29	GJ29		4 0 6 34	4 0 6 34		
	31	GJ29		2 2 8 0 03	2 6 8 6 37		
Nov.	3	GJ29	2 2 8 0 03		4 0 6 34		
	8	GJ30	4 0 6 34		0		

FICA Medicare Payable						Account No. 204	
Date		PR	Dr.	Cr.	Cr. Bal.		
201X							
Oct.	15	GJ28		1 0 6 74	1 0 6 74		
	25	GJ28	1 0 6 74		0		
	29*	GJ29		9 5 04	9 5 04		
	31	GJ29		5 3 3 23	6 2 8 27		
Nov.	3	GJ29	5 3 3 23		9 5 04		
	8	GJ30	9 5 04		0		

*This represents both the employee and employer deductions.

Notice several things about the ledger accounts. First, the entries on October 29 crediting the FICA OASDI Payable and FICA Medicare Payable accounts came from the general journal entries on this date because the payroll and payroll taxes were recorded on this date. These amounts represent both the employee and employer's shares of OASDI and Medicare. Also notice that the entries on November 8 debiting FICA OASDI Payable for $406.34 and FICA Medicare Payable for $95.04 came from the general journal. They are part of the payment that Travelwithus.com deposited with the Form 941 taxes. To summarize, journal entries crediting these accounts record tax liabilities, and journal entries debiting these accounts record payments of these taxes.

Completing the Employer's Quarterly Federal Tax Return, Form 941

Form 944, Employer's Annual Federal Tax Return The form used by employers to report FICA (OASDI and Medicare) taxes and FIT. This version will be filed by January 31 following the end of the year and can be used by employers who owe $1,000 or less for theses taxes and who have been told by the IRS that they must file this form.

The IRS requires all employers to complete tax returns reporting FICA OASDI, FICA Medicare, and FIT taxes. If these taxes total less than $1,000 for a calendar year, then employers will prepare Form 944, Employer's Annual Federal Tax Return. This form is due from employers by January 31 of the following year. Employers will complete this return only if the IRS notifies them that it is the form that they must use. If, however, taxes total more than $1,000 for a calendar year, then employers must instead complete Form 941, Employer's Quarterly Federal Tax Return, and submit it to the IRS for every quarter in a calendar year. Katherine Kurtz, the accountant for Travelwithus.com, used the worksheet in Figure 8.2 to prepare Form 941 for the last quarter of the year because Travelwithus.com's taxes exceeded $1,000.

The top section of Travelwithus.com's fourth quarter Form 941 in Figure 8.6 identifies the taxpayer, Travelwithus.com, and lists its address, the date that the quarter ended, and its EIN. Refer back to the worksheet in Figure 8.2 and use the letters below the column totals to follow amounts from this worksheet to the Form 941. Line-by-line instructions for completing the Form 941 are as follows:

Part 1:   *Answering questions that relate to the current quarter.*

Line 1:   This line is used to show how many employees were paid during the quarter.

2: This line is used to report total gross earnings for the quarter, which is $77,400.56 per column (a) of the worksheet in Figure 8.2.

3: Total income tax withheld is $12,852.03, which comes from column (b).

4: No entry is needed here; this line is only used for special situations.

5a, Column 1: The wages subject to FICA OASDI tax are the total taxable earnings of $75,900.56, which match column (c). The amount on this line is different from the line 2 amount because one employee reached the OASDI wage base limit of $106,800.

5a, Column 2: Katherine multiplies the amount on line 5a, Column 1, by 12.4%, which is the 6.2% rate for employees and the 6.2% rate for employers, to get the tax of $9,411.67 entered here. Notice that this amount matches column (e) of the worksheet.

5b: This line is used to report taxable tips that employees might have received. Travelwithus.com employees did not receive any tips, so this line is left blank.

5c, Column 1: The wages subject to Medicare tax are the total taxable earnings of $77,400.56, which match column (d). The amount on this line is the same as the line 2 amount because the Medicare tax has no wage base limit.

5c, Column 2: Katherine multiplies the amount on line 5c, Column 1, by 2.9%, which is the 1.45% rate for employees and the 1.45% rate for employers, to get the tax of $2,244.62 entered here. Notice that this amount matches column (f) of the worksheet.

FIGURE 8.6 Completed Form 941

Form **941 for 201X:** Employer's **QUARTERLY** Federal Tax Return

950110

(Rev. January 2010)   Department of the Treasury — Internal Revenue Service

OMB No. 1545-0029

(EIN)
Employer identification number   5 8 – 1 2 1 3 4 7 9

Name *(not your trade name)*   Travelwithus.com

Trade name *(if any)*

Address   10 Lovett Road
Number   Street   Suite or room number

Salem   MA   01970
City   State   ZIP code

Report for this Quarter of 2009
(Check one.)

☐ 1: January, February, March

☐ 2: April, May, June

☐ 3: July, August, September

☑ 4: October, November, December

Read the separate instructions before you complete Form 941. Type or print within the boxes.

Part 1: Answer these questions for this quarter.

1	Number of employees who received wages, tips, or other compensation for the pay period including: *Mar. 12* (Quarter 1), *June 12* (Quarter 2), *Sept. 12* (Quarter 3), *Dec. 12* (Quarter 4) **1**	6
2	Wages, tips, and other compensation **2**	77,400.56
3	Income tax withheld from wages, tips, and other compensation **3**	12,852.03
4	If no wages, tips, and other compensation are subject to social security or Medicare tax ☐ Check and go to line 6.	
5	Taxable social security and Medicare wages and tips:	

	Column 1		Column 2
5a Taxable social security wages	75,900.56	× .124 =	9,411.67
5b Taxable social security tips	.	× .124 =	.
5c Taxable Medicare wages & tips	77,400.56	× .029 =	2,244.62

	5d Total social security and Medicare taxes (*Column 2*, lines 5a + 5b + 5c = line 5d) . . **5d**	11,656.29
6	**Total taxes before adjustments** (lines 3 + 5d = line 6) **6**	24,508.32
7	**CURRENT QUARTER'S ADJUSTMENTS,** for example, a fractions of cents adjustment. See the instructions.	
	7a Current quarter's fractions of cents	.
	7b Current quarter's sick pay	.
	7c Current quarter's adjustments for tips and group-term life insurance	.
	7d TOTAL ADJUSTMENTS. Combine all amounts on lines 7a through 7c **7d**	.
8	**Total taxes after adjustments.** Combine lines 6 and 7d **8**	24,508.32
9	**Advance earned income credit (EIC) payments made to employees** **9**	.
10	**Total taxes after adjustment for advance EIC** (line 8 – line 9 = line 10) **10**	24,508.32
11	**Total deposits for this quarter,** including overpayment applied from a prior quarter and overpayment applied from Form 941-X or Form 944-X	24,508.32
12a	**COBRA premium assistance payments** (see instructions)	.
12b	**Number of individuals provided COBRA premium assistance reported on line 12a**	
13	**Add lines 11 and 12a** **13**	24,508.32
14	**Balance due.** If line 10 is more than line 13, write the difference here **14**	.
	For information on how to pay, see the instructions.	
15	**Overpayment.** If line 13 is more than line 10, write the difference here .	☐ Apply to next return. Check one ☐ Send a refund.

► You **MUST** complete both pages of Form 941 and **SIGN** it.   Next ➡

For Privacy Act and Paperwork Reduction Act Notice, see the back of the Payment Voucher.   Cat. No. 17001Z   Form **941** (Rev. 1-2010)

FIGURE 8.6 (*Continued*)

950210

Name (*not your trade name*)	**Employer identification number (EIN)**
Travelwithus.com	58-1213479

Part 2: Tell us about your deposit schedule and tax liability for this quarter.

If you are unsure about whether you are a monthly schedule depositor or a semiweekly schedule depositor, see *Pub. 15 (Circular E)*, section 11.

16 **M A** Write the state abbreviation for the state where you made your deposits OR write "MU" if you made your deposits in *multiple* states.

17 Check one: ☐ Line 10 is less than $2,500. Go to Part 3.

☐ You were a monthly schedule depositor for the entire quarter. Enter your tax liability for each month. Then go to Part 3.

Tax liability: Month 1 ☐ .

Month 2 ☐ .

Month 3 ☐ .

Total liability for quarter ☐ .   Total must equal line 10.

☑ You were a semiweekly schedule depositor for any part of this quarter. Complete *Schedule B (Form 941): Report of Tax Liability for Semiweekly Schedule Depositors,* and attach it to Form 941.

Part 3: Tell us about your business. If a question does NOT apply to your business, leave it blank.

18 If your business has closed or you stopped paying wages . . . . ☐ Check here, and

enter the final date you paid wages ☐ / / .

19 If you are a seasonal employer and you do not have to file a return for every quarter of the year . . ☐ Check here.

Part 4: May we speak with your third-party designee?

Do you want to allow an employee, a paid tax preparer, or another person to discuss this return with the IRS? See the instructions for details.

☐ Yes. Designee's name and phone number ☐   ( ) –

Select a 5-digit Personal Identification Number (PIN) to use when talking to the IRS. ☐ ☐ ☐ ☐ ☐

☑ No.

Part 5: Sign here. You MUST complete both pages of Form 941 and SIGN it.

Under penalties of perjury, I declare that I have examined this return, including accompanying schedules and statements, and to the best of my knowledge and belief, it is true, correct, and complete. Declaration of preparer (other than taxpayer) is based on all information of which preparer has any knowledge.

X **Sign your name here** *Katherine C. Kurtz*

Print your name here Katherine C. Kurtz

Print your title here Controller

Date 1 / 31 / 201X+1

Best daytime phone (978) 555 – 4040

Paid preparer's use only   Check if you are self-employed . . . . . ☐

Preparer's name		Preparer's SSN/PTIN	
Preparer's signature		Date	/ /
Firm's name (or yours if self-employed)		EIN	
Address		Phone	( ) –
City		State		ZIP code	

Form **941** (Rev. 1-2010)

5d: The total of OASDI tax of $9,411.67 and Medicare tax of $2,244.62 is $11,656.29.

6: This line is used to report the total income tax, OASDI tax, and Medicare tax withheld of $24,507.32. It is the sum of lines 3 and 5d. Notice that it matches column (g).

7a–h: These lines are used to report special tax adjustments. None apply to Travelwithus.com, so these lines are left blank.

8: This line reports total tax after adjustments, so it is the same as line 6.

9: If Travelwithus.com advanced any earned income credit to its employees, it would deduct these amounts on this line.

10: This line is the difference between lines 8 and 9.

11: This line shows the total of the Form 941 deposits that Travelwithus.com made for the last quarter, $24,508.32. This amount includes the last deposit that Travelwithus.com made for the quarter on Thursday, January 4, because it applies to the December 31 biweekly and monthly payrolls.

12 and 13: Travelwithus.com's deposits exactly total the Form 941 taxes for the quarter, which means it does not have any balance due, nor has it overpaid its taxes.

Part 2:   *Providing information about the deposit schedule.*

Line 14: Katherine indicates the abbreviation of the state in which Travelwithus.com has made its deposits.

Line 15: As a semiweekly depositor, Travelwithus.com checks this box and completes and attaches Schedule B: Report of Tax Liability for Semiweekly Schedule Depositors. By showing each day of the quarter, this schedule requires employers to present tax liability amounts on a day-by-day basis. The IRS requires employers to complete this schedule because, by comparing the dates of the tax liabilities to the dates that the deposits were made, it easily allows them to determine whether deposits were made on time. (Schedule B is not shown here.) The amounts for each day are added together to show the total for each month, and these monthly totals together should equal the total liability on line 10.

Part 3:   *Indicating specific situations that relate to the business.*

Lines 16 and 17: If a business has not closed and is not a seasonal employer, these lines do not apply. Katherine leaves them blank.

Part 4:   *Indicating whether the business would allow an employee, paid tax preparer, or another person to discuss the return with the IRS.. Katherine checks "No."*

Part 5:   *Signing the return.* Katherine signs the return on behalf of Travelwithus.com.

LEARNING UNIT 8-2 REVIEW

AT THIS POINT you should be able to do the following:

- Explain the purpose of Form SS-4.
- Explain which taxes are reported on Form 941.
- Understand how employers are classified as payroll tax depositors.
- Summarize Form 941 payroll tax deposit rules for monthly depositors.
- Summarize Form 941 payroll tax deposit rules for semiweekly depositors.
- Record the general journal entry to pay FIT, FICA OASDI, and FICA Medicare when a payroll tax deposit is made.
- Understand how the general journal entries recording FICA OASDI and FICA Medicare and the payment of these taxes are posted into the general ledger.
- Complete a Form 941, Employer's Quarterly Federal Tax Return, from a worksheet.

Instant Replay • Self-Review Quiz 8-2

Carol Ann's Import Chalet is a business that employs five full-time employees and four part-time employees. The accountant for Carol Ann's determined that the business is a monthly depositor. The accountant prepared a worksheet showing the following payroll tax liabilities for the month of October:

Payday	OASDI EE + ER	Medicare EE + ER	FIT
10/7	$486.56	$169.05	$829.00
10/14	$632.15	$165.01	$901.00
10/21	$579.43	$131.05	$734.00
10/28	$389.99	$142.24	$765.00
Totals	$2,088.13	$607.35	$3,229.00

1. What is the dollar amount of the Form 941 tax deposit that must be made, and when must it be made according to the monthly deposit rule? Use Figure 8.5 for the date.
2. Now assume that Carol Ann is classified as a semiweekly depositor. Please calculate the amount of each Form 941 tax deposit and its due date by completing the following table (use Figure 8.5 for the dates):

Payday	Date of Deposit	Amount of Deposit
10/7	?	?
10/14	?	?
10/21	?	?
10/28	?	?

Solutions to Instant Replay: Self-Review Quiz 8-2

COACHING TIP

The tax for Form 941 is
FICA OASDI: employee and employer
FICA Medicare: employee and employer
FIT: employee only

1. As a monthly depositor, Carol Ann's deposit date is Wednesday, November 15. The total amount of the deposit is $5,924.48 ($2,088.13 + $607.35 + $3,229.00).
2. As a semiweekly depositor, Carol Ann's deposit schedule is completed as follows:

Payday	Date of Deposit	Amount of Deposit	
10/7	10/13	$1,484.61	($486.56 + $169.05 + $829.00)
10/14	10/20	$1,698.16	
10/21	10/27	$1,444.48	
10/28	11/3	$1,297.23	

LEARNING UNIT 8-3 PREPARING FORMS W-2 AND W-3, PAYING FUTA TAX AND COMPLETING THE EMPLOYER'S ANNUAL UNEMPLOYMENT TAX RETURN, FORM 940, AND PAYING SUTA TAX AND WORKERS' COMPENSATION INSURANCE

Preparing Form W-2: Wage and Tax Statement

L04

The Internal Revenue Service requires that each calendar year employers complete a Form W-2, Wage and Tax Statement, a multipart form. The IRS requires Travelwithus.com to give or mail copies of Form W-2 to each person who worked for the company in the past year. These forms must be distributed by January 31 of the following year.

Employees use the amount on this form to prepare their income tax returns and calculate the amounts of income tax they owe. They must attach one copy of the form to their federal income tax return, and other copies are attached to any state or local income tax returns that they may be required to file. Taxpayers who file electronically do not attach a copy of their W-2 but must furnish a copy if requested by the IRS.

Figure 8.7 shows the W-2 that Stephanie Higuera received from Travelwithus.com. Travelwithus.com prepares the W-2s by using information from Stephanie's employee earnings record. Note that OASDI wages and taxes are shown separately from the amounts reported for Medicare wages and taxes because of the wage base limit for the OASDI tax that does not apply to the Medicare tax.

If an employee stops working for Travelwithus.com during the year, he or she may ask for a W-2 before the year ends. Travelwithus.com must provide the W-2 within 30 days of the last paycheck or the date of the request, whichever is later. Travelwithus.com must also give copies of the W-2s for all employees to the Social Security Administration and state and local governments. It will also keep a copy for its own records.

Form W-2, Wage and Tax Statement A form completed by the employer at the end of the calendar year to provide a summary of gross earnings and deductions to each employee. At least three copies go to the employee, one copy to the IRS, one copy to any state where employee income taxes have been withheld, one copy to the Social Security Administration, and one copy into the records of the business.

FIGURE 8.7 Completed Form W-2

Preparing Form W-3: Transmittal of Income and Tax Statements

The IRS also requires Travelwithus.com to prepare its Form W-3, Transmittal of Wage and Tax Statements. Employers such as Travelwithus.com send this form to the Social Security Administration along with copies of the W-2s for all employees (see Figure 8.8). Form W-3 reports the total amounts of wages, tips, and compensation paid to employees, the total OASDI and Medicare taxes withheld, and some other information. The information used to complete Form W-3 came from a summary of the individual employee earnings records that Katherine prepared soon after the year ended. (See Figure 8.9).

Form W-3, Transmittal of Income and Tax Statement A form completed by the employer to verify the number of W-2s and amounts withheld as shown on them. This form is sent to the Social Security Administration data processing center along with copies of each employee's W-2 forms.

FIGURE 8.8 Completed Form W-3

DO NOT STAPLE

a Control number	33333	For Official Use Only ▶ OMB No. 1545-0008		
b Kind of Payer	941 ☒ Military ☐ 943 ☐ 944 ☐ CT-1 ☐ Hshld. emp. ☐ Medicare govt. emp. ☐ Third-party sick pay ☐	1 Wages, tips, other compensation **286 425.30**		2 Federal income tax withheld **48 063.67**
		3 Social security wages **284 925.30**		4 Social security tax withheld **17655.37**
c Total number of Forms W-2 **6**	d Establishment number	5 Medicare wages and tips **286 425.30**		6 Medicare tax withheld **4153.17**
e Employer identification number (EIN) **58-1213479**		7 Social security tips	8 Allocated tips	
f Employer's name **TRAVELWITHUS.COM**		9 Advance EIC payments	10 Dependent care benefits	
		11 Nonqualified plans	12 Deferred compensation	
10 LOVETT ROAD SALEM, MA 01970		13 For third-party sick pay use only		
g Employer's address and ZIP code		14 Income tax withheld by payer of third-party sick pay		
h Other EIN used this year				
15 State **MA** Employer's state ID number **621-8966-4**		16 State wages, tips, etc. **286 425.30**		17 State income tax **22 914.02**
		18 Local wages, tips, etc.	19 Local income tax	
Contact person **KATHERINE C. KURTZ**		Telephone number **(978)555 4040**	For Official Use Only	
Email address **KKURTZ@TRAVELWITH.US**		Fax number **(978)555 4040**		

Under penalties of perjury, I declare that I have examined this return and accompanying documents, and, to the best of my knowledge and belief, they are true, correct, and complete.

Signature ▶ *Katherine C. Kurtz*   Title ▶ **CONTROLLER**   Date ▶ **2/28/201X**

Form **W-3** Transmittal of Wage and Tax Statements   **201X**   Department of the Treasury Internal Revenue Service

Send this entire page with the entire Copy A page of Form(s) W-2 to the Social Security Administration. Photocopies are not acceptable.

Do not send any payment (cash, checks, money orders, etc.) with Forms W-2 and W-3.

Employers send Form W-2 and Form W-3 to the Social Security Administration for FICA tax purposes. The Social Security Administration, under a special agreement with the IRS, makes all information found on individual W-2 forms electronically available to the IRS so that it can check the accuracy of the employer's 941 forms and individual employees' federal income tax returns.

L05 Paying FUTA Tax

If the total FUTA tax owed for the calendar year is less than $500, an employer must pay the tax to the IRS by the end of January of the next year. If the total amount owed is more than $500, then it is due by the end of the month following the end of the calendar quarter. If the employer is required to make Form 941 tax payments by EFTPS, then it must also deposit FUTA tax by this method.

By the end of the year, all of Travelwithus.com's employees earned more than the $7,000 wage base limit, so its total FUTA tax will be calculated as follows:

6 employees × $7,000 FUTA taxable earnings × 0.08%* FUTA tax rate = $336 FUTA tax

---

*Normal FUTA Tax credit 6.2%–5.4%.

FIGURE 8.9 W-3 Worksheet

Employee	Total Earnings	FICA Taxable Earnings		FICA Tax		FIT
		OASDI	Medicare	OASDI	Medicare	
Goldman, Ernie	103500 00	102000 00	103500 00	6324 00	1500 75	20097 00
Higuera, Stephanie	23723 40	23723 40	23723 40	1470 85	343 99	2241 86
Kurtz, Katherine	66448 16	66448 16	66448 16	4119 79	963 50	12625 15
Regan, Julia	58500 00	58500 00	58500 00	3627 00	848 25	9945 00
Sui, Annie	8287 14	8287 14	8287 14	513 80	120 16	1077 33
Taylor, Harold	25966 60	25966 60	25966 60	1609 93	376 52	2077 33
Total	286425 30	284925 30	286425 30	17665 37	4153 17	48063 67

TRAVELWITHUS.COM INC.
W-3 Amounts
YTD Totals

Because this amount is less than $500, Katherine does not need to make a deposit during the year and will deposit the taxes by the end of January of the following year. She then makes the following journal entry to record the payment of FUTA tax.

GENERAL JOURNAL

Date			PR	Dr.	Cr.
201X+1					
Jan.	31	FUTA Payable		336 00	
		Cash			336 00
		To record payment of the 201X FUTA			
		tax			

Completing the Employer's Annual Federal Unemployment (FUTA) Tax Return, Form 940

Businesses must complete Form 940, Employer's Annual Federal Unemployment (FUTA) Tax Return. Employers must file Form 940 by January 31 of the following year; however, if all taxes owed for the year were deposited by January 31, then the business has until February 10 to file its return.

To make sure that Travelwithus.com makes its FUTA deposits on time, Katherine keeps track of the amount of FUTA tax owed. Katherine prepared the worksheet in Figure 8.10 to determine the amount of FUTA taxes that Travelwithus.com owes for the first quarter of the year. Notice that she calculates the FUTA tax on the total wages because reporting the FUTA tax for each individual employee is not required. Also notice that Annie Sui has no earnings for the first quarter and therefore no earnings that are taxable for FUTA purposes because she was hired after the quarter began. Finally, notice that Ernie Goldman, Katherine Kurtz, and Julia Regan's first quarter earnings are greater than their FUTA taxable earnings because they earned more than $7,000 during the first quarter, and only the first $7,000 of earnings is taxable.

Although Travelwithus.com's other payroll amounts have been shown for the last quarter of the year, showing FUTA tax calculations for this quarter would not be very helpful. Almost all employees will have made more than the $7,000 FUTA limit by the start of the fourth quarter, and Travelwithus.com would only owe FUTA taxes for one employee, Annie Sui, who was hired just before the fourth quarter began.

Form 940, Employer's Annual Federal Unemployment Tax Return This form is used by employers at the end of the calendar year to report the amount of unemployment tax due for the year. If more than $500 is cumulatively owed at the end of a quarter, it should be paid one month after the end of that quarter. Normally, the report is due January 31 after the calendar year, or February 10 if an employer has already made all deposits.

At the end of the calendar year, Katherine prepares the Form 940 in Figure 8.11. Line-by-line instructions follow:

Part 1:

Line 1a: This line is used to show the state in which payments are made if only one state is involved.

1b is used by employers who pay state unemployment in more than one state.

Part 2: *Reporting taxable wages and FUTA tax.*

Line 3: Katherine shows the total wages and salaries paid during the year, $286,425.30, as shown on the W-3 worksheet.

4: This line is used to show any payments that are exempt from FUTA taxes, and does not apply to Travelwithus.com.

5: This line shows the amount of wages and salaries above the $7,000 limit, which is $244,425.30. Because the six employees all reached the $7,000 limit, the total limit is $42,000. Total wages and salaries of $286,425.30 minus taxable wages and salaries of $42,000 equals $244,425.30.

6: Katherine adds the total of lines 4 and 5 and gets $244,425.30.

7: Katherine subtracts line 6 from line 3 to determine the taxable amount of wages and salaries, $42,000.

8: Katherine multiplies line 7, $42,000, by the FUTA tax rate of .008 to get the total FUTA tax of $336.00 for the year.

Part 3 is used to determine adjustments to the FUTA tax calculated in line 8, if any.

Part 4 is used to calculate your FUTA tax.

12: This is the amount of FUTA tax less any adjustments made in Part 3. Travelwithus.com did not have any adjustments.

13: This line shows the amount of FUTA tax that Travelwithus.com paid for the year.

14 and 15: Travelwithus.com paid exactly the right amount of FUTA tax for the year; therefore, no balance is due and no overpayment was made.

Part 5: *Showing the tax liability by quarter.*

Katherine does not have to complete this section because Travelwithus. com's FUTA tax liability for the year was less than $500.

FIGURE 8.10
FUTA Worksheet

	TRAVELWITHUS.COM INC. FUTA Taxes 1st Quarter			
Employee	1st Quarter Earnings	FUTA Taxable Earnings	FUTA Tax Rate	FUTA Tax
Goldman, Ernie	23,925 00	7,000 00		
Higuera, Stephanie	5,928 00	5,928 00		
Kurtz, Katherine	16,612 04	7,000 00		
Regan, Julia	14,625 00	7,000 00		
Sui, Annie	—	—		
Taylor, Harold	5,325 59	5,325 59		
Total	66,415 63	32,253 59	0 008	258 03

FIGURE 8.11 Completed Form 940

Form **940 for 201X:** Employer's Annual Federal Unemployment (FUTA) Tax Return   850110

Department of the Treasury — Internal Revenue Service

OMB No. 1545-0028

(EIN)
Employer identification number   5 5 – 1 2 1 3 4 7 9

Name *(not your trade name)*   Travelwithus.com

Trade name *(if any)*

Address   10 Lovett Road
Number   Street   Suite or room number

Salem   MA   01970
City   State   ZIP code

Type of Return
(Check all that apply.)

☐ **a.** Amended
☐ **b.** Successor employer
☐ **c.** No payments to employees in 2010
☐ **d.** Final: Business closed or stopped paying wages

Read the separate instructions before you fill out this form. Please type or print within the boxes.

Part 1: Tell us about your return. If any line does NOT apply, leave it blank.

1   If you were required to pay your state unemployment tax in ...

1a One state only, write the state abbreviation . . . . **1a**   M A
- OR -
1b More than one state (You are a multi-state employer) . . . . **1b** ☐ Check here. Fill out Schedule A.

2   If you paid wages in a state that is subject to **CREDIT REDUCTION** . . . . **2** ☐ Check here. Fill out Schedule A (Form 940), Part 2.

Part 2: Determine your FUTA tax before adjustments for 2010. If any line does NOT apply, leave it blank.

3   Total payments to all employees **3**   286425.30

4   Payments exempt from FUTA tax . . . . **4**   0.

Check all that apply: **4a** ☐ Fringe benefits   **4c** ☐ Retirement/Pension   **4e** ☐ Other
4b ☐ Group-term life insurance   **4d** ☐ Dependent care

5   Total of payments made to each employee in excess of $7,000 . . . . **5**   244,425.30

6   Subtotal (line 4 + line 5 = line 6) **6**   244,425.00

7   Total taxable FUTA wages (line 3 – line 6 = line 7) **7**   42,000.00

8   FUTA tax before adjustments (line 7 × .008 = line 8) **8**   336.00

Part 3: Determine your adjustments. If any line does NOT apply, leave it blank.

9   If ALL of the taxable FUTA wages you paid were excluded from state unemployment tax, multiply line 7 by .054 (line 7 × .054 = line 9). Then go to line 12 . . . . . **9**   0.

10   If SOME of the taxable FUTA wages you paid were excluded from state unemployment tax, **OR** you paid ANY state unemployment tax late (after the due date for filing Form 940), fill out the worksheet in the instructions. Enter the amount from line 7 of the worksheet . . . . . **10**   0.

11   If credit reduction applies, enter the amount from line 3 of Schedule A (Form 940) . . . . **11**   .

Part 4: Determine your FUTA tax and balance due or overpayment for 2010. If any line does NOT apply, leave it blank.

12   Total FUTA tax after adjustments (lines 8 + 9 + 10 + 11 = line 12) **12**   336.00

13   FUTA tax deposited for the year, including any overpayment applied from a prior year . **13**   336.00

14   Balance due (If line 12 is more than line 13, enter the difference on line 14.)
- If line 14 is more than $500, you must deposit your tax.
- If line 14 is $500 or less, you may pay with this return. For more information on how to pay, see the separate instructions . . . . **14**   .

15   Overpayment (If line 13 is more than line 12, enter the difference on line 15 and check a box below.) . . . . **15**   .

Check one: ☐ Apply to next return.
☐ Send a refund.

▶ You **MUST** fill out both pages of this form and **SIGN** it.

Next ▶

For Privacy Act and Paperwork Reduction Act Notice, see the back of Form 940-V, Payment Voucher.   Cat. No. 11234O   Form **940** (2010)

FIGURE 8.11 (*Continued*)

850210

Name (not your trade name)	Employer identification number (EIN)
Travelwithus.com	58-1213479

Part 5: Report your FUTA tax liability by quarter only if line 12 is more than $500. If not, go to Part 6.

16 Report the amount of your **FUTA** tax liability for each quarter; do **NOT** enter the amount you deposited. If you had no liability for a quarter, leave the line blank.

16a **1st quarter** (January 1 – March 31) . . . . **16a** [.   ]

16b **2nd quarter** (April 1 – June 30) . . . . **16b** [.   ]

16c **3rd quarter** (July 1 – September 30) . . . . **16c** [.   ]

16d **4th quarter** (October 1 – December 31) . . . . **16d** [.   ]

17 Total tax liability for the year (lines 16a + 16b + 16c + 16d = line 17) **17** [.   ] **Total must equal line 12.**

Part 6: May we speak with your third-party designee?

Do you want to allow an employee, a paid tax preparer, or another person to discuss this return with the IRS? See the instructions for details.

☐ **Yes.**   Designee's name and phone number [   ] [   ]

Select a 5-digit Personal Identification Number (PIN) to use when talking to IRS [   ] [   ] [   ] [   ] [   ]

☑ **No.**

Part 7: Sign here. You MUST fill out both pages of this form and SIGN it.

Under penalties of perjury, I declare that I have examined this return, including accompanying schedules and statements, and to the best of my knowledge and belief, it is true, correct, and complete, and that no part of any payment made to a state unemployment fund claimed as a credit was, or is to be, deducted from the payments made to employees. Declaration of preparer (other than taxpayer) is based on all information of which preparer has any knowledge.

✗ **Sign your name here** *Katherine C. Kurtz*

Print your name here: **Katherine C. Kurtz**

Print your title here: **Controller**

Date: 2/10/201X+1

Best daytime phone: **(978) 555-4040**

Paid preparer use only   Check if you are self-employed . . . ☐

Preparer's name		PTIN
Preparer's signature		Date / /
Firm's name (or yours if self-employed)		EIN
Address		Phone
City	State	ZIP code

Paying SUTA Tax

State Unemployment Tax Act (SUTA) taxes are paid to the government of the state in which a business is located and are typically due by the end of the month following each calendar quarter. Employers also usually are required to complete a state unemployment tax report, much like they complete Form 940. Using the first quarter earnings (see Figure 8.10), Katherine calculates the SUTA tax due for the first quarter as follows:

$32,253.59 SUTA taxable earnings × 5.4% SUTA tax rate = $1,741.69

The journal entry to record the payment of SUTA follows:

State Unemployment Tax Act (SUTA) A tax usually paid only by employers to the state for employee unemployment insurance.

GENERAL JOURNAL					
Date		PR	Dr.	Cr.	
201X					
Apr. 30	SUTA Payable		1 7 4 1 69		
	Cash			1 7 4 1 69	
	To record payment of the SUTA				
	tax for the quarter ending March 31,				
	201X				

Paying Workers' Compensation Insurance

Remember from Chapter 7 that the premium for workers' compensation insurance is paid at the beginning of the year based on estimated gross payroll for the year, and the journal entry to record this payment is as follows:

Workers' compensation insurance Insurance paid, in advance by an employer to protect its employees against loss due to accidental death or injury incurred during employment.

GENERAL JOURNAL					
Date		PR	Dr.	Cr.	
201X					
Jan. 5	Prepaid Workers' Compensation Insurance		1 3 1 8 00		
	Cash			1 3 1 8 00	
	To record payment of the workers'				
	compensation insurance premium				
	for 201X				

Like any prepaid amount, this amount will gradually be transferred from the Prepaid Workers' Compensation Insurance account, an asset, to the Workers' Compensation Insurance Expense account in the month-end adjusting entries for 201X.

At the end of the year, if Travelwithus.com owes an additional premium because actual gross payroll was higher than estimated gross payroll, the payment of the additional premium would be recorded as follows:

GENERAL JOURNAL					
Date		PR	Dr.	Cr.	
201X					
Dec. 31	Workers' Compensation Insurance Expense		2 2 8 48		
	Cash			2 2 8 48	
	To record payment of the additional				
	workers' compensation insurance				
	premium for 201X				

LEARNING UNIT 8-3 REVIEW

AT THIS POINT you should be able to do the following:

- Prepare a Form W-2 and a Form W-3.
- Explain the difference between a Form W-2 and a Form W-3.
- Prepare Form 940.
- Explain when FUTA and SUTA taxes are paid.
- Explain when workers' compensation insurance premiums are paid.
- Record the payment of FUTA, SUTA, and workers' compensation insurance amounts.

Instant Replay ◉ Self-Review Quiz 8-3

Are the following statements true or false?

1. Employees must receive W-4s by January 31 of the following year.
2. Form W-3 is sent to the Social Security Administration yearly.
3. A Form 940 can only be prepared by a business that employs workers in only one state.
4. The Employer's Annual Federal Unemployment Tax Return reports the employer's FICA and FIT tax liabilities.
5. A FUTA tax liability of $500 or more must be paid 10 days after the quarter ends.
6. Premiums for workers' compensation insurance may be adjusted based on actual payroll figures.

COACHING TIP

Remember that the employee completes a W-4 when hired. The employer completes a W-2 for the employee at the end of the year.

Solutions to Instant Replay: Self-Review Quiz 8-3

1. False. W-2 forms must be sent to each employee by January 31 of the following year. The W-4 form is filled out by a new employee and is used for calculating federal and state income taxes.
2. True.
3. False. Form 940 can be prepared by a business that employs workers in one or more states.
4. False. The Employee's Annual Federal Unemployment Tax Return, Form 940, reports the FUTA tax liability. Form 941 reports the FICA and FIT tax liabilities.
5. False. A FUTA tax liability of $500 or more must be paid one month after the quarter ends.
6. True.

BLUEPRINT: FORM 941 TAX DEPOSIT RULES

Ten Frequently Asked Questions and Answers About Depositing OASDI, Medicare, and FIT to the Government

Here is a summary of questions and answers to help you understand the payroll tax deposit rules for Form 941 taxes:

1. **What are Form 941 taxes?** The term *Form 941 taxes* is used to describe the amount of FIT, OASDI, and Medicare paid by employees and the amount of OASDI and Medicare taxes that are matched and paid by an employer. The total of these taxes is known as Form 941 taxes because it is reported on Form 941 each quarter.

2. **When does an employer deposit Form 941 taxes?** How often an employer deposits Form 941 taxes depends on how the employer is classified for this purpose. The IRS usually classifies an employer as either a monthly or semiweekly depositor based on the amount of Form 941 taxes paid during a time period known as a look-back period.

3. **When is a look-back period?** A look-back period is a fiscal year that begins on July 1 and ends on June 30 of the year before the calendar year when the deposits will be made. For example, for the 2012 calendar year, an employer's look-back period will begin on July 1, 2010, and end on June 30, 2011.

4. **What is the dollar amount used to classify an employer for Form 941 tax deposits?** The key dollar amount used to determine whether an employer is a monthly or semiweekly depositor is $50,000 in Form 941 taxes. Two rules apply here:

   a. If the total amount deposited in Form 941 taxes is less than $50,000 during the look-back period, the employer is considered a monthly tax depositor.

   b. If the total amount deposited in Form 941 taxes is $50,000 or more during the look-back period, the employer is considered a semiweekly tax depositor.

5. **How do employers deposit Form 941 taxes?** Unless an employer pays Form 941 taxes of less than $2,500 per quarter the employer must utilize the Electronic Federal Tax Payment System (EFTPS) to deposit the Form 941 taxes. If the amount of Form 941 taxes owed is less than $2,500 per quarter, payment may be made by check at the time of the submission of the Form 941.

6. **When do monthly depositors make their deposits?** A monthly depositor will figure the total amount of Form 941 taxes owed in a calendar month and then pay this amount by the 15th of the next month. If an employer owes $3,125 in Form 941 taxes for the month of June, it will deposit this same amount no later than July 15 of the same year.

7. **When do semiweekly depositors make their deposits?** The rules for making deposits are a little more complicated for a semiweekly depositor. The depositor may have to make up to two Form 941 deposits each week. When a tax deposit is due depends on when the employees are paid. To keep the rules consistent, the IRS has taken a calendar week and divided it into two payday time periods. It is easiest to think of a two-week period of time when discussing these periods: Wednesday through Friday of week 1, and Saturday of week 1 through Tuesday of week 2.

   Two deposit rules apply to these two time periods. We can call these rules the Wednesday and Friday rules.

   a. Wednesday rule: If employees are paid during the Wednesday through Friday of week 1 period, the tax deposit will be due on Wednesday of week 2.

   b. Friday rule: If employees are paid anytime from Saturday of week 1 through Tuesday of week 2, the tax deposit will be due on Friday of week 2.

These rules mean that the payroll tax deposit will be due three banking days after the payday time period ends. For the Wednesday rule, the deposit is due three banking days after Friday of week 1, on the following Wednesday in week 2. For the Friday rule, the deposit is due three banking days after Tuesday of week 2, on Friday of week 2. The following illustration shows how this timing works.

	Week 1							Week 2						
	Sun	Mon	Tues	Wed	Thur	Fri	Sat	Sun	Mon	Tues	Wed	Thur	Fri	Sat
If payday is														
Then deposit is due														

8. **What is a banking day?** The term *banking day* refers to any day that banks are open to the public for business. Saturdays, Sundays, and legal holidays are not banking days.

9. **How do legal holidays affect payroll tax deposits?** If a legal holiday occurs after the last day of a payday time period, the employer will get one extra day to make its Form 941 tax deposit as follows:

    a. For monthly depositors: If the 15th of the month is a Saturday, Sunday, or legal holiday, the deposit will be due and payable on the next banking day.

    b. For semiweekly depositors: A deposit due on Wednesday will be due on Thursday of the same week, and a Friday deposit will be due on Monday of the following week. Remember that the employer will always have three banking days after the last day of either payday time period to make its payroll tax deposit.

10. **What happens if an employer is late with its Form 941 tax deposit?** If a Form 941 tax deposit is not made the day it should be deposited, the employer may be assessed a fine for lateness and may even be charged interest, depending on how late the deposit is.

ACCOUNTING COACH

The following Coaching Tips are from Learning Units 8-1 through 8-3. Take the Pre-Game Checkup and use the Check Your Score at the bottom of the page to see how you are doing. The Accounting Coach provides tips before each Checkup to help you avoid common accounting errors.

LU 8-1 Recording Payroll and Payroll Tax Expense and Paying the Payroll

Pre-Game Tips: The FICA (OASDI and Medicare) payable accounts contain both employee deductions and the employer's OASDI and Medicare payments.

Pre-Game Checkup

Answer true or false to the following statements.

1. The payroll register is the source of the data used to journalize the payroll in the general journal.
2. The FICA (OASDI and Medicare) payable accounts reflect the tax liability of only the employer.
3. Deductions for payroll withholding taxes represent a liability of the employees until the taxes are paid by the employer.
4. Workers' compensation insurance is paid by the employer to ensure that employees are compensated if they lose their job.
5. Very few companies use a special checking account for paying their payroll.

LU 8-2 Paying FIT and FICA Taxes and Completing the Employer's Quarterly Federal Tax Return, Form 941

Pre-Game Tips: Federal Form 941 reports the FIT, OASDI, and Medicare taxes withheld from employees, as well as reports the OASDI and Medicare taxes due from the employer.

Pre-Game Checkup

Answer true or false to the following statements.

1. If an employer owed less than $50,000 in total taxes during the look-back period it would be classified as a quarterly depositor.
2. The majority of businesses normally make their payroll tax deposits to pay their Form 941 taxes either monthly or semiweekly.

3. FIT, OASDI, Medicare, and FUTA taxes are known as Form 941 taxes.
4. Regardless of the amount of taxes owed, an employer must pay its Form 941 taxes using Electronic Federal Payment (EFTPS).
5. Journal entries crediting accounts OASDI Payable and FIT Payable record the payment of these taxes.

LU 8-3 Preparing Forms W-2 and W-3, Paying FUTA Tax and Completing the Employer's Annual Unemployment Tax Return, Form 940, and Paying SUTA Tax and Workers' Compensation Insurance

Pre-Game Tips: Employers send Form W-2 and Form W-3 to the Social Security Administration, which shares this information with the Internal Revenue Service (IRS).

Pre-Game Checkup

Answer true or false to the following statements.

1. If the amount of FUTA tax is less that $500 during a given quarter, no deposit is required until the FUTA tax liability reaches $500 or until the year ends.
2. The Employer's Annual Federal Unemployment (FUTA) Tax Return, Form 1040 is not due until January 31. However, the due date is extended to February 10 if all taxes owed were paid by January 31.
3. Form W-2s must be distributed to employees no later than February 10.
4. The cost of workers' compensation insurance is charged as an expense when it is paid at the beginning of the calendar year.
5. Employers send Form W-2s and Form W-3s to the Social Security Administration so employees' individual federal income tax returns may be checked.

CHECK YOUR SCORE: Answers to the Pre-Game Checkup

LU 8-1

1. True.
2. False—The FICA (OASDI and Medicare) payable accounts accumulate FICA taxes from both the employees and the employer.
3. False—The employee's liability for FICA (OASDI and Medicare) cease the moment the employer deducts the taxes from the employee's gross pay. Those taxes then become the responsibility of the employer.
4. False—Workers' compensation insurance premiums are paid by the employer to insure the employee against work-related injury or death.
5. False—Almost all large companies establish a special account for paying their payroll. It strengthens cash control, simplifies check reconciliation, and reduces the likelihood of an overdraft.

LU 8-2

1. False—If an employer owed less than $50,000 in total taxes during the look-back period it would be classified as a monthly depositor.
2. True.
3. False—FIT, OASDI, and Medicare taxes are known as Form 941 taxes. FUTA is not a Form 941 tax; it is paid using a Form 940, Employer's Annual Federal Unemployment (FUTA) Tax Return.
4. False—An employer is required to use EFTPS only if the employer owes more than $2,500 in a quarter.
5. False—Debits to the accounts OASDI Payable and FIT Payable record the payments of these taxes. Credits to these accounts record tax liabilities.

LU 8-3

1. True.
2. True.
3. False—Form W-2s must be distributed to employees by January 31.
4. False—When workers' compensation insurance premiums are paid at the beginning of the calendar year it is recorded as Prepaid Workers' Compensation Insurance, an asset. Like any prepaid account, Prepaid Workers' Compensation Insurance will be gradually adjusted over the course of the year to Workers' Compensation Insurance Expense.
5. True.

Chapter Summary

Here are all the key concepts and equations to help you understand the concepts of this chapter and prepare you for your exam. After completing this review, go to MyAccountingLab for more practice opportunities.

MyAccountingLab

Concepts You Should Know	Key Terms	
Recording payroll and payroll taxes. 1. The payroll register provides the data for journalizing the payroll in the general journal. 2. Deductions for payroll withholding taxes represent liabilities of the employer until paid. 3. The Accounts Charged columns in the payroll register indicate which accounts will be debited to record the total wages and salaries expense when a journal entry is prepared.	Payroll tax expense (p. 293)	🔴 **L01**
Recording the payroll and the paying of the payroll. 1. Paying a payroll results in debiting Wages and Salaries Payable and crediting Cash or Payroll Cash.	Employer identification number (EIN) (p. 296) Form SS-4 (p. 296)	🟢 **L02**
Recording employer taxes for FICA OASDI, FICA Medicare, FUTA, SUTA, and workers' compensation insurance. 1. The accounts FICA OASDI Payable and FICA Medicare Payable accumulate the tax liabilities of both the employer and the employee for OASDI and Medicare taxes.	Banking day (p. 297) Calendar quarter (p. 296) Federal Insurance Contributions Act (FICA) (p. 296) Federal Unemployment Tax Act (FUTA) (p. 296) Form 944, Employer's Annual Federal Tax Return (p. 300) Form 941, Employer's Quarterly Federal Tax Return (p. 297) Form 941 taxes (p. 297) Look-back period (p. 297) Monthly depositor (p. 297) Semiweekly depositor (p. 297)	🔵 **L03**

L04

Preparing Forms W-2, W-3, 941, and 940.

1. Federal Form 941 is prepared and filed no later than one month after the calendar quarter ends. It reports the amount of FIT, OASDI, and Medicare tax withheld from employees and the OASDI and Medicare taxes due from the employer for the calendar quarter.

2. FIT, OASDI, and Medicare taxes are known as Form 941 taxes.

3. The total amount of Form 941 taxes paid by a business during a specific period of time determines how often the business will have to make its payroll tax deposits. This time period is called a look-back period.

4. Businesses will normally make their payroll tax deposits to pay their Form 941 taxes either monthly or semiweekly.

5. Different deposit rules apply to monthly and semiweekly depositors and these rules determine when deposits are due.

6. Form 941 payroll tax deposits must be made by EFTPS unless the total tax liability for the quarter is <$2,500, in which case the employer can submit the payment together with Form 944.

7. Information to prepare W-2 forms can be obtained from the individual employee earnings records.

8. Form W-3 is used by the Social Security Administration in verifying that taxes have been withheld as reported on individual employee W-2 forms.

9. Form 940 is prepared by January 31, after the end of the previous calendar year. This form can be filed by February 10 if all required deposits have been made by January 31.

10. If the amount of FUTA taxes is equal to or more than $500 during any calendar quarter, the deposit must be made no later than one month after the quarter ends. If the amount is less than $500, no deposit is required until the liability reaches the $500 point or until the year ends, when any tax due must be paid by January 31 of the following year.

11. The premium for workers' compensation insurance based on estimated payroll for the year is paid at the beginning of the year by the employer to protect against potential losses to its employees due to accidental death or injury incurred while on the job. However, after the year is over and the exact amount of the payroll is known, the insurance premium is recalculated and there may be an adjustment in the year's insurance premium.

Form W-2, Wage and Tax Statement (p. 305)

Form W-3, Transmittal of Income and Tax Statements (p. 305)

L05

Paying FUTA, SUTA, and workers' compensation insurance.

1. FUTA is for federal unemployment and SUTA is for state unemployment. States will have different rates depending on their unemployment history.

Form 940, Employer's Annual Federal Unemployment Tax Return (p. 307)

State Unemployment Tax Act (SUTA) (p. 311)

Workers' compensation insurance (p. 311)

Discussion and Critical Thinking Questions/Ethical Case

1. What taxes are recorded when recording Payroll Tax Expense?

2. What is a calendar year?

3. An employer must always use a calendar year for payroll purposes. Agree or disagree?

4. Why does payroll information center on 13-week quarters?

5. How is an employer classified as a monthly or semiweekly depositor for Form 941 tax purposes?

6. How are Form 941 taxes paid to the Treasury Department?

7. How often is Form 941 completed?

8. Under what circumstance(s) does the amount on line 15 of Form 941 match the amount found on line 10?

9. Bill Smith leaves his job on July 9. He requests a copy of his W-2 form when he leaves. His boss tells him to wait until January of next year. Please discuss whether Bill's boss is correct in making this statement.

10. Why would one employer prepare a Form 940 completing Part 1, line 1a, but another would prepare a Form 940 Part 1, line 1b?

11. Employer A has a FUTA tax liability of $67.49 on March 31 of the current year. When does the employer have to make the deposit for this liability?

12. Employer B has a FUTA tax liability of $553.24 on January 31 of the current year. When does the employer have to make the deposit for this liability?

13. Who completes Form W-4? Form W-2? Form W-3? When is each form completed?

14. Why is the year-end adjusting entry needed for workers' compensation insurance?

15. Happy Carpet Cleaning, Inc., collects FIT, OASDI, and Medicare from its employees by withholding these taxes from its employees' pay. However, Happy does not pay these amounts to the federal government until the end of the calendar year so that it can maximize its cash during the year. Because it will be paying these amounts to the government, it believes that this practice does not affect its employees. Please comment on this practice.

Concept Check

MyAccountingLab

Account Classifications

1. Complete the following table. Indicate whether a debit or credit results in an increase to the account balance

● **L01** (10 MIN)

Accounts Affected	Category	↑↓	Rules
a. Payroll Tax Expense			
b. FICA OASDI Payable			
c. SIT Payable			
d. SUTA Payable			
e. Prepaid Workers' Compensation Insurance			

LO1, 2, 3 *(10 MIN)*   **Look-Back Periods**

2.   Label the following look-back periods for 200C by months.

A	B	C	D
200A		200B	

LO1, 2, 3 *(15 MIN)*   **Monthly versus Semiweekly Depositor**

3.   In December 200B, Mary is trying to find out whether she is a monthly or semiweekly depositor for FICA (OASDI and Medicare) and federal income tax for 200C. Please advise based on the following taxes owed:

200A	Quarter 3	$29,000
	Quarter 4	16,000
200B	Quarter 1	3,500
	Quarter 2	10,700

LO1, 2, 3 *(15 MIN)*   **Paying the Tax**

4.   Complete the following table:

Depositor	4-Quarter Look-Back Period Tax Liability	Payroll Paid	Tax Paid by
Monthly	$28,000	November	a.
Semiweekly	$66,000	On Wednesday	b.
		On Thursday	c.
		On Friday	d.
		On Saturday	e.
		On Sunday	f.
		On Monday	g.

LO1, 2, 3 *(15 MIN)*   **Payroll Account**

5.   Indicate which of the following items apply to the following account titles.

1.   An asset
2.   A liability
3.   An expense
4.   Appears on the income statement
5.   Appears on the balance sheet

_____ a. FICA OASDI Payable

_____ b. Office Salaries Expense

_____ c. Federal Income Tax Payable

_____ d. FICA Medicare Payable

_____ e. Wages and Salaries Payable

Exercises

MyAccountingLab

Set A

8A-1. Complete the table.

●●**L01, 2** *(10 MIN)*

Item	Account Category	Normal Balance	Account Appears on Which Financial Statements?
Medical Insurance Payable			
Wages and Salaries Payable			
Office Salaries Expense			
Market Wages Expense			
FICA OASDI Payable			
Federal Income Tax Payable			
State Income Tax Payable			

8A-2. The following amounts were taken from the weekly payroll register for the Wu Lake Company on September 9, 201X. Using the same account title headings used in this chapter, please prepare the general journal entry to record the payroll for the Wu Lake Company for September 9.

●●**L01, 2** *(20 MIN)*

Plant Wages Expense	$7,148.00
Office Salaries Expense	3,194.00
Deduction for FICA OASDI	538.24
Deduction for FICA Medicare	124.22
Deduction for federal income tax	2,168.55
Deduction for state income tax	502.64
Deduction for union dues	890.00

8A-3. Use the information from Exercise 8A-2 and the following information to prepare the general journal entry to record the payroll tax expense for the weekly payroll of September 9, 201X:

●●●**L01, 2, 3** *(20 MIN)*

Wages below the FUTA tax wage base limit	$900.00
FUTA tax rate	0.8%
Wages below the SUTA tax wage base limit	$900.00
SUTA tax rate	5.4%

8A-4. At the end of December 201X, the total amount of OASDI, $540, and Medicare, $180, was withheld as tax deductions from the employees of Falls, Inc. Federal income tax of $2,920 was also deducted from their paychecks. Falls is classified as a monthly depositor of Form 941 taxes. Indicate when this payroll tax deposit is due and provide a general journal entry to record the payment.

●●●**L01, 2, 3** *(20 MIN)*

LO1, 2 *(15 MIN)*   **8A-5.** The following payroll journal entry was prepared by Palmdale Company from its payroll register. Which columns of the payroll register have the data come from? How do the taxable earnings columns of the payroll register relate to this entry?

		GENERAL JOURNAL						
Date			PR	Dr.		Cr.		
201X								
Oct.	15	Customer Service Expense		1 2 0 0	00			
		FIT Payable				1 3 2	00	
		SIT Payable				7 2	00	
		FICA OASDI Payable				7 4	40	
		FICA Medicare Payable				1 7	40	
		Payroll Cash				9 0 4	20	
		To record payroll						

LO1, 2, 3 *(20 MIN)*   **8A-6.** Meghan's Grocery Store made the following Form 941 payroll tax deposits during the look-back period of July 1, 201A, through June 30, 201B:

Quarter Ended	Amount Paid in 941 Taxes
September 30, 201A	$15,780.31
December 31, 201A	13,892.45
March 31, 201B	13,600.12
June 30, 201B	14,020.42

Should Meghan's Grocery Store make Form 941 tax deposits monthly or semiweekly for 201C?

LO1, 2, 3 *(15 MIN)*   **8A-7.** If Meghan's Grocery Store downsized its operation during the second quarter of 201B and, as a result, paid only $6,119.83 in Form 941 taxes for the quarter that ended on June 30, 201B, should Meghan's Grocery make its Form 941 payroll tax deposits monthly or semiweekly for 201C?

LO1, 2, 3 *(15 MIN)*   **8A-8.** From the following T accounts, record the following: (a) the July 3 payment for FICA (OASDI and Medicare) and federal income taxes, (b) the July 30 payment of SUTA tax, and (c) the July 30 deposit of any FUTA tax that may be required.

FICA OASDI Payable 203	
	June 30 380 (EE)
	380 (ER)

FICA Medicare Payable 204	
	June 30 190 (EE)
	190 (ER)

FIT Payable 205	
	June 30 3,001

FUTA Tax Payable 206	
	June 30 143

SUTA Tax Payable 207	
	June 30 610

Set B

8B-1. Complete the table.

LO1, 2 *(10 MIN)*

Item	Account Category	Normal Balance	Account Appears on Which Financial Statements?
Health Insurance Payable			
Wages and Salaries Payable			
Office Salaries Expense			
Sales Salaries Expense			
FICA OASDI Payable			
Federal Income Tax Payable			
State Income Tax Payable			

8B-2. The following amounts were taken from the weekly payroll register for the Wu Vale Company on August 9, 201X. Please prepare the general journal entry to record the payroll for the Wu Vale Company for August 9.

LO1, 2 *(20 MIN)*

Plant Wages Expense	$7,128.00
Office Salaries Expense	3,114.00
Deduction for FICA OASDI	546.00
Deduction for FICA Medicare	100.30
Deduction for federal income tax	2,362.31
Deduction for state income tax	494.36
Deduction for union dues	920.00

8B-3. Use the information from Exercise 8B-2 and the following information to prepare the general journal entry to record the payroll tax expense for the weekly payroll of August 9, 201X.

LO1, 2, 3 *(20 MIN)*

Wages below the FUTA tax wage base limit	$900.00	Wages below the SUTA tax wage base limit	$900.00
FUTA tax rate	0.8%	SUTA tax rate	5.4%

8B-4. At the end of March 201X, the total amount of OASDI, $500, and Medicare, $220, was withheld as tax deductions from the employees of River, Inc. Federal income tax of $2,940 was also deducted from their paychecks. River is classified as a monthly depositor of Form 941 taxes. Indicate when this payroll tax deposit is due and provide a general journal entry to record the payment.

LO1, 2, 3 *(20 MIN)*

8B-5. The following payroll journal entry was prepared by Palmdale Company from its payroll register. Which columns of the payroll register have the data come from? How do the taxable earnings columns of the payroll register relate to this entry?

LO1, 2 *(15 MIN)*

General Journal				
Date	Accounts	PR	Debit	Credit
201X				
Oct. 15	Customer Service Expense		2,000.00	
	FIT Payable			220.00
	SIT Payable			120.00
	FICA OASDI Payable			124.00
	FICA Medicare Payable			29.00
	Payroll Cash			1,507.00
	To record payroll			

L01, 2, 3 *(20 MIN)*   **8B-6.**   Louise's Grocery Store made the following Form 941 payroll tax deposits during the look-back period of July 1, 201A, through June 30, 201B:

Quarter Ended	Amount Paid in 941 Taxes
September 30, 201A	$15,781.31
December 31, 201A	13,892.04
March 31, 201B	13,601.26
June 30, 201B	14,021.08

Should Louise's Grocery Store make Form 941 tax deposits monthly or semi-weekly for 201C?

L01, 2, 3 *(15 MIN)*   **8B-7.**   If Louise's Grocery Store downsized its operation during the second quarter of 201B and, as a result paid only $6,120.07 in Form 941 taxes for the quarter that ended on June 30, 201B, should Louise's Grocery Store make Form 941 tax deposits monthly or semi-weekly for 201C?

L01, 2, 3 *(15 MIN)*   **8B-8.**   From the following T-accounts, record the following: (a) the July 3 payment for FICA (OASDI and Medicare) and federal income taxes, (b) the July 30 payment of SUTA tax, and (c) the July 30 deposit of any FUTA tax that may be required.

FICA OASDI Payable 203		FICA Medicare Payable 204	
	June 30 450 (EE)		June 30 180 (EE)
	450 (ER)		180 (ER)

FIT Payable 205		FUTA Tax Payable 206	
	June 30 3,007		June 30 142

SUTA Tax Payable 207	
	June 30 606

MyAccountingLab   **Problems**

Set A

L01, 2, 3 *(30 MIN)*   **8A-1.**   For the biweekly pay period ending on April 10 at Eva's Pet Store, the following partial payroll summary was taken from the individual employee earnings records. Use it to do the following:

1. Complete the table. Use the federal income tax withholding table in Figure 7.2 to figure the amount of income tax withheld.
2. Prepare a journal entry to record the payroll tax expense for Eva's. Please show the calculations for FICA taxes.

Employee	Allowance and Marital Status	Gross	FICA OASDI	Medicare	Federal Income Tax
Apple Edge	S-1	$1,058			
Mike Johnson	S-0	912			
Nat Lane	S-2	1,000			
Derek Poole	S-0	1,266			
Dan Tarantino	S-2	1,580			

Check Figure:
Payroll Tax Expense
$694.85

Assume that the FICA tax rate for OASDI is 6.2% up to $106,800 in earnings (no one earned this much as of April 10), and Medicare is 1.45% on all earnings. The state unemployment tax rate is 5.1% on the first $7,000 of earnings, and the federal unemployment tax rate is 0.8% of the first $7,000 of earnings. (Only Dan Tarantino earned more than $7,000 as of April 10.) In cases where the amount of FICA tax calculates to one-half cent, round up to the next cent.

8A-2. The following is the monthly payroll of Johnson Company, owned by Dan Johnson. Employees are paid on the last day of each month.

●●● **L01, 2, 3** *(50 MIN)*

JANUARY

Employee	Monthly Earnings	YTD Earnings	FICA OASDI	Medicare	Federal Income Tax
Saul Fish	$1,940	$1,940	$120.28	$ 28.13	$ 258.00
Jade Bryant	3,250	3,250	201.50	47.13	363.00
Amy Hess	3,760	3,760	233.12	54.52	496.00
	$8,950	$8,950	$554.90	$129.78	$1,117.00

FEBRUARY

Employee	Monthly Earnings	YTD Earnings	FICA OASDI	Medicare	Federal Income Tax
Saul Fish	$2,110	$ 4,050	$130.82	$ 30.60	$ 302.00
Jade Bryant	3,370	6,620	208.94	48.87	319.00
Amy Hess	3,800	7,560	235.60	55.10	426.00
	$9,280	$18,230	$575.36	$134.57	$1,047.00

MARCH

Employee	Monthly Earnings	YTD Earnings	FICA OASDI	Medicare	Federal Income Tax
Saul Fish	$2,050	$ 6,100	$127.10	$ 29.73	$ 590.00
Jade Bryant	2,475	9,095	153.45	35.89	560.00
Amy Hess	4,150	11,710	257.30	60.18	543.00
	$8,675	$26,905	$537.85	$125.80	$1,693.00

Check Figure:
Deposit of SUTA Tax
$1,145.70

Johnson Company is located at 2 Square Street, Marblehead, Massachusetts 01945. Its employer identification number is 29-3458822. The FICA tax rate for Social Security is 6.2% up to $106,800 in earnings during the year, and Medicare is 1.45% on all earnings. The SUTA tax rate is 5.7% on the first $7,000. The FUTA tax rate is 0.8% on the first $7,000 of earnings. Johnson Company is classified as a monthly depositor for Form 941 taxes.

Your tasks are to do the following:

1. Journalize the entries to record the employer's payroll tax expense for each pay period in the general journal.

2. Journalize entries for the payment of each tax liability in the general journal.

●●● LO1, 2, 3 *(50 MIN)*

Check Figure:
Total Liability for
Quarter $7,973.52
○———————→

8A-3. John Andrews, the accountant for Johnson Company, must complete Form 941 for the first quarter of the current year. John gathered the needed data as presented in Problem 8A-2. Suddenly called away to an urgent budget meeting, John requested that you assist him by preparing the Form 941 for the first quarter. Please note that the difference in the tax liability, a few cents, should be adjusted on line 7a; this difference is due to the rounding of FICA tax amounts.

●●● LO1, 2, 3 *(60 MIN)*

[PT]

Check Figure:
Dec. 31 Payroll Tax
Expense $880.07
○———————→

8A-4. The following is the monthly payroll for the last three months of the year for Smith's Sporting Goods Shop, 2 Boat Road, Lynn, Massachusetts 01945. The shop is a sole proprietorship owned and operated by Bill Smith. The employer ID number for Smith's Sporting Goods is 28-9311893.

The employees at Smith's are paid once each month on the last day of the month. Paula Bush is the only employee who has contributed the maximum into Social Security. None of the other employees will reach the social security wage-base limit by the end of the year. Assume the rate for social security to be 6.2% with a wage-base maximum of $106,800, and the rate for Medicare to be 1.45% on all earnings. Smith's is classified as a monthly depositor for Form 941 payroll tax deposit purposes.

Your tasks are to do the following:

1. Journalize the entries to record the employer's payroll tax expense for each period in the general journal.

2. Journalize the payment of each tax liability in the general journal.

3. Complete Form 941 for the fourth quarter of the current year.

OCTOBER

Employee	Monthly Earnings	YTD Earnings	FICA OASDI	FICA Medicare	Federal Income Tax
Paula Bush	$ 2,820	$100,650	$174.84	$ 40.89	$ 530.00
Joe Lapine	3,540	39,700	219.48	51.33	422.00
Gina Vale	3,780	44,200	234.36	54.81	537.00
	$10,140	$184,550	$628.68	$147.03	$1,489.00

NOVEMBER

Employee	Monthly Earnings	YTD Earnings	FICA OASDI	FICA Medicare	Federal Income Tax
Paula Bush	$ 3,040	$103,690	$188.48	$ 44.08	$ 595.00
Joe Lapine	3,860	43,560	239.32	55.97	464.00
Gina Vale	3,660	47,860	226.92	53.07	556.00
	$10,560	$195,110	$654.72	$153.12	$1,615.00

DECEMBER

Employee	Monthly Earnings	YTD Earnings	FICA OASDI	FICA Medicare	Federal Income Tax
Paula Bush	$ 4,240	$107,930	$192.82	$ 61.48	$ 871.00
Joe Lapine	3,860	47,420	239.32	55.97	476.00
Gina Vale	4,320	52,180	267.84	62.64	708.00
	$12,420	$207,530	$699.98	$180.09	$2,055.00

8A-5. Using the information from Problem 8A-4, please complete a Form 940 for Smith's Sporting Goods for the current year. Additional information needed to complete the form is as follows:

   a. SUTA rate: 5.7%

   b. State reporting number: 025-319-2

   c. No FUTA tax deposits were made for this year.

   d. Smith's three employees for the year all earned over $7,000.

L04, 5 *(20 MIN)*

Check Figure:
Total Exempt Payments
$186,530

Set B

8B-1. For the biweekly pay period ending on April 10 at Clark's Pet Store, the following partial payroll summary is taken from the individual employee earnings records. Use it to do the following:

   1. Complete the table. Use the federal income tax withholding table in Figure 7.2 to figure the amount of income tax withheld.

   2. Prepare a journal entry to record the payroll tax expense for Clark's. Please show the calculations for FICA taxes.

L01, 2, 3 *(30 MIN)*

Check Figure:
Payroll Tax Expense
$694.57

Employee	Allowance and Marital Status	Gross	FICA OASDI	FICA Medicare	Federal Income Tax
Bill Apple	S-1	$ 1,042			
Homer Gomez	S-0	902			
William New	S-2	1,012			
John Taft	S-0	1,278			
Dan Tarantino	S-2	1,580			

Assume that the FICA tax rate for OASDI is 6.2% up to $106,800 in earnings (no one has earned this much as of April 10), and Medicare is 1.45% on all earnings. The state unemployment tax rate is 5.1% on the first $7,000 of earnings, and the federal unemployment tax rate is 0.8% of the first $7,000 of earnings. (Only Dan Tarantino earned more than $7,000 as of April 10.) In cases where the amount of FICA tax calculates to one-half cent, round up to the next cent.

8B-2. The following is the monthly payroll of Black Company, owned by Devin Black. Employees are paid on the last day of each month.

L01, 2, 3 *(50 MIN)*

Check Figure:
Deposit of SUTA tax
$1,154.54

JANUARY

Employee	Monthly Earnings	YTD Earnings	FICA OASDI	FICA Medicare	Federal Income Tax
Sam Fish	$1,970	$1,970	$122.14	$ 28.57	$ 264.00
Justine Bryant	3,210	3,210	199.02	46.55	357.00
Alison Pickens	3,800	3,800	235.60	55.10	506.00
	$8,980	$8,980	$556.76	$130.22	$1,127.00

FEBRUARY

Employee	Monthly Earnings	YTD Earnings	FICA OASDI	FICA Medicare	Federal Income Tax
Sam Fish	$2,110	$ 4,080	$130.82	$ 30.60	$ 296.00
Justine Bryant	3,360	6,570	208.32	48.72	327.00
Alison Pickens	3,850	7,650	238.70	55.83	418.00
	$9,320	$18,300	$577.84	$135.15	$1,041.00

MARCH

Employee	Monthly Earnings	YTD Earnings	FICA OASDI	FICA Medicare	Federal Income Tax
Sam Fish	$ 2,175	$ 6,255	$134.85	$ 31.54	$ 592.00
Justine Bryant	2,525	9,095	156.55	36.61	558.00
Alison Pickens	4,050	11,700	251.10	58.73	543.00
	$ 8,750	$27,050	$542.50	$126.88	$1,693.00

Black Company is located at 2 Square Street, Marblehead, Massachusetts 01945. Its employer identification number is 29-3458822. The FICA tax rate for Social Security is 6.2% up to $106,800 in earnings during the year, and Medicare is 1.45% on all earnings. The SUTA tax rate is 5.7% on the first $7,000 of earnings. The FUTA tax rate is 0.8% on the first $7,000 of earnings. Black Company is classified as a monthly depositor for Form 941 taxes.

Your tasks are to do the following:

1. Journalize the entries to record the employer's payroll tax expense for each pay period in the general journal.

2. Journalize entries for the payment of each tax liability in the general journal.

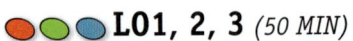 **LO1, 2, 3** *(50 MIN)*   **8B-3.**   Ted Chase, the accountant for Black Company, must complete Form 941 for the first quarter of the current year. Ted gathered the needed data as presented in Problem 8B-2. Suddenly called away to an urgent budget meeting, Ed requested that you assist him by preparing the Form 941 for the first quarter. Please note that the difference in the tax liability, a few cents, should be adjusted on line 7a; this difference is due to the rounding of FICA tax amounts.

Check Figure:
Liability for Quarter
$7,999.68

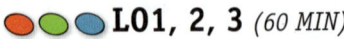 **LO1, 2, 3** *(60 MIN)*   **8B-4.**   The following is the monthly payroll for the last three months of the year for Brown's Sporting Goods Shop, 2 Boat Road, Lynn, Massachusetts 01945. The shop is a sole proprietorship owned and operated by Bill Brown. The employer ID number for Brown's Sporting Goods is 28-9311893.

The employees at Brown's are paid once each month on the last day of the month. David Clark is the only employee who has contributed the maximum into Social Security. None of the other employees will reach the Social Security wage-base limit by the end of the year. Assume the rate for Social Security to be 6.2% with a wage-base maximum of $106,800, and the rate for Medicare to be 1.45% on all earnings. Brown's is classified as a monthly depositor for Form 941 payroll tax deposit purposes.

Your tasks are to do the following:

1. Journalize the entries to record the employer's payroll tax expense for each period in the general journal.
2. Journalize the payment of each tax liability in the general journal.
3. Complete Form 941 for the fourth quarter of the current year.

OCTOBER

Employee	Monthly Earnings	YTD Earnings	FICA OASDI	FICA Medicare	Federal Income Tax
David Clark	$ 3,020	$101,800	$187.24	$ 43.79	$ 532.00
Jack Johnson	3,560	39,400	220.72	51.62	431.00
Hector Walker	3,800	43,900	235.60	55.10	531.00
	$10,380	$185,100	$643.56	$150.51	$1,494.00

NOVEMBER

Employee	Monthly Earnings	YTD Earnings	FICA OASDI	FICA Medicare	Federal Income Tax
David Clark	$ 2,950	$104,750	$182.90	$ 42.78	$ 596.00
Jack Johnson	3,780	43,180	234.36	54.81	470.00
Hector Walker	3,880	47,780	240.56	56.26	556.00
	$10,610	$195,710	$657.82	$153.85	$1,622.00

DECEMBER

Employee	Monthly Earnings	YTD Earnings	FICA OASDI	FICA Medicare	Federal Income Tax
David Clark	$ 4,160	$108,910	$127.10	$ 60.32	$ 870.00
Jack Johnson	3,740	46,920	231.88	54.23	843.00
Hector Walker	4,460	52,240	276.52	64.67	702.00
	$12,360	$208,070	$635.50	$179.22	$2,055.00

Check Figure:
Dec. 31 Payroll Tax Expense $814.72

8B-5. Using the information from Problem 8B-4, please complete a Form 940 for Brown's Sporting Goods for the current year. Additional information needed to complete the form is as follows:

a. SUTA rate: 5.7%
b. State reporting number: 025-319-2
c. No FUTA tax deposits were made for this year.
d. Brown's three employees for the year all earned over $7,000.

🟡🔵 **L04, 5** *(20 MIN)*

Check Figure:
Line 4 Total Exempt Payments $182,000

Financial Report Problem

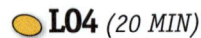 **LO4** *(20 MIN)*

Reading the Kellogg's Annual Report

Go to http://investor.kelloggs.com/annuals.cfm, to access the Kellogg's 2010 Annual Report. Go to Notes to Consolidated Financial Statements and find Note 8: Pension Benefits. How much did Kellogg's spend to fund the 401(k) plans and similar saving plans?

MyAccountingLab

SANCHEZ COMPUTER CENTER

In preparing for next year, on December 1 Tony Freedman hired two hourly employees to assist with some troubleshooting and repair work.

1. Prepare a payroll register for the three pay periods.

2. Record the following transactions in the general journal and post them to the general ledger.

Assume the following transactions:

Dec. 7 Paid employee wages: Lance Kumm, 38 hours, and Anthony Hall, 42 hours.

Dec. 14 Paid employee wages: Lance Kumm, 25 hours, and Anthony Hall, 36 hours.

Dec. 21 Paid employee wages: Lance Kumm, 26 hours, and Anthony Hall, 35 hours.

a. The following accounts have been added to the chart of accounts: Wages Payable #2010, FICA OASDI Payable #2020, FICA Medicare Payable #2030, FIT Payable #2040, State Income Tax Payable #2050, FUTA Tax Payable 2060, SUTA Tax Payable #2070, 2010 Wages Expense #5110, and Payroll Tax Expense #5120.

b. Assume FICA OASDI is taxed at 6.2% up to $106,800 in earnings and Medicare is taxed at at 1.45% on all earnings.

c. State income tax is 2% of gross pay.

d. None of the employees has federal income tax taken out of his or her pay.

e. Each employee earns $10 an hour and is paid 1½ times salary for hours worked in excess of 40 weekly.

As December comes to an end, Tony Freedman wants to take care of his payroll obligations. He will complete Form 941 for the fourth quarter of the current year and Form 940 for federal unemployment taxes. Tony will make the necessary deposits and payments associated with his payroll.

Assignment

1. Using the information in the Chapter 7 problem, record the December payrolls and the payment of the payrolls in the general journal and post them to the general ledger.

2. Using the information in this chapter, record the payroll tax expense for the fourth quarter in the general journal. Use December 31 as the date of the journal entry to record the payroll tax expense for the entire quarter. Post the entry to the general journal.

3. Record the payment of each tax liability in the general journal and post each entry to the general ledger. Sanchez Computer Center is classified as a quarterly depositor. The company wishes to pay all payroll taxes on December 31 even if no deposits are required.

4. Prepare Form 941 for the fourth quarter. Sanchez Computer Center's employer identification number is 35-4132588.

5. Complete Form 940 for Sanchez Computer Center. The FUTA tax ceiling is $7,000, and the SUTA tax ceiling is $7,000 in cumulative wages for each employee. The Sanchez Computer Center's FUTA rate is 0.8% and the SUTA rate is 2.7%. The state reporting number is 025-025-2.

Hint: Sometimes the amount of Social Security taxes paid by the employee for the quarter will not equal the employee's tax liability because of rounding. Any overage or difference should be reported on line 7a of Form 941.

SUBWAY CASE

Hold the Lettuce, Withhold the Taxes

 **L01, 2, 3, 4**
(30 MIN)

"As an employer, Stan, what are your tax responsibilities?" asked Angel Tavarez, president of the Los Palmos Kiwanis club. They were at one of the luncheons sponsored by the club every month, and Stan had been asked to join a discussion on the role of small business in the local economy. Fortunately, Angel had told the panelists the questions in advance, so Stan had his answers ready.

"Well, of course, I pay city, state, and U.S. government taxes myself. I also have to file city, state, and federal withholding taxes for each of my two employees. I have to withhold state unemployment taxes, as well as FICA, which is another name for OASDI and Medicare taxes, for each of them. I pay workers' compensation, too," said Stan.

"That's strange," said a voice from the audience. "My brother-in-law has a Subway restaurant in the southern part of the state, and he doesn't pay any city taxes. What's going on here?"

"Naturally, the situation is slightly different for Subway owners in different cities in our state—and across the country," said Stan confidently. "Not all cities have city income taxes. Different states have different regulations about workers' comp as well."

"Oh, right," said the voice, sounding embarrassed.

"So, Stan, how often do you have to pay taxes?" asked Angel Tavarez, shifting the topic diplomatically.

Stan picked up a piece of chalk and drew four large circles on the blackboard. Then he wrote the word "ASPIRIN" in each of the circles. A murmur of "Huh" and "What" went around the room.

"The average employee working for a company pays taxes once a year on April 15 and has one big tax headache. As an employer," Stan said, "I file tax returns on a quarterly basis, so I have four big tax headaches a year! Rather than filling out the 1040-EZ, I complete the Form 941, the Employer's Quarterly Federal Return, to report and pay payroll taxes to the IRS. Yet, while the form is due quarterly, I actually need to deposit the tax money into a Federal Reserve Bank once a month. In addition, I have to file the 940 at the end of each year to pay my federal and state unemployment taxes. Then, for each employee...."

"Stan," Angel interrupted, "I'm afraid time is running out for your segment of the panel discussion. We'll move on to Pamela Pudelle, who is going to tell us about advertising her new pet-grooming parlor."

Later, during the reception, Stan tapped Angel on the shoulder, "Sorry I went over my time limit," he said. "You didn't really go over," said Angel, "but you were getting a little too technical for the audience." While Stan was sorry to have let the discussion veer off course, he felt a little burst of pride: Who would have thought a year ago that he would be willing—and able—to expound about the tax burden of a small business owner!

Discussion Questions

1. What are the taxes called "Form 941 taxes"?
2. Why is Stan classified as a monthly depositor of Form 941 taxes?
3. Assume Stan owed $2,069.90 in Form 941 taxes for March. When would it be due? What would happen if that day were a Sunday?

PEACHTREE COMPUTER WORKSHOP

COMPUTERIZED ACCOUNTING APPLICATION FOR CHAPTER 8

Refresher on using Peachtree Complete Accounting

Before starting this assignment, you may want to refresh your memory by reading the following PDF documents in the multimedia library of the MyAccountingLab Web site. Remember to choose the PDF document for your version of Peachtree.

1. An Introduction to Peachtree Complete Accounting
2. Correcting Peachtree Transactions
3. How to Repeat or Restart a Peachtree Assignment
4. Backing Up and Restoring Your Work in Peachtree

You also should have completed the following workshops:

1. Workshop 1 Atlas Company from Chapter 3
2. Workshop 2 Zell Company from Chapter 4
3. Workshop 3 Sullivan Realty from Chapter 5

Workshop 4:

Payroll Mini Practice Set

In this workshop you will prepare January, February, and March payroll for Pete's Market using Peachtree. Tasks include entering payroll data, producing paychecks, and remitting payroll taxes. You will also print payroll reports.

Instructions and the data file for completing this assignment are in the multimedia library of the MyAccountingLab Web site. Open the *Workshop 4 Pete's Market* PDF document for your version of Peachtree and download the *Pete's Market* data file for your version of Peachtree.

QUICKBOOKS COMPUTER WORKSHOP

COMPUTERIZED ACCOUNTING APPLICATION FOR CHAPTER 8

Refresher on using QuickBooks Pro

Before starting this assignment, you may want to refresh your memory by reading the following PDF documents in the multimedia library of the MyAccountingLab Web site. Remember to choose the PDF document for your version of QuickBooks.

1. An Introduction to QuickBooks Pro
2. Correcting QuickBooks Transactions
3. How to Repeat or Restart a QuickBooks Assignment
4. Backing Up and Restoring Your Work in QuickBooks

You also should have completed the following workshops:

1. Workshop 1 Atlas Company from Chapter 3
2. Workshop 2 Zell Company from Chapter 4
3. Workshop 3 Sullivan Realty from Chapter 5

Workshop 4:

Payroll Mini Practice Set

In this workshop you will prepare January, February, and March payroll for Pete's Market using QuickBooks. Tasks include entering payroll data, producing paychecks, and remitting payroll taxes. You will also print payroll reports.

Instructions and the data file for completing this assignment are in the multimedia library of the MyAccountingLab Web site. Open the *Workshop 4 Pete's Market* PDF document for your version of QuickBooks and download the *Pete's Market* data file for your version of QuickBooks.

Sales and Cash Receipts

THE GAME PLAN

It's after the holidays. The lines to return or exchange gifts in stores are very long. Did you ever stop to think about how stores keep track of all the returns? How do they know what merchandise was discounted or not? Home Depot, like other companies, uses the accounting process to gather information about all sales made, whether cash or credit. Individual customer accounts are updated continually. Home Depot must monitor its inventory in order to ensure enough stock so that it does not run out of an item and miss the sales opportunity. In this chapter, in addition to accounting for returns, we will focus on how credit terms and sales tax may affect how we record the return.

LEARNING OBJECTIVES

- 1. Recording and posting sales transactions to the general and accounts receivable subsidiary ledger.
- 2. Preparing, journalizing, and posting a credit memorandum.
- 3. Recording and posting cash receipts transactions.
- 4. Recording to the accounts receivable subsidiary ledger.
- 5. Preparing a schedule of accounts receivable.

When you shop in Home Depot, a merchandise company, you will see a wide variety of products in the store. Let's first look at Chou's Toy Shop to get an overview of merchandise terms and journal entries.

LEARNING UNIT 9-1 CHOU'S TOY SHOP:
Seller's View of a Merchandise Company

Retailers Merchants who buy goods from wholesalers for resale to customers.

Merchandise Goods brought into a store for resale to customers.

Chou's Toy Shop, owned by Chou Li, is a retailer. It buys toys, games, bikes, and similar items from manufacturers and wholesalers and resells these goods (or merchandise) to its customers. The shelving, display cases, and so forth are called "fixtures" or "equipment." These items are not for resale.

Gross Sales

Each cash or charge sale made at Chou's Toy Shop is rung up at the register. Suppose the shop had $3,000 in sales on July 18. Of that amount, $1,800 was cash sales and $1,200 was charges. The account that recorded those sales would be

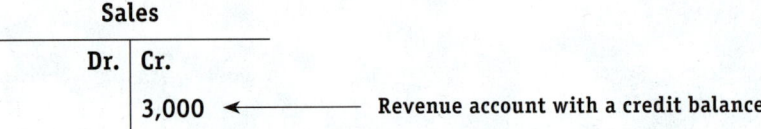

	Sales	
Dr.		Cr.
		3,000 ← ——— Revenue account with a credit balance

LO1

This account is a revenue account with a credit balance and will be found on the income statement. Figure 9.1 shows the journal entry for the day. *Note:* We talk about sales tax later. Lets look at a transaction analysis chart of this transaction before we journalize.

Accounts Affected	Category	↑↓	Rules	T Account Update
Cash	Asset	↑	Dr.	**Cash**
				1,800
Accounts Receivable	Asset	↑	Dr.	**Accounts Receivable**
				1,200
Sales	Revenue	↑	Cr.	**Sales**
				3,000

FIGURE 9.1
Recording Cash and Charge Sales for the Day

July	18	Cash	1 8 0 0 00		
		Accounts Receivable	1 2 0 0 00		
		Sales		3 0 0 0 00	
		Sales for July 18			

Sales Returns and Allowances

Sales Returns and Allowances (SRA) account A contra-revenue account that records price adjustments and allowances granted on merchandise that is defective and has been returned.

It would be great for Chou if all the customers were completely satisfied, but that rarely is the case. On July 19, Michelle Reese brought back a doll she bought on account for $50. She told Chou that the doll was defective and that she wanted either a price reduction or a new doll. They agreed on a $10 price reduction. Michelle now owes Chou $40. The account called Sales Returns and Allowances (SRA) would record this information.

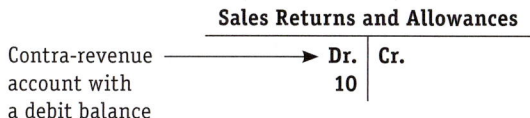

Sales Returns and Allowances

Contra-revenue ——————▶ **Dr.** | **Cr.**
account with   10 |
a debit balance

This account is a contra-revenue account with a debit balance. It will be recorded on the income statement. Figure 9.2 shows how the journal entry would look. Let's first look at a transaction analysis chart of this transaction before we journalize.

Accounts Affected	Category	↑↓	Rules	T Account Update
Sales Returns and Allowances	Contra-revenue	↑	Dr.	**Sales Ret. & Allow.** Dr. | Cr. 10 |
Accounts Receivable, Michelle Reese	Asset	↓	Cr.	**Accounts Receivable** Dr. | Cr. 1,200 | 10

Look at how the sales returns and allowances increase.

July	19	Sales Returns and Allowances		10 00	
		Accounts Receivable, Michelle Reese			10 00
		Issued credit memorandum			

FIGURE 9.2
Issuing a Credit Memorandum in the General Journal

Sales Discount

Chou gives a 2% sales discount to credit customers who pay their invoice early. He wants his customers to know about this policy, so he posted the following sign at the cash register:

Sales Discount Policy

2/10, n/30	**2% discount is allowed off price of bill if paid within the first 10 days or full amount is due within 30 days.**
n/10, EOM	**No discount. Full amount of bill is due within 10 days after the end of the month.**

Note that the discount period is the time when a discount is granted. The discount period is less time than the credit period, which is the length of time allowed to pay the amount owed on the invoice.

If Michelle pays her $40 bill early, she will get an $0.80 discount. This information is recorded in the Sales Discount account as follows:

Sales Discount

Contra-revenue ——————▶ **Dr.** | **Cr.**
account with a   0.80 |
debit balance

Sales discount Amount a customer is allowed to deduct from the bill total for paying a bill during the discount period.

Discount period A period shorter than the credit period when a discount is available to encourage early payment of bills.

Credit period Length of time allowed for payment of goods sold on account.

Sales Discount account A contra-revenue account that records cash discounts granted to customers for payments made within a specific period of time.

Michelle's discount is calculated as follows:

$$2\% \times \$40 = \$0.80$$

Michelle pays her bill on July 24. She is entitled to the discount because she paid her bill within 10 days. Figure 9.3 shows how Chou would record this payment on his books. Let's first look at a transaction analysis chart before we journalize.

COACHING TIP

Gross Sales

– Sales discount

– SRA

= Net sales

Accounts Affected	Category	↑↓	Rules	T Account Update
Cash	Asset	↑	Dr.	**Cash**
				Dr. 39.20 / **Cr.**
Sales Discount	Contra-revenue	↑	Dr.	**Sales Discount**
				Dr. 0.80 / **Cr.**
Accounts Receivable	Asset	↓	Cr.	**Accounts Receivable**
				Dr. 1,200 / **Cr.** 40

FIGURE 9.3
Recording Sales Discount

	July	24	Cash					3 9 20				
			Sales Discount					80				
			Accounts Receivable, Michelle Reese							4 0 00		
			Payment from Sale on Account									

Although Michelle pays $39.20, her Accounts Receivable is credited for the full amount, $40.

In the examples so far we have not shown any transactions with sales tax. Note that the actual or **net sales** for Chou would be **gross sales** less sales returns and allowances less any sales discounts. Let's look at how Chou would record his monthly sales if the sales tax were charged.

Net sales   Gross sales less sales returns and allowances less sales discounts.

Gross sales   The revenue earned from sale of merchandise to customers.

Sales Tax Payable

None of the preceding examples shows state sales tax. Still, like it or not, Chou must collect that tax from his customers and send it to the state. Sales tax represents a liability to Chou. The amount Chou must pay to the state is recorded in the Sales Tax Payable account.

Sales Tax Payable account   An account in the general ledger that accumulates the amount of sales tax owed. It has a credit balance.

Assume the state Chou's is located in charges a 5% sales tax. Remember that Chou's sales on July 18 were $3,000. Chou must figure out the sales tax on the purchases. For this purpose, let's assume only two sales were made on that date: the cash sale ($1,800) and the charge sale ($1,200).

The sales tax on the cash purchase is calculated as follows:

$$\$1,800 \times 0.05 = \$90 \text{ Tax}$$

$$\$1,800 + \$90 \text{ tax} = \$1,890 \text{ Cash}$$

Here is how the sales tax on the charge sale is computed:

$$\$1,200 \times 0.05 = \$60 \text{ Tax} + \$1,200 \text{ Charge} = \$1,260 \text{ Accounts Receivable}$$

It would be recorded as shown in Figure 9.4. Let's first look at a transaction analysis chart of this transaction before we journalize.

Accounts Affected	Category	↑↓	Rules	T Account Update

Cash — Asset — ↑ — Dr.

Cash

Dr.	Cr.
1,890	

Accounts Receivable — Asset — ↑ — Dr.

Accounts Receivable

Dr.	Cr.
1,260	

Sales Tax Payable — Liability — ↑ — Cr.

Sales Tax Payable

Dr.	Cr.
	90
	60

Sales — Revenue — ↑ — Cr.

Sales

Dr.	Cr.
	3,000

July	18	Cash	1 8 9 0 00			
		Accounts Receivable	1 2 6 0 00			
		Sales Tax Payable			1 5 0 00	
		Sales			3 0 0 0 00	
		July 18 Sales				

FIGURE 9.4
Sales with Sales Tax

In Learning Unit 9-2, we will look in detail at Art's Wholesale Company.

LEARNING UNIT 9-1 REVIEW

AT THIS POINT you should be able to do the following:

- Explain the purpose of a contra-revenue account.
- Explain how to calculate net sales.
- Define, journalize, and explain gross sales, sales returns and allowances, and sales discounts.
- Journalize an entry for a sale including sales tax payable.

Instant Replay ○ Self-Review Quiz 9-1

Respond true or false to the following:

1. Sales Returns and Allowances is a contra-asset account.
2. Sales Discount has a normal balance of a debit.
3. Sales Tax Payable is a liability.
4. Sales Discount is a contra-asset.
5. Accounts Receivable is a revenue.

Solutions to Instant Replay: Self-Review Quiz 9-1

1. False—it is a contra-revenue account.
2. True
3. True
4. False—it is a contra-revenue account.
5. False—it is an asset.

COACHING TIP

Sales: Revenue	↑	Cr.
SRA: Contra-revenue	↑	Dr.
SD: Contra-revenue	↑	Dr.

(Sale Discount)

LEARNING UNIT 9-2 RECORDING AND POSTING SALES TRANSACTIONS ON ACCOUNT* FOR ART'S WHOLESALE CLOTHING COMPANY:
Introduction to Subsidiary Ledgers and Credit Memorandum

Wholesalers Merchants who buy goods from suppliers and manufacturers for sale to retailers.

Art's Wholesale Clothing Company, as a **wholesaler**, buys merchandise from suppliers and sells the items to retailers, who in turn sell it to individual consumers.

The following transactions occurred in April for Art's Wholesale Clothing Company:

201X		
Apr.	3	Sold on account merchandise to Hal's Clothing, $800; terms 2/10, n/30.
	6	Sold on account merchandise to Bevan's Company, $1,600; terms 2/10, n/30.
	12	Credit memo #1 to Bevan's Company for returned merchandise, $600.
	18	Sold on account merchandise to Roe Company, $2,000; terms 2/10, n/30.
	24	Sold on account merchandise to Roe Company, $500; terms 2/10, n/30.
	28	Sold on account merchandise to Mel's Department Store, $900; terms 2/10, n/30.
	29	Sold on account merchandise to Mel's Department Store, $700; terms 2/10, n/30.

Sales invoice A bill sent to customer(s) reflecting a credit sale.

Let's look closer at the April 3 transaction of Art selling to Hal's Clothing. Figure 9.5 shows the actual bill on the **sales invoice** for this sale:

April 3   Sold on account merchandise to Hal's Clothing, $800. Terms 2/10, n/30.

Here is an analyis of the transaction by the transaction analysis chart.

Accounts Affected	Category	↑↓	Rules	Amount
Accounts Receivable, Hal's Clothing	Asset	↑	Dr.	$800
Sales	Revenue	↑	Cr.	$800

FIGURE 9.5
Sales Invoice

*At the end of Chapter 10, Appendix A shows an alternative method that uses a special journal to record transactions. Your instructor will let you know if this will be covered in your course.

The general journal is shown in Figure 9.6.

ART'S WHOLESALE CLOTHING COMPANY GENERAL JOURNAL				Page 2	
Date	Account Titles and Description	PR	Dr.	Cr.	
201X					
Apr. 3	Accounts Receivable, Hal's Clothing		80 00		
	Sales			80 00	
	Sale on account to Hal's				

FIGURE 9.6
Merchandise Sold and Accounts
Receivable

Accounts Receivable Subsidiary Ledgers

So far in this text, the only title we have used for recording amounts owed to the seller
has been Accounts Receivable. Art could have replaced the Accounts Receivable title
in the general ledger with the following list of customers who owe him money:

- Accounts Receivable, Bevans Company
- Accounts Receivable, Hal's Clothing
- Accounts Receivable, Mel's Department Store
- Accounts Receivable, Roe Company

As you can see, this system would not be manageable if Art had 1,000 credit customers. To solve this problem, Art sets up a separate accounts receivable subsidiary ledger.
Such a special ledger, often simply called a subsidiary ledger, contains a single type
of account, such as credit customers. An account is opened for each customer, and
the accounts are arranged alphabetically.

The diagram in Figure 9.7 shows how the accounts receivable subsidiary ledger
fits in with the general ledger. To clarify the difference in updating the general ledger
versus the subsidiary ledger, we will *post* to the general ledger and *record* to the subsidiary ledger. The word *post* refers to information that is moved from the journal to
the general ledger; the word *record* refers to information that is transferred from the
journal into the individual customer's account in the subsidiary ledger.

**Accounts receivable
subsidiary ledger** A book or file
that contains the individual records,
in alphabetical order, of amounts
owed by various credit customers.

Subsidiary ledger A ledger
that contains accounts of a single
type. Example: The accounts
receivable subsidiary ledger records
all credit customers.

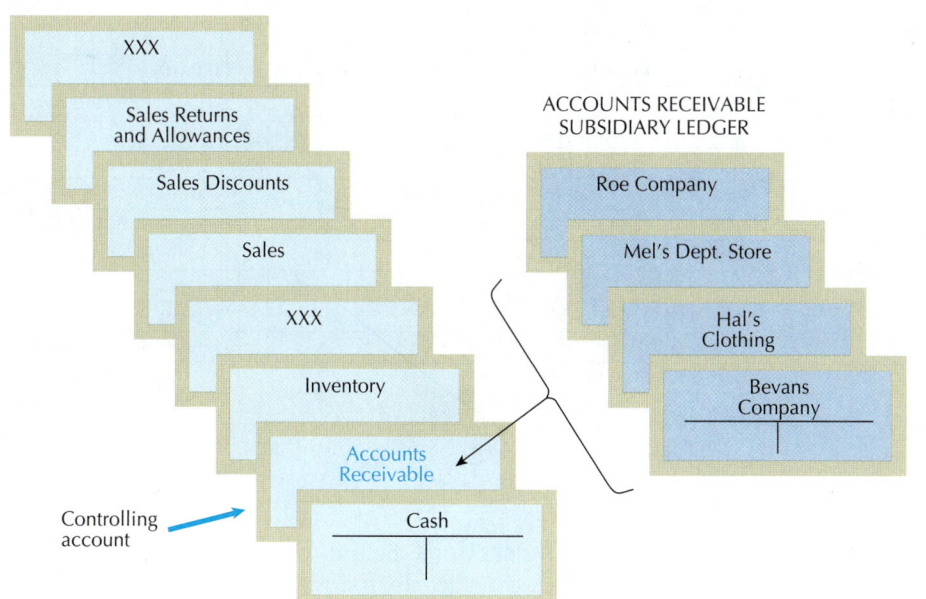

PARTIAL GENERAL LEDGER

ACCOUNTS RECEIVABLE
SUBSIDIARY LEDGER

Controlling
account

FIGURE 9.7
Partial General Ledger of Art's
Wholesale Clothing Company and
Accounts Receivable Subsidiary
Ledger

COACHING TIP

Proving: At the end of the
month, the sum of the accounts
receivable subsidiary ledger
will equal the ending balance
in Accounts Receivable, the
controlling account in the
general ledger.

The accounts receivable subsidiary ledger, or any other subsidiary ledger, can be in the form of a card file, a binder notebook, or computer tapes or disks. It will not have page numbers. The accounts receivable subsidiary ledger is organized alphabetically based on customers' names and addresses; new customers can be added and inactive customers deleted.

When using an accounts receivable subsidiary ledger, the account title Accounts Receivable in the general ledger is called the controlling account—Accounts Receivable because it summarizes or controls the accounts receivable subsidiary ledger. At the end of the month the total of the individual accounts in the accounts receivable ledger will equal the ending balance in Accounts Receivable in the general ledger.

Figure 9.8 shows how the general journal looks for Art before posting and recording this month's sales transactions on account.

FIGURE 9.8
Before Posting and Recording Sales Transactions

ART'S WHOLESALE CLOTHING COMPANY GENERAL JOURNAL					Page 2
Date		Account Titles and Description	PR	Dr.	Cr.
201X					
Apr.	3	Accounts Receivable, Hal's Clothing		8 0 0 00	
		Sales			8 0 0 00
		Sale on account to Hal's			
	6	Accounts Receivable, Bevan's Company		1 6 0 0 00	
		Sales			1 6 0 0 00
		Sale on account to Bevan's			
	12	Sales Returns and Allowances		6 0 0 00	
		Accounts Receivable, Bevan's Company			6 0 0 00
		Issued credit memo no. 1			
	18	Accounts Receivable, Roe Company		2 0 0 0 00	
		Sales			2 0 0 0 00
		Sale on account to Roe			
	24	Accounts Receivable, Roe Company		5 0 0 00	
		Sales			5 0 0 00
		Sale on account to Roe			
	28	Accounts Receivable, Mel's Dept. Store		9 0 0 00	
		Sales			9 0 0 00
		Sale on account to Mel's			
	29	Accounts Receivable, Mel's Dept. Store		7 0 0 00	
		Sales			7 0 0 00
		Sale on account to Mel's			

Posting and Recording Sales Transactions Before we post to the general ledger and record to the subsidiary ledger, consider the following T accounts, which show what each title would look like.

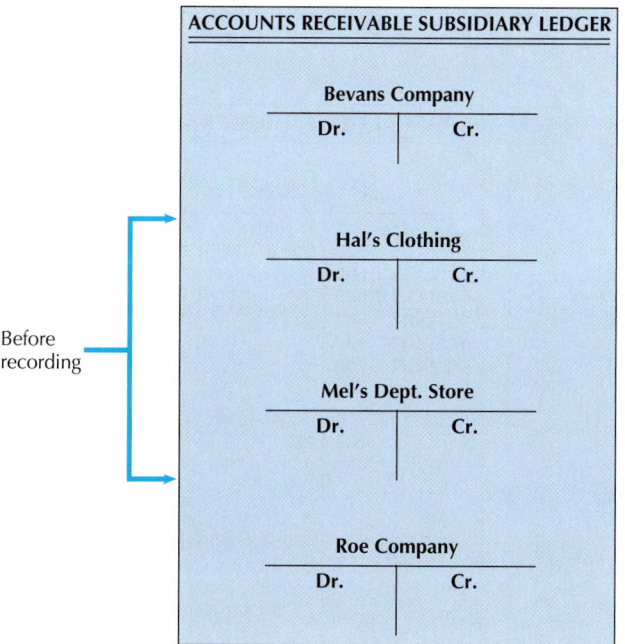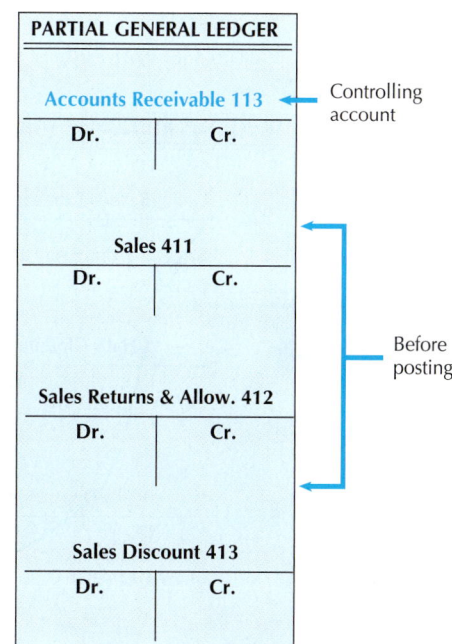

Figure 9.9 shows how the April 3 transaction is posted and recorded.

For this transaction we *post* to the general ledger Accounts Receivable and Sales accounts. Note how the account numbers of 113 and 411 are entered into the PR column of the general journal. We must also *record* to Hal's Clothing in the accounts receivable subsidiary ledger. The amount is placed on the debit side because Hal owed Art the money. When the subsidiary ledger is updated, a (✔) is placed in the PR column of the general journal. The following is how the accounts receivable subsidiary ledger and partial general ledger would look after postings.

	Date		Account Titles and Description	PR	Dr.	Cr.
	201X					
	Apr.	3	Accounts Receivable, Hal's Clothing	113✔	8000000	
			Sales	411		800000
			Sale on account to Hal's			

GENERAL JOURNAL — Page 2

FIGURE 9.9
Transaction for April 3 Posted and Recorded

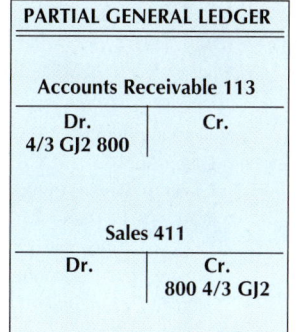

Now lets look at how the complete Accounts Receivable Subsidary Ledger and Partial General Ledger would look.

FIGURE 9.9 *(continued)*

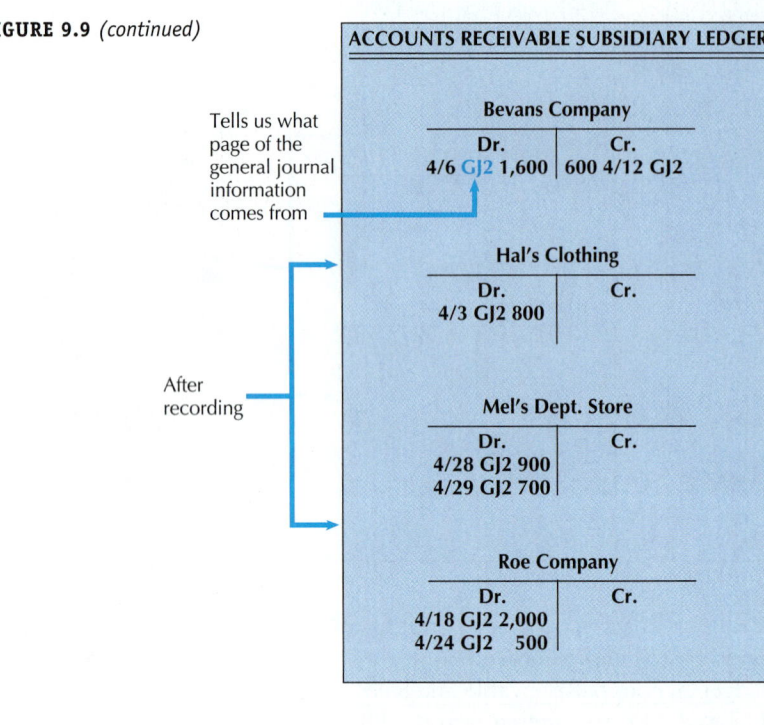

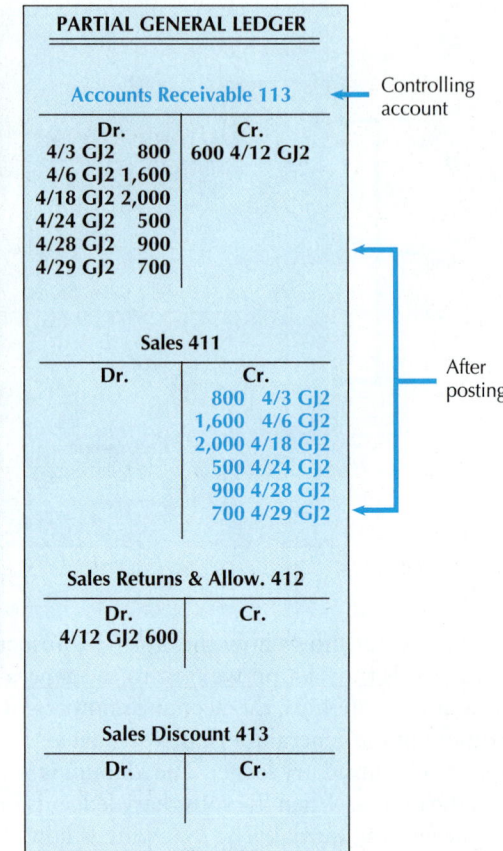

Tells us what page of the general journal information comes from

After recording

Controlling account

After posting

● **L02**

The Credit Memorandum

Credit memorandum A piece of paper sent by the seller to a customer who has returned merchandise previously purchased on credit. The credit memorandum indicates to the customer that the seller is reducing the amount owed by the customer.

Companies usually handle sales returns and allowances by means of a credit memorandum. Credit memoranda inform customers that the amount of the goods returned or the amount allowed for damaged goods has been subtracted (credited) from the customer's ongoing account with the company.

A sample credit memorandum from Art's Wholesale Clothing Company appears in Figure 9.10. It shows that on April 12, Credit Memorandum No. 1 was issued to Bevans Company for defective merchandise that had been returned.

FIGURE 9.10

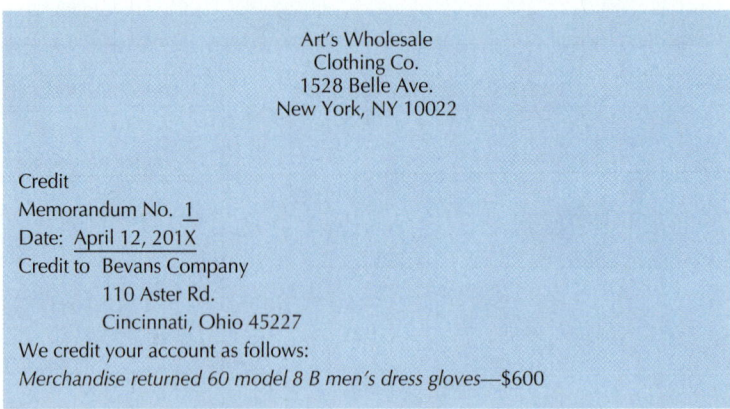

Art's Wholesale
Clothing Co.
1528 Belle Ave.
New York, NY 10022

Credit
Memorandum No. 1
Date: April 12, 201X
Credit to Bevans Company
                110 Aster Rd.
                Cincinnati, Ohio 45227
We credit your account as follows:
Merchandise returned 60 model 8 B men's dress gloves—$600

Let's look at a transaction analysis chart before we journalize, record, and post this transaction.

Accounts Affected	Category	↑↓	Rules
Sales Returns and Allowances	Contra-revenue account	↑	Dr.
Accounts Receivable, Bevans Co.	Asset	↓	Cr.

Journalizing, Recording, and Posting the Credit Memorandum

The credit memorandum results in two postings to the general ledger and one recording to the accounts receivable subsidiary ledger (see Figure 9.11).

Remember: Sales discounts are not taken on returns.

FIGURE 9.11
Postings and Recordings for the Credit Memorandum into the Subsidiary and General Ledgers

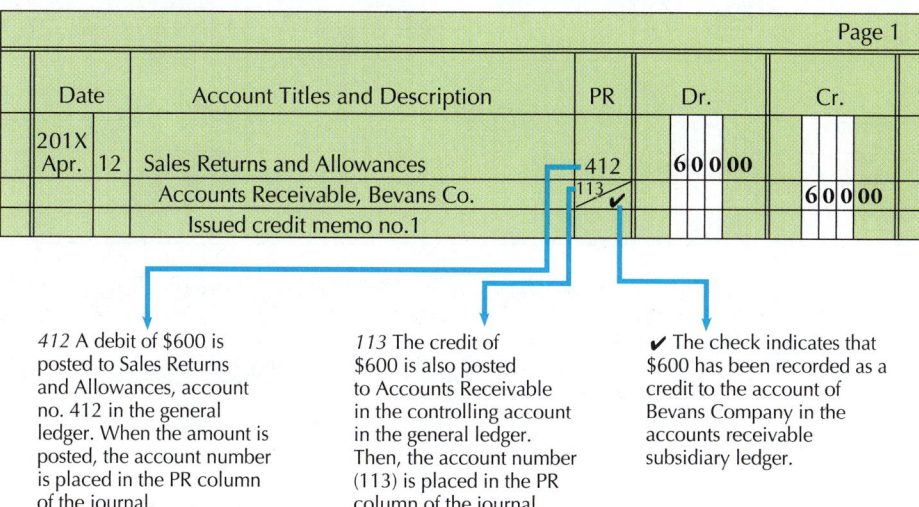

Note that in the PR column next to Accounts Receivable, Bevans Co., a diagonal line separates the account number 113 above and a ✔ below. This notation shows that the amount of $600 has been credited to Accounts Receivable in the controlling account in the general ledger *and* credited to the account of Bevans Company in the accounts receivable subsidiary ledger.

LEARNING UNIT 9-2 REVIEW

AT THIS POINT you should be able to do the following:

- Define and state the purposes of the accounts receivable subsidiary ledger.
- Define and state the purpose of the controlling account, Accounts Receivable.
- Journalize, record, or post sales on account to a general journal and its related accounts receivable and general ledgers.
- Explain, journalize, post, and record a credit memorandum.

Instant Replay ⊙ Self-Review Quiz 9-2

Journalize, post to the general ledger, and record to accounts receivable subsidiary ledger the following transactions of Bernie Company.

201X			
May	10	Sold merchandise on account to Ring Company, $600; terms 2/10, n/30.
	18	Sold merchandise on account to Lee Corp., $900; terms 2/10, n/30.
	25	Issued credit memo #1 to Ring Company for returned merchandise, $200.

Solution to Instant Replay: Self-Review Quiz 9-2

	BERNIE COMPANY GENERAL JOURNAL				Page 4	

Date		Account Titles and Description	PR	Dr.	Cr.	
201X						
May	10	Accounts Receivable, Ring Clothing	141 ✓	60000		
		Sales	310		60000	
		Sale on account to Ring Co.				
	18	Accounts Receivable, Lee Corp.	141 ✓	90000		
		Sales	310		90000	
		Sale on account to Lee Corp.				
	25	Sales Returns and Allowances	312	20000		
		Accounts Receivable, Ring Co.	141 ✓		20000	
		Issued credit memo no. 1				

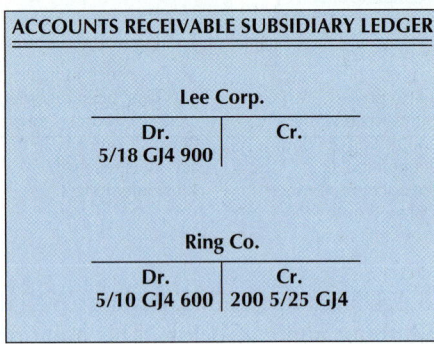

ACCOUNTS RECEIVABLE SUBSIDIARY LEDGER

Lee Corp.

Dr.	Cr.
5/18 GJ4 900	

Ring Co.

Dr.	Cr.
5/10 GJ4 600	200 5/25 GJ4

PARTIAL GENERAL LEDGER

Accounts Receivable 141

Dr.	Cr.
5/10 GJ4 600	200 5/25 GJ4
5/18 GJ4 900	

Sales 310

Dr.	Cr.
	600 5/10 GJ4
	900 5/18 GJ4

Sales Returns & Allow. 312

Dr.	Cr.
5/25 GJ4 200	

L03   LEARNING UNIT 9-3 RECORDING AND POSTING CASH RECEIPT TRANSACTIONS FOR ART'S WHOLESALE:

Schedule of Accounts Receivable

The following cash receipts transactions occurred for Art's Wholesale Clothing in April:

201X		
Apr.	1	Art Newner invested $8,000 in the business.
	4	Received check from Hal's Clothing for payment of invoice no. 1, less 2% discount.
	15	Cash sales for first half of April, $900.
	16	Received check from Bevans Company in settlement of invoice no. 2, less returns and 2% discount.
	22	Received check from Roe Company for payment of invoice no. 3, less 2% discount.
	27	Sold store equipment, $500.
	30	Cash sales for second half of April, $1,200.

Figure 9.12 provides a closer look at how the April 4 transaction would be journalized. Let's first look at the transaction analysis chart before showing the journalized transaction.

Accounts Affected	Category	↑↓	Rules	T Account Update
Cash	Asset	↑	Dr.	**Cash**
				Dr. 784 / Cr.
Sales Discount	Contra-revenue	↑	Dr.	**Sales Discount**
				Dr. 16 / Cr.
Accounts Receivable, Hal's Clothing	Asset	↓	Cr.	**Acc. Rec.** Dr. 800 / Cr. 800 **Hal's Clothing** Dr. 800 / Cr. 800

				Dr.	Cr.
Apr.	4	Cash		784 00	
		Sales Discount		16 00	
		Accounts Receivable, Hal's Clothing			800 00

COACHING TIP

Hal's Clothing is located in the accounts receivable subsidiary ledger.

FIGURE 9.12
Recording Sales Discount in General Journal

Figure 9.13 shows the complete set of April cash receipts transactions for Art's Wholesale journalized for the month, followed by a complete posting to the general ledger and recordings to the accounts receivable subsidiary ledger. (Remember from the past unit that we posted all the sales on account information.)

FIGURE 9.13
Journalized Cash Receipts Transactions

		GENERAL JOURNAL			Page 2

Date		Account Titles and Description	PR	Dr.	Cr.
201X					
Apr.	1	Cash	111	800 00	
		Art Newner, Capital	311		800 00
		Owner Investment			
	4	Cash	111	784 00	
		Sales Discount	413	16 00	
		Accounts Receivable, Hal's Clothing	113 ✔		800 00
		Hal's paid invoice no. 1			
	15	Cash	111	900 00	
		Sales	411		900 00
		Cash sales for first half of April			
	16	Cash	111	980 00	
		Sales Discount	413	20 00	
		Accounts Receivable, Bevan's Company	113 ✔		1000 00
		Bevan paid invoice no. 2			
	22	Cash	111	1960 00	
		Sales Discount	413	40 00	
		Accounts Receivable, Roe Co.	113 ✔		2000 00
		Roe paid invoice no. 3			

(continued)

FIGURE 9.13
(continued)

27	Cash	111	5 0 0 00			
	Store Equipment	121			5 0 0 00	
	Sold store equipment					
30	Cash	111	1 2 0 0 00			
	Sales	411			1 2 0 0 00	
	Cash sales for second half of April					

⬤ **LO4**

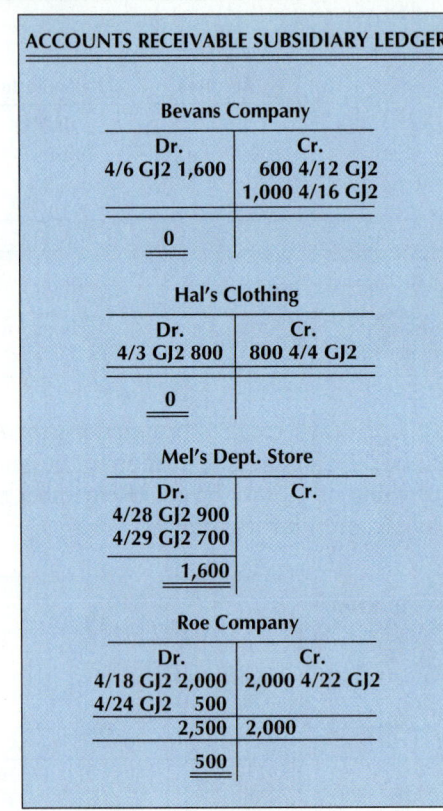

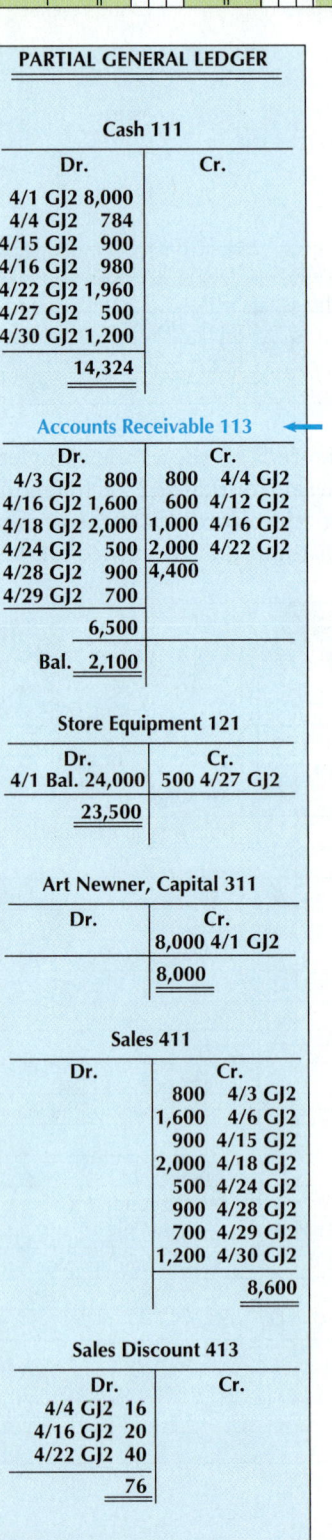

Controlling account

Schedule of Accounts Receivable

The schedule of accounts receivable is an alphabetical list of the companies that have an outstanding balance in the accounts receivable subsidiary ledger. This total should be equal to the balance of the Accounts Receivable controlling account in the general ledger at the end of the month.

Let's examine the schedule of accounts receivable for Art's Wholesale Clothing Company in Figure 9.14.

ART'S WHOLESALE CLOTHING COMPANY SCHEDULE OF ACCOUNTS RECEIVABLE APRIL 30, 201X	
Mel's Dept. Store	$1 6 0 0 00
Roe Company	5 0 0 00
Total Accounts Receivable	$2 1 0 0 00

The balance of the controlling account, Accounts Receivable ($2,100), in the general ledger does indeed equal the sum of the individual customer balances in the accounts receivable ledger ($2,100) as shown in the schedule of accounts receivable. The schedule of accounts receivable can help forecast potential cash inflows as well as possible credit and collection decisions.

L05

COACHING TIP

Schedule of Accounts Receivable is listed in alphabetical order.

FIGURE 9.14
Schedule of Accounts Receivable

Schedule of accounts receivable A list of the customers, in alphabetical order, that have an outstanding balance in the accounts receivable subsidiary ledger. This total should be equal to the balance of the Accounts Receivable controlling account in the general ledger at the end of the month.

LEARNING UNIT 9-3 REVIEW

AT THIS POINT you should be able to do the following:

- Journalize cash receipts transactions.
- Record and post cash receipts transactions to the accounts receivable subsidiary ledger and general ledger.
- Prepare a schedule of accounts receivable.

Instant Replay • Self-Review Quiz 9-3

Journalize, post to the general ledger, and record to the accounts receivable subsidiary ledger the following transactions of Mabel Corporation, given the following balances.

Accounts Receivable Subsidiary Ledger

Name	Balance	Invoice No.
Irene Welch	$500	1
Janis Fross	200	2

Partial General Ledger

	Acct. No.	Balance
Cash	110	$600
Accounts Receivable	120	700
Store Equipment	130	600
Sales	410	700
Sales Discount	420	

201X

May	1	Received check from Irene Welch for invoice no. 1, less 2% discount.
	8	Cash sales collected, $200.
	15	Received check from Janis Fross for invoice no. 2, less 2% discount.
	19	Sold store equipment at cost, $300.

Solution to Instant Replay: Self-Review Quiz 9-3

			PR	Dr.	Cr.
MABEL CORPORATION **GENERAL JOURNAL**					Page 3
Date					
201X					
May	1	Cash	110	490 00	
		Sales Discount	420	10 00	
		Accounts Receivable, Irene Welch	120 ✓		500 00
		Received payment from Irene Welch			
	8	Cash	110	200 00	
		Sales	410		200 00
		Cash sale			
	15	Cash	110	196 00	
		Sales Discount	420	4 00	
		Accounts Receivable, Janis Fross	120 ✓		200 00
		Received payment from Janis Fross			
	19	Cash	110	300 00	
		Store Equipment	130		300 00
		Sold store equipment			

ACCOUNTS RECEIVABLE SUBSIDIARY LEDGER

Janis Fross

Dr.	Cr.
Bal. 200	200 5/15 GJ3

Irene Welch

Dr.	Cr.
Bal. 500	500 5/1 GJ3

PARTIAL GENERAL LEDGER

Cash 110

Dr.	Cr.
Bal. 600	
5/1 GJ3 490	
5/8 GJ3 200	
5/15 GJ3 196	
5/19 GJ3 300	

Accounts Receivable 120

Dr.	Cr.
Bal. 700	500 5/1 GJ3
	200 5/15 GJ3

Store Equipment 130

Dr.	Cr.
Bal. 600	300 5/19 GJ3

Sales 410

Dr.	Cr.
	700 Bal.
	200 5/8 GJ3

Sales Discount 420

Dr.	Cr.
5/1 GJ3 10	
5/15 GJ3 4	

BLUEPRINT: TRANSFERRING INFORMATION FROM THE GENERAL JOURNAL

Post → General Ledger (account #)
Record → Subsidiary Ledger (✓)

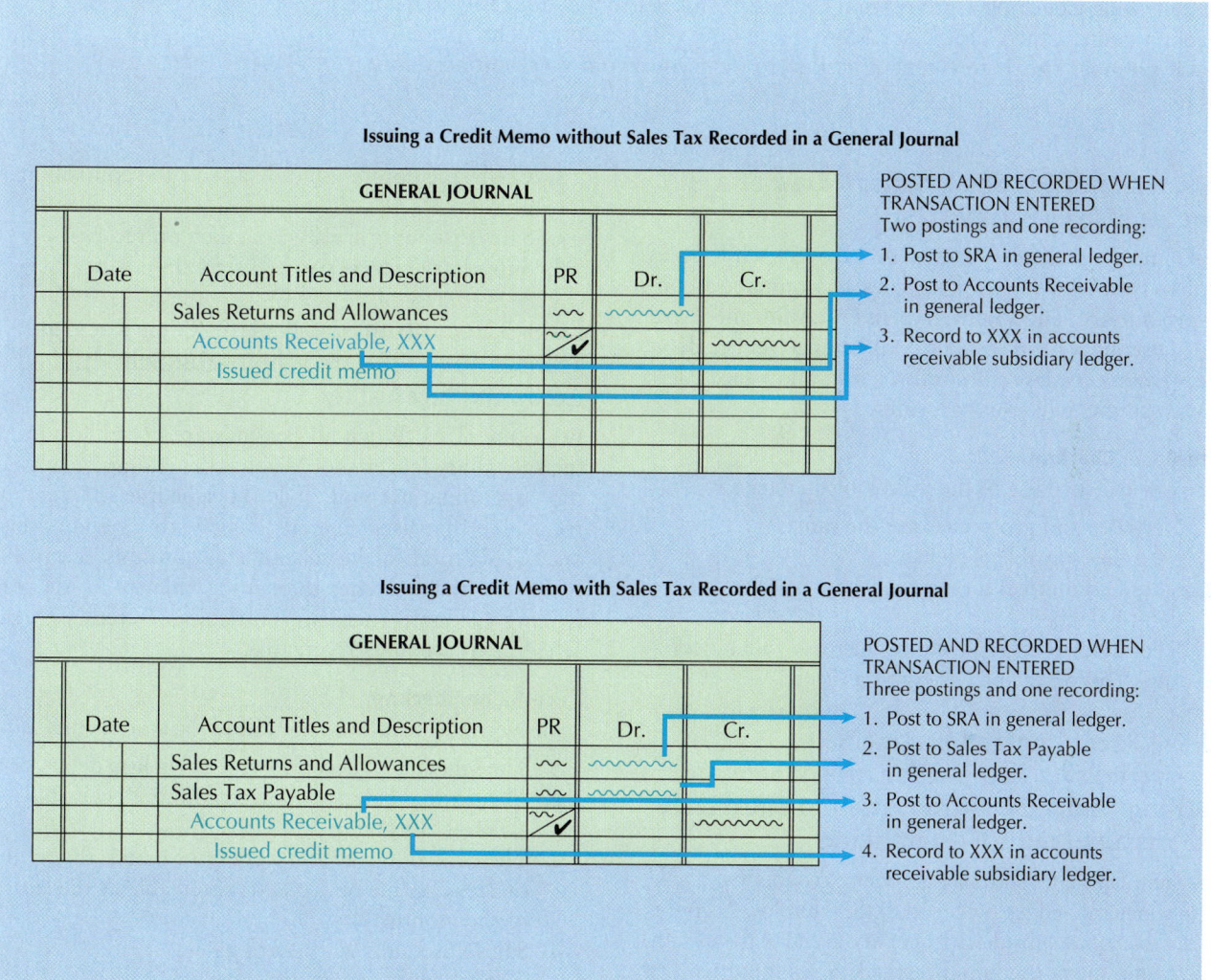

Issuing a Credit Memo without Sales Tax Recorded in a General Journal

	GENERAL JOURNAL			
Date	Account Titles and Description	PR	Dr.	Cr.
	Sales Returns and Allowances	∿	∿∿∿	
	Accounts Receivable, XXX	✓		∿∿∿
	Issued credit memo			

POSTED AND RECORDED WHEN TRANSACTION ENTERED
Two postings and one recording:
1. Post to SRA in general ledger.
2. Post to Accounts Receivable in general ledger.
3. Record to XXX in accounts receivable subsidiary ledger.

Issuing a Credit Memo with Sales Tax Recorded in a General Journal

	GENERAL JOURNAL			
Date	Account Titles and Description	PR	Dr.	Cr.
	Sales Returns and Allowances	∿	∿∿∿	
	Sales Tax Payable	∿	∿∿∿	
	Accounts Receivable, XXX	✓		∿∿∿
	Issued credit memo			

POSTED AND RECORDED WHEN TRANSACTION ENTERED
Three postings and one recording:
1. Post to SRA in general ledger.
2. Post to Sales Tax Payable in general ledger.
3. Post to Accounts Receivable in general ledger.
4. Record to XXX in accounts receivable subsidiary ledger.

ACCOUNTING COACH

The following Coaching Tips are from Learning Units 9-1 to 9-3. Take the Pre-Game Checkup and use the Check Your Score to see how you are doing. The Accounting Coach provides tips before each Checkup to help you avoid common accounting errors.

LU 9-1 Chou's Toy Shop: Seller's View of a Merchandise Company

Pre-Game Tips: Sales is a revenue account, while Sales Returns and Allowances and Sales Discounts are contra-revenue accounts. Sales Returns and Allowances and Sales Discounts have their normal balance on the debit side. Gross sales less sales returns and allowances, less sales discounts will equal net sales.

Pre-Game Checkup
Answer true or false to the following statements.

1. Net sales and gross sales are the same.
2. Sales Tax Payable is an asset.
3. Sales Discounts is a revenue account with a debit balance.
4. Sales Returns and Allowances increase with a debit.
5. Sales Discounts increase with a credit.

LU 9-2 Recording and Posting Sales Transactions on Account for Art's Wholesale Clothing Company: Introduction to Subsidiary Ledgers and Credit Memorandum

Pre-Game Tips: The controlling account, Accounts Receivable, in the general ledger will equal the sum of Accounts Receivable in the subsidiary ledger at the end of the month. If a credit memorandum is issued, Sales Returns and Allowances will increase with a debit, and an Accounts Receivable controlling account, as well as the specific subsidiary ledger, will be reduced. The normal balance of each account in the subsidiary ledger is a debit balance.

Pre-Game Checkup
Answer true or false to the following statements.

1. The controlling account is located in the subsidiary ledger.
2. A checkmark in the posting reference column means the controlling account has been updated.
3. Credit memorandum only affects the controlling account.
4. Sales discounts are always taken on returns.
5. Subsidiary ledgers can be listed alphabetically.

LU 9-3 Recording and Posting Cash Receipt Transactions for Arts Wholesale: Schedule of Accounts Receivable

Pre-Game Tips: When all postings are done the sum of the subsidiary ledger should equal the ending balance in the controlling account. It is the schedule of accounts receivable that lists each customer with its ending balance. This total in the schedule of accounts receivable is the one that matches the ending balance in the controlling account. There are no debits or credits on the schedule of accounts receivable.

Pre-Game Checkup
Answer true or false to the following statements.

1. The schedule of accounts receivable lists debits first.
2. The normal balance of an Accounts Receivable account is a credit.
3. The controlling account does not match the total of the schedule of accounts receivable at the end of the month.
4. Sales Discounts is a contra-asset.
5. The schedule of accounts receivable shows what we owe vendors.

CHECK YOUR SCORE: Answers to the Pre-Game Checkup

LU 9-1

1. False—Net sales is gross sales less allowances and any discounts.
2. False—Sales Tax Payable is a liability.
3. False—Sales Discounts is a contra-revenue account with a debit balance.
4. True.
5. False—Sales Discounts increase with a debit.

LU 9-2

1. False—The controlling account is located in the general ledger.
2. False—A checkmark in the posting reference column means the subsidiary ledger has been updated.
3. False—Credit memorandum affects both the controlling account and the subsidiary ledger.
4. False—Sales discounts are never taken on returns.
5. True.

LU 9-3

1. False—There are no debits on the schedule of accounts receivable.
2. False—The normal balance of an Accounts Receivable account is a debit.
3. False—The controlling account does match the total of the schedule of accounts receivable at the end of the month.
4. False—Sales Discounts is a contra-revenue account.
5. False—The schedule of accounts receivable shows the amount vendors owe the seller.

Chapter Summary

Here are all the key concepts and equations to help you understand the concepts of this chapter and prepare you for your exam. After completing this review, go to MyAccountingLab for more practice opportunities.

Concepts You Should Know	Key Terms
LO1 **Recording and posting sales transactions.** 1. Sales Returns and Allowances and Sales Discount are contra-revenue accounts. 2. Net Sales = Gross Sales – Sales Returns and Allowances – Sales Discounts. 3. Sales Tax Payable is a liability account.	Accounts receivable subsidiary ledger (p. 341) Controlling account— Accounts Receivable (p. 342) Credit period (p. 337) Discount period (p. 337) Gross sales (p. 338) Merchandise (p. 336) Net sales (p. 338) Retailers (p. 336) Sales discount (p. 337) Sales Discount account (p. 337) Sales invoice (p. 340) Sales Returns and Allowances (SRA) account (p. 336) Sales Tax Payable account (p. 338) Subsidiary ledger (p. 341) Wholesalers (p. 340)
LO2 **Preparing, journalizing, and posting a credit memorandum.** 1. When a credit memorandum is issued, the result is that Sales Returns and Allowances increases and Accounts Receivable decreases. 2. When we record this entry into the general journal, all parts of the transaction will be posted to the general ledger and recorded in the subsidiary ledger.	Credit memorandum (p. 344)
LO3 **Recording and posting cash receipts transactions.** 1. Sales result in an inflow of cash and/or accounts receivable. All cash receipts transactions result in an inward flow of cash.	

Recording to the accounts receivable subsidiary ledger. ○ **LO4**

1. The normal balance of the accounts receivable subsidiary ledger is a debit.

2. A ✓ in the PR of the general journal means that the subsidiary ledger has been updated.

3. The accounts receivable subsidiary ledger is not in the same book as Accounts Receivable, the controlling account in the general ledger.

Preparing a schedule of accounts receivable. ● **LO5**

1. The schedule of accounts receivable is an alphabetical list of companies with an outstanding balance.

2. At the end of the month, the total of all customers' ending balances in the accounts receivable subsidiary ledger should be equal to the ending balance in Accounts Receivable, the controlling account in the general ledger.

Schedule of accounts receivable (p. 349)

Discussion Questions and Critical Thinking Questions/Ethical Case

1. Explain the purpose of a contra-revenue account.

2. What is the normal balance of Sales Discount?

3. Give two examples of contra-revenue accounts.

4. What is the difference between a discount period and a credit period?

5. Explain the terms:

   a. 2/10, n/30

   b. n/10, EOM

6. What category is Sales Discount in?

7. Compare and contrast the Controlling Account—Accounts Receivable to the accounts receivable subsidiary ledger.

8. Why is the accounts receivable subsidiary ledger organized in alphabetical order?

9. When is a (✔) used?

10. What is an invoice? What purpose does it serve?

11. Why is sales tax a liability to the business?

12. Sales discounts are taken on sales tax. Agree or disagree? Explain why.

13. When a seller issues a credit memorandum (assume no sales tax), what accounts will be affected?

14. Amy Jak is the National Sales Manager of Land.com. To get sales up to the projection for the old year, Amy asked the accountant to put the first two weeks' sales in January back into December. Amy told the accountant that this secret would only be between them. Should Amy move the new sales into the old sales year? You make the call. Write down your specific recommendations to Amy.

Concept Checks

MyAccountingLab

● **LO1** *(5 MIN)*

Overview

1. Complete the following table for Sales, Sales Returns and Allowances, and Sales Discounts.

Accounts Affected	Category	Rules to Increase Account	Temporary or Permanent

● **LO1** *(5 MIN)*

Calculating Net Sales

2. Given the following, calculate net sales:

Gross Sales	$38
Sales Returns and Allowances	12
Sales Discounts	3

General Journal

LO1, 3, 4 *(10 MIN)*

3.   Match the following activities to the three business transactions (more than one number can be used).
   1. Record to the accounts receivable subsidiary ledger.
   2. Journalize the transaction.
   3. Post to the general ledger.
   a. _____ Sold merchandise on account to Lee Co., invoice no. 1, $60.
   b. _____ Sold merchandise on account to Flynn Co., invoice no. 2, $1,500.
   c. _____ Issued credit memorandum no. 1 to Flynn Co. for defective merchandise, $50.

Credit Memorandum

LO2 *(10 MIN)*

4.   Complete the transactional analysis box for the following transaction: Issued credit memorandum to Fox.com for defective merchandise, $206.

Journalize Transactions

LO1, 2, 3 *(15 MIN)*

5.   Journalize the following transactions:
   a. Sold merchandise on account to Weis Co., invoice no. 10, $32.
   b. Received check from Phair Co., $1000, less 2% discount.
   c. Cash Sales, $99.
   d. Issued credit memorandum no. 2 to Weis Co. for defective merchandise, $19.

6.   From the following, prepare a schedule of accounts receivable for Pine Co. for May 31, 201X.

LO5 *(15 MIN)*

Accounts Receivable Subsidiary Ledger

James Co.

	Dr.	Cr.
5/6 GJ1	99	

Noel Co.

	Dr.	Cr.	
5/20 GJ1	28	13	5/27 GJ1

Rose Co.

	Dr.	Cr.
5/9 GJ1	11	

General Ledger

Accounts Receivable

	Dr.	Cr.	
5/31 GJ1	138	13	5/31 GJ1

Exercises

Set A

●● **L01, 4** *(10 MIN)*

9A-1. From the general journal in Figure 9.15, record to the accounts receivable subsidiary ledger and post to the general ledger accounts as appropriate.

FIGURE 9.15
General Journal, Subsidiary Ledger, and Partial General Ledger

General Journal				
Date		PR	Dr.	Cr.
201X				
Nov. 18	Accounts Receivable, Wind Sail Co.		620 00	
	Sales			620 00
	Sold merchandise to Wind Sail Co.			
19	Accounts Receivable, Travel Co.		930 00	
	Sales			930 00
	Sold merchandise to Travel Co.			

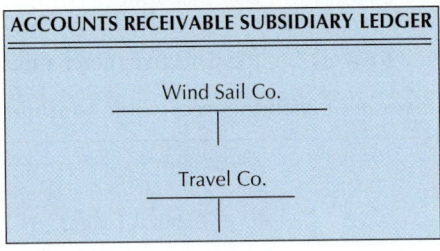

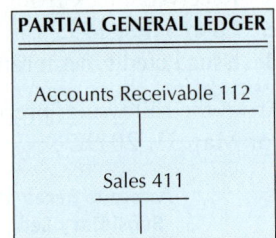

●●● **L01, 2, 4** *(10 MIN)*

9A-2. Journalize, record, and post when appropriate the following transactions in the general journal (all sales carry terms of 1/10, n/30):

201X		
May	16	Sold merchandise on account to Pearl Co., invoice no. 1, $900.
	18	Sold merchandise on account to Glenda Co., invoice no. 2, $1,900.
	20	Issued credit memorandum no. 1 to Glenda Co. for defective merchandise, $710.

Use the following account numbers: Accounts Receivable, 112; Sales, 411; Sales Returns and Allowances, 412.

●● **L03, 4** *(10 MIN)*

9A-3. From Exercise 9-2, journalize the receipt of a check from Pearl Co. for payment of invoice no. 1 on May 24.

●● **L04, 5** *(20 MIN)*

9A-4. From the following transactions for Andrew Co., journalize, record, post, and prepare a schedule of accounts receivable when appropriate. You will have to set up your own accounts receivable subsidiary ledger and partial general ledger as needed. All sales terms are 4/10, n/30.

201X		
Oct.	1	Andrew Albright invested $2,600 in the business.
	1	Sold merchandise on account to Greenfield Co., invoice no. 1, $750.
	2	Sold merchandise on account to Robert Co., invoice no. 2, $900.
	3	Cash sale, $215.
	8	Issued credit memorandum no. 1 to Greenfield Co. for defective merchandise, $150.
	10	Received check from Greenfield Co. for invoice no. 1, less returns and discount.
	15	Cash sale, $430.
	18	Sold merchandise on account to Greenfield Co., invoice no. 3, $650.

9A-5. From the following facts calculate what Cara Dock paid Hollow Co. for the purchase of a dining room set. Sale terms are 2/10, n/30.

    a. Sales ticket price before tax, $10,000, dated April 5.

    b. Sales tax, 8%.

    c. Returned one defective chair for credit of $800 on April 8.

    d. Paid bill on April 13.

🟢 **L02** *(10 MIN)*

Set B

9B-1. From the general journal in Figure 9.16, record to the accounts receivable subsidiary ledger and post to the general ledger accounts as appropriate.

🔴🟡 **L01, 4** *(10 MIN)*

FIGURE 9.16
The General Journal, Subsidiary Ledger, and Partial General Ledger

Date		Account Titles and Explanations	PR	Dr.	Cr.
201X					
Aug.	18	Accounts Receivable, Wind Sail Co.		5 6 0 00	
		Sales			
		Sold merchandise to Wind Sail Co.			5 6 0 00
	19	Accounts Receivable, Travel Co.		8 6 0 00	
		Sales			
		Sold merchandise to Travel Co.			8 6 0 00

General Journal

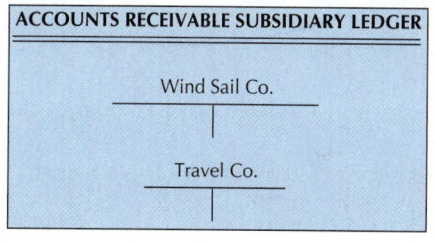

ACCOUNTS RECEIVABLE SUBSIDIARY LEDGER

Wind Sail Co.

Travel Co.

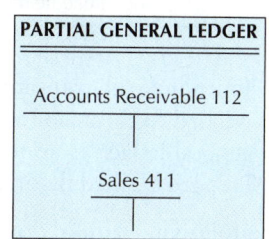

PARTIAL GENERAL LEDGER

Accounts Receivable 112

Sales 411

9B-2. Journalize, record, and post when appropriate the following transactions in the general journal (all sales carry terms of 5/10, n/30):

🔴🟢🟡 **L01, 2, 4** *(10 MIN)*

201X

Nov. 16   Sold merchandise on account to Pearl Co., invoice no. 1, $920.

      18   Sold merchandise on account to Glenda Co., invoice no. 2, $1,600.

      20   Issued credit memorandum no. 1 to Glenda Co. for defective merchandise, $690. Use the following account numbers: Accounts Receivable, 112; Sales, 411; Sales Returns and Allowances, 412.

9B-3. From Exercise 9B-2, journalize the receipt of a check from Pearl Co. for payment of invoice no.1 on November 24.

🔵🟡 **L03, 4** *(10 MIN)*

9B-4. From the following transactions for Andrew Co., journalize, record, post, and prepare a schedule of accounts receivable when appropriate. The accounts receivable subsidiary ledger and partial general ledger have been set up for you. All sales terms are 4/10, n/30.

🟡🔵 **L04, 5** *(20 MIN)*

201X

Oct. 1   Andrew Albright invested $3,200 in the business.

     1   Sold merchandise on account to Greenfield Co., invoice no. 1, $800.

     2   Sold merchandise on account to Robert Co., invoice no. 2, $920.

     3   Cash sale, $210.

     8   Issued credit memorandum no. 1 to Greenfield Co. for defective merchandise, $200.

    10   Received check from Greenfield Co. for invoice no. 1, less returns and discount.

    15   Cash sale, $420.

    18   Sold merchandise on account to Greenfield Co., invoice no. 3, $700.

 **LO2** *(10 MIN)*   **9B-5.** From the following facts calculate what Uriah Jones paid Jade Co. for the purchase of a dining room set. Sale terms are 1/10, n/30.

a. Sales ticket price before tax, $12,000, date April 5.

b. Sales tax 2%.

c. Returned one defective chair for credit of $500 on April 8.

d. Paid bill on April 13.

MyAccountingLab   ## Problems

Group A

 **LO1, 2, 4, 5**   **9A-1.** Bill Hass has opened Ciabatta and Whatnot, a wholesale grocery and bread
(40 MIN)   company. The following transactions occurred in January:

201X		
Jan.	1	Sold grocery merchandise to Cindi Co. on account, $500, invoice no. 1.
	4	Sold bread merchandise to Common Law Co. on account, $850, invoice no. 2.
	8	Sold grocery merchandise to Canadian Co. on account, $750, invoice no. 3.
	10	Issued credit memorandum no. 1 to Cindi Co. for $210 of grocery merchandise returned due to spoilage.
	15	Sold bread merchandise to Common Law Co. on account, $300, invoice no. 4.
	19	Sold grocery merchandise to Canadian Co. on account, $800, invoice no. 5.
	25	Sold bread merchandise to Cindi Co. on account, $150, invoice no. 6.

Check Figure:
Schedule of accounts
receivable $3,140

Required

1. Journalize the transactions.
2. Record to the accounts receivable subsidiary ledger and post to the general ledger as appropriate.
3. Prepare a schedule of accounts receivable for the end of January.

LO1, 2, 4, 5   **9A-2.** The following transactions of Jack's Auto Supply occurred in November
(50 MIN)   (Balances as of November 1 are given for general ledger and accounts receivable ledger accounts: Danielson $400 Dr.; Wallace $550 Dr.; Whitnall $400; Accounts Receivable $1,350 Dr.; Sales Tax Payable $1,900 Cr. Be sure to enter these balances in your working papers before beginning.):

201X		
Nov.	1	Sold auto parts merchandise to R. Danielson on account, $1,600, invoice no. 50, plus 6% sales tax.
	5	Sold auto parts merchandise to J. Wallace on account, $850, invoice no. 51, plus 6% sales tax.
	8	Sold auto parts merchandise to Lance Whitnall on account, $9,000, invoice no. 52, plus 6% sales tax.
	10	Issued credit memorandum no. 12 to R. Danielson for $850 for defective auto parts merchandise returned from Nov. 1 transaction. (Be careful to record the reduction in Sales Tax Payable as well.)
	12	Sold auto parts merchandise to J. Wallace on account, $750, invoice no. 53, plus 6% sales tax.

Check Figure:
Schedule of accounts
receivable $13,381

Required

1. Journalize the transactions.
2. Record to the accounts receivable subsidiary ledger and post to the general ledger as appropriate.
3. Prepare a schedule of accounts receivable for the end of November.

9A-3. Mike Patten owns Patten's Sneaker Shop. (Balances as of May 1 are provided for the accounts receivable and general ledger accounts as follows: Donati $375 Dr.; Lindall $850 Dr.; Pilar $550 Dr.; Zamora $650 Dr.; Cash $15,000 Dr.; Accounts Receivable $2,425 Dr.; sneaker rack equipment $850 Dr.; Mike Patten, Capital $39,000 Cr.; Sales $2,200 Cr. Be sure to put beginning balances in your working papers.) The following transactions occurred in May:

L01, 2, 3, 4, 5 *(70 MIN)*

201X		
May	1	Mike Patten invested an additional $14,500 in the sneaker store.
	3	Sold $900 of merchandise on account to B. Donati, sales ticket no. 60; terms 2/10, n/30.
	4	Sold $700 of merchandise on account to Ron Lindall, sales ticket no. 61; terms 2/10, n/30.
	9	Sold $400 of merchandise on account to Jim Zamora, sales ticket no. 62; terms 2/10, n/30.
	10	Received cash from B. Donati in payment of May 3 transaction, sales ticket no. 60, less discount.
	20	Sold $3,000 of merchandise on account to Pilar Pry, sales ticket no. 63; terms 2/10, n/30.
	22	Received cash payment from Ron Lindall in payment of May 4 transaction, sales ticket no. 61.
	23	Collected cash sales, $2,400.
	24	Issued credit memorandum no. 1 to Pilar Pry for $2,200 of merchandise returned from May 20 sales on account.
	26	Received cash from Pilar Pry in payment of May 20, sales ticket no. 63. (Don't forget about the credit memo and discount.)
	28	Collected cash sales, $6,800.
	30	Sold sneaker rack equipment for $350 cash. (Beware.)
	30	Sold merchandise priced at $4,000, on account to Ron Lindall, sales ticket no. 64; terms 2/10, n/30.
	31	Issued credit memorandum no. 2 to Ron Lindall for $700 of merchandise returned from May 30 transaction, sales ticket no. 64.

Check Figure:
Schedule of accounts
receivable $6,125

Required

1. Journalize the transactions.
2. Record to the accounts receivable subsidiary ledger and post to the general ledger as needed.
3. Prepare a schedule of accounts receivable for the end of May.

L01, 2, 3, 4, 5 *(75 MIN)*

PT/QB

Check Figure:
Schedule of accounts
receivable $2,173

9A-4. Gary Wilcox opened Gary's Cosmetic Market on October 1. A 6% sales tax is calculated and added to all cosmetic sales. Gary offers no sales discounts. The following transactions occurred in October:

201X		
Oct.	1	Gary Wilcox invested $8,500 in the Cosmetic Market from his personal savings account.
	5	From the cash register tapes, lipstick cash sales were $4,800, plus sales tax.
	5	From the cash register tapes, eye shadow cash sales were $2,500, plus sales tax.
	8	Sold lipstick on account to Fione Tay Co., $500, sales ticket no. 1, plus sales tax.
	9	Sold eye shadow on account to Marika Sanford Co., $1,500, sales ticket no. 2, plus sales tax.
	15	Issued credit memorandum no. 1 to Fione Tay Co. for $300 for lipstick returned. (Be sure to reduce Sales Tax Payable for Gary's.)
	19	Marika Sanford Co. paid half the amount owed from sales ticket no. 2, dated October 9.
	21	Sold lipstick on account to Mary Ruvolo Co., $550, sales ticket no. 3, plus sales tax.
	24	Sold eye shadow on account to Peter Melnyk Co., $700, sales ticket no. 4, plus sales tax.
	25	Issued credit memorandum no. 2 to Mary Ruvolo Co. for $150 for lipstick returned from sales ticket no. 3, dated October 21.
	29	Cash sales taken from the cash register tape showed the following: 1. Lipstick: $1,300 + $78 sales tax collected. 2. Eye shadow: $2,600 + $156 sales tax collected.
	29	Sold lipstick on account to Marika Sanford Co., $500, sales ticket no. 5, plus sales tax.
	30	Received payment from Marika Sanford Co. of sales ticket no. 5, dated October 29.

Required

1. Journalize the transactions.
2. Record to the accounts receivable subsidiary ledger and post to the general ledger when appropriate.
3. Prepare a schedule of accounts receivable for the end of October.

MyAccountingLab

L01, 2, 4, 5
(40 MIN)

Group B

9B-1. Bill Haas has opened Ciabatta and Whatnot, a wholesale grocery and bread company. The following transactions occurred in January:

201X		
Jan.	1	Sold grocery merchandise to Cindi Co. on account, $900, invoice no. 1.
	4	Sold bread merchandise to Common Law Co. on account, $550, invoice no. 2.
	8	Sold grocery merchandise to Canadian Co. on account, $1,000, invoice no. 3.
	10	Issued credit memorandum no. 1 to Cindi Co. for $160 of grocery merchandise returned due to spoilage.
	15	Sold bread merchandise to Common Law Co. on account, $300, invoice no. 4.
	19	Sold grocery merchandise to Canadian Co. on account, $400, invoice no. 5.
	25	Sold bread merchandise to Cindi Co. on account, $500, invoice no. 6.

Check Figure:
Schedule of accounts
receivable $3,490

Required

1. Journalize the transactions.
2. Record to the accounts receivable subsidiary ledger and post to the general ledger as appropriate.
3. Prepare a schedule of accounts receivable for the end of January.

9B-2. The following transactions of Jack's Auto Supply occurred in November (Balances as of November 1 are given for general ledger and accounts receivable ledger accounts: Danielson $1,100 Dr.; Wallace $250 Dr.; Whitnall $500; Accounts Receivable $1,850 Dr.; Sales Tax Payable $2,000 Cr. Be sure to enter these balances in your working papers before beginning.):

LO1, 2, 4, 5
(50 MIN)

201X		
Nov.	1	Sold auto parts merchandise to R. Danielson on account, $600, invoice no. 30, plus 8% sales tax.
	5	Sold auto parts merchandise to J. Wallace on account, $900, invoice no. 31, plus 8% sales tax.
	8	Sold auto parts merchandise to Lance Whitnall on account, $9,000, invoice no. 32, plus 8% sales tax.
	10	Issued credit memorandum no. 12 to R. Danielson for $450 for defective auto parts merchandise returned from January 1 transaction. (Be careful to record the reduction in Sales Tax Payable as well.)
	12	Sold auto parts merchandise to J. Wallace on account, $450, invoice no. 33, plus 8% sales tax.

Required

1. Journalize the transactions.
2. Record to the accounts receivable subsidiary ledger and post to the general ledger as appropriate.
3. Prepare a schedule of accounts receivable for the end of November.

Check Figure:
Schedule of accounts
receivable $13,190

9B-3. Mike Pattern owns Pattern's Sneaker Shop. (Balances as of May 1 are provided for the accounts receivable and general ledger accounts as follows: Donati $325 Dr.; Lindall $800 Dr.; Pry $500 Dr.; Zamora $700 Dr.; Cash $14,000 Dr.; Accounts Receivable $2,325 Dr.; sneaker rack equipment $1,300 Dr.; Mike Pattern, Capital $39,000 Cr.; Sales $2,500 Cr. Be sure to put them in your working papers.) The following transactions occurred in May:

LO1, 2, 3, 4, 5 *(70 MIN)*

201X		
May	1	Mike Pattern invested an additional $11,000 in the sneaker store.
	3	Sold $800 of merchandise on account to B. Donati, sales ticket no. 70; terms 1/10, n/30.
	4	Sold $600 of merchandise on account to Ron Lindall, sales ticket no. 71; terms 1/10, n/30.
	9	Sold $300 of merchandise on account to Jim Zamora, sales ticket no. 72; terms 1/10, n/30.
	10	Received cash from B. Donati in payment of May 3 transaction, sales ticket no. 70, less discount.
	20	Sold $2,000 of merchandise on account to Pilar Pry, sales ticket no. 73; terms 1/10, n/30.
	22	Received cash payment from Ron Lindall in payment of May 4 transaction, sales ticket no. 71.
	23	Collected cash sales, $2,000.
	24	Issued credit memorandum no. 1 to Pilar Pry for $1,800 of merchandise returned from May 20 sales on account.
	26	Received cash from Pilar Pry in payment of May 20 sales ticket no. 73. (Don't forget about the credit memo and discount.)
	28	Collected cash sales, $7,000.
	30	Sold sneaker rack equipment for $150 cash. (Beware.)
	30	Sold merchandise priced at $5,000 on account to Ron Lindall, sales ticket no. 74, terms 1/10, n/30.
	31	Issued credit memorandum no. 2 to Ron Lindall for $875 of merchandise returned from May 30 transaction, sales ticket no. 74.

Required

1. Journalize the transactions.
2. Record to the accounts receivable subsidiary ledger and post to the general ledger as needed.
3. Prepare a schedule of accounts receivable for the end of May.

L01, 2, 3, 4, 5 *(75 MIN)*

9B-4. Gary Wilcox opened Gary's Cosmetic Market on October 1. A 4% sales tax is calculated and added to all cosmetic sales. Gary offers no sales discounts. The following transactions occurred in April:

201X		
Oct.	1	Gary Wilcox invested $9,500 in the Cosmetic Market from his personal savings account.
	5	From the cash register tapes, lipstick cash sales were $4,900, plus sales tax.
	5	From the cash register tapes, eye shadow cash sales were $2,500, plus sales tax.
	8	Sold lipstick on account to Fione Tay Co., $500, sales ticket no. 1, plus sales tax.
	9	Sold eye shadow on account to Marika Sanford Co., $600, sales ticket no. 2, plus sales tax.
	15	Issued credit memorandum no. 1 to Marika Sanford Co. for $50 for lipstick returned. (Be sure to reduce Sales Tax Payable for Gary's.)
	19	Marika Sanford Co. paid half the amount owed from sales ticket no. 2, dated October 9.
	21	Sold lipstick on account to Mary Ruvolo Co., $500, sales ticket no. 3, plus sales tax.
	24	Sold eye shadow on account to Peter Melnyk Co., $800, sales ticket no. 4, plus sales tax.
	25	Issued credit memorandum no. 2 to Mary Ruvolo Co. for $300 for lipstick returned from sales ticket no. 3, dated October 21.
	29	Cash sales taken from the cash register tape showed the following: 1. Lipstick: $700 + $28 sales tax collected. 2. Eye shadow: $3,500 + $140 sales tax collected.
	29	Sold lipstick on account to Marika Sanford Co., $500, sales ticket no. 5, plus sales tax.
	30	Received payment from Marika Sanford Co. of sales ticket no. 5, dated October 29.

Required

1. Journalize, record, and post as appropriate.
2. Prepare a schedule of accounts receivable for the end of October.

L01 *(15 MIN)*   **Reading the Kellogg's Annual Report**

Go to http://investor.kelloggs.com/annuals.cfm, to access the Kellogg's 2010 Annual Report, Note 1, Revenue Recognition, and find out what account records the promotional package inserts.

MyAccountingLab

SANCHEZ COMPUTER CENTER

To assist you in recording these transactions for the month of January, at the end of this problem is the schedule of accounts receivable as of December 31 and an updated chart of accounts with the current balance listed for each account.

Assignment

1. Journalize the transactions.
2. Record in the accounts receivable subsidiary ledger and post to the general ledger as appropriate. A partial subsidiary ledger is included in the working papers that accompany this text.

3. The following accounts have been added to the chart of accounts: Sales #4010, Sales Returns and Allowances #4020, and Sales Discounts #4030.
4. Prepare a schedule of accounts receivable as of January 31, 201X.

The January transactions are as follows:

Jan.	1	Sold $700 worth of merchandise to Taylor Golf on credit, sales invoice no. 5000; terms 2/10, n/30.
	10	Sold $3,000 worth of merchandise on account to Anthony Pitale, sales invoice no. 5001; terms 2/10, n/30.
	11	Received $3,000 from Accu Pac, Inc., toward payment of its balance; no discount allowed.
	12	Collected $2,000 cash sales.
	19	Sold $4,000 worth of merchandise on account to Vita Needle, sales invoice no. 5002; terms 4/10, n/30.
	20	Collected balance in full from invoice no. 5001, Anthony Pitale.
	29	Issued credit memorandum to Taylor Golf for $400 worth of merchandise returned, invoice no. 5000.
	29	Collected full payment from Vita Needle, invoice no. 5002.

Schedule of Accounts Receivable
Sanchez Computer Center
December 31, 201X

Taylor Golf	$ 2,900.00
Vita Needle	6,800.00
Accu Pac	3,900.00
Total Amount Due	$13,600.00

Chart of Accounts and Current Balances as of 12/31/1X

Account #	Account Name	Debit Balance	Credit Balance
1000	Cash	$ 3,336.64	
1010	Petty Cash	100	
1020	Accounts Receivable	13,600	
1025	Prepaid Rent	1,600	
1030	Supplies	90	
1040	Merchandise Inventory	0	
1080	Computer Shop Equipment	3,800	
1081	Accumulated Dep., C.S. Equip.		$ 99
1090	Office Equipment	1,050	
1091	Accumulated Dep., Office Equip.		20
2000	Accounts Payable		2,050
2010	Wages Payable		0
2020	FICA—Social Security Payable		0
2030	FICA—Medicare Payable		0
2040	FIT Payable		0
2050	SIT Payable		0
2060	FUTA Payable		0
2070	SUTA Payable		0
3000	Freedman, Capital		7,406
3010	Freedman, Withdrawals	2,015	

(continued)

Chart of Accounts and Current Balances as of 12/31/1X

Account #	Account Name	Debit Balance	Credit Balance
3020	Income Summary		0
4000	Service Revenue		18,500
4010	Sales		0
4020	Sales Returns and Allowances	0	
4030	Sales Discounts	0	
5010	Advertising Expense	0	
5020	Rent Expense	0	
5030	Utilities Expense	0	
5040	Phone Expense	150	
5050	Supplies Expense	42	
5060	Insurance Expense	0	
5070	Postage Expense	25	
5080	Dep. Exp., C.S. Equipment	0	
5090	Dep. Exp., Office Equipment	0	
5100	Miscellaneous Expense	10	
5110	Wage Expense	2,030	
5120	Payroll Tax Expense	226.36	
5130	Interest Expense	0	
5140	Bad Debt Expense	0	
6000	Purchases	0	
6010	Purchases Returns and Allowances		0
6020	Purchases Discounts		0
6030	Freight In	0	

Purchases and Cash Payments

THE GAME PLAN

So you have decided to buy a Sony high-definition, 3D television. You know the exact model you want; however, there is only a limited supply available. You visit Best Buy and ask the salesperson if this model is in stock. The salesperson goes to the computer and searches the inventory. Yes, there is one left in stock. You buy it and now that item is reported temporarily out of stock. In this chapter you will learn how inventory is accounted for when purchased by the company and sold to a buyer.

LEARNING OBJECTIVES

- **1.** Recording and posting purchase transactions.
- **2.** Recording to accounts payable subsidiary ledger.
- **3.** Preparing, journalizing, and posting a debit memorandum.
- **4.** Recording and posting cash payment transactions.
- **5.** Preparing a schedule of accounts payable.
- **6.** Journalizing transactions for a perpetual accounting system.

LO1

LEARNING UNIT 10-1 CHOU'S TOY SHOP:
Buyer's View of a Merchandise Company

Purchases

Purchases Merchandise for resale. It is a cost.

When you go into your local Target do you ever wonder how a store records all of the merchandise it purchases from a company like Sony? First, let us look at Chou's Toy Shop. Chou brings merchandise into his toy store for resale to customers. The account that records the cost of this merchandise is called Purchases. Suppose Chou buys $4,000 worth of Barbie dolls on account from Mattel Manufacturing on July 6. The Purchases account records all merchandise bought for resale.

	Purchases	
Purchases is a cost.	Dr.	Cr.
The rules work the same as an expense.	4,000	

This account has a debit balance and is classified as a cost. Purchases represent costs that are directly related to bringing merchandise into the store for resale to customers. The July 6 entry would be analyzed and journalized as in Figure 10.1.

COACHING TIP

If Chou's purchased a new display case for the store, it would not show up in the Purchases account. The case is considered equipment that is not for resale to customers.

Accounts Affected	Category	↑↓	Rules	T Account Update
Purchases	Cost	↑	Dr.	**Purchases** Dr. 4,000 | Cr.
Accounts Payable, Mattel	Liability	↑	Cr.	**Acc. Payable** Dr. | Cr. 4,000 **Mattel** Dr. | Cr. 4,000

Keep in mind that we would have to record to Mattel in the accounts payable subsidiary ledger. We talk about the subsidiary ledger in Learning Unit 10-2.

FIGURE 10.1
Purchased Merchandise on Account

Jul.	6	Purchases			4 0 0 0 00		
		Accounts Payable, Mattel				4 0 0 0 00	
		Purchases on account					

Purchases Returns and Allowances

Purchases Returns and Allowances A contra-cost account in the ledger that records the amount of defective or unacceptable merchandise returned to suppliers and/or price reductions given for defective items.

Chou noticed that some of the dolls he received were defective, and he notified the manufacturer of the defects. On July 9, Mattel issued a credit memorandum indicating that Chou would get a $500 reduction from the original selling price. Chou then agreed to keep the dolls. The account that records a decrease to a buyer's cost is a contra-cost account called Purchases Returns and Allowances. The account lowers the cost of purchases.

Purchases Returns and Allowances	
Dr.	Cr.
	500 ← **Normal balance is a credit.**

Let's analyze this reduction to cost and prepare a general journal entry (Figure 10.2).

Accounts Affected	Category	↑↓	Rules	T Account Update				
Accounts Payable, Mattel	Liability	↓	Dr.	**Acc. Payable**			**Mattel**	
				Dr.	Cr.		Dr.	Cr.
				500	4,000		500	4,000
Purchases Returns and Allowances	Contra-cost	↑	Cr.	**Purchases Ret. & Allow.**				
				Dr.	Cr.			
					500			

When posted to general ledger accounts as well as recorded to Mattel in the accounts payable subsidiary ledger, Chou owes $500 less.

Jul.	9	Accounts Payable, Mattel		500 00		
		Purchases Returns and Allowances			500 00	
		Received credit memorandum				

FIGURE 10.2
Credit Memorandum Received

Purchases Discount Now let's look at the analysis and journal entry when Chou pays Mattel. Mattel offers a 2% cash discount if the invoice is paid within 10 days. To take advantage of this cash discount, Chou sent a check to Mattel on July 15. The discount is taken after the allowance.

$4,000
− 500 allowance

$3,500 × 0.02 = $70 purchases discount

The account that records this discount is called Purchases Discount. It, too, is a contra-cost account because it lowers the cost of purchases.

Purchases Discount

Dr.	Cr.
	70	← Normal balance is a credit.

Let's analyze and prepare a general journal entry (Figure 10.3).

Jul.	15	Accounts Payable, Mattel		3 500 00		
		Purchases Discount			70 00	
		Cash			3 430 00	
		Paid Mattel balance owed				

COACHING TIP

Remember: For Chou it is a purchases discount, whereas for Mattel it is a sales discount.

Purchases Discount A contra-cost account in the general ledger that records discounts offered by vendors of merchandise for prompt payment of purchases by buyers.

COACHING TIP

Remember: Purchases are debits; purchases discounts are credits.

FIGURE 10.3
Purchase Discount Journalized

Accounts Affected	Category	↑↓	Rules	T Account Update				
Accounts Payable, Mattel	Liability	↓	Dr.	**Acc. Payable**			**Mattel**	
				Dr.	Cr.		Dr.	Cr.
				500	4,000		500	4,000
				3,500			3,500	
Purchases Discount	Contra-cost	↑	Cr.	**Purchases Discount**				
				Dr.	Cr.			
					70			
Cash	Asset	↓	Cr.	**Cash**				
				Dr.	Cr.			
					3,430			

After the journal entry is posted and recorded to Mattel, the result will show that Chou saved $70 and totally reduced what he owed to Mattel. The actual—or net—cost of his purchase is $3,430, calculated as follows:

Purchases	$4,000
− Purchases Returns and Allowances	500
− Purchases Discounts	70
= Net Purchases	$3,430

F.O.B. destination *Seller* pays or is responsible for the cost of freight to purchaser's location or destination.

Freight charges are not taken into consideration in calculating net purchases. Still, they are important. If the seller is responsible for paying the shipping cost until the goods reach their destination, the freight charges are F.O.B. destination. (F.O.B. stands for "free on board" the carrier.) For example, if a seller located in Boston sold goods F.O.B. destination to a buyer in New York, the seller would have to pay the cost of shipping the goods to the buyer.

F.O.B. shipping point *Purchaser* pays or is responsible for the shipping costs from seller's shipping point to purchaser's location.

If the buyer is responsible for paying the shipping costs, the freight charges are F.O.B. shipping point. In this situation, the seller will sometimes prepay the freight charges as a matter of convenience and will add it to the invoice of the purchaser, as in the following example:

Bill amount ($800 + $80 prepaid freight)	$880
Less 5% cash discount (0.05 × $800)	40
Amount to be paid by buyer	$840

Purchases discounts are not taken on freight. The discount is based on the purchase price.

If the seller ships goods F.O.B. shipping point, legal ownership (title) passes to the buyer *when the goods are shipped*. If goods are shipped by the seller F.O.B. destination, title will change *when goods have reached their destination*. (See Exhibit 10.1.)

EXHIBIT 10.1

FOB shipping point

FOB destination

FOB shipping point: Title changes hands at the shipping point, and buyer owns the goods while they are in transit. So, the buyer pays the shipping costs.

FOB destination: Title changes hands at the destination point, and seller owns the goods while they are in transit. So, the seller, not the buyer, pays the shipping costs.

LEARNING UNIT 10-1 REVIEW

AT THIS POINT you should be able to do the following:

- Explain and calculate purchases, purchases returns and allowances, and purchases discounts.
- Calculate net purchases.
- Explain why purchases discounts are not taken on freight.
- Compare and contrast F.O.B. destination with F.O.B. shipping point.

Instant Replay ◉ Self-Review Quiz 10-1

Respond true or false to the following:

1. Net purchases = Purchases − Purchases Returns and Allowances − Purchases Discount.
2. Purchases is a contra-cost.
3. F.O.B. destination means the seller covers shipping cost and retains title until goods reach their destination.
4. Purchases discounts are not taken on freight.
5. Purchases Discount is a contra-cost account.

Solutions to Instant Replay: Self-Review Quiz 10-1

1. True   2. False   3. True   4. True   5. True

LEARNING UNIT 10-2 RECORDING AND POSTING PURCHASES TRANSACTIONS ON ACCOUNT FOR ART'S WHOLESALE CLOTHING COMPANY:

Introduction to Subsidiary Ledgers and Debit Memorandum

201X			
Apr.	3	Purchased merchandise on account, $5,000, and freight, $50, from Abby Blake Co.; terms 2/10, n/60.	
	4	Purchased equipment on account, $4,000, from Joe Francis Co.	
	6	Purchased merchandise on account, $800, from Thorpe Co.; terms 1/10, n/30.	
	7	Purchased merchandise on account, $980, from John Sullivan Co.; terms n/10, EOM.	
	9	Art's issued debit memo #1, $200, to Thorpe for defective merchandise.	
	12	Purchased merchandise on account, $600, from Abby Blake Co.; terms 1/10, n/30.	
	25	Purchased $500 of supplies on account from John Sullivan Co.	

Let's look at the steps Art's Wholesale Clothing Company took when it ordered goods from Abby Blake Company on April 3.

Step 1: Prepare a Purchase Requisition at Art's Wholesale Clothing Company The inventory clerk notes a low inventory level of ladies' jackets for resale, so the clerk sends a purchase requisition to the purchasing department. A duplicate copy is sent to the accounting department. A third copy remains with the department that initiated the request to be used as a check on the purchasing department.

Purchase requisition A form used within a business by the requesting department asking the purchasing department of the business to buy specific goods.

Step 2: Purchasing Department of Art's Wholesale Clothing Company Prepares a Purchase Order After checking various price lists and suppliers' catalogs, the purchasing department fills out a form called a purchase order. This form gives Abby Blake Company the authority to ship the ladies' jackets ordered by Art's Wholesale Clothing Company (see Figure 10.4).

Purchase order A form used in business to place an order for the buying of goods from a seller.

FIGURE 10.4
Purchase Order

PURCHASE ORDER NO. 1
ART'S WHOLESALE CLOTHING COMPANY
1528 BELLE AVE.
NEW YORK, NY 10022

Purchased From:	Abby Blake Company 12 Foster Road Englewood Cliffs, NJ 07632		Date: April 1, 201X Shipped VIA: Freight Truck Terms: 2/10, n/60 FOB: Englewood Cliffs
Quantity	Description	Unit Price	Total
100	Ladies' Jackets Code 14-0	$50	$5,000

Art's Wholesale
By: Bill Joy

Purchase order number must appear on all invoices.

Step 3: Sales Invoice Prepared by Abby Blake Company Abby Blake Company receives the purchase order and prepares a sales invoice. The sales invoice for the seller is the purchase invoice for the buyer. A sales invoice is shown in Figure 10.5.

The invoice shows that the goods will be shipped F.O.B. Englewood Cliffs. Thus, Art's Wholesale Clothing Company is responsible for paying the shipping costs.

The sales invoice also shows a freight charge. Thus, Abby Blake prepaid the shipping costs as a matter of convenience. Art's will repay the freight charges when it pays the invoice.

Purchase invoice The seller's sales invoice, which is sent to the purchaser.

Step 4: Receiving the Goods When goods are received, Art's Wholesale inspects the shipment and completes a receiving report. The receiving report verifies that the exact merchandise that was ordered was received in good condition.

Receiving report A business form used to notify the appropriate people of the ordered goods received along with the quantities and specific condition of the goods.

FIGURE 10.5
Sales Invoice

SALES INVOICE NO. 228
ABBY BLAKE COMPANY
12 FOSTER ROAD
ENGLEWOOD, CLIFFS, NJ 07632

Sold To:	Art's Wholesale Clothing Co. 1528 Belle Ave. New York, NY 10022		Date: April 3, 201X Shipped VIA: Freight Truck Terms: 2/10, n/60 Your Order No: 1 FOB: Englewood Cliffs
Quantity	Description	Unit Price	Total
100	Ladies' Jackets Code 14-0 Freight	$50	$5,000 50 $5,050

Step 5: Verifying the Numbers Before the invoice is approved for recording and payment, the accounting department must check the purchase order, invoice, and receiving report to make sure that all are in agreement and that no steps have been omitted. The form used for checking and approval is an invoice approval form (see Figure 10.6).

INVOICE APPROVAL FORM Art's Wholesale Clothing Co.	
Purchase Order #	_____
Requisition check	_____
Purchase Order check	_____
Receiving Report check	_____
Invoice check	_____
Approved for Payment	_____

Invoice approval form Used by the accounting department in checking the invoice and finally approving it for recording and payment.

FIGURE 10.6
Invoice Approval Form

Keep in mind that Art's Wholesale Clothing Company does not record this purchase until the *invoice is approved for recording and payment*. Abby Blake Company records this transaction in its records when the sales invoice is prepared, however.

Let's look closer at the April 3 transaction.

201X

Apr. 3 Purchased merchandise on account, $5,000, plus freight, $50, from Abby Blake Co.

THE ANALYSIS			
Accounts Affected	**Category**	**↑↓**	**Rules of Dr. and Cr.**
Purchases	Cost	↑	Dr. $5,000
Freight-In	Cost	↑	Dr. $50
Accounts Payable, Abby Blake Co.	Liability	↑	Cr. $5,050

Figure 10.7 shows how the general journal would look.

						Page 2
Apr.	3	Purchases		5 0 0 0 00		
		Freight-In		5 0 00		
		Accounts Payable, Abby Blake Co.			5 0 5 0 00	
		Purchased merchandise on account				
		from Abby Blake				

COACHING TIP

	Buyer			Seller	
Purchase	Dr.	Cost	Sale	Cr.	Revenue
PRA	Cr.	Contra-cost	SRA	Dr.	Contra-revenue
PD	Cr.	Contra-cost	SD	Dr.	Contra-revenue

FIGURE 10.7
Merchandise Purchase, Plus Freight Cost

Accounts Payable Subsidiary Ledger

L02

In the last chapter we saw the accounts receivable subsidiary ledger. It listed customers owing Art's money from sales on account. Now we look at Art's, the buyer, and an accounts payable subsidiary ledger. See Figure 10.8.

Note that the normal balance is a credit for Accounts Payable and its subsidiary ledger, whereas in the last chapter Accounts Receivable had a debit normal balance.

Accounts Payable is the controlling account in the ledger and at the end of the month the sum of the individual amount owed to the creditors should equal the balance in Accounts Payable at the end of the month.

Accounts payable subsidiary ledger A book or file that contains, in alphabetical order, the name of the creditor and amount owed from purchases on account.

Figure 10.9 shows how the general journal looks for Art's before posting and recording this month's purchases on account.

FIGURE 10.8

Partial General Ledger of Art's Wholesale Clothing Company and Accounts Payable Subsidiary Ledger

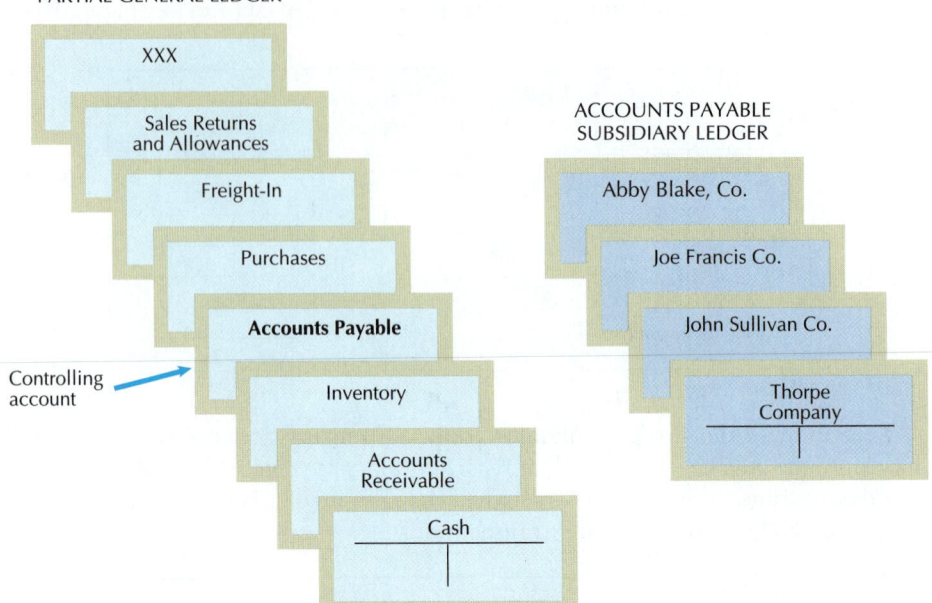

PARTIAL GENERAL LEDGER

XXX

Sales Returns and Allowances

Freight-In

Purchases

Accounts Payable

Controlling account →

Inventory

Accounts Receivable

Cash

ACCOUNTS PAYABLE SUBSIDIARY LEDGER

Abby Blake, Co.

Joe Francis Co.

John Sullivan Co.

Thorpe Company

FIGURE 10.9

		GENERAL JOURNAL			Page 2
Date		Account Titles and Description	PR	Dr.	Cr.
201X					
Apr.	3	Purchases		5 0 0 00	
		Freight-In		5 0 00	
		Accounts Payable, Abby Blake Co.			5 0 5 0 00
		Purchased merchandise on account, Blake			
	4	Equipment		4 0 0 0 00	
		Accounts Payable, Joe Francis			4 0 0 0 00
		Purchased equipment on account, Francis			
	6	Purchases		8 0 0 00	
		Accounts Payable, Thorpe Company			8 0 0 00
		Purchased merchandise on account, Thorpe			
	7	Purchases		9 8 0 00	
		Accounts Payable, John Sullivan Co.			9 8 0 00
		Purchased merchandise on account, Sullivan			
	9	Accounts Payable, Thorpe Company		2 0 0 00	
		Purchases Returns and Allowances			2 0 0 00
		Debit memo no. 1			
	12	Purchases		6 0 0 00	
		Accounts Payable, Abby Blake Co.			6 0 0 00
		Purchased merchandise on account, Blake			
	25	Supplies		5 0 0 00	
		Accounts Payable, John Sullivan Co.			5 0 0 00
		Purchased supplies on account, Sullivan			

Posting and Recording Purchases Transactions Before we post to the general ledger and record to the subsidiary ledger, let's first examine the T accounts and what each one would look like.

(Before Recordings)

ACCOUNTS PAYABLE SUBSIDIARY LEDGER

Abby Blake Co.
Dr. | Cr.

Joe Francis Co.
Dr. | Cr.

John Sullivan Co.
Dr. | Cr.

Thorpe Co.
Dr. | Cr.

(Before Postings)

PARTIAL GENERAL LEDGER

Supplies 115
Dr. | Cr.

Purchases 511
Dr. | Cr.

Equipment 121
Dr. | Cr.

Purchases Returns and Allowances 513
Dr. | Cr.

Freight-In 514
Dr. | Cr.

Accounts Payable 211
Dr. | Cr.

Controlling account

Now let's look at how to post and record the April 3 transaction.

FIGURE 10.10

	Date		Account Titles and Description	PR	Dr.	Cr.
	201X					
	Apr.	3	Purchases	511	5 0 0 00	
			Freight-In	514	5 0 00	
			Accounts Payable, Abby Blake Co.	211 ✓		5 0 5 0 00
			Purchased merchandise on account, Blake			

GENERAL JOURNAL — Page 2

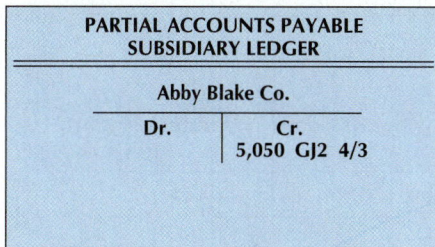

PARTIAL ACCOUNTS PAYABLE SUBSIDIARY LEDGER

Abby Blake Co.
Dr. | Cr.
     | 5,050 GJ2 4/3

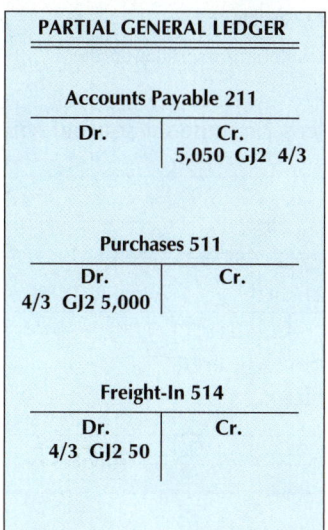

PARTIAL GENERAL LEDGER

Accounts Payable 211
Dr. | Cr.
     | 5,050 GJ2 4/3

Purchases 511
Dr. | Cr.
4/3 GJ2 5,000 |

Freight-In 514
Dr. | Cr.
4/3 GJ2 50 |

For this transaction we post to the general ledger accounts Purchases, Freight-In, and Accounts Payable. Note how the account numbers 511, 514, and 211 are entered into the PR column of the general journal. We must also *record* to Abby Blake Co. in the accounts payable subsidiary ledger. Note that it is placed on the credit side because we owe Abby the money. When the subsidiary ledger is updated, a (✔) is placed in the PR column of the general journal. Figure 10.10 shows how the accounts payable subsidiary ledger and the partial general ledger would look after posting and recording.

Before concluding this unit, let's take a closer look at the April 9 transaction when Art's issues a debit memorandum to Thorpe Company. We analyze the transaction and show how to post and record it.

● L03   Debit Memorandum

Debit memorandum A memo issued by a purchaser to a seller, indicating that some Purchases Returns and Allowances have occurred and therefore the purchaser now owes less money on account.

In Chapter 9, Art's Wholesale Clothing Company had to handle returned goods as a seller. It did so by issuing credit memoranda to customers who returned or received an allowance on the price. In this chapter, Art's must handle returns as a buyer. It does so by using debit memoranda. A debit memorandum is a piece of paper issued by a customer to a seller. It indicates that a return or allowance has occurred.

On April 6, Art's Wholesale had purchased men's hats for $800 from Thorpe Company. On April 9, 20 hats valued at $200 were found to have defective brims. Art's issued a debit memorandum to Thorpe Company, as shown in Figure 10.11. At some point in the future, Thorpe will issue Art's a credit memorandum. Let's look at how Art's Wholesale Clothing Company handles such a transaction in its accounting records.

FIGURE 10.11
Debit Memorandum

DEBIT MEMORANDUM		No. 1
Art's Wholesale Clothing Company 1528 Belle Ave. New York, NY 10022		
TO: Thorpe Company 3 Access Road Beverly, MA 01915		April 9, 201X
WE DEBIT your account as follows:		

Quantity		Unit Cost	Total
20	Men's Hats Code 827 – defective brims	$10	$200

COACHING TIP

Result of debit memo: debits or reduces Accounts Payable. On seller's books, accounts affected would include Sales Returns and Allowances and Accounts Receivable.

Journalizing and Posting the Debit Memo First, let's look at a transactional analysis chart.

Accounts Affected	Category	↑↓	Rules
Accounts Payable	Liability	↓	Dr.
Purchases Returns and Allowances	Contra-cost	↑	Cr.

Next, let's examine the journal entry for the debit memorandum (Figure 10.12).

FIGURE 10.12
Debit Memorandum Journalized and Posted

		GENERAL JOURNAL			
					Page 2
	Date	Account Titles and Description	PR	Dr.	Cr.
	Apr. 9	Accounts Payable, Thorpe Company	211 ✔	2 0 0 00	
		Purchases Returns and Allowances	513		2 0 0 00
		Debit memo no.1			

The two postings and one recording are the following:

1. **211:** Post to Accounts Payable as a debit in the general ledger (account no. 211). When done, place in the PR column the account number, 211, above the diagonal on the same line as Accounts Payable in the journal.

2. **✓:** Record to Thorpe Co. in the accounts payable subsidiary ledger to show that Art's doesn't owe Thorpe as much money. When done, place a ✓ in the journal in the PR column below the diagonal line on the same line as Accounts Payable in the journal.

3. **513:** Post to Purchases Returns and Allowances as a credit in the general ledger (account no. 513). When done, place the account number, 513, in the PR column of the journal on the same line as Purchases Returns and Allowances. (If equipment was returned that was not merchandise for resale, we would credit Equipment and not Purchases Returns and Allowances.)

COACHING TIP

PURCHASES RETURNS AND ALLOWANCES

Dr.	Cr.
−	+

The following are the completed accounts payable subsidiary ledger and general ledger for Art's.

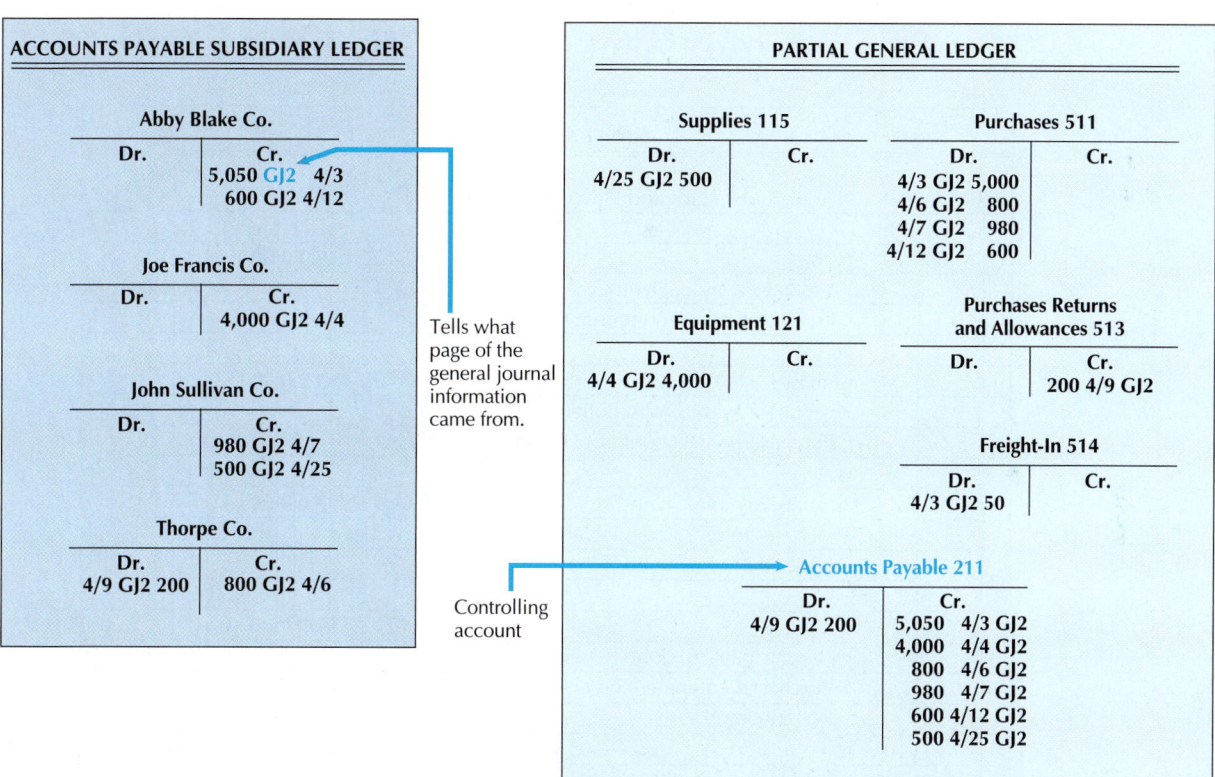

LEARNING UNIT 10-2 REVIEW

AT THIS POINT you should be able to do the following:

- Explain the relationship between a purchase requisition, a purchase order, and a purchase invoice.
- Explain for what purpose a typical invoice approval form may be used.
- Journalize transactions for purchase and cash payments.
- Explain how to record to the accounts payable subsidiary ledger and post to the general ledger from a general journal.
- Explain a debit memorandum and be able to journalize an entry resulting from its issuance.

Instant Replay ◉ Self-Review Quiz 10-2

Journalize and post the following transactions:

201X		
May	5	Bought merchandise on account from Flynn Co., invoice no. 512, dated May 6, $900; terms 1/10, n/30.
	7	Bought merchandise from John Butler Company, invoice no. 403, dated May 7, $1,000; terms n/10 EOM.
	13	Issued debit memo no. 1 to Flynn Co. for merchandise returned, $300, from invoice no. 512.
	17	Purchased $400 of equipment on account from John Butler Company, invoice no. 413, dated May 18.

Solution to Instant Replay: Self-Review Quiz 10-2

GENERAL JOURNAL					Page 1
Date	Account Titles and Description	PR	Dr.	Cr.	
201X					
May 5	Purchases	512	900 00		
	Accounts Payable, Flynn Co.	212 ✔		900 00	
	Purchased on account from Flynn				
7	Purchases	512	1000 00		
	Accounts Payable, John Butler Co.	212 ✔		1000 00	
	Purchased on account from Butler				
13	Accounts Payable, Flynn Co.	212 ✔	300 00		
	Purchases returns and allowances	513		300 00	
	Issued debit memo no. 1				
17	Equipment	121	400 00		
	Accounts Payable, John Butler Co.	212 ✔		400 00	
	Purchased equipment on account				
	from Butler				

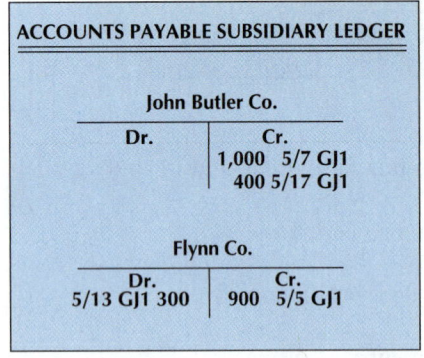

ACCOUNTS PAYABLE SUBSIDIARY LEDGER

John Butler Co.
Dr.	Cr.
	1,000 5/7 GJ1
	400 5/17 GJ1

Flynn Co.
Dr.	Cr.
5/13 GJ1 300	900 5/5 GJ1

PARTIAL GENERAL LEDGER

Equipment 121
Dr.	Cr.
5/17 GJ1 400	

Accounts Payable 212
Dr.	Cr.
5/13 GJ1 300	900 5/5 GJ1
	1,000 5/7 GJ1
	400 5/17 GJ1

Purchases 512
Dr.	Cr.
5/5 GJ1 900	
5/7 GJ1 1,000	

Purchases Returns and Allowances 513
Dr.	Cr.
	300 5/13 GJ1

LEARNING UNIT 10-3 RECORDING AND POSTING CASH PAYMENTS TRANSACTIONS FOR ART'S WHOLESALE:
Schedule of Accounts Payable

The following cash payment transactions occurred for Art's Wholesale Clothing Company in April.

201X		
Apr.	2	Issued check no. 1 to Pete Blum for insurance paid in advance, $900.
	7	Issued check no. 2 to Joe Francis Company in payment of its April 4 invoice no. 388.
	9	Issued check no. 3 to Rick Flo Co. for merchandise purchased for cash, $800.
	12	Issued check no. 4 to Thorpe Company in payment of its April 6 invoice no. 414, less the return and 1% discount.
	28	Issued check no. 5, $700, for salaries paid.

Figure 10.13 provides a closer look at how the April 12 transaction would be journalized.

Accounts Affected	Category	↑↓	Rules	T Account Update
Cash	Asset	↓	Cr.	**Cash** Dr. | Cr. | 594
Purchases Discount	Contra-cost	↑	Cr.	**Purchases Discount** Dr. | Cr. | 6
Account Payable, Thorpe Co.	Liability	↓	Dr.	**Accounts Payable** Dr. | Cr. 600 | 600 **Thorpe Co.** Dr. | Cr. 600 | 600

Apr.	12	Accounts Payable, Thorpe Co.			600 00		
		Purchases Discount					6 00
		Cash					594 00
		Paid invoice no. 414					

FIGURE 10.13

Figure 10.14 (p. 380) shows the complete set of cash payments transactions journalized for the month, followed by a complete posting to the general ledger and recordings to the accounts payable subsidiary ledger (remember from the past unit that we posted all the purchases on account).

FIGURE 10.14

GENERAL JOURNAL					Page 2
Date	Account Titles and Description	PR	Dr.	Cr.	
201X					
Apr. 2	Prepaid Insurance	116	9 0 0 00		
	Cash	111		9 0 0 00	
	Paid for insurance in advance				
7	Accounts Payable, Joe Francis Co.	211 ✓	4 0 0 00		
	Cash	111		4 0 0 00	
	Paid invoice no. 388				
9	Purchases	511	8 0 0 00		
	Cash	111		8 0 0 00	
	Cash purchases				
12	Accounts Payable, Thorpe Co.	211 ✓	6 0 0 00		
	Purchases Discount	512		6 00	
	Cash	111		5 9 4 00	
	Paid invoice no. 414				
28	Salaries Expense	611	7 0 0 00		
	Cash	111		7 0 0 00	
	Paid salaries				

(continued on next page)

 **L05**

Controlling account The account in the general ledger that summarizes or controls a subsidiary ledger. Example: The Accounts Payable account in the general ledger is the controlling account for the accounts payable subsidiary ledger. After postings are complete, it shows the total amount owed from purchases made on account.

Now let's prove that the sum of the accounts payable subsidiary ledger at the end of the month is equal to the controlling account, Accounts Payable, at the end of April for Art's Wholesale Clothing Company. To do so, creditors with an ending balance in Art's accounts payable subsidiary ledger must be listed in the schedule of accounts payable (see Figure 10.15). At the end of the month, the total owed ($7,130) in Accounts Payable, the controlling account in the general ledger, should equal the sum owed the individual creditors that are listed on the schedule of accounts payable. If it doesn't, the journalizing, posting, and recording must be checked to ensure that they are complete. Also, the balances of each title should be checked.

LEARNING UNIT 10-3 REVIEW

AT THIS POINT you should be able to do the following:

- Journalize, post, and record cash payments transactions.
- Prepare a schedule of accounts payable.

Instant Replay ◉ Self-Review Quiz 10-3

For the following transactions, journalize, post to the general ledger, and record to the accounts payable subsidiary ledger.

Accounts Payable Subsidiary Ledger

Name	Balance	Invoice No.
Bob Finkelstein	$300	488
Al Jeep	200	410

(Continued on following page spread on p. 382)

FIGURE 10.14 (*Continued*)

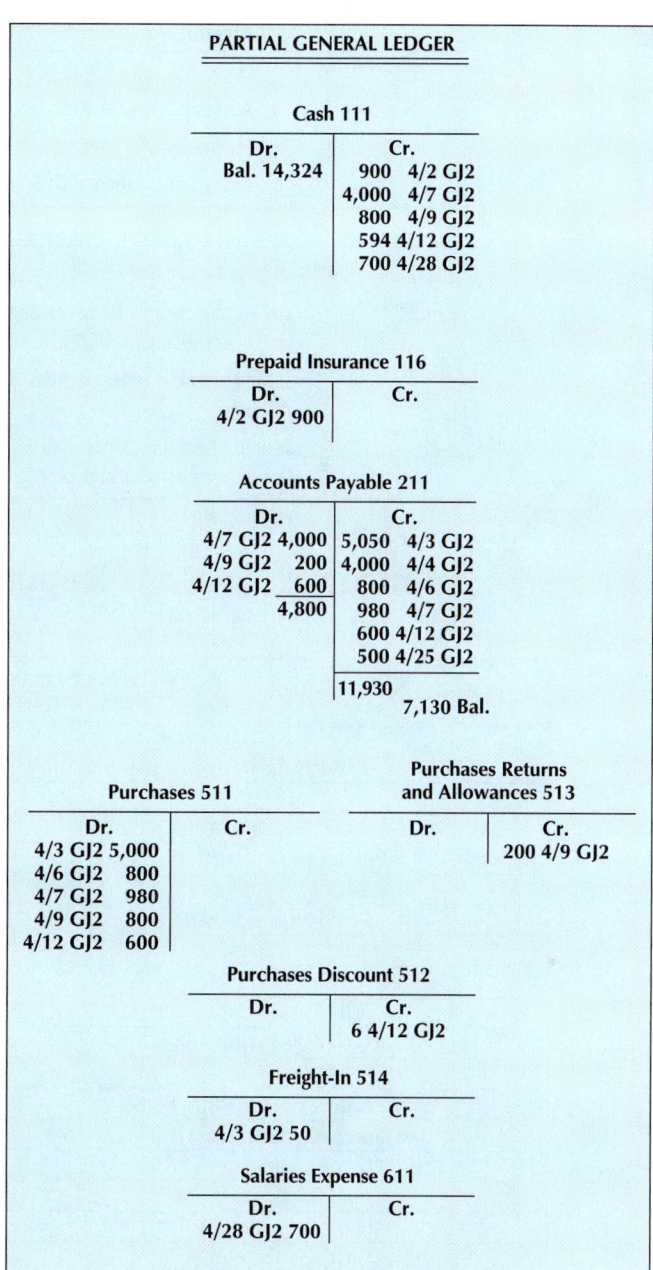

ACCOUNTS PAYABLE SUBSIDIARY LEDGER

Abby Blake Co.

Dr.	Cr.
	5,050 4/3 GJ2
	600 4/12 GJ2

Joe Francis Co.

Dr.	Cr.
4/7 GJ2 4,000	4,000 4/4 GJ1

John Sullivan Co.

Dr.	Cr.
	980 4/7 GJ2
	500 4/25 GJ2

Thorpe Co.

Dr.	Cr.
4/9 GJ1 200	800 4/6 GJ2
4/12 GJ1 600	

PARTIAL GENERAL LEDGER

Cash 111

Dr.	Cr.
Bal. 14,324	900 4/2 GJ2
	4,000 4/7 GJ2
	800 4/9 GJ2
	594 4/12 GJ2
	700 4/28 GJ2

Prepaid Insurance 116

Dr.	Cr.
4/2 GJ2 900	

Accounts Payable 211

Dr.	Cr.
4/7 GJ2 4,000	5,050 4/3 GJ2
4/9 GJ2 200	4,000 4/4 GJ2
4/12 GJ2 600	800 4/6 GJ2
4,800	980 4/7 GJ2
	600 4/12 GJ2
	500 4/25 GJ2
	11,930
	7,130 Bal.

Purchases 511

Dr.	Cr.
4/3 GJ2 5,000	
4/6 GJ2 800	
4/7 GJ2 980	
4/9 GJ2 800	
4/12 GJ2 600	

Purchases Returns and Allowances 513

Dr.	Cr.
	200 4/9 GJ2

Purchases Discount 512

Dr.	Cr.
	6 4/12 GJ2

Freight-In 514

Dr.	Cr.
4/3 GJ2 50	

Salaries Expense 611

Dr.	Cr.
4/28 GJ2 700	

FIGURE 10.15
Schedule of Accounts Payable

ART'S WHOLESALE CLOTHING COMPANY SCHEDULE OF ACCOUNTS PAYABLE APRIL 30, 201X		
Abby Blake Co.	$5 6 5 0	00
John Sullivan Co.	1 4 8 0	00
Total Accounts Payable	$7 1 3 0	00

Partial General Ledger

Account No.	Balance
Cash 110	$700
Accounts Payable 210	500
Purchases Discount 511	—
Advertising Expense 610	—

201X

Jun.   1   Issued check no. 15 to Al Jeep in payment of its May 25 invoice no. 410, less purchases discount of 2%.

8   Issued check no. 16 to Moss Advertising Co. to pay advertising bill due, $75, no discount.

9   Issued check no. 17 to Bob Finkelstein in payment of its May 28 invoice no. 488, less purchases discount of 2%.

Solution to Instant Replay: Self-Review Quiz 10-3

MELISSA COMPANY
GENERAL JOURNAL   Page 2

Date		Account Titles and Description	PR	Dr.	Cr.
201X					
Jun.	1	Accounts Payable, Al Jeep	210 ✓	2 0 0 00	
		Purchases Discount	110		4 00
		Cash			1 9 6 00
		Paid invoice no. 410			
	8	Advertising Expense	610	7 5 00	
		Cash	110		7 5 00
		Paid Advertising Bill			
	9	Accounts Payable, Bob Finkelstein	210 ✓	3 0 0 00	
		Purchases Discount	110		6 00
		Cash			2 9 4 00
		Paid invoice no. 488			

ACCOUNTS PAYABLE SUBSIDIARY LEDGER

Bob Finkelstein

Dr.	Cr.
6/1 GJ2 300	300 Bal.

Al Jeep

Dr.	Cr.
6/9 GJ2 200	200 Bal.

PARTIAL GENERAL LEDGER

Cash 110

Dr.	Cr.
Bal. 700	196 6/1 GJ2
	75 6/8 GJ2
	294 6/9 GJ2

Purchases Discount 511

Dr.	Cr.
	4 6/1 GJ2
	6 6/9 GJ2

Accounts Payable 210

Dr.	Cr.
6/1 GJ2 200	500 Bal.
6/9 GJ2 300	

Advertising Expense 610

Dr.	Cr.
6/8 GJ2 75	

LEARNING UNIT 10-4 INTRODUCTION TO A MERCHANDISE COMPANY USING A PERPETUAL INVENTORY SYSTEM

● L06

Introduction to the Merchandise Cycle

In this learning unit we will focus on recording transactions using a perpetual inventory system. This is an inventory system that continually monitors its levels of inventory. The previous units were based on a periodic inventory system. This means that at the end of each accounting period the cost of unsold goods is calculated. There is no continual tracking of inventory.

Let's use Walmart as an example as both the buyer and seller. We know that Walmart must buy inventory from suppliers to sell to you, the customer. This inventory is called merchandise inventory. It is an asset sold to you for cash or accounts receivable and represents *sales revenue* or sales for Walmart.

What did it cost Walmart to bring the inventory into the store? The cost of goods sold is the total cost of merchandise inventory brought into the store and sold. These costs do not include any operating expenses such as heat, advertising, and salaries. To find Walmart's profit before operating expenses, we take the sales revenue less cost of goods sold. Figure 10.16 is called *gross profit on sales.*

Perpetual inventory system An inventory system that keeps *continual track* of each type of inventory by recording units on hand at beginning, units sold, and the current balance after each sale or purchase.

Periodic inventory system An inventory system that, at the *end* of each accounting period, calculates the cost of the unsold goods on hand by taking the cost of each unit times the number of units of each product on hand.

Merchandise Inventory An asset and perpetual inventory system account that records purchases of merchandise. Discounts and returns are recorded in this account for the buyer.

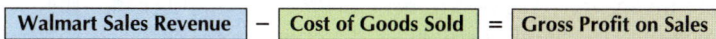

| Walmart Sales Revenue | − | Cost of Goods Sold | = | Gross Profit on Sales |

FIGURE 10.16
Calculating Gross Profit on Sales

For example, if Walmart sells a TV for $500 that cost $300 to bring into the store, its gross profit is $200. To find its net income or net loss, Walmart would subtract its operating expenses. Figure 10.17 shows how a merchandiser calculates its net income or net loss.

Note: In step 1 the sales provide an inflow of cash or accounts receivable. Step 2 shows that when the inventory is sold, it is recognized as a cost (cost of goods sold). By subtracting sales less cost of goods sold, we arrive at the gross profit in step 3. Step 4 shows that operating expenses subtracted from gross profit result in a net income or net loss in step 5.

Cost of goods sold In a perpetual inventory system, an account that records the cost of merchandise inventory used to make the sale.

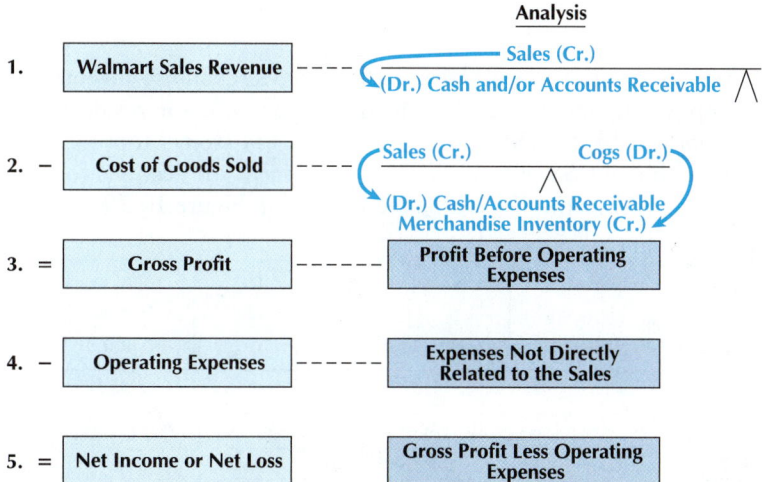

Analysis

FIGURE 10.17
Introduction to Perpetual Inventory for a Merchandise Company

What Inventory System Walmart Uses

When you pay at Walmart you see the use of bar codes and optical scanners. Walmart keeps detailed records of the inventory it brings into the store and what inventory is sold. With this method, Walmart keeps track of what it costs to make the sale (cost of goods sold) by matching revenues and costs (see Figure 10.18).

FIGURE 10.18
Matching Revenues and Costs

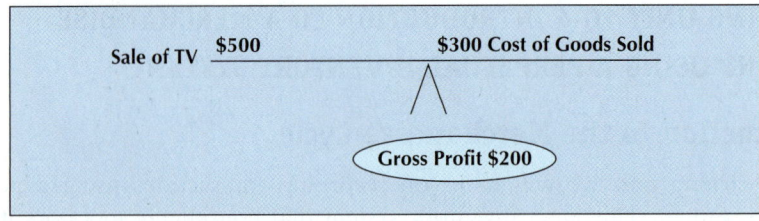

More and more companies, large or small, are using the perpetual inventory system due to increasing computerization. Walmart knows that using the perpetual inventory system will help control stocks of inventory as well as lost or stolen goods.

Recording Merchandise Transactions

Now let's look at Walmart as both a buyer and seller. Let's first focus on Walmart the buyer.

Walmart: The Buyer When Walmart brings merchandise inventory into the stores from suppliers it is recorded in the *Merchandise Inventory account.* Think of this account as purchases of merchandise—for cash or on account—that is for resale to customers. Each order is documented by an invoice for Walmart. Keep in mind that Merchandise Inventory is the cost of bringing the merchandise into the store, not the price at which the merchandise will be sold to customers. Let's assume that on July 9 Walmart bought flat-screen TVs from Sony Corp. for $7,000 with terms 2/10, n/30. Walmart would record the purchase as shown in Figure 10.19.

FIGURE 10.19
Purchase Inventory on Account

Analysis:	Merchandise Inventory	A	↑	Dr.	$7,000
	Accounts Payable	L	↑	Cr.	$7,000

Journal Entry:	Jul.	9	Merchandise Inventory		7 0 0 0 00	
			Accounts Payable/Sony			7 0 0 0 00
			Purchased inventory on account			
			from Sony 2/10, n/30			

Keep in mind that not all purchases will go to Merchandise Inventory. Walmart will buy supplies, equipment, and so forth that are not for resale to customers. These amounts will be debited to the specific account from Moore Co. For example, if Walmart bought $5,000 of shelving equipment on account for its store on November 9, the transaction would be recorded as in Figure 10.20.

FIGURE 10.20
Purchasing of Equipment on Account

Analysis:	Shelving Equipment	A	↑	Dr.	$5,000
	Accounts Payable	L	↑	Cr.	$5,000

Journal Entry:	Nov.	9	Shelving Equipment		5 0 0 0 00	
			Accounts Payable/Moore Co.			5 0 0 0 00
			Purchased equipment on account			

What happens if Walmart finds a defective TV among its purchase from Sony?

Recording Purchases Returns and Allowances Because on July 14 Walmart noticed a damaged TV in the shipment, it issues a debit memorandum. This document notifies Sony, the supplier, that Walmart is reducing what is owed Sony by $600, the cost of the TV (to bring it into the store) and that the TV is being returned. On Walmart's books the analysis and journal entry in Figure 10.21 results.

Analysis:	Accounts Payable	L	↓	Dr.	$600
	Merchandise Inventory	A	↓	Cr.	$600

FIGURE 10.21
Recording a Debit Memorandum

Journal Entry:		Jul.	14	Accounts Payable/Sony	6 0 0 00		
				Merchandise Inventory		6 0 0 00	
				To record debit memo no. 10			

Note that the cost of merchandise inventory has been reduced by $600 due to the return. In the perpetual inventory system there is no purchases, returns, and allowances title. The reduction in cost from the return is recorded *directly* into the Merchandise Inventory account. Let's now look at how Walmart would record any cash discounts it receives due to payment of the Sony bill within the discount period.

Recording Purchase Discounts   Let's assume that Walmart pays Sony within the first 10 days. Keep in mind that we take no discounts on returned goods (the $600 return). The amount of purchase discount will be recorded as a reduction to the cost of merchandise inventory. Figure 10.22 shows the analysis and journal entry on July 16. A discount lowers the cost of inventory.

Analysis:	Accounts Payable	L	↓	Dr.	$6,400
	Cash	A	↓	Cr.	$6,272
	Merchandise Inventory	A	↓	Cr.	$ 128

FIGURE 10.22
Recording a Purchase Discount

($7,000 – $600 Return)

Journal Entry:		Jul.	16	Accounts Payable/Sony	6 4 0 0 00		
				Cash		6 2 7 2 00	
				Merchandise Inventory		1 2 8 00	

2% × $6,400

Keep in mind that had Walmart missed the discount period, it would have debited $6,400 to Accounts Payable and credited Cash for $6,400. Merchandise Inventory would not be reduced.

Recording Cost of Freight   The cost of freight ($300) is to be paid by Walmart. When the purchaser is responsible for cost of freight, it is added to the cost of merchandise inventory. If the cost of freight is paid by the seller, it could be recorded in an operating expense account called Freight-Out. Figure 10.23 is the analysis and journal entry for freight on July 10.

Analysis:	Merchandise Inventory	A	↑	Dr.	$300
	Cash	A	↓	Cr.	$300

FIGURE 10.23
Recording Cost of Freight

Freight Cost added to Merchandise Inventory

Journal Entry:		Jul.	10	Merchandise Inventory	3 0 0 00		
				Cash		3 0 0 00	
				Payment of freight			

Walmart: The Seller   Now let's look at Walmart as the *seller* of merchandise.

Recording Sales at Walmart   Sales revenues are earned at Walmart when the goods are transferred to the buyer. The earned revenue can be for cash and/or credit. Let's look at the following example of the sale of a TV at Walmart for $950 on credit to customer Jones on August 10, which cost Walmart $600. Keep in mind when using the perpetual inventory system that at the time of the earned sale Walmart will do the following:

At selling price ⟶	1. Record the sales (cash and/or credit).
At cost ⟶	2. Record the cost of the inventory sold and the reduction in inventory.

First, let's analyze the transaction in Figure 10.24. Note that we will have two entries, one to record the sale and one to show a new cost and less inventory on hand.

FIGURE 10.24
Recording Sales and Cost of Goods Sold

Selling Price <	Accounts Receivable	Asset	↑	Dr.	$950
	Sales	Revenue	↑	Cr.	$950
Cost to < Make sale	Cost of Goods Sold	Cost	↑	Dr.	$600
	Merchandise Inventory	Asset	↓	Cr.	$600

Journal Entries:

Aug.	10	Accounts Receivable/Jones	950 00	
		Sales		950 00
		Charge sales		
	10	Cost of Goods Sold	600 00	
		Merchandise Inventory		600 00
		To record cost of		
		merchandise sold on account		

Be sure to go back to steps 1 and 2 of Figure 10.17. These two steps reinforce the preceding journal entries. Remember that if the sale were a cash sale, we would have debited Cash instead of Accounts Receivable. Note also that the Sales account only records sales of goods held for resale.

How Walmart Records Sales Returns Allowances and Sales Discounts   Keep in mind that we are now looking at how the *seller* of merchandise records a transaction giving the customer a credit due to an allowance or a return of goods from a previous sale. Usually, the seller will issue a *credit memorandum*, a document informing the customer of the adjustment due to the return or allowance. For example, let's look at a customer, Smith Co., who returned a $950 TV on August 15 that had been purchased at Walmart. On Walmart's books, the analysis and journal entry in Figure 10.25 resulted.

The first entry records the return at the original selling price using the contra-revenue account Sales Returns and Allowances. The second entry records putting the inventory back in Walmart's books at cost and reducing its Cost of Goods Sold because the inventory was not sold. Remember that we only record the Cost of Goods Sold when the sale has been earned. Keep in mind that if the customer kept the TV but at a reduced price, no entry affecting Merchandise Inventory and Cost of Goods Sold would be needed.

FIGURE 10.25
Return of Goods

The Analysis: at Selling Price	Sales Returns and Allowances	Contra-Revenue	↑	Dr.	$950
	Accounts Receivable	Asset	↓	Cr.	$950
At Cost	Merchandise Inventory	Asset	↑	Dr.	$600
	Costs of Goods Sold	Cost	↓	Cr.	$600

Journal Entries:

Aug.	15	Sales Returns and Allowances		9 5 0 00			
		Accounts Receivable*/Smith Co.				9 5 0 00	
		Returned goods					
	15	Merchandise Inventory		6 0 0 00			
		Cost of Goods Sold				6 0 0 00	

*If it were a *cash* customer, cash would be credited.

Let's assume a customer, Smith Co., on August 25 gets a 2% discount for paying for a $950 TV early. The analysis and entry in Figure 10.26 would result on the seller's book:

FIGURE 10.26
Recording Sales Discount

The Analysis:	Cash	Asset	↑	Dr.	$931
	Sales Discount	Contra-Revenue	↑	Dr.	$ 19
	Accounts Receivable	Asset	↓	Cr.	$950

Journal Entry:

Aug.	25	Cash		9 3 1 00			
		Sales Discount		1 9 00			
		Accounts Receivable/Smith Co.				9 5 0 00	

Now let's summarize (Figure 10.27) all the entries for both the buyer and the seller (in this case, Walmart).

FIGURE 10.27

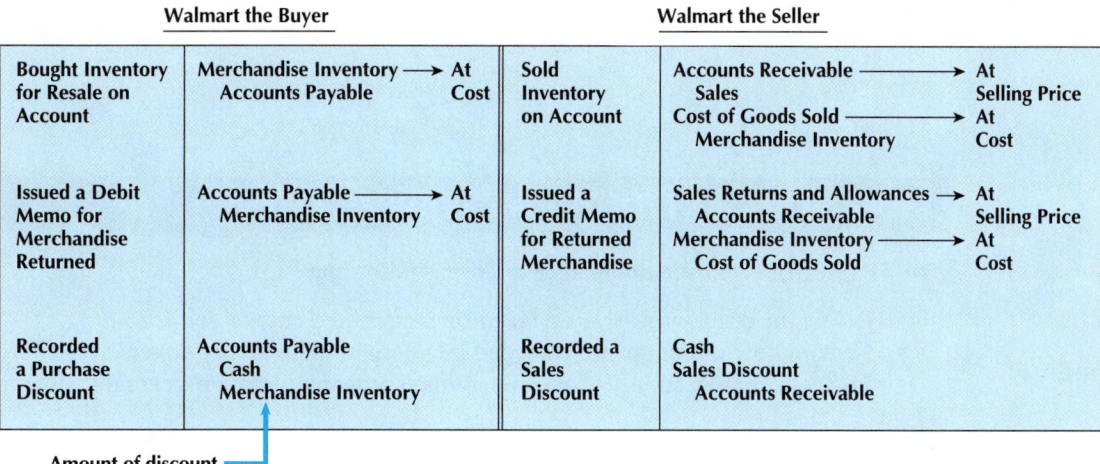

	Walmart the Buyer			Walmart the Seller	
Bought Inventory for Resale on Account	Merchandise Inventory → At Accounts Payable Cost		Sold Inventory on Account	Accounts Receivable ────→ At Sales Selling Price Cost of Goods Sold ──→ At Merchandise Inventory Cost	
Issued a Debit Memo for Merchandise Returned	Accounts Payable ───→ At Merchandise Inventory Cost		Issued a Credit Memo for Returned Merchandise	Sales Returns and Allowances → At Accounts Receivable Selling Price Merchandise Inventory ───→ At Cost of Goods Sold Cost	
Recorded a Purchase Discount	Accounts Payable Cash Merchandise Inventory		Recorded a Sales Discount	Cash Sales Discount Accounts Receivable	

Amount of discount ──→

Figure 10.28 shows a comparison of Perpetual and Periodic Systems.

FIGURE 10.28 Comparison of Perpetual and Periodic Systems

Transaction	Perpetual System	Periodic System
(A) Sold merchandise that cost $8,000 on account for $20,000.	Accts. Receivable 20 000 00 Sales 20 000 00 Cost of Goods Sold 8 000 00 Merch. Inventory 8 000 00	Accts. Receivable 20 000 00 Sales 20 000 00
(B) Purchased $900 of merchandise on account.	Merch. Inventory 9 00 00 Accts. Payable 9 00 00	Purchases 9 00 00 Accts. Payable 9 00 00
(C) Paid $50 freight charges.	Merch. Inventory 50 00 Cash 50 00	Freight-In 50 00 Cash 50 00
(D) Cash customer returned $200 of merchandise. Cost of merchandise was $100.	Sales Ret. & Allow. 2 00 00 Cash* 2 00 00 Merch. Inventory 1 00 00 Cost of Goods Sold 1 00 00	Sales Ret. & Allow. 2 00 00 Cash* 2 00 00
(E) Returned $400 of merchandise previously bought on account because of defects.	Accts. Payable 4 00 00 Merch. Inventory 4 00 00	Accts. Payable 4 00 00 Pur. Ret. & Allow. 4 00 00

* or Accounts Receivable if made to charge customers

LEARNING UNIT 10-4 REVIEW

AT THIS POINT you should be able to do the following:

- Define the terms *merchandise inventory*, *sales*, and *cost of goods sold*.
- Explain how discounts are recorded in a perpetual inventory system.
- Journalize transactions for a merchandise company using a perpetual system.

Instant Replay ◉ Self-Review Quiz 10-4

Pete's Clock Shops completed the following merchandise transactions in the month of June:

201X			
Jun.	1	Purchased merchandise on account from Clock Suppliers, $4,000; terms 2/10, n/30.	
	3	Sold merchandise on account, $2,000; terms 2/10, n/30. The cost of the merchandise sold was $1,200.	
	4	Received credit from Clock Suppliers for merchandise returned, $400.	
	10	Received collections in full, less discounts, from June 3 sales.	
	11	Paid Clock Suppliers in full, less discount.	
	14	Purchased office equipment for cash, $500.	
	15	Purchased $2,800 of merchandise from Abe's Distribution for cash.	
	16	Received a refund because of defective merchandise from supplier on cash purchase of $400.	
	17	Purchased merchandise from Rose Corp., $6,000, free on board shipping point (buyer pays freight); terms 2/10, n/30. Freight to be paid on June 20.	
	18	Sold merchandise for $3,000 cash; the cost of the merchandise sold was $1,600.	
	20	Paid freight on June 17 purchase, $180.	
	25	Purchased merchandise from Lee Co., $1,400, free on board destination (seller pays freight); terms 2/10, n/30.	
	26	Paid Rose Corp. in full, less discount.	
	27	Made refunds to cash customers for returned clocks, $300. The cost of the defective clocks was $120.	

Pete's Clock Shop accounts included the following:

Cash, 101; Accounts Receivable, 112; Merchandise Inventory, 120; Office Equipment, 124; Accounts Payable, 201; P. Rings, Capital, 301; Sales, 401; Sales Returns and Allowances, 411; Sales Discount, 412; Cost of Goods Sold, 501.

Journalize the transactions using a perpetual inventory system.

Solution to Instant Replay: Self-Review Quiz 10-4

	Date		Account Titles and Description	PR	Dr.	Cr.
			GENERAL JOURNAL			Page 2
201X						
Jun.	1		Merchandise Inventory		4 0 0 0 00	
			Accounts Payable			4 0 0 0 00
	3		Accounts Receivable		2 0 0 0 00	
			Sales			2 0 0 0 00
			Cost of Goods Sold		1 2 0 0 00	
			Merchandise Inventory			1 2 0 0 00
	4		Accounts Payable		4 0 0 00	
			Merchandise Inventory			4 0 0 00
	10		Cash		1 9 6 0 00	
			Sales Discount		4 0 00	
			Accounts Receivable			2 0 0 0 00
	11		Accounts Payable		3 6 0 0 00	
			Cash			3 5 2 8 00
			Merchandise Inventory			7 2 00
	14		Office Equipment		5 0 0 00	
			Cash			5 0 0 00
	15		Merchandise Inventory		2 8 0 0 00	
			Cash			2 8 0 0 00
	16		Cash		4 0 0 00	
			Merchandise Inventory			4 0 0 00
	17		Merchandise Inventory		6 0 0 0 00	
			Accounts Payable			6 0 0 0 00
	18		Cash		3 0 0 0 00	
			Sales			3 0 0 0 00
			Cost of Goods Sold		1 6 0 0 00	
			Merchandise Inventory			1 6 0 0 00
	20		Merchandise Inventory		1 8 0 00	
			Cash			1 8 0 00
	25		Merchandise Inventory		1 4 0 0 00	
			Accounts Payable			1 4 0 0 00
	26		Accounts Payable		6 0 0 0 00	
			Cash			5 8 8 0 00
			Merchandise Inventory			1 2 0 00
	27		Sales Returns and Allowances		3 0 0 00	
			Cash*			3 0 0 00
			Merchandise Inventory		1 2 0 00	
			Cost of Goods Sold			1 2 0 00

* If this were a charge customer it would have been Accounts Receivable.

BLUEPRINT: PERIODIC VERSUS PERPETUAL

Periodic	Perpetual
Purchases	Merchandise Inventory
Purchase Discounts	Merchandise Inventory
Sales/Accounts Receivable	Sales/Accounts Receivable Cost of Goods Sold/Merchandise Inventory
Freight-In	Merchandise Inventory
Sales Discounts	Sales Discounts
Sales Returns and Allowances	Sales Returns and Allowances

ACCOUNTING COACH

CHAPTER 10

The following Coaching Tips are from Learning Units 10-1 to 10-4. Take the Pre-Game Checkup and use the Check Your Score at the bottom of the page to see how you are doing. The Accounting Coach provides tips before each Checkup to help you avoid common accounting errors.

LU 10-1 Chou's Toy Shop: Buyers View of a Merchandise Company

Pre-Game Tips: Merchandise for resale to customers is called a purchase. The Purchases account is a cost that will be shown on the income statement. This cost works just like expenses but is directly related to bringing the goods for resale into the store. Purchases Returns and Allowances and Purchases Discounts are contra-cost accounts that will be recorded on the income statement. If shipping terms are FOB destination the seller will pay the cost of freight.

Pre-Game Checkup

Answer true or false to the following statements.

1. The normal balance of Purchases is a debit.
2. Purchases Discounts is a cost.
3. F.O.B. shipping point means that the seller of the goods is responsible for covering the shipping costs.
4. An increase in Purchases Returns and Allowances is a credit.
5. A credit memorandum received will result in an increase in Accounts Payable.

LU 10-2 Recording and Posting Purchases Transactions on Account for Art's Wholesale Clothing Company; Introduction to Subsidiary Ledgers and Debit Memorandum

Pre-Game Tips: The accounts payable subsidiary ledger lists the amounts owed to each customer. It is just the opposite of the accounts receivable subsidiary ledger. The normal balance of the accounts payable subsidiary ledger is a credit. The controlling account, Accounts Payable, is located in the general ledger. The cost of freight is recorded in the Freight-In account, which represents a cost of freight. It has a debit balance. A debit memorandum means the buyer does not owe as much and thus Accounts Payable is reduced and a purchases returns and allowances results. The debit memorandum also reduces what is owed to the customer in the subsidiary ledger.

Pre-Game Checkup

Answer true or false to the following statements.

1. Purchases Returns and Allowances is increased by a debit.
2. Freight-In is a cost that will be shown on the income statement.
3. The controlling account, Accounts Payable, is located in the subsidiary ledger.
4. The normal balance of each customer in the accounts payable subsidiary ledger is a credit.
5. Debit memorandums are issued by the seller.

LU 10-3 Recording and Posting Cash Payments Transactions for Art's Wholesale: Schedule of Accounts Payable

Pre-Game Tips: When a cash payment is made within the discount period from a charge purchase the result is a debit to Accounts Payable and the Subsidiary account and a credit to Purchases Discounts and Cash. Remember that Purchases Discounts is a contra-cost account with a normal credit balance. At the end of the month the total from the schedule of accounts payable should equal the ending balance in Accounts Payable, the controlling account.

Pre-Game Checkup

Answer true or false to the following statements.

1. Purchases Discounts is a contra-revenue account.
2. The schedule of accounts payable is listed by debits and credits.
3. An increase in Purchases Discounts is made by debiting the account.
4. Purchases Discounts are shown on the balance sheet.
5. The normal balance of each customer in the accounts payable subsidiary ledger is a debit.

LU 10-4 Introduction to a Merchandise Company Using a Perpetual Inventory System

Pre-Game Tips: In a perpetual inventory system, all purchases of inventory are recorded in an asset account called Merchandise Inventory. The cost of selling inventory is recorded in the Cost of Goods Sold account. When a sale is made, the company gets cash and/or accounts receivable and a sale is shown. At the same time, the company records the cost of goods to Inventory Sold along with a reduction in Merchandise Inventory since it is sold. Returns to the seller will increase the Merchandise Inventory account. If a seller pays for the cost of freight, it is added to the cost of merchandise inventory.

Pre-Game Checkup

Answer true or false to the following statements.

1. In the perpetual system there are no Purchases, Purchases Discounts, or Purchases Returns and Allowances accounts.

2. The Sales Discount account is not used in a perpetual accounting system.
3. Cost of freight results in a decrease to Merchandise Inventory.
4. Sales plus cost of goods sold equals gross profit.
5. Perpetual systems do not record cash sales.

CHECK YOUR SCORE: Answers to the Pre-Game Checkup

LU 10-1

1. True.
2. False—Purchases Discounts is a contra-cost.
3. False—F.O.B. shipping point means that the buyer of the goods is responsible for covering the shipping costs.
4. True.
5. False—A credit memorandum received by the purchaser will result in a decrease in Accounts Payable.

LU 10-2

1. False—Purchases Returns and Allowances is increased by a credit.
2. True.
3. False—The controlling account, Accounts Payable, is located in the general ledger.
4. True.
5. False—Debit memorandums are issued by the buyer.

LU 10-3

1. False—Purchases Discounts is a contra-cost account.
2. False—The schedule of accounts payable contains no debits or credits.
3. False—An increase in Purchases Discounts is made by crediting the account.
4. False—Purchases Discounts are shown on the income statement.
5. False—The normal balance of each customer in the accounts payable subsidiary ledger is a credit.

LU 10-4

1. True.
2. False—The Sales Discount account is used in a perpetual accounting system.
3. False—Cost of freight results in an increase to Merchandise Inventory because it increases the cost of the inventory.
4. False—Sales minus cost of goods sold equals gross profit.
5. False—Perpetual systems record both cash and charge sales.

Chapter Summary

MyAccountingLab

Here are all the key concepts and equations to help you understand the concepts of this chapter and prepare you for your exam. After completing this review, go to MyAccountingLab for more practice opportunities.

Concepts You Should Know	Key Terms
L01 **Recording and posting purchase transactions.** 1. Purchases are merchandise for resale. The Purchases account is a cost. 2. Purchases Returns and Allowances and Purchases Discounts are contra-costs. 3. F.O.B. shipping point means that the purchaser of the goods is responsible for covering the shipping costs. 4. Purchases discounts are not taken on freight.	F.O.B. destination (p. 370) F.O.B. shipping point (p. 370) Invoice approval form (p. 373) Purchases (p. 368) Purchases Discount (p. 369) Purchase order (p. 372) Purchase invoice (p. 372) Purchases Returns and Allowances (p. 368) Purchase requisition (p. 372) Receiving report (p. 372)

L02 **Recording to accounts payable subsidiary ledger.**
 	
1. The steps for buying merchandise from a company may include the following:
  a. The requesting department prepares a purchase requisition.
  b. The purchasing department prepares a purchase order.
  c. The seller receives the order and prepares a sales invoice (a purchase invoice from the buyer).
  d. The buyer receives the goods and prepares a receiving report.
  e. The accounting department verifies and approves the invoice for payment.
2. The accounts payable subsidiary ledger, organized in alphabetical order, is not in the same book as Accounts Payable, the controlling account in the general ledger.
	Accounts payable subsidiary ledger (p. 373)

L03 **Preparing, journalizing, and posting a debit memorandum.** 1. A debit memorandum (issued by the buyer) indicates that the amount owed from a previous purchase is being reduced because some goods were defective or not up to a specific standard and thus were returned or an allowance requested.	Debit memorandum (p. 376)

Recording and posting cash payment transactions.   ● **L04**

1. All payments of cash (check) are recorded in the general journal.

2. At the end of the month, the schedule of accounts payable, a list of ending amounts owed individual creditors, should equal the ending balance in Accounts Payable, the controlling account in the general ledger.

Preparing a schedule of accounts payable.   Controlling account   ● **L05**
                                                        (p. 380)

1. The schedule of accounts payable is a list of ending amounts owed individual creditors.

2. At the end of the month, the total amount on the schedule should equal the ending balance in Accounts Payable, the controlling account in the general ledger.

Journalizing transactions for a perpetual accounting system.   Cost of goods sold   ● **L06**
                                                                    (p. 383)

1. In a perpetual inventory system, whenever a sale is recognized, the cost of goods sold and merchandise inventory must be updated.   **Merchandise Inventory** (p. 383)

2. Purchases discounts or returns are reflected directly in the Merchandise Inventory account (a debit) for a perpetual inventory system.   **Periodic inventory system** (p. 383)

Perpetual inventory system (p. 383)

Discussion Questions and Critical Thinking/Ethical Case

1. Explain how net purchases is calculated.

2. What is the normal balance of Purchases Discount?

3. What is a contra-cost?

4. Explain the difference between F.O.B. shipping point and F.O.B. destination.

5. F.O.B. destination means that title to the goods will switch to the buyer when goods are shipped. Do you agree or disagree? Why?

6. What is the normal balance of each creditor in the accounts payable subsidiary ledger?

7. Why could the balance of the controlling account, Accounts Payable, equal the sum of the accounts payable subsidiary ledger during the month?

8. What is the relationship between a purchase requisition and a purchase order?

9. What purpose could a typical invoice approval form serve?

10. Explain the difference between merchandise and equipment.

11. Why would the purchaser issue a debit memorandum?

12. Explain why a trade discount is not a cash discount.

13. What new account is used in a perpetual system compared to the periodic system?

14. What is the normal balance of cost of goods sold?

15. How are discounts recorded in a perpetual system?

16. Spring Co. bought merchandise from All Co. with terms 2/10, n/30. Joanne Ring, the bookkeeper, forgot to pay the bill within the first 10 days. She went to Mel Ryan, the head accountant, who told her to backdate the check so that it looked like the bill was paid within the discount period. Joanne told Mel that she thought they could get away with it. Should Joanne and Mel backdate the check to take advantage of the discount? You make the call. Write down your specific recommendations to Joanne.

MyAccountingLab

Concept Checks

Questions 1–6 are based on a periodic inventory system.

Questions 7–10 are based on a perpetual inventory system.

⬤⬤⬤ **L01, 2, 3** *(10 MIN)*   **Accounts for Purchase Activities**

1. Complete the following table:

To the Seller		To the Buyer
Sales	↔	a. *Purchases*
Sales returns and allowances	↔	b. *Purchase Returns + Allow*
Sales discount	↔	c. *Purchase Discount*
Credit memorandum	↔	d. *Debit Memo*
Schedule of accounts receivable	↔	e. *Sched. of Accts Payable*
Accounts receivable subsidiary ledger	↔	f. *Accts Payable sub ledger*

✳ *Cost of Goods Sold = Expense*

Accounts

● **LO1** *(5 MIN)*

2. Complete the following table:

Account	Category	↑↓	Temporary or Permanent
Purchases			
Purchases Returns and Allowances			
Purchases Discount			

Calculating Net Purchases

● **LO1** *(5 MIN)*

3. Calculate Net Purchases from the following: Purchases, $30; Purchases Returns and Allowances, $4; Purchases Discounts, $1.

General Journal, Recording, and Posting

●●● **LO1, 2, 3** *(10 MIN)*

4. Match the following to the three business transactions (more than one number can be used).

   1. Recorded to the accounts payable subsidiary ledger.

   2. Recorded to the general journal.

   3. Posted to the general ledger.

   _____ a. Bought merchandise on account from Strong.com, invoice no. 12, $160.

   _____ b. Bought equipment on account from Lee Co., invoice no. 13, $150.

   _____ c. Issued debit memo no. 1 to Strong.com for merchandise returned, $60, from invoice no. 12.

Journalizing Transactions

●● **LO1, 5** *(15 MIN)*

5. Journalize the following transactions:
   a. Issued credit memo no. 2, $44, to Pam Co.
   b. Cash sales, $184.
   c. Received check from Mark Co., $50, less 1% discount.
   d. Bought merchandise on account from Mellow Co., $36, invoice no. 20; terms 1/10, n/30.
   e. Cash purchase of merchandise, $230.
   f. Issued debit memo to Mellow Co., $12, for merchandise returned from invoice no. 20.

● **LO5** *(10 MIN)*

6. From the following prepare a schedule of Accounts Payable for Matthews.com for May 31, 201X:

Accounts Payable Subsidiary Ledger

Robertson Co.

Dr.	Cr.	
	55	5/7 GJ1

Brian Co.

	Dr.	Cr.	
5/25 GJ1	8	47	5/20 GJ1

General Ledger

Accounts Payable

	Dr.	Cr.	
5/31 GJ1	8	102	5/31 GJ1

● **LO6** *(15 MIN)*

7. Draw a seesaw similar to the one shown in Figure 10.18 and show a sale of $1,000 that cost the store $450. Be sure to label all the accounts.

L06 *(10 MIN)*   **8.** Bailey C. paid $190 to Porter Co. and received a $25 purchases discount. Journalize the entry.

L06 *(10 MIN)*   **9.** Pavel Morse returned $310 of merchandise to Lazlo Co. What would be the journal entry on the books of both the buyer and seller?

L06 *(10 MIN)*   **10.** Vintage Co. paid the cost of freight, $90. Journalize the transaction. Assume that Vintage Co. is the buyer.

MyAccountingLab

EXERCISES

Set A

Exercises 10A-1–10A-6 are based on a periodic inventory system.
    Exercises 10A-7–10A-10 are based on a perpetual inventory system.

L01 *(15 MIN)*   **10A-1.** From the general journal in Figure 10.29, record to the accounts payable subsidiary ledger and post to general ledger accounts as appropriate.

FIGURE 10.29

		GENERAL JOURNAL			Page 2
Date			PR	Dr.	Cr.
201X					
Jun. 3	Purchases			850 00	
		Accounts Payable, Avril.com			850 00
		Purchased merchandise on account			
	4	Purchases		600 00	
		Accounts Payable, Jill.com			600 00
		Purchased merchandise on account			
	8	Equipment		170 00	
		Accounts Payable, Pearl.com			170 00
		Bought equipment on account			

Partial Accounts Payable Subsidiary Ledger

Avril.com

Dr.	Cr.

Jill.com

Dr.	Cr.

Pearl.com

Dr.	Cr.

Partial General Ledger

Equipment 120

Dr.	Cr.

Accounts Payable 210

Dr.	Cr.

Purchases 510

Dr.	Cr.

L03 *(15 MIN)*   **10A-2.** On June 10, 201X, Even Co. issued debit memorandum no. 1 for $360 to Mango Co. for merchandise returned from invoice no. 312. Your task is to journalize, record, and post this transaction as appropriate.

L04, 5 *(20 MIN)*   **10A-3.** Journalize, record, and post when appropriate the following transactions into the general journal (p. 2) for Kaden's Clothing. All purchases discounts are 4/10, n/30. If using working papers, be sure to put in beginning balances.

Accounts Payable Subsidiary Ledger

Name	Balance	Invoice No.
A. Jenkins	$1,400	522
B. Foss	700	488
J. Lee	800	562
B. Rodgers	450	821

Partial General Ledger

Account	Balance
Cash 110	$3,500
Accounts Payable 210	3,350
Purchases Discount 511	
Advertising Expense 610	

201X

Apr. 1 Issued check no. 20 to A. Jenkins Company in payment of its March 28 invoice no. 522.

8 Issued check no. 21 to Fios Advertising in payment of its advertising bill, $98, no discount.

15 Issued check no. 22 to B. Foss in payment of his March 25 invoice no. 488.

10A-4. From Exercise 10A-3, prepare a schedule of accounts payable and verify that the total of the schedule equals the amount in the controlling account. ● **L05** *(10 MIN)*

10A-5. Record the following transaction in a transaction analysis chart for the buyer: Bought merchandise for $8,600 on account. Shipping terms were F.O.B. destination. The cost of shipping was $490. ● **L01** *(10 MIN)*

10A-6. Lucy Adams bought merchandise with a list price of $3,600. Lucy was entitled to a 25% trade discount as well as a 3% cash discount. What was Lucy's actual cost of buying this merchandise after the cash discount? ● **L01** *(10 MIN)*

10A-7. Journalize the following transactions: ● **L06** *(15 MIN)*

201X

Apr. 8 Purchased merchandise on account from Collins Supplies, $10,000; terms 2/10, n/30.

15 Sold merchandise on account, $6,500; terms 2/10, n/30. The cost of merchandise was $5,000.

20 Received credit from Collins Suppliers for merchandise returned, $110.

10A-8. Journalize the following transactions: ● **L06** *(15 MIN)*

201X

Jan. 4 Sold merchandise for $300 cash. The cost of merchandise was $250.

9 Purchased merchandise from Red Co., $3,500, free on board shipping (buyer pays freight); terms 3/10, n/30. Freight to be paid on January 20.

20 Paid freight on January 9 purchase, $70.

LO6 *(15 MIN)*

10A-9. Journalize the following transactions:

201X		
Apr.	5	Sold merchandise for $1,050 cash. The cost of the merchandise was $600.
	16	Made refunds to cash customers for defective merchandise, $90. The cost of defective merchandise was $30.

LO6 *(15 MIN)*

10A-10. Journalize the following transactions:

201X		
Jul.	8	Sold merchandise on account, $580, Ring; terms 4/10, n/30. Cost of merchandise was $310.
	12	Purchased office equipment on account from NHB Co., $1,900.
	13	Made refunds to cash customers, $240, for defective merchandise. The cost of defective merchandise was $40.

Set B

LO1 *(15 MIN)*

10B-1. From the general journal in Figure 10.30, record to the accounts payable subsidiary ledger and post to the general ledger accounts as appropriate.

FIGURE 10.30

	Journal Entry			
Date	Accounts	PR	Debit	Credit
201X				
Jun. 3	Purchases		910	
	Accounts Payable, Avril.com			910
	Purchased merchandise on account			
4	Purchases		590	
	Accounts Payable, Jill.com			590
	Purchased merchandise on account			
8	Equipment		150	
	Accounts Payable, Pearl.com			150
	Bought equipment on account			

Partial Accounts Payable Subsidiary Ledger

Avril.com

Dr.	Cr.

Jill.com

Dr.	Cr.

Pearl.com

Dr.	Cr.

Partial General Ledger

Equipment 120

Dr.	Cr.

Accounts Payable 210

Dr.	Cr.

Purchases 510

Dr.	Cr.

10B-2. On October 10, 201X, Barney Co. issued debit memorandum no. 1 for $420 to Mango Co. for merchandise returned from invoice no. 312. Your task is to journalize, record, and post this transaction as appropriate. Use the periodic inventory system.

L03 *(15 MIN)*

10B-3. Journalize, record, and post when appropriate the following transactions into the general journal for Kaden's Clothing. All purchases discounts are 3/10, n/30. Assume the periodic inventory system. If using working papers, be sure to put in beginning balances.

L04, 5 *(20 MIN)*

201X		
Apr.	1	Issued check no. 20 to A. Jenkins Company in payment of its March 28 invoice no. 522.
	8	Issued check no. 21 to Fios Advertising in payment of its advertising bill, $97, no discount.
	15	Issued check no. 22 to B. Foss in payment of its March 25 invoice no. 488.

Accounts Payable Subsidiary Ledger

Name	Balance	Invoice No.
A. Jenkins	$500	522
B. Foss	100	488
J. Lee	400	562
B. Rodgers	50	821

Partial General Ledger

Account	Balance
Cash 110	$2,800
Accounts Payable 210	1,050
Purchases Discount 511	
Advertising Expense 610	

10B-4. From Exercise 10B-3, prepare a schedule of accounts payable and verify that the total of the schedule equals the amount in the controlling account.

L05 *(10 MIN)*

10B-5. Record the following transaction in a transaction analysis chart for the buyer: Bought merchandise for $9,100 on account. Shipping terms were F.O.B. destination. The cost of shipping was $460. Assume the periodic inventory system.

L01 *(10 MIN)*

10B-6. Mike Dolan bought merchandise with a list price of $3,000. Angie was entitled to a 30% trade discount as well as a 4% cash discount. What was Mike's actual cost of buying this merchandise after the cash discount?

L01 *(10 MIN)*

10B-7. Journalize the following transactions. Assume a perpetual inventory system.

L06 *(15 MIN)*

201X		
Apr.	8	Purchased merchandise on account from Young Supplies, $20,000; terms 4/10, n/30.
	15	Sold merchandise on account, $4,000; terms 4/10, n/30. The cost of merchandise was $2,500.
	20	Received credit from Young Supplies for merchandise returned, $200.

● **LO6** *(15 MIN)*

10B-8. Journalize the following transactions. Assume the perpetual inventory system.

201X		
Jan.	4	Sold merchandise for $750 cash. The cost of merchandise was $200.
	9	Purchased merchandise from Rare Co., $2,700, free on board shipping (buyer pays freight); terms 1/10, n/30. Freight to be paid on January 20.
	20	Paid freight on January 9 purchase, $70.

● **LO6** *(15 MIN)*

10B-9. Journalize the following transactions. Assume the perpetual inventory system.

201X		
Apr.	5	Sold merchandise for $1,450 cash. The cost of the merchandise was $725.
	16	Made refunds to cash customers for defective merchandise, $65. The cost of defective merchandise was $30.

● **LO6** *(15 MIN)*

10B-10. Journalize the following transactions. Assume a perpetual inventory system.

201X		
Jul.	8	Sold merchandise on account, $640, Ring; terms 2/10, n/30. Cost of merchandise was $380.
	12	Purchased office equipment on account from TRE Co., $1,300.
	13	Made refunds to cash customers, $150, for defective merchandise. The cost of defective merchandise was $35.

Problems

Set A

●● **LO1, 2** *(30 MIN)*

10A-1. Rodney Fey recently opened Rodney's Skate Shop. As the bookkeeper of the company, please journalize, record, and post when appropriate the following transactions (account numbers are Store Supplies, 115; Store Equipment, 121; Accounts Payable, 210; Purchases, 510):

Check Figure:
Accounts payable ending Bal. $8,200
○————————————→

201X		
Jun.	4	Bought $800 of merchandise on account from Adams Co., invoice no. 442, dated June 5; terms 7/10, n/30.
	5	Bought $4,800 of store equipment from Norton Co., invoice no. 502, dated June 6.
	8	Bought $1,200 of merchandise on account from Rolo Co., invoice no. 401, dated June 9; terms 7/10, n/30.
	14	Bought $1,400 of store supplies on account from Adams Co., invoice no. 419, dated June 14.

●●● **LO1, 2, 5** *(45 MIN)*

10A-2. The following transactions occurred for Rachel's Natural Food. If using working papers, be sure to put in beginning balances.

201X		
Aug.	8	Purchased $800 of merchandise on account from Airon Co., invoice no. 400, dated August 9; terms 6/10, n/60.
	10	Purchased $1,100 of merchandise on account from Bixby Co., invoice no. 420, dated August 11; terms 6/10, n/60.

12   Purchased $500 of store supplies on account from Mixon Co., invoice no. 510, dated August 13.

14   Issued debit memo no. 8 to Airon Co. for merchandise returned, $400, from invoice no. 400.

17   Purchased $620 of office equipment on account from Ryan Co., invoice no. 810, dated August 18.

24   Purchased $500 of additional store supplies on account from Mixon Co., invoice no. 516, dated August 25; terms 6/10, n/30.

Check Figure:
Total schedule of accounts payable $5,470

Your tasks are to do the following:

1.   Journalize the transactions.
2.   Post and record as appropriate.
3.   Prepare a schedule of accounts payable.

Accounts Payable Subsidiary Ledger

Name	Balance
Airon Co.	$ 450
Bixby Co.	400
Mixon Co.	1,250
Ryan Co.	250

Partial General Ledger

Account	Number	Balance
Store Supplies	110	$ —
Office Equipment	120	—
Accounts Payable	210	2,350
Purchases	510	$16,000
Purchases Returns and Allowances	512	—

Check Figure:
Total of schedule of accounts payable $2,175

10A-3. Wendy Ellis operates a wholesale computer center. The account balances as of October 1, 201X, are as follows. If using working papers, be sure to put in beginning balances.

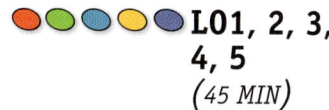**L01, 2, 3, 4, 5**
(45 MIN)

Accounts Payable Subsidiary Ledger

Name	Balance
Andrews Co.	$1,050
Hitch Co.	1,600
Seakale Co.	650
Zeke Co.	1,000

Check Figure:
Total of schedule of accounts payable $2,175

Partial General Ledger

Account	Number	Balance
Cash	110	$18,000
Delivery Truck	150	—
Accounts Payable	210	4,300
Computer Purchases	510	—
Computer Purchases Discount	511	—
Rent Expense	610	—
Utilities Expense	620	—

Your tasks are to do the following:

1. Journalize the following transactions.
2. Record to the accounts payable subsidiary ledger and post to the general ledger as appropriate.
3. Prepare a schedule of accounts payable.

201X		
Oct.	1	Paid half the amount owed Hitch Co. from previous purchases of appliances on account, less a 5% purchases discount, check no. 21.
	3	Bought a delivery truck for $9,500 cash, check no. 22, payable to Bill Brown Co.
	6	Bought computer merchandise from Lectro Co., check no. 23, $2,600.
	18	Bought additional computer merchandise from Proton Co., check no. 24, $900.
	24	Paid Zeke Co. the amount owed, less a 5% purchases discount, check no. 25.
	28	Paid rent expense to Prince's Realty Trust, check no. 26, $1,700.
	29	Paid utilities expense to Pumice Utility Co., check no. 27, $290.
	30	Paid half the amount owed Seakale Co., no discount, check no. 28.

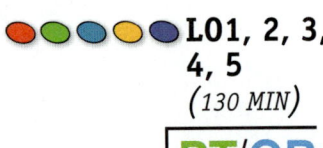

LO1, 2, 3, 4, 5

(130 MIN)

PT/QB

10A-4. Allison Cooper opened Allison's Toy House. As her newly hired accountant, your tasks are to do the following:

1. Journalize the transactions for the month of October.
2. Record to subsidiary ledgers and post to the general ledger as appropriate.
3. Prepare a schedule of accounts receivable and a schedule of accounts payable.

The following is the partial chart of accounts for Allison's Toy House:

Allison's Toy House Chart of Accounts

Assets		Revenue	
110	Cash	410	Toy Sales
112	Accounts Receivable	412	Sales Returns and Allowances
114	Prepaid Rent	414	Sales Discounts
121	Delivery Truck	**Cost of Goods**	
Liabilities		510	Toy Purchases
210	Accounts Payable	512	Purchases Returns and Allowances
Owner's Equity		514	Purchases Discount
310	A. Cooper, Capital	**Expenses**	
		610	Salaries Expense
		612	Cleaning Expense

Check Figures:
Total of accounts receivable account. $6,900
Total of accounts payable account. $9,200

201X		
Oct.	1	Allison Cooper invested $8,200 in the toy store.
	1	Paid three months' rent in advance, check no. 1, $3,000.
	1	Purchased merchandise from Sarah Harmitz Company on account, $3,800, invoice no. 410, dated October 2; terms 7/10, n/30.
	3	Sold merchandise to Robert Gibbs on account, $1,100, invoice no. 1; terms 7/10, n/30.
	6	Sold merchandise to Inez Tenenbaum on account, $700, invoice no. 2; terms 7/10, n/30.

8   Purchased merchandise from Sarah Harmitz Co. on account, $1,500, invoice no. 415, dated October 9; terms 7/10, n/30.

9   Sold merchandise to Robert Gibbs on account, $600, invoice no. 3; terms 7/10, n/30.

9   Paid cleaning service, check no. 2, $200.

10   Inez Tenenbaum returned merchandise that cost $300 to Allison's Toy House. Allison issued credit memorandum no. 1 to Inez Tenenbaum for $300.

10   Purchased merchandise from Lane Chipkin on account, $4,000, invoice no. 311, dated October 11; terms 6/15, n/60.

12   Paid Sarah Harmitz Co. invoice no. 410, dated October 2, check no. 3.

13   Sold $1,600 of toy merchandise for cash.

13   Paid salaries, $900, check no. 4.

14   Returned merchandise to Lane Chipkin in the amount of $1,500. Allison's Toy House issued debit memorandum no. 1 to Lane Chipkin.

15   Sold merchandise for $3,800 cash.

16   Received payment from Inez Tenenbaum, invoice no. 2 (less returned merchandise) less discount.

16   Robert Gibbs paid invoice no. 1.

16   Sold toy merchandise to Amanda Reader on account, $3,900, invoice no. 4; terms 7/10, n/30.

20   Purchased delivery truck on account from Sam Katz Garage, $3,100, invoice no. 111, dated October 21 (no discount).

22   Sold to Robert Gibbs merchandise on account, $1,000, invoice no. 5; terms 7/10, n/30.

23   Paid Lane Chipkin balance owed, check no. 5.

24   Sold toy merchandise on account to Amanda Reader, $1,700, invoice no. 6; terms 7/10, n/30.

25   Purchased toy merchandise, $500, check no. 6.

26   Purchased toy merchandise from William Smith on account, $4,600, invoice no. 211, dated October 27; terms 7/10, n/30.

28   Robert Gibbs paid invoice no. 5, dated October 22.

28   Amanda Reader paid invoice no. 6, dated October 24.

28   Allison invested an additional $5,500 in the business.

28   Purchased merchandise from Sarah Harmitz Co., $1,600, invoice no. 436, dated October 29; terms 7/10, n/30.

30   Paid Sarah Harmitz Co. invoice no. 436, check no. 7.

30   Sold merchandise to Bonnie Flow Company on account, $2,400, invoice no. 7; terms 7/10, n/30.

10A-5.   Jasmine's Toy Shop completed the following merchandise transactions in the month of April: ● **L06** *(40 MIN)*

201X

Apr.   2   Purchased merchandise on account from Westland Suppliers, $1,000; terms 1/10, n/30.

4   Sold merchandise on account, $600; terms 1/10, n/30. The cost of the merchandise sold was $300.

4   Received credit from Westland Suppliers for merchandise returned, $100.

10   Received collections in full, less discounts, from April 4 sales.

11   Paid Westland Suppliers in full, less discount.

(continued on next page)

14	Purchased store equipment for cash, $270.
15	Purchased $1,500 of merchandise from Collins Distribution for cash.
16	Received a refund due to defective merchandise from supplier on cash purchase of $100.
17	Purchased merchandise from Brown Corp., $5,000, free on board shipping point (buyer pays freight); terms 1/10, n/30. Freight to be paid on April 21.
18	Sold merchandise for $2,500 cash; the cost of merchandise sold was $1,500.
21	Paid freight on April 17 purchase, $90.
25	Purchased merchandise from Aster Co., $1,120, free on board destination (seller pays freight); terms 1/10, n/30.
26	Paid Brown Corp. in full, less discount.
27	Made refunds to cash customers for defective toys, $160. The cost of the defective toys was $90.

Jasmine's Toy Shop accounts included the following: Cash, 101; Accounts Receivable, 112; Merchandise Inventory, 120; Store Equipment; 124; Accounts Payable, 201; J. Jasmine, Capital, 301; Sales, 401; Sales Discounts, 412; Sales Returns and Allowances, 414; Cost of Goods Sold, 501.

Assignment
Journalize the transactions using a perpetual inventory system.

Set B

 **L01, 2** *(30 MIN)*   **10B-1.**   Rodney Fey recently opened Rodney's Skate Shop. As the bookkeeper of the company, please journalize, record, and post when appropriate the following transactions:

201X		
Jun.	4	Bought $700 of merchandise on account from Adams.com, invoice no. 442, dated June 5; terms 5/10, n/30.
	5	Bought $4,600 of store equipment from Norton Co., invoice no. 502, dated June 6.
	8	Bought $2,000 of merchandise on account from Rolo Co., invoice no. 401, dated June 9 terms 5/10, n/30.
	14	Bought $1,600 of store supplies on account from Adam.Com, invoice no. 419, dated June 14.

L01, 2, 5   **10B-2.**   As the accountant of Rachel's Natural Food Store (1) journalize the fol-
(45 MIN)   lowing transactions into the general journal (p. 2), (2) record and post as appropriate, and (3) prepare a schedule of accounts payable. If using working papers, be sure to put in the following balances: Airon Co. $250; Bixby Co. $750; Mixon Co. $1,200; Ryan Co. $400; Accounts Payable $2,600; Purchases $1,900.

201X		
Aug.	8	Purchased $700 of merchandise on account from Airon Co., invoice no. 400, dated August 9; terms 6/10, n/60.
	10	Purchased $1,350 of merchandise on account from Bixby Co., invoice no. 420, dated August 11; terms 6/10, n/60.
	12	Purchased $550 of store supplies on account from Mixon Co., invoice no. 510, dated August 13.
	14	Issued debit memo no. 8 to Airon Co. for merchandise returned, $450, from invoice no. 400.

17	Purchased $560 of office equipment on account from Ryan Co., invoice no. 810, dated August 18.
24	Purchased $850 of additional store supplies on account from Mixon Co., invoice no. 516, dated August 25; terms 6/10, n/30.

10B-3. Wendy Ellis operates a wholesale computer center and has hired you as her bookkeeper to record the following transactions. She would like you to (1) journalize the following transactions, (2) record to the accounts payable subsidiary ledger and post to the general ledger as appropriate, and (3) prepare a schedule of accounts payable. If using working papers, be sure to put in the following beginning balances: Andrews Co. $1,350; Hitch Co. $1,200; Seakate Co. $700; Cash $17,000; Accounts Receivable $4,650.

○○○○○**L01, 2, 3, 4, 5**
(45 MIN)

201X

Oct.	1	Paid half the amount owed Hitch Co. from previous purchases of appliances on account, less a 5% purchases discount, check no. 21.
	3	Bought a delivery truck for $6,500 cash, check no. 22, payable to Bob Singer Co.
	6	Bought computer merchandise from Lossy Co., check no. 23, $3,100.
	18	Bought additional computer merchandise from Proton Co., check no. 24, $650.
	24	Paid Zeke Co. the amount owed, less a 5% purchases discount, check no. 25.
	28	Paid rent expense to King's Realty Trust, check no. 26, $2,400.
	29	Paid utilities expense to Gravel Utility Co., check no. 27, $280.
	30	Paid half the amount owed Seakate Co., no discount, check no. 28.

Check Figure:
Total of schedule of accounts payable $2,300

10B-4. Allison Cooper opened Allison's Toy House. As her newly hired accountant, your tasks are to do the following:

1. Journalize the transactions for the month of October.
2. Record to subsidiary ledgers and post to the general ledger as appropriate.
3. Prepare a schedule of accounts receivable and a schedule of accounts payable.

(Use the same chart of accounts as in Problem 10A-4. The working papers that accompany this text have all the forms you need to complete this problem.)

○○○○○**L01, 2, 3, 4, 5**
(130 MIN)

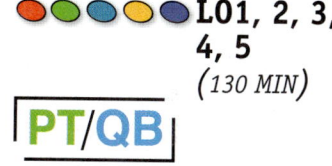

201X

Oct.	1	Allison Cooper invested $7,400 in the toy store.
	1	Paid three months' rent in advance, check no. 1, $2,900.
	1	Purchased merchandise from Sarah Harmitz Company on account, $3,700, invoice no. 410, dated October 2; terms 7/10, n/30.
	3	Sold merchandise to Robert Gibbs on account, $120, invoice no. 1; terms 7/10, n/30.
	6	Sold merchandise to Inez Tenenbaum on account, $800, invoice no. 2; terms 2/10, n/30.
	8	Purchased merchandise from Sarah Harmitz Co., $900, invoice no. 415, dated October 9; terms 7/10, n/30.
	9	Sold merchandise to Robert Gibbs on account, $100, invoice no. 3; terms 7/10, n/30.
	9	Paid cleaning service, check no. 2, $225.
	10	Inez Tenenbaum returned merchandise that cost $200 to Allison's Toy House. Allison issued credit memorandum no. 1 to Inez Tenenbaum for $200.

Check Figure:
Total of schedule of accounts receivable $7,600; of accounts payable $9,400

(continued on next page)

10	Purchased merchandise from Lane Chipkin on account, $3,700, invoice no. 311, dated October 11; terms 5/15, n/60.
12	Paid Lane Chipkin Co. invoice no. 410, dated October 2, check no. 3.
13	Sold $1,000 of toy merchandise for cash.
13	Paid salaries, $800, check no. 4.
14	Returned merchandise to Lane Chipkin in the amount of $1,400. Allison's Toy House issued debit memorandum no. 1 to Lane Chipkin.
15	Sold merchandise for $3,700 cash.
16	Received payment from Inez Tenenbaum, invoice no. 2 (less returned merchandise), less discount.
16	Robert Gibbs paid invoice no. 1.
16	Sold toy merchandise to Amanda Reader on account, $4,500, invoice no. 4; terms 7/10, n/30.
20	Purchased delivery truck on account from Sam Katz Garage, $3,100, invoice no. 111, dated October 21 (no discount).
22	Sold to Robert Gibbs merchandise on account, $500, invoice no. 5; terms 7/10, n/30.
23	Paid Lane Chipkin balance owed, check no. 5.
24	Sold toy merchandise on account to Amanda Reader, $1,600, invoice no. 6; terms 7/10, n/30.
25	Purchased toy merchandise, $1,200, check no. 6.
26	Purchased toy merchandise from Sanya Burger on account, $5,400, invoice no. 211, dated October 27; terms 7/10, n/30.
28	Robert Gibbs paid invoice no. 5, dated October 22.
28	Amanda Reader paid invoice no. 6, dated October 24.
28	Allison invested an additional $7,500 in the business.
28	Purchased merchandise from Sarah Harmitz Co., $1,500, invoice no. 436, dated October 29; terms 7/10, n/30.
30	Paid Sarah Harmitz Co. invoice no. 436, check no. 7.
30	Sold merchandise to Bonnie Flow Company on account, $3,000, invoice no. 7; terms 7/10, n/30.

⬤⬤⬤⬤⬤ **LO1, 2, 3, 4, 5**
(40 MIN)

10B-5. Julie's Toy Shop completed the following merchandise transactions in the month of April:

201X

Apr.		
	2	Purchased merchandise on account from Beech Suppliers, $4,000; terms 1/10, n/30.
	4	Sold merchandise on account $500; terms 1/10, n/30. The cost of the merchandise sold was $200.
	4	Received credit from Beech Suppliers for merchandise returned, $500.
	10	Received collections in full, less discounts, from April 4 sales.
	11	Paid Beech Suppliers in full, less discount.
	14	Purchased office equipment for cash, $350.
	15	Purchased $1,600 of merchandise from Kelly Distribution for cash.
	16	Received a refund due for defective merchandise from supplier on cash purchase of $115.
	17	Purchased merchandise from Roy Corp., $3,000, free on board shipping point (buyer pays freight); terms 1/10, n/30. Freight to be paid on April 21.
	18	Sold merchandise for $2,800 cash; the cost of the merchandise sold was $1,700.

Check Figure:
Journal entry for Apr. 21 transaction.

Dr. Merchandise inventory	$125
Cr. Cash	$125

21	Paid freight on April 17 purchase, $125.
25	Purchased merchandise from Roland Co., $1,150, free on board destination (seller pays freight); terms 1/10, n/30.
26	Paid Roy Corp., in full, less discount.
27	Made refunds to cash customers for defective toys, $210. The cost of the defective toys was $110.

Julie's Toy Shop accounts included the following: Cash, 101; Accounts Receivable, 112; Merchandise Inventory, 120; Office Equipment, 124; Accounts Payable, 201; B. Julie, Capital, 301; Sales, 401; Sales Discounts, 412; Sales Returns and Allowances, 414; Cost of Goods Sold, 501.

Assignment
Journalize the transactions using the perpetual inventory system.

Financial Report Problem

Reading the Kellogg's Annual Report
Go to http://investor.kelloggs.com/annuals.cfm, to access the Kellogg's 2010 Annual Report, and locate the balance sheet. How much has merchandise inventory increased from 2009 to 2010?

 **LO1** *(15 MIN)*

 **ON the Job**

MyAccountingLab

SANCHEZ COMPUTER CENTER

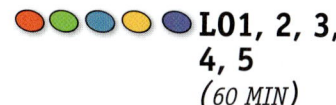 **LO1, 2, 3, 4, 5**
(60 MIN)

The following is an updated schedule of accounts payable as of January 31, 201X.

Schedule of Accounts Payable	
Office Depot	$ 50
System Design Furniture	1,400
Pac Bell	150
Multi Systems, Inc.	450
Total Accounts Payable	$ 2,050

Assignment

1. Journalize the transactions.

2. Record in the accounts payable subsidiary ledger and post to the general ledger as appropriate. A partial general ledger is included in the working papers that accompany this text.

3. The following accounts have been added to the chart of accounts: Purchases #6000, Purchase Returns and Allowances #6010, and Purchase Discounts #6020.

4. Prepare a schedule of accounts payable as of February 28, 201X.

The transactions for the month of February are as follows:

201X

Feb.

1	Prepaid the rent for the months of February, March, and April, $1,200, check #2585.
4	Bought merchandise on account from Multi Systems, Inc., purchase order no. 4010, $450; terms 3/10, n/30.
8	Bought office supplies on account from Office Depot, purchase order no. 4011, $250; terms n/30.
9	Purchased merchandise on account from Computer Connection, purchase order no. 4012, $500; terms 1/30, n/60.
15	Paid purchase order no. 4010 in full to Multi Systems, Inc., check #2586.
21	Issued debit memorandum no. 10 to Computer Connection for merchandise returned from purchase order no. 4012, $100.
27	Paid for office supplies, $50, check #2587.

PEACHTREE COMPUTER WORKSHOP

COMPUTERIZED ACCOUNTING APPLICATION FOR CHAPTER 10

Refresher on using Peachtree Complete Accounting

Before starting this assignment, you may want to refresh your memory by reading the following PDF documents in the multimedia library of the MyAccountingLab Web site. Remember to choose the PDF document for your version of Peachtree.

1. An Introduction to Peachtree Complete Accounting
2. Correcting Peachtree Transactions
3. How to Repeat or Restart a Peachtree Assignment
4. Backing Up and Restoring Your Work in Peachtree

You also should have completed the following workshops:

1. Workshop 1 Atlas Company from Chapter 3
2. Workshop 2 Zell Company from Chapter 4
3. Workshop 3 Sullivan Realty from Chapter 5
4. Workshop 4 Pete's Market from Chapter 8

Workshop 5:

PART A: Recording Transactions in the Sales, Receipts, Purchases, and Payments Journals

PART B: Accounting Cycle Mini Practice Set with Sales and Purchasing

PART A: In this part of the workshop, you will learn to record customer sales on account, customer credit memos, customer cash receipts, purchases from vendors on account, and payments to vendors for Mars Company using Peachtree. You will also print the aged receivables and aged payables reports and the sales journal, cash receipts journal, purchasing journal, and cash disbursement journals.

Instructions and the data file for completing Part A of the assignment are in the multimedia library of the MyAccountingLab Web site. Open the *Workshop 5 Part A Mars Company* PDF document for your version of Peachtree and download the *Mars Company* data file for your version of Peachtree.

PART B: In this part of the workshop you will complete a mini practice set of March accounting transactions for Abby's Toy House using Peachtree. Transactions include customer sales on account, customer credit memos, customer cash receipts, purchases from vendors on account, payments to vendors, and general journal entries in Peachtree. You will also print the aged receivables and aged payables reports and the general journal and general ledger reports.

Instructions and the data file for completing Part B of the assignment are in the multimedia library of the MyAccountingLab Web site. Open the *Workshop 5 Part B Abby's Toy House* PDF document for your version of Peachtree and download the *Abby's Toy House* data file for your version of Peachtree.

QUICKBOOKS COMPUTER WORKSHOP

COMPUTERIZED ACCOUNTING APPLICATION FOR CHAPTER 10

Refresher on Using QuickBooks Pro

Before starting this assignment, you may want to refresh your memory by reading the following PDF documents in the multimedia library of the MyAccountingLab Web site. Remember to choose the PDF document for your version of QuickBooks.

1. An Introduction to QuickBooks Pro
2. Correcting QuickBooks Transactions
3. How to Repeat or Restart a QuickBooks Assignment
4. Backing Up and Restoring Your Work in QuickBooks

You also should have completed the following workshops:

1. Workshop 1 Atlas Company from Chapter 3
2. Workshop 2 Zell Company from Chapter 4
3. Workshop 3 Sullivan Realty from Chapter 5
4. Workshop 4 Pete's Market from Chapter 8

Workshop 5:

PART A: Recording Transactions in the Sales, Receipts, Purchases, and Payments Journals

PART B: Accounting Cycle Mini Practice Set with Sales and Purchasing

PART A: In this part of the workshop, you will learn to record customer sales on account, customer credit memos, customer cash receipts, purchases from vendors on account, and payments to vendors for Mars Company using QuickBooks. You will also print the aged receivables and aged payables reports and the sales journal, cash receipts journal, purchasing journal, and cash disbursement journals.

Instructions and the data file for completing Part A of the assignment are in the multimedia library of the MyAccountingLab Web site. Open the *Workshop 5 Part A Mars Company* PDF document for your version of QuickBooks and download the *Mars Company* data file for your version of QuickBooks.

PART B: In this part of the workshop, you will complete a mini practice set of March accounting transactions for Abby's Toy House using QuickBooks. Transactions include customer sales on account, customer credit memos, customer cash receipts, purchases from vendors on account, payments to vendors, and general journal entries in Peachtree. You will also print the aged receivables and aged payables reports and the general journal and general ledger reports.

Instructions and the data file for completing Part B of the assignment are in the multimedia library of the MyAccountingLab Web site. **Open the Workshop 5 Part B Abby's Toy House** PDF document for your version of QuickBooks and download the *Abby's Toy House* data file for your version of QuickBooks.

Appendix A

SPECIAL JOURNALS WITH PROBLEM MATERIAL

LEARNING OBJECTIVES

● **1.** Identify which special journal or general journal will record a transaction.

● **2.** Record transactions in special journals or a general journal and post to subsidiary and general ledger accounts.

CLASSROOM DEMONSTRATION PROBLEM:
Periodic Method

●● **L01, 2**

DEMONSTRATION PROBLEM

Journalizing Transactions to Special Journals*; Posting to Subsidiary and General Ledger Accounts from Special Journals

All credit sales are 2/10, n/30. All merchandise purchased on account has 3/10, n/30 credit terms. Assume Periodic Inventory System. Ignore Sales Tax. The company uses Sales Journal, Purchases Journal, Cash Receipt and Cash Payment Journals as well as a General Journal.

Requirements:

1. Identify which special journal or if the general journal will be used to record a transaction.
2. Journalize transactions and post to subsidiary ledgers and general ledgers as appropriate.

201X

Mar.		
	1	J. Ling invested $2,000 into the business.
	1	Sold merchandise on account to Balder Co., $500, invoice no. 1.
	2	Purchased merchandise on account from Case Co., $500.
	4	Sold $2,000 of merchandise for cash.
	6	Paid Case Co. from previous purchases on account, check no. 1.
	8	Sold merchandise on account to Lewis Co., $1,000, invoice no. 2.
	10	Received payment from Balder for invoice no. 1.
	12	Issued a credit memorandum to Lewis Co. for $200 for faulty merchandise.
	14	Received payment from Lewis Co.
	16	Purchased merchandise on account from Noone Co., $1,000.
	17	Purchased equipment on account from Case Co., $300.
	18	Issued a debit memorandum to Noone Co. for $500 for defective merchandise.
	20	Paid salaries, $300, check no. 2.
	24	Paid Noone balance owed, check no. 3.

---

*All sales on account will go in a Sales Journal. Purchases on account will go in a Purchases Journal. Cash received will go in the Cash Receipts Journal and money paid out will go in the Cash Payments Journal. Transactions that do not fit into these special journals will go into the General Journal.

Demonstration Problem Solution

Part 1	Part 2	Demonstration Problem Complete

Identify which special journal or general journal will record a transaction.

Transaction	What to Do Step-by-Step

201X

Mar.

1   *Money Received:* Record in cash receipts journal. Post immediately to J. Ling, Capital, because it is in sundry.

1   *Sale on Account:* Record in sales journal. Record immediately to Balder Co. in accounts receivable subsidiary ledger. Place a ✓ in Post. Ref. column of sales journal when subsidiary is updated.

2   *Buy Merchandise on Account:* Record in purchases journal. Record to Case Co. immediately in the accounts payable subsidiary ledger.

4   *Money In:* Record in cash receipts journal. No posting needed (put an ✕ in Post. Ref. column).

6   *Money Out:* Record in cash payments journal. Save $15, which is a Purchases Discount. Record immediately to Case Co. in accounts payable subsidiary ledger (the full amount of $500).

8   *Sales on Account:* Record in sales journal. Update immediately to Lewis in accounts receivable subsidiary ledger.

10   *Money In:* Record in cash receipts journal. Because Balder pays within 10 days, it gets a $10 discount. Record the full amount immediately to Balder in the accounts receivable subsidiary ledger.

12   *Returns:* Record in general journal. Seller issues credit memo resulting in higher sales returns and customers owing less. All postings and recordings are done immediately.

14   *Money In:* Record in cash receipts journal:

$$\$1,000 - \$200 \text{ returns} = \$800$$
$$\times\ 0.02$$
$$\$\ 16 \text{ discount}$$

Record immediately the $800 to Lewis in the accounts receivable subsidiary ledger.

16   *Buy Now, Pay Later:* Record in purchases journal. Record immediately to Noone Co. in the accounts payable subsidiary ledger.

17   *Buy Now, Pay Later:* Record in purchases journal in Sundry. This item is not merchandise for resale. Record and post immediately.

18   *Returns:* Record in general ledger. Buyer issues a debit memo reducing the Accounts Payable due to purchases return and allowances. Post and record immediately.

20   *Salaries:* Record in cash payments journal, sundry column. Post immediately to Salaries Expense.

24   *Money Out:* Record in cash payments journal. Save 3% ($15), a purchases discount. Record immediately to accounts payable subsidiary ledger that you reduce Noone by $500.

Requirement 2

Record transactions in special journals or general journal and post to subsidiary and general ledger accounts.

Part 1	Part 2	Demonstration Problem Complete

Record accounts receivable subsidiary ledger immediately.

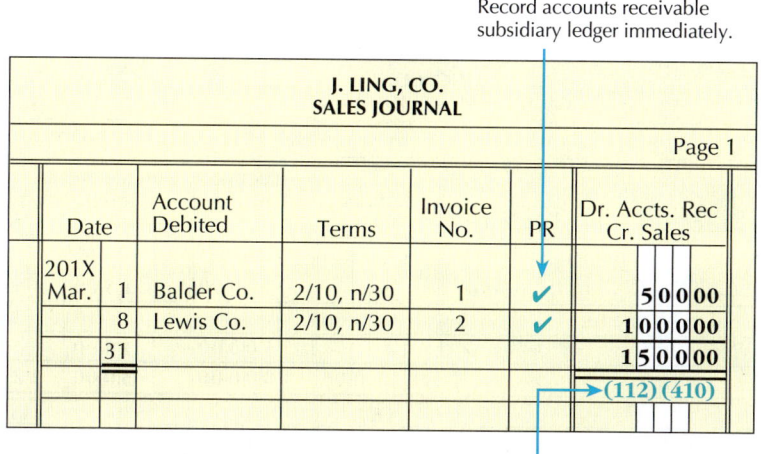

Total posted at end of month to these accounts.

COACHING TIP

Remember, the sales journal only records sales on account.

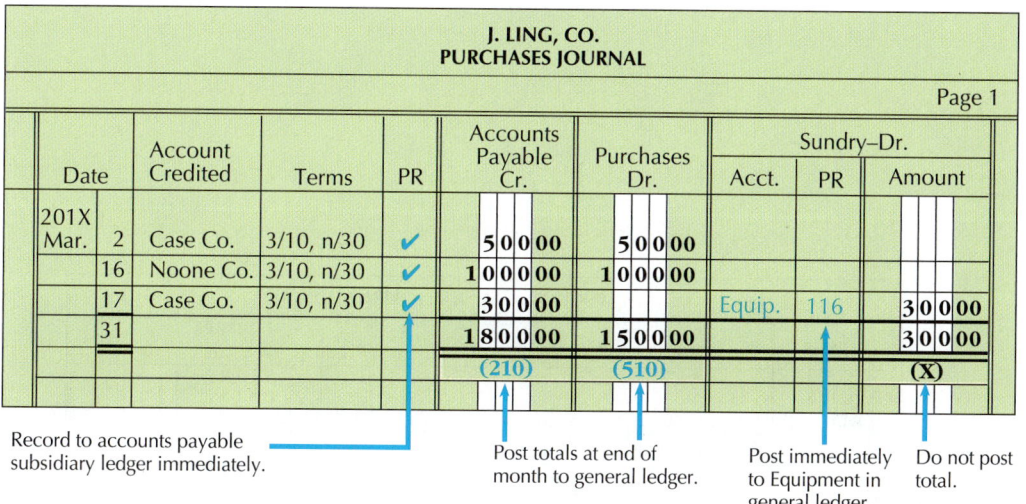

Record to accounts payable subsidiary ledger immediately.

Post totals at end of month to general ledger.

Post immediately to Equipment in general ledger.

Do not post total.

FIGURE A.2
Purchases Journal

COACHING TIP

Remember, the purchases journal records buy now, pay later transactions. Purchases are merchandise for resale, while equipment is not for resale.

Post to capital immediately.

FIGURE A.3
Cash Receipts Journal

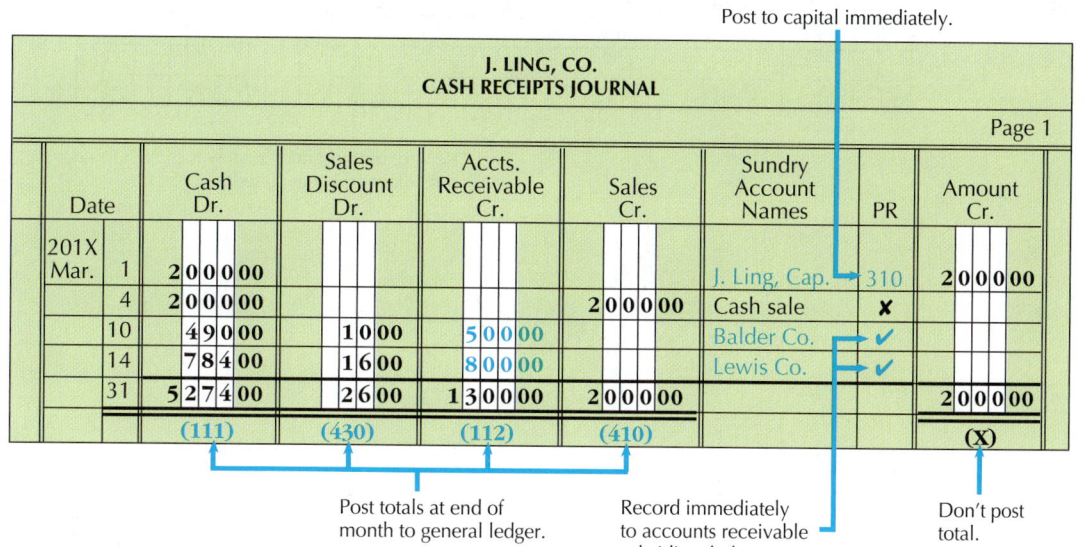

Post totals at end of month to general ledger.

Record immediately to accounts receivable subsidiary ledger.

Don't post total.

COACHING TIP

Remember, the cash receipts journal records any transaction that involves the receipt of cash.

FIGURE A.4
Cash Payments Journal

Record immediately to accounts
payable subsidiary ledger.

COACHING TIP

Remember, the cash
payment records only
transactions that result in
the payment of cash.

J. LING, CO. CASH PAYMENTS JOURNAL

Page 1

Date		Ck. No.	Account Debited	PR.	Sundry Dr.	Accounts Payable Dr.	Purchases Discount Cr.	Cash Cr.
201X Mar.	6	1	Case Co	✔		500 00	15 00	485 00
	20	2	Salaries Expense	610	300 00			300 00
	24	3	Noone Co.	✔		500 00	15 00	485 00
	31				300 00	1000 00	30 00	1270 00
					(X)	(210)	(530)	(111)

Post immediately to
Salaries Expense.

Do not
post total.

Post totals at end of month
to the general ledger.

FIGURE A.5
General Journal

COACHING TIP

Remember, transactions not fitting
into the four special journals are
recorded in the general journal.

J. LING, CO. GENERAL JOURNAL

Page 1

Date		Account Titles and Description	PR	Dr.	Cr.
201X Mar.	12	Sales Returns and Allowances	420	200 00	
		Accounts Receivable, Lewis Co.	112 ✔		200 00
		Issued credit memo			
	18	Accounts Payable, Noone Co.	210 ✔	500 00	
		Purchases Returns and Allowances	520		500 00
		Issued debit memo			

Record and post immediately to
subsidiary and general ledgers.

ACCOUNTS RECEIVABLE SUBSIDIARY LEDGER

Balder Company

Date	PR	Dr.	Cr.	Dr. Bal.
201X 3/1	SJ1	500		500
3/10	CRJ1		500	——

Lewis Company

Date	PR	Dr.	Cr.	Dr. Bal.
201X 3/8	SJ1	1,000		1,000
3/12	GJ1		200	800
3/14	CPJ1		800	——

ACCOUNTS PAYABLE SUBSIDIARY LEDGER

Case Company

Date	PR	Dr.	Cr.	Cr. Bal.
201X 3/2	PJ1		500	500
3/6	CPJ1	500		——
3/17	PJ1		300	300

Noone Company

Date	PR	Dr.	Cr.	Cr. Bal.
201X 3/16	PJ1		1,000	1,000
3/18	GJ1	500		500
3/24	CPJ1	500		——

FIGURE A.6
Subsidiary and General Ledgers

COACHING TIP

Note that in the accounts receivable subsidiary ledger (Dr. balance) customers owe the seller, while in the accounts payable subsidiary ledger (Cr. balance) the seller owes the vendors it purchased items from.

GENERAL LEDGER

Cash 111
3/31 CRJ1 5,274	1,270 3/31 CPJ1
Bal. 4,004	

Accounts Receivable 112
3/31 SJ1 1,500	200 3/12 GJ1
Bal. 0	1,300 3/31 CRJ1

Equipment 116
3/17 PJ1 300	

Accounts Payable 210
3/18 GJ1 500	1,800 3/31 PJ1
3/31 CPJ1 1,000	300 Bal.

J. Ling, Capital 310
	2,000 3/1 CRJ1

Sales 410
	1,500 3/31 SJ1
	2,000 3/31 CRJ1
	3,500 Bal.

Sales Returns and Allowances 420
3/12 GJ1 200	

Sales Discount 430
3/31 CRJ1 26	

Purchases 510
3/31 PJ1 1,500	

Purchase Returns and Allowances 520
	500 3/18 GJ1

Purchase Discount 530
	30 3/31 CPJ1

Salaries Expense 610
3/20 CPJ1 300	

COACHING TIP

Remember, in the General Ledger Accounts Receivable and Accounts Payable are the controlling accounts.

SUMMARY OF SOLUTION TIPS

Seller	Buyer
Sales journal	Purchases journal
Cash receipts journal	Cash payments journal
Sales (Cr.)	Purchases (Dr.)
Sales Returns and Allowances (Dr.)	Purchase Returns and Allowances (Cr.)
Sales Discounts (Dr.)	Purchase Discounts (Cr.)
Accounts Receivable (Dr.)	Accounts Payable (Cr.)
Accounts receivable subsidiary ledger	Accounts payable subsidiary ledger
Schedule of accounts receivable	Schedule of accounts payable
Issue a credit memo or receive a debit memo	Receive a credit memo or issue a debit memo

End of Month Post totals (except sundry) of special journal to the general ledger.

Note: In this problem at the end of the month, (1) Accounts Receivable in the general ledger, the controlling account, has a zero balance, as does each title in the accounts receivable subsidiary ledger, and (2) the balance in Accounts Payable (the controlling account) is $300. In the accounts payable subsidiary ledger, J. Ling owes Case $300. The sum of the accounts payable subsidiary ledger does equal the balance in the controlling account at the end of the month.

Part 1	Part 2	Demonstration Problem Complete

Appendix A Problems

A-1. Jill Blue opened Food.com, a wholesale grocery and pizza company. Since Jill Blue only sells to retailers, she does not have to charge sales tax to her customers. Jill Blue uses a sales journal for sales on account. The following transactions occurred in June:

201X

June	1	Sold grocery merchandise to Duncan Co. on account, $500, invoice no. 1.
	4	Sold pizza merchandise to Sue Moore Co. on account, $600, invoice no. 2.
	8	Sold grocery merchandise to Long Co. on account, $700, invoice no. 3.
	10	Issued credit memorandum no. 1 to Duncan Co. for $150 of grocery merchandise returned due to spoilage.
	15	Sold pizza merchandise to Sue Moore Co. on account, $160, invoice no. 4.
	19	Sold grocery merchandise to Long Co. on account, $300, invoice no. 5.
	25	Sold pizza merchandise to Duncan Co. on account, $1,200, invoice no. 6.

Check Figure:
Schedule of accounts
receivable $3,310

Required

1. Journalize the transactions in the appropriate journals.
2. Record to the accounts receivable subsidiary ledger and post to the general ledger as appropriate.
3. Prepare a schedule of accounts receivable.

A-2. The following transactions of Ted's Auto Supply occurred in November. Ted uses a sales journal to record sales on account (your working papers have balances as of November 1 for certain general ledger and accounts receivable ledger accounts):

201X

Nov.   1   Sold auto parts merchandise to R. Volan on account, $1,000, invoice no. 60, plus 5% sales tax.

      5   Sold auto parts merchandise to J. Seth on account, $800, invoice no. 61, plus 5% sales tax.

      8   Sold auto parts merchandise to Lance Corner on account, $9,000, invoice no. 62, plus 5% sales tax.

   10   Issued credit memorandum no. 12 to R. Volan for $500 for defective auto parts merchandise returned from Nov. 1 transaction. (Be careful to record the reduction in Sales Tax Payable as well.)

   12   Sold auto parts merchandise to J. Seth on account, $600, invoice no. 63, plus 5% sales tax.

Required

1. Journalize the transactions in the appropriate journals.
2. Record to the accounts receivable subsidiary ledger and post to the general ledger as appropriate.
3. Prepare a schedule of accounts receivable.

Check Figure:
Schedule of accounts receivable $13,045

A-3. Abby Kim recently opened Skates.com. Abby uses a purchases journal to record purchases on account. As the bookkeeper of her company, please journalize, record, and post when appropriate the following transactions (account numbers are Store Supplies, 115; Store Equipment, 121; Accounts Payable, 210; Purchases, 510):

201X

June   4   Bought $700 of merchandise on account from Mail.com, invoice no. 442, dated June 5; terms 2/10, n/30.

      5   Bought $4,000 of store equipment from Norton Co., invoice no. 502, dated June 6.

      8   Bought $1,400 of merchandise on account from Rolo Co., invoice no. 401, dated June 9; terms 2/10, n/30.

   14   Bought $900 of store supplies on account from Mail.com, invoice no. 419, dated June 14.

Check Figure:
Total of purchases column in purchases journal: $2,100

A-4. Mabel's Natural Food Store uses a purchases journal and a general journal to record the following transactions (continued from April):

201X

May   8   Purchased $600 of merchandise on account from Aton Co., invoice no. 400, dated May 9; terms 2/10, n/60.

   10   Purchased $1,200 of merchandise on account from Broward Co., invoice no. 420, dated May 11; terms 2/10, n/60.

   12   Purchased $500 of store supplies on account from Midden Co., invoice no. 510, dated May 13.

   14   Issued debit memo no. 8 to Aton Co., for merchandise returned, $400, from invoice no. 400.

   17   Purchased $560 of office equipment on account from Relar Co., invoice no. 810, dated May 18.

   24   Purchased $650 of additional store supplies on account from Midden Co., invoice no. 516, dated May 25; terms 2/10, n/30.

Check Figure:
Total schedule of accounts payable $5,810

The food store decided to keep a separate column for the purchases of supplies in the purchases journal. Your tasks are to do the following:

1. Journalize the transactions.
2. Post and record as appropriate.
3. Prepare a schedule of accounts payable.

A-5. Abby Ellen opened Abby's Toy House. As her newly hired accountant, your tasks are to do the following:

1. Journalize the transactions for the month of March. Abby uses special journals for sales on account, purchases on account, cash receipts and cash payments, as well as a general journal.
2. Record to subsidiary ledgers and post to the general ledger as appropriate.
3. Total and rule the journals.
4. Prepare a schedule of accounts receivable and a schedule of accounts payable.
5. Ignore Sales Tax.

The following is the partial chart of accounts for Abby's Toy House:

Check Figures:
Total of schedule of accounts receivable $7,600
Total of schedule of accounts payable $9,000

Abby's Toy House Chart of Accounts

Assets		Revenue	
110	Cash	410	Toy Sales
112	Accounts Receivable	412	Sales Returns and Allowances
114	Prepaid Rent	414	Sales Discounts
121	Delivery Truck	**Cost of Goods**	
Liabilities		510	Toy Purchases
210	Accounts Payable	512	Purchases Returns and Allowances
Owner's Equity		514	Purchases Discount
310	A. Ellen, Capital	**Expenses**	
		610	Salaries Expense
		612	Cleaning Expense

201X

Mar.

1 Abby Ellen invested $8,000 in the toy store.

1 Paid three months' rent in advance, check no. 1, $3,000.

1 Purchased merchandise from Earl Miller Company on account, $4,000, invoice no. 410, dated March 2; terms 2/10, n/30.

3 Sold merchandise to Bill Burton on account, $1,000, invoice no. 1; terms 2/10, n/30.

6 Sold merchandise to Jim Rex on account, $700, invoice no. 2; terms 2/10, n/30.

8 Purchased merchandise from Earl Miller Co. on account, $1,200, invoice no. 415, dated March 9; terms 2/10, n/30.

9 Sold merchandise to Bill Burton on account, $600, invoice no. 3; terms 2/10, n/30.

9 Paid cleaning service, check no. 2, $300.

10 Jim Rex returned merchandise that cost $300 to Abby's Toy House. Abby issued credit memorandum no. 1 to Jim Rex for $300.

10 Purchased merchandise from Minnie Katz on account, $4,000, invoice no. 311, dated March 11; terms 1/15, n/60.

12 Paid Earl Miller Co. invoice no. 410, dated March 2, check no. 3.

13 Sold $1,300 of toy merchandise for cash.

13 Paid salaries, $600, check no. 4.

14 Returned merchandise to Minnie Katz in the amount of $1,000. Abby's Toy House issued debit memorandum no. 1 to Minnie Katz.

15 Sold merchandise for $4,000 cash.

16 Received payment from Jim Rex, invoice no. 2 (less returned merchandise) less discount.

16 Bill Burton paid invoice no. 1.

16 Sold toy merchandise to Amy Rose on account, $4,000, invoice no. 4; terms 2/10, n/30.

20 Purchased delivery truck on account from Sam Katz Garage, $3,000, invoice no. 111, dated March 21 (no discount).

22 Sold to Bill Burton merchandise on account, $900, invoice no. 5; terms 2/10, n/30.

23 Paid Minnie Katz balance owed, check no. 5.

24 Sold toy merchandise on account to Amy Rose, $1,100, invoice no. 6; terms 2/10, n/30.

25 Purchased toy merchandise, $600, check no. 6.

26 Purchased toy merchandise from Woody Smith on account, $4,800, invoice no. 211, dated March 27; terms 2/10, n/30.

28 Bill Burton paid invoice no. 5, dated March 22.

28 Amy Rose paid invoice no. 6, dated March 24.

28 Abby invested an additional $5,000 in the business.

28 Purchased merchandise from Earl Miller Co., $1,400, invoice no. 436, dated March 29; terms 2/10, n/30.

30 Paid Earl Miller Co. invoice no. 436, check no. 7.

30 Sold merchandise to Bonnie Flow Company on account, $3,000, invoice no. 7; terms 2/10, n/30.

SALES AND CASH RECEIPTS JOURNAL USING A PERPETUAL INVENTORY SYSTEM FOR ART'S WHOLESALE CLOTHING

ART'S WHOLESALE CLOTHING COMPANY SALES JOURNAL						
						Page 1
Date	Account Debited	Terms	Invoice No.	Post. Ref.	Dr. Acc. Rec Cr. Sales	Cost of Goods Sold Dr. Merchandise Inventory Cr.
201X Apr. 3	Hal's Clothing	2/10, n/30	1	✔	800 00	560 00
6	Bevans Company	2/10, n/30	2	✔	1600 00	1120 00
18	Roe Company	2/10, n/30	3	✔	2000 00	1400 00
24	Roe Company	2/10, n/30	4	✔	500 00	350 00
28	Mel's Dept. Store	2/10, n/30	5	✔	900 00	630 00
29	Mel's Dept. Store	2/10, n/30	6	✔	700 00	490 00
30						
					6500 00	4550 00
					(113) (411)	(510) (114)

FIGURE A.7
A Sales Journal under a Perpetual System

What's new:

In the sales journal: New columns for Cost of Goods Sold (Dr.) and Inventory (Cr.). Each time a charge sale is earned, the Cost of Goods Sold increases and the amount of Inventory at cost is reduced.

In the general ledger: New ledger accounts for Inventory and Cost of Goods Sold. Example: On April 3, Art's Wholesale sold Hal's Clothing $800 of merchandise on account. This sale cost Art's $560 to bring this merchandise into the store.

FIGURE A.8
A Cash Receipts Journal under a
Perpetual System

Date	Cash Dr.	Sales Discount Dr.	Accounts Receivable Cr.	Sales Cr.	Sundry Account Name	Post. Ref.	Amount Cr.	Costs of Goods Sold Dr. Merchandise Inventory Cr.
ART'S WHOLESALE CLOTHING COMPANY **CASH RECEIPTS JOURNAL**								Page 1
201X Apr. 1	8000.00				Art Newner, Capital	311	8000.00	
4	784.00	16.00	800.00		Hal's Clothing	✔		
15	900.00			900.00	Cash Sales	x		630.00
16	980.00	20.00	1000.00		Bevans Company	✔		
22	1960.00	40.00	2000.00		Roe Company	✔		
27	500.00				Store Equipment	121	500.00	
30	1200.00			1200.00	Cash Sales	x		840.00
	14324.00	76.00	3800.00	2100.00			8500.00	1470.00
	(111)	(413)	(113)	(411)			(X)	(510) (114)

What's new:

In the cash receipts journal: New columns for Cost of Goods Sold (Dr.) and Inventory (Cr.). Each time a cash sale is earned, the Cost of Goods Sold increases and the amount of Inventory at cost is reduced.

Preparing a Worksheet for a Merchandise Company

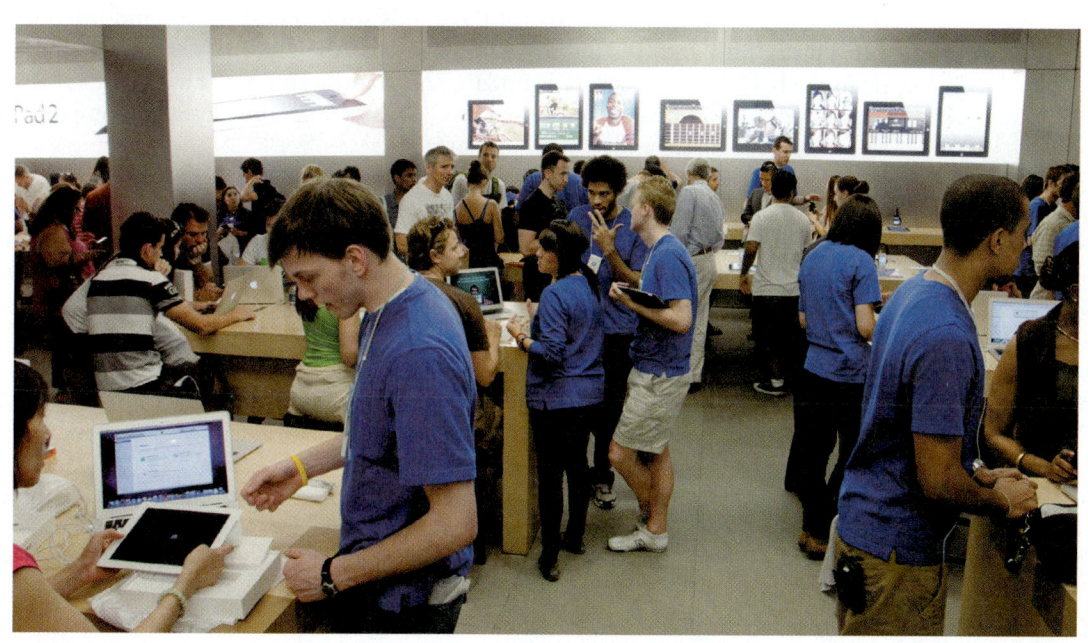

THE GAME PLAN

Do you ever need to adjust your work schedule so you can do better in class? Companies often have to make adjustments to better serve their customers. For example, when you visit an Apple store, Apple makes adjustments to the inventory so customer demand can be met. In addition, Apple makes other adjustments that customers may not be aware of. These adjustments include supplies, rent, the number of employees, and depreciation. Like the preparation of worksheets of non-merchandising companies that you learned in Chapter 4, to make these adjustments, many merchandise companies will also use a worksheet with some differences. In this chapter you will learn how a merchandising company prepares a worksheet and how it flows to the financial statements.

LEARNING OBJECTIVES

1. Figuring adjustments for merchandise inventory, unearned rent, supplies used, insurance expired, depreciation expense, and salaries accrued.

2. Preparing a worksheet for a merchandise company.

When you shop at the Apple Store, do you ever wonder how Apple controls its inventory? In Chapters 9 and 10 we discussed the subsidiary ledgers as well as entries for a merchandise company. Additional material provided an introduction to perpetual inventory. Now we shift our attention to recording adjustments and completing a worksheet for a merchandise company. Note that the appendix at the end of the chapter shows worksheets for a perpetual system.

🔴 **LO1**

LEARNING UNIT 11-1 ADJUSTMENTS FOR MERCHANDISE INVENTORY AND UNEARNED RENT

Cost of goods sold Total cost of the goods which were sold to customers.

The Merchandise Inventory account shows the goods that a merchandise company has available to sell to customers. Companies have several ways to keep track of the cost of goods sold (the total cost of the goods sold to customers) and the quantity of inventory on hand. In this chapter we discuss the periodic inventory system, in which the balance in inventory is updated only at the end of the accounting period.*
This system is used by companies, such as Art's Wholesale Clothing Company, that sell a variety of merchandise with low unit prices.

Periodic inventory system An inventory system that, at the *end* of each accounting period, calculates the cost of the unsold goods on hand by taking the cost of each unit times the number of units on hand of each product.

Assume that Art's Wholesale Clothing Company started the year with $19,000 worth of merchandise. This merchandise is called beginning merchandise inventory or simply beginning inventory. The balance of beginning inventory in the merchandise inventory account never changes during the accounting period. Any purchases of merchandise are recorded in a separate account, the Purchases account. During the accounting period $52,000 worth of such purchases were made and recorded in the Purchases accounts by Art's Wholesale.

Beginning merchandise inventory (beginning inventory) The cost of goods on hand in a company to *begin* an accounting period.

At the end of the period, the company takes a physical count of the merchandise in stock; this amount is called ending merchandise inventory or simply ending inventory. It is calculated on an inventory sheet as shown in Figure 11.1. This $4,000 is the ending inventory for this period and will become the beginning inventory for the next period.

Ending merchandise inventory (ending inventory) The cost of goods that remain unsold at the *end* of the accounting period. It is an asset on the new balance sheet.

When the income statement is prepared, the cost of goods sold section requires two distinct numbers for inventory. The beginning inventory adds to the cost of goods sold, and the ending inventory is subtracted from the cost of goods sold. Remember that the two figures for beginning and ending inventory were calculated months apart. Thus, combining these amounts to come up with one inventory figure would not be accurate.

Freight-In A cost of goods sold account that records the shipping cost to the buyer.

Note that in the calculation (in the margin) of cost of goods sold a title called Freight-In is shown.

Cost of goods sold

       Beginning inventory

   +   Net purchases

   +   Freight-in

   −   Ending inventory
   _____

   =   Cost of goods sold

FIGURE 11.1
Ending Inventory Sheet

ART'S WHOLESALE CLOTHING COMPANY ENDING INVENTORY SHEET AS OF DECEMBER 31, 201X			
Amount	Explanation	Unit Cost	Total
20	Ladies' Jackets code 14-0	$50	$1,000
10	Men's Hats code 327	10	100
90	Men's Shirts code 423	10	900
100	Ladies' Blouses code 481	20	2,000
			$4,000
Counted by _____ Checked and priced by _____			

Perpetual inventory system An inventory system that keeps *continual track* of each type of inventory by recording units on hand at the beginning, units sold, and the current balance after each sale or purchase.

_____
*For a discussion of the perpetual inventory system, see Chapter 10, Learning Unit 10-4.

Freight-In is a cost of goods sold account that records the shipping cost to the buyer. Note that net sales (gross sales less sales returns and allowances and sales discounts) less cost of goods sold equals gross profit. Subtracting operating expenses from gross profits equals net income.

Gross profit Net sales less cost of goods sold.

Adjustments A and B: Merchandise Inventory, $19,000 Adjusting the Merchandise Inventory account is a two-step process because we must record the beginning inventory and ending inventory amounts separately. The first step deals with beginning merchandise inventory.

Given: Beginning Inventory, $19,000 Our first adjustment removes the old outdated beginning inventory from the asset account (Merchandise Inventory) and transfers it to Income Summary. We do so by crediting Merchandise Inventory for $19,000 and debiting Income Summary for the same amount. This adjustment (A) is shown in the following T account form and on a transaction analysis chart.

COACHING TIP

Note that Income Summary has no normal balance of debit or credit.

Merchandise Inventory 114		Income Summary 313	
Bal. 19,000 | Adj. 19,000		Adj. 19,000 |	

Adjustment (A)

Accounts Affected	Category	↑↓	Rules
Income Summary	—	—	Dr.
Merchandise Inventory	Asset	↓	Cr.

(This, as well as the following adjusting entries would be recorded first on the worksheet and then in the general journal.)

The second step is entering the amount of ending inventory ($4,000) in the Merchandise Inventory account. This step is done to record the up-to-date amount of goods on hand at the end of the period as an asset and to subtract this amount from the cost of goods sold (because we have not sold this inventory yet). To do so, we debit Merchandise Inventory for $4,000 and credit Income Summary for the same amount. This adjustment (B) is shown in the following T account form.

COACHING TIP

Second adjustment updates Inventory account with a new figure for ending inventory.

Merchandise Inventory 114		Income Summary 313	
Bal. 19,000 | Adj. 19,000		Adj. 19,000 | Adj. 4,000	
Adj. 4,000 |			

Adjustment (B)

COACHING TIP

Beginning inventory	$19,000
+ Net cost of purchases*	50,910
= Cost of goods available for sale	$69,910
– Ending inventory	4,000
= Cost of goods sold	$65,910

*$52,000 Purchases – $860 PD – $680 PRA + $450 Freight-In

Let's look at how this process or method of recording merchandise inventory is reflected in the balance sheet and income statement (see Figure 11.2). Note that the $19,000 of beginning inventory is assumed sold and is shown on the income statement as part of the cost of goods sold. The ending inventory of $4,000 is assumed not to be sold and is subtracted from the cost of goods sold on the income statement. The ending inventory becomes next month's beginning inventory on the balance sheet. When the income statement is prepared, we will need a figure for beginning inventory as well as a figure for ending inventory. The goal of this adjustment is to wipe out the old inventory (a cost) and show the new inventory (not yet a cost).

Adjustment C: Unearned Rent Another new account we have not seen before is a liability called Unearned Rent or Rent Received in Advance. This account records the amount collected for rent before the service (renting the space) has been provided.

FIGURE 11.2
Recording Inventory on a
Partial Balance Sheet and
Income Statement

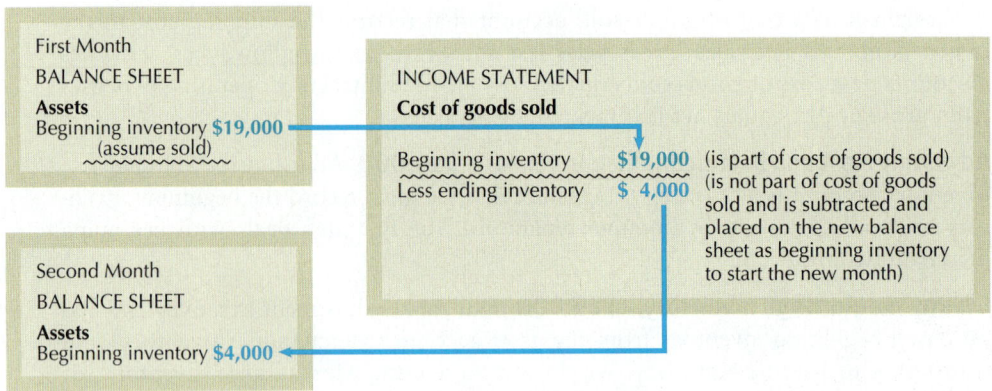

First Month
BALANCE SHEET
Assets
Beginning inventory **$19,000**
(assume sold)

INCOME STATEMENT
Cost of goods sold

Beginning inventory $19,000 (is part of cost of goods sold)
Less ending inventory $ 4,000 (is not part of cost of goods sold and is subtracted and placed on the new balance sheet as beginning inventory to start the new month)

Second Month
BALANCE SHEET
Assets
Beginning inventory **$4,000**

COACHING TIP

Received cash for renting space in future:

Cash	Asset	↑	Dr.
Unearned Rent	Liab.	↑	Cr.

COACHING TIP

The adjustment when rental income is earned:

Unearned Rent	Liab.	↓	Dr.
Rental Income	Rev.	↑	Cr.

Suppose Art's Wholesale Clothing Company is subletting a portion of its space to Jesse Company for $200 per month. Jesse Company sends Art's cash for $600 for three months' rent paid in advance. This unearned rent ($600) is a liability on the balance sheet because Art's Wholesale owes Jesse Company three months' worth of occupancy.

When Art's Wholesale fulfills a portion of the rental agreement—when Jesse Company has been in the space for a period of time—this liability account will be reduced and the Rental Income account will be increased. Rental income is another type of revenue for Art's Wholesale.

Remember that under accrual accounting, revenue is recognized when it is earned, whether payment is received then or not. Here, Art's Wholesale collected cash in advance for a service that it has not yet performed. A liability called Unearned Rent is the result. Art's Wholesale may have the cash, but the rental income is not recorded until it is earned. Examples of other types of unearned revenue besides unearned rent include prepaid subscriptions for magazines, legal fees collected before the work is performed, and prepaid insurance.

LEARNING UNIT 11-1 REVIEW

AT THIS POINT you should be able to do the following:

- Define the periodic system of inventory accounting.
- Explain why beginning and ending inventory are two separate figures in the cost of goods sold section on the income statement.
- Calculate net sales, cost of goods sold, gross profit, and net income.
- Show how to calculate a figure for ending merchandise inventory.
- Explain why Unearned Rent is a *liability* account.

⬐ Instant Replay ⊙ Self-Review Quiz 11-1

Given the following, prepare the two *adjusting* entries for Merchandise Inventory on 12/31/1X.

Merchandise Inventory, 1/1/1X	$ 8,000
Purchases	9,000
Purchases Returns and Allowances	3,000
Merchandise Inventory, 12/31/1X	4,000
Cost of Goods Sold	10,000
Unearned Magazine Subscriptions	8,000

Solution to Instant Replay: Self-Review Quiz 11-1

Dec.	31	Income Summary	8 00 00			
		Merchandise Inventory			8 00 00	
	31	Merchandise Inventory	4 00 00			
		Income Summary			4 00 00	

FIGURE 11.3
Merchandise Inventory Adjustments

COACHING TIP

Note that Unearned Magazine Subscriptions is a liability and is not involved in the adjustment for Merchandise Inventory.

LEARNING UNIT 11-2 COMPLETING THE WORKSHEET

LO2

In this unit we prepare a worksheet for Art's Wholesale Clothing Company. For convenience, we reproduce the company's chart of accounts in Figure 11.4.

Figure 11.5 (p. 428) shows the trial balance that was prepared on December 31, 201X, from Art's Wholesale ledger. (Note that it is placed directly in the first two columns of the worksheet.)

In looking at the trial balance, we see many new titles that did not appear in the trial balance which we completed for a service company in Chapter 5. Let's look specifically at these new titles shown in Table 11.1.

Note the following:

- **Mortgage Payable** is a liability account that records the increases and decreases in the amount of debt owed on a mortgage. We discuss this account more in the next chapter, when financial reports are prepared.

Mortgage Payable A liability account showing amount owed on a mortgage.

FIGURE 11.4
Art's Wholesale Clothing Company Chart of Accounts

CHART OF ACCOUNTS

Assets 100–199
111   Cash
112   Petty Cash
113   Accounts Receivable
114   Merchandise Inventory
115   Supplies
116   Prepaid Insurance
121   Store Equipment
122   Accum. Depreciation, Store Equipment

Liabilities 200–299
211   Accounts Payable
212   Salaries Payable
213   Federal Income Tax Payable
214   FICA—Social Security Payable
215   FICA—Medicare Payable
216   State Income Tax Payable
217   SUTA Tax Payable
218   FUTA Tax Payable
219   Unearned Rent*
220   Mortgage Payable

Owner's Equity 300–399
311   Art Newner, Capital
312   Art Newner, Withdrawals
313   Income Summary

Revenue 400–499
411   Sales
412   Sales Returns and Allowances
413   Sales Discount
414   Rental Income

Cost of Goods Sold 500–599
511   Purchases
512   Purchases Discount
513   Purchases Returns and Allowances
514   Freight-In

Expenses 600–699
611   Salaries Expense
612   Payroll Tax Expense
613   Depreciation Expense, Store Equipment
614   Supplies Expense
615   Insurance Expense
616   Postage Expense
617   Miscellaneous Expense
618   Interest Expense
619   Cleaning Expense
620   Delivery Expense

*Although Unearned Rent is the only term under Liabilities not using payable, it is a liability.

FIGURE 11.5
Trial Balance Section of the Worksheet

	Trial Balance	
	Dr.	Cr.
Cash	12 9 2 0 00	
Petty Cash	1 0 0 00	
Accounts Receivable	14 5 0 0 00	
Merchandise Inventory	19 0 0 0 00	
Supplies	8 0 0 00	
Prepaid Insurance	9 0 0 00	
Store Equipment	4 0 0 0 00	
Acc. Dep., Store Equipment		4 0 0 00
Accounts Payable		17 9 0 0 00
Federal Income Tax Payable		8 0 0 00
FICA—Soc. Sec. Payable		4 5 4 00
FICA—Medicare Payable		1 0 6 00
State Income Tax Payable		2 0 0 00
SUTA Tax Payable		1 0 8 00
FUTA Tax Payable		3 2 00
Unearned Rent		6 0 0 00
Mortgage Payable		2 3 2 0 00
Art Newner, Capital		7 9 0 5 00
Art Newner, Withdrawals	8 6 0 0 00	
Income Summary		
Sales		95 0 0 0 00
Sales Returns and Allowances	9 5 0 00	
Sales Discount	6 7 0 00	
Purchases	52 0 0 0 00	
Purchases Discount		8 6 0 00
Purchases Returns and Allowances		6 8 0 00
Freight-In	4 5 0 00	
Salaries Expense	11 7 0 0 00	
Payroll Tax Expense	4 2 0 00	
Postage Expense	2 5 00	
Miscellaneous Expense	3 0 00	
Interest Expense	3 0 0 00	
	127 3 6 5 00	127 3 6 5 00

Interest Expense The cost of borrowing money.

Unearned Revenue A liability account that records amount owed for goods or services in advance of delivery. The Cash account would record the receipt of cash.

- **Interest Expense** represents a nonoperating expense for Art's Wholesale and thus is categorized as Other Expense. We look at this expense in the next chapter.
- **Unearned Revenue** is a liability account that records receipt of payment for goods and services in advance of delivery. Unearned Rent is a particular example of this general type of account.

We already discussed the adjustments that make up the two-step process involved in adjusting Merchandise Inventory at the end of the accounting period. Now we show T accounts and transaction analysis charts for other adjustments that need to be made at this point for a merchandise firm, just as they must be made for a service company.

Adjustment C: Rental Income Earned by Art's Wholesale, $200 A month ago, Cash was increased by $600, as was a liability, Unearned Rent. Art's Wholesale received payment in advance but had not earned the rental income.

TABLE 11.1 Summary of New Account Titles

Title	Category	Account Reported on	Normal Balance	Temporary or Permanent
Petty Cash	Asset	Balance Sheet	Dr.	Permanent
Merchandise Inventory* (When sold)	Asset	Balance Sheet from prior period	Dr.	Permanent
	Cost of Goods Sold	Income Statement of current period		
Federal Income Tax Payable	Liability	Balance Sheet	Cr.	Permanent
FICA—Social Security Payable	Liability	Balance Sheet	Cr.	Permanent
FICA—Medicare Payable	Liability	Balance Sheet	Cr.	Permanent
State Income Tax Payable	Liability	Balance Sheet	Cr.	Permanent
SUTA Tax Payable	Liability	Balance Sheet	Cr.	Permanent
FUTA Tax Payable	Liability	Balance Sheet	Cr.	Permanent
Unearned Rent[†]	Liability	Balance Sheet	Cr.	Permanent
Mortgage Payable	Liability	Balance Sheet	Cr.	Permanent
Sales	Revenue	Income Statement	Cr.	Temporary
Sales Returns and Allowances	Contra-Revenue	Income Statement	Dr.	Temporary
Sales Discount	Contra-Revenue	Income Statement	Dr.	Temporary
Purchases[§]	Cost of Goods Sold	Income Statement	Dr.	Temporary
Purchases Discount	Contra-Cost of Goods Sold	Income Statement	Cr.	Temporary
Purchases Returns and Allowances	Contra-Cost of Goods Sold	Income Statement	Cr.	Temporary
Freight-In	Cost of Goods Sold	Income Statement	Dr.	Temporary
Payroll Tax Expense	Expense	Income Statement	Dr.	Temporary
Postage Expense	Expense	Income Statement	Dr.	Temporary
Interest Expense	Other Expense	Income Statement	Dr.	Temporary

*The ending inventory of current period is a contra-cost of goods sold on the income statement and will be an asset on the balance sheet for the next period.
[†]Referred to as Unearned Revenue.
[§]Note that the categories for Purchases and Freight-In are Cost of Goods Sold, whereas Purchases Discounts and Purchases Returns and Allowances are Contra-Cost of Goods Sold.

Now, because $200 has been earned, the liability is reduced and Rental Income can be recorded for the $200. This step is shown as follows:

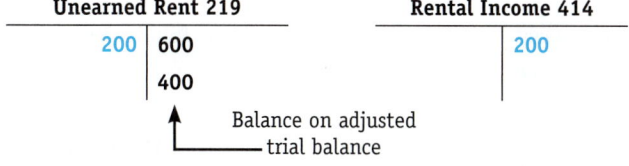

Unearned Rent	Liability	↓	Dr.	$200
Rental Income	Revenue	↑	Cr.	$200

Adjustment D: Supplies on Hand, $300 Because $500 worth of supplies were used up, Supplies Expense is increased, and the asset Supplies is decreased.

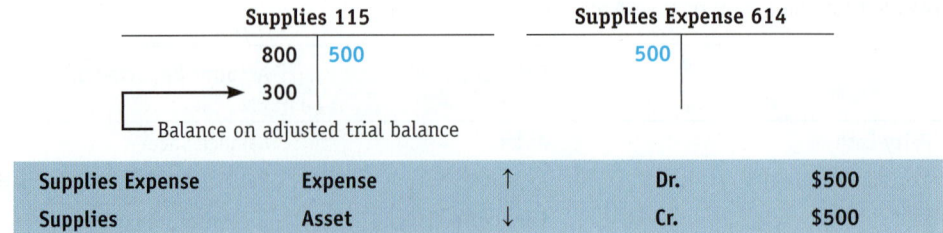

| Supplies Expense | Expense | ↑ | Dr. | $500 |
| Supplies | Asset | ↓ | Cr. | $500 |

Adjustment E: Insurance Expired, $300 Because insurance has expired by $300, Insurance Expense is increased by $300 and the asset Prepaid Insurance is decreased by $300.

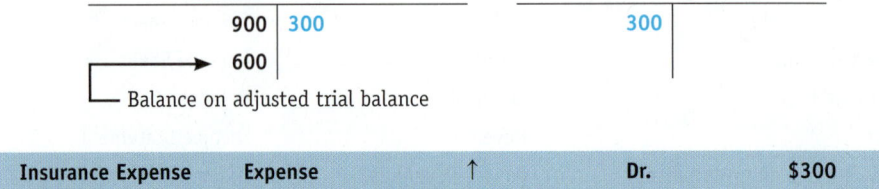

| Insurance Expense | Expense | ↑ | Dr. | $300 |
| Prepaid Insurance | Asset | ↓ | Cr. | $300 |

Adjustment F: Depreciation Expense, $50 When depreciation is taken, Depreciation Expense and Accumulated Depreciation are both increased by $50. Note that the cost of the store equipment remains the same.

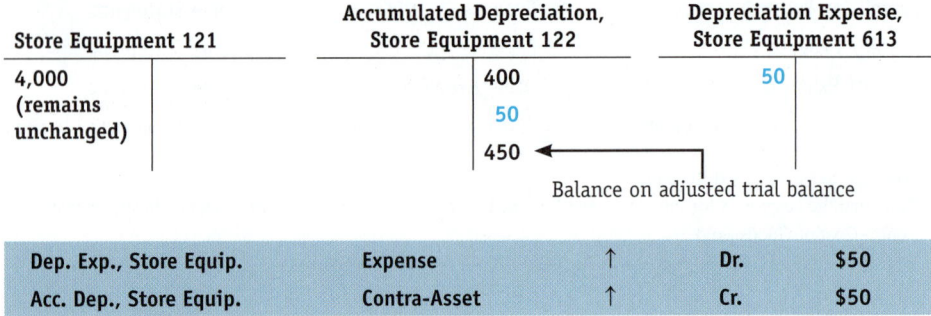

| Dep. Exp., Store Equip. | Expense | ↑ | Dr. | $50 |
| Acc. Dep., Store Equip. | Contra-Asset | ↑ | Cr. | $50 |

Adjustment G: Salaries Accrued, $600 The $600 in accrued salaries causes an increase in Salaries Expense and Salaries Payable.

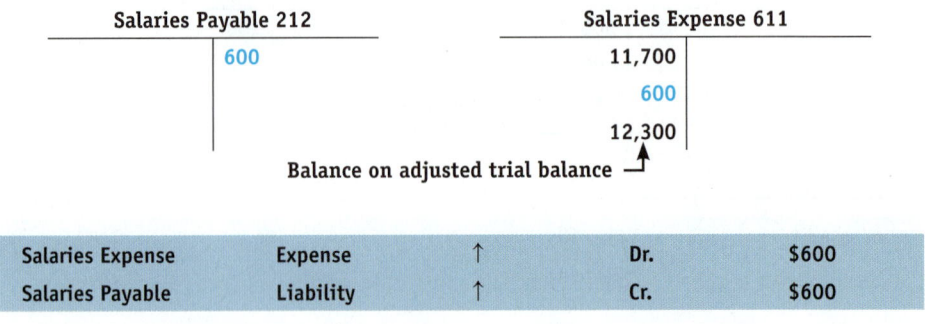

| Salaries Expense | Expense | ↑ | Dr. | $600 |
| Salaries Payable | Liability | ↑ | Cr. | $600 |

Figure 11.6 shows the worksheet with the adjustments and adjusted trial balance columns filled out. Note that the adjustment numbers in the Income Summary from beginning and ending inventory are also carried over to the adjusted trial balance and are not combined.

FIGURE 11.6
Worksheet with Three Columns Filled Out

	Trial Balance Dr.	Trial Balance Cr.	Adjustments Dr.	Adjustments Cr.	Adjusted Trial Balance Dr.	Adjusted Trial Balance Cr.
Cash	1292000				1292000	
Petty Cash	10000				10000	
Accounts Receivable	1450000		(B)	(A)	1450000	
Merchandise Inventory	1900000		400000	1900000	400000	
Supplies	80000			(D)50000	30000	
Prepaid Insurance	90000			(E)30000	60000	
Store Equipment	400000				400000	
Acc. Dep., Store Equipment		40000		(F) 5000		45000
Accounts Payable		1790000				1790000
Federal Income Tax Payable		80000				80000
FICA—Soc. Sec. Payable		45400				45400
FICA—Medicare Payable		10600				10600
State Income Tax Payable		20000				20000
SUTA Tax Payable		10800				10800
FUTA Tax Payable		3200				3200
Unearned Rent		60000	(C)20000			40000
Mortgage Payable		232000				232000
Art Newner, Capital		790500				790500
Art Newner, Withdrawals	860000		(A)	(B)	860000	
Income Summary			1900000	400000	1900000	400000
Sales		9500000				9500000
Sales Returns and Allowances	95000				95000	
Sales Discount	67000				67000	
Purchases	5200000				5200000	
Purchases Discount		86000				86000
Purchases Returns and Allowances		68000				68000
Freight-In	45000				45000	
Salaries Expense	1170000		(G)60000		1230000	
Payroll Tax Expense	42000				42000	
Postage Expense	2500				2500	
Miscellaneous Expense	3000				3000	
Interest Expense	30000				30000	
	12736500	12736500				
Rental Income				(C)20000		20000
Supplies Expense			(D)50000		50000	
Insurance Expense			(E)30000		30000	
Depreciation Expense, Store Equip.			(F) 5000		5000	
Salaries Payable				(G)60000		60000
			2465000	2465000	13201500	13201500

The next step in completing the worksheet is to fill out the income statement columns from the adjusted trial balance, as shown in Figure 11.7.

COACHING TIP

Remember: We do not combine the $19,000 and $4,000 in Income Summary. When we prepare the cost of goods sold section for the formal income statement, we will need both a beginning and an ending figure for inventory.

FIGURE 11.7
Income Statement Section of the Worksheet

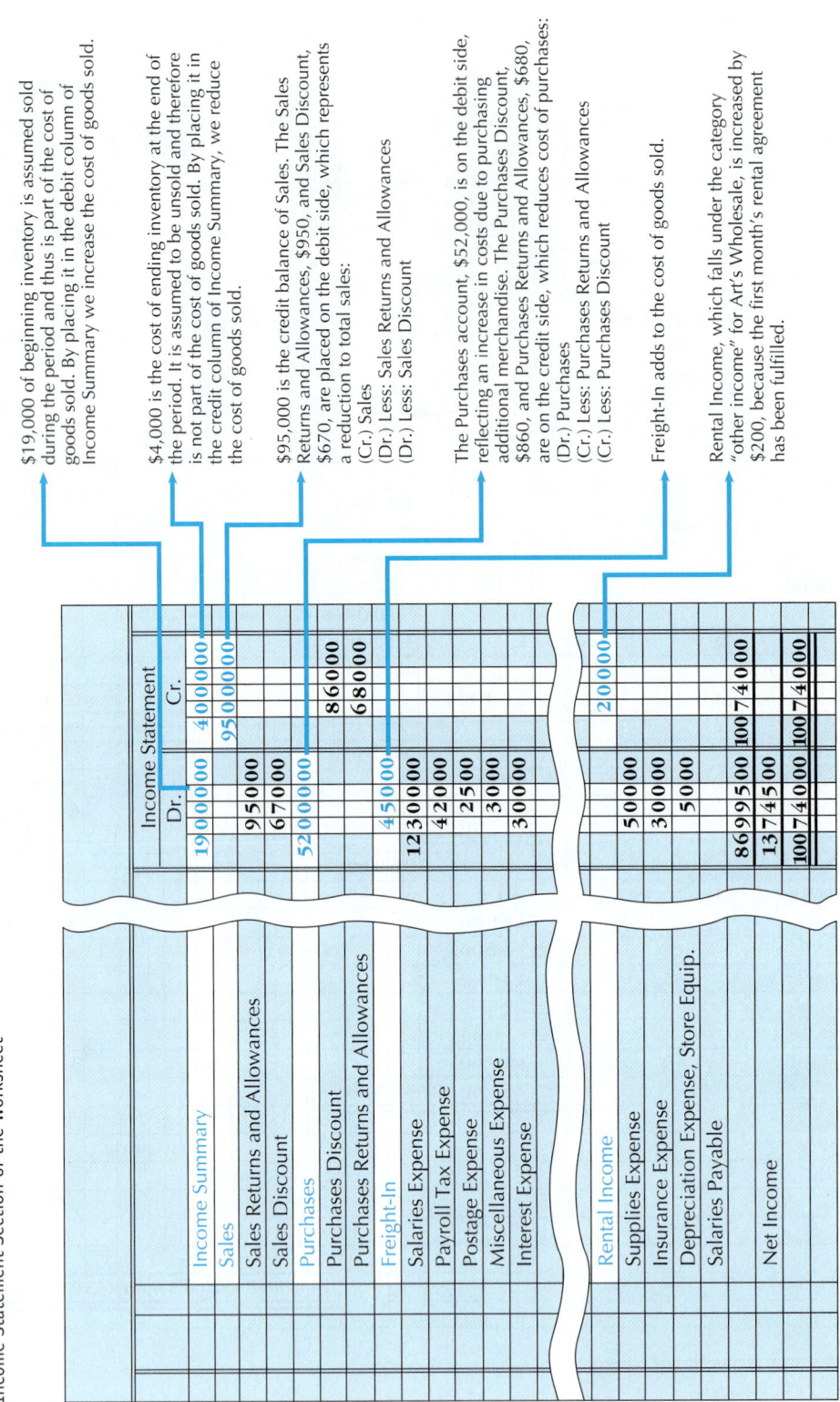

The next step in completing the worksheet is to fill out the balance sheet columns (Figure 11.8). Note how ending inventory is carried over to the balance sheet from the adjusted trial balance column. Take time also to look at the placement of the payroll tax liabilities as well as Unearned Rent on the worksheet.

Figure 11.9 (p. 434) is the completed worksheet.

FIGURE 11.8
Balance Sheet Section of the Worksheet

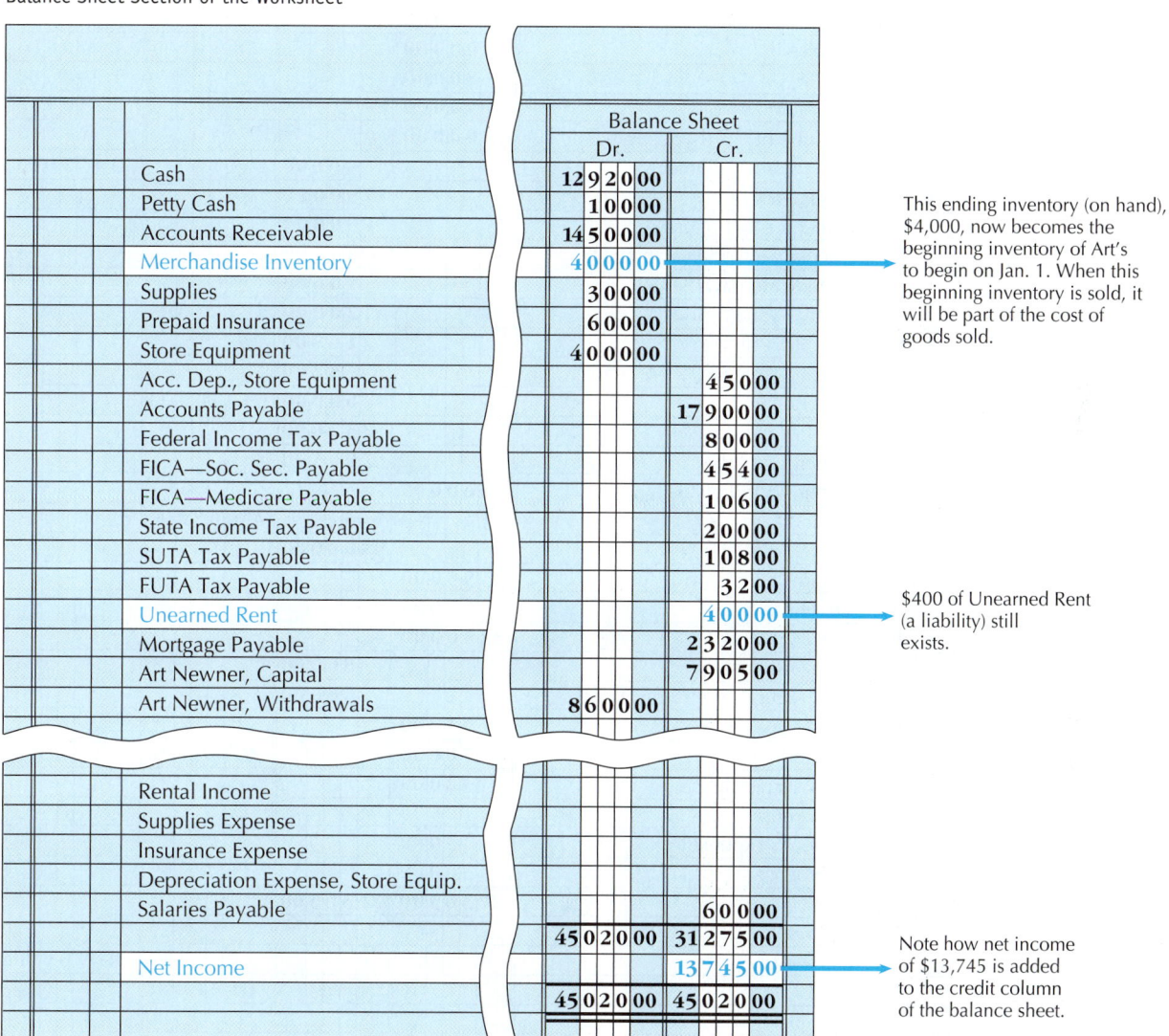

	Balance Sheet	
	Dr.	Cr.
Cash	12 9 2 0 00	
Petty Cash	1 0 0 00	
Accounts Receivable	14 5 0 0 00	
Merchandise Inventory	4 0 0 0 00	
Supplies	3 0 0 00	
Prepaid Insurance	6 0 0 00	
Store Equipment	4 0 0 0 00	
Acc. Dep., Store Equipment		4 5 0 00
Accounts Payable		17 9 0 0 00
Federal Income Tax Payable		8 0 0 00
FICA—Soc. Sec. Payable		4 5 4 00
FICA—Medicare Payable		1 0 6 00
State Income Tax Payable		2 0 0 00
SUTA Tax Payable		1 0 8 00
FUTA Tax Payable		3 2 00
Unearned Rent		4 0 0 00
Mortgage Payable		2 3 2 0 00
Art Newner, Capital		7 9 0 5 00
Art Newner, Withdrawals	8 6 0 0 00	
Rental Income		
Supplies Expense		
Insurance Expense		
Depreciation Expense, Store Equip.		
Salaries Payable		6 0 0 00
	45 0 2 0 00	31 2 7 5 00
Net Income		13 7 4 5 00
	45 0 2 0 00	45 0 2 0 00

This ending inventory (on hand), $4,000, now becomes the beginning inventory of Art's to begin on Jan. 1. When this beginning inventory is sold, it will be part of the cost of goods sold.

$400 of Unearned Rent (a liability) still exists.

Note how net income of $13,745 is added to the credit column of the balance sheet.

FIGURE 11.9
Completed Worksheet

	Trial Balance Dr.	Trial Balance Cr.	Adjustments Dr.	Adjustments Cr.
WORKSHEET				
FOR YEAR ENDED DECEMBER 31, 201X				
Cash	12 920 00			
Petty Cash	100 00			
Accounts Receivable	14 500 00			
Merchandise Inventory	19 000 00		(B) 4 000 00	(A) 19 000 00
Supplies	800 00			(D) 500 00
Prepaid Insurance	900 00			(E) 300 00
Store Equipment	4 000 00			
Acc. Dep., Store Equipment		400 00		(F) 50 00
Accounts Payable		17 900 00		
Federal Income Tax Payable		800 00		
FICA—Social Security Payable		454 00		
FICA—Medicare Payable		106 00		
State Income Tax Payable		200 00		
SUTA Tax Payable		108 00		
FUTA Tax Payable		32 00		
Unearned Rent		600 00	(C) 200 00	
Mortgage Payable		2 320 00		
Art Newner, Capital		7 905 00		
Art Newner, Withdrawals	8 600 00			
Income Summary			(A) 19 000 00	(B) 4 000 00
Sales		95 000 00		
Sales Returns and Allowances	950 00			
Sales Discount	670 00			
Purchases	52 000 00			
Purchases Discount		860 00		
Purchases Returns and Allowances		680 00		
Freight-In	450 00			
Salaries Expense	11 700 00		(G) 600 00	
Payroll Tax Expense	420 00			
Postage Expense	25 00			
Miscellaneous Expense	30 00			
Interest Expense	300 00			
	127 365 00	127 365 00		
Rental Income				(C) 200 00
Supplies Expense			(D) 500 00	
Insurance Expense			(E) 300 00	
Depreciation Expense, Store Equip.			(F) 50 00	
Salaries Payable				(G) 600 00
			24 650 00	24 650 00
Net Income				

FIGURE 11.9
(continued)

Adjusted Trial Bal. Dr.	Adjusted Trial Bal. Cr.	Income Statement Dr.	Income Statement Cr.	Balance Sheet Dr.	Balance Sheet Cr.
12 9 20 00				12 9 20 00	
1 00 00				1 00 00	
14 5 00 00				14 5 00 00	
4 0 00 00				4 0 00 00	
3 00 00				3 00 00	
6 00 00				6 00 00	
4 0 00 00				4 0 00 00	
	4 50 00				4 50 00
	17 9 00 00				17 9 00 00
	8 00 00				8 00 00
	4 54 00				4 54 00
	1 06 00				1 06 00
	2 00 00				2 00 00
	1 08 00				1 08 00
	32 00				32 00
	4 00 00				4 00 00
	2 3 20 00				2 3 20 00
	7 9 05 00				7 9 05 00
8 6 00 00				8 6 00 00	
19 0 00 00	4 0 00 00	19 0 00 00	4 0 00 00		
	95 0 00 00		95 0 00 00		
9 50 00		9 50 00			
6 70 00		6 70 00			
52 0 00 00		52 0 00 00			
	8 60 00		8 60 00		
	6 80 00		6 80 00		
4 50 00		4 50 00			
12 3 00 00		12 3 00 00			
4 20 00		4 20 00			
25 00		25 00			
30 00		30 00			
3 00 00		3 00 00			
	2 00 00		2 00 00		
5 00 00		5 00 00			
3 00 00		3 00 00			
50 00		50 00			
	6 00 00				6 00 00
132 0 15 00	132 0 15 00	86 9 95 00	100 7 40 00	45 0 20 00	31 2 75 00
		13 7 45 00			13 7 45 00
		100 7 40 00	100 7 40 00	45 0 20 00	45 0 20 00

LEARNING UNIT 11-2 REVIEW

AT THIS POINT you should be able to do the following:

- Complete adjustments for a merchandise company.
- Complete a worksheet.

Instant Replay ◉ Self-Review Quiz 11-2

From the trial balance shown in Figure 11.10, complete a worksheet for Ray Company. Additional data include the following: (A and B) On December 31, 201X, ending inventory was calculated at $200; (C) Storage Fees Now Earned, $516; (D) Prepaid Rent Expired, $100; (E) Depreciation Expense, Office Equipment, $60; (F) Salaries Accrued, $200.

FIGURE 11.10
Trial Balance of Ray Company

Account Title	Trial Balance Dr.	Trial Balance Cr.
Cash	2 4 8 6 00	
Merchandise Inventory	8 2 4 00	
Prepaid Rent	1 1 5 2 00	
Prepaid Insurance	6 0 00	
Office Equipment	2 1 6 0 00	
Accumulated Depreciation, Office Equipment		5 6 0 00
Unearned Storage Fees		2 5 1 6 00
Accounts Payable		1 0 0 00
B. Ray, Capital		1 9 3 2 00
Income Summary	—	—
Sales		1 1 0 4 0 00
Sales Returns and Allowances	5 4 6 00	
Sales Discount	2 1 6 00	
Purchases	5 2 5 6 00	
Purchases Returns and Allowances		1 6 8 00
Purchases Discount		1 0 2 00
Salaries Expense	2 0 1 6 00	
Insurance Expense	1 3 9 2 00	
Utilities Expense	9 6 00	
Plumbing Expense	2 1 4 00	
	1 6 4 1 8 00	1 6 4 1 8 00

COACHING TIP

The ending inventory of $200 becomes next month's beginning inventory.

Solution to Instant Replay: Self-Review Quiz 11-2

The solution is shown in Figure 11.11.

FIGURE 11.11
Worksheet for Ray Company

RAY COMPANY
WORKSHEET
FOR YEAR ENDED DECEMBER 31, 201X

Account	Trial Balance Dr.	Trial Balance Cr.	Adjustments Dr.	Adjustments Cr.	Adjusted Trial Balance Dr.	Adjusted Trial Balance Cr.	Income Statement Dr.	Income Statement Cr.	Balance Sheet Dr.	Balance Sheet Cr.
Cash	248600				248600				248600	
Merchandise Inventory	82400		(B) 20000	(A) 82400	20000				20000	
Prepaid Rent	115200			(D) 10000	105200				105200	
Prepaid Insurance	6000				6000				6000	
Office Equipment	216000				216000				216000	
Acc. Dep., Office Equipment		56000		(E) 6000		62000				62000
Unearned Storage Fees		251600	(C) 51600			200000				200000
Accounts Payable		10000				10000				10000
B. Ray, Capital		193200				193200				193200
Income Summary			(A) 82400	(B) 20000	82400	20000	82400	20000		
Sales		1104000				1104000		1104000		
Sales Returns and Allowances	54600				54600		54600			
Sales Discount	21600				21600		21600			
Purchases	525600				525600		525600			
Purchases Returns and Allowances		16800				16800		16800		
Purchases Discount		10200				10200		10200		
Salaries Expense	201600		(F) 20000		221600		221600			
Insurance Expense	139200				139200		139200			
Utilities Expense	9600				9600		9600			
Plumbing Expense	21400				21400		21400			
	1641800	1641800								
Storage Fees Earned				(C) 51600		51600		51600		
Rent Expense			(D) 10000		10000		10000			
Depreciation Expense, Equipment			(E) 6000		6000		6000			
Salaries Payable				(F) 20000		20000				20000
			190000	190000	1687800	1687800	1092000	1202600	595800	485200
Net Income							110600			110600
							1202600	1202600	595800	595800

BLUEPRINT: A WORKSHEET FOR A MERCHANDISE COMPANY

Account Titles	Adjustments Dr.	Adjustments Cr.	Adjusted Trial Balance Dr.	Adjusted Trial Balance Cr.	Income Statement Dr.	Income Statement Cr.	Balance Sheet Dr.	Balance Sheet Cr.
Cash			X				X	
Petty Cash			X				X	
Accounts Receivable			X				X	
Merchandise Inventory	X-E	X-B	X-E				X-E	
Supplies			X				X	
Equipment			X				X	
Acc. Dep., Store Equipment				X				X
Accounts Payable				X				X
Federal Income Tax Payable				X				X
FICA—Social Security Payable				X				X
FICA—Medicare Payable				X				X
State Income Tax Payable				X				X
SUTA Tax Payable				X				X
FUTA Tax Payable				X				X
Unearned Sales				X				X
Mortgage Payable				X				X
A. Flynn, Capital				X				X
A. Flynn, Withdrawals			X				X	
Income Summary*	X-B	X-E	X-B	X-E	X-B	X-E		
Sales				X		X		
Sales Returns and Allow.			X		X			
Sales Discount			X		X			
Purchases			X		X			
Purchases Ret. and Allow.				X		X		
Purchases Discount				X		X		
Freight-In			X		X			
Salaries Expense			X		X			
Payroll Tax Expense			X		X			
Insurance Expense			X		X			
Depreciation Expense			X		X			
Salaries Payable				X				X
Rental Income				X		X		

* Note that the figures for beginning (X-B) and ending inventory (X-E) are never combined on the Income Summary line of the worksheet. When the formal income statement is prepared, two distinct figures for inventory will be used to explain and calculate cost of goods sold. Beginning inventory adds to cost of goods sold; ending inventory reduces cost of goods sold.

ACCOUNTING COACH

The following Coaching Tips are from Learning Units 11-1 and 11-2. Take the Pre-Game Checkup and use the Check Your Score at the bottom of the page to see how you are doing. The Accounting Coach provides tips before each Checkup to help you avoid common accounting errors.

LU 11-1 Adjustments for Merchandise Inventory and Unearned Rent

Pre-Game Tips: The purpose of the adjustment for Merchandise Inventory is to wipe out the beginning inventory and bring on the ending inventory. We assume that the beginning inventory is sold and is part of the cost of goods sold. The ending inventory is not sold and is not part of the cost of goods sold. The ending inventory becomes the new figure for beginning inventory. Unearned Rent is not a revenue account. It is a liability. Revenue will only be recognized when it is earned.

Pre-Game Checkup
Answer true or false to the following statements.

1. Freight-In is a cost of goods sold account.
2. Beginning inventory is subtracted from cost of goods sold.
3. Income Summary is not used to adjust Merchandise Inventory.
4. When unearned rent is earned the liability will go up.
5. The ending inventory of one period can never be the new inventory of the next period.

LU 11-2 Completing the Worksheet

Pre-Game Tips: Before you complete the worksheet, make sure you review this table:

Sales	Revenue	Credit Balance	Income Statement
SRA	Contra Revenue	Debit Balance	Income Statement
Unearned	Liability	Credit Balance	Balance Sheet
Purchases	Cost	Debit Balance	Income Statement
PRA	Contra Cost	Credit Balance	Income Statement

Pre-Game Checkup
Answer true or false to the following statements.

1. Ending inventory goes in the credit column of the balance sheet section of the worksheet.
2. Freight-In goes in the debit column of the balance sheet section of the worksheet.
3. Unearned Rent goes in the debit column of the balance sheet section of the worksheet.
4. Accumulated Depreciation goes in the credit column of the balance sheet section of the worksheet.
5. Income Summary for the beginning inventory goes in the credit column of the income statement.

CHECK YOUR SCORE: Answers to the Pre-Game Checkup

LU 11-1
1. True.
2. False—Beginning inventory is added to cost of goods sold.
3. False—Income Summary is used to adjust Merchandise Inventory.
4. False—When unearned rent is earned the liability will go down.
5. False—The ending inventory of one period always becomes new inventory of the next period.

LU 11-2
1. False—Ending inventory goes in the debit column of the balance sheet section of the worksheet.
2. True—Freight-In goes in the debit column of the income statement.
3. False—Unearned Rent goes in the credit column of the balance sheet section of the worksheet.
4. True.
5. True.

Chapter Summary

Here are all the key concepts and equations to help you understand the concepts of this chapter and prepare you for your exam. After completing this review, go to MyAccountingLab for more practice opportunities.

Concepts You Should Know	Key Terms
L01 Figuring adjustments for merchandise inventory, unearned rent, supplies used, insurance expired, depreciation expense, and salaries accrued. 1. The periodic inventory system updates the record of goods on hand only at the end of the accounting period. 2. In the periodic inventory system, additional purchases of merchandise during the accounting period will be recorded in the Purchases account. The amount in beginning inventory will remain unchanged during the accounting period. At the end of the period, a new figure for ending inventory will be calculated. 3. Beginning inventory from the start of the accounting period becomes part of the cost of goods sold, whereas ending inventory is a reduction to cost of goods sold. 4. The perpetual inventory system keeps a continuous record of inventory. 5. Net sales less cost of goods sold equals gross profit. Gross profit less operating expenses equals net income. 6. Unearned Revenue is a liability account that accumulates revenue that has not been earned yet, although the cash has been received. It represents a liability to the seller until the service or product is performed or delivered.	**Beginning merchandise inventory (beginning inventory)** (p. 424) **Cost of goods sold** (p. 424) **Ending merchandise inventory (ending inventory)** (p. 424) **Freight-In** (p. 424) **Gross profit** (p. 425) **Periodic inventory system** (p. 424) **Perpetual inventory system** (p. 424)
L02 Preparing a worksheet for a merchandise company. 1. Both the beginning and ending figures for merchandise inventory are shown in the Merchandise Inventory account and Income Summary. The balance sheet debit column shows the ending figure for inventory. 2. Unearned Revenue is a liability on the balance sheet credit column.	**Interest Expense** (p. 428) **Mortgage Payable** (p. 427) **Unearned Revenue** (p. 428)

Discussion Questions and Critical Thinking/Ethical Case

1. What is the function of the Purchases account?

2. Explain why Unearned Revenue is a liability account.

3. In a periodic system of inventory, the balance of beginning inventory will remain unchanged during the period. True or false?

4. What is the purpose of an inventory sheet?

5. Why do many Unearned Revenue accounts have to be adjusted?

6. Explain why figures for beginning and ending inventory are not combined on the Income Summary line of the worksheet.

7. Jim Heary is the custodian of petty cash. Jim, who is short of personal cash, decided to pay his home electrical and phone bills from petty cash. He plans to pay it back next month. Do you feel Jim should do so? You make the call. Write down your specific recommendations to Jim.

Concept Checks

MyAccountingLab

Adjustment for Merchandise Inventory

● **L01** (10 MIN)

1. Given the following, journalize the adjusting entries for Merchandise Inventory. Note that ending inventory has a balance of $21,000.

Merchandise Inventory 114	Income Summary 313
54,000	

Adjustment for Unearned Fees

● **L01** (15 MIN)

2. a. Given the following, journalize the adjusting entry. By December 31, $230 of the unearned dog walking fees were earned.

Unearned Dog Walking Fees 225		Earned Dog Walking Fees 441	
890	12/1/1X	5,100	12/1/1X

   b. What is the category of unearned dog walking fees?

Worksheet

● **L02** (10 MIN)

3. Match the following:
   1. Located on the Income Statement debit column of the worksheet.
   2. Located on the Income Statement credit column of the worksheet.
   3. Located on the Balance Sheet debit column of the worksheet.
   4. Located on the Balance Sheet credit column of the worksheet.

   _____ a. Beginning Merchandise Inventory (amount)
   _____ b. Sales Returns and Allowance
   _____ c. Salaries Payable
   _____ d. Sales
   _____ e. Accounts Receivable

LO1 *(10 MIN)*   **Merchandise Inventory Adjustment**

4.   Given beginning merchandise inventory of $1,500 and ending merchandise inventory of $45, what would be the adjusting entries?

LO2 *(10 MIN)*   **Income Summary on the Worksheet**

5.   Given a figure of beginning inventory of $440 and a $920 figure for ending inventory, place these numbers on the Income Summary line of this partial worksheet.

	Adj.		ATB		Income Statement	
	Dr.	Cr.	Dr.	Cr.	Dr.	Cr.
Income Summary	A	B	C	D	E	F

Exercises

Set A

LO1 *(10 MIN)*   **11A-1.** Indicate the normal balance and category of each of the following accounts:

   a. Unearned Revenue
   b. Merchandise Inventory (beginning of period)
   c. Freight-In
   d. Payroll Tax Expense
   e. Purchases Discount
   f. Sales Discount
   g. FICA—Social Security Payable
   h. Purchases Returns and Allowances

LO1 *(15 MIN)*   **11A-2.** From the following, calculate (a) net sales, (b) cost of goods sold, (c) gross profit, and (d) net income: Sales, $21,800; Sales Discount, $500; Sales Returns and Allowances, $270; Beginning Inventory, $660; Net Purchases, $13,100; Ending Inventory, $560; Operating Expenses, $3,700.

LO1 *(10 MIN)*   **11A-3.** Autumn Co. had the following balances on December 31, 201X:

Cash		Unearned Janitorial Service	
2,600			590

Janitorial Service	
7,700	

The accountant for Autumn has asked you to make an adjustment because $390 of janitorial services has just been performed for customers who had paid for two months. Construct a transaction analysis chart.

LO1, 2 *(15 MIN)*   **11A-4.** Dixon Co. purchased merchandise costing $430,000. Calculate the cost of goods sold under the following situations:

   a. Beginning inventory $37,000 and no ending inventory
   b. Beginning inventory $46,000 and a $62,000 ending inventory
   c. No beginning inventory and a $31,000 ending inventory

LO2 *(20 MIN)*   **11A-5.** Prepare a worksheet for Morin Co. from the following information using Figure 11.12:

a/b. Merchandise Inventory, ending	9
c. Store Supplies on hand	2
d. Depreciation on Store Equipment	3
e. Accrued Salaries	2

FIGURE 11.12
Trial Balance for Morin Co.

MORIN CO. TRIAL BALANCE DECEMBER 31, 201X	Dr.	Cr.
Cash	7 00	
Accounts Receivable	2 00	
Merchandise Inventory	13 00	
Store Supplies	8 00	
Store Equipment	20 00	
Accumulated Depreciation, Store Equipment		8 00
Accounts Payable		7 00
J. Morin, Capital		38 00
Income Summary		
Sales		44 00
Sales Returns and Allowances	6 00	
Purchases	19 00	
Purchases Discount		5 00
Freight-In	2 00	
Salaries Expense	13 00	
Advertising Expense	12 00	
Totals	102 00	102 00

Set B

11B-1. Indicate the normal balance and category of each of the following accounts: ● **L01** *(10 MIN)*

 a. Salaries Payable
 b. Merchandise Inventory (beginning of period)
 c. Freight-In
 d. Payroll Tax Expense
 e. Purchases Returns and Allowances
 f. Sales Returns and Allowance
 g. FICA—Social Security Payable
 h. Purchases Discounts

11B-2. From the following, calculate (a) net sales, (b) cost of goods sold, (c) gross profit, and (d) net income: Sales, $22,700; Sales Discount, $400; Sales Returns and Allowances, $370; Beginning Inventory, $760; Net Purchases, $12,100; Ending Inventory, $460; Operating Expenses, $2,700. ● **L01** *(15 MIN)*

11B-3. Bates Co. had the following balances on December 31, 201X: ● **L01** *(10 MIN)*

The accountant for Bates has asked you to make an adjustment because $430 of janitorial services has just been performed for customers who had paid for two months. Construct a transaction analysis chart.

Cash		Unearned Janitorial Service	
1,800			620

Janitorial Service	
7,500	

11B-4. Edmond Co. purchased merchandise costing $350,000. Calculate the cost of goods sold under the following situations: ●● **L01, 2** *(15 MIN)*

 a. Beginning inventory $37,000 and no ending inventory
 b. Beginning inventory $49,000 and a $64,000 ending inventory
 c. No beginning inventory and a $25,000 ending inventory

LO2 *(20 MIN)*   **11B-5.** Prepare a worksheet for Mitchell Co. from the following information using Figure 11.13.

FIGURE 11.13
Trial Balance for Mitchell Co.

MITCHELL CO. TRIAL BALANCE DECEMBER 31, 201X	Dr.	Cr.
Cash	6 00	
Accounts Receivable	4 00	
Merchandise Inventory	11 00	
Store Supplies	9 00	
Store Equipment	18 00	
Accumulated Depreciation, Store Equipment		6 00
Accounts Payable		5 00
J. Mitchell, Capital		32 00
Income Summary		
Sales		66 00
Sales Returns and Allowances	12 00	
Purchases	21 00	
Purchases Discount		2 00
Freight-In	4 00	
Salaries Expense	11 00	
Advertising Expense	15 00	
Totals	111 00	111 00

a/b. Merchandise Inventory, ending   12
 c. Store Supplies on hand   2
 d. Depreciation on Store Equipment   6
 e. Accrued Salaries   1

Problems

Set A

You can also use the foldout worksheets at the end of the working papers that accompany this text.

LO1 *(30 MIN)*   **11A-1.** Based on the following accounts, calculate the following:

Check Figure:
Net income $2,103

 a. Net sales
 b. Cost of goods sold
 c. Gross profit
 d. Net income

Accounts Payable	$ 5,900
Operating Expenses	2,100
Kiln Co., Capital	19,800
Purchases	1,700
Freight-In	91
Ending Merchandise Inventory, Dec. 31, 201X	61
Sales	6,300
Accounts Receivable	540
Cash	790
Purchases Discount	54
Sales Returns and Allowances	320
Beg. Merchandise Inventory, Jan. 1, 201X	82
Purchases Returns and Allowances	74
Sales Discount	93

11A-2 From the trial balance in Figure 11.14, complete a worksheet for Jack's Hardware. Assume the following:

    a/b. Ending inventory on December 31 is calculated at $320.
    c. Insurance expired, $150.
    d. Depreciation on store equipment, $50.
    e. Accrued wages, $110.

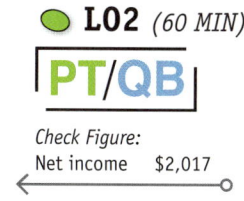

● **L02** *(60 MIN)*

Check Figure:
Net income $2,017

FIGURE 11.14
Trial Balance for Jack's Hardware

JACK'S HARDWARE TRIAL BALANCE DECEMBER 31, 201X	Dr.	Cr.
Cash	786 00	
Accounts Receivable	1152 00	
Merchandise Inventory	650 00	
Prepaid Insurance	720 00	
Store Equipment	2170 00	
Accumulated Depreciation, Store Equipment		640 00
Accounts Payable		525 00
Jack Spool, Capital		1656 00
Income Summary	—	—
Hardware Sales		11134 00
Hardware Sales Returns and Allowances	524 00	
Hardware Sales Discount	240 00	
Purchases	5244 00	
Purchases Discount		160 00
Purchases Returns and Allowances		126 00
Wages Expense	1756 00	
Rent Expense	784 00	
Telephone Expense	107 00	
Miscellaneous Expense	108 00	
Total	14241 00	14241 00

● **L02** *(60 MIN)*

Check Figure:
Net income $5,175

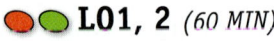

11A-3. The owner of Sonata Company asked you to prepare a worksheet from the trial balance in Figure 11.15.

Additional Data

a/b. Ending merchandise inventory on December 31, $1,845.

  c. Office supplies used up, $240.

  d. Rent expired, $235.

  e. Depreciation expense on office equipment, $575.

  f. Office salaries earned but not paid, $320.

FIGURE 11.15
Trial Balance for Sonata Company

SONATA COMPANY TRIAL BALANCE DECEMBER 31, 201X	Dr.	Cr.
Cash	5 2 5 4 00	
Petty Cash	2 0 0 00	
Accounts Receivable	2 4 0 9 00	
Beginning Merchandise Inventory, Jan. 1	4 9 7 2 00	
Prepaid Rent	6 4 9 00	
Office Supplies	9 6 6 00	
Office Equipment	9 1 8 0 00	
Accumulated Depreciation, Office Equipment		7 6 0 0 00
Accounts Payable		5 9 8 2 00
K. Sonata, Capital		5 4 7 6 00
K. Sonata, Withdrawals	5 1 0 0 00	
Income Summary		
Sales		5 2 2 1 8 00
Sales Returns and Allowances	1 0 5 00	
Sales Discount	2 2 0 0 00	
Purchases	2 9 4 2 8 00	
Purchases Discount		1 4 00
Purchases Returns and Allowances		3 4 8 00
Office Salaries Expense	7 3 0 4 00	
Insurance Expense	2 4 7 5 00	
Advertising Expense	8 0 0 00	
Utilities Expense	5 9 6 00	
Total	7 1 6 3 8 00	7 1 6 3 8 00

●● **L01, 2** *(60 MIN)*

Check Figure:
Net loss $3,574

11A-4. From the trial balance in Figure 11.16 (p. 447) and additional data, complete the worksheet for John's Wholesale Clothing Company.

Additional Data

a/b. Ending merchandise inventory on December 31, $5,500.

  c. Supplies on hand, $450.

  d. Insurance expired, $450.

  e. Depreciation on store equipment, $450.

  f. Storage fees earned, $156.

JOHN'S WHOLESALE CLOTHING COMPANY TRIAL BALANCE DECEMBER 31, 201X		
	Dr.	Cr.
Cash	4 3 5 0 00	
Petty Cash	3 0 0 00	
Accounts Receivable	7 1 0 0 00	
Merchandise Inventory	9 1 0 0 00	
Supplies	9 0 0 00	
Prepaid Insurance	8 9 0 00	
Store Equipment	2 8 0 0 00	
Acc. Dep., Store Equipment		1 2 0 0 00
Accounts Payable		11 0 1 5 00
Federal Income Tax Payable		1 1 0 0 00
FICA—Social Security Payable		4 6 2 00
FICA—Medicare Payable		1 3 0 00
State Income Tax Payable		1 5 0 00
SUTA Tax Payable		1 0 0 00
FUTA Tax Payable		3 6 00
Unearned Storage Fees		2 7 5 00
John Win, Capital		14 0 0 0 00
John Win, Withdrawals	4 2 0 0 00	
Income Summary		
Sales		45 9 0 0 00
Sales Returns and Allowances	1 5 0 0 00	
Sales Discount	1 4 0 5 00	
Purchases	27 0 0 0 00	
Purchases Discount		3 5 0 00
Purchases Returns and Allowances		3 0 0 00
Freight-In	1 5 0 00	
Salaries Expense	14 0 0 0 00	
Payroll Tax Expense	4 1 0 00	
Interest Expense	8 6 5 00	
Total	74 9 7 0 00	74 9 7 0 00

FIGURE 11.16
Trial Balance for John's Wholesale Clothing Company

Set B

MyAccountingLab

11B-1. Based on the following accounts, calculate (a) net sales, (b) cost of goods sold, (c) gross profit, and (d) net income.

● **L01** (30 MIN)

Accounts Payable	$ 6,400
Operating Expenses	1,500
Market Co., Capital	19,200
Purchases	1,300
Freight-In	89
Ending Merchandise Inventory, Dec. 31, 201X	65
Sales	5,500
Accounts Receivable	540
Cash	770
Purchases Discounts	50
Sales Returns and Allowances	290
Beginning Merchandise Inventory, Jan 1, 201X	82
Purchases Returns and Allowances	69
Sales Discount	85

Check Figure:
Net income $2,338

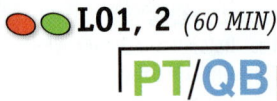

LO1, 2 *(60 MIN)*

11B-2. From the trial balance in Figure 11.17 as well as additional data, complete a worksheet for Jabar's Hardware.

Additional Data

a/b. Ending inventory on December 31 is calculated at $300.
   c. Insurance expired, $170.
   d. Depreciation on store equipment, $70.
   e. Accrued wages, $80.

FIGURE 11.17
Trial Balance for Jabar's Hardware

JABAR'S HARDWARE TRIAL BALANCE DECEMBER 31, 201X	Dr.	Cr.
Cash	7 9 1 00	
Accounts Receivable	1 1 7 7 00	
Merchandise Inventory	5 7 5 00	
Prepaid Insurance	6 7 5 00	
Store Equipment	2 1 9 0 00	
Accumulated Depreciation, Store Equipment		6 6 0 00
Accounts Payable		4 9 3 00
Jabar Spool, Capital		1 6 0 8 00
Income Summary	—	—
Hardware Sales		1 1 0 5 2 00
Hardware Sales Returns and Allowances	5 6 8 00	
Hardware Sales Discount	2 1 6 00	
Purchases	5 2 3 2 00	
Purchases Discounts		2 0 0 00
Purchases Returns and Allowances		9 6 00
Wages Expense	1 7 0 8 00	
Rent Expense	7 7 6 00	
Telephone Expense	9 3 00	
Miscellaneous Expense	1 0 8 00	
Total	14 1 0 9 00	14 1 0 9 00

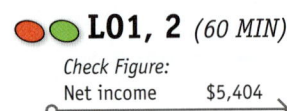

LO1, 2 *(60 MIN)*

11B-3. The owner of Ballad Company asked you to prepare a worksheet from the trial balance shown in Figure 11.18 (p. 449) and additional data.

Additional Data

a/b. Ending merchandise inventory on December 31, $1,785.
   c. Office supplies used up, $200.
   d. Rent expired, $185.
   e. Depreciation expense on office equipment, $450.
   f. Office salaries earned but not paid, $280.

BALLAD COMPANY TRIAL BALANCE DECEMBER 31, 201X	Dr.	Cr.
Cash	5 3 2 1 00	
Petty Cash	2 2 0 00	
Accounts Receivable	2 6 0 8 00	
Beginning Merchandise Inventory, Jan. 1	4 9 5 1 00	
Prepaid Rent	6 4 9 00	
Office Supplies	9 0 0 00	
Office Equipment	9 2 5 0 00	
Accumulated Depreciation, Office Equipment		7 9 0 0 00
Accounts Payable		5 9 1 2 00
K. Ballad, Capital		5 5 0 2 00
K. Ballad, Withdrawals	5 1 0 0 00	
Income Summary	—	—
Sales		52 7 3 3 00
Sales Returns and Allowances	9 4 00	
Sales Discount	2 3 0 0 00	
Purchases	29 3 1 6 00	
Purchases Discounts		2 4 00
Purchases Returns and Allowances		3 0 0 00
Office Salaries Expense	7 8 2 4 00	
Insurance Expense	2 4 5 0 00	
Advertising Expense	8 0 0 00	
Utilities Expense	5 8 8 00	
Total	72 3 7 1 00	72 3 7 1 00

FIGURE 11.18
Trial Balance for Ballad Company

11B-4. From the trial balance in Figure 11.19 and additional data, complete the worksheet for Sean's Wholesale Clothing Company.

Additional Data

a/b. Ending merchandise inventory on December 31, $5,900.
 c. Supplies on hand, $250.
 d. Insurance expired, $600.
 e. Depreciation on store equipment, $500.
 f. Storage fees earned, $216.

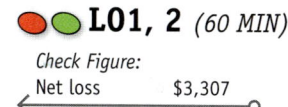

L01, 2 *(60 MIN)*

Check Figure:
Net loss $3,307

FIGURE 11.19
Trial Balance for Sean's Wholesale
Clothing Company

SEAN'S WHOLESALE CLOTHING COMPANY TRIAL BALANCE DECEMBER 31, 201X		
	Dr.	Cr.
Cash	4 8 9 0 00	
Petty Cash	1 0 0 00	
Accounts Receivable	7 5 0 0 00	
Merchandise Inventory	9 1 0 0 00	
Supplies	7 0 0 00	
Prepaid Insurance	8 3 0 00	
Store Equipment	2 8 0 0 00	
Accumulated Depreciation, Store Equipment		1 3 0 0 00
Accounts Payable		10 9 6 5 00
FIT Payable		1 0 0 00
FICA—Social Security Payable		4 5 2 00
FICA—Medicare Payable		1 1 4 00
SIT Payable		1 1 0 00
SUTA Tax Payable		1 1 8 00
FUTA Tax Payable		3 4 00
Unearned Storage Fees		4 0 0 00
Sean Win, Capital		14 0 0 0 00
Sean Win, Withdrawals	3 8 0 0 00	
Income Summary		
Sales		43 3 2 2 00
Sales Returns and Allowances	1 5 2 5 00	
Sales Discount	1 4 0 5 00	
Purchases	25 5 0 0 00	
Purchases Discount		5 0 0 00
Purchases Returns and Allowances		3 5 0 00
Freight-In	2 0 0 00	
Salaries Expense	13 0 0 0 00	
Payroll Tax Expense	4 0 0 00	
Interest Expense	9 1 5 00	
	72 6 6 5 00	72 6 6 5 00

○ **L01** *(10 MIN)*   **Financial Report Problem**

Reading the Kellogg's Annual Report
Go to http://investor.kelloggs.com/annuals.cfm, to access the Kellogg's 2010 Annual Report and find the Consolidated Statement of Earnings. What is the cost of goods sold in 2010?

MyAccountingLab   **ON the JOB**

○○ **L01, 2** *(60 MIN)*   **SANCHEZ COMPUTER CENTER**

The first six months of the year have concluded for Sanchez Computer Center, and Tony wants to make the necessary adjustments to his accounts to prepare accurate financial statements.

Assignment

To prepare these adjustments, use the trial balance in Figure 11.20 and the following inventory that Tony took at the end of March:

Supplies

10 dozen 1/4 " screws at a cost of $10 a dozen

5 dozen 1/2 " screws at a cost of $7 a dozen

2 feet of coaxial cable at a cost of $5 per foot

Merchandise Inventory

A physical inventory taken on March 31 indicated that merchandise inventory was valued at $300.

Depreciation of Computer Equipment

Computer depreciates at $33 a month; purchased July 5.

Computer workstations depreciate at $20 per month; purchased September 17.

Shop benches depreciate at $25 per month; purchased November 5.

Depreciation of Office Equipment

Office equipment depreciates at $10 per month; purchased July 17.

Fax machine depreciates at $10 per month; purchased November 20.

Expiration of Prepaid Rent

Six months' worth of rent at a rental rate of $400 per month has expired. The following accounts have been added to the chart of accounts: Merchandise Inventory #1050, and Income Summary #3020.

Remember: If any long-term asset is purchased in the first 15 days of the month, Tony will charge depreciation for the full month. If an asset is purchased later than the 15th, he will not charge depreciation in the month it was purchased.

Complete the 10-column worksheet for the six months ended March 31, 201X.

	Sanchez Computer Trial Balance March 31, 201X	
	Trial Balance	
Account Titles	Dr.	Cr.
Cash	13,416.64	
Petty Cash	100.00	
Accounts Receivable	10,900.00	
Prepaid Rent	2,800.00	
Supplies	390.00	
Computer Shop Equipment	3,800.00	
Accum. Dep., C.S. Equip.		99.00
Office Equipment	1,050.00	
Accum. Dep., Office Equip.		20.00
Accounts Payable		2,700.00
T. Freedman, Capital		7,406.00
T. Freedman, Withdrawals	2,015.00	

FIGURE 11.20

Trial Balance for Sanchez Computer March 31, 201X

(continued)

Sanchez Computer
Trial Balance
March 31, 201X

Income Summary		
Service Revenue		18,500.00
Sales		9,700.00
Sales Returns and Allowances	400.00	
Sales Discounts	220.00	
Advertising Expense		
Rent Expense		
Utilities Expense		
Phone Expense	150.00	
Supplies Expense	42.00	
Insurance Expense		
Postage Expense	25.00	
Miscellaneous Expense	10.00	
Wages Expense	2,030.00	
Payroll Tax Expense	226.36	
Purchases	950.00	
Purchase Returns		100.00
Total	38,525.00	38,525.00

Appendix

A Worksheet for Art's Wholesale Clothing Co. Using a Perpetual Inventory System

What's New: The Merchandise Inventory account (in Figure A.1) does not need to be adjusted. The $4,000 figure for merchandise is the up-to-date balance in the account. The difference between beginning inventory and ending inventory will be part of a new account called *Cost of Goods Sold* on the worksheet.

How the $65,910 of Cost of Goods Sold was calculated from a periodic setup:

	Purchases	$52,000	← **Assumed sold; part of cost**
+	Merchandise Inventory	$15,000	← **Beg. Inv. – Ending Inv.** **$19,000 – $4,000**
–	Purchases Discount	860	→ **Reduces costs**
–	Purchases Returns and Allowances	680	↗
+	Freight-In	450	→ **Adds to cost**
		$65,910	**Cost of Goods Sold**

What's Deleted from the Periodic Worksheet: Account titles for Purchases, Purchases Discounts, Purchases Returns and Allowances, and Freight-In.

Note: Net income is the same on the periodic and the perpetual worksheets.

Problem for Appendix

Using the solution to Instant Replay Self-Review Quiz 11-2 (p. 436) about Ray Company, convert this worksheet to a perpetual inventory system worksheet.

FIGURE A.1
Worksheet for Art's Wholesale Clothing Co. Using a Perpetual Inventory System

ART'S WHOLESALE CLOTHING CO.
WORKSHEET
FOR YEAR ENDED DECEMBER 31, 201X

Account Titles	Trial Balance Dr.	Trial Balance Cr.	Adjustments Dr.	Adjustments Cr.	Adjusted Trial Balance Dr.	Adjusted Trial Balance Cr.	Income Statement Dr.	Income Statement Cr.	Balance Sheet Dr.	Balance Sheet Cr.
Cash	129200 00				129200 00				129200 00	
Petty Cash	100 00				100 00				100 00	
Accounts Receivable	14500 00				14500 00				14500 00	
Merchandise Inventory	4000 00				4000 00				4000 00	
Supplies	800 00			(B) 500 00	300 00				300 00	
Prepaid Insurance	900 00			(C) 300 00	600 00				600 00	
Store Equipment	4000 00				4000 00				4000 00	
Acc. Dep., Store Equip.		400 00		(D) 50 00		450 00				450 00
Accounts Payable		17900 00				17900 00				17900 00
Federal Income Tax		800 00				800 00				800 00
FICA—Social Security		454 00				454 00				454 00
FICA—Medicare		106 00				106 00				106 00
State Income Tax		200 00				200 00				200 00
SUTA Tax		108 00				108 00				108 00
FUTA Tax Payable		32 00				32 00				32 00
Unearned Rent		600 00	(A) 200 00			400 00				400 00
Mortgage Payable		2320 00				2320 00				2320 00
Art Newner, Capital		7905 00				7905 00				7905 00
Art Newner, Withdrawal	860 00				860 00				860 00	
Sales		95000 00				95000 00		95000 00		
Sales Returns and Allow.	950 00				950 00		950 00			
Sales Discount	670 00				670 00		670 00			
Cost of Goods Sold	65910 00				65910 00		65910 00			
Salaries Expense	11700 00		(E) 600 00		12300 00		12300 00			
Payroll Tax Expense	420 00				420 00		420 00			
Postage Expense	25 00				25 00		25 00			
Miscellaneous Expense	30 00				30 00		30 00			
Interest Expense	30 00				30 00		30 00			
	125825 00	125825 00								
Rental Income				(A) 200 00		200 00		200 00		
Supplies Expense			(B) 500 00		500 00		500 00			
Insurance Expense			(C) 300 00		300 00		300 00			
Dep. Exp., Store Equip.			(D) 50 00		50 00		50 00			
Salaries Payable				(E) 600 00		600 00				600 00
			1650 00	1650 00	126475 00	126475 00	81455 00	95200 00	45020 00	31275 00
Net Income							13745 00			13745 00
							95200 00	95200 00	45020 00	45020 00

FIGURE A.2
Worksheet for Ray Company Using a Perpetual Inventory System

RAY COMPANY
WORKSHEET
FOR YEAR ENDED DECEMBER 31, 201X

Account Titles	Trial Balance Dr.	Trial Balance Cr.	Adjustments Dr.	Adjustments Cr.	Adjusted Trial Balance Dr.	Adjusted Trial Balance Cr.	Income Statement Dr.	Income Statement Cr.	Balance Sheet Dr.	Balance Sheet Cr.
Cash	248600				248600				248600	
Merchandise Inventory	20000				20000				20000	
Prepaid Rent	115200			(B)10000	105200				105200	
Prepaid Insurance	6000				6000				6000	
Office Equipment	216000				216000				216000	
Accumulated Dep., Off. Equip.		56000		(C)6000		62000				62000
Unearned Storage Fees		251600	(A)51600			200000				200000
Accounts Payable		10000				10000				10000
B. Ray, Capital		193200				193200				193200
Sales		1104000				1104000		1104000		
Sales Returns and Allowances	54600				54600		54600			
Sales Discounts	21600				21600		21600			
COGS*	561000				561000		561000			
Salaries Expense	201600		(D)20000		221600		221600			
Insurance Expense	139200				139200		139200			
Utilities Expense	9600				9600		9600			
Plumbing Expense	21400				21400		21400			
	1614800	1614800								
Storage Fees Earned				(A)51600		51600		51600		
Rent Expense			(B)10000		10000		10000			
Dep. Expense, Equip.			(C)6000		6000		6000			
Salaries Payable				(D)20000		20000				20000
			87600	87600	1640800	1640800	1045000	1155600	595800	485200
Net Income							110600			110600
							1155600	1155600	595800	595800

*$624 ($824 − $200) + $5,256 − $168 − $102.

Completion of the Accounting Cycle for a Merchandise Company

THE GAME PLAN

Have you noticed the high price of electronic games for children? Prices seem to be increasing month by month. Stores like Toys"R"Us try to be competitive but they have to make sure that they make a profit as well. Each year, companies prepare financial statements to see how their profit-making operations are performing. Two of the financial statements that they prepare are called the income statement and the balance sheet. In this chapter, you will learn to prepare these two financial statements. The income statement will look at the company's revenues, amount of returns, cost of goods sold, and operating expenses. The balance sheet will provide a look at the company's assets, liabilities, and stockholders' equity on a certain date. The preparation of these financial statements allows stakeholders, such as creditors and investors, to evaluate whether or not they want to do business with a company, whether lending it money or investing in the company stock. Financial statements are an important barometer of a company's success.

LEARNING OBJECTIVES

1. Preparing financial statements for a merchandise company.
2. Recording adjusting and closing entries for a merchandise company.
3. Preparing a post-closing trial balance for a merchandise company.
4. Completing reversing entries.

When you buy a toy at Toys"R"Us just keep in mind all the steps Toys"R"Us must take to complete its accounting cycle. In this chapter we discuss the steps involved in completing the accounting cycle for a merchandise company. These steps include preparing financial reports, journalizing and posting adjusting and closing entries, preparing a post-closing trial balance, and reversing entries.

LEARNING UNIT 12-1 PREPARING FINANCIAL STATEMENTS

As we discussed in Chapter 5, when we were dealing with a service company rather than a merchandise company, the three financial statements can be prepared from the worksheet. Let's begin by looking at how Art's Wholesale Clothing Company prepares the income statement.

● LO1   The Income Statement

Art is interested in knowing how well his shop performed for the year ended December 31, 201X. What were its net sales? What was the level of returns of goods from dissatisfied customers? What was the cost of the goods brought into the store versus the selling price received? How many goods were returned to suppliers? What is the cost of the goods that have not been sold? What was the cost of the Freight-In? The income statement in Figure 12.1 is prepared from the income statement columns of the worksheet. Note that no debit or credit columns appear on the formal income statement; the inside columns in financial reports are used for subtotaling, not for debit and credit.

The income statement is broken down into several sections. Remembering the sections can help you set it up correctly on your own. The income statement shows the following:

	Net Sales
−	Cost of Goods Sold
=	Gross Profit
−	Operating Expenses
=	Net Income from Operations
+	Other Income
−	Other Expenses
=	Net Income

Let's take these sections one at a time and see where the figures come from on the worksheet.

Revenue Section

Net Sales The first major category of the income statement shows net sales. The figure here—$93,380—is not on the worksheet. Instead, the accountant must combine the amounts for gross sales, sales returns and allowances, and sales discount found on the worksheet to arrive at a figure for net sales. Thus these individual amounts are not summarized in a single figure for net sales until the formal income statement is prepared.

Cost of Goods Sold Section The figures for Merchandise Inventory are shown separately on the worksheet. The $19,000 represents the beginning inventory of the period, and the $4,000, calculated from an inventory sheet, is the ending inventory. Note that on the financial report the cost of goods sold section uses two separate figures for inventory.

Note that the following numbers are not found on the worksheet but are shown on the formal income statement (they are combined by the accountant in preparing the income statement):

- Net Purchases: $50,460 (Purchases – Purchases Discount – Purchases Returns and Allowances)
- Net Cost of Purchases: $50,910 (Net Purchases + Freight-In)
- Cost of Goods Available for Sale: $69,910 (Beginning Inventory + Net Cost of Purchases)
- Cost of Goods Sold: $65,910 (Cost of Goods Available for Sale – Ending Inventory)

COACHING TIP

	Sales
−	Sales Ret. & Allow.
−	Sales Discount
=	Net Sales

COACHING TIP

	Beg. Inventory
+	Net Cost of Purchases
−	Ending Inventory
=	Cost of Goods Sold

FIGURE 12.1
Partial Worksheet and Income Statement

ART'S WHOLESALE CLOTHING COMPANY
INCOME STATEMENT
FOR YEAR ENDED DECEMBER 31, 201X

Revenue:				
Gross Sales				$95 000 00
Less: Sales Ret. and Allow.			$ 95000	
Sales Discount			67000	162000
Net Sales				$93 380 00
Cost of Goods Sold:				
Merchandise Inventory, 1/1/1X			$19 000 00	
Purchases		$52 000 00		
Less: Purch. Discount	$ 86000			
Purch. Ret. and Allow.	68000	154000		
Net Purchases		$50 460 00		
Add: Freight-In		45000		
Net Cost of Purchases			50 910 00	
Cost of Goods Available for Sale			$69 910 00	
Less: Merch. Inv., 12/31/1X			40 000 00	
Cost of Goods Sold				65 910 00
Gross Profit				$27 470 00
Operating Expenses:				
Salaries Expense			$123 00 00	
Payroll Tax Expense			42000	
Dep. Exp., Store Equip.			5000	
Supplies Expense			50000	
Insurance Expense			30000	
Postage Expense			2500	
Miscellaneous Expense			3000	
Total Operating Expenses				13 625 00
Net Income from Operations				$13 845 00
Other Income:				
Rental Income			$ 20000	
Other Expenses:				
Interest Expense			30000	10000
Net Income				$13 745 00

ART'S WHOLESALE CLOTHING COMPANY
PARTIAL WORKSHEET
FOR YEAR ENDED DECEMBER 31, 201X

	Income Statement	
	Dr.	Cr.
Income Summary	19 000 00	40 000 00
Sales		95 000 00
Sales Returns and Allowances	95000	
Sales Discount	67000	
Purchases	52 000 00	
Purchases Discount		86000
Purchases Returns and Allowances		68000
Freight-In	45000	
Salaries Expense	123 000 00	
Payroll Tax Expense	42000	
Postage Expense	2500	
Miscellaneous Expense	3000	
Interest Expense	30000	
Rental Income		20000
Supplies Expense	50000	
Insurance Expense	30000	
Depreciation Expense, Store Equip.	5000	
Salaries Payable		
	86 995 00	100 740 00
Net Income	13 745 00	
	100 740 00	100 740 00

Gross Profit Gross profit ($27,470) is calculated by subtracting the cost of goods sold from net sales ($93,380 – $65,910). This amount is not found on the worksheet.

Operating Expenses Section Like the other figures we have discussed, the business's operating expenses do not appear on the worksheet. To get this figure ($13,625), the accountant adds up all the expenses from the worksheet.

Many operating companies break expenses down into those directly related to the selling activity of the company (selling expenses) and those related to administrative or office activity (administrative expenses or general expenses). Here's a sample list (not connected to example for Art's Wholesale) broken down into these two categories:

Operating Expenses

- Selling Expenses:

    Sales Salaries Expense

    Delivery Expense

    Advertising Expense

    Depreciation Expense, Store Equipment

    Insurance Expense

      Total Selling Expenses

- Administrative Expenses:

    Rent Expense

    Office Salaries Expense

    Utilities Expense

    Office Supplies Expense

    Depreciation Expense, Office Equipment

      Total Administrative Expenses

        Total Operating Expenses

Other Income (or Other Revenue) Section The other income, or other revenue, section is used to record any revenue other than revenue from sales. For example, Art's Wholesale makes a profit from subletting a portion of a building. The $200 of rental income the company earns from this is recorded in the other income section.

Other Expenses Section The other expenses section is used to record nonoperating expenses, that is, expenses that are not related to the main operating activities of the business. For example, Art's Wholesale owes $300 interest on money it has borrowed. That expense is shown in the other expenses section.

Statement of Owner's Equity

The information used to prepare the statement of owner's equity comes from the balance sheet columns of the worksheet. Keep in mind that the capital account in the ledger should be checked to see whether any additional investments occurred during the period. Figure 12.2 shows how the worksheet aids in this step. The ending figure of $13,050 for Art Newner, Capital is carried over to the balance sheet, which is the final report we look at in this chapter.

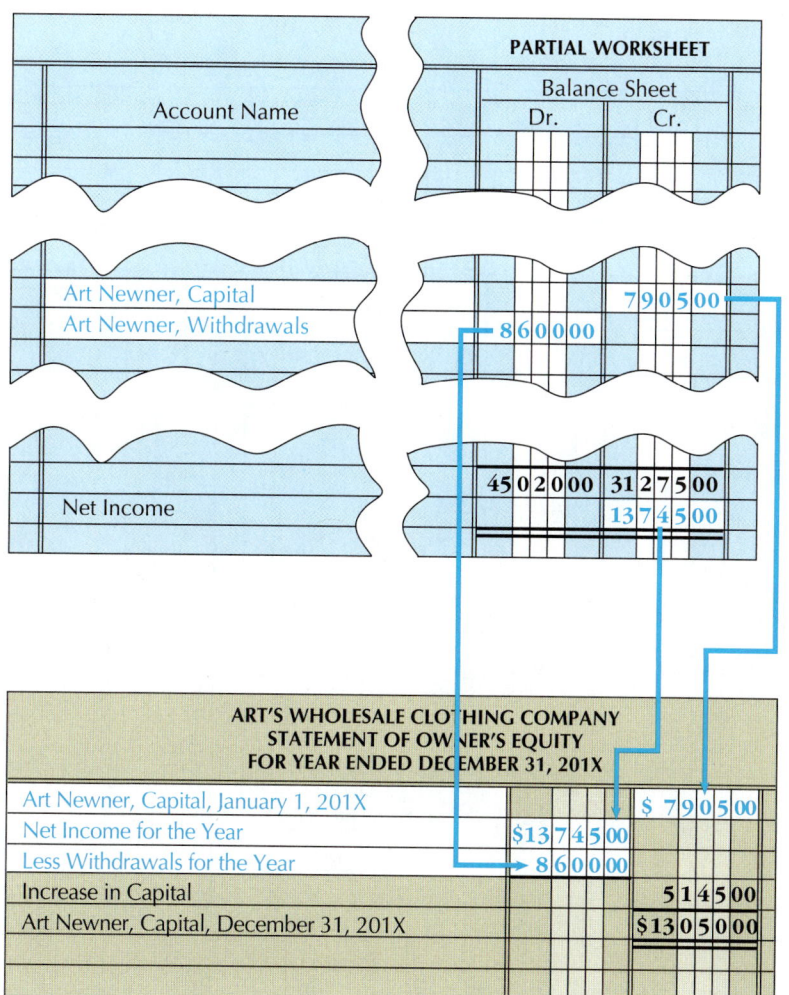

FIGURE 12.2
Preparing Statement of Owner's Equity from the Worksheet

COACHING TIP

Any additional investment by the owner would be added to his or her beginning capital amount.

The Balance Sheet

Figure 12.3 shows how a worksheet is used to aid in the preparation of a classified balance sheet. A classified balance sheet breaks down the assets and liabilities into more detail. Classified balance sheets provide management, owners, creditors, and suppliers with more information about the company's ability to pay current and long-term debts. They also provide a more complete financial picture of the firm.

The categories on the classified balance sheet are as follows:

- Current assets are defined as cash and assets that will be converted into cash or used up during the normal operating cycle of the company or one year, whichever is longer. (Think of the operating cycle as the time period it takes a company to buy and sell merchandise and then collect accounts receivable.)

  Accountants list current assets in order of how easily they can be converted into cash (called *liquidity*). In most cases, Accounts Receivable can be turned into cash more quickly than Merchandise Inventory. For example, it can be quite difficult to sell an outdated computer in a computer store or to sell last year's model car this year.

- Plant and equipment are long-lived assets that are used in the production or sale of goods or services. Art's Wholesale has only one plant asset, store equipment; other plant assets could include buildings and land. The assets are usually listed in order according to how long they will last; the shortest-lived assets are listed first. Land is always the last asset listed (and—keep in mind—land is never depreciated). Note that we still show the cost of the asset less its accumulated depreciation.

Classified balance sheet A balance sheet that categorizes assets as current assets or plant and equipment and groups liabilities as current or long-term liabilities.

Current assets Assets that can be converted into cash or used within one year or the normal operating cycle of the business, whichever is longer.

Operating cycle Average time it takes to buy and sell merchandise and then collect accounts receivable.

Plant and equipment Long-lived assets such as equipment, buildings or land that are used in the production or sale of goods or services.

FIGURE 12.3
Partial Worksheet and Classified Balance Sheet

ART'S WHOLESALE CLOTHING COMPANY
WORKSHEET
FOR YEAR ENDED DECEMBER 31, 201X

	Balance Sheet	
	Dr.	Cr.
Cash	12920 00	
Petty Cash	100 00	
Accounts Receivable	14500 00	
Merchandise Inventory	4000 00	
Supplies	300 00	
Prepaid Insurance	600 00	
Store Equipment	4000 00	
Acc. Dep., Store Equipment		450 00
Accounts Payable		17900 00
Federal Income Tax Payable		800 00
FICA—Social Security Payable		454 00
FICA—Medicare Payable		106 00
State Income Tax Payable		200 00
SUTA Tax Payable		108 00
FUTA Tax Payable		32 00
Unearned Rent		400 00
Mortgage Payable		2320 00
Art Newner, Capital		7905 00
Salaries Payable		600 00
	45020 00	31275 00
Net Income		13745 00
	45020 00	45020 00

ART'S WHOLESALE CLOTHING COMPANY
CLASSIFIED BALANCE SHEET
FOR YEAR ENDED DECEMBER 31, 201X

Assets

Current Assets:			
Cash	$12920 00		
Petty Cash	100 00		
Accounts Receivable	14500 00		
Merchandise Inventory	4000 00		
Supplies	300 00		
Prepaid Insurance	600 00		
Total Current Assets		$32420 00	
Plant and Equipment:			
Store Equipment	$4000 00		
Less: Accum. Depreciation	450 00	3550 00	
Total Assets		$35970 00	

Liabilities

Current Liabilities:			
Mortgage Payable (current portion)	$ 320 00		
Accounts Payable	17900 00		
Federal Income Tax Payable	800 00		
FICA—Social Security Payable	454 00		
FICA—Medicare Payable	106 00		
State Income Tax Payable	200 00		
SUTA Tax Payable	108 00		
FUTA Tax Payable	32 00		
Salaries Payable	600 00		
Unearned Rent	400 00		
Total Current Liabilities		$20920 00	
Long-Term Liabilities			
Mortgage Payable		2000 00	
Total Liabilities		$22920 00	
Owner's Equity			
Art Newner, Capital, December 31, 201X		13050 00	
Total Liabilities and Owner's Equity		$35970 00	

- **Current liabilities** are the debts or obligations of Art's Wholesale that must be paid within one year or one operating cycle. The order of listing accounts in this section is not always the same; many times companies will list their liabilities in the order they expect to pay them off. Note that the current portion of the mortgage, $320 (that portion due within one year), is listed before Accounts Payable.

- **Long-term liabilities** are debts or obligations that are not due and payable for a comparatively long period, usually for more than one year. For Art's Wholesale the only long-term liability is Mortgage Payable. The long-term portion of the mortgage is listed here; the current portion, due within one year, is listed under current liabilities.

Current liabilities Obligations that will come due within one year or within the operating cycle, whichever is longer.

COACHING TIP

Mortgage Payable:

$2,320

– 320 current portion
_____

$2,000 long-term liability

Long-term liabilities Obligations that are not due or payable for a long time, usually for more than a year.

LEARNING UNIT 12-1 REVIEW

AT THIS POINT you should be able to do the following:

- Prepare a detailed income statement from the worksheet.
- Explain the difference between selling and administrative expenses.
- Prepare a statement of owner's equity from the worksheet.
- Explain as well as compare current assets with plant and equipment.
- Explain the difference between current and long-term liabilities.
- Prepare a classified balance sheet from a worksheet.

 Instant Replay ◉ Self-Review Quiz 12-1

Using the worksheet from Self-Review Quiz 11-2 in Chapter 11 (p. 436), prepare in proper form (1) an income statement, (2) a statement of owner's equity, and (3) a classified balance sheet for Ray Company.

Solutions to Instant Replay: Self-Review Quiz 12-1

1

FIGURE 12.4
Income Statement for Ray Company

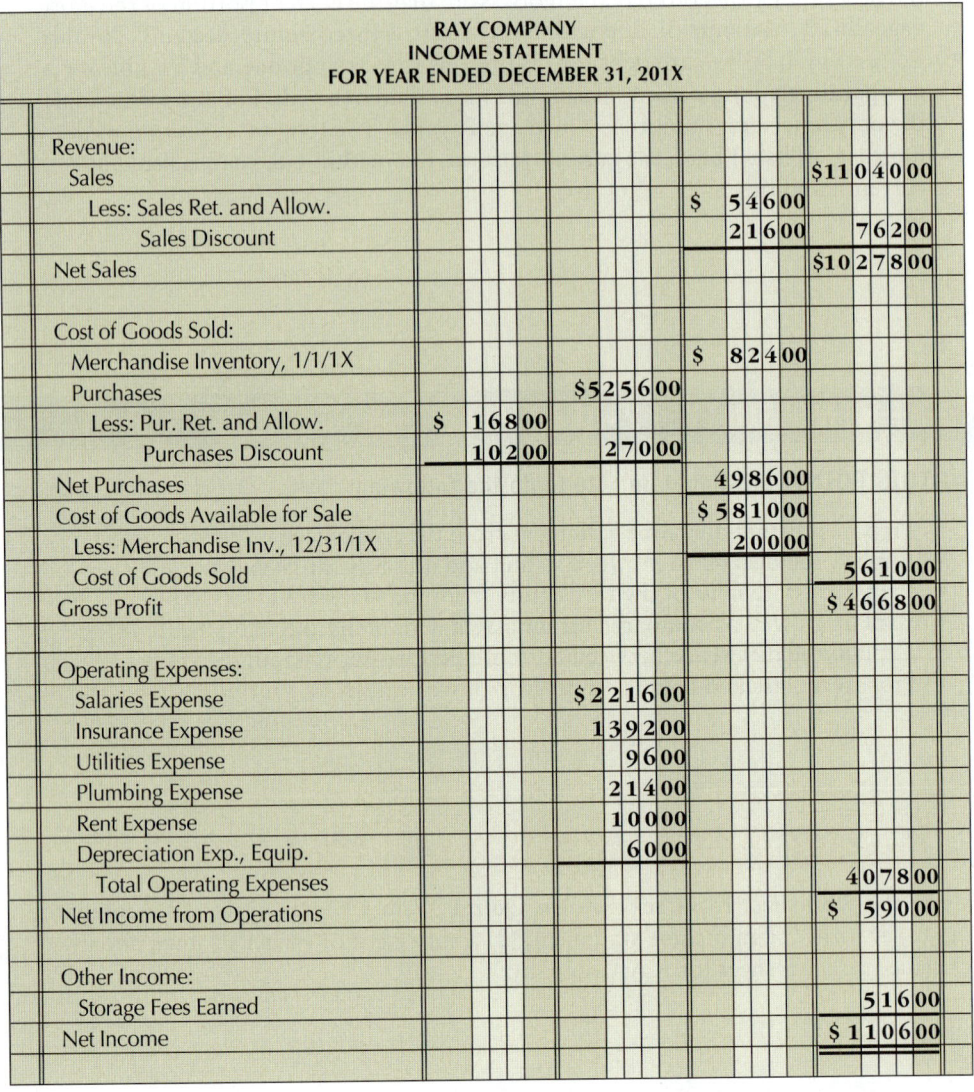

RAY COMPANY INCOME STATEMENT FOR YEAR ENDED DECEMBER 31, 201X				
Revenue:				
Sales				$110 400 00
Less: Sales Ret. and Allow.			$ 5 460 00	
Sales Discount			2 160 00	7 620 00
Net Sales				$102 780 00
Cost of Goods Sold:				
Merchandise Inventory, 1/1/1X			$ 8 240 00	
Purchases		$52 560 00		
Less: Pur. Ret. and Allow.	$ 1 680 00			
Purchases Discount	1 020 00	2 700 00		
Net Purchases			49 860 00	
Cost of Goods Available for Sale			$ 58 100 00	
Less: Merchandise Inv., 12/31/1X			2 000 00	
Cost of Goods Sold				56 100 00
Gross Profit				$ 46 680 00
Operating Expenses:				
Salaries Expense		$ 22 160 00		
Insurance Expense		13 920 00		
Utilities Expense		96 00		
Plumbing Expense		2 140 00		
Rent Expense		1 000 00		
Depreciation Exp., Equip.		600 00		
Total Operating Expenses				40 780 00
Net Income from Operations				$ 5 900 00
Other Income:				
Storage Fees Earned				5 160 00
Net Income				$ 11 060 00

2

FIGURE 12.5
Statement of Owner's Equity for Ray Company

RAY COMPANY STATEMENT OF OWNER'S EQUITY FOR YEAR ENDED DECEMBER 31, 201X	
B. Ray, Capital, 1/1/1X	$ 19 320 0
Net Income for the Year	11 060 0
B. Ray, Capital, 12/31/1X	$ 30 380 0

3

RAY COMPANY BALANCE SHEET DECEMBER 31, 201X				
Assets				
Current Assets:				
Cash		$ 2 4 8 6 00		
Merchandise Inventory		2 0 0 00		
Prepaid Rent		1 0 5 2 00		
Prepaid Insurance		6 0 00		
Total Current Assets			$ 3 7 9 8 00	
Plant and Equipment:				
Office Equipment		$ 2 1 6 0 00		
Less: Accumulated Depreciation		6 2 0 00	1 5 4 0 00	
Total Assets			$ 5 3 3 8 00	
Liabilities				
Current Liabilities				
Accounts Payable	$ 1 0 0 00			
Salaries Payable		2 0 0 00		
Unearned Storage Fees		2 0 0 0 00		
Total Liabilities			$ 2 3 0 0 00	
Owner's Equity				
B. Ray, Capital, December 31, 201X			3 0 3 8 00	
Total Liabilities and Owner's Equity			$ 5 3 3 8 00	

FIGURE 12.6
Balance Sheet for Ray Company

LEARNING UNIT 12-2 JOURNALIZING AND POSTING ADJUSTING AND CLOSING ENTRIES; PREPARING THE POST-CLOSING TRIAL BALANCE

● LO2

Journalizing and Posting Adjusting Entries

From the worksheet of Art's Wholesale (repeated in Figure 12.7 for your convenience), the adjusting entries can be journalized from the adjustments column and posted to the ledger. Keep in mind that the adjustments have been placed only on the worksheet, not in the journal or in the ledger. At this point, the journal does not reflect adjustments and the ledger still contains only unadjusted amounts.

Partial Ledger

Merchandise Inventory 114			Income Summary 313	
Dr.	Cr.		Dr.	Cr.
19,000	19,000 (A)		(A) 19,000	4,000 (B)
(B) 4,000				

FIGURE 12.7
Completed Worksheet

ART'S WHOLESALE CLOTHING CO.
WORKSHEET
FOR YEAR ENDED DECEMBER 31, 201X

	Trial Balance Dr.	Trial Balance Cr.	Adjustments Dr.	Adjustments Cr.
Cash	12 920 00			
Petty Cash	100 00			
Accounts Receivable	14 500 00			
Merchandise Inventory	19 000 00		(B) 4 000 00	(A) 19 000 00
Supplies	800 00			(D) 500 00
Prepaid Insurance	900 00			(E) 300 00
Store Equipment	4 000 00			
Acc. Dep., Store Equipment		400 00		(F) 5 00
Accounts Payable		17 900 00		
Federal Income Tax Payable		800 00		
FICA—Social Security Payable		454 00		
FICA—Medicare Payable		106 00		
State Income Tax Payable		200 00		
SUTA Tax Payable		108 00		
FUTA Tax Payable		32 00		
Unearned Rent		600 00	(C) 200 00	
Mortgage Payable		2 320 00		
Art Newner, Capital		7 905 00		
Art Newner, Withdrawals	8 600 00			
Income Summary			(A) 19 000 00	(B) 4 000 00
Sales		95 000 00		
Sales Returns and Allowances	950 00			
Sales Discount	670 00			
Purchases	52 000 00			
Purchases Discount		860 00		
Purchases Returns and Allowances		680 00		
Freight-In	450 00			
Salaries Expense	11 700 00		(G) 600 00	
Payroll Tax Expense	420 00			
Postage Expense	25 00			
Miscellaneous Expense	30 00			
Interest Expense	300 00			
	127 365 00	127 365 00		
Rental Income				(C) 200 00
Supplies Expense			(D) 500 00	
Insurance Expense			(E) 300 00	
Depreciation Expense, Store Equip.			(F) 5 00	
Salaries Payable				(G) 600 00
			24 650 00	24 650 00
Net Income				

FIGURE 12.7
(continued)

Account	Adjusted Trial Bal. Dr.	Adjusted Trial Bal. Cr.	Income Statement Dr.	Income Statement Cr.	Balance Sheet Dr.	Balance Sheet Cr.
Cash	1292000				1292000	
Petty Cash	10000				10000	
Accounts Receivable	1450000				1450000	
Merchandise Inventory	400000				400000	
Supplies	30000				30000	
Prepaid Insurance	60000				60000	
Store Equipment	400000				400000	
Acc. Dep., Store Equipment		45000				45000
Accounts Payable		1790000				1790000
Federal Income Tax Payable		80000				80000
FICA—Social Security Payable		45400				45400
FICA—Medicare Payable		10600				10600
State Income Tax Payable		20000				20000
SUTA Tax Payable		10800				10800
FUTA Tax Payable		3200				3200
Unearned Rent		40000				40000
Mortgage Payable		232000				232000
Art Newner, Capital		790500				790500
Art Newner, Withdrawals	860000				860000	
Income Summary	1900000	400000	1900000	400000		
Sales		9500000		9500000		
Sales Returns and Allowances	95000		95000			
Sales Discount	67000		67000			
Purchases	5200000		5200000			
Purchases Discount		86000		86000		
Purchases Returns and Allowances		68000		68000		
Freight-In	45000		45000			
Salaries Expense	1230000		1230000			
Payroll Tax Expense	42000		42000			
Postage Expense	2500		2500			
Miscellaneous Expense	3000		3000			
Interest Expense	30000		30000			
Rental Income		20000		20000		
Supplies Expense	50000		50000			
Insurance Expense	30000		30000			
Depreciation Expense, Store Equip.	5000		5000			
Salaries Payable		60000				60000
	13201500	13201500	8699500	10074000	4502000	3127500
Net Income			1374500			1374500
			10074000	10074000	4502000	4502000

Supplies 115			Supplies Expense 614	
Dr.	Cr.		Dr.	Cr.
800	500 (D)		(D) 500	

Prepaid Insurance 116			Insurance Expense 615	
Dr.	Cr.		Dr.	Cr.
900	300 (E)		(E) 300	

Accum. Dep., Store Equipment 122			Dep. Expense, Store Equip. 613	
Dr.	Cr.		Dr.	Cr.
	400		(F) 50	
	50 (F)			

Salaries Payable 212			Salaries Exp. 611	
Dr.	Cr.		Dr.	Cr.
	600 (G)		11,700	
			(G) 600	

Unearned Rent 219			Rental Income 414	
Dr.	Cr.		Dr.	Cr.
(C) 200	600			200 (C)

The journalized and posted adjusting entries are shown in Figure 12.8. Note that the liability Unearned Rent is reduced by $200 and Rental Income has increased by $200.

FIGURE 12.8
Journalized and Posted
Adjusting Entries

ART'S WHOLESALE CLOTHING CO.
GENERAL JOURNAL

Page 2

Date		Account Titles and Description	PR	Dr.	Cr.
		Adjusting Entries			
	31	Income Summary	313	1900000	
		Merchandise Inventory	114		1900000
		Transferred beginning inventory			
		to Income Summary			
	31	Merchandise Inventory	114	400000	
		Income Summary	313		400000
		Records cost of ending inventory			
	31	Unearned Rent	219	20000	
		Rental Income	414		20000
		Rental income earned			
	31	Supplies Expense	614	50000	
		Supplies	115		50000
		Supplies consumed			
	31	Insurance Expense	615	30000	
		Prepaid Insurance	116		30000
		Insurance expired			
	31	Dep. Exp., Store Equipment	613	5000	
		Acc. Dep., Store Equipment	122		5000
		Depreciation on equipment			
	31	Salaries Expense	611	60000	
		Salaries Payable	212		60000
		Accrued salaries			

	Income Summary 313		
	Dr.	Cr.	
Adj.	19,000	4,000	Adj.
Clos.	67,995	96,740	Clos.
	86,995	100,740	
Net Income → Clos.	13,745		

COACHING TIP

Note that Income Summary before the closing process contains the adjustments for Merchandise Inventory. The end result is that the net income of $13,745 is closed to the Capital account.

Journalizing and Posting Closing Entries

In Chapter 5, we discussed the closing process for a service company. The goals of closing are the same for a merchandise company. These goals are (1) to clear all temporary accounts in the ledger to zero and (2) to update capital in the ledger to its latest balance. The company must use the worksheet and the steps listed here to complete the closing process.

STEP 1 Close all balances on the income statement credit column of the worksheet, except Income Summary, by debits.
Then credit the total to the Income Summary account.

STEP 2 Close all balances on the income statement debit column of the worksheet, except Income Summary, by credits.
Then debit the total to the Income Summary account.

STEP 3 Transfer the balance of the Income Summary account to the Capital account.

STEP 4 Transfer the balance of the owner's Withdrawals account to the Capital account.

Let's look now at the journalized closing entries in Figure 12.9. When these entries are posted, all the temporary accounts will have zero balances in the ledger, and the Capital account will be updated with a new balance.

Let's take a moment to look at the Income Summary account in T account form:

The Post-Closing Trial Balance

● **LO3**

The post-closing trial balance shown in Figure 12.10 (on the following page spread to the right) is prepared from the general ledger. Note first that all temporary accounts have been closed and thus are not shown on this post-closing trial balance. Note also that the ending inventory figure of the last accounting period, $4,000, becomes the beginning inventory figure on January 1, 201X.

FIGURE 12.9
General Journal Closing Entries

ART'S WHOLESALE CLOTHING CO.
GENERAL JOURNAL

Page 2

Date	Account Titles and Description	PR	Dr.	Cr.
	Closing Entries			
31	Sales	411	95 00 0 00	
	Rental Income	414	2 0 0 00	
	Purchases Discount	512	8 6 0 00	
	Purchases Ret. and Allow.	513	6 8 0 00	
	Income Summary	313		96 7 4 0 00
	Transfers credit account balances			
	on income statement column of			
	worksheet to Income Summary			
31	Income Summary	313	67 9 9 5 00	
	Sales Returns and Allowances	412		9 5 0 00
	Sales Discount	413		6 7 0 00
	Purchases	511		52 0 0 0 00
	Freight-In	514		4 5 0 00
	Salaries Expense	611		12 3 0 0 00
	Payroll Tax Expense	612		4 2 0 00
	Postage Expense	616		2 5 00
	Miscellaneous Expense	617		3 0 00
	Interest Expense	618		3 0 0 00
	Supplies Expense	614		5 0 0 00
	Insurance Expense	615		3 0 0 00
	Depreciation Expense, Store Equip.	613		5 0 00
	Transfers all expenses, and			
	deductions to Sales are			
	closed to Income Summary			
31	Income Summary	313	13 7 4 5 00	
	A. Newner, Capital	311		13 7 4 5 00
	Transfer of net income to			
	Capital from Income Summary			
31	A. Newner, Capital	311	8 6 0 0 00	
	A. Newner, Withdrawals	312		8 6 0 0 00
	Closes withdrawals to			
	Capital Account			

LEARNING UNIT 12-2 REVIEW

AT THIS POINT you should be able to do the following:

- Journalize and post adjusting entries for a merchandise company.
- Explain the relationship of the worksheet to the adjusting and closing process.
- Complete the closing process for a merchandise company.
- Prepare a post-closing trial balance and explain why ending Merchandise Inventory is not a temporary account.

Instant Replay ● Self-Review Quiz 12-2

Using the worksheet from Self-Review Quiz 11-2 in Chapter 11 (p. 436), journalize the closing entries.

FIGURE 12.10
Post-Closing Trial Balance for Art's Wholesale Clothing Company

ART'S WHOLESALE CLOTHING COMPANY POSTCLOSING TRIAL BALANCE DECEMBER 31, 201X	Dr.	Cr.
Cash	12 9 2 0 00	
Petty Cash	1 0 0 00	
Accounts Receivable	14 5 0 0 00	
Merchandise Inventory	4 0 0 0 00	
Supplies	3 0 0 00	
Prepaid Insurance	6 0 0 00	
Store Equipment	4 0 0 0 00	
Accum. Depreciation, Store Equipment		4 5 0 00
Accounts Payable		17 9 0 0 00
Federal Income Tax Payable		8 0 0 00
FICA—Social Security Payable		4 5 4 00
FICA—Medicare Payable		1 0 6 00
State Income Tax Payable		2 0 0 00
SUTA Tax Payable		1 0 8 00
FUTA Tax Payable		3 2 00
Salary Payable		6 0 0 00
Unearned Rent		4 0 0 00
Mortgage Payable		2 3 2 0 00
Art Newner, Capital		13 0 5 0 00
	36 4 2 0 00	36 4 2 0 00

Solution to Instant Replay Self-Review Quiz 12-2

FIGURE 12.11
Closing Entries Journalized

					Page 2
Date		Account Titles and Description	PR	Dr.	Cr.
		Closing Entries			
Dec.	31	Sales		11 0 4 0 00	
		Storage Fees Earned		5 1 6 00	
		Purchases Returns and Allowances		1 6 8 00	
		Purchases Discount		1 0 2 00	
		Income Summary			11 8 2 6 00
	31	Income Summary		10 0 9 6 00	
		Sales Returns and Allowances			5 4 6 00
		Sales Discount			2 1 6 00
		Purchases			5 2 5 6 00
		Salaries Expense			2 2 1 6 00
		Insurance Expense			1 3 9 2 00
		Utilities Expense			9 6 00
		Plumbing Expense			2 1 4 00
		Rent Expense			1 0 0 00
		Depreciation Exp., Equipment			6 0 00
	31	Income Summary		1 1 0 6 00	
		B. Ray, Capital			1 1 0 6 00

⬤ **LO4**

LEARNING UNIT 12-3 REVERSING ENTRIES (OPTIONAL SECTION)

Reversing entries Optional bookkeeping technique in which certain adjusting entries are reversed or switched on the first day of the new accounting period so that transactions in the new period can be recorded without referring back to prior adjusting entries.

The accounting cycle for Art's Wholesale Clothing Company is completed. Now let's look at reversing entries, an optional way of handling some adjusting entries. Reversing entries are general journal entries that are the opposite of adjusting entries. Reversing entries help reduce potential errors and simplify the recordkeeping process. If Art's accountant makes reversing entries, routine transactions can be made in the usual steps.

To help explain the concept of reversing entries, let's look at these two adjustments that could be reversed:

1. When an increase occurs in an asset account (no previous balance).

    Example: Interest Receivable

    Interest Income

    (Interest earned but not collected is covered in later chapters.)

2. When an increase occurs in a liability account (no previous balance).

    Example: Salaries Expense

    Salaries Payable

With the exception of businesses in their first year of operation, accounts such as Accumulated Depreciation or Inventory cannot be reduced because they have previous balances.

Art's bookkeeper handles an entry without reversing for salaries at the end of the year (see Figure 12.12). Note that the permanent account, Salaries Payable, carries over to the new accounting period a $600 balance. Remember that the $600 was an expense of the prior year.

FIGURE 12.12
Reversing Entries Not Used

❶ On December 31, an adjusting entry was journalized and posted for $600 of salaries incurred but not paid.

ADJUSTING JOURNAL ENTRY		
Salaries Expense	600 00	
Salaries Payable		600 00

T ACCOUNT UPDATE

Salaries Exp.	Salaries Pay.
11,700	600
600	

❷ On January 8 after closing entries have been journalized and posted, Salaries Expense has a zero balance.

CLOSING JOURNAL ENTRY		
Income Summary	XXX	
Salaries Expense		12 300 00

Salaries Exp.		Salaries Pay.
11,700	12,300	600
600		

On January 8 of the new year, the payroll to be paid is $2,000. If the optional reversing entry is *not* used, the bookkeeper must make the following compound Journal journal entry as shown in Figure 12.13.

FIGURE 12.13
Entry When Optional Reversing Entry Is Not Used

Salaries Payable	600 00	
Salaries Expense	1 400 00	
Cash		2 000 00

Salaries Exp.	Salaries Pay.	Cash
1,400	600 | 600	| 2,000

To do so, the bookkeeper has to refer back to the adjustment on December 31 to determine how much of the salary of $2,000 is indeed a new salary expense and what portion was shown in the old year although not paid. It is easy to see how potential errors can result if the bookkeeper pays the payroll but forgets about the adjustment in the previous year. In this way, reversing entries can help avoid potential errors.

Figure 12.14 shows the four steps the bookkeeper would take if reversing entries were used. Note that steps 1 and 2 are the same whether the accountant uses reversing entries or not.

FIGURE 12.14
Reversing Entries Used

❶
On December 31, an adjustment for salary was recorded.

Salaries Exp.		Salaries Pay.	
11,700			600
600			

❷
Closing entry on December 31.

Salaries Exp.		Salaries Pay.	
11,700	12,300		600
600			

❸
On January 1 (first day of the following fiscal period), a reverse adjusting entry was made for salary on December 31 (by "flipping" the previous adjustment).

Jan.	1	Salaries Payable	600 00		
		Salaries Expense		600 00	

Salaries Exp.		Salaries Pay.	
	600	600	600

This way, the liability is reduced to 0. We know it will be paid in this new period, but the Salaries Expense has a credit balance of $600 until the payroll is paid. When the payroll of $2,000 is paid, the following results:

❹
Paid Payroll $2,000.

Jan.	1	Salaries Expense	2000 00		
		Cash		2000 00	

Salaries Exp.		Cash	
2,000	600		2,000

Note that the balance of Salaries Expense is indeed only $1,400, the *true* expense in the new year. Reversing results in switching the adjustment the first day of the new period. Also note that each of the accounts ends up with the same balance no matter which method is chosen. Using a reversing entry for salaries, however, allows the accountant to make the normal entry when it is time to pay salaries.

LEARNING UNIT 12-3 REVIEW

AT THIS POINT you should be able to do the following:

- Explain the purpose of reversing entries.
- Complete a reversing entry.
- Explain when reversing entries can be used.

Instant Replay ⊙ Self-Review Quiz 12-3

Explain which of the following situations could be reversed:

1

Supplies Exp.		Supplies	
	200	800	200

2

Wages Exp.		Wages Payable	
3,200			200
200			

3

Sales		Unearned Sales	
	4,000	50	200
	50		

Solutions to Instant Replay: Self-Review Quiz 12-3

1. Not reversed: Asset Supplies is decreasing, not increasing.
2. Reversed: Liability is increasing and no previous balance exists.
3. Not reversed: Liability is decreasing and a previous balance exists.

Blueprint: Financial Statements

(1) INCOME STATEMENT

Revenue:				
Sales				$ XXX
Less: Sales Ret. and Allow.			$ XXX	
Sales Discount			XXX	XXX
Net Sales				$ XXXX
Cost of Goods Sold:				
Merchandise Inventory, 1/1/1X			$ XXX	
Purchases		$XXX		
Less: Purchases Discount	$XXX			
Purch. Ret. and Allow.	XXX	XXX		
Net Purchases		XXX		
Add: Freight-In		XXX		
Net Cost of Purchases			XXX	
Cost of Goods Avail. for Sale			$XXXX	
Less: Merch. Inv., 12/31/1X			XXX	
Cost of Goods Sold				XXXX
Gross Profit				$XXXX
Operating Expenses:				
~~			$XXX	
~~			XXX	
~~			XXX	
Total Operating Expenses				XXX
Net Income from Operations				$ XXX
Other Income:				
Rental Income			$ XXX	
Storage Fees Income			XXX	
Total Other Income			$ XXX	
Other Expenses:				
Interest Expenses			XXX	XXX
Net Income:				$ XXX

(2) STATEMENT OF OWNER'S EQUITY

Beginning Capital			$XXX
Additional Investments			XXX
Total Investment			$XXX
Net Income		$XXX	
Less: Withdrawals		XXX	
Increase in Capital			XXX
Ending Capital			$XXX

(3) BALANCE SHEET				
Assets				
Current Assets:				
Cash		$ XXXX		
Acccounts Receivable		XXXX		
Merchandise Inventory		XXXX		
Prepaid Insurance		XXX		
Total Current Assets			$ XXXX	
Plant and Equipment:				
Store Equipment	$XXXX			
Less Accumulated Depreciation	XXXX	$XXXX		
Office Equipment	$XXXX			
Less Accumulated Depreciation	XXX	XXX		
Total Plant and Equipment			XXXX	
Total Assets			$XXXX	
Liabilities				
Current Liabilities:				
Unearned Revenue		$XXX		
Mortgage Payable (current portion)		XXX		
Accounts Payable		XXX		
Salaries Payable		XX		
FICA—Social Security Payable		XX		
FICA—Medicare Payable		XX		
Income Taxes Payable		XX		
Total Current Liabilities			$XXX	
Long-Term Liabilities				
Mortgage Payable			$XXX	
Total Liabilities			$XXXX	
Owner's Equity				
Capital*			XXXX	
Total Liabilities and Owner's Equity			$XXXX	

* From statement of owner's equity

ACCOUNTING COACH

The following Coaching Tips are from Learning Units 12-1 to 12-3. Take the Pre-Game Checkup and use the Check Your Score at the bottom of the page to see how you are doing. The Accounting Coach provides tips before each Checkup to help you avoid common accounting errors.

LU 12-1 Preparing Financial Statements

Pre-Game Tips: The financial statements do not have debits and credits. The inside columns are for subtotaling. The totals on the financial statements will not always equal the same total amounts on the worksheet. Net Income will always be the same on the worksheet and income statement.

Purchases along with Merchandise Inventory will be added to Cost of Goods Sold, while Ending Inventory will be subtracted. Revenue less Cost of Goods Sold equals Gross Profit. To get Net Income from Operations, we subtract Gross Profit from Operating Expenses.

Pre-Game Checkup
Answer true or false to the following statements.

1. Freight-In is subtracted from Net Purchases.
2. Sales on the formal income statement has a credit balance.
3. Rental Income is shown on the balance sheet.
4. Accumulated Depreciation is a contra-asset on the balance sheet.
5. Unearned Rent is a revenue on the income statement.

LU 12-2 Journalizing and Posting Adjusting and Closing Entries; Preparing the Post-Closing Trial Balance

Pre-Game Tips: All adjustments can be taken from the adjustments column on the worksheet. Keep in mind that we adjust Inventory through Income Summary. We assume that old inventory is sold and is a cost and that the ending inventory is not a cost until it is sold. Income Summary is a temporary account and will not appear on the post-closing trial balance. The closing process transfers all temporary accounts through Income Summary except Withdrawals, which is closed directly to Capital.

Pre-Game Checkup
Answer true or false to the following statements.

1. Some temporary accounts will go on the post-closing trial balance.
2. Merchandise Inventory (ending) is listed as a debit on the post-closing trial balance.
3. Unearned Rent is a permanent account.
4. The Capital amount on the post-closing trial balance is listed before the closing process.
5. Purchases is listed on the post-closing trial balance.

LU 12-3 Reversing Entries (Optional Section)

Pre-Game Tips: Reversing entries is a way of handling some adjusting entries. By making a reversing entry, the accountant does not have to worry about the past adjustment and will make the normal entry when a transaction occurs. Reversing entries can be done when an increase occurs in an asset (no previous balance) or when an increase occurs in a liability account (no previous balance).

Pre-Game Checkup
Answer true or false to the following statements.
1. Reversing entries are required.
2. Interest Income and Interest Receivables may sometimes use a reversing entry.
3. Reversing entries are made in the old year, not the new.
4. Reversing entries for Salary will show true salary expense in the new year.
5. Regardless of whether reversing entries are used, the same balances will end up in each account.

CHECK YOUR SCORE: Answers to the Pre-Game Checkup

LU 12-1
1. False—Freight-In is added to Net Purchases.
2. False—Sales on the formal income statement has no debits or credits.
3. False—Rental Income is shown on the income statement.
4. True.
5. False—Unearned Rent is a liability on the balance sheet.

LU 12-2
1. False—No temporary accounts will go on the post-closing trial balance.
2. True.
3. True.
4. False—The Capital account on the post-closing trial balance is listed after the closing process.
5. False—Purchases is a temporary account and will not appear on the post-closing trial balance.

LU 12-3
1. False—Reversing entries are optional.
2. True.
3. False—Reversing entries are made in the new year.
4. True.
5. True.

Chapter Summary

Here are all the key concepts and equations to help you understand the concepts of this chapter and prepare you for your exam. After completing this review, go to MyAccountingLab for more practice opportunities.

Concepts You Should Know	Key Equations and Terms
L01 **Preparing financial statements for a merchandise company.** 1. The formal income statement can be prepared from the income statement columns of the worksheet. 2. No debit or credit columns are used on the formal income statement. 3. The cost of goods sold section has a figure for beginning inventory and a separate figure for ending inventory. 4. Operating expenses could be broken down into selling and administrative expenses of owner's equity. 5. A classified balance sheet breaks assets into current assets and plant and equipment. Liabilities are broken down into current and long term liabilities.	**Administrative expenses (general expenses)** (p. 458) **Classified balance sheet** (p. 459) **Current assets** (p. 459) **Current liabilities** (p. 461) **Long-term liabilities** (p. 461) **Operating cycle** (p. 459) **Other expenses** (p. 458) **Other income** (p. 458) **Plant and equipment** (p. 459) **Selling expenses** (p. 458)
L02 **Recording adjusting and closing entries.** 1. The information for journalizing, adjusting, and closing entries can be obtained from the worksheet. 2. In the closing process, the balance of all temporary accounts will be zero and the Capital account is brought up to its new balance. 3. Inventory is not a temporary account. The ending inventory, along with other permanent accounts, will be listed in the post-closing trial balance.	
L03 **Preparing a post-closing trial balance.** 1. Merchandise Inventory is a permanent account. 2. The ending inventory, along with other permanent accounts, will be listed in the post-closing trial balance.	
L04 **Completing reversing entries.** 1. Reversing entries are optional. They can aid in reducing potential errors and simplify the recordkeeping process. 2. The reversing entry "flips" the previous adjustment on the first day of a new fiscal period. 3. Reversing entries are only used if (a) assets are increasing and have no previous balance or (b) liabilities are increasing and have no previous balance.	**Reversing entries** (p. 470)

Discussion Questions and Critical Thinking/Ethical Case

1. Which columns of the worksheet aid in the preparation of the income statement?

2. Explain the components of cost of goods sold.

3. Explain how operating expenses can be broken down into different categories.

4. What is the difference between current assets and plant and equipment?

5. What is an operating cycle?

6. Why journalize adjusting entries *after* the formal reports in a manual system have been prepared?

7. Explain the steps of closing for a merchandise company.

8. Temporary accounts could appear on a post-closing trial balance. Agree or disagree?

9. What is the purpose of using reversing entries? Are they mandatory? When should they be used?

10. Janet Flynn, owner of Reel Company, plans to apply for a bank loan at Petro National Bank. Because the company has a lot of debt on its balance sheet, Janet does not plan to show the loan officer the balance sheet. She plans only to bring the income statement. Do you feel that this move is a sound financial move by Janet? You make the call. Write down your specific recommendations to Janet.

Concept Checks

MyAccountingLab

Calculate Net Sales

● **L01** *(5 MIN)*

1. From the following, calculate net sales:

Purchases	$101	Sales Discount	$21
Gross Sales	176	Operating Expenses	48
Sales Returns and Allowances	18		

Calculate Cost of Goods Sold

● **L01** *(5 MIN)*

2. Calculate Cost of Goods Sold:

Freight-In	$ 8	Ending Inventory	$ 7
Beginning Inventory	16	Net Purchases	67

Calculate Gross Profit and Net Income

● **L01** *(10 MIN)*

3. Using Exercises 1 and 2, calculate the following:
   a. Gross profit
   b. Net income or net loss

LO1, 2 *(15 MIN)*   **Classification of Accounts**

4.   Match the following categories to each account listed.

1. Current Asset
2. Plant and Equipment
3. Current Liabilities
4. Long-Term Liabilities

_____ **a.** Petty Cash   _____ **f.** Mortgage Payable (Current)
_____ **b.** Accounts Receivable   _____ **g.** SUTA Payable
_____ **c.** Prepaid Rent   _____ **h.** Accumulated Depreciation
_____ **d.** FICA Payable   _____ **i.** Computer Equipment
_____ **e.** Store Supplies   _____ **j.** Unearned Rent

LO4 *(10 MIN)*   **Reversing Entries**

5.   **a.** On January 1, prepare a reversing entry. On January 8, journalize the entry to record the paying of salary expense, $820.
       b. What will be the balance in Salaries Expense on January 8 (after posting)?

December 31:

Salaries Expense			Salaries Payable	
Dr.	Cr.		Dr.	Cr.
820	1,170 closing			350 Adj.
Adj. 350				

MyAccountingLab   # Exercises

Set A

LO1 *(15 MIN)*   **12A-1.** From the following accounts, prepare a cost of goods sold section in proper form: Merchandise Inventory, 12/31/1X, $9,040; Purchases Discount, $860; Merchandise Inventory, 12/01/1X, $4,400; Purchases, $60,000; Purchases Returns and Allowances, $1,040; Freight-In, $330.

LO1 *(10 MIN)*   **12A-2.** Give the category, the classification, and the report(s) on which each of the following appears (for example: Cash—asset, current asset, balance sheet):

a. Salaries Payable
b. Accounts Payable
c. Mortgage Payable
d. Unearned Legal Fees
e. SIT Payable
f. Office Equipment
g. Land

LO2 *(10 MIN)*   **12A-3.** From the partial worksheet in Figure 12.15, journalize the closing entries for December 31 for G. Jackson Co.

LO1 *(15 MIN)*   **12A-4.** From the worksheet in Exercise 12A-3, prepare the assets section of a classified balance sheet.

LO2, 4 *(30 MIN)*   **12A-5.** On December 31, 2012, $290 of salaries has been accrued. (Salaries before the accrued amount totaled $28,000.) The next payroll to be paid will be on February 3, 2013, for $5,700. Please do the following:

a. Journalize and post the adjusting entry (use T accounts).
b. Journalize and post the reversing entry on January 1.
c. Journalize and post the payment of the payroll. Cash has a balance of $17,000 before the payment of payroll on February 3.

G. JACKSON CO.
WORKSHEET
FOR YEAR ENDED DECEMBER 31, 201X

Account Titles	Income Statement Dr.	Income Statement Cr.	Balance Sheet Dr.	Balance Sheet Cr.
Cash			1 8 8 00	
Merchandise Inventory			4 5 2 00	
Prepaid Advertising			5 6 4 00	
Prepaid Insurance			3 1 00	
Office Equipment			1 0 6 2 00	
Accum. Dep., Office Equip.				2 1 2 00
Accounts Payable				2 5 1 00
G. Jackson, Capital				9 6 2 00
Income Summary	3 5 8 00	4 5 2 00		
Sales		5 4 9 6 00		
Sales Returns and Allowances	2 2 6 00			
Sales Discount	1 0 7 00			
Purchases	2 6 2 8 00			
Purchases Returns and Allow.		3 8 00		
Purchases Discount		5 3 00		
Salaries Expense	1 0 8 6 00			
Insurance Expense	6 9 4 00			
Utilities Expense	4 7 00			
Plumbing Expense	5 5 00			
Advertising Expense	1 0 00			
Dep. Expenses, Office Equip.	2 8 00			
Salaries Payable				7 2 00
	5 2 3 9 00	6 0 3 9 00	2 2 9 7 00	1 4 9 7 00
Net Income	8 0 0 00			8 0 0 00
	6 0 3 9 00	6 0 3 9 00	2 2 9 7 00	2 2 9 7 00

FIGURE 12.15
Worksheet for G. Jackson Co.

Set B

12B-1. From the following accounts, prepare a cost of goods sold section in proper form: Merchandise Inventory, 12/31/1X, $8,990; Purchases Discount, $850; Merchandise Inventory, 12/01/1X, $4,200; Purchases, $64,000; Purchases Returns and Allowances, $960; Freight-In $280.

● **LO1** *(15 MIN)*

12B-2. Give the category, the classification, and the report(s) on which each of the following appears (for example: Cash—asset, current asset, balance sheet):

● **LO1** *(10 MIN)*

    a. Wages Payable
    b. Accounts Payable
    c. Notes Payable
    d. Unearned Revenue
    e. FIT Payable
    f. Office Furniture
    g. Land

LO2 *(10 MIN)*   **12B-3.** From the partial worksheet in Figure 12.16, journalize the closing entries for December 31 for G. Jackson Co.

FIGURE 12.16
Worksheet for G. Jackson Co.

	G. JACKSON CO. WORKSHEET FOR YEAR ENDED DECEMBER 31, 201X				
Account	Income Statement Debit	Income Statement Credit	Balance Sheet Debit	Balance Sheet Credit
Cash			1 9 2 00	
Merchandise Inventory			4 4 8 00	
Prepaid Advertising			5 5 5 00	
Prepaid Insurance			2 8 00	
Office Equipment			1 0 8 3 00	
Accum. Dep., Office Equipment				2 0 7 00
Accounts Payable				2 5 2 00
G. Jackson, Capital				9 8 6 00
Income Summary	3 6 2 00	4 4 8 00		
Sales		5 5 1 8 00		
Sales Returns and Allowances	2 2 3 00			
Sales Discounts	1 0 9 00			
Purchases	2 6 2 1 00			
Purchases Returns and Allowances		3 2 00		
Purchases Discount		4 7 00		
Salaries Expense	1 0 8 6 00			
Insurance Expense	6 9 6 00			
Utilities Expense	4 3 00			
Plumbing Expenses	5 4 00			
Advertising Expense	1 4 00			
Dep. Expenses, Office Equip.	3 0 00			
Salaries Payable				7 2 00
	5 2 3 8 00	6 0 4 5 00	2 3 0 6 00	1 4 9 9 00
Net Income	8 0 7 00			8 0 7 00
	6 0 4 5 00	6 0 4 5 00	2 3 0 6 00	2 3 0 6 00

LO1 *(15 MIN)*   **12B-4.** From the worksheet in Exercise 12B-3, prepare the assets section of a classified balance sheet.

LO2, 4 *(30 MIN)*   **12B-5.** On December 31, 2012, $330 of salaries has been accrued. (Salaries before the accrued amount totaled $28,500.) The next payroll to be paid will be on February 3, 2013, for $6,400. Please do the following:

a. Journalize and post the adjusting entry (use T accounts).
b. Journalize and post the reversing entry on January 1.
c. Journalize and post the payment of the payroll. Cash has a balance of $14,500 before the payment of payroll on February 3.

MyAccountingLab   **Problems**

Set A

LO1 *(30 MIN)*   **12A-1.** Prepare a formal income statement from the partial worksheet for Rose Co. in Figure 12.17.

Check Figure:
Net Income from
operations $659

Account Titles	ROSE CO. PARTIAL WORKSHEET FOR YEAR ENDED DECEMBER 31, 201X Income Statement	
	Dr.	Cr.
Income Summary	3 9 0 00	2 5 0 00
Sales		2 6 5 0 00
Sales Returns and Allowances	1 1 9 00	
Sales Discount	6 0 00	
Purchases	8 7 0 00	
Purchases Returns and Allow.		1 6 3 00
Purchases Discount		1 3 1 00
Freight-In	1 0 6 00	
Salaries Expense	2 0 0 00	
Insurance Expense	2 4 0 00	
Advertising Expense	1 1 5 00	
Rental Income		2 3 0 00
Rent Expense	2 4 5 00	
Dep. Exp., Store Equip.	1 9 0 00	
Salaries Payable		
	2 5 3 5 00	3 4 2 4 00
Net Income	8 8 9 00	
	3 4 2 4 00	3 4 2 4 00

FIGURE 12.17
Partial Worksheet for Rose Co.

LO1 *(40 MIN)*

12A-2. Prepare a statement of owner's equity and a classified balance sheet from the worksheet for John's Company in Figure 12.18. (*Note:* Of the Mortgage Payable, $220 is due within one year.)

FIGURE 12.18
Partial Worksheet for John's Company

Check Figure:
Total Assets $32,195

JOHN'S COMPANY
WORKSHEET
FOR YEAR ENDED DECEMBER 31, 201X

Account Titles	Balance Sheet	
	Dr.	Cr.
Cash	2300000	
Petty Cash	12000	
Accounts Receivable	135000	
Merchandise Inv.	390000	
Supplies	37500	
Prepaid Insurance	45000	
Store Equipment	270000	
Acc. Dep., Store Eq.		90000
Automobile	150000	
Acc. Dep., Auto.		30000
Accounts Payable		260000
Taxes Payable		235000
Unearned Rent		1950000
Mortgage Payable		60000
H. Johns, Capital		1200000
H. Johns, With.	15000	
Salaries Payable		60000
	3354500	3885000
Net Loss	530500	
	3885000	3885000

LO1, 2 *(90 MIN)*

Check Figure:
Net Income $4,570

12A-3. a Complete the worksheet for Joe's Supplies in Figure 12.19 (p. 483).
b. Prepare an income statement, a statement of owner's equity, and a classified balance sheet. (*Note:* The amount of the mortgage due the first year is $820.)
c. Journalize the adjusting and closing entries.

FIGURE 12.19
Worksheet for Joe's Supplies

JOE'S SUPPLIES
WORKSHEET
FOR YEAR ENDED DECEMBER 31, 201X

Account Titles	Trial Balance Dr.	Trial Balance Cr.	Adjustments Dr.	Adjustments Cr.
Cash	1800 00			
Accounts Receivable	3300 00			
Merch. Inventory, 1/1/1X	11300 00	(B)	10100 00	11300 00 (A)
Prepaid Insurance	1900 00			490 00 (E)
Equipment	3700 00			
Accum. Dep., Equipment		1010 00		360 00 (D)
Accounts Payable		5100 00		
Unearned Training Fees		2090 00	(C) 270 00	
Mortgage Payable		1180 00		
P. Joe, Capital		10560 00		
P. Joe, Withdrawals	4290 00			
Income Summary		(A)	11300 00	10100 00 (B)
Sales		95500 00		
Sales Returns and Allowances	3200 00			
Sales Discount	2630 00			
Purchases	63100 00			
Purchases Returns and Allow.		13900 00		
Purchases Discount		3220 00		
Freight-In	2640 00			
Advertising Expense	11400 00			
Rent Expense	9600 00			
Salaries Expense	13700 00			
	132560 00	132560 00		
Training Fees Earned				270 00 (C)
Dep. Exp., Equipment			(D) 360 00	
Insurance Expense			(E) 490 00	
			22520 00	22520 00

12A-4. Using the ledger balances and additional data given, do the following for Cross Lumber for the year ended December 31, 201X:

1. Prepare the worksheet.
2. Prepare the income statement, statement of owner's equity, and balance sheet.

L01, 2, 3, 4
(150 MIN)

Check Figure:
Net Income $4,466

(continued on page 484)

3. Journalize and post adjusting and closing entries. (Be sure to put beginning balances in the ledger first.)
4. Prepare a post-closing trial balance.
5. Journalize the reversing entry for wages accrued.

Account Balances for Cross Lumber

Acct. No.		
110	Cash	$ 1,390
111	Accounts Receivable	1,380
112	Merchandise Inventory	4,500
113	Lumber Supplies	279
114	Prepaid Insurance	223
121	Lumber Equipment	3,000
122	Accum. Dep., Lumber Equipment	500
220	Accounts Payable	1,190
221	Wages Payable	—
330	J. Cross, Capital	7,097
331	J. Cross, Withdrawals	2,700
332	Income Summary	—
440	Sales	23,000
441	Sales Returns and Allowances	250
550	Purchases	15,100
551	Purchases Discount	305
552	Purchases Returns and Allowances	320
660	Wages Expense	2,300
661	Advertising Expense	430
662	Rent Expense	860
663	Dep. Expense, Lumber Equipment	—
664	Lumber Supplies Expense	—
665	Insurance Expense	—

Additional Data

a./b.	Merchandise inventory, December 31	$5,000
c.	Lumber supplies on hand, December 31	90
d.	Insurance expired	160
e.	Depreciation for the year	270
f.	Accrued wages on December 31	100

Set B

12B-1. From the partial worksheet for Rose Co. shown in Figure 12.20, prepare a formal income statement.

MyAccountingLab

● **L01** *(70 MIN)*

PT/QB

FIGURE 12.20
Partial Worksheet of Rose Co.

Check Figure:
Net income from
operations $975

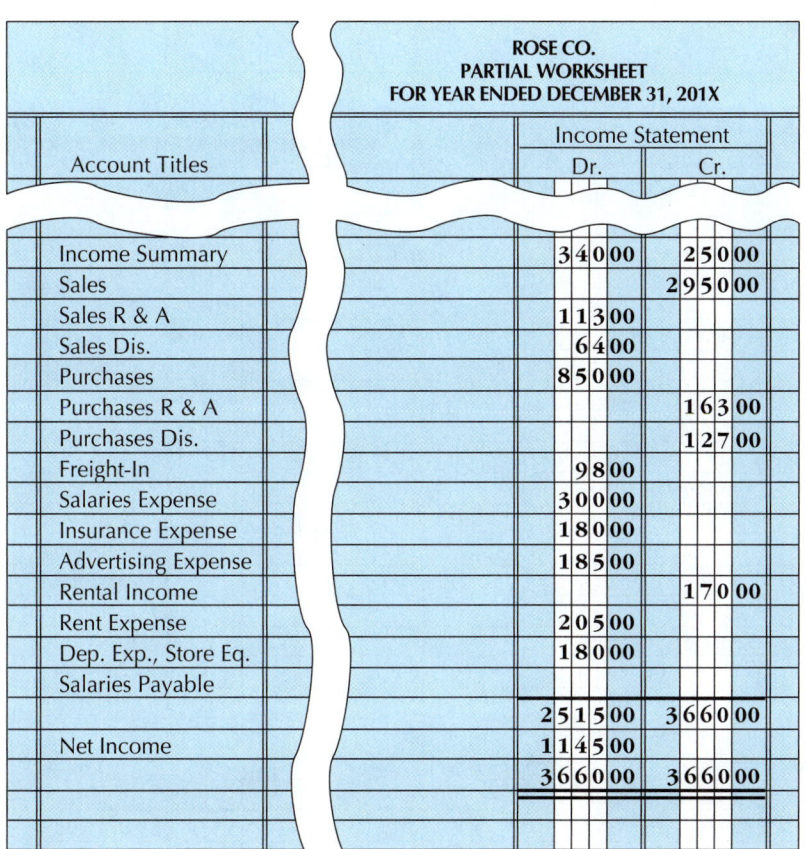

ROSE CO.
PARTIAL WORKSHEET
FOR YEAR ENDED DECEMBER 31, 201X

Account Titles	Income Statement Dr.	Income Statement Cr.
Income Summary	3 4 0 00	2 5 0 00
Sales		2 9 5 0 00
Sales R & A	1 1 3 00	
Sales Dis.	6 4 00	
Purchases	8 5 0 00	
Purchases R & A		1 6 3 00
Purchases Dis.		1 2 7 00
Freight-In	9 8 00	
Salaries Expense	3 0 0 00	
Insurance Expense	1 8 0 00	
Advertising Expense	1 8 5 00	
Rental Income		1 7 0 00
Rent Expense	2 0 5 00	
Dep. Exp., Store Eq.	1 8 0 00	
Salaries Payable		
	2 5 1 5 00	3 6 6 0 00
Net Income	1 1 4 5 00	
	3 6 6 0 00	3 6 6 0 00

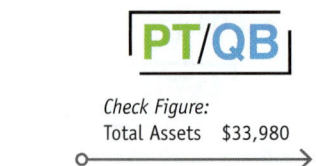

L01 *(40 MIN)*

PT/QB

Check Figure:
Total Assets $33,980

FIGURE 12.21
Worksheet for John's Company

12B-2. From the worksheet shown for John's Company in Figure 12.21, complete the following:

a. Statement of owner's equity
b. Classified balance sheet

(*Note:* Of the Mortgage Payable, $190 is due within one year.)

JOHN'S COMPANY
WORKSHEET
FOR YEAR ENDED DECEMBER 31, 201X

Account Titles	Balance Sheet Dr.	Cr.
Cash	2 4 0 0 00	
Petty Cash	1 3 0 00	
Accts. Receivable	1 5 0 0 00	
Merch. Inventory	3 7 0 0 00	
Supplies	2 7 5 00	
Prepaid Ins.	5 0 0 00	
Store Equip.	3 0 0 0 00	
Acc. Dep., Store Eq.		9 0 0 00
Automobile	2 0 0 0 00	
Acc. Dep., Auto.		2 2 5 00
Accts. Payable		2 9 0 0 00
Taxes Payable		2 4 5 0 00
Unearned Rent		1 9 0 0 0 00
Mortgage Payable		6 5 0 00
H. Johns, Capital		1 2 2 0 0 00
H. Johns, Withd.	5 0 00	
Salaries Payable		7 5 0 00
	35 1 5 5 00	39 0 7 5 00
Net Loss	3 9 2 0 00	
	39 0 7 5 00	39 0 7 5 00

12B-3. From the partial worksheet for Joe's Supplies in Figure 12.22, do the following:

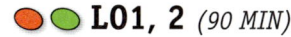
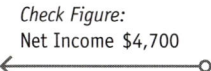

L01, 2 *(90 MIN)*

1. Complete the worksheet.
2. Prepare the income statement, statement of owner's equity, and classified balance sheet. (*Note:* The amount of the mortgage due the first year is $890.)
3. Journalize the adjusting and closing entries.

Check Figure:
Net Income $4,700

FIGURE 12.22
Worksheet for Joe's Supplies

JOE'S SUPPLIES
WORKSHEET
FOR YEAR ENDED DECEMBER 31, 201X

Account Titles	Trial Balance Dr.	Trial Balance Cr.	Adjustments Dr.	Adjustments Cr.
Cash	2 5 0 0 00			
Accounts Receivable	3 1 0 0 00			
Merch. Inventory, 1/1/1X	11 0 0 0 00		(B)10 6 0 0 00	11 0 0 0 00 (A)
Prepaid Insurance	1 9 2 0 00			5 5 0 00 (E)
Equipment	3 1 0 0 00			
Accum. Dep., Equipment		1 0 1 0 00		4 4 0 00 (D)
Accounts Payable		5 0 7 0 00		
Unearned Training Fees		2 1 7 00	(C) 3 0 0 00	
Mortgage Payable		1 3 3 0 00		
P. Joe, Capital		10 5 0 0 00		
P. Joe, Withdrawals	4 2 5 0 00			
Income Summary			(A)11 0 0 0 00	10 6 0 0 00 (B)
Sales		95 6 8 0 00		
Sales Returns and Allowances	3 1 7 0 00			
Sales Discount	2 6 0 0 00			
Purchases	64 1 0 0 00			
Purchases Returns and Allow.		1 3 3 0 00		
Purchases Discounts		3 2 4 0 00		
Freight-In	2 6 6 0 00			
Advertising Expense	1 1 3 0 00			
Rent Expense	9 5 0 0 00			
Salaries Expense	13 1 0 0 00			
	132 3 0 0 00	132 3 0 0 00		
Training Fees Earned				3 0 0 00 (C)
Dep. Exp., Equipment			(D) 4 4 0 00	
Insurance Expense			(E) 5 5 0 00	
			22 8 9 0 00	22 8 9 0 00

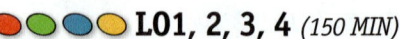 **L01, 2, 3, 4** *(150 MIN)*

Check Figure:
Net Income $5,608

12B-4. From the ledger balances and additional data given, do the following for Cross Lumber for the year ended December 31, 201X.

1. Prepare the worksheet.
2. Prepare the income statement, statement of owner's equity, and balance sheet.
3. Journalize and post adjusting and closing entries. (Be sure to put beginning balances in the ledger first.)
4. Prepare a post-closing trial balance.
5. Journalize the reversing entry for wages accrued.

Account Balances of Cross Lumber		
Acct. No.		
110	Cash	$ 1,300
111	Accounts Receivable	1,280
112	Merchandise Inventory	4,300
113	Lumber Supplies	267
114	Prepaid Insurance	209
121	Lumber Equipment	3,300
122	Acc. Dep., Lumber Equipment	530
220	Accounts Payable	1,200
221	Wages Payable	—
330	J. Cross, Capital	5,761
331	J. Cross, Withdrawals	2,700
332	Income Summary	—
440	Sales	23,200
441	Sales Returns and Allowances	230
550	Purchases	14,500
551	Purchases Discount	325
552	Purchases Returns and Allowances	340
660	Wages Expense	2,120
661	Advertising Expense	370
662	Rent Expense	780
663	Dep. Exp., Lumber Equipment	—
664	Lumber Supplies Expense	—
665	Insurance Expense	—

Additional Data

a./b.	Merchandise inventory, December 31	$4,700
c.	Lumber supplies on hand, December 31	75
d.	Insurance expired	120
e.	Depreciation for the year	210
f.	Accrued wages on December 31	135

Financial Report Problem

L02, 3 *(5 MIN)*

Reading the Kellogg's Annual Report

Go to http://investor.kelloggs.com/annuals.cfm, to access the Kellogg's 2010 Annual Report and locate the consolidated statement of earnings. How much has Selling and General Administrative Expense increased from 2009 to 2010?

ON the JOB ||||||||||||||||||||||||||||

MyAccountingLab

●●L01, 2 *(60 MIN)*

SANCHEZ COMPUTER CENTER

Using the worksheet in Chapter 11 for Sanchez Computer Center, journalize and post the adjusting entries and prepare the financial statements.

Mini Practice Set

The Corner Dress Shop

Reviewing the Accounting Cycle for a Merchandise Company

This practice set will help you review all the key concepts of a merchandise company, along with the integration of payroll, including the preparation of Form 941.

Because you are the bookkeeper of the Corner Dress Shop, we have gathered the following information for you. It will be your task to complete the accounting cycle for March.

THE CORNER DRESS SHOP POST-CLOSING TRIAL BALANCE FEBRUARY 28, 201X	1	2
Cash	2 1 9 3 90	
Accounts Receivable	2 2 0 0 00	
Petty Cash	3 5 00	
Merchandise Inventory	5 6 0 0 00	
Prepaid Rent	1 8 0 0 00	
Delivery Truck	6 0 0 0 00	
Accumulated Depreciation, Truck		1 5 0 0 00
Accounts Payable		1 9 0 0 00
FIT Payable		9 7 5 00
FICA—OASDI Payable		1 3 3 9 20
FICA—Medicare Payable		3 1 3 20
SIT Payable		7 5 6 00
SUTA Payable		9 7 9 20
FUTA Payable		1 6 3 20
Unearned Rent		8 0 0 00
B. Loeb, Capital		9 1 0 3 10
Total	17 8 2 8 90	17 8 2 8 90

Balances in subsidiary ledgers as of March 1 are as follows:

Accounts Receivable		Accounts Payable	
Bing Co.	$2,200	Blew Co.	$1,900
Blew Co.	—	Jones Co.	—
Ronald Co.	—	Moe's Garage	—
		Morris Co.	—

Payroll is paid monthly:

FICA rate	OASDI 6.2% on $106,800
	Medicare 1.45% on all earnings
SUTA rate	4.8% on $7,000
FUTA rate	.8% on $7,000
SIT rate	7%
FIT	Use the table provided at the end of this practice set.

The payroll register for January and February is provided. In March, salaries are as follows:

Mel Case	$3,325
Jane Holl	4,120
Jackie Moore	4,760

Your tasks are to do the following:

1. Set up a general ledger, accounts receivable subsidiary ledger and accounts payable subsidiary ledger, auxiliary petty cash record, and payroll register. (Be sure to update ledger accounts based on information given in the post-closing trial balance for February 28 before beginning.)
2. Journalize the transactions, and prepare the payroll register.
3. Update the accounts payable and accounts receivable subsidiary ledgers.
4. Post to the general ledger.
5. Prepare a trial balance on a worksheet and complete the worksheet.
6. Prepare an income statement, statement of owner's equity, and classified balance sheet.
7. Journalize the adjusting and closing entries.
8. Post the adjusting and closing entries to the ledger.
9. Prepare a post-closing trial balance.
10. Complete Form 941 and sign it as of the last day in April.

**Chart of Accounts for the
Corner Dress Shop**

Assets	**Revenue**
110 Cash	410 Sales
111 Accounts Receivable	412 Sales Returns and Allowances
112 Petty Cash	414 Sales Discount
114 Merchandise Inventory	416 Rental Income
116 Prepaid Rent	
120 Delivery Truck	**Cost of Goods Sold**
121 Accumulated Depreciation, Truck	510 Purchases
	512 Purchases Returns and Allowances
Liabilities	514 Purchases Discount
210 Accounts Payable	
212 Salaries Payable	**Expenses**
214 Federal Income Tax Payable	610 Sales Salaries Expense
216 FICA—OASDI Payable	611 Office Salaries Expense
218 FICA—Medicare Payable	612 Payroll Tax Expense
220 State Income Tax Payable	614 Cleaning Expense
222 SUTA Tax Payable	616 Depreciation Expense, Truck
224 FUTA Tax Payable	618 Rent Expense
226 Unearned Rent	620 Postage Expense
	622 Delivery Expense
Owner's Equity	624 Miscellaneous Expense
310 B. Loeb, Capital	
320 B. Loeb, Withdrawals	
330 Income Summary	

THE CORNER DRESS SHOP
PAYROLL REGISTER
JANUARY AND FEBRUARY 201X

Employees	Allow. and Marital Status	Cum. Earnings	Salary	Earnings Reg.	O/T	Gross	Cum. Earnings
Mel Case	M – 2		3 3 0 0 00	3 3 0 0 00		3 3 0 0 00	3 3 0 0 00
Jane Holl	M – 1		3 4 0 0 00	3 4 0 0 00		3 4 0 0 00	3 4 0 0 00
Jackie Moore	M – 0		4 1 0 0 00	4 1 0 0 00		4 1 0 0 00	4 1 0 0 00
Totals for Jan.			10 8 0 0 00	10 8 0 0 00		10 8 0 0 00	10 8 0 0 00
Mel Case	M – 2	3 3 0 0 00	3 3 0 0 00	3 3 0 0 00		3 3 0 0 00	6 6 0 0 00
Jane Holl	M – 1	3 4 0 0 00	3 4 0 0 00	3 4 0 0 00		3 4 0 0 00	6 8 0 0 00
Jackie Moore	M – 0	4 1 0 0 00	4 1 0 0 00	4 1 0 0 00		4 1 0 0 00	8 2 0 0 00
Totals for Feb.		10 8 0 0 00	10 8 0 0 00	10 8 0 0 00		10 8 0 0 00	21 6 0 0 00

PAYROLL REGISTER

Taxable Earnings Unemp.	FICA Soc. Sec.	FICA Medicare	Deductions OASDI	Medicare	FIT	SIT	Net Pay	Ck. No.	Office Salary Expense	Sales Salary Expense
3 3 0 0 00	3 3 0 0 00	3 3 0 0 00	2 0 4 60	4 7 85	2 3 3 00	2 3 1 00	2 5 8 3 55		3 3 0 0 00	
3 4 0 0 00	3 4 0 0 00	3 4 0 0 00	2 1 0 80	4 9 30	2 9 7 00	2 3 8 00	2 6 0 4 90			3 4 0 0 00
4 1 0 0 00	4 1 0 0 00	4 1 0 0 00	2 5 4 20	5 9 45	4 4 5 00	2 8 7 00	3 0 5 4 90			4 1 0 0 00
10 8 0 0 00	10 8 0 0 00	10 8 0 0 00	6 6 9 60	1 5 6 60	9 7 5 00	7 5 6 00	8 2 4 2 80		3 3 0 0 00	7 5 0 0 00
3 3 0 0 00	3 3 0 0 00	3 3 0 0 00	2 0 4 60	4 7 85	2 3 3 00	2 3 1 00	2 5 8 3 55		3 3 0 0 00	
3 4 0 0 00	3 4 0 0 00	3 4 0 0 00	2 1 0 80	4 9 30	2 9 7 00	2 3 8 00	2 6 0 4 90			3 4 0 0 00
2 9 0 0 00	4 1 0 0 00	4 1 0 0 00	2 5 4 20	5 9 45	4 4 5 00	2 8 7 00	3 0 5 4 90			4 1 0 0 00
9 6 0 0 00	10 8 0 0 00	10 8 0 0 00	6 6 9 60	1 5 6 60	9 7 5 00	7 5 6 00	8 2 4 2 80		3 3 0 0 00	7 5 0 0 00

201X

Mar. 1 Bing paid balance owed, no discount.

2 Purchased merchandise from Morris Company on account, $10,000; terms 2/10, n/30.

2 Paid $6 from the petty cash fund for cleaning package, voucher no. 18 (consider it a cleaning expense).

3 Sold merchandise to Ronald Company on account, $7,000, invoice no. 51; terms 2/10, n/30.

5 Paid $3 from the petty cash fund for postage, voucher no. 19.

6 Sold merchandise to Ronald Company on account, $5,000, invoice no. 52; terms 2/10, n/30.

8 Paid $10 from the petty cash fund for first aid emergency, voucher no. 20.

9 Purchased merchandise from Morris Company on account, $5,000; terms 2/10, n/30.

9 Paid $5 for delivery expense from petty cash fund, voucher no. 21.

9 Sold more merchandise to Ronald Company on account, $3,000, invoice no. 53; terms 2/10, n/30.

9 Paid cleaning service, $300, check no. 110.

(Continued)

(Continued)

10   Ronald Company returned merchandise costing $1,000 from invoice no. 52; the Corner Dress shop issued credit memo no. 10 to Ronald Company for $1,000.

11   Purchased merchandise from Jones Company on account, $10,000; terms 1/15, n/60.

12   Paid Morris Company invoice dated March 2, check no. 111.

13   Sold $7,000 of merchandise for cash.

14   Returned merchandise to Jones Company in amount of $2,000; the Corner Dress Shop issued debit memo no. 4 to Jones Company.

14   Paid $5 from the petty cash fund for delivery expense, voucher no. 22.

15   Paid taxes due for FICA (OASDI and Medicare) and FIT for February payroll, check no. 112.

15   Sold Merchandise for $29,000 cash.

15   Betty withdrew $100 for her own personal expenses, check no. 113.

15   Paid state income tax for February payroll, check no. 114.

16   Received payment from Ronald Company for invoice no. 52, less discount.

16   Ronald Company paid invoice no. 51, $7,000.

16   Sold merchandise to Bing Company on account, $3,200, invoice no. 54; terms 2/10, n/30.

21   Purchased delivery truck on account from Moe's Garage, $17,200.

22   Sold merchandise to Ronald Company on account, $4,000, invoice no. 55; terms 2/10, n/30.

23   Paid Jones Company the balance owed, check no. 115.

24   Sold merchandise to Bing Company on account, $2,000, invoice no. 56; terms 2/10, n/30.

25   Purchased merchandise for $1,000 check no. 116.

27   Purchased merchandise from Blew Company on account, $6,000; terms 2/10, n/30.

27   Paid $2 postage from the petty cash fund, voucher no. 23.

28   Ronald Company paid invoice no. 55 dated March 22, less discount.

28   Bing Company paid invoice no. 54 dated March 16.

29   Purchased merchandise from Morris Company on account, $9,000; terms 2/10, n/30.

30   Sold merchandise to Blew Company on account, $10,000, invoice no. 57; terms 2/10, n/30.

30   Issued check no. 117 to replenish to the same level the petty cash fund.

30   Recorded payroll in payroll register.

30   Journalized payroll entry (to be paid on 31st).

30   Journalized employer's payroll tax expense.

31   Paid payroll checks no. 118, no. 119, and no. 120.

Additional Data

a./b. Ending merchandise inventory, $13,515.

c. During March, rent expired, $600.

d. Truck depreciated, $150.

e. Rental income earned, $200 (one month's rent from subletting).

f. Betty Loeb's dress shop is located at 1 Milgate Rd., Marblehead, MA 01945. Its identification number is 33-4158215.

MARRIED Persons—MONTHLY Payroll Period

(For Wages Paid through December 201X)

And the wages are—		And the number of withholding allowances claimed is—										
At least	But less than	0	1	2	3	4	5	6	7	8	9	10
		The amount of income tax to be withheld is—										
$ 0	$680	$0	$0	$0	$0	$0	$0	$0	$0	$0	$0	$0
680	720	4	0	0	0	0	0	0	0	0	0	0
720	760	8	0	0	0	0	0	0	0	0	0	0
760	800	12	0	0	0	0	0	0	0	0	0	0
2,600	2,640	223	177	135	104	73	42	11	0	0	0	0
2,640	2,680	229	183	139	108	77	46	15	0	0	0	0
2,680	2,720	235	189	143	112	81	50	19	0	0	0	0
2,720	2,760	241	195	149	116	85	54	23	0	0	0	0
2,760	2,800	247	201	155	120	89	58	27	0	0	0	0
2,800	2,840	253	207	161	124	93	62	31	0	0	0	0
2,840	2,880	259	213	167	128	97	66	35	4	0	0	0
2,880	2,920	265	219	173	132	101	70	39	8	0	0	0
2,920	2,960	271	225	179	136	105	74	43	12	0	0	0
2,960	3,000	277	231	185	140	109	78	47	16	0	0	0
3,000	3,040	283	237	191	145	113	82	51	20	0	0	0
3,040	3,080	289	243	197	151	117	86	55	24	0	0	0
3,080	3,120	295	249	203	157	121	90	59	28	0	0	0
3,120	3,160	301	255	209	163	125	94	63	32	2	0	0
3,160	3,200	307	261	215	169	129	98	67	36	6	0	0
3,200	3,240	313	267	221	175	133	102	71	40	10	0	0
3,240	3,280	319	273	227	181	137	106	75	44	14	0	0
3,280	3,320	325	279	233	187	141	110	79	48	18	0	0
3,320	3,360	331	285	239	193	146	114	83	52	22	0	0
3,360	3,400	337	291	245	199	152	118	87	56	26	0	0
$3,400	$3,440	$343	$297	$251	$205	$158	$122	$91	$60	$30	$0	$0
3,440	3,480	349	303	257	211	164	126	95	64	34	3	0
3,480	3,520	355	309	263	217	170	130	99	68	38	7	0
3,520	3,560	361	315	269	223	176	134	103	72	42	11	0
3,560	3,600	367	321	275	229	182	138	107	76	46	15	0
3,600	3,640	373	327	281	235	188	142	111	80	50	19	0
3,640	3,680	379	333	287	241	194	148	115	84	54	23	0
3,680	3,720	385	339	293	247	200	154	119	88	58	27	0
3,720	3,760	391	345	299	253	206	160	123	92	62	31	0
3,760	3,800	397	351	305	259	212	166	127	96	66	35	4
3,800	3,840	403	357	311	265	218	172	131	100	70	39	8
3,840	3,880	409	363	317	271	224	178	135	104	74	43	12
3,880	3,920	415	369	323	277	230	184	139	108	78	47	16
3,920	3,960	421	375	329	283	236	190	144	112	82	51	20
3,960	4,000	427	381	335	289	242	196	150	116	86	55	24
4,000	4,040	433	387	341	295	248	202	156	120	90	59	28
4,040	4,080	439	393	347	301	254	208	162	124	94	63	32
4,080	4,120	445	399	353	307	260	214	168	128	98	67	36
4,120	4,160	451	405	359	313	266	220	174	132	102	71	40
4,160	4,200	457	411	365	319	272	226	180	136	106	75	44
4,200	4,240	463	417	371	325	278	232	186	140	110	79	48
4,240	4,280	469	423	377	331	284	238	192	146	114	83	52
4,280	4,320	475	429	383	337	290	244	198	152	118	87	56
4,320	4,360	481	435	389	343	296	250	204	158	122	91	60
4,360	4,400	487	441	395	349	302	256	210	164	126	95	64
4,400	4,440	493	447	401	355	308	262	216	170	130	99	68
4,440	4,480	499	453	407	361	314	268	222	176	134	103	72
4,480	4,520	505	459	413	367	320	274	228	182	138	107	76
4,520	4,560	511	465	419	373	326	280	234	188	142	111	80
4,560	4,600	517	471	425	379	332	286	240	194	147	115	84
4,600	4,640	523	477	431	385	338	292	246	200	153	119	88
4,640	4,680	529	483	437	391	344	298	252	206	159	123	92
4,680	4,720	535	489	443	397	350	304	258	212	165	127	96
4,720	4,760	541	495	449	403	356	310	264	218	171	131	100
4,760	4,800	547	501	455	409	362	316	270	224	177	135	104
4,800	4,840	553	507	461	415	368	322	276	230	183	139	108
4,840	4,880	559	513	467	421	374	328	282	236	189	143	112
4,880	4,920	565	519	473	427	380	334	288	242	195	149	116
4,920	4,960	571	525	479	433	386	340	294	248	201	155	120
4,960	5,000	577	531	485	439	392	346	300	254	207	161	124
5,000	5,040	583	537	491	445	398	352	306	260	213	167	128
5,040	5,080	589	543	497	451	404	358	312	266	219	173	132
5,080	5,120	595	549	503	457	410	364	318	272	225	179	136
5,120	5,160	601	555	509	463	416	370	324	278	231	185	140
5,160	5,200	607	561	515	469	422	376	330	284	237	191	145

PEACHTREE COMPUTER WORKSHOP

COMPUTERIZED ACCOUNTING APPLICATION FOR CHAPTER 12

Refresher on using Peachtree Complete Accounting

Before starting this assignment, you may want to refresh your memory by reading the following PDF documents in the multimedia library of the MyAccountingLab Web site. Remember to choose the PDF document for your version of Peachtree.

1. An Introduction to Peachtree Complete Accounting
2. Correcting Peachtree Transactions
3. How to Repeat or Restart a Peachtree Assignment
4. Backing Up and Restoring Your Work in Peachtree

You also should have completed the following workshops:

1. Workshop 1 Atlas Company from Chapter 3
2. Workshop 2 Zell Company from Chapter 4
3. Workshop 3 Sullivan Realty from Chapter 5
4. Workshop 4 Pete's Market from Chapter 8
5. Workshop 5 Part A Mars Company from Chapter 10
6. Workshop 5 Part B Abby's Toy House from Chapter 10

Workshop 6:

Accounting Cycle for a Merchandising Company

In this workshop you complete an accounting cycle for a merchandising business owned by the Corner Dress Shop using Peachtree. Tasks include maintaining inventory, recording sales on account, merchandise returns, merchandise purchases, vendor payments, and payroll. You will also prepare inventory reports, aged receivables and aged payable reports, general journal and general ledger reports, a trial balance, and financial statements. Finally, you will close the accounting period.

Instructions and the data file for completing this assignment are in the multimedia library of the MyAccountingLab Web site. Open the *Workshop 6 The Corner Dress Shop* PDF document for your version of Peachtree and download *The Corner Dress Shop* data file for your version of Peachtree.

QUICKBOOKS COMPUTER WORKSHOP

COMPUTERIZED ACCOUNTING APPLICATION FOR CHAPTER 12

Refresher on using QuickBooks Pro

Before starting this assignment, you may want to refresh your memory by reading the following PDF documents in the multimedia library of the MyAccountingLab Web site. Remember to choose the PDF document for your version of QuickBooks.

1. An Introduction to QuickBooks Pro
2. Correcting QuickBooks Transactions
3. How to Repeat or Restart a QuickBooks Assignment
4. Backing Up and Restoring Your Work in QuickBooks

You also should have completed the following workshops:

1. Workshop 1 Atlas Company from Chapter 3
2. Workshop 2 Zell Company from Chapter 4
3. Workshop 3 Sullivan Realty from Chapter 5
4. Workshop 4 Pete's Market from Chapter 8
5. Workshop 5 Part A Mars Company from Chapter 10
6. Workshop 5 Part B Abby's Toy House from Chapter 10

Workshop 6:

Accounting Cycle for a Merchandising Company

In this workshop you complete an accounting cycle for a merchandising business owned by the Corner Dress Shop using QuickBooks. Tasks include maintaining inventory, recording sales on account, merchandise returns, merchandise purchases, vendor payments, and payroll. You will also prepare inventory reports, aged receivables and aged payable reports, general journal and general ledger reports, a trial balance, and financial statements. Finally, you will close the accounting period.

Instructions and the data file for completing this assignment are in the multimedia library of the MyAccountingLab Web site. Open the *Workshop 6 The Corner Dress Shop* PDF document for your version of Quickbooks and download the *The Corner Dress Shop* data file for your version of Quickbooks.

GLINDEX   A Combined Glossary and Subject Index

A

Account. An accounting device used in bookkeeping to record increases and decreases of business transactions relating to individual assets, liabilities, capital, withdrawals, revenue, expenses, and so on, 40. *See also* Standard account

account categories, 130

Accounts Receivable, 342

Accumulated Depreciation, 124

adjustments to. *See* Adjustments

balancing, 40–41, 43

Capital, 93, 169–170

Cash, 92

Cash Short and Over, 241–243, 247

chart of. *See* Chart of Accounts

contra-cost accounts, 394

contra-revenue accounts, 337, 354

Cost of Goods Sold, 383, 456

Income Summary, 168–169

ledger, 40

Merchandise Inventory, 384, 424–426

Mortgage Payable, 427

normal balance of, 43, 65

Office Salaries, 92

Office Supplies, 121–122

Payroll Cash, 294

Prepaid Rent, 122–123

Purchases Returns and Allowances, 368–369

Purchases, 368, 392

Purchases Discount, 369–370, 392, 394

Revenue, 1

Salaries Accrued, 126–128, 135, 430, 440

Sales Discount, 337–338

Sales Returns and Allowances, 336–337, 352, 354

Sales Tax Payable, 338–339

Supplies on Hand, 135, 429, 440

T accounts, 40, 42–44, 64–65

temporary (nominal), 166

Unearned Rent, 425–426

Word Processing Equipment, 123–126

Accounting. A system that measures the business's activities in financial terms, provides written reports and financial statements about those activities, and communicates these reports to decision makers and others, 2–4

compared to bookkeeping, 4

Accounting cycle. For each accounting period, the process that begins with the recording of business transactions or procedures into a journal and ends with the completion of a post-closing trial balance, 77–78

analyzing and recording transactions, 78–83

blueprint for, 146

journalizing, 78–83, 166–171, 463–467, 475–476

post-closing trial balance, 176–177, 467, 475–476

posting adjusting entries, 463–467, 475–476

posting closing entries, 166–171, 467, 475–476

posting to the ledger, 86–87, 92, 103

preparing the financial statements, 18–21, 53, 55, 64, 136–138, 456–461, 475–476

preparing the trial balance, 93–96, 103

preparing the worksheet, 120, 147

recording journal entries from worksheet, 162–164

Accounting equation

and balance sheet, 9

balancing, 43

basic, 5–7. *See also* Basic accounting equation

expanded, 11–17, 166

and T account entries, 42–44

Accounting period. The period of time for which an income statement is prepared, 78

Accounting process. *See* Accounting

Accounting software, 4

Accounts payable. Amounts owed to creditors that result from the purchase of goods or services on account—a liability, 7, 17, 92, 417. *See also* Schedule of Accounts Payable

Accounts payable subsidiary ledger. A book or file that contains, in alphabetical order, the name of the creditor and amount owed from purchases on account, 373, 394

Accounts receivable. An asset that indicates amounts owed by customers, 12–13, 17, 417. *See also* Schedule of Accounts Receivable

Accounts receivable subsidiary ledger. A book or file that contains the individual records, in alphabetical order, of amounts owed by various credit customers, 341–344, 355, 417

Accrued salaries payable. Salaries that are earned by employees but unpaid and unrecorded during the period (and thus need to be recorded by an adjustment) and will not come due for payment until the next accounting period, 126–127

Accumulated depreciation. A contra-asset account that summarizes or accumulates the amount of depreciation that has been taken on an asset, 124

Adjusting. The process of calculating the latest up-to-date balance of each account at the end of an accounting period, 121, 148. *See also* Adjustments

adjusting entries, journalizing and posting, 463–467, 475–476

Adjusting journal entries. Journal entries that are needed in order to update specific ledger accounts to reflect correct balances at the end of an accounting period, 162–165

Adjustments. *See also* Adjusting

to Office Supplies, 121–122, 135

to Prepaid Rent, 122–123, 135

to Salaries Accrued account, 126–128, 135

to Word Processing Equipment account, 123–125, 135

Administrative expenses (general expenses). Operating expenses such as general office expenses that are incurred indirectly in the selling of goods, 458

Allowances (also called *exemptions*). Certain dollar amounts of a person's income tax that will be considered nontaxable for income tax withholding purposes, 263

Assets. Properties (resources) of value owned by a business (cash, supplies, equipment, land), 5. *See also* Current assets

petty cash as, 236–237

rent paid in advance as, 80

rules for, 43

shift in, 6. *See also* Shift in Assets

ATM. Automatic teller machine that allows for depositing, withdrawal and advanced banking transactions, 231–233, 245

Auxiliary petty cash record. A supplementary record for summarizing petty cash information, 238

B

Balance sheet. Also known as *Statement of financial position*, 9, 19–21, 23, 141. *See also* Classified balance sheet

affected by adjustments, 163

heading of, 9

for a merchandising company, 459–461

section of worksheet, 131, 136, 148, 433

Bank reconciliation. The process of reconciling the checkbook balance with the bank balance given on the bank statement, 222, 228–231, 233–234, 245–246

Bank statement. A report sent by a bank to a customer indicating the previous balance, ATM transactions, nonsufficient funds, individual checks processed, individual deposits received, service charges, and ending bank balance, 230

reconciliation of. *See* Bank reconciliation

Banking, online, 228, 231–233, 245–246

advantages of, 232

disadvantages of, 233

and security, 233

Banking day. A banking day is any day that a bank is open to the public for business. Generally, a banking day will end at 2:00 or 3:00 P.M. local

time. Banking business transacted after this time
is usually considered to be the next day's business.
Saturdays, Sundays, and federal holidays are
usually not considered banking days, 297, 314

Basic accounting equation. Assets = Liabilities +
Owner's Equity, 5

**Beginning merchandise inventory (beginning
inventory).** The cost of goods on hand in a
company to begin an accounting period, 424, 440

Blank endorsement, 223

Book of final entry. Book that receives information
about business transactions from a book of
original entry (a journal). Example: a ledger, 78

Book of original entry. Book that records the first
formal information about business transactions.
Example: a journal, 78, 103

Book value. Cost of asset (for example, equipment)
less accumulated depreciation, 125

Bookkeeping. The recording function of the
accounting process, 4. *See also* Double–entry
bookkeeping

compared to accounting, 4

Business organizations, 2–3

C

Calendar quarter. A three-month, 13-week time
period. Four calendar quarters occur during a
calendar year that runs from January 1 through
December 31. The first quarter is January through
March, the second is April through June, the
third is July through September, and the fourth is
October through December, 296

Calendar year. (1) A one-year period beginning
on January 1 and ending on December 31.
Employers must use a calendar year for payroll
purposes, even if the employer uses a fiscal year
for financial statements and for any other reason.
(2) The 12-month period a business chooses for
its accounting year. Alternatively known as *fiscal
year* and *natural business year*, 78, 266

Call centers (banking), 232

Cancelled check. A check that has been processed by a
bank and is no longer negotiable, 228

Capital. The owner's investment of equity in the
company, 6, 8. *See also* Ending capital

Capital Account, 93, 169–170

Cash. *See also* Cash receipts; Change fund; Petty cash
monitoring, 222

Cash Account, 92

Cash payment transactions, 379–380, 392, 395
recording, 416

Cash receipts, 354
journal for, 421–422

Cash Short and Over. The account that records cash
shortages and overages. If the ending balance is
a debit, it is recorded on the income statement
as a miscellaneous expense; if it is a credit, it is
recorded as miscellaneous income, 241–243, 247

Change fund. Fund made up of various denominations
that are used to make change for customers, 236,
241, 245, 247

Chart of accounts. A numbering system of accounts
that lists the account titles and account numbers
to be used by a company, 44, 65
relationship with journal, 78–79
use for journalizing, 103

Check. A form used to indicate a specific amount of
money that is to be paid by the bank to a named
person or company, 226. *See also* Cancelled check;
NSF (Nonsufficient funds); Outstanding checks
endorsement of, 223
payroll, 294

Check truncation (safekeeping). Procedure whereby
checks are not returned to the drawer with the
bank statement but are instead kept at the bank
for a certain amount of time before being first
transferred to microfilm and then destroyed, 233

Checkbooks, 226–228

Checking accounts, 222–223, 245–246
deposits to, 223

Classified balance sheet. A balance sheet that
categorizes assets as current assets or plant and
equipment and groups liabilities as current or
long-term liabilities, 459

Closing journal entries. Journal entries that are
prepared to (a) reset all temporary accounts to
a zero balance and (b) update Capital to a new
balance, 166, 175–176
journalizing and posting, 467

Compound entry. A transaction involving more than one debit or credit, 45, 65

Compound journal entry. A journal entry that affects more than two accounts, 80, 103

Computer software, banking, 228

Controlling account—Accounts Receivable. The Accounts Receivable account in the general ledger, after postings are complete, shows a firm the total amount of money owed to it. This figure is broken down in the accounts receivable subsidiary ledger, where it indicates specifically who owes the money, 342

Corporation. A type of business organization that is owned by stockholders. Stockholders usually are not personally liable for the corporation's debts, 3

Corrections

    to account titles, 94

    of entries to wrong accounts, 95–96

    to entry errors, 95

    made after posting, 95

    to numerical errors, 95

Cost of freight, 370, 385, 394

Cost of goods sold. (1) In a perpetual inventory system, an account that records the cost of merchandise inventory used to make the sale. (2) Total cost of the goods which were sold to customers, 383, 424, 456

Credit. The right-hand side of any account. A number entered on the right side of any account is said to be credited to an account, 40, 64–65

    from bank, 231

    purchases discounts as, 369

    rules for, 43–44, 53

    and the trial balance, 93

Credit cards, 225–226

Credit memorandum. (1) A piece of paper sent by the seller to a customer who has returned merchandise previously purchased on credit. The credit memorandum indicates to the customer that the seller is reducing the amount owed by the customer. (2) Increase in depositor's balance, 230, 344–345, 352, 354

Credit period. Length of time allowed for payment of goods sold on account, 337

Creditor. Someone who has a claim to assets, 5–6

Cross-referencing. Adding to the PR column of the journal the account number of the ledger account that was updated from the journal, 86, 93

Current assets. Assets that can be converted into cash or used within one year or the normal operating cycle of the business, whichever is longer, 459

Current liabilities. Obligations that will come due within one year or within the operating cycle, whichever is longer, 461

Custodian, of petty cash account, 236–237

D

Debit. The left-hand side of any account. A number entered on the left side of any account is said to be debited to an account, 40, 64–65

    ending debit balance, 54

    purchases as, 369

    rules for, 43–44, 53

    and the trial balance, 93

Debit cards, 225–226, 232

Debit memorandum. (1) A memo issued by a purchaser to a seller, indicating that some Purchases Returns and Allowances have occurred and therefore the purchaser now owes less money on account. (2) Decrease in depositor's balance, 230, 376, 392, 394

    journalizing and posting, 376–377

Delivery expense, 370, 385, 394

Deposit slip. A form provided by the bank for use in depositing money or checks into a checking account, 223

Deposits, to bank account, 223, 230

Deposits in transit. Deposits that were made by customers of a bank but did not reach, or were not processed by, the bank before the preparation of the bank statement, 230–231, 245–246

Depreciation. The allocation (spreading) of the cost of an asset (such as an auto or equipment) over its expected useful life, 123–125, 135. *See also* Accumulated depreciation; Depreciation Expense

    accumulated, 124

    expense of, 430, 440

Discount period. A period shorter than the credit period when a discount is available to encourage early payment of bills, 337

Dollar sign, use of, 10, 55

Double-entry bookkeeping. An accounting system in which the recording of each transaction affects two or more accounts and the total of the debits is equal to the total of the credits, 45, 65

Drawee. Bank that drawer has an account with, 226, 246

Drawer. A person who writes a check, 226, 246

E

e-Banks, 232

Electronic Federal Tax Payment System (EFTPS), 299

Electronic funds transfer (EFT). An electronic system that transfers funds without the use of paper checks, 231

EFT number, 299

Employee earnings record. *See* Individual employee earnings record

Employer identification number (EIN). A number assigned by the IRS that is used by an employer when recording and paying payroll and income taxes, 296

Employer payroll tax expense, 270, 272–273, 276, 304, 317

Employer's Annual Federal Unemployment Tax Return. *See* Form 940, Employer's Annual Federal Unemployment Tax Return

Employer's Quarterly Federal Tax Return. *See* Form 944, Employer's Annual Federal Tax Return

Ending balance. The difference between footings in a T account, 41

Ending capital. Beginning Capital + Additional Investments + Net Income Withdrawals = Ending Capital. Or: Beginning Capital + Additional Investments – Net Loss – Withdrawals = Ending Capital, 20

Ending merchandise inventory (ending inventory). The cost of goods that remain unsold at the end of the accounting period. It is an asset on the new balance sheet, 424

Endorsement. *Blank:* Could be further endorsed. *Full:* Restricts further endorsement to only the person or company named. *Restrictive:* Restricts any further endorsement, 223, 246

Equities. The rights or financial claim of creditors (liabilities) and owners (owner's equity) who supply the assets to a firm, 5

Errors

correcting, 94–96

in trial balance, 93–95

Ethical cases

backdating checks, 396

borrowing from petty cash, 441

bribes from suppliers, 192

concealing debt, 477

copying software, 106

employee classification, 280

following GAAP, 149

moving new sales into old sales year, 356

padding expense account, 30

paying employee withholding tax to government, 319

reporting bank errors, 248

using fictional figures, 66

Expanded accounting equation. Assets = Liabilities + Capital – Withdrawals + Revenue – Expenses, 12

Expense. A cost incurred in running a business by consuming goods or services in producing revenue. A subdivision of owner's equity, 12–13, 17

dating of, 81

F

F.O.B. destination. *Seller* pays or is responsible for the cost of freight to purchaser's location or destination, 370

F.O.B. shipping point. *Purchaser* pays or is responsible for the shipping costs from seller's shipping point to purchaser's location, 370, 394

Fair Labor Standards Act (Federal Wage and Hour Law). A law the majority of employers must follow that contains rules stating the minimum hourly rate of pay and the maximum number of hours a worker will work before being paid time and a half for overtime hours worked. This law also has other rules and regulations that employers must follow for payroll purposes, 261

Federal Income Tax (FIT) withholding. Amount of federal income tax withheld by the employer from the employee's gross pay; the amount withheld is determined by the employee's gross pay, the pay period, the number of allowances claimed by the employee on the W-4 form, and the marital status indicated on the W-4 form, 262–263, 296–300, 313, 315, 317. *See also* Form 941 taxes

Federal Insurance Contributions Act (FICA). (1)Part of the Social Security law that requires employees and employers to pay OASDI taxes and Medicare taxes. (2)Part of the Social Security Act of 1935, this law taxes both the employer and employee up to a certain maximum rate and wage base for OASDI tax purposes. It also taxes both the employer and employee for Medicare purposes, but this tax has no wage base maximum, 266, 296

Medicare tax, 267, 272, 276, 295–296, 304, 313, 317

OASDI, 266–267, 272, 276, 295–296, 304, 315, 313, 317

FICA taxes, paying, 296–300, 315, 317

Federal Tax Deposit Coupon, 299

Federal Unemployment Tax Act (FUTA). A tax paid by employers to the federal government. The current rate is 0.8% on the first $7,000 of earnings of each employee after the normal SUTA tax credit is applied, 272–273, 296

Financial reports, 75

Financial statements

for a merchandising company, 456–461

preparation of, 18–21, 53, 55, 64, 136–138, 456–461, 475–476

preparing from worksheet, 136–138, 147–148

Fiscal year, 77, 161. *See also* Accounting cycle; Calendar year

journalizing at end of, 177

posting adjusting and closing entries at end of, 177

Footings. The totals of each side of a T account, 41, 54, 65

Form 940, Employer's Annual Federal Unemployment Tax Return. This form is used by employers at the end of the calendar year to report the amount of unemployment tax due for the year. If more than $500 is cumulatively owed at the end of a quarter, it should be paid one month after the end of that quarter. Normally, the report is due January 31 after the calendar year, or February 10 if an employer has already made all deposits, 306–307, 315, 317–318

completing, 307–310.

Form 941, Employer's Quarterly Federal Tax Return. A tax report that a business will complete after the end of each calendar quarter indicating the total FICA (OASDI and Medicare) taxes owed plus the amount of FIT withheld from employees' pay for the quarter. If federal tax deposits have been made correctly and on time, the total amount deposited should equal the amount due on Form 941. Any difference results in a payment due or a refund, 297, 318

completing, 300–303

Form 941 taxes. Another term used to describe FIT, OASDI, and Medicare. This name comes from the form used to report these taxes, 297–300, 304, 315, 317

deposit rules, 313–314, 315, 317

fines for late payment, 314

Form 944, Employer's Annual Federal Tax Return. The form used by employers to report FICA (OASDI and Medicare) taxes and FIT. This version will be filed by January 31 following the end of the year and can be used by employers who owe $1,000 or less for these taxes and who have been told by the IRS that they must file this form, 300

Form SS-4. The form filled out by an employer to get an EIN. The form is sent to the IRS, which assigns the number to the business, 296

Form W-2, Wage and Tax Statement. A form completed by the employer at the end of the calendar year to provide a summary of gross earnings and deductions to each employee. At least three copies go to the employee, one copy to the IRS, one copy to any state where employee income taxes have been withheld, one copy to the Social Security Administration, and one copy into the records of the business, 304–305, 315, 318

Form W-3, Transmittal of Income and Tax Statement. A form completed by the employer to verify the number of W-2s and amounts withheld as shown on them. This form is sent to the Social Security Administration data processing center along with copies of each employee's W-2 forms, 305, 315, 318

preparing, 305–306

Form W-4 (Employee's Withholding Allowance Certificate). A form filled out by employees and used by employers to supply needed information about the number of allowances claimed, marital status, and so forth. The form is used for payroll purposes to determine federal income tax withholding from an employee's paycheck, 263

Four-column account. A running balance account that records debits and credits and has a column for an ending balance (debit or credit). It replaces the standard two-column account we used earlier, 86

Fraud, prevention of, 2. *See also* Internal control system

Freight charges, 370, 385, 394

Freight-In. A cost of goods sold account that records the shipping cost to the buyer, 424–425

Full endorsement, 223

FUTA. *See* Form 940, Employer's Annual Federal Unemployment Tax Return

G

General journal, 351. *See also* Journal

General ledger, 342

    partial, 92

General Ledger Accounts

    posting to from special journals, 413–418

Generally accepted accounting principles (GAAP). The procedures and guidelines that must be followed during the accounting process, 4

Gross earnings (gross pay). Amount of pay received before any deductions, 261–262

Gross profit. Net sales less cost of goods sold, 425, 440, 458

Gross sales. The revenue earned from sale of merchandise to customers, 338, 352, 354

H

Historical cost. The actual cost of an asset at time of purchase, 123

Hourly employees, 261

I

Income statement. An accounting statement that details the performance of a firm (revenue minus expenses) for a specific period of time, 18, 23, 141

    affected by adjustments, 163

    of a merchandising company, 456

    preparing from worksheet, 136–138, 141

Income Summary. A temporary account in the ledger that summarizes revenue and expenses and transfers the balance (net income or net loss) to Capital. This account does not have a normal balance, i.e., it could have a debit or a credit balance, 166, 168–169, 425

Income tax

    city, 264

    county, 264

    federal, 262–263, 296–300, 313, 315, 317

    state, 263–264

Individual employee earnings record. An accounting document that summarizes the total amount of wages paid and the deductions for the calendar year. It aids in preparing governmental reports. A new record is prepared for each employee each year, 270–271, 276

Insurance Expired, 135, 430, 440

Interest Expense. The cost of borrowing money, 428

Interim reports. Financial statements that are prepared for a month, quarter, or some other portion of the fiscal year, 78

Internal control system. Procedures and methods to control a firm's assets as well as monitor its operations, 2, 222

Internal Revenue Service (IRS), 262

International Financial Reporting Standards (IFRS). A group of accounting standards and procedures that if adopted by the US, could replace GAAP, 4

Internet banking. *See* Banking, online

Interstate commerce. A test that is applied to determine whether an employer must follow the rules of the Fair Labor Standards Act. If an employer communicates or does business with another business in some other state, it is usually considered to be involved in interstate commerce, 261

Inventories. *See also* Beginning merchandise inventory; Ending merchandise inventory

    merchandise, 383–384, 456

Invoice approval form. Used by the accounting department in checking the invoice and finally approving it for recording and payment, 373

IRS Circular E. An IRS tax publication of tax tables, 263

IRS forms. *See* Form 940, Employer's Annual Federal Unemployment Tax Return; Form 941, Employer's Quarterly Federal Tax Return; Form 944, Employer's Annual Federal Tax Return; Form SS-4; Form W-2, Wage and Tax Statement; Form W-3, Transmittal of Income and Tax Statement; Form W-4 (Employee's Withholding Allowance Certificate)

J

Journal. A listing of business transactions in chronological order. The journal links on one page the debit and credit parts of transactions. Alternatively known as *general journal*, 78

    relationship with chart of accounts, 78–79

    sales journal, 421

    special, 413-418

Journal entry. The transaction (debits and credits) that is recorded into a journal once it is analyzed, 78. *See also* Adjusting journal entries; Closing journal entries; Compound journal entry

    adjusting, 162–164, 190–191

    closing, 166–170, 190–191

    protocol for, 79

Journalizing. The process of recording a transaction entry into the journal, 78

    using Chart of Accounts, 103

L

Ledger. A group of accounts that records data from business transactions, 40, 42, 65, 103. *See also* Subsidiary ledger

    adjusting, 165

    posting to, 86–87, 92, 103. *See also* Posting

Ledger accounts, 40

Legal holidays, 314

Liabilities. Obligations that come due in the future. Liabilities are the financial rights or claims of creditors to assets, 5. *See also* Current liabilities; Long-term liabilities

    rules for, 43

Limited Liability Corporations, 3

Long-term liabilities. Obligations that are not due or payable for a long time, usually for more than a year, 461

Look-back period. A period of time used to determine whether a business should make its Form 941 tax deposits on a monthly or semiweekly basis. The IRS defines this period as July 1 through June 30 of the year prior to the year in which Form 941 tax deposits will be made, 297, 313

M

Manufacturer. Business that makes a product and sells it to its customers, 3–4

Medical insurance. Health care insurance for which premiums may be paid through a deduction from an employee's paycheck, 267

    withholding for, 267

Medicare tax. *See also* Form 941 taxes

    calculating employer payments, 272

    as employer payroll tax, 295–296, 304, 315, 317

    FAQs, 313–314

    wage base amounts, 266–267, 276

Merchandise. Goods brought into a store for resale to customers, 336

Merchandise company. Business that buys a product from a manufacturing company to sell to its customers, 3–4

    financial statement for, 456–461

    income statement for, 456

Merchandise inventory. An asset and perpetual inventory system account that records purchases of merchandise. Discounts and returns are recorded in this account for the buyer, 383–384, 456

    adjustments for, 439–440, 424–426

Monthly depositor. A business classified as a monthly depositor will make its payroll tax deposits only once each month for the amount of Form 941 taxes due from the prior month, 297, 313

Mortgage Payable. A liability account showing amount owed on a mortgage, 427

N

Natural business year. *See* Calendar year

Net income. When revenue totals more than expenses, the result is net income, 12, 19–20

Net loss. When expenses total more than revenue, the result is net loss, 12, 19

Net pay. Gross earnings, less deductions. Net pay, or take-home pay, is what the worker actually takes home, 267

Net sales. Gross sales less sales returns and allowances less sales discounts, 338, 352, 354, 456

Normal balance of an account. The side of an account that increases by the rules of debit and credit, 43, 65

NSF (nonsufficient funds). Notation indicating that a check has been written on an account that lacks sufficient funds to back it up, 230, 246

O

OASDI taxes. *See also* Form 941 taxes

employer payment for, 270, 272

as employer payroll tax, 295–296, 304, 315, 317

FAQs, 313–314

wage base amounts, 266–267, 276

withholding for, 266–267

Office Salaries Expense, 92

Office Supplies Account, 121–122

adjustments to, 121–122, 135

Online banking. *See* Banking, online

Operating cycle. Average time it takes to buy and sell merchandise and then collect accounts receivable, 459

Operating expenses, 458

Other expenses. Non-operating expenses that do not relate to the main operating activities of the business; they appear in a separate section on the income statement. One example given in the text is Interest Expense, interest owed on money borrowed by the company, 458

Other income. Any revenue other than revenue from sales. It appears in a separate section on the income statement. Examples: Rental Income and Storage Fees, 458

Outstanding checks. Checks written by a company or person that were not received or not processed by the bank before the preparation of the bank statement, 230–231, 246

Overtime earnings, 261–262

Owner's drawing account. *See* Withdrawals

Owner's equity. Rights or financial claims to the assets of a business (in the accounting equation, assets minus liabilities), 5, 12, 17

subdivisions of, 15, 17

and withdrawals, 82

P

Partnership. A form of business organization that has at least two owners. The partners usually are personally liable for the partnership's debts, 2–3

Pay or payroll period. A length of time used by an employer to calculate the amount of an employee's earnings. Pay periods can be daily, weekly, biweekly (once every two weeks), semimonthly (twice each month), monthly, quarterly, or annual, 261

Payee. One to whom a note is payable. The person or company to whom a check is payable, 226, 246

Payroll. *See also* Gross earnings; Net pay

overtime earnings, 261–262

paying, 293–294, 315, 317

process, 259–260

recording, 291–293, 315, 317

recording payment of, 293–294, 315, 317

Payroll laws, state, 261

Payroll register. A multicolumn form that is used to record payroll data, 268, 270, 276

Payroll taxes, 262–263

   employer, 295, 315, 313

   recording expenses, 293, 315, 317

   types of depositors, 297–298

Payroll withholdings, other than taxes, 267

Periodic inventory system. (1)An inventory system that, at the *end* of each accounting period, calculates the cost of the unsold goods on hand by taking the cost of each unit times the number of units on hand of each product. (2)An inventory system that counts inventory only at the end of the accounting period, 383, 424, 440

   calculations using, 452

Periodic method, 413–418

Permanent (real) accounts. Accounts whose balances are carried over to the next accounting period. Examples: Assets, Liabilities, Capital, 166

Perpetual accounting system, 395

Perpetual inventory system. An inventory system that keep *continual track* of each type of inventory by recording units on hand at the beginning, units sold, and the current balance after each sale or purchase, 383, 392–393, 421–422, 424, 440

   calculations using, 452

Personal identification number (PIN), 232–233

Petty cash, 223

Petty cash fund. Fund (source) that allows payment of small amounts without the writing of checks, 236, 245, 247

   auxiliary record, 238

   making payments from, 237

   replenishing, 239

Petty cash voucher. A petty cash form to be completed when money is taken out of petty cash, 237–238

Phishing. Fake e-mails that attempt to obtain information about online banking customers, 233

Plant and equipment. Long-lived assets such as equipment, buildings, or land that are used in the production or sale of goods or services, 459

Point-of-sale cash registers, 256–257

POS terminals. *See* Point-of-sale cash registers

Post-closing trial balance. The final step in the accounting cycle that lists only permanent accounts in the ledger and their balances after adjusting and closing entries have been posted, 176, 178, 190–191, 467

Posting. The transferring, copying, or recording of information from a journal to a ledger, 86, 92

   adjusting entries, 162–165, 190–191

   closing entries, 166–170, 190–191

   to the ledger, 103

Posting references, 80, 87. *See also* Cross-referencing

Prepaid Rent Account, 122–123

   adjustments to, 121–122, 135

Purchase Discounts, recording, 385–387

Purchase invoice. The seller's sales invoice, which is sent to the purchaser, 372

Purchase order. A form used in business to place an order for the buying of goods from a seller, 372

Purchase requisition. A form used within a business by the requesting department asking the purchasing department of the business to buy specific goods, 372

Purchase transactions, recording and posting, 394

Purchases. Merchandise for resale. It is a cost, 368, 394, 415

Purchases accounts, 368, 392

Purchases Discount. A contra-cost account in the general ledger that records discounts offered by vendors of merchandise for prompt payment of purchases by buyers, 369–370, 392, 394

Purchases Returns and Allowances. A contra-ledger that records the amount of defective or unacceptable merchandise returned to suppliers and/or price reductions given for defective items, 368, 392, 394

   recording, 384–387

Purchases Transactions on Account, recording and posting, 375–376, 392

R

Receiving report. A business form used to notify the appropriate people of the ordered goods received along with the quantities and specific condition of the goods, 372

Rent, prepaid

    as asset, 80

    as expense, 103

Residual value. Estimated value of an asset after all the allowable depreciation has been taken, 124

Restrictive endorsement, 223, 246

Retailers. Merchants who buy goods from wholesalers for resale to customers, 336

Revenue. An amount earned by performing services for customers or selling goods to customers; it can be in the form of cash or accounts receivable. A subdivision of owner's equity: As revenue increases, owner's equity increases, 11, 17

    dating of, 82

    revenue accounts, 1

Reversing entries. Optional bookkeeping technique in which certain adjusting entries are reversed or switched on the first day of the new accounting period so that transactions in the new period can be recorded without referring back to prior adjusting entries, 470–471, 475–476

Rubber stamp, used for endorsements, 223

S

Salaried employees, 261

Salaries Accrued account, 126–128, 135, 430, 440. *See also* Accrued salaries payable

    adjustments to, 126–128, 135

Sales. *See also* Gross sales; Net sales

    gross profit on, 383

    recording, 386

Sales discount. Amount a customer is allowed to deduct from the bill total for paying a bill during the discount period, 337, 345, 352, 354

Sales Discount account. A contra-revenue account that records cash discounts granted to customers for payments made within a specific period of time, 337–338. *See also* Purchases Discount

Sales invoice. A bill sent to customer(s) reflecting a credit sale, 340

Sales Returns and Allowances (SRA) account. A contra-revenue account that records price adjustments and allowances granted on merchandise that is defective and has been returned, 336–337, 352, 354

Sales revenue, 383

Sales Tax Payable account. An account in the general ledger that accumulates the amount of sales tax owed. It has a credit balance, 338–339

Sarbanes-Oxley Act, 2

Schedule of accounts payable, 379–380, 392, 395

Schedule of accounts receivable. A list of the customers, in alphabetical order, that have an outstanding balance in the accounts receivable subsidiary ledger. This total should be equal to the balance of the Accounts Receivable controlling account in the general ledger at the end of the month, 349, 352, 355

Selling expenses. Operating expenses directly related to the sale of goods excluding Cost of Goods Sold, 458

Semiweekly depositor. A business classified as a semiweekly depositor may have to make its payroll tax deposits up to twice in one week, depending on when payroll is paid, 297–298, 313–314

Service charges, 230–231

Service company. Business that provides a service, 3–4, 11

Shift in assets. A shift that occurs when the composition of the assets has changed but the total of the assets remains the same, 6, 8, 14

Shipping costs, 370, 394

Signature card. A form signed by a bank customer that the bank uses to verify signature authenticity on all checks, 222

Slide. The error that results in adding or deleting zeros in the writing of a number. Example: 79,000 → 7,920, 94

Social Security taxes. *See* OASDI taxes

Sole proprietorship. A type of business organization that has one owner. The owner is personally liable for paying the business's debts, 2–3

Standard account. A formal account that includes columns for date, explanation, posting reference, debit, and credit, 40, 65

State Income Tax (SIT) withholding. Amount of state income tax withheld by the employer from the employee's gross pay, 263

State Unemployment Tax Act (SUTA). A tax usually paid only by employers to the state for employee unemployment insurance, 272–273, 311, 315, 317

Statement of account, from bank, 228

Statement of cash flows. A financial report that provides a detailed breakdown of the specific increases and decreases in cash during an accounting period. It helps readers of the statement evaluate past performance as well as predict future cash flows of the business, 20

Statement of financial position, 9. *See also* Balance sheet

Statement of owner's equity. A financial statement that reveals the change in capital. The ending figure for capital is then placed on the balance sheet, 18, 23, 141

for a merchandising company, 458

preparing from worksheet, 138

Subsidiary ledger. A ledger that contains accounts of a single type. Example: The accounts receivable subsidiary ledger records all credit customers, 341, 352, 392

posting to from special journals, 413–418

Supplies. One type of asset acquired by a firm; it has a much shorter life than equipment, 6

as expense, 81

Supplies on Hand, 135, 429, 440

SUTA. *See* State Unemployment Tax Act

T

T account. A skeleton version of a standard account, used for demonstration purposes, 40, 64–65

T account entries, 42–44

Taxable earnings. Shows amount of earnings subject to a tax. The tax itself is not shown, 267

Taxes. *See also* Federal Income Tax (FIT) withholding, paying; Form 941 taxes; IRS Circular E; IRS Forms; Payroll taxes; State Income Tax (SIT) withholding; State Unemployment Tax Act (SUTA); Tax Act of 1989

employee, 304, 313, 315, 317

employer taxes, 313, 315, 317

income tax, 262–264

Medicare tax, 267, 272, 276, 295–296, 304

OASDI taxes, 266–267, 272, 276, 295–296, 304

Temporary (nominal) accounts. Accounts whose balances at the end of an accounting period are not carried over to the next accounting period, 166

Total, distinguishing, 10

Transactions

analysis of, 44–50, 52–53, 65

journalizing, 79–83, 96

merchandise transactions, 384–388

recording, 64

sales transactions on account, 340

Transit number, ABA, 223, 235

Transmittal of Income and Tax Statement. *See* Form W-3, Transmittal of Income and Tax Statement

Transposition. The accidental rearrangement of digits of a number. Example: 152 → 125, 94

Trial balance. (1)A list of the ending balances of all the accounts in a ledger. (2)An informal listing of the ledger accounts and their balances in the ledger to aid in proving the equality of debits and credits, The total of the debits should equal the total of the credits. 53–54, 64–65, 93

indentation of titles on, 58

post-closing, 176

preparation of, 93–96, 103

Truncation. *See* Check truncation

U

Unearned Rent Account, 425–426

adjustments to, 439–440

Unearned Revenue. A liability account that records amount owed for goods or services in advance of delivery. The Cash account would record the receipt of cash, 428, 440

Unemployment taxes, 272–273

V

Virtual banks, 232

W

Wage bracket table. One of various charts in IRS Circular E that provides information about deductions for federal income tax based on earnings and data supplied on the W-4 form, 263, 265

Wholesalers. Merchants who buy goods from suppliers and manufacturers for sale to retailers, 340

Withdrawals. A subdivision of owner's equity that records money or other assets an owner withdraws from a business for personal use, 12, 15, 19, 50

and owner's equity, 82

Word Processing Equipment Account, 123–126

adjustments to, 123–125, 135

Workers' compensation insurance. (1)A benefit plan required by federal regulations in which employers must purchase insurance to protect their employees against losses due to injury or death incurred while on the job. (2)Insurance paid, in advance by an employer to protect its employees against loss due to accidental death or injury incurred during employment, 273–274, 276, 311

Worksheet. A columnar device used by accountants to aid them in completing the accounting cycle— often just referred to as "spreadsheet." It is not a formal report, 120, 148

account title column, 135

adjusted trial balance section, 128–129, 136

adjustments section, 120–128, 135–136

balance sheet section, 131, 136, 148, 433

blueprint for preparing, 146

and the closing process, 167

income statement section, 128–131, 136, 148

for merchandise company, 427–436, 439–440

preparing, 120, 147

recording journal entries from 162–164

trial balance section, 120, 136

Workweek. A seven-day (168-hour) period used to determine overtime hours for employees, A workweek can begin on any given day, but must end seven days later, 261

CREDITS

Chapter 1, page 1, © Iain Masterton / Alamy

Chapter 2, page 39, © dbimages / Alamy; page 76, Courtesy Subway Restaurants

Chapter 3, page 77, © PSL Images / Alamy

Chapter 4, page 119, © izmostock / Alamy; page 135, © sonya etchison/Shutterstock.com; page 159, Courtesy Subway Restaurants

Chapter 5, page 161, ZUMA Press/Newscom; page 176, © iStockphoto.com/Katja Bone; page 178, © Racheal Grazias/Shutterstock.com; page 203, Courtesy Subway Restaurants

Chapter 6, page 221, © Jeff Greenberg / Alamy; page 256, Courtesy Subway Restaurants

Chapter 7, page 259, © Daisy-Daisy / Alamy; page 287, Courtesy Subway Restaurants

Chapter 8, page 289, © VIEW Pictures Ltd / Alamy; page 331, Courtesy Subway Restaurants

Chapter 9, page 335, © Michael Newman / Photo Edit

Chapter 10, page 367, James Berglie/ZUMA Press/ Newscom

Chapter 11, page 423, © Cindy Hopkins / Alamy

Chapter 12, page 455, Andreas Gebert/dpa/ picture-alliance/Newscom

STUDY GUIDE AND WORKING PAPERS CHAPTERS 1–12

COLLEGE ACCOUNTING
A Practical Approach

Twelfth Edition

Jeffrey Slater

*North Shore Community College
Danvers, Massacusetts*

PEARSON

Boston Columbus Indianapolis New York San Francisco Upper Saddle River
Amsterdam Cape Town Dubai London Madrid Milan Munich Paris Montreal Toronto
Delhi Mexico City Sao Paulo Sydney Hong Kong Seoul Singapore Taipei Tokyo

VP/Editorial Director: Sally Yagan
Acquisitions Editor: Lacey Vitetta
Development Editor: Mignon Tucker
Editorial Project Managers: Nicole Sam and Christina Rumbaugh
Editorial Assistants: Jane Avery and Lauren Zanedis
Director of Marketing: Maggie Moylan Leen
Marketing Assistants: Ian Gold and Kimberly Lovato
Senior Managing Editor: Nancy Fenton
Senior Production Project Manager: Roberta Sherman

Manufacturing Buyer: Carol Melville
Cover Designer: Anthony Gemmellaro
Media Project Manager, Production: John Cassar
Media Project Manager: Sarah Peterson
Full-Service Project Management: GEX Publishing Services
Composition: GEX Publishing Services
Printer/Binder: Courier/Kendallville
Cover Printer: Lehigh-Phoenix Color/Hagerstown
Text Font: Times Roman 10/12

www.pearsonhighered.com

10 9 8 7 6 5 4 3 2 1
ISBN 10: 0-13-277215-9
ISBN 13: 978-0-13-277215-0

Contents

STUDY GUIDE AND WORKING PAPERS CHAPTERS 1–12

Chapter 1   Introduction to Accounting Concepts and Procedures SG-1

Chapter 2   Debits and Credits: Analyzing and Recording
Business Transactions SG-24

Chapter 3   Beginning the Accounting Cycle: Journalizing, Posting,
and the Trial Balance SG-50

Chapter 4   The Accounting Cycle Continued: Preparing Worksheets
and Financial Statements SG-97

Chapter 5   The Accounting Cycle Completed: Adjusting, Closing,
and the Post-Closing Trial Balance SG-117

Chapter 6   Banking Procedures and Control of Cash SG-186

Chapter 7   Payroll Concepts and Procedures—Employee Taxes SG-213

Chapter 8   The Employer's Tax Responsibilities:
Principles and Procedures SG-231

Chapter 9   Sales and Cash Receipts SG-257

Chapter 10   Purchases and Cash Payments SG-297

Appendix 10A Appendix Forms SG-351

Chapter 11   Preparing a Worksheet for a Merchandise Company SG-377

Chapter 12   Completion of the Accounting Cycle
for a Merchandise Company SG-385

1

INTRODUCTION TO ACCOUNTING CONCEPTS AND PROCEDURES

INSTANT REPLAY: SELF-REVIEW QUIZ 1-1

GRACIE RYAN REAL ESTATE

	ASSETS			=	LIABILITIES	+	OWNER'S EQUITY
	Cash	+	Computer Equipment	=	Accounts Payable	+	Gracie Ryan, Capital
TRANSACTION 1							
NEW BALANCE				=			
TRANSACTION 2							
NEW BALANCE				=			
TRANSACTION 3							
ENDING BALANCE		+		=		+	
				=			

INSTANT REPLAY: SELF-REVIEW QUIZ 1-2

_____

_____

_____

ASSETS					LIABILITIES AND OWNER'S EQUITY				

INSTANT REPLAY: SELF-REVIEW QUIZ 1-3

B. BING CO.

	ASSETS			=	LIABILITIES	+		OWNER'S EQUITY				
	Cash	+ Accounts Receivable	+ Cleaning Equipment	=	Accounts Payable	+	B. Bing, Capital	− B. Bing Withd.	+	Revenue	−	Expenses
Beg. Balance	$10,000	+ $2,500	+ $6,500	=	$1,000	+	$11,800	− $800	+	$9,000	−	$2,000
1.												
Balance												
2.												
Balance												
3.												
Balance												
4.												
Balance												
5.												
Ending Balance	+	+	=			+		−	+		−	

INSTANT REPLAY: SELF-REVIEW QUIZ 1-4

(1)

_____
_____
_____

(2)

_____
_____
_____

(3)

_____
_____
_____

ASSETS						LIABILITIES AND OWNER'S EQUITY					

FORMS FOR DEMONSTRATION PROBLEM

(1)

MICHAEL BROWN, ATTORNEY AT LAW

	ASSETS			= LIABILITIES +		OWNER'S EQUITY				
	Cash	+ Accounts Receivable	+ Office Equipment	= Accounts Payable	+ M. Brown, Capital	– M. Brown, Withd.	+ Legal fees	– Expenses		
A.										
Balance										
B.										
Balance										
C.										
Balance										
D.										
Balance										
E.										
Balance										
F.										
Balance										
G.										
Balance										
H.										
Balance										
I.										
Ending Balance										

DEMONSTRATION PROBLEM (CONTINUED)

(2A)

MICHAEL BROWN, ATTORNEY AT LAW
INCOME STATEMENT
FOR MONTH ENDED JUNE 30, 201X

(2B)

MICHAEL BROWN, ATTORNEY AT LAW
STATEMENT OF OWNER'S EQUITY
FOR MONTH ENDED JUNE 30, 201X

(3C)

MICHAEL BROWN, ATTORNEY AT LAW
BALANCE SHEET
JUNE 30, 201X

ASSETS	LIABILITIES AND OWNER'S EQUITY

CHAPTER 1
CONCEPT CHECK

1. A. _____
   B. _____
   C. _____
   D. _____
   E. _____
   F. _____

2. A. _____
   B. _____
   C. _____

3. A. _____
   B. _____

4. _____
   _____
   _____

5. _____
   _____
   _____
   _____
   _____

6. _____
   _____
   _____
   _____

7. A. _____
   B. _____
   C. _____
   D. _____

8. A. _____
   B. _____
   C. _____
   D. _____
   E. _____
   F. _____
   G. _____
   H. _____

9. A. _____
   B. _____
   C. _____
   D. _____

PROBLEM 1A-3 OR PROBLEM 1B-3

RICK FOX
TYPING SERVICE

	ASSETS				= LIABILITIES +		OWNER'S EQUITY				
	Cash	+	Accounts Receivable	+	Office Equipment	=	Accounts Payable	+	R. Ferlito, Capital	–	R. Ferlito, Withd.	+	Typing Revenue	–	Expenses
A.												
BALANCE												
B.												
BALANCE												
C.												
BALANCE												
D.												
BALANCE												
E.												
BALANCE												
F.												
BALANCE												
G.												
BALANCE												
H.												
ENDING BALANCE												

PROBLEM 1A-4 OR PROBLEM 1B-4

(A)

WHELDON STENCILING SERVICE
INCOME STATEMENT
FOR MONTH ENDED NOVEMBER 30, 201X

(B)

WHELDON STENCILING SERVICE
STATEMENT OF OWNER'S EQUITY
FOR MONTH ENDED NOVEMBER 30, 201X

PROBLEM 1A-4 OR PROBLEM 1B-4 (CONCLUDED)

(C)

WHELDON STENCILING SERVICE
BALANCE SHEET
NOVEMBER 30, 201X

ASSETS				LIABILITIES AND OWNER'S EQUITY			

PROBLEM 1A-5 OR PROBLEM 1B-5

TRICKETT'S CATERING SERVICE

	ASSETS				=	LIABILITIES	+					OWNER'S EQUITY				
	Cash	+	Accounts Receivable	+	Equipment	=	Accounts Payable	+	J. Trickett, Capital	−	J. Trickett, Withd.	+	Catering Revenue	−	Expenses
10/25															
BALANCE															
10/27															
BALANCE															
10/28															
BALANCE															
10/29															
BALANCE															
11/1															
BALANCE															
11/5															
BALANCE															
11/8															
BALANCE															
11/10															
BALANCE															
11/15															
BALANCE															
11/17															
BALANCE															
11/20															
BALANCE															
11/25															
BALANCE															
11/28															
BALANCE															
11/30															
END. BAL.															

(A)

Name _____ Class _____ Date _____

PROBLEM 1A-5 OR PROBLEM 1B-5 (CONTINUED)

(B)

TRICKETT'S CATERING SERVICE
BALANCE SHEET
MARCH 31, 201X

ASSETS   LIABILITIES AND OWNER'S EQUITY

(C)

TRICKETT'S CATERING SERVICE
INCOME STATEMENT
FOR MONTH ENDED APRIL 30, 201X

PROBLEM 1A-5 OR PROBLEM 1B-5 (CONCLUDED)

(D)

TRICKETT'S CATERING SERVICE
STATEMENT OF OWNER'S EQUITY
FOR MONTH ENDED APRIL 30, 201X

(E)

TRICKETT'S CATERING SERVICE
BALANCE SHEET
APRIL 30, 201X

ASSETS   **LIABILITIES AND OWNER'S EQUITY**

CHAPTER 1
SUMMARY PRACTICE TEST:
INTRODUCTION TO ACCOUNTING CONCEPTS AND PROCEDURES

Part I Instructions

Fill in the blank(s) to complete the statement.

1. _____ was passed to prevent corporate fraud.

2. _____ – Liabilities = Owner's Equity

3. The owner's current investment or equity in the assets of a business is called _____.

4. A list of assets, liabilities, and owner's equity as of a particular date is reported on a(n) _____ _____.

5. _____ create an outward or potential outward flow of assets.

6. Revenue earned not on account creates an asset entitled _____.

7. _____ record personal expenses that are not related to the business. They are a subdivision of owner's equity.

8. The _____ _____ reports how well a business performs for a period of time.

9. The _____ _____ _____ _____ is a report that shows changes in capital.

10. The ending figure for capital from the statement of owner's equity is placed on the _____ _____.

Part II Instructions

Answer true or false to the following statements.

1. Accounts Receivable is a liability.
2. Liabilities produce revenue.
3. Revenue is an asset.
4. Capital means cash.
5. Bookkeeping is 50% of accounting.
6. The balance sheet lists assets, revenue, and owner's equity.
7. The balance sheet shows where we are now for a specific period of time.
8. Revenue creates an outward flow of assets.
9. Expenses are a subdivision of owner's equity.
10. Withdrawals are the only subdivision of owner's equity.
11. Withdrawals are listed on the income statement.
12. Revenue is a subdivision of owner's equity.
13. Revenues and withdrawals are listed on the income statement.
14. The income statement helps update the statement of owner's equity, and the statement of owner's equity helps update the balance sheet.
15. Withdrawals are listed on the statement of owner's equity.

Part III Instructions

In column B, record the appropriate code(s) that result from recording the transaction in column A.

1.	Increase in assets	5.	Increase in capital
2.	Decrease in assets	6.	Increase in revenues
3.	Increase in liabilities	7.	Increase in expenses
4.	Decrease in liabilities	8.	Increase in withdrawals

COLUMN A	COLUMN B
1. EXAMPLE: Pete Smith invested $5,000 in his business.	1,5
2. Bought computer equipment on account for $600.	_____
3. Paid salaries of $70.	_____
4. Bought additional computer equipment for $750 cash.	_____
5. Paid rent expense of $90.	_____
6. Received $5,000 in cash from revenue earned.	_____
7. Paid heat expense of $15.	_____
8. Earned revenue of $500 that will not be received until next month.	_____
9. Paid amount owed on equipment previously purchased on account.	_____
10. Paid for cleaning supplies expense, $15.	_____
11. Customers paid $10 of amount previously owed.	_____
12. Bought additional equipment of $1,000, half paid in cash and half charged.	_____
13. Charged customer $100 for services performed.	_____
14. Pete paid home phone bill from the company's cash.	_____
15. Advertising expense incurred but not to be paid until next month.	_____

CHAPTER 1 SOLUTIONS TO SUMMARY PRACTICE TEST

Part I

1.	The Sarbanes-Oxley Act	5.	Expenses	9.	statement of owner's equity
2.	Assets	6.	Cash	10.	balance sheet
3.	capital	7.	Withdrawals		
4.	balance sheet	8.	income statement		

Part II

1.	false	**6.**	false	**11.**	false
2.	false	**7.**	false	**12.**	true
3.	false	**8.**	false	**13.**	false
4.	false	**9.**	true	**14.**	true
5.	false	**10.**	false	**15.**	true

Part III

1.	1,5	**6.**	1,6	**11.**	1,2
2.	1,3	**7.**	7,2	**12.**	1,2,3
3.	7,2	**8.**	1,6	**13.**	1,6
4.	1,2	**9.**	4,2	**14.**	8,2
5.	7,2	**10.**	7,2	**15.**	7,3

Name _____ Class _____ Date _____

CONTINUING PROBLEM—ON THE JOB FOR CHAPTER 1

SANCHEZ COMPUTER CENTER

	ASSETS				= LIABILITIES +		OWNER'S EQUITY		
	Cash	+ Supplies	+ Computer Shop Equipment	+ Office Equipment	= Accounts Payable	+ Freedman Capital	− Freedman, Withdrawals	+ Revenue	− Expenses
a									
BALANCE									
b									
BALANCE									
c									
BALANCE									
d									
BALANCE									
e									
BALANCE									
f									
BALANCE									
g									
BALANCE									
h									
BALANCE									
i									
BALANCE									
j									
END BAL.									

SG-22

C.	1. Accounts Affected	2. Category	3. ↑↓	4. Rules	5. T Account Update

D.	1. Accounts Affected	2. Category	3. ↑↓	4. Rules	5. T Account Update

E.	1. Accounts Affected	2. Category	3. ↑↓	4. Rules	5. T Account Update

INSTANT REPLAY: SELF-REVIEW QUIZ 2-3

Cash	111
4,500	300
2,000	100
1,000	1,200
300	1,300
	2,600

Accounts Payable	211
300	700

Salon Fees	411
	3,500
	1,000

Accounts Receivable	121
1,000	300

Pam Jay, Capital	311
	4,000

Rent Expense	511
1,200	

Salon Equipment	131
700	

Pam Jay, Withdrawals	321
100	

Salon Supplies Exp.	521
1,300	

Salaries Expense	531
2,600	

Name _____ Class _____ Date _____

(1)

_____
_____
_____

(2)

_____
_____
_____

(3)

(4)

FORMS FOR DEMONSTRATION PROBLEM

(1,2,3)

| Advertising Expense 511 | Gas Expense 512 | Salaries Expense 513 | Telephone Expense 514 |

| Accounts Payable 211 | Mel Free, Capital 311 | Mel Free, Withdrawals 312 | Delivery Fees Earned 411 |

| Cash 111 | Accounts Receivable 112 | Office Equipment 121 | Delivery Trucks 122 |

FORMS FOR DEMONSTRATION PROBLEM (CONTINUED)

(4)

MEL'S DELIVERY SERVICE
TRIAL BALANCE
JULY 31, 201X

	Dr.	Cr.

(5A)

MEL'S DELIVERY SERVICE
INCOME STATEMENT
FOR MONTH ENDED JULY 31, 201X

FORMS FOR DEMONSTRATION PROBLEM (CONCLUDED)

(5B)

MEL'S DELIVERY SERVICE
STATEMENT OF OWNER'S EQUITY
FOR MONTH ENDED JULY 31, 201X

(5C)

MEL'S DELIVERY SERVICE
BALANCE SHEET
JULY 31, 201X

ASSETS   LIABILITIES AND OWNER'S EQUITY

CHAPTER 2
CONCEPT CHECK

1.

2. A. _____ _____ _____ _____
    B. _____ _____ _____ _____
    C. _____ _____ _____ _____
    D. _____ _____ _____ _____
    E. _____ _____ _____ _____
    F. _____ _____ _____ _____
    G. _____ _____ _____ _____

3.

4. _____

5. A. _____
    B. _____
    C. _____
    D. _____
    E. _____
    F. _____
    G. _____
    H. _____
    I. _____
    J. _____
    K. _____

PROBLEM 2A-2 OR PROBLEM 2B-2

Cash 111	Brian Pud, Withdrawals 312

Office Equipment 121	Consulting Fees Earned 411

Accounts Payable 211	Advertising Expense 511

Brian Pud, Capital 311	Rent Expense 512

PROBLEM 2A-3 OR PROBLEM 2B-3

(A)

| Cash   111 | | Accounts Payable   211 | | Fees Earned   411 |

| Office Equipment   121 | | Brad Joy, Capital   311 | | Rent Expense   511 |

| | | Brad Joy, Withdrawals   312 | | Utilities Expense   512 |

(B)

BRAD'S CLEANING SERVICE
TRIAL BALANCE
OCTOBER 31, 201X

	Dr.	Cr.

PROBLEM 2A-4 OR PROBLEM 2B-4

(A)

GAIL LUCAS, ATTORNEY AT LAW
INCOME STATEMENT
FOR MONTH ENDED MAY 31, 201X

(B)

GAIL LUCAS, ATTORNEY AT LAW
STATEMENT OF OWNER'S EQUITY
FOR MONTH ENDED MAY 31, 201X

PROBLEM 2A-4 OR PROBLEM 2B-4 (CONCLUDED)

(C)

GAIL LUCAS, ATTORNEY AT LAW
BALANCE SHEET
MAY 31, 201X

ASSETS

LIABILITIES AND OWNER'S EQUITY

PROBLEM 2A-5 OR PROBLEM 2B-5

(1,2,3)

Advertising Expense   511

_____|_____

Gas Expense   512

_____|_____

Salaries Expense   513

_____|_____

Telephone Expense   514

_____|_____

Accounts Payable   211

_____|_____

Avery Annis, Capital   311

_____|_____

Avery Annis, Withdrawals   312

_____|_____

Delivery Fees Earned   411

_____|_____

Cash   111

_____|_____

Accounts Receivable   112

_____|_____

Office Equipment   121

_____|_____

Delivery Trucks   122

_____|_____

PROBLEM 2A-5 OR PROBLEM 2-B5 (CONTINUED)

(4)

ANNIS'S DELIVERY SERVICE
TRIAL BALANCE
AUGUST 31, 201X

		Dr.	Cr.

(5A)

ANNIS'S DELIVERY SERVICE
INCOME STATEMENT
FOR MONTH ENDED AUGUST 31, 201X

PROBLEM 2A-5 OR PROBLEM 2B-5 (CONCLUDED)

(5B)

ANNIS'S DELIVERY SERVICE
STATEMENT OF OWNER'S EQUITY
FOR MONTH ENDED AUGUST 31, 201X

(5C)

ANNIS'S DELIVERY SERVICE
BALANCE SHEET
AUGUST 31, 201X

ASSETS				LIABILITIES AND OWNER'S EQUITY			

CHAPTER 2
SUMMARY PRACTICE TEST:
DEBITS AND CREDITS: ANALYZING AND RECORDING
BUSINESS TRANSACTIONS

Part I Instructions

Fill in the blank(s) to complete the statement.

1. Financial reports do not contain _____ or _____.
2. The right side of any T account is called the _____ _____.
3. Assets are increased by _____.
4. The process of balancing an account involves _____.
5. Transaction analysis charts are an aid in recording _____ _____.
6. The _____ _____ _____ indicates the names and numbering system of accounts.
7. A(n) _____ is a group of accounts.
8. A(n) _____ _____ is an informal report that lists accounts and their balances.
9. Withdrawals are increased by _____.
10. The income statement, statement of owner's equity, and balance sheet may be prepared from a(n) _____ _____.
11. Cash, Accounts Receivable, and Equipment are examples of _____.
12. Increasing expenses ultimately cause owner's equity to _____.
13. An increase in rent expense is a(n) _____ by the rules of debits and credits.
14. A debit to one asset and a credit to another asset for the same transaction reflect a(n) _____ in assets.
15. The category of accounts receivable is a(n) _____.

Part II Instructions

Bea Paul opened a shuttle service company. From the following chart of accounts, indicate in column B (by account number) which account (s) will be debited or credited as related to the transaction in column A.

Chart of Accounts

ASSETS	LIABILITIES	EXPENSES
10 Cash	50 Accounts Payable	80 Advertising
20 Accounts Receivable		90 Gas
30 Equipment	OWNER'S EQUITY	100 Salaries
40 Shuttle Bus	60 B. Paul, Capital	110 Telephone
	62 B. Paul, Withdrawals	
	REVENUE	
	70 Taxi Fees Earned	

COLUMN A   **COLUMN B**

		DEBIT(S)	CREDIT(S)
1.	EXAMPLE: Bea Paul invested $40,000 in the shuttle service.	10	60
2.	Purchased a shuttle bus on account for $25,000.	_____	_____
3.	Bought equipment on account for $3,000.	_____	_____
4.	Advertising bill received, but not paid until next month, $60.	_____	_____
5.	Bea paid home telephone bill from company checkbook, $20.	_____	_____
6.	Collected $100 in cash from daily shuttle fees earned.	_____	_____
7.	Customer charged a shuttle ride of $20.	_____	_____
8.	Received partial payment for Transaction #7 of $10.	_____	_____
9.	Paid business telephone bill, $32.	_____	_____
10.	Purchased additional equipment for cash, $550.	_____	_____
11.	Paid shuttle driver salaries of $150.	_____	_____
12.	Drove customer on account to local train station for $6.	_____	_____
13.	Received $5 from customer who hired a shuttle for ride across town.	_____	_____
14.	Collected from past charged revenue, $15.	_____	_____
15.	Bought office equipment on account for $110.	_____	_____

Part III Instructions

Answer true or false to the following statements.

1. There are no debit and credit columns found on the three financial statements.
2. A trial balance could balance but be wrong.
3. Withdrawals are listed on the credit column of the trial balance.
4. Double entry bookkeeping results in a system where the sum of all the debits is equal to the sum of all the credits.
5. The ledger is numbered like a textbook.

6. Withdrawals are always increased by credits.

7. An expense could create a liability.

8. A shift in assets means the total of assets must change.

9. The rules of debit and credit are constantly changing.

10. The transaction analysis chart is a teaching device.

11. The chart of accounts makes locating and identifying accounts easier.

12. The left side of any account is a credit.

13. A debit means all accounts are decreasing.

14. Financial statements are prepared from a trial balance.

15. The statement of owner's equity is prepared before the income statement.

16. Liabilities increase by credits.

17. Footings aid in balancing accounts.

18. Withdrawals are listed on the income statement.

19. The balance sheet contains the old figure for capital.

20. Think of a credit as always meaning something good.

CHAPTER 2
SOLUTIONS TO SUMMARY PRACTICE TEST

Part I

1.	debits/credits	**6.**	chart of accounts	**11.**	assets
2.	credit side	**7.**	ledger (general)	**12.**	decrease
3.	debits	**8.**	trial balance	**13.**	debit
4.	footings	**9.**	debits	**14.**	shift
5.	business transactions	**10.**	trial balance	**15.**	asset

Part II

	Debit	Credit			Debit	Credit			Debit	Credit
1.	10	60	**6.**		10	70	**11.**	100	10
2.	40	50	**7.**		20	70	**12.**	20	70
3.	30	50	**8.**		10	20	**13.**	10	70
4.	80	50	**9.**		110	10	**14.**	10	20
5.	62	10	**10.**		30	10	**15.**	30	50

Part III

1.	true	**6.**	false	**11.**	true	**16.**	true
2.	true	**7.**	true	**12.**	false	**17.**	true
3.	false	**8.**	false	**13.**	false	**18.**	false
4.	true	**9.**	false	**14.**	true	**19.**	false
5.	false	**10.**	true	**15.**	false	**20.**	false

SANCHEZ COMPUTER CENTER
STATEMENT OF OWNER'S EQUITY
FOR THE TWO MONTHS ENDED AUGUST 31, 201X

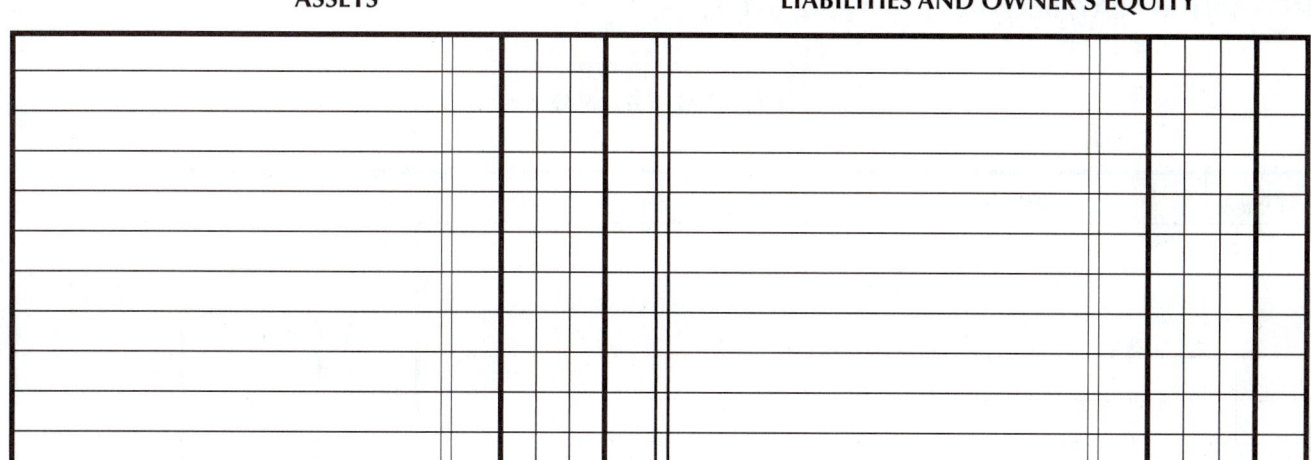

SANCHEZ COMPUTER CENTER
BALANCE SHEET
AUGUST 31, 201X

ASSETS   **LIABILITIES AND OWNER'S EQUITY**

BEGINNING THE ACCOUNTING CYCLE: JOURNALIZING, POSTING, AND THE TRIAL BALANCE

INSTANT REPLAY: SELF-REVIEW QUIZ 3-1

LOWE'S REPAIR SERVICE
GENERAL JOURNAL

PAGE 1

Date		Account Titles and Description	PR	Dr.			Cr.		

LOWE'S REPAIR SERVICE
GENERAL JOURNAL

Date	Account Titles and Description	PR	Dr.	Cr.

INSTANT REPLAY: SELF-REVIEW QUIZ 3-2

CLARK'S WORD PROCESSING SERVICES
GENERAL JOURNAL

PAGE 1

Date 201X		Account Titles and Description	PR	Dr.				Cr.			
May	1	Cash		10	0	0	0	00				
		Brenda Clark, Capital						10	0	0	0	00
		Initial investment of cash by owner										
	1	Word Processing Equipment		6	0	0	0	00				
		Cash							1	0	0	0	00
		Accounts Payable							5	0	0	0	00
		Purchase of equip. from Ben Co.										
	1	Prepaid Rent		1	2	0	0	00				
		Cash							1	2	0	0	00
		Rent paid in advance (3 months)										
	3	Office Supplies			6	0	0	00				
		Accounts Payable								6	0	0	00
		Purchase of supplies on acct. from Norris										
	7	Cash		3	0	0	0	00				
		Word Processing Fees							3	0	0	0	00
		Cash received for services rendered										
	13	Office Salaries Expense			6	5	0	00				
		Cash								6	5	0	00
		Payment of office salaries										
	18	Advertising Expense			2	5	0	00				
		Accounts Payable								2	5	0	00
		Bill received but not paid from Al's News										
	20	Brenda Clark, Withdrawals			6	2	5	00				
		Cash								6	2	5	00
		Personal withdrawal of cash										
	22	Accounts Receivable		5	0	0	0	00				
		Word Processing Fees							5	0	0	0	00
		Billed Morris Co. for fees earned										

CLARK'S WORD PROCESSING SERVICES
GENERAL JOURNAL

PAGE 2

Date 201X		Account Titles and Description	PR			Dr.				Cr.			
May	27	Office Salaries Expense			6	5	0	00					
		Cash								6	5	0	00
		Payment of office salaries											
	28	Accounts Payable		2	5	0	0	00					
		Cash								2	5	0	0	00
		Paid half the amount owed Ben Co.											
	29	Telephone Expense			2	2	0	00					
		Cash								2	2	0	00
		Paid telephone bill											

PARTIAL LEDGER OF CLARK'S WORD PROCESSING SERVICE

CASH   ACCOUNT NO. 111

Date	Explanation	Post Ref.	Debit	Credit	Balance	
					Debit	Credit

ACCOUNTS RECEIVABLE   ACCOUNT NO. 112

Date	Explanation	Post Ref.	Debit	Credit	Balance	
					Debit	Credit

OFFICE SUPPLIES   ACCOUNT NO. 114

Date		Explanation	Post Ref.	Debit	Credit	Balance Debit	Balance Credit

PREPAID RENT   ACCOUNT NO. 115

Date		Explanation	Post Ref.	Debit	Credit	Balance Debit	Balance Credit

WORD PROCESSING EQUIPMENT   ACCOUNT NO. 121

Date		Explanation	Post Ref.	Debit	Credit	Balance Debit	Balance Credit

ACCOUNTS PAYABLE   ACCOUNT NO. 211

Date		Explanation	Post Ref.	Debit	Credit	Balance Debit	Balance Credit

BRENDA CLARK, CAPITAL   ACCOUNT NO. 311

Date	Explanation	Post Ref.	Debit	Credit	Balance Debit	Balance Credit

BRENDA CLARK, WITHDRAWALS   ACCOUNT NO. 312

Date	Explanation	Post Ref.	Debit	Credit	Balance Debit	Balance Credit

WORD PROCESSING FEES   ACCOUNT NO. 411

Date	Explanation	Post Ref.	Debit	Credit	Balance Debit	Balance Credit

OFFICE SALARIES EXPENSE   ACCOUNT NO. 511

Date	Explanation	Post Ref.	Debit	Credit	Balance Debit	Balance Credit

ADVERTISING EXPENSE   ACCOUNT NO. <u>512</u>

Date	Explanation	Post Ref.	Debit	Credit	Balance Debit	Balance Credit

TELEPHONE EXPENSE   ACCOUNT NO. <u>513</u>

Date	Explanation	Post Ref.	Debit	Credit	Balance Debit	Balance Credit

INSTANT REPLAY: SELF-REVIEW QUIZ 3-3

1. _____

GENERAL JOURNAL

2. PAGE 4

Date		Account Titles and Description	PR		Dr.			Cr.	

END OF CHAPTER PROBLEMS

PROBLEM 3A-1 OR PROBLEM 3B-1

JAROME'S CLEANING SERVICE
GENERAL JOURNAL

PAGE 1

Date		Account Titles and Description	PR	Dr.	Cr.

PROBLEM 3A-1 OR PROBLEM 3B-1 (CONCLUDED)

JAROME'S CLEANING SERVICE
GENERAL JOURNAL

PAGE 2

Date	Account Titles and Description	PR	Dr.	Cr.

PROBLEM 3A-2 OR PROBLEM 3B-2
(A, B)

BARBIE'S ART STUDIO
GENERAL JOURNAL

PAGE 1

Date	Account Titles and Description	PR	Dr.	Cr.

PROBLEM 3A-2 OR PROBLEM 3B-2 (CONTINUED)

GENERAL LEDGER OF BARBIE'S ART STUDIO

CASH   ACCOUNT NO. 111

Date	Explanation	Post Ref.	Debit	Credit	Balance Debit	Balance Credit

ACCOUNTS RECEIVABLE   ACCOUNT NO. 112

Date	Explanation	Post Ref.	Debit	Credit	Balance Debit	Balance Credit

PREPAID RENT   ACCOUNT NO. 114

Date	Explanation	Post Ref.	Debit	Credit	Balance Debit	Balance Credit

ART SUPPLIES   ACCOUNT NO. 121

Date	Explanation	Post Ref.	Debit	Credit	Balance Debit	Balance Credit

PROBLEM 3A-2 OR PROBLEM 3B-2 (CONTINUED)

EQUIPMENT   ACCOUNT NO. 131

Date	Explanation	Post Ref.	Debit	Credit	Balance	
					Debit	Credit

ACCOUNTS PAYABLE   ACCOUNT NO. 211

Date	Explanation	Post Ref.	Debit	Credit	Balance	
					Debit	Credit

BARBIE RILEY, CAPITAL   ACCOUNT NO. 311

Date	Explanation	Post Ref.	Debit	Credit	Balance	
					Debit	Credit

BARBIE RILEY, WITHDRAWALS   ACCOUNT NO. 312

Date	Explanation	Post Ref.	Debit	Credit	Balance	
					Debit	Credit

PROBLEM 3A-2 OR PROBLEM 3B-2 (CONTINUED)

ART FEES EARNED　　　　　　　　　　　　　　**ACCOUNT NO. 411**

Date	Explanation	Post Ref.	Debit	Credit	Balance Debit	Balance Credit

ELECTRICAL EXPENSE　　　　　　　　　　　　**ACCOUNT NO. 511**

Date	Explanation	Post Ref.	Debit	Credit	Balance Debit	Balance Credit

SALARIES EXPENSE　　　　　　　　　　　　　**ACCOUNT NO. 521**

Date	Explanation	Post Ref.	Debit	Credit	Balance Debit	Balance Credit

TELEPHONE EXPENSE　　　　　　　　　　　　**ACCOUNT NO. 531**

Date	Explanation	Post Ref.	Debit	Credit	Balance Debit	Balance Credit

PROBLEM 3A-2 OR PROBLEM 3B-2 (CONCLUDED)

(C)

BARBIE'S ART STUDIO
TRIAL BALANCE
NOVEMBER 30, 201X

	Dr.	Cr.

PROBLEM 3A-3 OR PROBLEM 3B-3
(A, B)

A. GLOVER'S PLACEMENT AGENCY
GENERAL JOURNAL

PAGE 1

Date	Account Titles and Description	PR	Dr.	Cr.

PROBLEM 3A-3 OR PROBLEM 3B-3 (CONTINUED)

GENERAL LEDGER OF A. GLOVER'S PLACEMENT AGENCY

CASH   **ACCOUNT NO. 111**

Date	Explanation	Post Ref.	Debit	Credit	Balance	
					Debit	Credit

ACCOUNTS RECEIVABLE   **ACCOUNT NO. 112**

Date	Explanation	Post Ref.	Debit	Credit	Balance	
					Debit	Credit

SUPPLIES   **ACCOUNT NO. 131**

Date	Explanation	Post Ref.	Debit	Credit	Balance	
					Debit	Credit

EQUIPMENT   **ACCOUNT NO. 141**

Date	Explanation	Post Ref.	Debit	Credit	Balance	
					Debit	Credit

PROBLEM 3A-3 OR PROBLEM 3B-3 (CONTINUED)

ACCOUNTS PAYABLE   ACCOUNT NO. 211

Date	Explanation	Post Ref.	Debit	Credit	Balance Debit	Balance Credit

A. GLOVER, CAPITAL   ACCOUNT NO. 311

Date	Explanation	Post Ref.	Debit	Credit	Balance Debit	Balance Credit

A. GLOVER, WITHDRAWALS   ACCOUNT NO. 312

Date	Explanation	Post Ref.	Debit	Credit	Balance Debit	Balance Credit

PLACEMENT FEES EARNED   ACCOUNT NO. 411

Date	Explanation	Post Ref.	Debit	Credit	Balance Debit	Balance Credit

PROBLEM 3A-3 OR PROBLEM 3B-3 (CONTINUED)

WAGE EXPENSE   ACCOUNT NO. 511

Date		Explanation	Post Ref.	Debit	Credit	Balance	
						Debit	Credit

TELEPHONE EXPENSE   ACCOUNT NO. 521

Date		Explanation	Post Ref.	Debit	Credit	Balance	
						Debit	Credit

ADVERTISING EXPENSE   ACCOUNT NO. 531

Date		Explanation	Post Ref.	Debit	Credit	Balance	
						Debit	Credit

PROBLEM 3A-3 OR PROBLEM 3B-3 (CONCLUDED)

(C)

A. GLOVER'S PLACEMENT AGENCY
TRIAL BALANCE
NOVEMBER 30, 201X

		Dr.		Cr.	

CHAPTER 3
SUMMARY PRACTICE TEST:
BEGINNING THE ACCOUNTING CYCLE: JOURNALIZING, POSTING, AND THE TRIAL BALANCE

Part I Instructions

Fill in the blank(s) to complete the statement.

1. A fiscal year runs for _____ months.

2. _____ _____ are prepared for parts of a fiscal year (monthly, quarterly, etc.).

3. The _____ _____ _____ eliminates the need for footings.

4. The positive balance of each account is referred to as its _____ _____ .

5. The process of recording transactions in a journal is called _____ .

6. Entries are journalized in _____ _____ .

7. A ledger is often called a(n) _____ _____ _____ _____ .

8. The _____ portion of a journal entry is indented and placed below the _____ portion.

9. A journal entry requiring three or more accounts is called a(n) _____ _____ _____ .

10. Accounts receivable is a(n) _____ on the balance sheet.

11. When supplies are used up or consumed they become a(n) _____ .

12. The book of original entry usually refers to a(n) _____ .

13. The process of transferring information from a journal to a ledger is called _____ .

14. _____ _____ deals with the process of updating the PR of the journal from the account number of the ledger to indicate to which account in the ledger information has been posted.

15. Recording $995.00 as $99.50 is an example of a(n) _____ .

Name _____ Class _____ Date _____

Part II Instructions

Match the term in column A to the definition, example, or phrase in column B. Be sure to use a letter only once.

COLUMN A

  __g__ 1. EXAMPLE: Book of original entry
  _____ 2. Non-Business Expense
  _____ 3. Slide
  _____ 4. Transposition
  _____ 5. Posting
  _____ 6. General Journal
  _____ 7. Cross-reference
  _____ 8. Journalizing
  _____ 9. Balance Sheet prepared monthly
  _____ 10. A fiscal year

COLUMN B

a. 243 — 2430
b. Transferring information from a general journal to a ledger
c. Chronological order
d. Increased by a credit
e. Withdrawal
f. Compound journal entry
g. General journal
h. Rearrangement of digits of a number by accident
i. Updating PR column of journal from ledger account
j. Trial balance
k. Place to record transactions
l. Accounting cycle
m. Accounting period
n. Interim statements

Part III Instructions

Answer true or false to the following statements.

1. A slide cannot affect position of numbers.
2. The totals of a trial balance may possibly not balance due to transpositions.
3. Withdrawals has a normal balance of a credit.
4. The running balance of an account can be kept in a four-column account.
5. The journal links debits and credits in alphabetical order.
6. The ledger accumulates information from the journal.
7. The post reference column of a ledger records the account number of that account.
8. An accounting cycle must be from January 1 to December 31.
9. The ledger is the book of original entry.
10. The income statement is prepared for a specific accounting period.
11. Interim statements are prepared for an entire fiscal year.
12. A calendar year could be a fiscal year.
13. 390 written by mistake as 3,900 is an example of a slide.

THE ACCOUNTING CYCLE COMPLETED: ADJUSTING, CLOSING, AND THE POST-CLOSING TRIAL BALANCE

5

INSTANT REPLAY: SELF-REVIEW QUIZ 5-1

(1)

Date	Account Titles and Description	PR	Dr.	Cr.

(2) Partial Ledger

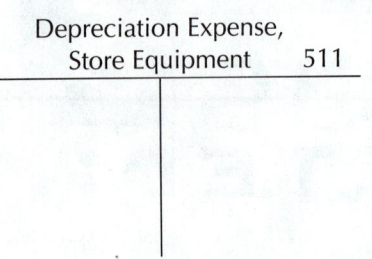

Depreciation Expense,
Store Equipment   511

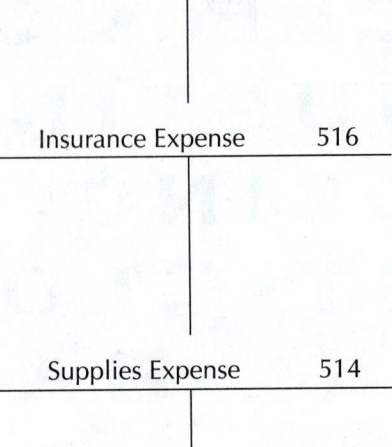

Accumulated Depreciation,
Store Equipment   122

4

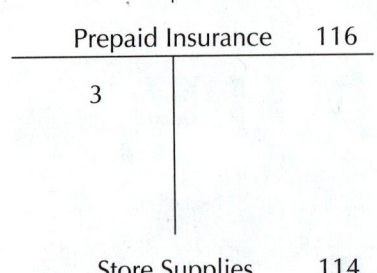

Prepaid Insurance   116

3

Insurance Expense   516

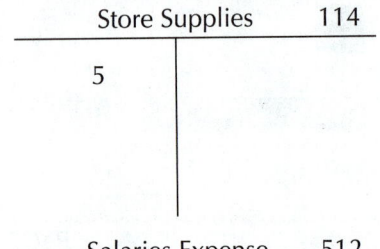

Store Supplies   114

5

Supplies Expense   514

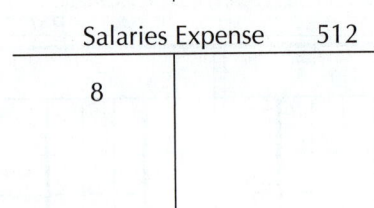

Salaries Expense   512

8

Salaries Payable   212

INSTANT REPLAY: SELF-REVIEW QUIZ 5-2
(1)

_____
_____
_____

P. Logan, Capital 310	Revenue from Clients 410	Supplies Expense 514
14	25	4

P. Logan, Withdrawals 311	Depreciation Expense, Store Equipment 510	Insurance Expense 516
3	1	2

Income Summary 312	Salaries Expense 512	Rent Expense 518
	11	2

(2) _____

_____

_____

INSTANT REPLAY: SELF-REVIEW QUIZ 5-3

FORMS FOR DEMONSTRATION PROBLEM

Use one of the blank fold-out worksheets that accompanied your textbook.

ROLO COMPANY
GENERAL JOURNAL

PAGE 1

Date	Account Titles and Description	PR	Dr.	Cr.

FORMS FOR DEMONSTRATION PROBLEM (CONTINUED)

ROLO COMPANY
GENERAL JOURNAL

PAGE 2

Date	Account Titles and Description	PR	Dr.	Cr.

FORMS FOR DEMONSTRATION PROBLEM (CONTINUED)

CASH   **ACCOUNT NO. 111**

Date		Explanation	Post Ref.	Debit	Credit	Balance Debit	Balance Credit

ACCOUNTS RECEIVABLE   **ACCOUNT NO. 112**

Date		Explanation	Post Ref.	Debit	Credit	Balance Debit	Balance Credit

PREPAID RENT   **ACCOUNT NO. 114**

Date		Explanation	Post Ref.	Debit	Credit	Balance Debit	Balance Credit

OFFICE SUPPLIES   **ACCOUNT NO. 115**

Date		Explanation	Post Ref.	Debit	Credit	Balance Debit	Balance Credit

FORMS FOR DEMONSTRATION PROBLEM (CONTINUED)

OFFICE EQUIPMENT   ACCOUNT NO. 121

Date		Explanation	Post Ref.	Debit	Credit	Balance	
						Debit	Credit

ACCUMULATED DEPRECIATION, OFFICE EQUIPMENT   ACCOUNT NO. 122

Date		Explanation	Post Ref.	Debit	Credit	Balance	
						Debit	Credit

ACCOUNTS PAYABLE   ACCOUNT NO. 211

Date		Explanation	Post Ref.	Debit	Credit	Balance	
						Debit	Credit

FORMS FOR DEMONSTRATION PROBLEM (CONTINUED)

SALARIES PAYABLE   ACCOUNT NO. 212

Date		Explanation	Post Ref.	Debit	Credit	Balance	
						Debit	Credit

ROLO KERN, CAPITAL   ACCOUNT NO. 311

Date		Explanation	Post Ref.	Debit	Credit	Balance	
						Debit	Credit

ROLO KERN, WITHDRAWALS   ACCOUNT NO. 312

Date		Explanation	Post Ref.	Debit	Credit	Balance	
						Debit	Credit

INCOME SUMMARY   ACCOUNT NO. 313

Date		Explanation	Post Ref.	Debit	Credit	Balance	
						Debit	Credit

FEES EARNED   ACCOUNT NO. 411

Date		Explanation	Post Ref.	Debit	Credit	Balance	
						Debit	Credit

FORMS FOR DEMONSTRATION PROBLEM (CONTINUED)

SALARIES EXPENSE   ACCOUNT NO. 511

Date	Explanation	Post Ref.	Debit	Credit	Balance Debit	Balance Credit

ADVERTISING EXPENSE   ACCOUNT NO. 512

Date	Explanation	Post Ref.	Debit	Credit	Balance Debit	Balance Credit

RENT EXPENSE   ACCOUNT NO. 513

Date	Explanation	Post Ref.	Debit	Credit	Balance Debit	Balance Credit

OFFICE SUPPLIES EXPENSE   ACCOUNT NO. 514

Date	Explanation	Post Ref.	Debit	Credit	Balance Debit	Balance Credit

DEPRECIATION EXPENSE, OFFICE EQUIPMENT   ACCOUNT NO. 515

Date	Explanation	Post Ref.	Debit	Credit	Balance Debit	Balance Credit

FORMS FOR DEMONSTRATION PROBLEM (CONTINUED)

ROLO COMPANY
INCOME STATEMENT
FOR MONTH ENDED JANUARY 31, 201X

ROLO COMPANY
STATEMENT OF OWNER'S EQUITY
FOR MONTH ENDED JANUARY 31, 201X

FORMS FOR DEMONSTRATION PROBLEM (CONTINUED)

ROLO COMPANY
BALANCE SHEET
JANUARY 31, 201X

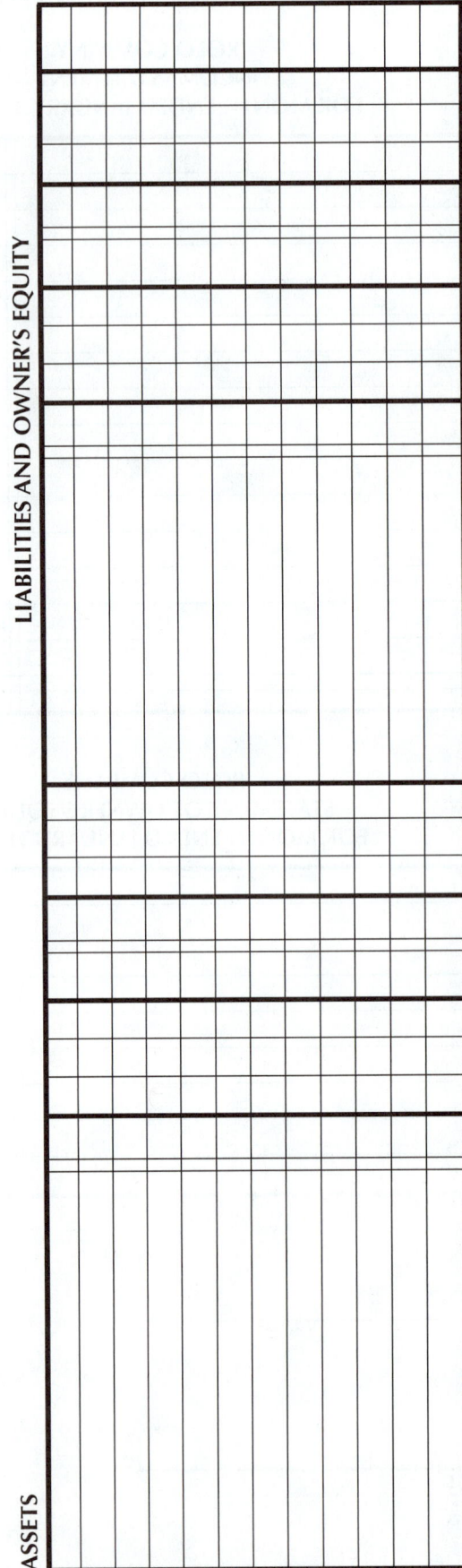

ASSETS

LIABILITIES AND OWNER'S EQUITY

FORMS FOR DEMONSTRATION PROBLEM (CONCLUDED)

ROLO COMPANY
POST-CLOSING TRIAL BALANCE
JANUARY 31, 201X

	Dr.	Cr.

CHAPTER 5
CONCEPT CHECK

GENERAL JOURNAL

1.

Date	Account Titles and Description	PR	Dr.	Cr.

Prepaid Insurance 115	Insurance Expense 510
Store Supplies 116	Depreciation Expense, Store Equipment 512
Accumulated Depreciation Store Equipment 119	Supplies Expense 514
Salaries Payable 210	Salaries Expense 516

2. _____

_____

_____

_____

_____

_____

_____

_____

END OF CHAPTER PROBLEMS

PROBLEM 5A-1 OR PROBLEM 5B-1

Use one of the blank fold-out worksheets that accompanied your textbook.

(2)

DAISY'S DANCE STUDIO
GENERAL JOURNAL

PAGE 3

Date	Account Titles and Description	PR	Dr.	Cr.

PROBLEM 5A-2 OR PROBLEM 5B-2

(1)

PALMER'S CLEANING SERVICE
GENERAL JOURNAL

PAGE 2

Date	Account Titles and Description	PR	Dr.	Cr.

PROBLEM 5A-2 OR PROBLEM 5B-2 (CONTINUED)

CASH   ACCOUNT NO. 112

Date		Explanation	Post Ref.	Debit	Credit	Balance	
						Debit	Credit

PREPAID INSURANCE   ACCOUNT NO. 114

Date		Explanation	Post Ref.	Debit	Credit	Balance	
						Debit	Credit

CLEANING SUPPLIES   ACCOUNT NO. 115

Date		Explanation	Post Ref.	Debit	Credit	Balance	
						Debit	Credit

AUTO   ACCOUNT NO. 121

Date		Explanation	Post Ref.	Debit	Credit	Balance	
						Debit	Credit

ACCUMULATED DEPRECIATION, AUTO   ACCOUNT NO. 122

Date		Explanation	Post Ref.	Debit	Credit	Balance	
						Debit	Credit

PROBLEM 5A-2 OR PROBLEM 5B-2 (CONTINUED)

ACCOUNTS PAYABLE   ACCOUNT NO. 212

Date	Explanation	Post Ref.	Debit	Credit	Balance	
					Debit	Credit

SALARIES PAYABLE   ACCOUNT NO. 213

Date	Explanation	Post Ref.	Debit	Credit	Balance	
					Debit	Credit

B. PALMER, CAPITAL   ACCOUNT NO. 312

Date	Explanation	Post Ref.	Debit	Credit	Balance	
					Debit	Credit

B. PALMER, WITHDRAWALS   ACCOUNT NO. 313

Date	Explanation	Post Ref.	Debit	Credit	Balance	
					Debit	Credit

INCOME SUMMARY   ACCOUNT NO. 314

Date	Explanation	Post Ref.	Debit	Credit	Balance	
					Debit	Credit

PROBLEM 5A-2 OR PROBLEM 5B-2 (CONTINUED)

CLEANING FEES   ACCOUNT NO. 412

Date		Explanation	Post Ref.	Debit	Credit	Balance	
						Debit	Credit

SALARIES EXPENSE   ACCOUNT NO. 513

Date		Explanation	Post Ref.	Debit	Credit	Balance	
						Debit	Credit

TELEPHONE EXPENSE   ACCOUNT NO. 514

Date		Explanation	Post Ref.	Debit	Credit	Balance	
						Debit	Credit

ADVERTISING EXPENSE   ACCOUNT NO. 515

Date		Explanation	Post Ref.	Debit	Credit	Balance	
						Debit	Credit

GAS EXPENSE   ACCOUNT NO. 516

Date		Explanation	Post Ref.	Debit	Credit	Balance	
						Debit	Credit

PROBLEM 5A-2 OR PROBLEM 5B-2 (CONTINUED)

INSURANCE EXPENSE   ACCOUNT NO. 517

Date	Explanation	Post Ref.	Debit	Credit	Balance Debit	Balance Credit

CLEANING SUPPLIES EXPENSE   ACCOUNT NO. 518

Date	Explanation	Post Ref.	Debit	Credit	Balance Debit	Balance Credit

DEPRECIATION EXPENSE, AUTO   ACCOUNT NO. 519

Date	Explanation	Post Ref.	Debit	Credit	Balance Debit	Balance Credit

PROBLEM 5A-2 OR PROBLEM 5B-2 (CONCLUDED)

(2)

PALMER'S CLEANING SERVICE
POST-CLOSING TRIAL BALANCE
JANUARY 31, 201X

	Dr.	Cr.

PROBLEM 5A-3 OR PROBLEM 5B-3

Use one of the blank fold-out worksheets that accompanied your textbook.

PROBLEM 5A-3 OR PROBLEM 5B-3 (CONTINUED)

PARKER'S PLOWING
GENERAL JOURNAL

PAGE 1

Date	Account Titles and Description	PR	Dr.	Cr.

PROBLEM 5A-3 OR PROBLEM 5B-3 (CONTINUED)

PARKER'S PLOWING
GENERAL JOURNAL

PAGE 2

Date	Account Titles and Description	PR	Dr.	Cr.

PROBLEM 5A-3 OR PROBLEM 5B-3 (CONTINUED)

PARKER'S PLOWING
GENERAL JOURNAL

PAGE 3

Date	Account Titles and Description	PR	Dr.	Cr.

PROBLEM 5A-3 OR PROBLEM 5B-3 (CONTINUED)

CASH　　　　　　　　　　　　**ACCOUNT NO. 111**

Date	Explanation	Post Ref.	Debit	Credit	Balance Debit	Balance Credit

ACCOUNTS RECEIVABLE　　　　**ACCOUNT NO. 112**

Date	Explanation	Post Ref.	Debit	Credit	Balance Debit	Balance Credit

PREPAID RENT　　　　　　　　**ACCOUNT NO. 114**

Date	Explanation	Post Ref.	Debit	Credit	Balance Debit	Balance Credit

SNOW SUPPLIES　　　　　　　**ACCOUNT NO. 115**

Date	Explanation	Post Ref.	Debit	Credit	Balance Debit	Balance Credit

PROBLEM 5A-3 OR PROBLEM 5B-3 (CONTINUED)

OFFICE EQUIPMENT   ACCOUNT NO. 121

Date	Explanation	Post Ref.	Debit	Credit	Balance Debit	Balance Credit

ACCUMULATED DEPRECIATION, OFFICE EQUIPMENT   ACCOUNT NO. 122

Date	Explanation	Post Ref.	Debit	Credit	Balance Debit	Balance Credit

SNOW EQUIPMENT   ACCOUNT NO. 123

Date	Explanation	Post Ref.	Debit	Credit	Balance Debit	Balance Credit

ACCUMULATED DEPRECIATION, SNOW EQUIPMENT   ACCOUNT NO. 124

Date	Explanation	Post Ref.	Debit	Credit	Balance Debit	Balance Credit

ACCOUNTS PAYABLE   ACCOUNT NO. 211

Date	Explanation	Post Ref.	Debit	Credit	Balance Debit	Balance Credit

PROBLEM 5A-3 OR PROBLEM 5B-3 (CONTINUED)

SALARIES PAYABLE   **ACCOUNT NO. 212**

Date	Explanation	Post Ref.	Debit	Credit	Balance Debit	Balance Credit

PARKER MURONEY, CAPITAL   **ACCOUNT NO. 311**

Date	Explanation	Post Ref.	Debit	Credit	Balance Debit	Balance Credit

PARKER MURONEY, WITHDRAWALS   **ACCOUNT NO. 312**

Date	Explanation	Post Ref.	Debit	Credit	Balance Debit	Balance Credit

INCOME SUMMARY   **ACCOUNT NO. 313**

Date	Explanation	Post Ref.	Debit	Credit	Balance Debit	Balance Credit

PLOWING FEES   **ACCOUNT NO. 411**

Date	Explanation	Post Ref.	Debit	Credit	Balance Debit	Balance Credit

PROBLEM 5A-3 OR PROBLEM 5B-3 (CONTINUED)

SALARIES EXPENSE ACCOUNT NO. <u>511</u>

Date		Explanation	Post Ref.	Debit	Credit	Balance	
						Debit	Credit

ADVERTISING EXPENSE ACCOUNT NO. <u>512</u>

Date		Explanation	Post Ref.	Debit	Credit	Balance	
						Debit	Credit

TELEPHONE EXPENSE ACCOUNT NO. <u>513</u>

Date		Explanation	Post Ref.	Debit	Credit	Balance	
						Debit	Credit

RENT EXPENSE ACCOUNT NO. <u>514</u>

Date		Explanation	Post Ref.	Debit	Credit	Balance	
						Debit	Credit

SNOW SUPPLIES EXPENSE ACCOUNT NO. <u>515</u>

Date		Explanation	Post Ref.	Debit	Credit	Balance	
						Debit	Credit

PROBLEM 5A-3 OR PROBLEM 5B-3 (CONTINUED)

DEPRECIATION EXPENSE, OFFICE EQUIPMENT   ACCOUNT NO. 516

Date		Explanation	Post Ref.	Debit	Credit	Balance	
						Debit	Credit

DEPRECIATION EXPENSE, SNOW EQUIPMENT   ACCOUNT NO. 517

Date		Explanation	Post Ref.	Debit	Credit	Balance	
						Debit	Credit

PROBLEM 5A-3 OR PROBLEM 5B-3 (CONTINUED)

PARKER'S PLOWING
INCOME STATEMENT
FOR MONTH ENDED JANUARY 31, 201X

PARKER'S PLOWING
STATEMENT OF OWNER'S EQUITY
FOR MONTH ENDED JANUARY 31, 201X

PROBLEM 5A-3 OR PROBLEM 5B-3 (CONTINUED)

PARKER'S PLOWING
BALANCE SHEET
JANUARY 31, 201X

ASSETS

LIABILITIES AND OWNER'S EQUITY

PROBLEM 5A-3 OR PROBLEM 5B-3 (CONCLUDED)

PARKER'S PLOWING
POST-CLOSING TRIAL BALANCE
JANUARY 31, 201X

		Dr.	Cr.

CHAPTER 5
SUMMARY PRACTICE TEST:
THE ACCOUNTING CYCLE COMPLETED:
ADJUSTING, CLOSING, AND
THE POST-CLOSING TRIAL BALANCE

Part I Instructions

Fill in the blank(s) to complete the statement.

1. After the closing process only _____ accounts remain with balances.
2. Revenue, Expenses, and Withdrawals are examples of _____ _____.
3. _____ in temporary accounts will not be carried over to the next accounting period.
4. After closing entries are posted, owner's Capital in the ledger will contain the _____ _____.
5. Revenue is closed to Income Summary by a(n) _____ to each revenue account and a(n) _____ to Income Summary.
6. Expenses are closed to Income Summary by _____ the individual expenses and _____ Income Summary.
7. If the balance of Income Summary is a credit, it will be closed by _____ Income Summary and _____ owner's Capital.
8. The balance of Withdrawals is closed by a(n) _____ and the amount transferred to owner's Capital by a(n) _____.
9. At the end of the closing process, all temporary accounts in the ledger will have a(n) _____ balance.
10. The _____ _____ _____ _____ contains a list of permanent accounts after the adjusting and closing entries have been posted to the ledger from a journal.
11. Closing entries can be prepared from a(n) _____.
12. After closing entries are posted, Income Summary will have a(n) _____ balance.
13. Journalizing adjustments can be done from the _____.
14. Cash, Equipment, and Supplies are not part of the _____ process.
15. Income Summary is a(n) _____ account.

Part II Instructions

The following is a chart of accounts for Al's Auto Shop. From the chart, indicate in Column B (by account number) which accounts will be debited or credited as related to the transactions in Column A.

CHART OF ACCOUNTS

ASSETS	OWNER'S EQUITY
112 Cash	340 A. Jones, Capital
114 Accounts Receivable	341 A. Jones, Withdrawals
116 Prepaid Rent	342 Income Summary
118 Auto Supplies	
120 Delivery Truck	REVENUE
121 Accumulated Depreciation, Delivery Truck	450 Fees Earned
LIABILITIES	EXPENSES
230 Accounts Payable	560 Salaries
232 Salaries Payable	562 Advertising
	564 Rent
	566 Auto Supplies
	568 Depreciation Expense, Delivery Truck

	COLUMN A	COLUMN B	
		Debit(s)	Credit(s)
1.	Closed balance in revenue account to Income Summary.	_____	_____
2.	Closed balance in individual expenses to Income Summary.	_____	_____
3.	Closed balance in Income Summary to owner's Capital. (Assume that it is a net income.)	_____	_____
4.	Closed Withdrawals to owner's Capital.	_____	_____
5.	Recorded auto supplies used up.	_____	_____
6.	Recorded depreciation on delivery truck.	_____	_____
7.	Brought Salaries Expense up to date (an adjustment).	_____	_____

Part III Instructions

Answer true or false to the following statements.

1. Closing entries are done every other month.
2. Adjustments are journalized before preparing the worksheet.
3. Closing entries can only clear permanent accounts.
4. Income summary is a temporary account.
5. Interim statements can be prepared from worksheets.
6. To clear expenses in the closing process, a compound entry is appropriate.
7. Withdrawals is a temporary account on the income statement.
8. Income Summary helps update withdrawals.

9. Accumulated Depreciation is a permanent account on the income statement.
10. Cash, Rent Expense, and Accounts Receivable need to be closed at the end of the period.
11. Closing entries do not relate to the worksheet.
12. Revenue is closed by a credit.
13. Expenses are placed on the debit side of the Income Summary account.
14. A post-closing trial balance closely resembles the ending balance sheet.
15. Accumulated Depreciation never has to be adjusted.
16. Interim statements are always prepared monthly.
17. A post-closing trial balance is prepared before adjustments are journalized.
18. Income Summary is shown on the balance sheet.
19. The process of closing entries will help update owner's Capital.
20. The normal balance of the Income Summary is a debit.
21. The normal balance of the Income Summary is a credit.
22. The income statement is listed in terms of debits and credits.
23. Closing updates only permanent accounts.
24. The completion of financial statements means that the Capital account in the ledger has been updated.
25. Withdrawals is closed to Income Summary.

SOLUTIONS TO SUMMARY PRACTICE TEST

Part I

1. permanent
2. temporary accounts
3. Balances
4. ending figure (balance)
5. debit, credit
6. crediting, debiting
7. debiting, crediting
8. credit, debit
9. zero
10. post-closing trial balance
11. worksheet
12. zero
13. worksheet
14. closing
15. temporary

Part II

	Debit	Credit
1.	450	342
2.	342	560, 562, 564, 566, 568
3.	342	340
4.	340	341
5.	566	118
6.	568	121
7.	560	232

Part III

1.	false	**7.**	false	**13.**	true	**19.**	true	**25.**	false
2.	false	**8.**	false	**14.**	true	**20.**	false		
3.	false	**9.**	false	**15.**	false	**21.**	false		
4.	true	**10.**	false	**16.**	false	**22.**	false		
5.	true	**11.**	false	**17.**	false	**23.**	false		
6.	true	**12.**	false	**18.**	false	**24.**	false		

MINI PRACTICE SET
SULLIVAN REALTY

SULLIVAN REALTY
GENERAL JOURNAL

PAGE 1

Date	Account Titles and Description	PR	Dr.	Cr.

MINI PRACTICE SET
SULLIVAN REALTY

SULLIVAN REALTY
GENERAL JOURNAL

PAGE 2

Date	Account Titles and Description	PR	Dr.	Cr.

MINI PRACTICE SET
SULLIVAN REALTY

SULLIVAN REALTY
GENERAL JOURNAL

PAGE 3

Date	Account Titles and Description	PR	Dr.	Cr.

MINI PRACTICE SET
SULLIVAN REALTY

SULLIVAN REALTY
GENERAL JOURNAL

PAGE 4

Date	Account Titles and Description	PR	Dr.	Cr.

MINI PRACTICE SET
SULLIVAN REALTY

SULLIVAN REALTY
GENERAL JOURNAL

PAGE 5

Date	Account Titles and Description	PR	Dr.	Cr.

MINI PRACTICE SET
SULLIVAN REALTY

SULLIVAN REALTY
GENERAL JOURNAL

PAGE 6

Date	Account Titles and Description	PR	Dr.	Cr.

Name _____ Class _____ Date _____

MINI PRACTICE SET
SULLIVAN REALTY

CASH   **ACCOUNT NO. 111**

Date	Explanation	Post Ref.	Debit	Credit	Balance Debit	Credit

MINI PRACTICE SET
SULLIVAN REALTY

ACCOUNTS RECEIVABLE   ACCOUNT NO. 112

Date	Explanation	Post Ref.	Debit	Credit	Balance	
					Debit	Credit

PREPAID RENT   ACCOUNT NO. 114

Date	Explanation	Post Ref.	Debit	Credit	Balance	
					Debit	Credit

OFFICE SUPPLIES   ACCOUNT NO. 115

Date	Explanation	Post Ref.	Debit	Credit	Balance	
					Debit	Credit

OFFICE EQUIPMENT   ACCOUNT NO. 121

Date	Explanation	Post Ref.	Debit	Credit	Balance	
					Debit	Credit

MINI PRACTICE SET: SULLIVAN REALTY

ACCUMULATED DEPRECIATION, OFFICE EQUIPMENT   ACCOUNT NO. 122

Date	Explanation	Post Ref.	Debit	Credit	Balance Debit	Balance Credit

AUTOMOBILE   ACCOUNT NO. 123

Date	Explanation	Post Ref.	Debit	Credit	Balance Debit	Balance Credit

ACCUMULATED DEPRECIATION, AUTOMOBILE   ACCOUNT NO. 124

Date	Explanation	Post Ref.	Debit	Credit	Balance Debit	Balance Credit

ACCOUNTS PAYABLE   ACCOUNT NO. 211

Date	Explanation	Post Ref.	Debit	Credit	Balance Debit	Balance Credit

SALARIES PAYABLE   ACCOUNT NO. 212

Date	Explanation	Post Ref.	Debit	Credit	Balance Debit	Balance Credit

MINI PRACTICE SET
SULLIVAN REALTY

JOHN SULLIVAN, CAPITAL   ACCOUNT NO. 311

Date	Explanation	Post Ref.	Debit	Credit	Balance Debit	Balance Credit

JOHN SULLIVAN, WITHDRAWALS   ACCOUNT NO. 312

Date	Explanation	Post Ref.	Debit	Credit	Balance Debit	Balance Credit

INCOME SUMMARY   ACCOUNT NO. 313

Date	Explanation	Post Ref.	Debit	Credit	Balance Debit	Balance Credit

MINI PRACTICE SET
SULLIVAN REALTY

COMMISSIONS EARNED   ACCOUNT NO. 411

Date	Explanation	Post Ref.	Debit	Credit	Balance Debit	Balance Credit

RENT EXPENSE   ACCOUNT NO. 511

Date	Explanation	Post Ref.	Debit	Credit	Balance Debit	Balance Credit

SALARIES EXPENSE   ACCOUNT NO. 512

Date	Explanation	Post Ref.	Debit	Credit	Balance Debit	Balance Credit

MINI PRACTICE SET
SULLIVAN REALTY

GAS EXPENSE   ACCOUNT NO. 513

Date		Explanation	Post Ref.	Debit	Credit	Balance	
						Debit	Credit

REPAIRS EXPENSE   ACCOUNT NO. 514

Date		Explanation	Post Ref.	Debit	Credit	Balance	
						Debit	Credit

TELEPHONE EXPENSE   ACCOUNT NO. 515

Date		Explanation	Post Ref.	Debit	Credit	Balance	
						Debit	Credit

ADVERTISING EXPENSE   ACCOUNT NO. 516

Date		Explanation	Post Ref.	Debit	Credit	Balance	
						Debit	Credit

MINI PRACTICE SET
SULLIVAN REALTY

OFFICE SUPPLIES EXPENSE   ACCOUNT NO. 517

Date	Explanation	Post Ref.	Debit	Credit	Balance Debit	Balance Credit

DEPRECIATION EXPENSE, OFFICE EQUIPMENT   ACCOUNT NO. 518

Date	Explanation	Post Ref.	Debit	Credit	Balance Debit	Balance Credit

DEPRECIATION EXPENSE, AUTOMOBILE   ACCOUNT NO. 519

Date	Explanation	Post Ref.	Debit	Credit	Balance Debit	Balance Credit

MISCELLANEOUS EXPENSE   ACCOUNT NO. 524

Date	Explanation	Post Ref.	Debit	Credit	Balance Debit	Balance Credit

MINI PRACTICE SET
SULLIVAN REALTY

Use the blank fold-out worksheets that accompanied your textbook.

SULLIVAN REALTY
INCOME STATEMENT
FOR MONTH ENDED JUNE 30, 201X

MINI PRACTICE SET
SULLIVAN REALTY

SULLIVAN REALTY
STATEMENT OF OWNER'S EQUITY
FOR MONTH ENDED JUNE 30, 201X

MINI PRACTICE SET
SULLIVAN REALTY

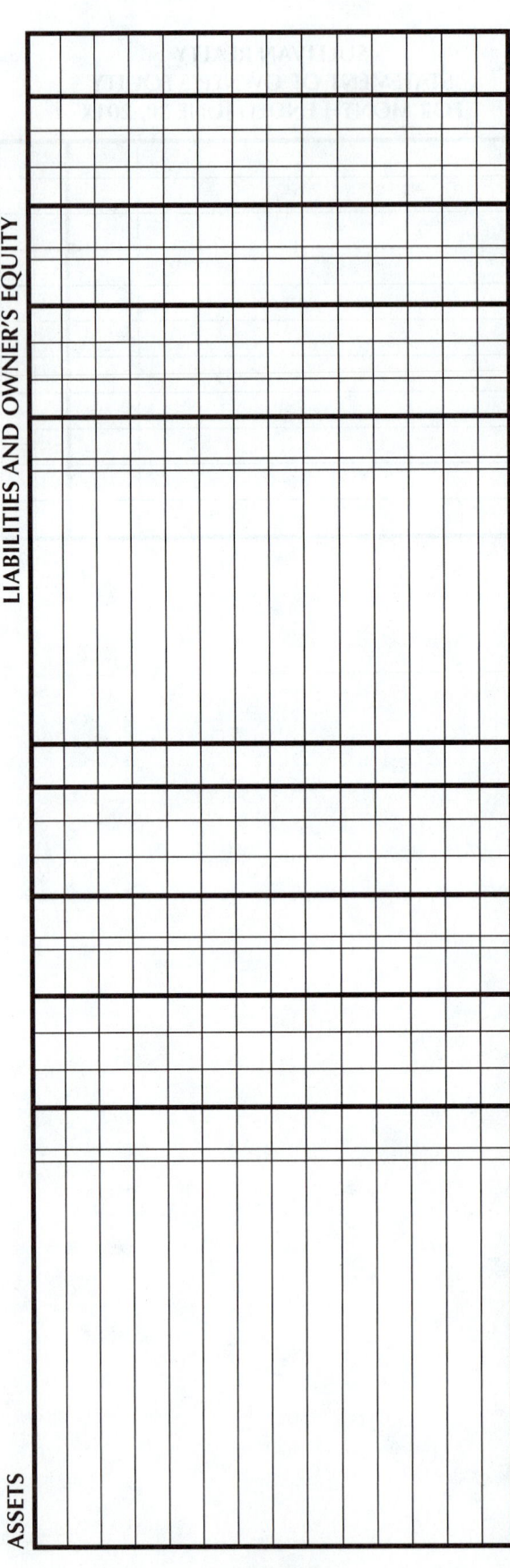

SULLIVAN REALTY
BALANCE SHEET
JUNE 30, 201X

ASSETS

LIABILITIES AND OWNER'S EQUITY

MINI PRACTICE SET
SULLIVAN REALTY

SULLIVAN REALTY
POST-CLOSING TRIAL BALANCE
JUNE 30, 201X

	Dr.	Cr.

You can find the worksheet for July with the blank fold-out worksheets that accompanied your textbook.

**MINI PRACTICE SET
SULLIVAN REALTY**

SULLIVAN REALTY
INCOME STATEMENT
FOR MONTH ENDED JULY 31, 201X

MINI PRACTICE SET
SULLIVAN REALTY

SULLIVAN REALTY
STATEMENT OF OWNER'S EQUITY
FOR MONTH ENDED JULY 31, 201X

MINI PRACTICE SET
SULLIVAN REALTY

SULLIVAN REALTY
BALANCE SHEET
JULY 31, 201X

ASSETS

LIABILITIES AND OWNER'S EQUITY

FORMS FOR EXERCISES A OR B

6A-1 OR 6B-1

KING CO.
BANK RECONCILIATION AS OF MARCH 31, 201X

CHECKBOOK BALANCE		BALANCE PER BANK	
Ending Checkbook Balance	_____	Ending Bank Statement Balance	_____
Deduct:	_____	Add:	_____
Bank Service Charge	_____	Deposit in Transit	_____
	_____		_____
	_____	Deduct:	_____
	_____	Outstanding Checks	_____
	_____		_____
Reconciled Balance	_____	Reconciled Balance	_____

6A-2 OR 6B-2

6A-3 OR 6B-3

EXERCISES (CONCLUDED)

6A-4 OR 6B-4

6A-5 OR 6B-5

    Beg. Change Fund
+Cash Register Total
=Cash should have on hand
–Counted Cash
= Cash Shortage

PROBLEM 6A-3 OR PROBLEM 6B-3

JOYOUS CO.
GENERAL JOURNAL

Date	Account Titles and Description	PR	Dr.	Cr.

PROBLEM 6A-3 OR PROBLEM 6B-3 (CONCLUDED)

JOYOUS CO.
AUXILIARY PETTY CASH RECORD

Date	Voucher No.	Description	Receipts	Payment	Category of Payment				
					Postage Expense	Office Supplies Expense	Account	Sundry Amount	

SOLUTIONS TO SUMMARY PRACTICE TEST

Part I

1.	increasing	6.	change fund
2.	debit card	7.	miscellaneous income
3.	journal entries	8.	Checks outstanding
4.	asset	9.	increase
5.	journal	10.	Safekeeping

Part II

1.	b, d, e	6.	a, d
2.	c	7.	b, d
3.	c	8.	c
4.	a, d	9.	a, d
5.	c	10.	b, d

Part III

1.	false	6.	false	11.	true	16.	false	21.	false
2.	false	7.	false	12.	true	17.	true	22.	false
3.	false	8.	false	13.	true	18.	true	23.	false
4.	false	9.	true	14.	false	19.	false		
5.	true	10.	false	15.	false	20.	false		

Part IV

LOGAN CO.			BANK BALANCE		
Checkbook Balance		$5,263.08	Bank Balance		$7,980.00
ADD:			ADD:		
			Deposit		
Interest	$ 42		in Transit		2,558.22
Collection of note	4,200	4,242.00			$9,038.22
		8,005.08			
DEDUCT:			DEDUCT:		
Service Chg.	$ 29.76		Check outstanding		$3,762.90
Error	2,700.00	2,729.76			
Reconciled Balance		$6,775.32	Reconciled Balance		$6,775.32

CONTINUING PROBLEM—ON THE JOB FOR CHAPTER 6

SANCHEZ COMPUTER CENTER
GENERAL JOURNAL

PAGE 3

Date		Account Titles and Description	PR	Dr.	Cr.

CASH   ACCOUNT NO. <u>1000</u>

Date		Explanation	Post Ref.	Debit	Credit	Balance					
						Debit				Credit	
9/30	1X	Balance forward	✔			1	6	4	5	00	

PETTY CASH   ACCOUNT NO. <u>1010</u>

Date		Explanation	Post Ref.	Debit	Credit	Balance	Credit
						Debit	Credit

ACCOUNTS RECEIVABLE   ACCOUNT NO. 1020

Date		Explanation	Post Ref.	Debit	Credit	Balance	
						Debit	Credit
9/30	1X	Balance forward	✔			2 6 0 0 00	

PREPAID RENT   ACCOUNT NO. 1025

Date		Explanation	Post Ref.	Debit	Credit	Balance	
						Debit	Credit
9/30	1X	Balance forward	✔			4 0 0 00	

SUPPLIES   ACCOUNT NO. 1030

Date		Explanation	Post Ref.	Debit	Credit	Balance	
						Debit	Credit
9/30	1X	Balance forward	✔			9 0 00	

COMPUTER SHOP EQUIPMENT   ACCOUNT NO. 1080

Date		Explanation	Post Ref.	Debit	Credit	Balance	
						Debit	Credit
9/30	1X	Balance forward	✔			2 4 0 0 00	

ACCUMULATED DEPRECIATION, COMPUTER SHOP EQUIPMENT   ACCOUNT NO. 1081

Date		Explanation	Post Ref.	Debit	Credit	Balance	
						Debit	Credit
9/30	1X	Balance forward	✔				9 9 00

OFFICE EQUIPMENT   ACCOUNT NO. 1090

Date		Explanation	Post Ref.	Debit	Credit	Balance	
						Debit	Credit
9/30	1X	Balance forward	✔			6 0 0 00	

ACCUMULATED DEPRECIATION, OFFICE EQUIPMENT   ACCOUNT NO. 1091

Date		Explanation	Post Ref.	Debit	Credit	Balance	
						Debit	Credit
9/30	1X	Balance forward	✔				2 0 00

ACCOUNTS PAYABLE   ACCOUNT NO. 2000

Date		Explanation	Post Ref.	Debit	Credit	Balance	
						Debit	Credit
9/30	1X	Balance forward	✔				2 1 0 00

T. FREEDMAN, CAPITAL   ACCOUNT NO. 3000

Date		Explanation	Post Ref.	Debit	Credit	Balance	
						Debit	Credit
9/30	1X	Balance forward	✔				7 4 0 6 00

T. FREEDMAN, WITHDRAWALS   ACCOUNT NO. 3010

Date		Explanation	Post Ref.	Debit	Credit	Balance	
						Debit	Credit

INCOME SUMMARY   ACCOUNT NO. 3020

Date		Explanation	Post Ref.	Debit	Credit	Balance	
						Debit	Credit

SERVICE REVENUE   ACCOUNT NO. 4000

Date	Explanation	Post Ref.	Debit	Credit	Balance	
					Debit	Credit

ADVERTISING EXPENSE   ACCOUNT NO. 5010

Date	Explanation	Post Ref.	Debit	Credit	Balance	
					Debit	Credit

RENT EXPENSE   ACCOUNT NO. 5020

Date	Explanation	Post Ref.	Debit	Credit	Balance	
					Debit	Credit

UTILITIES EXPENSE   ACCOUNT NO. 5030

Date		Explanation	Post Ref.	Debit	Credit	Balance	
						Debit	Credit

PHONE EXPENSE   ACCOUNT NO. 5040

Date		Explanation	Post Ref.	Debit	Credit	Balance	
						Debit	Credit

SUPPLIES EXPENSE   ACCOUNT NO. 5050

Date		Explanation	Post Ref.	Debit	Credit	Balance	
						Debit	Credit

INSURANCE EXPENSE   ACCOUNT NO. 5060

Date		Explanation	Post Ref.	Debit	Credit	Balance	
						Debit	Credit

POSTAGE EXPENSE   ACCOUNT NO. 5070

Date		Explanation	Post Ref.	Debit	Credit	Balance	
						Debit	Credit

DEPRECIATION EXPENSE, COMPUTER SHOP EQUIPMENT   ACCOUNT NO. 5080

Date		Explanation	Post Ref.	Debit	Credit	Balance	
						Debit	Credit

DEPRECIATION EXPENSE, OFFICE EQUIPMENT   ACCOUNT NO. 5090

Date		Explanation	Post Ref.	Debit	Credit	Balance	
						Debit	Credit

MISCELLANEOUS EXPENSE   ACCOUNT NO. 5100

Date		Explanation	Post Ref.	Debit	Credit	Balance	
						Debit	Credit

SANCHEZ COMPUTER CENTER
TRIAL BALANCE
OCTOBER 31, 201X

AUXILIARY PETTY CASH RECORD

Date	Voucher No.	Description	Receipts	Payment	Category of Payment				
					Postage Expense	Supplies Expense	Account	Sundry	Amount

SANCHEZ COMPUTER CENTER
BANK RECONCILIATION AS OF SEPTEMBER 30, 201X

BALANCE PER BANK   **CHECKBOOK BALANCE**

Bank Statement Balance   Checkbook Balance

 Add: _____   Add:

 Deduct: _____   _____

                         _____   Deduct:

                                                                 _____

Reconciled Balance   _____   Reconciled Balance   _____

PAYROLL CONCEPTS AND PROCEDURES— EMPLOYEE TAXES

7

INSTANT REPLAY: SELF-REVIEW QUIZ 7-1

REGULAR EARNINGS

OVERTIME

GROSS EARNINGS

INSTANT REPLAY: SELF-REVIEW QUIZ 7-2

FIT

SIT

FICA - OASDI

FICA - Medicare

NET PAY

INSTANT REPLAY: SELF-REVIEW QUIZ 7-3

FICA - OASDI _____

FICA - Medicare _____

FUTA _____

SUTA _____

CONTINUING PROBLEM—ON THE JOB FOR CHAPTER 7

(1)

SANCHEZ COMPUTER CENTER
GENERAL JOURNAL

PAGE 4

Date	Account Titles and Description	PR	Dr.	Cr.

SANCHEZ COMPUTER CENTER
GENERAL JOURNAL

Date		Account Titles and Description	PR	Dr.		Cr.	

CASH   ACCOUNT NO. 1000

Date		Explanation	Post Ref.	Debit	Credit	Balance Debit	Balance Credit
10/31	1X	Balance forward	✔			4 2 9 3 00	

PETTY CASH   ACCOUNT NO. 1010

Date		Explanation	Post Ref.	Debit	Credit	Balance Debit	Balance Credit
10/31	1X	Balance forward	✔			1 0 0 00	

ACCOUNTS RECEIVABLE   ACCOUNT NO. 1020

Date		Explanation	Post Ref.	Debit	Credit	Balance Debit	Balance Credit
10/31	1X	Balance forward	✔			4 2 0 0 00	

PREPAID RENT   ACCOUNT NO. 1025

| Date | | Explanation | Post Ref. | Debit | Credit | Balance | |
						Debit	Credit
10/31	1X	Balance forward	✓			1 6 0 0 00	

SUPPLIES   ACCOUNT NO. 1030

| Date | | Explanation | Post Ref. | Debit | Credit | Balance | |
						Debit	Credit
10/31	1X	Balance forward	✓			9 0 00	

COMPUTER SHOP EQUIPMENT   ACCOUNT NO. 1080

| Date | | Explanation | Post Ref. | Debit | Credit | Balance | |
						Debit	Credit
10/31	1X	Balance forward	✓			2 4 0 0 00	

ACCUMULATED DEPRECIATION, COMPUTER SHOP EQUIPMENT   ACCOUNT NO. 1081

| Date | | Explanation | Post Ref. | Debit | Credit | Balance | |
						Debit	Credit
10/31	1X	Balance forward	✓				9 9 00

OFFICE EQUIPMENT

ACCOUNT NO. **1090**

Date		Explanation	Post Ref.	Debit	Credit	Balance Debit	Balance Credit
10/31	1X	Balance forward	✓			6 0 0 00	

ACCUMULATED DEPRECIATION, OFFICE EQUIPMENT

ACCOUNT NO. **1091**

Date		Explanation	Post Ref.	Debit	Credit	Balance Debit	Balance Credit
10/31	1X	Balance forward	✓				2 0 00

ACCOUNTS PAYABLE

ACCOUNT NO. **2000**

Date		Explanation	Post Ref.	Debit	Credit	Balance Debit	Balance Credit
10/31	1X	Balance forward	✓				5 0 00

WAGES PAYABLE

ACCOUNT NO. **2010**

Date	Explanation	Post Ref.	Debit	Credit	Balance Debit	Balance Credit

FICA—OASDI PAYABLE   ACCOUNT NO. 2020

Date	Explanation	Post Ref.	Debit	Credit	Balance Debit	Balance Credit

FICA—MEDICARE PAYABLE   ACCOUNT NO. 2030

Date	Explanation	Post Ref.	Debit	Credit	Balance Debit	Balance Credit

FIT PAYABLE   ACCOUNT NO. 2040

Date	Explanation	Post Ref.	Debit	Credit	Balance Debit	Balance Credit

SIT PAYABLE   ACCOUNT NO. 2050

Date	Explanation	Post Ref.	Debit	Credit	Balance Debit	Balance Credit

T. FREEDMAN CAPITAL

ACCOUNT NO. **3000**

Date		Explanation	Post Ref.	Debit	Credit	Balance Debit	Balance Credit
10/31	1X	Balance forward	✔				7 4 0 6 00

T. FREEDMAN WITHDRAWALS

ACCOUNT NO. **3010**

Date		Explanation	Post Ref.	Debit	Credit	Balance Debit	Balance Credit
10/31	1X	Balance forward	✔			2 0 1 5 00	

SERVICE REVENUE

ACCOUNT NO. **4000**

Date		Explanation	Post Ref.	Debit	Credit	Balance Debit	Balance Credit
10/31	1X	Balance forward	✔				7 8 0 0 00

ADVERTISING EXPENSE

ACCOUNT NO. **5010**

Date	Explanation	Post Ref.	Debit	Credit	Balance Debit	Balance Credit

RENT EXPENSE

ACCOUNT NO. **5020**

Date	Explanation	Post Ref.	Debit	Credit	Balance Debit	Balance Credit

UTILITIES EXPENSE   ACCOUNT NO. 5030

Date		Explanation	Post Ref.	Debit	Credit	Balance	
						Debit	Credit

PHONE EXPENSE   ACCOUNT NO. 5040

Date		Explanation	Post Ref.	Debit	Credit	Balance	
						Debit	Credit

SUPPLIES EXPENSE   ACCOUNT NO. 5050

Date		Explanation	Post Ref.	Debit	Credit	Balance	
						Debit	Credit
10/31	1X		✔			4 2 00	

INSURANCE EXPENSE   ACCOUNT NO. 5060

Date		Explanation	Post Ref.	Debit	Credit	Balance	
						Debit	Credit

POSTAGE EXPENSE   ACCOUNT NO. 5070

Date		Explanation	Post Ref.	Debit	Credit	Balance	
						Debit	Credit
10/31	1X	Balance forward	✔			2 5 00	

DEPRECIATION EXPENSE C. S. EQUIPMENT   ACCOUNT NO. 5080

Date	Explanation	Post Ref.	Debit	Credit	Balance Debit	Balance Credit

DEPRECIATION EXPENSE OFFICE EQUIPMENT   ACCOUNT NO. 5090

Date	Explanation	Post Ref.	Debit	Credit	Balance Debit	Balance Credit

MISCELLANEOUS EXPENSE   ACCOUNT NO. 5100

Date	Explanation	Post Ref.	Debit	Credit	Balance Debit	Balance Credit
10/31 1X	Balance forward	✔			1 0 00	

WAGES EXPENSE   ACCOUNT NO. 5110

Date	Explanation	Post Ref.	Debit	Credit	Balance Debit	Balance Credit

(2) Use the fold-out payroll register that accompanied your textbook.

(3)

SANCHEZ COMPUTER CENTER
TRIAL BALANCE
NOVEMBER 30, 201X

		Dr.		Cr.	

CHAPTER 8

CONCEPT CHECK

1.

A.			
B.			
C.			
D.			
E.			

2.

A. _____

B. _____

C. _____

D. _____

3.

_____

_____

_____

_____

4.

A. _____

B. _____

C. _____

D. _____

E. _____

F. _____

G. _____

5.

A. _____

B. _____

C. _____

D. _____

E. _____

FORMS FOR EXERCISES A OR B

8A-1 OR 8B-1.

ACCOUNT	CATEGORY	DR/CR	STATEMENT FOUND ON

8A-2 OR 8B-2.

8A-3 OR 8B-3.

Name _____ Class _____ Date _____

EXERCISES (CONCLUDED)

8A-4 OR 8B-4.

_____
_____
_____
_____
_____
_____
_____
_____
_____

8A-5 OR 8B-5.

_____
_____
_____
_____

8A-6 OR 8B-6.

_____
_____

8A-7 OR 8B-7.

_____
_____
_____

8A-8 OR 8B-8.

END OF CHAPTER PROBLEMS

PROBLEM 8A-1 OR PROBLEM 8B-1

Employee	Allowance & Marital Status	Gross	FICA		Federal Income Tax
			OASDI	Medicare	

(2)

PROBLEM 8A-2 OR PROBLEM 8B-2

Date	Account Titles and Description	PR	Dr.	Cr.

PROBLEM 8A-2 OR PROBLEM 8B-2 (CONCLUDED)

Date		Account Titles and Description	PR		Dr.		Cr.

PROBLEM 8A-3 OR PROBLEM 8B-3

Form **941 for 201X:** **Employer's QUARTERLY Federal Tax Return**

(Rev. January 201X)

950110

Department of the Treasury — Internal Revenue Service

OMB No. 1545-0029

(EIN)
Employer identification number ☐☐ – ☐☐☐☐☐☐☐

Name *(not your trade name)* _____

Trade name *(if any)* _____

Address _____
Number   Street   Suite or room number

_____
City   State   ZIP code

Report for this Quarter of 2009
(Check one.)

☐ **1:** January, February, March

☐ **2:** April, May, June

☐ **3:** July, August, September

☐ **4:** October, November, December

Read the separate instructions before you complete Form 941. Type or print within the boxes.

Part 1: Answer these questions for this quarter.

1 Number of employees who received wages, tips, or other compensation for the pay period including: *Mar. 12 (Quarter 1), June 12 (Quarter 2), Sept. 12 (Quarter 3), Dec. 12 (Quarter 4)*   **1** _____

2 Wages, tips, and other compensation . . . . **2** _____

3 Income tax withheld from wages, tips, and other compensation . . . . **3** _____

4 If no wages, tips, and other compensation are subject to social security or Medicare tax   ☐ Check and go to line 6.

5 Taxable social security and Medicare wages and tips:

	Column 1		Column 2
5a Taxable social security wages	_____	× .124 =	_____
5b Taxable social security tips	_____	× .124 =	_____
5c Taxable Medicare wages & tips	_____	× .029 =	_____

5d Total social security and Medicare taxes (*Column 2,* lines 5a + 5b + 5c = line 5d) . . **5d** _____

6 Total taxes before adjustments (lines 3 + 5d = line 6) . . . . **6** _____

7 CURRENT QUARTER'S ADJUSTMENTS, for example, a fractions of cents adjustment. See the instructions.

7a Current quarter's fractions of cents . . . . _____

7b Current quarter's sick pay . . . . _____

7c Current quarter's adjustments for tips and group-term life insurance _____

7d TOTAL ADJUSTMENTS. Combine all amounts on lines 7a through 7c . . . . **7d** _____

8 Total taxes after adjustments. Combine lines 6 and 7d . . . . **8** _____

9 Advance earned income credit (EIC) payments made to employees . . . . **9** _____

10 Total taxes after adjustment for advance EIC (line 8 – line 9 = line 10) . . . . . **10** _____

11 Total deposits for this quarter, including overpayment applied from a prior quarter and overpayment applied from Form 941-X or Form 944-X . . . . _____

12a COBRA premium assistance payments (see instructions) . . . . . _____

12b Number of individuals provided COBRA premium assistance reported on line 12a . . . . _____

13 Add lines 11 and 12a . . . . **13** _____

14 Balance due. If line 10 is more than line 13, write the difference here . . . **14** _____
For information on how to pay, see the instructions.

15 Overpayment. If line 13 is more than line 10, write the difference here _____ ☐ Apply to next return.   Check one ☐ Send a refund.

▶ You **MUST** complete both pages of Form 941 and **SIGN** it.

Next ➡

For Privacy Act and Paperwork Reduction Act Notice, see the back of the Payment Voucher.   Cat. No. 17001Z   Form **941** (Rev. 1-201X)

PROBLEM 8A-3 OR PROBLEM 8B-3 (CONCLUDED)

950210

Name *(not your trade name)*	Employer identification number (EIN)

Part 2: Tell us about your deposit schedule and tax liability for this quarter.

If you are unsure about whether you are a monthly schedule depositor or a semiweekly schedule depositor, see *Pub. 15 (Circular E)*, section 11.

16 ☐☐ Write the state abbreviation for the state where you made your deposits OR write "MU" if you made your deposits in *multiple* states.

17 Check one: ☐ Line 10 is less than $2,500. Go to Part 3.

☐ You were a monthly schedule depositor for the entire quarter. Enter your tax liability for each month. Then go to Part 3.

Tax liability: Month 1 ☐

Month 2 ☐

Month 3 ☐

Total liability for quarter ☐ Total must equal line 10.

☐ You were a semiweekly schedule depositor for any part of this quarter. Complete *Schedule B (Form 941): Report of Tax Liability for Semiweekly Schedule Depositors,* and attach it to Form 941.

Part 3: Tell us about your business. If a question does NOT apply to your business, leave it blank.

18 If your business has closed or you stopped paying wages . . . . ☐ Check here, and

enter the final date you paid wages ☐ / / .

19 If you are a seasonal employer and you do not have to file a return for every quarter of the year . . ☐ Check here.

Part 4: May we speak with your third-party designee?

Do you want to allow an employee, a paid tax preparer, or another person to discuss this return with the IRS? See the instructions for details.

☐ Yes. Designee's name and phone number ☐ ( ) –

Select a 5-digit Personal Identification Number (PIN) to use when talking to the IRS. ☐☐☐☐☐

☐ No.

Part 5: Sign here. You MUST complete both pages of Form 941 and SIGN it.

Under penalties of perjury, I declare that I have examined this return, including accompanying schedules and statements, and to the best of my knowledge and belief, it is true, correct, and complete. Declaration of preparer (other than taxpayer) is based on all information of which preparer has any knowledge.

X Sign your name here ☐

Print your name here ☐

Print your title here ☐

Date / /

Best daytime phone ( ) –

Paid preparer's use only

Check if you are self-employed . . . . ☐

Preparer's name		Preparer's SSN/PTIN	
Preparer's signature		Date	/ /
Firm's name (or yours if self-employed)		EIN	
Address		Phone	( ) –
City	State	ZIP code	

PROBLEM 8A-4 OR PROBLEM 8B-4

PROBLEM 8A-4 OR PROBLEM 8B-4 (CONTINUED)

Form **941 for 201X:** Employer's QUARTERLY Federal Tax Return

(Rev. January 201X)   Department of the Treasury — Internal Revenue Service

950110

OMB No. 1545-0029

(EIN)
Employer identification number   ☐☐ – ☐☐☐☐☐☐☐

Name *(not your trade name)* _____

Trade name *(if any)* _____

Address _____
Number   Street   Suite or room number

_____
City   State   ZIP code

Report for this Quarter of 2009
(Check one.)

☐ **1:** January, February, March

☐ **2:** April, May, June

☐ **3:** July, August, September

☐ **4:** October, November, December

Read the separate instructions before you complete Form 941. Type or print within the boxes.

Part 1: Answer these questions for this quarter.

1 Number of employees who received wages, tips, or other compensation for the pay period including: *Mar. 12* (Quarter 1), *June 12* (Quarter 2), *Sept. 12* (Quarter 3), *Dec. 12* (Quarter 4) **1** ☐

2 Wages, tips, and other compensation . . . . **2** ☐

3 Income tax withheld from wages, tips, and other compensation . . . . **3** ☐

4 If no wages, tips, and other compensation are subject to social security or Medicare tax ☐ Check and go to line 6.

5 Taxable social security and Medicare wages and tips:

	Column 1		Column 2
5a Taxable social security wages	☐	× .124 =	☐
5b Taxable social security tips	☐	× .124 =	☐
5c Taxable Medicare wages & tips	☐	× .029 =	☐

5d Total social security and Medicare taxes (*Column 2,* lines 5a + 5b + 5c = line 5d) . **5d** ☐

6 Total taxes before adjustments (lines 3 + 5d = line 6) . . . . **6** ☐

7 **CURRENT QUARTER'S ADJUSTMENTS,** for example, a fractions of cents adjustment. See the instructions.

7a Current quarter's fractions of cents . . . . ☐

7b Current quarter's sick pay . . . . ☐

7c Current quarter's adjustments for tips and group-term life insurance ☐

7d **TOTAL ADJUSTMENTS.** Combine all amounts on lines 7a through 7c . . . . . . **7d** ☐

8 Total taxes after adjustments. Combine lines 6 and 7d . . . . **8** ☐

9 Advance earned income credit (EIC) payments made to employees . . . . . . **9** ☐

10 Total taxes after adjustment for advance EIC (line 8 – line 9 = line 10) . . . . **10** ☐

11 Total deposits for this quarter, including overpayment applied from a prior quarter and overpayment applied from Form 941-X or Form 944-X . . . . ☐

12a COBRA premium assistance payments (see instructions) . . . . . ☐

12b Number of individuals provided COBRA premium assistance reported on line 12a . . . . ☐

13 Add lines 11 and 12a . . . . **13** ☐

14 **Balance due.** If line 10 is more than line 13, write the difference here . . . . **14** ☐
For information on how to pay, see the instructions.

15 **Overpayment.** If line 13 is more than line 10, write the difference here ☐ Check one ☐ Apply to next return. ☐ Send a refund.

▶ You **MUST** complete both pages of Form 941 and **SIGN** it.   Next ➡

For Privacy Act and Paperwork Reduction Act Notice, see the back of the Payment Voucher.   Cat. No. 17001Z   Form **941** (Rev. 1-201X)

PROBLEM 8A-4 OR PROBLEM 8B-4 (CONCLUDED)

950210

Name *(not your trade name)*   Employer identification number (EIN)

Part 2: Tell us about your deposit schedule and tax liability for this quarter.

If you are unsure about whether you are a monthly schedule depositor or a semiweekly schedule depositor, see *Pub. 15 (Circular E)*, section 11.

16 ☐☐ Write the state abbreviation for the state where you made your deposits OR write "MU" if you made your deposits in *multiple* states.

17 Check one: ☐ Line 10 is less than $2,500. Go to Part 3.

☐ You were a monthly schedule depositor for the entire quarter. Enter your tax liability for each month. Then go to Part 3.

Tax liability: Month 1 [_____ .]

Month 2 [_____ .]

Month 3 [_____ .]

Total liability for quarter [_____ .] Total must equal line 10.

☐ You were a semiweekly schedule depositor for any part of this quarter. Complete *Schedule B (Form 941): Report of Tax Liability for Semiweekly Schedule Depositors*, and attach it to Form 941.

Part 3: Tell us about your business. If a question does NOT apply to your business, leave it blank.

18 If your business has closed or you stopped paying wages . . . . ☐ Check here, and

enter the final date you paid wages [/   /   ] .

19 If you are a seasonal employer and you do not have to file a return for every quarter of the year . . ☐ Check here.

Part 4: May we speak with your third-party designee?

Do you want to allow an employee, a paid tax preparer, or another person to discuss this return with the IRS? See the instructions for details.

☐ Yes. Designee's name and phone number [_____]   (___) ___ – ____

Select a 5-digit Personal Identification Number (PIN) to use when talking to the IRS. ☐☐☐☐☐

☐ No.

Part 5: Sign here. You MUST complete both pages of Form 941 and SIGN it.

Under penalties of perjury, I declare that I have examined this return, including accompanying schedules and statements, and to the best of my knowledge and belief, it is true, correct, and complete. Declaration of preparer (other than taxpayer) is based on all information of which preparer has any knowledge.

X **Sign your name here** [_____]   Print your name here [_____]

Print your title here [_____]

Date [/   /   ]   Best daytime phone (___) ___ – ____

Paid preparer's use only   Check if you are self-employed . . . . ☐

Preparer's name	Preparer's SSN/PTIN
Preparer's signature	Date / /
Firm's name (or yours if self-employed)	EIN
Address	Phone ( ) –
City State	ZIP code

PROBLEM 8A-5 OR PROBLEM 8B-5

Continuing Problem for Chapter 8- Sanchez Computer Center

Form **940 for 201X:** Employer's Annual Federal Unemployment (FUTA) Tax Return

850110

Department of the Treasury — Internal Revenue Service

OMB No. 1545-0028

(EIN)
Employer identification number ☐☐ – ☐☐☐☐☐☐☐

Name *(not your trade name)*

Trade name *(if any)*

Address

Number   Street   Suite or room number

City   State   ZIP code

Type of Return
(Check all that apply.)

☐ **a.** Amended

☐ **b.** Successor employer

☐ **c.** No payments to employees in 2010

☐ **d.** Final: Business closed or stopped paying wages

Read the separate instructions before you fill out this form. Please type or print within the boxes.

Part 1: Tell us about your return. If any line does NOT apply, leave it blank.

1   If you were required to pay your state unemployment tax in ...

    1a One state only, write the state abbreviation . . . . **1a** ☐☐
    - OR -
    1b More than one state (You are a multi-state employer) . . . . **1b** ☐ Check here. Fill out Schedule A.

2   If you paid wages in a state that is subject to **CREDIT REDUCTION** . . . . **2** ☐ Check here. Fill out Schedule A (Form 940), Part 2.

Part 2: Determine your FUTA tax before adjustments for 2010. If any line does NOT apply, leave it blank.

3   Total payments to all employees . . . . **3** ☐

4   Payments exempt from FUTA tax . . . . . . **4** ☐

    Check all that apply: **4a** ☐ Fringe benefits   **4c** ☐ Retirement/Pension   **4e** ☐ Other
    4b ☐ Group-term life insurance   **4d** ☐ Dependent care

5   Total of payments made to each employee in excess of $7,000 . . . . **5** ☐

6   Subtotal (line 4 + line 5 = line 6) . . . . **6** ☐

7   Total taxable FUTA wages (line 3 – line 6 = line 7) . . . . **7** ☐

8   FUTA tax before adjustments (line 7 × .008 = line 8) . . . . **8** ☐

Part 3: Determine your adjustments. If any line does NOT apply, leave it blank.

9   If ALL of the taxable FUTA wages you paid were excluded from state unemployment tax, multiply line 7 by .054 (line 7 × .054 = line 9). Then go to line 12 . . . . **9** ☐

10   If SOME of the taxable FUTA wages you paid were excluded from state unemployment tax, OR you paid ANY state unemployment tax late (after the due date for filing Form 940), fill out the worksheet in the instructions. Enter the amount from line 7 of the worksheet . . . . . **10** ☐

11   If credit reduction applies, enter the amount from line 3 of Schedule A (Form 940) . . . . **11** ☐

Part 4: Determine your FUTA tax and balance due or overpayment for 2010. If any line does NOT apply, leave it blank.

12   Total FUTA tax after adjustments (lines 8 + 9 + 10 + 11 = line 12) . . . . **12** ☐

13   FUTA tax deposited for the year, including any overpayment applied from a prior year . **13** ☐

14   Balance due (If line 12 is more than line 13, enter the difference on line 14.)
    • If line 14 is more than $500, you must deposit your tax.
    • If line 14 is $500 or less, you may pay with this return. For more information on how to pay, see the separate instructions   **14** ☐

15   Overpayment (If line 13 is more than line 12, enter the difference on line 15 and check a box below.) . . . . **15** ☐

Check one: ☐ Apply to next return.
☐ Send a refund.

▶ You **MUST** fill out both pages of this form and **SIGN** it.

Next ▶

For Privacy Act and Paperwork Reduction Act Notice, see the back of Form 940-V, Payment Voucher.   Cat. No. 11234O   Form **940** (201X)

CONTINUING PROBLEM—ON THE JOB FOR CHAPTER 8
SANCHEZ COMPUTER CENTER

SANCHEZ COMPUTER CENTER
GENERAL JOURNAL

PAGE 5

Date	Account Titles and Description	PR	Dr.	Cr.

CONTINUING PROBLEM FOR CHAPTER 8
SANCHEZ COMPUTER CENTER

SANCHEZ COMPUTER CENTER
GENERAL JOURNAL

PAGE 6

Date	Account Titles and Description	PR	Dr.	Cr.

CONTINUING PROBLEM FOR CHAPTER 8
SANCHEZ COMPUTER CENTER

Mini Practice Set

Form 941 for 201X: Employer's QUARTERLY Federal Tax Return

(Rev. January 201X)

Department of the Treasury — Internal Revenue Service

950110

OMB No. 1545-0029

(EIN)
Employer identification number ☐☐ — ☐☐☐☐☐☐☐

Name *(not your trade name)*

Trade name *(if any)*

Address

Number   Street   Suite or room number

City   State   ZIP code

Report for this Quarter of 2009
(Check one.)

☐ **1:** January, February, March

☐ **2:** April, May, June

☐ **3:** July, August, September

☐ **4:** October, November, December

Read the separate instructions before you complete Form 941. Type or print within the boxes.

Part 1: Answer these questions for this quarter.

1   Number of employees who received wages, tips, or other compensation for the pay period including: *Mar. 12* (Quarter 1), *June 12* (Quarter 2), *Sept. 12* (Quarter 3), *Dec. 12* (Quarter 4)   **1** ☐

2   Wages, tips, and other compensation . . . .   **2** ☐

3   Income tax withheld from wages, tips, and other compensation . . . .   **3** ☐

4   If no wages, tips, and other compensation are subject to social security or Medicare tax   ☐ Check and go to line 6.

5   Taxable social security and Medicare wages and tips:

	Column 1		Column 2
5a Taxable social security wages	☐	× .124 =	☐
5b Taxable social security tips	☐	× .124 =	☐
5c Taxable Medicare wages & tips	☐	× .029 =	☐

5d   Total social security and Medicare taxes (*Column 2*, lines 5a + 5b + 5c = line 5d) .   **5d** ☐

6   Total taxes before adjustments (lines 3 + 5d = line 6) . . . .   **6** ☐

7   CURRENT QUARTER'S ADJUSTMENTS, for example, a fractions of cents adjustment. See the instructions.

7a   Current quarter's fractions of cents . . . . . .   ☐

7b   Current quarter's sick pay . . . .   ☐

7c   Current quarter's adjustments for tips and group-term life insurance   ☐

7d   TOTAL ADJUSTMENTS. Combine all amounts on lines 7a through 7c . . . . .   **7d** ☐

8   Total taxes after adjustments. Combine lines 6 and 7d . . . . .   **8** ☐

9   Advance earned income credit (EIC) payments made to employees . . . . .   **9** ☐

10   Total taxes after adjustment for advance EIC (line 8 – line 9 = line 10) . . . . .   **10** ☐

11   Total deposits for this quarter, including overpayment applied from a prior quarter and overpayment applied from Form 941-X or Form 944-X . . . .   **11** ☐

12a   COBRA premium assistance payments (see instructions) . . . . .   **12a** ☐

12b   Number of individuals provided COBRA premium assistance reported on line 12a .   ☐

13   Add lines 11 and 12a . . . .   **13** ☐

14   Balance due. If line 10 is more than line 13, write the difference here . . . .   **14** ☐
For information on how to pay, see the instructions.

15   Overpayment. If line 13 is more than line 10, write the difference here   ☐   Check one ☐ Apply to next return. ☐ Send a refund.

▶ You **MUST** complete both pages of Form 941 and **SIGN** it.   Next ➡

For Privacy Act and Paperwork Reduction Act Notice, see the back of the Payment Voucher.   Cat. No. 17001Z   Form **941** (Rev. 1-201X)

CONTINUING PROBLEM FOR CHAPTER 8
SANCHEZ COMPUTER CENTER
Mini Practice Set (Continued)

9502010

Name *(not your trade name)*	Employer identification number (EIN)

Part 2: Tell us about your deposit schedule and tax liability for this quarter.

If you are unsure about whether you are a monthly schedule depositor or a semiweekly schedule depositor, see *Pub. 15 (Circular E)*, section 11.

16 ☐☐ Write the state abbreviation for the state where you made your deposits OR write "MU" if you made your deposits in *multiple* states.

17 Check one: ☐ Line 10 is less than $2,500. Go to Part 3.

☐ You were a monthly schedule depositor for the entire quarter. Enter your tax liability for each month. Then go to Part 3.

Tax liability: Month 1 [.]

Month 2 [.]

Month 3 [.]

Total liability for quarter [.] Total must equal line 10.

☐ You were a semiweekly schedule depositor for any part of this quarter. Complete *Schedule B (Form 941): Report of Tax Liability for Semiweekly Schedule Depositors*, and attach it to Form 941.

Part 3: Tell us about your business. If a question does NOT apply to your business, leave it blank.

18 If your business has closed or you stopped paying wages . . . . ☐ Check here, and

enter the final date you paid wages [/ /] .

19 If you are a seasonal employer and you do not have to file a return for every quarter of the year . . ☐ Check here.

Part 4: May we speak with your third-party designee?

Do you want to allow an employee, a paid tax preparer, or another person to discuss this return with the IRS? See the instructions for details.

☐ Yes. Designee's name and phone number [ ] ( ) –

Select a 5-digit Personal Identification Number (PIN) to use when talking to the IRS. ☐ ☐ ☐ ☐ ☐

☐ No.

Part 5: Sign here. You MUST complete both pages of Form 941 and SIGN it.

Under penalties of perjury, I declare that I have examined this return, including accompanying schedules and statements, and to the best of my knowledge and belief, it is true, correct, and complete. Declaration of preparer (other than taxpayer) is based on all information of which preparer has any knowledge.

X Sign your name here [ ]

Print your name here [ ]

Print your title here [ ]

Date [/ /]

Best daytime phone ( ) –

Paid preparer's use only	Check if you are self-employed . . . . ☐
Preparer's name	Preparer's SSN/PTIN
Preparer's signature	Date / /
Firm's name (or yours if self-employed)	EIN
Address	Phone ( ) –
City	State	ZIP code

Continuing Problem for Chapter 8- Sanchez Computer Center

Form **940 for 201X:** **Employer's Annual Federal Unemployment (FUTA) Tax Return**   850110

Department of the Treasury — Internal Revenue Service

OMB No. 1545-0028

(EIN)
Employer identification number ☐☐ – ☐☐☐☐☐☐☐

Name *(not your trade name)* _____

Trade name *(if any)* _____

Address _____
Number   Street   Suite or room number
_____
City   State   ZIP code

Type of Return
(Check all that apply.)

☐ **a.** Amended

☐ **b.** Successor employer

☐ **c.** No payments to employees in 2010

☐ **d.** Final: Business closed or stopped paying wages

Read the separate instructions before you fill out this form. Please type or print within the boxes.

Part 1: Tell us about your return. If any line does NOT apply, leave it blank.

1   If you were required to pay your state unemployment tax in ...

    1a **One state only,** write the state abbreviation . . . . **1a** ☐☐

    - OR -

    1b **More than one state** (You are a multi-state employer) . . . . **1b** ☐ Check here. Fill out Schedule A.

2   If you paid wages in a state that is subject to **CREDIT REDUCTION** . . . . **2** ☐ Check here. Fill out Schedule A (Form 940), Part 2.

Part 2: Determine your FUTA tax before adjustments for 2010. If any line does NOT apply, leave it blank.

3   Total payments to all employees . . . . **3** ☐

4   Payments exempt from FUTA tax . . . . **4** ☐

    Check all that apply: **4a** ☐ Fringe benefits   **4c** ☐ Retirement/Pension   **4e** ☐ Other
    4b ☐ Group-term life insurance   **4d** ☐ Dependent care

5   Total of payments made to each employee in excess of $7,000 . . . . **5** ☐

6   **Subtotal** (line 4 + line 5 = line 6) . . . . **6** ☐

7   Total taxable FUTA wages (line 3 – line 6 = line 7) . . . . **7** ☐

8   FUTA tax before adjustments (line 7 × .008 = line 8) . . . . **8** ☐

Part 3: Determine your adjustments. If any line does NOT apply, leave it blank.

9   If ALL of the taxable FUTA wages you paid were excluded from state unemployment tax, multiply line 7 by .054 (line 7 × .054 = line 9). Then go to line 12 . . . **9** ☐

10   If SOME of the taxable FUTA wages you paid were excluded from state unemployment tax, OR you paid ANY state unemployment tax late (after the due date for filing Form 940), fill out the worksheet in the instructions. Enter the amount from line 7 of the worksheet . . . . . **10** ☐

11   If credit reduction applies, enter the amount from line 3 of Schedule A (Form 940) . . . . **11** ☐

Part 4: Determine your FUTA tax and balance due or overpayment for 2010. If any line does NOT apply, leave it blank.

12   Total FUTA tax after adjustments (lines 8 + 9 + 10 + 11 = line 12) . . . . **12** ☐

13   FUTA tax deposited for the year, including any overpayment applied from a prior year . **13** ☐

14   Balance due (If line 12 is more than line 13, enter the difference on line 14.)
    • If line 14 is more than $500, you must deposit your tax.
    • If line 14 is $500 or less, you may pay with this return. For more information on how to pay, see the separate instructions . . . . **14** ☐

15   Overpayment (If line 13 is more than line 12, enter the difference on line 15 and check a box below.) . . . . **15** ☐

Check one: ☐ Apply to next return.
    ☐ Send a refund.

▶ You **MUST** fill out both pages of this form and **SIGN** it.

Next ▶

For Privacy Act and Paperwork Reduction Act Notice, see the back of Form 940-V, Payment Voucher.   Cat. No. 11234O   Form **940** (201X)

Continuing Problem for Chapter 8- Sanchez Computer Center (Continued)

850210

Name *(not your trade name)*	Employer identification number (EIN)

Part 5: Report your FUTA tax liability by quarter only if line 12 is more than $500. If not, go to Part 6.

16 Report the amount of your FUTA tax liability for each quarter; do NOT enter the amount you deposited. If you had no liability for a quarter, leave the line blank.

    16a 1st quarter (January 1 – March 31) . . . . 16a [.   ]

    16b 2nd quarter (April 1 – June 30) . . . . 16b [.   ]

    16c 3rd quarter (July 1 – September 30) . . . . 16c [.   ]

    16d 4th quarter (October 1 – December 31) . . . . . . 16d [.   ]

17 Total tax liability for the year (lines 16a + 16b + 16c + 16d = line 17) 17 [.   ] **Total must equal line 12.**

Part 6: May we speak with your third-party designee?

Do you want to allow an employee, a paid tax preparer, or another person to discuss this return with the IRS? See the instructions for details.

☐ **Yes.** Designee's name and phone number [   ] [   ]

         Select a 5-digit Personal Identification Number (PIN) to use when talking to IRS [ ][ ][ ][ ][ ]

☐ **No.**

Part 7: Sign here. You MUST fill out both pages of this form and SIGN it.

Under penalties of perjury, I declare that I have examined this return, including accompanying schedules and statements, and to the best of my knowledge and belief, it is true, correct, and complete, and that no part of any payment made to a state unemployment fund claimed as a credit was, or is to be, deducted from the payments made to employees. Declaration of preparer (other than taxpayer) is based on all information of which preparer has any knowledge.

✗ **Sign your name here** [   ]

Print your name here [   ]

Print your title here [   ]

Date [/   /   ]

Best daytime phone [   ]

Paid preparer use only   Check if you are self-employed . . . ☐

Preparer's name	[ ]	PTIN	[ ]
Preparer's signature	[ ]	Date	[/ /]
Firm's name (or yours if self-employed)	[ ]	EIN	[ ]
Address	[ ]	Phone	[ ]
City	[ ]	State	[ ]	ZIP code	[ ]

Mini Practice Set

Form **941 for 201X:** **Employer's QUARTERLY Federal Tax Return**

(Rev. January 201X)

Department of the Treasury — Internal Revenue Service

950110

OMB No. 1545-0029

(EIN)
Employer identification number ☐☐ — ☐☐☐☐☐☐☐

Name (not your trade name) _____

Trade name (if any) _____

Address _____
Number   Street   Suite or room number

_____
City   State   ZIP code

Report for this Quarter of 2009
(Check one.)

☐ **1:** January, February, March

☐ **2:** April, May, June

☐ **3:** July, August, September

☐ **4:** October, November, December

Read the separate instructions before you complete Form 941. Type or print within the boxes.

Part 1: Answer these questions for this quarter.

1 Number of employees who received wages, tips, or other compensation for the pay period including: *Mar. 12 (Quarter 1)*, *June 12 (Quarter 2)*, *Sept. 12 (Quarter 3)*, *Dec. 12 (Quarter 4)* **1** _____

2 Wages, tips, and other compensation . . . . **2** _____ . __

3 Income tax withheld from wages, tips, and other compensation . . . . **3** _____ . __

4 If no wages, tips, and other compensation are subject to social security or Medicare tax   ☐ Check and go to line 6.

5 Taxable social security and Medicare wages and tips:

	Column 1		Column 2
5a Taxable social security wages	_____ . __	× .124 =	_____ . __
5b Taxable social security tips	_____ . __	× .124 =	_____ . __
5c Taxable Medicare wages & tips	_____ . __	× .029 =	_____ . __

5d Total social security and Medicare taxes (*Column 2*, lines 5a + 5b + 5c = line 5d) . . **5d** _____ . __

6 Total taxes before adjustments (lines 3 + 5d = line 6) . . . . **6** _____ . __

7 **CURRENT QUARTER'S ADJUSTMENTS,** for example, a fractions of cents adjustment. See the instructions.

7a Current quarter's fractions of cents . . . . _____ . __

7b Current quarter's sick pay . . . . _____ . __

7c Current quarter's adjustments for tips and group-term life insurance _____ . __

7d **TOTAL ADJUSTMENTS.** Combine all amounts on lines 7a through 7c . . . . . . **7d** _____ . __

8 Total taxes after adjustments. Combine lines 6 and 7d . . . . **8** _____ . __

9 Advance earned income credit (EIC) payments made to employees . . . . **9** _____ . __

10 Total taxes after adjustment for advance EIC (line 8 – line 9 = line 10) . . . . . . **10** _____ . __

11 Total deposits for this quarter, including overpayment applied from a prior quarter and overpayment applied from Form 941-X or Form 944-X . . . . _____ . __

12a COBRA premium assistance payments (see instructions) . . . . . _____ . __

12b Number of individuals provided COBRA premium assistance reported on line 12a . . . . _____

13 Add lines 11 and 12a . . . . **13** _____ . __

14 Balance due. If line 10 is more than line 13, write the difference here . . . . **14** _____ . __
For information on how to pay, see the instructions.

15 Overpayment. If line 13 is more than line 10, write the difference here _____ . __   Check one ☐ Apply to next return.   ☐ Send a refund.

▶ You **MUST** complete both pages of Form 941 and **SIGN** it.

Next ➡

For Privacy Act and Paperwork Reduction Act Notice, see the back of the Payment Voucher.   Cat. No. 17001Z   Form **941** (Rev. 1-201X)

Mini Practice Set (Continued)

9502010

Name *(not your trade name)*	Employer identification number (EIN)

Part 2: Tell us about your deposit schedule and tax liability for this quarter.

If you are unsure about whether you are a monthly schedule depositor or a semiweekly schedule depositor, see *Pub. 15 (Circular E),* section 11.

16 ☐☐ Write the state abbreviation for the state where you made your deposits OR write "MU" if you made your deposits in *multiple* states.

17 Check one: ☐ Line 10 is less than $2,500. Go to Part 3.

☐ You were a monthly schedule depositor for the entire quarter. Enter your tax liability for each month. Then go to Part 3.

Tax liability: Month 1 ▯ .

Month 2 ▯ .

Month 3 ▯ .

Total liability for quarter ▯ . Total must equal line 10.

☐ You were a semiweekly schedule depositor for any part of this quarter. Complete *Schedule B (Form 941): Report of Tax Liability for Semiweekly Schedule Depositors,* and attach it to Form 941.

Part 3: Tell us about your business. If a question does NOT apply to your business, leave it blank.

18 If your business has closed or you stopped paying wages . . . . ☐ Check here, and

enter the final date you paid wages ▯ / / .

19 If you are a seasonal employer and you do not have to file a return for every quarter of the year . . ☐ Check here.

Part 4: May we speak with your third-party designee?

Do you want to allow an employee, a paid tax preparer, or another person to discuss this return with the IRS? See the instructions for details.

☐ Yes. Designee's name and phone number ▯ ( ) –

Select a 5-digit Personal Identification Number (PIN) to use when talking to the IRS. ☐☐☐☐☐

☐ No.

Part 5: Sign here. You MUST complete both pages of Form 941 and SIGN it.

Under penalties of perjury, I declare that I have examined this return, including accompanying schedules and statements, and to the best of my knowledge and belief, it is true, correct, and complete. Declaration of preparer (other than taxpayer) is based on all information of which preparer has any knowledge.

X **Sign your name here** ▯

Print your name here ▯

Print your title here ▯

Date / /

Best daytime phone ( ) –

Paid preparer's use only

Check if you are self-employed . . . . . ☐

Preparer's name		Preparer's SSN/PTIN	
Preparer's signature		Date	/ /
Firm's name (or yours if self-employed)		EIN	
Address		Phone	( ) –
City	State	ZIP code	

Form **941** (Rev. 1-201X)

9

SALES AND CASH RECEIPTS

INSTANT REPLAY: SELF-REVIEW QUIZ 9-1

1. _____ 2. _____ 3. _____ 4. _____ 5. _____

INSTANT REPLAY:
SELF-REVIEW QUIZ 9-2

BERNIE COMPANY
GENERAL JOURNAL

PAGE 1

Date	Account Titles and Description	PR	Dr.	Cr.

ACCOUNTS RECEIVABLE SUBSIDIARY LEDGER

NAME LEE CORP.

ADDRESS 118 MORRIS RD., BOSTON, MA 01935

Date	Explanation	Post Ref.	Debit	Credit	Dr. Balance

NAME RING COMPANY

ADDRESS 31 NORRIS ROAD, BOSTON, MA 01935

Date	Explanation	Post Ref.	Debit	Credit	Dr. Balance

PARTIAL GENERAL LEDGER

ACCOUNT RECEIVABLE   ACCOUNT NO. 141

Date		Explanation	Post Ref.	Debit	Credit	Balance	
						Debit	Credit

SALES   ACCOUNT NO. 310

Date		Explanation	Post Ref.	Debit	Credit	Balance	
						Debit	Credit

SALES RETURNS AND ALLOWANCES   ACCOUNT NO. 312

Date		Explanation	Post Ref.	Debit	Credit	Balance	
						Debit	Credit

INSTANT REPLAY: SELF-REVIEW QUIZ 9-3

MABEL CORPORATION
GENERAL JOURNAL

PAGE 3

Date	Account Titles and Description	PR	Dr.	Cr.

PARTIAL GENERAL LEDGER

CASH — ACCOUNT NO. 110

Date 201X		Explanation	Post Ref.	Debit	Credit	Balance Debit	Balance Credit
May	1	Balance	✓			600 00	

ACCOUNTS RECEIVABLE — ACCOUNT NO. 120

Date 201X		Explanation	Post Ref.	Debit	Credit	Balance Debit	Balance Credit
May	1	Balance	✓			700 00	

STORE EQUIPMENT — ACCOUNT NO. 130

Date 201X		Explanation	Post Ref.	Debit	Credit	Balance Debit	Balance Credit
May	1	Balance	✓			600 00	

SALES — ACCOUNT NO. 410

Date 201X		Explanation	Post Ref.	Debit	Credit	Balance Debit	Balance Credit
May	1	Balance	✓				700 00

SALES DISCOUNT **ACCOUNT NO. 420**

Date 201X		Explanation	Post Ref.	Debit	Credit	Balance Debit	Balance Credit

NAME **JANIS FROSS**

ADDRESS **81 FOSTER RD., BEVERLY, MA 09125**

Date 201X		Explanation	Post Ref.	Debit	Credit	Dr. Balance
May	1	Balance	✔			2 0 0 00

ACCOUNTS RECEIVABLE SUBSIDIARY LEDGER

NAME **IRENE WELCH**

ADDRESS **10 RONG RD., BEVERLY, MA 01215**

Date 201X		Explanation	Post Ref.	Debit	Credit	Dr. Balance
May	1	Balance	✔			5 0 0 00

CHAPTER 9
CONCEPT CHECK

1.

2.

3.

A. _____   _____   _____

B. _____   _____   _____

C. _____   _____   _____

4.

5.

Date		Account Titles and Description	PR	Dr.			Cr.		

6.

PINE CO.
SCHEDULE OF ACCOUNTS RECEIVABLE
MAY 31, 201X

Name _____ Class _____ Date _____

FORMS FOR EXERCISES A OR B

9A-1 OR 9B-1.

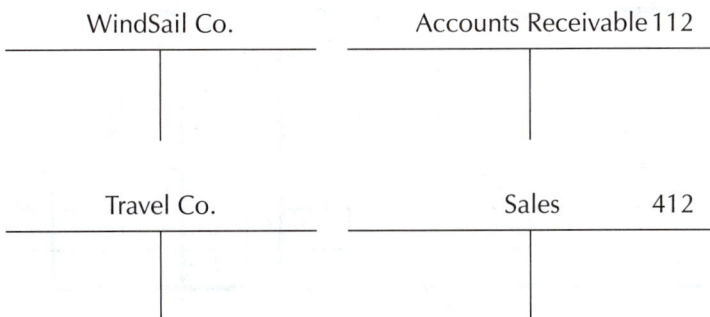

WindSail Co.   Accounts Receivable 112

Travel Co.   Sales   412

9A-2 OR 9B-2.

GENERAL JOURNAL

Date	Account Titles and Description	PR	Dr.	Cr.

Glenda Co.   Sales   411

Pearl Co.   Accounts Receivable 112   Sales Returns & Allowances   412

EXERCISES (CONTINUED)

9A-3 OR 9B-3.

9A-4 OR 9B-4.

ANDREW CO.
GENERAL JOURNAL

PAGE 1

Date	Account Titles and Description	PR	Dr.	Cr.

EXERCISES (CONCLUDED)

GENERAL JOURNAL (CONTINUED)   PAGE 1

Date	Account Titles and Description	PR	Dr.	Cr.

ACCOUNTS RECEIVABLE SUBSIDIARY LEDGER

Greenfield Co.
_____|_____

Robert Co.
_____|_____

PARTIAL GENERAL LEDGER

Cash   111
_____|_____

Accounts Receivable   113
_____|_____

Andrew Albright, Capital   311
_____|_____

Sales   411
_____|_____

Sales Returns &
Allowances   412
_____|_____

Sales Discount   413
_____|_____

ANDREW CO.
SCHEDULE OF ACCOUNTS RECEIVABLE
October 31, 201X

_____
_____
_____
_____

9A-5 OR 9B-5. _____

_____
_____
_____
_____

END OF CHAPTER PROBLEMS

PROBLEM 9A-1 OR PROBLEM 9B-1

CIABATTA AND WHATNOT
GENERAL JOURNAL

PAGE 1

Date	Account Titles and Description	PR	Dr.	Cr.

PROBLEM 9A-1 OR PROBLEM 9B-1 (CONTINUED)

ACCOUNTS RECEIVABLE SUBSIDIARY LEDGER

NAME   CANADIAN CO.

ADDRESS   942 MOSE ST., REVERE, MA 01938

Date		Explanation	Post Ref.	Debit	Credit	Dr. Balance

NAME   CINDI CO.

ADDRESS   8 JOSS AVE., LYNN, MA 01947

Date		Explanation	Post Ref.	Debit	Credit	Dr. Balance

NAME   COMMON LAW CO.

ADDRESS   10 LOST RD., TOPSFIELD, MA 01998

Date		Explanation	Post Ref.	Debit	Credit	Dr. Balance

PROBLEM 9A-1 OR PROBLEM 9B-1 (CONTINUED)

CIABATTA AND WHATNOT
GENERAL LEDGER

ACCOUNTS RECEIVABLE　　　　　　　**ACCOUNT NO. 112**

Date	Explanation	Post Ref.	Debit	Credit	Balance Debit	Balance Credit

BREAD SALES　　　　　　　**ACCOUNT NO. 410**

Date	Explanation	Post Ref.	Debit	Credit	Balance Debit	Balance Credit

GROCERY SALES　　　　　　　**ACCOUNT NO. 411**

Date	Explanation	Post Ref.	Debit	Credit	Balance Debit	Balance Credit

SALES RETURNS AND ALLOWANCES　　　　　**ACCOUNT NO. 412**

Date	Explanation	Post Ref.	Debit	Credit	Balance Debit	Balance Credit

PROBLEM 9A-2 OR PROBLEM 9B-2 (CONTINUED)

JACK'S AUTO SUPPLY
PARTIAL GENERAL LEDGER

ACCOUNTS RECEIVABLE   **ACCOUNT NO. 110**

Date	Explanation	Post Ref.	Debit	Credit	Balance Debit	Balance Credit

SALES TAX PAYABLE   **ACCOUNT NO. 210**

Date	Explanation	Post Ref.	Debit	Credit	Balance Debit	Balance Credit

AUTO PARTS SALES   **ACCOUNT NO. 410**

Date	Explanation	Post Ref.	Debit	Credit	Balance Debit	Balance Credit

SALES RETURNS AND ALLOWANCES   **ACCOUNT NO. 420**

Date	Explanation	Post Ref.	Debit	Credit	Balance Debit	Balance Credit

PROBLEM 9A-2 OR PROBLEM 9B-2 (CONCLUDED)

(3)

JACK'S AUTO SUPPLY
SCHEDULE OF ACCOUNTS RECEIVABLE
NOVEMBER 30, 201X

PROBLEM 9A-4 OR PROBLEM 9B-4 (CONTINUED)

GARY'S COSMETIC MARKET
GENERAL JOURNAL

PAGE 2

Date	Account Titles and Description	PR	Dr.	Cr.

PROBLEM 9A-4 OR PROBLEM 9B-4 (CONTINUED)

ACCOUNTS RECEIVABLE SUBSIDIARY LEDGER

NAME   PETER MELNYK CO.

ADDRESS   2 RYAN RD., BUFFALO, NY 09113

Date		Explanation	Post Ref.	Debit	Credit	Debit Balance

PROBLEM 9A-4 OR PROBLEM 9B-4 (CONTINUED)

ACCOUNTS RECEIVABLE SUBSIDIARY LEDGER

NAME   MARIKA SANFORD CO.

ADDRESS   4 REEL RD., LANCASTER, PA 04332

Date	Explanation	Post Ref.	Debit	Credit	Debit Balance

NAME   MARY RUVOLO CO.

ADDRESS   14 BONE DR., ENGLEWOOD CLIFFS, NJ 07632

Date	Explanation	Post Ref.	Debit	Credit	Debit Balance

NAME   FIONE TAY CO.

ADDRESS   2 MARION RD., BOSTON, MA 01981

Date	Explanation	Post Ref.	Debit	Credit	Debit Balance

PROBLEM 9A-4 OR PROBLEM 9B-4 (CONTINUED)

GARY'S COSMETIC MARKET
GENERAL LEDGER

CASH   ACCOUNT NO. **10**

Date	Explanation	Post Ref.	Debit	Credit	Balance Debit	Balance Credit

ACCOUNTS RECEIVABLE   ACCOUNT NO. **12**

Date	Explanation	Post Ref.	Debit	Credit	Balance Debit	Balance Credit

PROBLEM 9A-4 OR PROBLEM 9B-4 (CONTINUED)

SALES TAX PAYABLE　　　　　　　　　　　　　**ACCOUNT NO. 20**

Date	Explanation	Post Ref.	Debit	Credit	Balance Debit	Balance Credit

GARY WILCOX, CAPITAL　　　　　　　　　　　**ACCOUNT NO. 30**

Date	Explanation	Post Ref.	Debit	Credit	Balance Debit	Balance Credit

LIPSTICK SALES　　　　　　　　　　　　　　**ACCOUNT NO. 40**

Date	Explanation	Post Ref.	Debit	Credit	Balance Debit	Balance Credit

PROBLEM 9A-4 OR PROBLEM 9B-4 (CONCLUDED)

SALES RETURNS & ALLOWANCES, LIPSTICK   ACCOUNT NO. 42

Date	Explanation	Post Ref.	Debit	Credit	Balance Debit	Balance Credit

EYE SHADOW SALES   ACCOUNT NO. 44

Date	Explanation	Post Ref.	Debit	Credit	Balance Debit	Balance Credit

(3)

GARY'S COSMETIC MARKET
SCHEDULE OF ACCOUNTS RECEIVABLE
OCTOBER 31, 201X

Part II

	Dr.	Cr.
1.	10	40
2.	44	20
3.	20	40
4.	10	20
	42	

Part III

1.	false	**11.**	true
2.	true	**12.**	true
3.	false	**13.**	false
4.	false	**14.**	false
5.	false	**15.**	false
6.	false	**16.**	false
7.	true	**17.**	true
8.	false	**18.**	true
9.	false	**19.**	false
10.	true		

CONTINUING PROBLEM—ON THE JOB FOR CHAPTER 9

SANCHEZ COMPUTER CENTER
GENERAL JOURNAL

PAGE 7

Date	Account Titles and Description	PR	Dr.	Cr.

SANCHEZ COMPUTER CENTER
SCHEDULE OF ACCOUNTS RECEIVABLE
1/31/1X

_____
_____
_____
_____

CASH   **ACCOUNT NO. 1000**

Date		Explanation	Post Ref.	Debit	Credit	Balance	
						Debit	Credit
1/1	1X	Balance Forward	✔			3 3 3 6 64	

SANCHEZ COMPUTER CENTER
PARTIAL GENERAL LEDGER

ACCOUNTS RECEIVABLE   **ACCOUNT NO. 1020**

Date		Explanation	Post Ref.	Debit	Credit	Balance Debit	Balance Credit
1/1	1X	Balance Forward	✓			13 600 00	

SALES   **ACCOUNT NO. 4010**

Date		Explanation	Post Ref.	Debit	Credit	Balance Debit	Balance Credit

SALES RETURNS & ALLOWANCES   **ACCOUNT NO. 4020**

Date		Explanation	Post Ref.	Debit	Credit	Balance Debit	Balance Credit

SALES DISCOUNTS   ACCOUNT NO. <u>4030</u>

Date		Explanation	Post Ref.	Debit	Credit	Balance	
						Debit	Credit

ACCOUNTS RECEIVABLE
SUBSIDIARY LEDGER

NAME   TAYLOR GOLF   **ACCOUNT NO. 100**

ADDRESS   1010 MOCKINGBIRD LANE, CARLSBAD, CA 92008

Date		Explanation	Post Ref.	Debit	Credit	Dr. Balance
1/1	1X	Balance forward	✔			2 9 0 0 00

NAME   VITA NEEDLE   **ACCOUNT NO. 101**

ADDRESS   144 CANTATA, IRVINE, CA 92606

Date		Explanation	Post Ref.	Debit	Credit	Dr. Balance
1/1	1X	Balance	✔			6 8 0 0 00

ACCOUNTS RECEIVABLE SUBSIDIARY LEDGER

NAME   ACCU PAC   ACCOUNT NO. **103**

ADDRESS   1717 JORDAN ST., SAN CLEMENTE, CA 91607

Date		Explanation	Post Ref.	Debit	Credit	Dr. Balance
1/1	1X	Balance	✔			3 9 0 0 00

NAME   ANTHONY J. PITALE   ACCOUNT NO. **104**

ADDRESS   600 NEWPORT BEACH, NEWPORT, CA 91600

Date	Explanation	Post Ref.	Debit	Credit	Dr. Balance

10

PURCHASES AND CASH PAYMENTS

INSTANT REPLAY: SELF-REVIEW QUIZ 10-1

1. _____ 2. _____ 3. _____ 4. _____ 5. _____

INSTANT REPLAY: SELF-REVIEW QUIZ 10-2

MUNROE CO.
GENERAL JOURNAL

PAGE 1

Date	Account Titles and Description	PR	Dr.	Cr.

ACCOUNTS PAYABLE SUBSIDIARY LEDGER

NAME   JOHN BUTLER COMPANY

ADDRESS   18 REED RD., HOMEWOOD, IL 60430

Date		Explanation	Post Ref.	Debit	Credit	Cr. Balance

NAME   FLYNN COMPANY

ADDRESS   15 FOSS AVE., ENGLEWOOD CLIFFS, NJ 07632

Date		Explanation	Post Ref.	Debit	Credit	Cr. Balance

PARTIAL GENERAL LEDGER

EQUIPMENT   **ACCOUNT NO. 121**

Date		Explanation	Post Ref.	Debit	Credit	Balance Debit	Balance Credit

ACCOUNTS PAYABLE   ACCOUNT NO. 212

Date		Explanation	Post Ref.	Debit	Credit	Balance	
						Debit	Credit

PURCHASES   ACCOUNT NO. 512

Date		Explanation	Post Ref.	Debit	Credit	Balance	
						Debit	Credit

PURCHASES RETURNS AND ALLOWANCES   ACCOUNT NO. 513

Date		Explanation	Post Ref.	Debit	Credit	Balance	
						Debit	Credit

INSTANT REPLAY: SELF-REVIEW QUIZ 10-3

MELISSA COMPANY
GENERAL JOURNAL

Date	Account Titles and Description	PR	Dr.	Cr.

ACCOUNTS PAYABLE SUBSIDARY LEDGER

NAME   **BOB FINKELSTEIN**

ADDRESS   **112 FLYING HIGHWAY, TRENTON, NJ 00861**

Date 201X		Explanation	Post Ref.	Debit	Credit	Cr. Balance
June	1	Balance	✔			3 0 0 00

NAME   **AL JEEP**

ADDRESS   **118 WANG RD., SAUGUS, MA 01432**

Date 201X		Explanation	Post Ref.	Debit	Credit	Cr. Balance
June	1	Balance	✔			2 0 0 00

PARTIAL GENERAL LEDGER

CASH   **ACCOUNT NO. 110**

Date 201X		Explanation	Post Ref.	Debit	Credit	Balance Debit	Balance Credit
June	1	Balance	✔			7 0 0 00	

ACCOUNTS PAYABLE   **ACCOUNT NO. 210**

Date 201X		Explanation	Post Ref.	Debit	Credit	Balance Debit	Balance Credit
June	1	Balance	✔				5 0 0 00

PURCHASES DISCOUNT   **ACCOUNT NO. 511**

Date		Explanation	Post Ref.	Debit	Credit	Balance Debit	Balance Credit

ADVERTISING EXPENSE   **ACCOUNT NO. 610**

Date		Explanation	Post Ref.	Debit	Credit	Balance Debit	Balance Credit

INSTANT REPLAY: SELF-REVIEW QUIZ 10-4

PETE'S CLOCK SHOP
GENERAL JOURNAL

PAGE 2

Date	Account Titles and Description	PR	Dr.	Cr.

PETE'S CLOCK SHOP
GENERAL JOURNAL

Date		Account Titles and Description	PR	Dr.	Cr.

CHAPTER 10
CONCEPT CHECK

1. A. _____   D. _____

   B. _____   E. _____

   C. _____   F. _____

2.

3. _____

   _____

   _____

   _____

   _____

   _____

   _____

   _____

   _____

   _____

4. A. _____

   B. _____

   C. _____

5.

6.

MATTHEW.COM
SCHEDULE OF ACCOUNTS PAYABLE
MAY 31, 201X

7.

_____

_____

8, 9, 10

Date		Account Titles and Description	PR		Dr.		Cr.	

FORMS FOR EXERCISES A OR B

10A-1 OR 10B-1.

Avril.com		Equipment	120

Jill.com		Accounts Payable	210

Pearl.com		Purchases	510

10A-2 OR 10B-2.

PAGE 1

Mango Co.		Accounts Payable	211		Purchases Returns and Allowances	513

EXERCISES (CONTINUED)

10A-3 OR 10B-3.   PAGE 2

Date	Account Titles and Description	PR	Dr.	Cr.

ACCOUNTS PAYABLE SUBSIDIARY LEDGER   **PARTIAL GENERAL LEDGER**

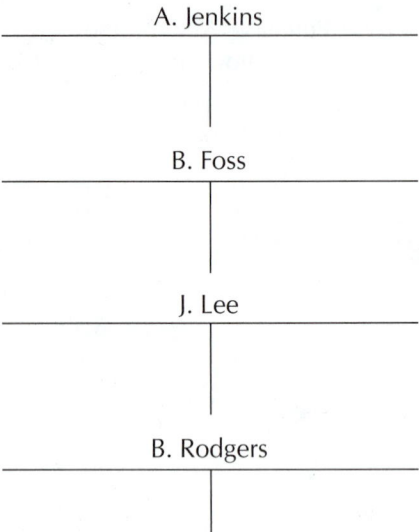

A. Jenkins   Cash   110

B. Foss   Accounts Payable   210

J. Lee   Purchases Discount   511

B. Rodgers   Advertising Expense   610

EXERCISES (CONTINUED)

10A-4 OR 10B-4.

KADEN'S CLOTHING
SCHEDULE OF ACCOUNTS PAYABLE
APRIL 30, 201X

_____

_____

_____

_____

_____ Accounts Payable   210 _____

10A-5 OR 10B-5.

Accounts Affected	Category	↑↓	Rules

10A-6 OR 10B-6.

_____

_____

_____

_____

_____

FORM FOR EXERCISES 10A-7 OR 10B-7, 10A-8 OR 10B-8, 10A-9 OR 10B-9, 10A-10 OR 10B-10

Date	Account Titles and Description	PR	Dr.	Cr.

FORM FOR EXERCISES 10A-7 OR 10B-7, 10A-8 OR 10B-8, 10A-9 OR 10B-9, 10A-10 OR 10B-10 (CONTINUED)

Date		Account Titles and Description	PR		Dr.			Cr.	

CALCULATIONS PAGE

END OF CHAPTER PROBLEMS

PROBLEM 10A-1 OR PROBLEM 10B-1

RODNEY'S SKATE SHOP
GENERAL JOURNAL

PAGE 2

Date	Account Titles and Description	PR	Dr.	Cr.

PROBLEM 10A-1 OR PROBLEM 10B-1 (CONTINUED)

ACCOUNTS PAYABLE SUBSIDIARY LEDGER

NAME   ADAMS.COM

ADDRESS   12 SMITH ST., DEARBORN, MI 09113

Date		Explanation	Post Ref.	Debit	Credit	Cr. Balance

NAME   NORTON CO.

ADDRESS   1 RANTOUL RD., CHARLOTTE, NC 01114

Date		Explanation	Post Ref.	Debit	Credit	Cr. Balance

NAME   ROLO CO.

ADDRESS   2 WEST RD., LYNN, MA 01471

Date		Explanation	Post Ref.	Debit	Credit	Cr. Balance

PARTIAL GENERAL LEDGER

STORE SUPPLIES   **ACCOUNT NO. 115**

Date		Explanation	Post Ref.	Debit	Credit	Balance Debit	Balance Credit

PROBLEM 10A-1 OR PROBLEM 10B-1 (CONCLUDED)

STORE EQUIPMENT   ACCOUNT NO. 121

Date		Explanation	Post Ref.	Debit	Credit	Balance	
						Debit	Credit

ACCOUNTS PAYABLE   ACCOUNT NO. 210

Date		Explanation	Post Ref.	Debit	Credit	Balance	
						Debit	Credit

PURCHASES   ACCOUNT NO. 510

Date		Explanation	Post Ref.	Debit	Credit	Balance	
						Debit	Credit

PROBLEM 10A-2 OR PROBLEM 10B-2

RACHEL'S NATURAL FOOD

Date	Account Titles and Description	PR	Dr.	Cr.

PROBLEM 10A-2 OR PROBLEM 10B-2 (CONTINUED)

ACCOUNTS PAYABLE SUBSIDIARY LEDGER

NAME   AIRON CO.

ADDRESS   11 LYNNWAY AVE., NEWPORT, RI 03112

Date	Explanation	Post Ref.	Debit	Credit	Cr. Balance

NAME   BIXBY CO.

ADDRESS   21 RIVER ST., ANAHEIM, CA 43110

Date	Explanation	Post Ref.	Debit	Credit	Cr. Balance

NAME   MIXON CO.

ADDRESS   10 ASTER RD., DUBUQUE, IA 80021

Date	Explanation	Post Ref.	Debit	Credit	Cr. Balance

NAME   RYAN CO.

ADDRESS   22 GERALD RD., SMITH, CO 43138

Date	Explanation	Post Ref.	Debit	Credit	Cr. Balance

PROBLEM 10A-2 OR PROBLEM 10B-2 (CONTINUED)

PARTIAL GENERAL LEDGER

STORE SUPPLIES   ACCOUNT NO. <u>110</u>

Date	Explanation	Post Ref.	Debit	Credit	Balance Debit	Balance Credit

OFFICE EQUIPMENT   ACCOUNT NO. <u>120</u>

Date	Explanation	Post Ref.	Debit	Credit	Balance Debit	Balance Credit

ACCOUNTS PAYABLE   ACCOUNT NO. <u>210</u>

Date	Explanation	Post Ref.	Debit	Credit	Balance Debit	Balance Credit

PURCHASES   ACCOUNT NO. <u>510</u>

Date	Explanation	Post Ref.	Debit	Credit	Balance Debit	Balance Credit

PROBLEM 10A-2 OR PROBLEM 10B-2 (CONCLUDED)

PURCHASES RETURNS AND ALLOWANCES   **ACCOUNT NO. 512**

Date		Explanation	Post Ref.	Debit	Credit	Balance	
						Debit	Credit

RACHEL'S NATURAL FOOD

SCHEDULE OF ACCOUNTS PAYABLE
AUGUST 31, 201X

PROBLEM 10A-3 OR PROBLEM 10B-3

Date	Account Titles and Description	PR	Dr.	Cr.

PROBLEM 10A-3 OR PROBLEM 10B-3 (CONTINUED)

ACCOUNTS PAYABLE SUBSIDIARY LEDGER

NAME ANDREWS CO.

ADDRESS 1 REACH RD., IPSWICH, MA 01932

Date		Explanation	Post Ref.	Debit	Credit	Cr. Balance

NAME HITCH CO.

ADDRESS 1 RALPH RD., REVERE, MA 01321

Date		Explanation	Post Ref.	Debit	Credit	Cr. Balance

NAME SEAKATE CO.

ADDRESS 7 PLYMOUTH AVE., GLENN, NH 01218

Date		Explanation	Post Ref.	Debit	Credit	Cr. Balance

NAME ZEKE CO.

ADDRESS 22 REY RD., BOCA RATON, FL 99132

Date		Explanation	Post Ref.	Debit	Credit	Cr. Balance

PROBLEM 10A-3 OR PROBLEM 10B-3 (CONTINUED)

PARTIAL GENERAL LEDGER

CASH   ACCOUNT NO. 110

Date	Explanation	Post Ref.	Debit	Credit	Balance Debit	Balance Credit

DELIVERY TRUCK   ACCOUNT NO. 150

Date 201X	Explanation	Post Ref.	Debit	Credit	Balance Debit	Balance Credit

ACCOUNTS PAYABLE   ACCOUNT NO. 210

Date	Explanation	Post Ref.	Debit	Credit	Balance Debit	Balance Credit

COMPUTER PURCHASES   ACCOUNT NO. 510

Date 201X	Explanation	Post Ref.	Debit	Credit	Balance Debit	Balance Credit

PROBLEM 10A-3 OR PROBLEM 10B-3 (CONCLUDED)

COMPUTER PURCHASES DISCOUNT   ACCOUNT NO. 511

Date	Explanation	Post Ref.	Debit	Credit	Balance Debit	Balance Credit

RENT EXPENSE   ACCOUNT NO. 610

Date	Explanation	Post Ref.	Debit	Credit	Balance Debit	Balance Credit

UTILITIES EXPENSE   ACCOUNT NO. 620

Date	Explanation	Post Ref.	Debit	Credit	Balance Debit	Balance Credit

ELLIS COMPUTER CENTER
SCHEDULE OF ACCOUNTS PAYABLE
OCTOBER 31, 201X

PROBLEM 10A-4 OR PROBLEM 10B-4

(1)

ALLISON'S TOY HOUSE
GENERAL JOURNAL

PAGE 1

Date	Account Titles and Description	PR	Dr.	Cr.

PROBLEM 10A-4 OR PROBLEM 10B-4 (CONTINUED)

Date		Account Titles and Description	PR		Dr.			Cr.	

PROBLEM 10A-4 OR PROBLEM 10B-4 (CONTINUED)

Date	Account Titles and Description	PR	Dr.	Cr.

PROBLEM 10A-4 OR PROBLEM 10B-4 (CONTINUED)

Date		Account Titles and Description	PR	Dr.			Cr.		

PROBLEM 10A-4 OR PROBLEM 10B-4 (CONTINUED)

Date	Account Titles and Description	PR	Dr.	Cr.

PROBLEM 10A-4 OR PROBLEM 10B-4 (CONTINUED)

(2)   ACCOUNTS PAYABLE SUBSIDIARY LEDGER

NAME   LANE CHIPKIN

ADDRESS   87 GARFIELD AVE., REVERE, MA 01245

Date		Explanation	Post Ref.	Debit	Credit	Cr. Balance

NAME   SAM KATZ GARAGE

ADDRESS   22 REGIS RD., BOSTON, MA 01950

Date		Explanation	Post Ref.	Debit	Credit	Cr. Balance

NAME   SARAH HARMITZ CO.

ADDRESS   22 RETTER ST., SAN DIEGO, CA 01211

Date		Explanation	Post Ref.	Debit	Credit	Cr. Balance

NAME   WILLIAM SMITH

ADDRESS   2 SPRING ST., WEERS, ND 02118

Date		Explanation	Post Ref.	Debit	Credit	Cr. Balance

PROBLEM 10A-4 OR PROBLEM 10B-4 (CONTINUED)

ACCOUNTS RECEIVABLE SUBSIDIARY LEDGER

NAME   ROBERT GIBBS

ADDRESS   24 RYAN RD., BUIKE, OH 02183

Date		Explanation	Post Ref.	Debit	Credit	Dr. Balance

NAME   BONNIE FLOW CO.

ADDRESS   2 SMITH RD., DALLAS, TX 22210

Date		Explanation	Post Ref.	Debit	Credit	Dr. Balance

NAME   INEZ TENENBAUM

ADDRESS   1 SCHOOL ST., CLEVELAND, OH 22441

Date		Explanation	Post Ref.	Debit	Credit	Dr. Balance

PROBLEM 10A-4 OR PROBLEM 10B-4 (CONTINUED)

NAME   AMANDA READER

ADDRESS   18 VEEK RD., CHESTER, CT 80111

Date		Explanation	Post Ref.	Debit	Credit	Dr. Balance

GENERAL LEDGER

CASH   ACCOUNT NO. 110

Date		Explanation	Post Ref.	Debit	Credit	Balance Debit	Balance Credit

PROBLEM 10A-4 OR PROBLEM 10B-4 (CONTINUED)

ACCOUNTS RECEIVABLE   ACCOUNT NO. 112

Date		Explanation	Post Ref.	Debit	Credit	Balance	
						Debit	Credit

PREPAID RENT   ACCOUNT NO. 114

Date		Explanation	Post Ref.	Debit	Credit	Balance	
						Debit	Credit

DELIVERY TRUCK   ACCOUNT NO. 121

Date		Explanation	Post Ref.	Debit	Credit	Balance	
						Debit	Credit

PROBLEM 10A-4 OR PROBLEM 10B-4 (CONTINUED)

ACCOUNTS PAYABLE ACCOUNT NO. <u>210</u>

Date	Explanation	Post Ref.	Debit	Credit	Balance Debit	Balance Credit

A. COOPER, CAPITAL ACCOUNT NO. <u>310</u>

Date	Explanation	Post Ref.	Debit	Credit	Balance Debit	Balance Credit

TOY SALES ACCOUNT NO. <u>410</u>

Date	Explanation	Post Ref.	Debit	Credit	Balance Debit	Balance Credit

PROBLEM 10A-4 OR PROBLEM 10B-4 (CONTINUED)

SALES RETURNS AND ALLOWANCES   ACCOUNT NO. 412

Date	Explanation	Post Ref.	Debit	Credit	Balance Debit	Balance Credit

SALES DISCOUNTS   ACCOUNT NO. 414

Date	Explanation	Post Ref.	Debit	Credit	Balance Debit	Balance Credit

TOY PURCHASES   ACCOUNT NO. 510

Date	Explanation	Post Ref.	Debit	Credit	Balance Debit	Balance Credit

PURCHASES RETURNS AND ALLOWANCES   ACCOUNT NO. 512

Date	Explanation	Post Ref.	Debit	Credit	Balance Debit	Balance Credit

PROBLEM 10A-4 OR PROBLEM 10B-4 (CONTINUED)

PURCHASES DISCOUNT　　　　　　　　　　**ACCOUNT NO. 514**

Date	Explanation	Post Ref.	Debit	Credit	Balance Debit	Balance Credit

SALARIES EXPENSE　　　　　　　　　　**ACCOUNT NO. 610**

Date	Explanation	Post Ref.	Debit	Credit	Balance Debit	Balance Credit

CLEANING EXPENSE　　　　　　　　　　**ACCOUNT NO. 612**

Date	Explanation	Post Ref.	Debit	Credit	Balance Debit	Balance Credit

PROBLEM 10A-4 OR PROBLEM 10B-4 (CONCLUDED)

(3)

ALLISON'S TOY HOUSE
SCHEDULE OF ACCOUNTS RECEIVABLE
OCTOBER 31, 201X

(3)

ALLISON'S TOY HOUSE
SCHEDULE OF ACCOUNTS PAYABLE
OCTOBER 31, 201X

PROBLEM 10A-5 OR PROBLEM 10B-5

Date	Account Titles and Description	PR	Dr.	Cr.

Part II

1.	cost	Dr	Cr	Income Statement
2.	contra-cost	Cr	Dr	Income Statement
3.	asset	Dr	Cr	Balance Sheet
4.	cost	Dr	Cr	Income Statement
5.	expense	Dr	Cr	Income Statement
6.	liability	Cr	Dr	Balance Sheet
7.	contra-cost	Cr	Dr	Income Statement
8.	asset	Dr	Cr	Balance Sheet
9.	asset	Dr	Cr	Balance Sheet
10.	contra-revenue	Dr	Cr	Income Statement

Part III

1.	false		**11.**	false
2.	false		**12.**	false
3.	true		**13.**	false
4.	true		**14.**	true
5.	false		**15.**	true
6.	true		**16.**	true
7.	true		**17.**	false
8.	false		**18.**	true
9.	true		**19.**	true
10.	true		**20.**	false

CONTINUING PROBLEM—ON THE JOB FOR CHAPTER 10

SANCHEZ COMPUTER CENTER
GENERAL JOURNAL

PAGE 7

Date	Account Titles and Description	PR	Dr.	Cr.

PARTIAL GENERAL LEDGER

CASH   ACCOUNT NO. 1000

Date		Explanation	Post Ref.	Debit	Credit	Balance Debit	Balance Credit
2/1	1X	Balance forward	✔			15 1 6 6 65	

SUPPLIES   ACCOUNT NO. 1030

Date		Explanation	Post Ref.	Debit	Credit	Balance Debit	Balance Credit
2/1	1X	Balance forward	✔			9 0 00	

MERCHANDISE INVENTORY   ACCOUNT NO. 1040

Date		Explanation	Post Ref.	Debit	Credit	Balance Debit	Balance Credit

PREPAID RENT   ACCOUNT NO. **1025**

Date		Explanation	Post Ref.	Debit	Credit	Balance	
						Debit	Credit
2/1	1X	Balance forward	✔			1 6 0 0 00	

ACCOUNTS PAYABLE   ACCOUNT NO. **2000**

Date		Explanation	Post Ref.	Debit	Credit	Balance	
						Debit	Credit
2/1	1X	Balance forward	✔				2 0 5 0 00

PURCHASES   ACCOUNT NO. **6000**

Date		Explanation	Post Ref.	Debit	Credit	Balance	
						Debit	Credit

PURCHASE RETURNS AND ALLOWANCES   ACCOUNT NO. **6010**

Date		Explanation	Post Ref.	Debit	Credit	Balance	
						Debit	Credit

PURCHASE DISCOUNTS   ACCOUNT NO. **6020**

Date		Explanation	Post Ref.	Debit	Credit	Balance	
						Debit	Credit

SANCHEZ COMPUTER CENTER
SCHEDULE OF ACCOUNTS PAYABLE
2/28/1X

ACCOUNTS PAYABLE SUBSIDIARY LEDGER

NAME   MULTI SYSTEMS, INC.   # 6A3

ADDRESS   1919 MORAN ST., ANAHEIM, CA 92606

Date		Explanation	Post Ref.	Debit	Credit	Cr. Balance
2/1	1X	Balance forward	✓			4 5 0 00

NAME   OFFICE DEPOT   # 6A4

ADDRESS   460 ESCONDIDO BLVD., ESCONDIDO, CA 92025

Date		Explanation	Post Ref.	Debit	Credit	Cr. Balance
2/1	1X	Balance forward	✓			5 0 00

NAME   **SAN DIEGO ELECTRIC**   **# 6A5**

ADDRESS   **606 INDUSTRIAL ST., SAN DIEGO, CA 92121**

Date		Explanation	Post Ref.	Debit	Credit	Cr. Balance

NAME   **PAC BELL**   **# 6A6**

ADDRESS   **101 BELL AVE., SAN DIEGO, CA 92101**

Date		Explanation	Post Ref.	Debit	Credit	Cr. Balance
2/1	1X	Balance forward	✔			1 5 0 00

NAME   **COMPUTER CONNECTION**   **# 6A7**

ADDRESS   **1020 WIL LANE, LOS ANGELES, CA 92405**

Date		Explanation	Post Ref.	Debit	Credit	Cr. Balance

NAME   **SYSTEM DESIGN FURNITURE**   **# 6A8**

ADDRESS   **2070 FIRST ST., SAN DIEGO, CA 92101**

Date		Explanation	Post Ref.	Debit				Credit				Cr. Balance				
2/1	1X	Balance forward	✔									1	4	0	0	00

APPENDIX 10A
FORMS FOR CLASSROOM DEMONSTRATION PROBLEM — SPECIAL JOURNALS

J. LING CO.
SALES JOURNAL

PAGE 1

Date		Account Debited	Terms	Invoice No.	Post Ref.	Dr. Acc. Receivable Cr. Sales	

CASH RECEIPTS JOURNAL   PAGE 1

Date		Cash Dr.		Sales Discounts Dr.		Accounts Receivable Cr.		Sales Cr.		Sundry			
										Account Name	PR	Amount Cr.	

PURCHASES JOURNAL   PAGE 1

Date	Account Credited	Terms	PR	Accounts Payable Cr.		Purchases Dr.		Sundry Dr.			
								Account	PR	Amount	

CASH PAYMENTS JOURNAL   PAGE 1

Date	Check No.	Accounts Debited	PR	Sundry Account Dr.		Accounts Payable Dr.		Purchases Discounts Cr.		Cash Cr.	

DEMO DOC PROBLEM (CONTINUED)

GENERAL JOURNAL

Date	Account Titles and Description	PR	Dr.	Cr.

ACCOUNTS RECEIVABLE SUBSIDIARY LEDGER

NAME   **BALDER CO.**

ADDRESS   **1 ROCK RD., DENVER, CO 66083**

Date	Explanation	Post Ref.	Debit	Credit	Dr. Balance

NAME   **LEWIS CO.**

ADDRESS   **15 SMITH AVE., REVERE, MA 01545**

Date	Explanation	Post Ref.	Debit	Credit	Dr. Balance

DEMO DOC PROBLEM (CONCLUDED)

ACCOUNTS PAYABLE SUBSIDIARY LEDGER

NAME   CASE CO.

ADDRESS   1 LONG RD., MARLBOROUGH, MA 01545

Date	Explanation	Post Ref.	Debit	Credit	Cr. Balance

NAME   NOONE CO.

ADDRESS   11 MILL RD., MALDEN, OK 01143

Date	Explanation	Post Ref.	Debit	Credit	Cr. Balance

PARTIAL GENERAL LEDGER

Cash   111

Sales   410

Purchases Discounts   530

Accounts Receivable   112

Sales Returns & Allowances   420

Salaries Expense   610

Equipment   116

Sales Discount   430

Accounts Payable   210

Purchases   510

J. Ling, Capital   310

Purchases Returns & Allowances   520

CHAPTER 10A APPENDIX FORMS

PROBLEM A-1

(1, 2)

FOOD.COM
SALES JOURNAL

PAGE 1

Date	Account Debited	Invoice No.	PR	Accounts Receivable Dr.	Pizza Sales Cr.	Grocery Sales Cr.

(1, 2)

FOOD.COM
GENERAL JOURNAL

PAGE 1

Date	Account Titles and Description	PR	Dr.	Cr.

PROBLEM A-1 (CONTINUED)

ACCOUNTS RECEIVABLE SUBSIDIARY LEDGER

NAME   DUNCAN CO.

ADDRESS   942 MOSE ST., REVERE, MA 01938

Date	Explanation	Post Ref.	Debit	Credit	Dr. Balance

NAME   LONG CO.

ADDRESS   8 JOSS AVE., LYNN, MA 01947

Date	Explanation	Post Ref.	Debit	Credit	Dr. Balance

NAME   SUE MOORE CO.

ADDRESS   10 LOST RD., TOPSFIELD, MA 01998

Date	Explanation	Post Ref.	Debit	Credit	Dr. Balance

PROBLEM A-1 (CONTINUED)

FOOD.COM
GENERAL LEDGER

ACCOUNTS RECEIVABLE   **ACCOUNT NO. 112**

Date		Explanation	Post Ref.	Debit	Credit	Balance	
						Debit	Credit

PIZZA SALES   **ACCOUNT NO. 410**

Date		Explanation	Post Ref.	Debit	Credit	Balance	
						Debit	Credit

GROCERY SALES   **ACCOUNT NO. 411**

Date		Explanation	Post Ref.	Debit	Credit	Balance	
						Debit	Credit

SALES RETURNS AND ALLOWANCES   **ACCOUNT NO. 412**

Date		Explanation	Post Ref.	Debit	Credit	Balance	
						Debit	Credit

PROBLEM A-1 (CONCLUDED)

FOOD.COM
SCHEDULE OF ACCOUNTS RECEIVABLE
JUNE 30, 201X

PROBLEM A-2

(1, 2)

TED'S AUTO SUPPLY
SALES JOURNAL

PAGE 4

Date	Customer's Name Account Receivable	Invoice No.	PR	Accounts Receivable Dr.	Sales Tax Payable Cr.	Auto Parts Sales Cr.

PROBLEM A-2 (CONTINUED)

(1, 2)

TED'S AUTO SUPPLY
GENERAL JOURNAL

PAGE 2

Date	Account Titles and Description	PR	Dr.	Cr.

PROBLEM A-2 (CONTINUED)

ACCOUNTS RECEIVABLE SUBSIDIARY LEDGER

NAME   LANCE CORNER

ADDRESS   9 ROE ST., BARTLETT, NH 01382

Date 201X		Explanation	Post Ref.	Debit	Credit	Dr. Balance
Nov	1	Balance	✔			4 0 0 00

NAME   J. SETH

ADDRESS   22 REESE ST., LACONIA, NH 04321

Date 201X		Explanation	Post Ref.	Debit	Credit	Dr. Balance
Nov	1	Balance	✔			2 0 0 00

NAME   R. VOLAN

ADDRESS   12 ASTER RD., MERRIMACK, NH 02134

Date 201X		Explanation	Post Ref.	Debit	Credit	Dr. Balance
Nov	1	Balance	✔			1 0 0 0 00

PROBLEM A-2 (CONTINUED)

TED'S AUTO SUPPLY
GENERAL JOURNAL

ACCOUNTS RECEIVABLE ACCOUNT NO. 110

Date 201X		Explanation	Post Ref.	Debit	Credit	Balance Debit	Balance Credit
Nov	1	Balance	✔			1 6 0 0 00	

SALES TAX PAYABLE ACCOUNT NO. 210

Date 201X		Explanation	Post Ref.	Debit	Credit	Balance Debit	Balance Credit
Nov	1	Balance	✔				1 6 0 0 00

AUTO PARTS SALES ACCOUNT NO. 410

Date		Explanation	Post Ref.	Debit	Credit	Balance Debit	Balance Credit

SALES RETURNS AND ALLOWANCES ACCOUNT NO. 420

Date		Explanation	Post Ref.	Debit	Credit	Balance Debit	Balance Credit

PROBLEM A-2 (CONCLUDED)

(3)

TED'S AUTO SUPPLY
SCHEDULE OF ACCOUNTS RECEIVABLE
NOVEMBER 30, 201X

PROBLEM A-3

SKATES.COM
PURCHASES JOURNAL

Date	Account Credited	Date of Invoice	Inv. No.	Terms	PR	Accounts Payable Cr.	Purchases Dr.	Sundry Dr.		
								Account	PR	Amount

PROBLEM A-3 (CONTINUED)

ACCOUNTS PAYABLE SUBSIDIARY LEDGER

NAME   MAIL.COM

ADDRESS   12 SMITH ST., DEARBORN, MI 09113

Date		Explanation	Post Ref.	Debit	Credit	Cr. Balance

NAME   NORTON CO.

ADDRESS   1 RANTOUL RD., CHARLOTTE, NC 01114

Date		Explanation	Post Ref.	Debit	Credit	Cr. Balance

NAME   ROLO CO.

ADDRESS   2 WEST RD., LYNN, MA 01471

Date		Explanation	Post Ref.	Debit	Credit	Cr. Balance

PARTIAL GENERAL LEDGER

STORE SUPPLIES   **ACCOUNT NO. 115**

Date		Explanation	Post Ref.	Debit	Credit	Balance	
						Debit	Credit

PROBLEM A-3 (CONCLUDED)

STORE EQUIPMENT   **ACCOUNT NO. 121**

Date	Explanation	Post Ref.	Debit	Credit	Balance Debit	Balance Credit

ACCOUNTS PAYABLE   **ACCOUNT NO. 210**

Date	Explanation	Post Ref.	Debit	Credit	Balance Debit	Balance Credit

PURCHASES   **ACCOUNT NO. 510**

Date	Explanation	Post Ref.	Debit	Credit	Balance Debit	Balance Credit

PROBLEM A-4

PAGE 10

MABEL'S NATURAL FOOD STORE
PURCHASES JOURNAL

Date	Account Credited	Date of Invoice	Inv. No.	Terms	PR	Accounts Payable Cr.	Purchases Dr.	Store Supplies Dr.	Sundry Dr. Account	PR	Amount

PROBLEM A-4 (CONTINUED)

ACCOUNTS PAYABLE SUBSIDIARY LEDGER

NAME   ATON CO.

ADDRESS   11 LYNNWAY AVE., NEWPORT, RI 03112

Date 201X		Explanation	Post Ref.	Debit	Credit	Cr. Balance
May	1	Balance	✔			4 0 0 00

NAME   BROWARD CO.

ADDRESS   21 RIVER ST., ANAHEIM, CA 43110

Date 201X		Explanation	Post Ref.	Debit	Credit	Cr. Balance
May	1	Balance	✔			6 0 0 00

NAME   MIDDEN CO.

ADDRESS   10 ASTER RD., DUBUQUE, IA 80021

Date 201X		Explanation	Post Ref.	Debit	Credit	Cr. Balance
May	1	Balance	✔			1 2 0 0 00

NAME   RELAR CO.

ADDRESS   22 GERALD RD., SMITH, CO 43138

Date 201X		Explanation	Post Ref.	Debit	Credit	Cr. Balance
May	1	Balance	✔			5 0 0 00

PROBLEM A-4 (CONTINUED)

PARTIAL GENERAL LEDGER

STORE SUPPLIES ACCOUNT NO. **110**

Date	Explanation	Post Ref.	Debit	Credit	Balance Debit	Balance Credit

OFFICE EQUIPMENT ACCOUNT NO. **120**

Date	Explanation	Post Ref.	Debit	Credit	Balance Debit	Balance Credit

ACCOUNTS PAYABLE ACCOUNT NO. **210**

Date 201X	Explanation	Post Ref.	Debit	Credit	Balance Debit	Balance Credit
May 1	Balance	✔				2 7 0 0 00

PURCHASES ACCOUNT NO. **510**

Date 201X	Explanation	Post Ref.	Debit	Credit	Balance Debit	Balance Credit
May 1	Balance	✔			16 7 0 0 00	

PROBLEM A-4 (CONCLUDED)

PURCHASES RETURNS AND ALLOWANCES   ACCOUNT NO. 512

Date	Explanation	Post Ref.	Debit	Credit	Balance Debit	Balance Credit

GENERAL JOURNAL   PAGE 2

Date	Account Titles and Description	PR	Dr.	Cr.

MABEL'S NATURAL FOOD STORE
SCHEDULE OF ACCOUNTS PAYABLE
MAY 31, 201X

PROBLEM A-5

(1,3)

ABBY'S TOY HOUSE
PURCHASES JOURNAL

PAGE 1

Date	Account Credited	Date of Inv.	Inv. No.	Terms	PR	Accounts Payable Cr.	Toy Purchases Dr.	Sundry Dr.		
								Accounts	PR	Amount

PROBLEM A-5 (CONTINUED)

ABBY'S TOY HOUSE
CASH RECEIPTS JOURNAL

PAGE 1

Date	Cash Dr.	Sales Discounts Dr.	Accounts Receivable Cr.	Toy Sales Cr.	Sundry Account	PR	Amount Cr.

PROBLEM A-5 (CONTINUED)

ABBY'S TOY HOUSE
CASH PAYMENTS JOURNAL

PAGE 1

Date	Check No.	Account Debited	PR	Sundry Dr.	Accounts Payable Dr.	Purchases Discount Cr.	Cash Cr.

PROBLEM A-5 (CONTINUED)

ABBY'S TOY HOUSE
SALES JOURNAL
MARCH 31, 201X

Date	Account Debited	Invoice No.	Terms	PR	Accounts Rec. – Dr. Toy Sales – Cr.			

ABBY'S TOY HOUSE
GENERAL JOURNAL
MARCH 31, 201X

Date	Account Titles and Description	PR	Dr.			Cr.		

PROBLEM A-5 (CONTINUED)

(2)   ACCOUNTS PAYABLE SUBSIDIARY LEDGER

NAME   MINNIE KATZ

ADDRESS   87 GARFIELD AVE., REVERE, MA 01245

Date		Explanation	Post Ref.	Debit	Credit	Cr. Balance

NAME   SAM KATZ GARAGE

ADDRESS   22 REGIS RD., BOSTON, MA 01950

Date		Explanation	Post Ref.	Debit	Credit	Cr. Balance

NAME   EARL MILLER CO.

ADDRESS   22 RETTER ST., SAN DIEGO, CA 01211

Date		Explanation	Post Ref.	Debit	Credit	Cr. Balance

NAME   WOODY SMITH

ADDRESS   2 SPRING ST., WEERS, ND 02118

Date		Explanation	Post Ref.	Debit	Credit	Cr. Balance

PROBLEM A-5 (CONTINUED)

ACCOUNTS RECEIVABLE SUBSIDIARY LEDGER

NAME   **BILL BURTON**

ADDRESS   **24 RYAN RD., BUIKE, OH 02183**

Date	Explanation	Post Ref.	Debit	Credit	Dr. Balance

NAME   **BONNIE FLOW CO.**

ADDRESS   **2 SMITH RD., DALLAS, TX 22210**

Date	Explanation	Post Ref.	Debit	Credit	Dr. Balance

NAME   **JIM REX**

ADDRESS   **1 SCHOOL ST., CLEVELAND, OH 22441**

Date	Explanation	Post Ref.	Debit	Credit	Dr. Balance

PROBLEM A-5 (CONTINUED)

NAME   AMY ROSE

ADDRESS   18 VEEK RD., CHESTER, CT 80111

Date		Explanation	Post Ref.	Debit	Credit	Dr. Balance

GENERAL LEDGER

CASH   **ACCOUNT NO. 110**

Date		Explanation	Post Ref.	Debit	Credit	Balance Debit	Balance Credit

ACCOUNTS RECEIVABLE   **ACCOUNT NO. 112**

Date		Explanation	Post Ref.	Debit	Credit	Balance Debit	Balance Credit

PREPAID RENT   **ACCOUNT NO. 114**

Date		Explanation	Post Ref.	Debit	Credit	Balance Debit	Balance Credit

PROBLEM A-5 (CONTINUED)

DELIVERY TRUCK   ACCOUNT NO. 121

Date		Explanation	Post Ref.	Debit	Credit	Balance	
						Debit	Credit

ACCOUNTS PAYABLE   ACCOUNT NO. 210

Date		Explanation	Post Ref.	Debit	Credit	Balance	
						Debit	Credit

A. ELLEN, CAPITAL   ACCOUNT NO. 310

Date		Explanation	Post Ref.	Debit	Credit	Balance	
						Debit	Credit

TOY SALES   ACCOUNT NO. 410

Date		Explanation	Post Ref.	Debit	Credit	Balance	
						Debit	Credit

PROBLEM A-5 (CONTINUED)

SALES RETURNS AND ALLOWANCES   ACCOUNT NO. 412

Date	Explanation	Post Ref.	Debit	Credit	Balance Debit	Balance Credit

SALES DISCOUNTS   ACCOUNT NO. 414

Date	Explanation	Post Ref.	Debit	Credit	Balance Debit	Balance Credit

TOY PURCHASES   ACCOUNT NO. 510

Date	Explanation	Post Ref.	Debit	Credit	Balance Debit	Balance Credit

PURCHASES RETURNS AND ALLOWANCES   ACCOUNT NO. 512

Date	Explanation	Post Ref.	Debit	Credit	Balance Debit	Balance Credit

PROBLEM A-5 (CONTINUED)

PURCHASES DISCOUNT   ACCOUNT NO. 514

Date		Explanation	Post Ref.	Debit	Credit	Balance	
						Debit	Credit

SALARIES EXPENSE   ACCOUNT NO. 610

Date		Explanation	Post Ref.	Debit	Credit	Balance	
						Debit	Credit

CLEANING EXPENSE   ACCOUNT NO. 612

Date		Explanation	Post Ref.	Debit	Credit	Balance	
						Debit	Credit

PROBLEM A-5 (CONCLUDED)

(4)

ABBY'S TOY HOUSE
SCHEDULE OF ACCOUNTS RECEIVABLE
MARCH 31, 201X

(4)

ABBY'S TOY HOUSE
SCHEDULE OF ACCOUNTS PAYABLE
MARCH 31, 201X

PREPARING A WORKSHEET FOR A MERCHANDISE COMPANY

11

INSTANT REPLAY: SELF-REVIEW QUIZ 11-1

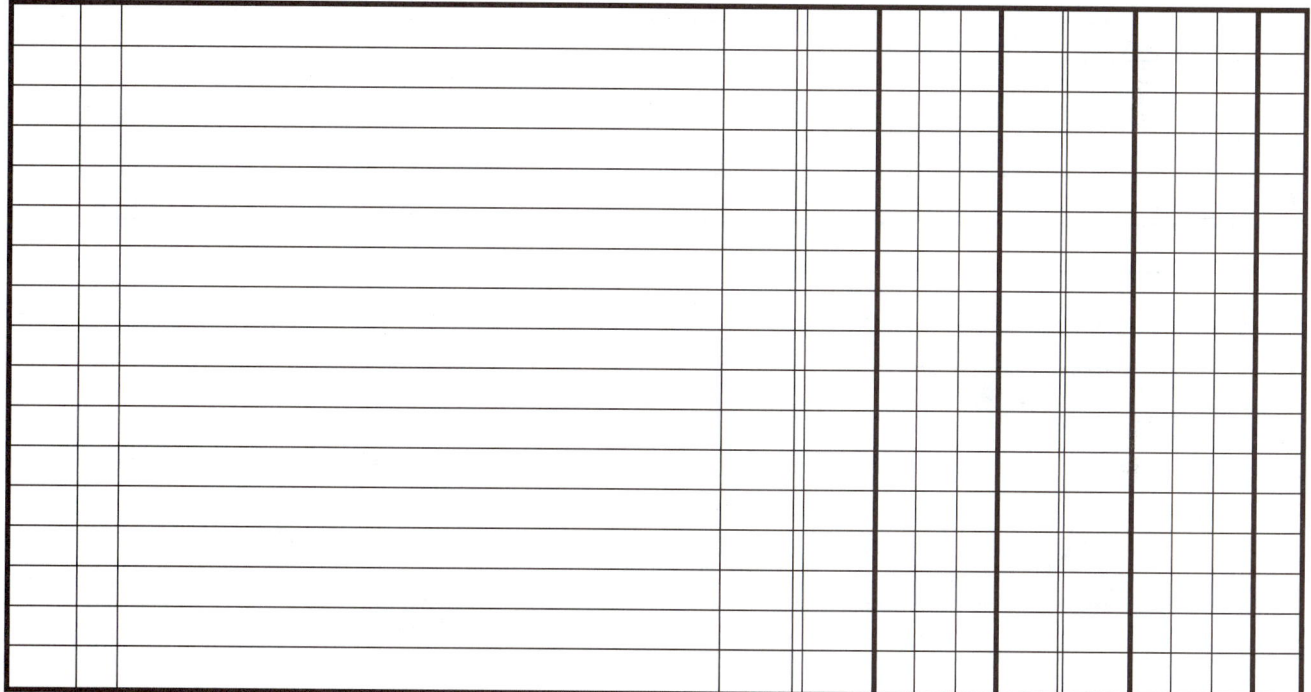

INSTANT REPLAY: SELF-REVIEW QUIZ 11-2

Use one of the blank fold-out worksheets that accompanied your textbook.

CHAPTER 11
CONCEPT CHECK

1.													
2.													

3.　　A. _____　　　　E. _____
　　　　B. _____　　　　F. _____
　　　　C. _____
　　　　D. _____

4. _____

_____

_____

_____

_____

_____

_____

5.

A. _____ B. _____ C. _____ D. _____ E. _____ F. _____

FORMS FOR EXERCISES A OR B

11A-1 OR 11B-1.

A. _____
B. _____
C. _____
D. _____
E. _____
F. _____
G. _____
H. _____

11A-2 OR 11B-2.

A. _____
_____
_____

B. _____
_____
_____

C. _____
_____
_____

D. _____
_____
_____

11A-3 OR 11B-3.

Accounts Affected	Category	↑↓	Rules

11A-4 OR 11B-4.

A. _____
B. _____
C. _____

11A-5 OR 11B-5.

Use one of the blank fold-out worksheets that accompanied your textbook.

END OF CHAPTER PROBLEMS

PROBLEM 11A-1 OR PROBLEM 11B-1

	A.	
	B.	
	C.	
	D.	

PROBLEM 11A-2 OR PROBLEM 11B-2;
PROBLEM 11A-3 OR PROBLEM 11B-3;
PROBLEM 11A-4 OR PROBLEM 11B-4

Use blank fold-out worksheets that accompanied your textbook.

CHAPTER 11
SUMMARY PRACTICE TEST:
PREPARING A WORKSHEET
FOR A MERCHANDISE COMPANY

Part I Instructions

Fill in the blank(s) to complete the statement.

1. The _____ _____ system keeps a continual track of the quantity and cost of the inventory on hand.

2. In the periodic inventory system, new inventories bought is recorded in the _____ account.

3. A continuous record of inventory is kept in a(n) _____ _____ system.

4. When using the periodic system, _____ _____ will remain unchanged.

5. _____ _____ represents a liability on the balance sheet and records money received for a sale or service not yet performed.

6. Freight-in is _____ to the cost of goods sold.

7. Net Sales less Cost of Goods Sold equals _____ _____.

8. _____ _____ equals Gross Sales less Sales Discounts and Sales Returns and Allowances.

9. Net Purchases equals Purchases less _____ _____ and _____ _____ _____ _____.

10. A(n) _____ _____ helps calculate ending inventory.

11. Ending inventory is _____ from the cost of goods available for sale.

12. Net purchases are _____ to Beginning Inventory to get the cost of goods available for sale.

13. Gross Profit less _____ equals Net Income.

14. Purchase discounts _____ the total cost of merchandise sold.

15. Beginning inventory at the end of the period is assumed to be _____, and thus a _____.

16. The ending inventory of one period becomes the _____ _____ next period.

17. Ending inventory represents goods not _____.

18. The inventory account is _____ at the end of the period.

19. Purchases are increased by a(n) _____.

20. Sales returns and allowances are used in calculating _____ _____.

21. Beginning Inventory plus Net Purchases equals _____ _____ _____ _____ _____ _____.

22. Beginning Inventory and Ending Inventory are never _____ on the worksheet.

Part II Instructions

Answer true or false to the following statements.

1. Unearned Revenue is a liability.
2. Perpetual inventory keeps a continuous record of inventory.
3. Purchases increase cost of goods sold.
4. Freight-in is added to cost of goods sold.
5. Figures for Beginning and Ending Inventory are combined on the worksheet.
6. A periodic system is used by companies with low volume and high unit prices.
7. Merchandise Inventory is an asset.
8. Unearned Revenue is a liability on the income statement.
9. Inventory is always taken 10 times per year.
10. Purchases replace ending inventory in a periodic system.
11. A trial balance may be placed directly on a worksheet.
12. The adjustment process updates the inventory account.
13. A post-closing trial balance has no temporary accounts.
14. Sales Discounts is a permanent account.
15. Gross sales are located on the balance sheet.
16. The Sales Returns and Allowances account has a normal balance of a credit.
17. Ending inventory of one period is the beginning inventory of the following period.
18. Net income always means cash.
19. Ending inventory increases cost of goods sold.
20. Net purchases is always the same as total purchases.
21. Gross profit plus expenses equals net income.
22. Unearned Storage Fees is a liability.
23. Merchandise inventory that is sold is assumed to be a cost.
24. Accumulated Depreciation is increased by a debit.
25. Merchandise Inventory can never be listed on a trial balance.
26. Ending Merchandise Inventory can only be found on a balance sheet.
27. The amount of rent expired is used in the adjustment process.
28. Adjustments help update individual ledger accounts.
29. Purchases Returns and Allowances is found on a balance sheet.
30. Beginning Merchandise Inventory found on the balance sheet from the prior period will also be placed in the cost of goods sold section of the balance sheet.
31. Sales always means cash received.
32. Ending Merchandise Inventory of the current period is found only on the balance sheet.
33. Purchases adds to the cost of goods sold.
34. Purchases discounts reduce the cost of purchases on the balance sheet.
35. Beginning inventory can never be assumed sold by the end of a period.

36. Ending inventory in one period becomes beginning inventory for the next two periods.

37. The ending inventory may be calculated from an inventory sheet.

38. Income Summary is used in the adjustment of merchandise inventory.

39. Ending inventory not sold is only placed in the credit column of the balance sheet section on the worksheet.

40. Purchases Discount is recorded in the credit column of the income statement section on the worksheet.

41. Gross profit and net income mean the same.

42. All companies must give sales discounts.

43. A merchandise company does not need a cost of goods sold section on the income statement.

44. Cost of goods available to sell less ending inventory equals cost of goods not sold.

SOLUTIONS TO SUMMARY PRACTICE TEST

Part I

1. perpetual inventory
2. Purchases
3. perpetual inventory
4. beginning inventory
5. Unearned Revenue
6. added
7. Gross Profit
8. Net sales
9. Purchases Discounts, Purchases Returns and Allowances
10. Inventory sheet (record)
11. subtracted
12. added
13. Expenses
14. reduce
15. sold, cost
16. begining inventory
17. sold
18. adjusted
19. debit
20. net sales
21. Cost of Goods Available for Sale
22. combined

Part II

1. true	**12.** true	**23.** true	**34.** false
2. true	**13.** true	**24.** false	**35.** false
3. true	**14.** false	**25.** false	**36.** false
4. true	**15.** false	**26.** false	**37.** true
5. false	**16.** false	**27.** true	**38.** true
6. false	**17.** true	**28.** true	**39.** false
7. true	**18.** false	**29.** false	**40.** true
8. false	**19.** false	**30.** false	**41.** false
9. false	**20.** false	**31.** false	**42.** false
10. false	**21.** false	**32.** false	**43.** false
11. true	**22.** true	**33.** true	**44.** false

CONTINUING PROBLEM—ON THE JOB FOR CHAPTER 11

Use the blank fold-out worksheet that accompanied your textbook.

COMPLETION OF THE ACCOUNTING CYCLE FOR A MERCHANDISE COMPANY

12

INSTANT REPLAY: SELF-REVIEW QUIZ 12-1

(1)

(2)

(3)

INSTANT REPLAY: SELF-REVIEW QUIZ 12-2

GENERAL JOURNAL   PAGE 2

Date		Account Titles and Description		PR	Dr		Cr.

INSTANT REPLAY: SELF-REVIEW QUIZ 12-3

Situation 1

Situation 2

Situation 3

Name _____ Class _____ Date _____

CHAPTER 12
CONCEPT CHECK

1.

_____
_____
_____
_____

2.

_____
_____
_____
_____
_____
_____

3.

_____
_____
_____
_____
_____
_____

4. A. _____   F. _____
B. _____   G. _____
C. _____   H. _____
D. _____   I. _____
E. _____   J. _____

5.

FORMS FOR EXERCISES A or B

12A-1 OR 12B-1.

COST OF GOODS SOLD

Merchandise Inv. 12/01/1X _____
Purchases _____
Less: Purchases Disc. _____
           Purch. R. & A. _____
_____
 Net Purchases _____
         Add: Freight-in _____
Net Cost of Purchases _____
Cost of Goods Available for Sale _____
Less: Merchandise Inv. 12/31/1X _____
         Cost of Goods Sold _____

12A-2 OR 12B-2.

A. _____

B. _____

C. _____

D. _____

E. _____

F. _____

G. _____

12A-3 OR 12B-3.

EXERCISES (CONCLUDED)

12A-4 OR 12B-4.

G. JACKSON
PARTIAL BALANCE SHEET
DECEMBER 31, 201X

12A-5 OR 12B-5.

(A)

Salaries Expense	Salaries Payable

(B)

Salaries Expense	Salaries Expense

(C)

Salaries Expense	Cash

END OF CHAPTER PROBLEMS

PROBLEM 12A-1 OR PROBLEM 12B-1

ROSE CO.
INCOME STATEMENT
FOR YEAR ENDED DECEMBER 31, 201X

PROBLEM 12A-2 OR PROBLEM 12B-2

JOHN'S CO.
STATEMENT OF OWNER'S EQUITY
FOR MONTH ENDED DECEMBER 31, 201X

PROBLEM 12A-2 OR PROBLEM 12B-2 (CONCLUDED)

JOHN'S CO.
BALANCE SHEET
DECEMBER 31, 201X

PROBLEM 12A-3 OR PROBLEM 12B-3

Use one of the blank fold-out worksheets that accompanied your textbook.

JOE'S SUPPLIES
INCOME STATEMENT
FOR YEAR ENDED DECEMBER 31, 201X

PROBLEM 12A-3 OR PROBLEM 12B-3 (CONTINUED)

JOE'S SUPPLIES
STATEMENT OF OWNER'S EQUITY
FOR YEAR ENDED DECEMBER 31, 201X

Name _____ Class _____ Date _____

PROBLEM 12A-3 OR PROBLEM 12B-3 (CONTINUED)

JOE'S SUPPLIES
BALANCE SHEET
DECEMBER 31, 201X

PROBLEM 12A-3 OR PROBLEM 12B-3 (CONTINUED)

GENERAL JOURNAL

PAGE 2

Date		Account Titles and Description	PR		Dr.			Cr.	

PROBLEM 12A-3 OR PROBLEM 12B-3 (CONCLUDED)

GENERAL JOURNAL

PAGE 3

Date		Account Titles and Description	PR		Dr.		Cr.	

PROBLEM 12A-4 OR PROBLEM 12B-4

Use one of the blank fold-out worksheets that accompanied your textbook.

CROSS LUMBER
INCOME STATEMENT
FOR YEAR ENDED DECEMBER 31, 201X

PROBLEM 12A-4 OR PROBLEM 12B-4 (CONTINUED)

Use one of the blank fold-out worksheets that accompanied your textbook.

CROSS LUMBER
STATEMENT OF OWNER'S EQUITY
FOR YEAR ENDED DECEMBER 31, 201X

PROBLEM 12A-4 OR PROBLEM 12B-4 (CONTINUED)

CROSS LUMBER
BALANCE SHEET
DECEMBER 31, 201X

PROBLEM 12A-4 OR PROBLEM 12B-4 (CONTINUED)

GENERAL JOURNAL

PAGE 2

Date	Account Titles and Description	PR	Dr.	Cr.

PROBLEM 12A-4 OR PROBLEM 12B-4 (CONTINUED)

CROSS LUMBER
GENERAL LEDGER

CASH   **ACCOUNT NO. 110**

Date	Explanation	Post Ref.	Debit	Credit	Balance Debit	Balance Credit

ACCOUNTS RECEIVABLE   **ACCOUNT NO. 111**

Date	Explanation	Post Ref.	Debit	Credit	Balance Debit	Balance Credit

MERCHANDISE INVENTORY   **ACCOUNT NO. 112**

Date	Explanation	Post Ref.	Debit	Credit	Balance Debit	Balance Credit

LUMBER SUPPLIES   **ACCOUNT NO. 113**

Date	Explanation	Post Ref.	Debit	Credit	Balance Debit	Balance Credit

PROBLEM 12A-4 OR PROBLEM 12B-4 (CONTINUED)

PREPAID INSURANCE   ACCOUNT NO. 114

Date	Explanation	Post Ref.	Debit	Credit	Balance Debit	Balance Credit

LUMBER EQUIPMENT   ACCOUNT NO. 121

Date	Explanation	Post Ref.	Debit	Credit	Balance Debit	Balance Credit

ACCUMULATED DEPRECIATION, LUMBER EQUIPMENT   ACCOUNT NO. 122

Date	Explanation	Post Ref.	Debit	Credit	Balance Debit	Balance Credit

ACCOUNTS PAYABLE   ACCOUNT NO. 220

Date	Explanation	Post Ref.	Debit	Credit	Balance Debit	Balance Credit

WAGES PAYABLE   ACCOUNT NO. 221

Date	Explanation	Post Ref.	Debit	Credit	Balance Debit	Balance Credit

PROBLEM 12A-4 OR PROBLEM 12B-4 (CONTINUED)

J. CROSS, CAPITAL   ACCOUNT NO. 330

Date		Explanation	Post Ref.	Debit	Credit	Balance	
						Debit	Credit

J. CROSS, WITHDRAWALS   ACCOUNT NO. 331

Date		Explanation	Post Ref.	Debit	Credit	Balance	
						Debit	Credit

INCOME SUMMARY   ACCOUNT NO. 332

Date		Explanation	Post Ref.	Debit	Credit	Balance	
						Debit	Credit

SALES   ACCOUNT NO. 440

Date		Explanation	Post Ref.	Debit	Credit	Balance	
						Debit	Credit

SALES RETURNS AND ALLOWANCES   ACCOUNT NO. 441

Date		Explanation	Post Ref.	Debit	Credit	Balance	
						Debit	Credit

PROBLEM 12A-4 OR PROBLEM 12B-4 (CONTINUED)

PURCHASES   ACCOUNT NO. 550

Date		Explanation	Post Ref.	Debit	Credit	Balance Debit	Balance Credit

PURCHASES DISCOUNT   ACCOUNT NO. 551

Date		Explanation	Post Ref.	Debit	Credit	Balance Debit	Balance Credit

PURCHASES RETURNS AND ALLOWANCES   ACCOUNT NO. 552

Date		Explanation	Post Ref.	Debit	Credit	Balance Debit	Balance Credit

WAGES EXPENSE   ACCOUNT NO. 660

Date		Explanation	Post Ref.	Debit	Credit	Balance Debit	Balance Credit

ADVERTISING EXPENSE   ACCOUNT NO. 661

Date		Explanation	Post Ref.	Debit	Credit	Balance Debit	Balance Credit

PROBLEM 12A-4 OR PROBLEM 12B-4 (CONTINUED)

RENT EXPENSE — ACCOUNT NO. 662

Date	Explanation	Post Ref.	Debit	Credit	Balance Debit	Balance Credit

DEPRECIATION EXPENSE, LUMBER EQUIPMENT — ACCOUNT NO. 663

Date	Explanation	Post Ref.	Debit	Credit	Balance Debit	Balance Credit

LUMBER SUPPLIES EXPENSE — ACCOUNT NO. 664

Date	Explanation	Post Ref.	Debit	Credit	Balance Debit	Balance Credit

INSURANCE EXPENSE — ACCOUNT NO. 665

Date	Explanation	Post Ref.	Debit	Credit	Balance Debit	Balance Credit

PROBLEM 12A-4 OR PROBLEM 12B-4 (CONCLUDED)

CROSS LUMBER
POST-CLOSING TRIAL BALANCE
DECEMBER 31, 201X

		Dr.		Cr.	

CHAPTER 12
SUMMARY PRACTICE TEST:
COMPLETION OF THE ACCOUNTING
CYCLE FOR A MERCHANDISE COMPANY

Part I Instructions

Fill in the blank(s) to complete the statement.

1. There are no debits or credits on _____ _____.

2. The formal income statement uses _____ _____ figures for inventory.

3. The gross profit figure _____ (is/is not) found on the worksheet.

4. _____ expenses are related to the general activity.

5. _____ _____ are related to the administrative function.

6. _____ _____ could be broken down into selling and administrative expenses.

7. The _____ figure for capital is not found on the worksheet.

8. _____ _____ are cash or other assets that will be converted into cash during the normal operating cycle of the company or one year, whichever is longer.

9. _____ and _____ are long-lived assets used for the production or sale of other assets or services.

10. Debts or obligations that are to be paid with current assets within one year or one operating cycle are called _____ _____.

11. Mortgage Payable is an example of a(n) _____ _____ _____.

12. Ending merchandise inventory is a(n) _____ _____.

13. By the adjusting process, the beginning inventory of the period is transferred to _____ _____.

14. The _____ _____ _____ _____ contains no temporary accounts.

15. A reversing entry involves certain _____ entries.

16. Reversing entries are used only if assets are _____ and have no previous balance and liabilities are _____ and have no balance.

Part II Instructions

Match the term in the last column to the definition, example, or phrase in the right column. Be sure to use a letter only once.

__d__	**1.** EXAMPLE: Computer Equipment	a. Subtotaling
_____	**2.** Net Sales-Cost of Goods Sold	b. Unearned Revenue
_____	**3.** Operating Cycle	c. Current asset
_____	**4.** Inside Columns of Financial Reports	d. Plant and Equipment
_____	**5.** Gross Profit-Operating Expenses	e. Reversing Entry
_____	**6.** Operating Expenses	f. Time Period
_____	**7.** Temporary Account	g. Net Income
_____	**8.** OASDI	h. Current Liability
_____	**9.** Result of an adjusting entry	i. When earned reduced by a debit
_____	**10.** Petty Cash	j. Gross Profit
_____	**11.** An asset that is adjsuted	k. Merchandise Inventory
_____	**12.** Ending Capital	l. Debit Balance
_____	**13.** A Liability showing revenue no earned	m. Not found on worksheet
_____	**14.** Unearned training fees	n. Income Summary
		o. Selling and Administrative

Part III Instructions

Answer true or false to the following statements.

1. A balance sheet records all revenue.
2. Cost of goods sold contains only ending inventory.
3. Net sales less cost of goods sold equals gross profit.
4. Operating expenses can only be administrative.
5. Supplies is part of Plant and Equipment.
6. Unearned Rent is an asset.
7. An operating cycle of a business must be one year.
8. Accumulated Depreciation is a current asset.
9. Long-term liabilities are due within one year.
10. Merchandise Inventory is a temporary account.
11. The normal balance of merchandise inventory is a debit.
12. The post-closing trial balance will not contain any unearned revenue accounts.
13. Ending inventory is closed directly to Capital.
14. Reversing entries cannot be applied to all adjustments.
15. Reversing entries are optional at the end of each month before the close of the year.
16. Reversing entries switch closing entries on the first day of the new period.
17. An adjusting entry with an asset decreasing with no prevoius balance cannot be reversed.
18. Closing entries will update the merchandise inventory account.
19. Beginning merchandise inventory of a period is assumed sold by the end of the period.
20. An adjusting entry for Accrued Wages can be reversed.

CHAPTER 12
SOLUTIONS TO SUMMARY PRACTICE TEST

Part I

1. financial reports
2. two separate
3. is not
4. General
5. Administrative expenses
6. Operating expenses
7. ending
8. Current assets
9. Plant, Equipment
10. current liabilities
11. long-term liability
12. permanent account
13. Income Summary
14. post-closing trial balance
15. adjusting
16. increasing, increasing

Part II

1. d
2. j
3. f
4. a
5. g
6. o
7. n
8. h
9. e
10. l
11. k
12. m
13. b
14. i

Part III

1. false
2. false
3. true
4. false
5. false
6. false
7. false
8. false
9. false
10. false
11. true
12. false
13. false
14. true
15. false
16. false
17. true
18. false
19. true
20. true

CONTINUING PROBLEM—ON THE JOB FOR CHAPTER 12

SANCHEZ COMPUTER CENTER
GENERAL JOURNAL   PAGE 8

Date	Account Titles and Description	PR	Dr.	Cr.

SANCHEZ COMPUTER CENTER
GENERAL LEDGER

CASH   ACCOUNT NO. **1000**

Date		Explanation	Post Ref.	Debit	Credit	Balance Debit	Balance Credit
3/1	1X	Balance forward	✔			13 4 1 6 64	

PETTY CASH   ACCOUNT NO. **1010**

Date		Explanation	Post Ref.	Debit	Credit	Balance Debit	Balance Credit
3/1	1X	Balance forward	✔			1 0 0 00	

ACCOUNTS RECEIVABLE   ACCOUNT NO. **1020**

Date		Explanation	Post Ref.	Debit	Credit	Balance Debit	Balance Credit
3/1	1X	Balance forward	✔			10 9 0 0 00	

PREPAID RENT   ACCOUNT NO. **1025**

Date		Explanation	Post Ref.	Debit	Credit	Balance Debit	Balance Credit
3/1	1X	Balance forward	✔			2 8 0 0 00	

SUPPLIES   ACCOUNT NO. 1030

Date		Explanation	Post Ref.	Debit	Credit	Balance Debit	Balance Credit
3/1	1X	Balance forward	✔			3 9 0 00	

MERCHANDISE INVENTORY   ACCOUNT NO. 1040

Date		Explanation	Post Ref.	Debit	Credit	Balance Debit	Balance Credit

COMPUTER SHOP EQUIPMENT   ACCOUNT NO. 1080

Date		Explanation	Post Ref.	Debit	Credit	Balance Debit	Balance Credit
3/1	1X	Balance forward	✔			3 8 0 0	

ACCUMULATED DEPRECIATION, C.S. EQUIPMENT   ACCOUNT NO. 1081

Date		Explanation	Post Ref.	Debit	Credit	Balance Debit	Balance Credit
3/1	1X	Balance forward	✔				9 9 00

OFFICE EQUIPMENT   ACCOUNT NO. 1090

Date		Explanation	Post Ref.	Debit	Credit	Balance Debit	Balance Credit
3/1	1X	Balance forward	✔			1 0 5 0 00	

ACCUMULATED DEPRECIATION, OFFICE EQUIPMENT   ACCOUNT NO. <u>1091</u>

Date		Explanation	Post Ref.	Debit	Credit	Balance Debit	Balance Credit
3/1	1X	Balance forward	✔				2 0 00

ACCOUNTS PAYABLE   ACCOUNT NO. <u>2000</u>

Date		Explanation	Post Ref.	Debit	Credit	Balance Debit	Balance Credit
3/1	1X	Balance forward	✔				2 7 0 0 00

WAGES PAYABLE   ACCOUNT NO. <u>2010</u>

Date		Explanation	Post Ref.	Debit	Credit	Balance Debit	Balance Credit

FICA OASDI PAYABLE   ACCOUNT NO. <u>2020</u>

Date		Explanation	Post Ref.	Debit	Credit	Balance Debit	Balance Credit

FICA MEDICARE PAYABLE   ACCOUNT NO. <u>2030</u>

Date		Explanation	Post Ref.	Debit	Credit	Balance Debit	Balance Credit

FIT PAYABLE   ACCOUNT NO. 2040

Date		Explanation	Post Ref.	Debit	Credit	Balance	
						Debit	Credit

SIT PAYABLE   ACCOUNT NO. 2050

Date		Explanation	Post Ref.	Debit	Credit	Balance	
						Debit	Credit

FUTA PAYABLE   ACCOUNT NO. 2060

Date		Explanation	Post Ref.	Debit	Credit	Balance	
						Debit	Credit

SUTA PAYABLE   ACCOUNT NO. 2070

Date		Explanation	Post Ref.	Debit	Credit	Balance	
						Debit	Credit

T. FREEDMAN, CAPITAL   ACCOUNT NO. 3000

Date		Explanation	Post Ref.	Debit	Credit	Balance	
						Debit	Credit
3/1	1X	Balance forward	✓				7 4 0 6 00

T. FREEDMAN WITHDRAWALS   ACCOUNT NO. 3010

Date		Explanation	Post Ref.	Debit	Credit	Balance	
						Debit	Credit
3/1	1X	Balance forward	✔			2 0 1 5 00	

INCOME SUMMARY   ACCOUNT NO. 3020

Date		Explanation	Post Ref.	Debit	Credit	Balance	
						Debit	Credit

SERVICE REVENUE   ACCOUNT NO. 4000

Date		Explanation	Post Ref.	Debit	Credit	Balance	
						Debit	Credit
3/1	1X	Balance forward	✔				18 5 0 0 00

SALES   ACCOUNT NO. 4010

Date		Explanation	Post Ref.	Debit	Credit	Balance	
						Debit	Credit
3/1	1X	Balance forward	✔				9 7 0 0 00

GENERAL LEDGER

SALES RETURNS AND ALLOWANCES   **ACCOUNT NO. 4020**

Date		Explanation	Post Ref.	Debit	Credit	Balance Debit	Balance Credit
3/1	1X	Balance forward	✔			4 0 0 00	

SALES DISCOUNTS   **ACCOUNT NO. 4030**

Date		Explanation	Post Ref.	Debit	Credit	Balance Debit	Balance Credit
3/1	1X	Balance forward	✔			2 2 0 00	

ADVERTISING EXPENSE   **ACCOUNT NO. 5010**

Date	Explanation	Post Ref.	Debit	Credit	Balance Debit	Balance Credit
	Balance forward					

RENT EXPENSE   **ACCOUNT NO. 5020**

Date	Explanation	Post Ref.	Debit	Credit	Balance Debit	Balance Credit

UTILITIES EXPENSE   **ACCOUNT NO. 5030**

Date	Explanation	Post Ref.	Debit	Credit	Balance Debit	Balance Credit
	Balance forward					

PHONE EXPENSE   ACCOUNT NO. 5040

Date		Explanation	Post Ref.	Debit	Credit	Balance	
						Debit	Credit
3/1	1X	Balance forward	✔			1 5 0 00	

SUPPLIES EXPENSE   ACCOUNT NO. 5050

Date		Explanation	Post Ref.	Debit	Credit	Balance	
						Debit	Credit
3/1	1X		✔			4 2 00	

INSURANCE EXPENSE   ACCOUNT NO. 5060

Date		Explanation	Post Ref.	Debit	Credit	Balance	
						Debit	Credit

POSTAGE EXPENSE   ACCOUNT NO. 5070

Date		Explanation	Post Ref.	Debit	Credit	Balance	
						Debit	Credit
3/1	1X	Balance forward	✔			2 5 00	

DEPRECIATION EXPENSE C.S. EQUIPMENT   ACCOUNT NO. 5080

Date		Explanation	Post Ref.	Debit	Credit	Balance	
						Debit	Credit

DEPRECIATION EXPENSE OFFICE EQUIPMENT   ACCOUNT NO. 5090

Date	Explanation	Post Ref.	Debit	Credit	Balance Debit	Balance Credit

MISCELLANEOUS EXPENSE   ACCOUNT NO. 5100

Date		Explanation	Post Ref.	Debit	Credit	Balance Debit	Balance Credit
3/1	1X	Balance forward	✔			1 0 00	

WAGE EXPENSE   ACCOUNT NO. 5110

Date		Explanation	Post Ref.	Debit	Credit	Balance Debit	Balance Credit
3/1	1X	Balance forward	✔			2 0 3 0 00	

PAYROLL TAX EXPENSE   ACCOUNT NO. 5120

Date		Explanation	Post Ref.	Debit	Credit	Balance Debit	Balance Credit
3/1	1X	Balance forward	✔			2 2 6 36	

INTEREST EXPENSE   ACCOUNT NO. 5130

Date	Explanation	Post Ref.	Debit	Credit	Balance Debit	Balance Credit

BAD DEBT EXPENSE   ACCOUNT NO. 5140

Date		Explanation	Post Ref.	Debit	Credit	Balance Debit	Balance Credit

PURCHASES   ACCOUNT NO. 6000

Date		Explanation	Post Ref.	Debit	Credit	Balance Debit	Balance Credit
3/1	1X	Balance forward	✔			9 5 0 00	

PURCHASE RETURNS AND ALLOWANCES   ACCOUNT NO. 6010

Date		Explanation	Post Ref.	Debit	Credit	Balance Debit	Balance Credit
3/1	1X	Balance forward	✔				1 0 0 00

PURCHASE DISCOUNTS   ACCOUNT NO. 6020

Date		Explanation	Post Ref.	Debit	Credit	Balance Debit	Balance Credit

FREIGHT IN   ACCOUNT NO. 6030

Date		Explanation	Post Ref.	Debit	Credit	Balance Debit	Balance Credit

SANCHEZ COMPUTER CENTER
INCOME STATEMENT
FOR THE SIX MONTHS ENDED MARCH 31, 201X

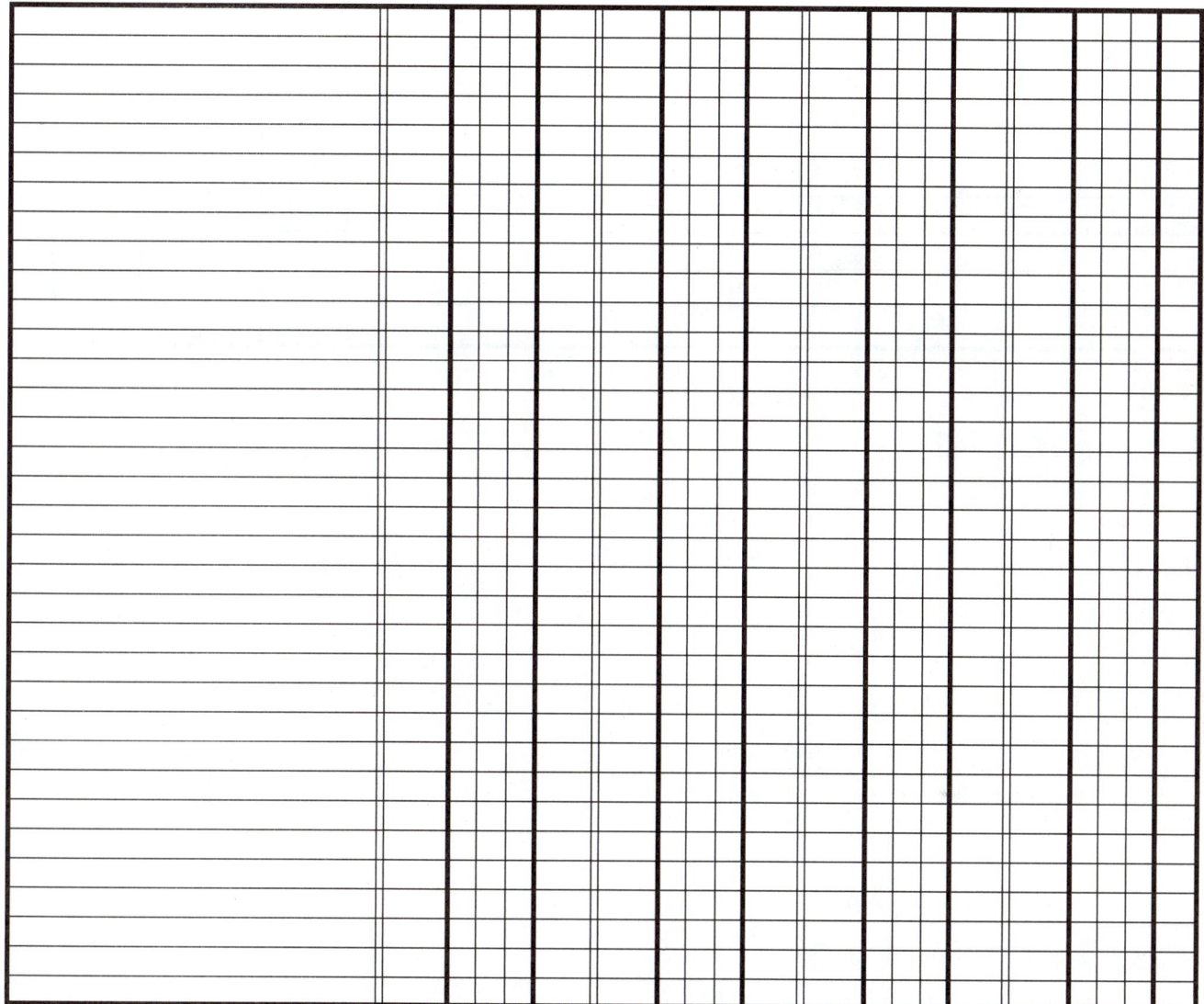

SANCHEZ COMPUTER CENTER
STATEMENT OF OWNER'S EQUITY
FOR THE SIX MONTHS ENDED MARCH 31, 201X

SANCHEZ COMPUTER CENTER
BALANCE SHEET
MARCH 31, 201X

MINI PRACTICE SET

THE CORNER DRESS SHOP
GENERAL JOURNAL

Date	Account Titles and Description	PR	Dr.	Cr.

THE CORNER DRESS SHOP

Use a blank fold-out worksheet and a blank payroll register that accompanied your textbook.

MINI PRACTICE SET
Use the blank fold-out worksheets that accompanied your textbook.

THE CORNER DRESS SHOP
GENERAL JOURNAL

PAGE 5

Date		Account Titles and Description	PR		Dr.		Cr.	

MINI PRACTICE SET

THE CORNER DRESS SHOP
GENERAL JOURNAL

PAGE 6

Date	Account Titles and Description	PR	Dr.	Cr.

MINI PRACTICE SET

THE CORNER DRESS SHOP
GENERAL JOURNAL

Date	Account Titles and Description	PR	Dr.	Cr.

MINI PRACTICE SET

THE CORNER DRESS SHOP
GENERAL JOURNAL

Date	Account Titles and Description	PR	Dr.	Cr.

MINI PRACTICE SET

THE CORNER DRESS SHOP
GENERAL JOURNAL

PAGE 9

Date	Account Titles and Description	PR	Dr.	Cr.

MINI PRACTICE SET

THE CORNER DRESS SHOP
AUXILIARY PETTY CASH RECORD

Date	Voucher No.	Description	Receipts	Payment	Category of Payment				
					Postage Expense	Delivery Expense	Sundry		
							Account	Amount	

MINI PRACTICE SET

ACCOUNTS PAYABLE SUBSIDIARY LEDGER

NAME   BLEW CO. _____

Date 201X		Explanation	Post Ref.	Debit	Credit	Credit Balance
Mar	1	Balance	✓			1 9 0 0 00

NAME   JONES CO. _____

Date 201X	Explanation	Post Ref.	Debit	Credit	Credit Balance

NAME   MOE'S GARAGE _____

Date 201X	Explanation	Post Ref.	Debit	Credit	Credit Balance

MINI PRACTICE SET

NAME MORRIS CO. _____

Date 201X		Explanation	Post Ref.	Debit	Credit	Credit Balance

ACCOUNTS RECEIVABLE SUBSIDIARY LEDGER

NAME BING CO. _____

Date 201X		Explanation	Post Ref.	Debit	Credit	Debit Balance
Mar	1	Balance	✔			2 2 0 0 00

NAME BLEW CO. _____

Date 201X		Explanation	Post Ref.	Debit	Credit	Debit Balance

MINI PRACTICE SET

NAME   RONALD CO. _____

Date 201X		Explanation	Post Ref.	Debit	Credit	Debit Balance

GENERAL LEDGER

CASH   **ACCOUNT NO. 110**

Date 201X		Explanation	Post Ref.	Debit	Credit	Balance Debit	Balance Credit
Mar	1	Balance	✔			2 2 3 1 90	

MINI PRACTICE SET

ACCOUNTS RECEIVABLE   ACCOUNT NO. 111

Date 201X		Explanation	Post Ref.	Debit	Credit	Balance Debit	Balance Credit
Mar	1	Balance	✔			2 2 0 0 00	

PETTY CASH   ACCOUNT NO. 112

Date 201X		Explanation	Post Ref.	Debit	Credit	Balance Debit	Balance Credit
Mar	1	Balance	✔			3 5 00	

MERCHANDISE INVENTORY   ACCOUNT NO. 114

Date 201X		Explanation	Post Ref.	Debit	Credit	Balance Debit	Balance Credit
Mar	1	Balance	✔			5 6 0 0 00	

MINI PRACTICE SET

PREPAID RENT   ACCOUNT NO. 116

Date 201X		Explanation	Post Ref.	Debit	Credit	Balance	
						Debit	Credit
Mar	1	Balance	✔			1 8 0 0 00	

DELIVERY TRUCK   ACCOUNT NO. 120

Date 201X		Explanation	Post Ref.	Debit	Credit	Balance	
						Debit	Credit
Mar	1	Balance	✔			6 0 0 0 00	

ACCUMULATED DEPRECIATION, TRUCK   ACCOUNT NO. 121

Date 201X		Explanation	Post Ref.	Debit	Credit	Balance	
						Debit	Credit
Mar	1	Balance	✔				1 5 0 0 00

MINI PRACTICE SET

ACCOUNTS PAYABLE   ACCOUNT NO. 210

Date 201X		Explanation	Post Ref.	Debit	Credit	Balance Debit	Balance Credit
Mar	1	Balance	✔				1 9 0 0 00

SALARIES PAYABLE   ACCOUNT NO. 212

Date 201X	Explanation	Post Ref.	Debit	Credit	Balance Debit	Balance Credit

FIT PAYABLE   ACCOUNT NO. 214

Date 201X		Explanation	Post Ref.	Debit	Credit	Balance Debit	Balance Credit
Mar	1	Balance	✔				1 0 1 3 00

MINI PRACTICE SET

FICA-OASDI PAYABLE   ACCOUNT NO. 216

Date 201X		Explanation	Post Ref.	Debit	Credit	Balance	
						Debit	Credit
Mar	1	Balance	✔				1 3 3 9 20

FICA-MEDICARE PAYABLE   ACCOUNT NO. 218

Date 201X		Explanation	Post Ref.	Debit	Credit	Balance	
						Debit	Credit
Mar	1	Balance	✔				3 1 3 20

SIT PAYABLE   ACCOUNT NO. 220

Date 201X		Explanation	Post Ref.	Debit	Credit	Balance	
						Debit	Credit
Mar	1	Balance	✔				7 5 6 00

SUTA TAX PAYABLE   ACCOUNT NO. 222

Date 201X		Explanation	Post Ref.	Debit	Credit	Balance	
						Debit	Credit
Mar	1	Balance	✔				9 7 9 20

FUTA TAX PAYABLE   ACCOUNT NO. 224

Date 201X		Explanation	Post Ref.	Debit	Credit	Balance	
						Debit	Credit
Mar	1	Balance	✔				1 6 3 20

UNEARNED RENT   ACCOUNT NO. 226

Date 201X		Explanation	Post Ref.	Debit	Credit	Balance	
						Debit	Credit
Mar	1	Balance	✔				8 0 0 00

MINI PRACTICE SET

B. LOEB, CAPITAL   ACCOUNT NO. 310

Date 201X	Explanation	Post Ref.	Debit	Credit	Balance Debit	Balance Credit
Mar 1	Balance	✔				9 1 0 3 10

B. LOEB, WITHDRAWALS   ACCOUNT NO. 320

Date 201X	Explanation	Post Ref.	Debit	Credit	Balance Debit	Balance Credit

INCOME SUMMARY   ACCOUNT NO. 330

Date 201X	Explanation	Post Ref.	Debit	Credit	Balance Debit	Balance Credit

SALES   ACCOUNT NO. 410

Date 201X	Explanation	Post Ref.	Debit	Credit	Balance Debit	Balance Credit

SALES RETURNS AND ALLOWANCES   ACCOUNT NO. 412

Date 201X	Explanation	Post Ref.	Debit	Credit	Balance Debit	Balance Credit

MINI PRACTICE SET

SALES DISCOUNT   ACCOUNT NO. 414

Date 201X	Explanation	Post Ref.	Debit	Credit	Balance Debit	Balance Credit

RENTAL INCOME   ACCOUNT NO. 416

Date 201X	Explanation	Post Ref.	Debit	Credit	Balance Debit	Balance Credit

PURCHASES   ACCOUNT NO. 510

Date 201X	Explanation	Post Ref.	Debit	Credit	Balance Debit	Balance Credit

PURCHASES RETURNS AND ALLOWANCES   ACCOUNT NO. 512

Date 201X	Explanation	Post Ref.	Debit	Credit	Balance Debit	Balance Credit

PURCHASES DISCOUNT   ACCOUNT NO. 514

Date 201X	Explanation	Post Ref.	Debit	Credit	Balance Debit	Balance Credit

MINI PRACTICE SET

SALES SALARY EXPENSE   ACCOUNT NO. 610

Date 201X	Explanation	Post Ref.	Debit	Credit	Balance Debit	Balance Credit

OFFICE SALARY EXPENSE   ACCOUNT NO. 611

Date 201X	Explanation	Post Ref.	Debit	Credit	Balance Debit	Balance Credit

PAYROLL TAX EXPENSE   ACCOUNT NO. 612

Date 201X	Explanation	Post Ref.	Debit	Credit	Balance Debit	Balance Credit

CLEANING EXPENSE   ACCOUNT NO. 614

Date 201X	Explanation	Post Ref.	Debit	Credit	Balance Debit	Balance Credit

DEPRECIATION EXPENSE, TRUCK   ACCOUNT NO. 616

Date 201X	Explanation	Post Ref.	Debit	Credit	Balance Debit	Balance Credit

MINI PRACTICE SET

RENT EXPENSE   ACCOUNT NO. 618

Date 201X	Explanation	Post Ref.	Debit	Credit	Balance Debit	Balance Credit

POSTAGE EXPENSE   ACCOUNT NO. 620

Date 201X	Explanation	Post Ref.	Debit	Credit	Balance Debit	Balance Credit

DELIVERY EXPENSE   ACCOUNT NO. 622

Date 201X	Explanation	Post Ref.	Debit	Credit	Balance Debit	Balance Credit

MISCELLANEOUS EXPENSE   ACCOUNT NO. 624

Date 201X	Explanation	Post Ref.	Debit	Credit	Balance Debit	Balance Credit

MINI PRACTICE SET

THE CORNER DRESS SHOP
SCHEDULE OF ACCOUNTS RECEIVABLE
MARCH 31, 201X

THE CORNER DRESS SHOP
SCHEDULE OF ACCOUNTS PAYABLE
MARCH 31, 201X

MINI PRACTICE SET

THE CORNER DRESS SHOP
INCOME STATEMENT
FOR MONTH ENDED MARCH 31, 201X

MINI PRACTICE SET

THE CORNER DRESS SHOP
STATEMENT OF OWNER'S EQUITY
FOR MONTH ENDED MARCH 31, 201X

MINI PRACTICE SET

THE CORNER DRESS SHOP
BALANCE SHEET
MARCH 31, 201X

MINI PRACTICE SET

THE CORNER DRESS SHOP
POST-CLOSING TRIAL BALANCE
MARCH 31, 201X

Name _____ Class _____ Date _____

MINI PRACTICE SET

Form **941 for 201X:** **Employer's QUARTERLY Federal Tax Return**

(Rev. January 2006)

Department of the Treasury — Internal Revenue Service

990106

OMB No. 1545-0029

(EIN)
Employer identification number

☐☐ — ☐☐☐☐☐☐☐

Name (not your trade name)

Trade name (if any)

Address

Number   Street   Suite or room number

City   State   ZIP code

Report for this Quarter ...
(Check one.)

☐ **1:** January, February, March

☐ **2:** April, May, June

☐ **3:** July, August, September

☐ **4:** October, November, December

Read the separate instructions before you fill out this form. Please type or print within the boxes.

Part 1: Answer these questions for this quarter.

1 Number of employees who received wages, tips, or other compensation for the pay period including: *Mar. 12* (Quarter 1), *June 12* (Quarter 2), *Sept. 12* (Quarter 3), *Dec. 12* (Quarter 4)   **1** ☐

2 Wages, tips, and other compensation . . . .   **2** ☐ .

3 Total income tax withheld from wages, tips, and other compensation . . . .   **3** ☐ .

4 If no wages, tips, and other compensation are subject to social security or Medicare tax . . ☐ Check and go to line 6.

5 Taxable social security and Medicare wages and tips:

Column 1   Column 2

5a Taxable social security wages   ☐ .   × .124 =   ☐ .

5b Taxable social security tips   ☐ .   × .124 =   ☐ .

5c Taxable Medicare wages & tips ☐ .   × .029 =   ☐ .

5d Total social security and Medicare taxes (*Column 2,* lines 5a + 5b + 5c = line 5d) . . **5d** ☐ .

6 Total taxes before adjustments (lines 3 + 5d = line 6) . . . . **6** ☐ .

7 TAX ADJUSTMENTS (Read the instructions for line 7 before completing lines 7a through 7h.):

7a Current quarter's fractions of cents . . . .   ☐ .

7b Current quarter's sick pay . . . .   ☐ .

7c Current quarter's adjustments for tips and group-term life insurance   ☐ .

7d Current year's income tax withholding (attach Form 941c) . . . .   ☐ .

7e Prior quarters' social security and Medicare taxes (attach Form 941c)   ☐ .

7f Special additions to federal income tax (attach Form 941c) . . .   ☐ .

7g Special additions to social security and Medicare (attach Form 941c)   ☐ .

7h TOTAL ADJUSTMENTS (Combine all amounts: lines 7a through 7g.) . . . . **7h** ☐ .

8 Total taxes after adjustments (Combine lines 6 and 7h.) . . . . **8** ☐ .

9 Advance earned income credit (EIC) payments made to employees . . . . **9** ☐ .

10 Total taxes after adjustment for advance EIC (line 8 – line 9 = line 10) . . . . . . **10** ☐ .

11 Total deposits for this quarter, including overpayment applied from a prior quarter . . . **11** ☐ .

12 Balance due (If line 10 is more than line 11, write the difference here.) . . . . . . **12** ☐ .
Make checks payable to *United States Treasury.*

13 Overpayment (If line 11 is more than line 10, write the difference here.)   ☐ .   Check one ☐ Apply to next return.
                                                                                              ☐ Send a refund.

▶ You **MUST** fill out both pages of this form and **SIGN** it.

Next ➡

For Privacy Act and Paperwork Reduction Act Notice, see the back of the Payment Voucher.   Cat. No. 17001Z   Form **941** (Rev. 1-2006)

MINI PRACTICE SET

990206

Name *(not your trade name)*	Employer identification number (EIN)

Part 2: Tell us about your deposit schedule and tax liability for this quarter.

If you are unsure about whether you are a monthly schedule depositor or a semiweekly schedule depositor, see *Pub. 15 (Circular E)*, section 11.

14 ☐ ☐ Write the state abbreviation for the state where you made your deposits OR write "MU" if you made your deposits in *multiple* states.

15 Check one: ☐ Line 10 is less than $2,500. Go to Part 3.

☐ You were a monthly schedule depositor for the entire quarter. Fill out your tax liability for each month. Then go to Part 3.

Tax liability: Month 1 [_____.__]

Month 2 [_____.__]

Month 3 [_____.__]

Total liability for quarter [_____.__] Total must equal line 10.

☐ You were a semiweekly schedule depositor for any part of this quarter. Fill out *Schedule B (Form 941): Report of Tax Liability for Semiweekly Schedule Depositors,* and attach it to this form.

Part 3: Tell us about your business. If a question does NOT apply to your business, leave it blank.

16 If your business has closed or you stopped paying wages . . . . ☐ Check here, and

enter the final date you paid wages [___/___/___] .

17 If you are a seasonal employer and you do not have to file a return for every quarter of the year . . ☐ Check here.

Part 4: May we speak with your third-party designee?

Do you want to allow an employee, a paid tax preparer, or another person to discuss this return with the IRS? See the instructions for details.

☐ Yes. Designee's name [_____]

Phone (____) ____ – _____   Personal Identification Number (PIN) ☐ ☐ ☐ ☐ ☐

☐ No.

Part 5: Sign here. You MUST fill out both sides of this form and SIGN it.

Under penalties of perjury, I declare that I have examined this return, including accompanying schedules and statements, and to the best of my knowledge and belief, it is true, correct, and complete.

X Sign your name here [_____]

Print name and title [_____]

Date [___/___/___]   Phone (____) ____ – _____

Part 6: For PAID preparers only *(optional)*

Paid Preparer's Signature			
Firm's name			
Address		EIN	
		ZIP code	
Date ___/___/___ Phone (___) ___ – ___		SSN/PTIN	

☐ Check if you are self-employed.

Form **941** (Rev. 1-2006)